EIGHTEEN
WOM

Roger Lonsdale is a Fello
English Literature in the
editor of *The New Oxford Book of Eighteen*
(also available as an Oxford Paperback).

EIGHTEENTH CENTURY WOMEN POETS

An Oxford Anthology

Edited by

ROGER LONSDALE

Oxford   New York

OXFORD UNIVERSITY PRESS

1990

Oxford University Press, Walton Street, Oxford OX2 6DP

Oxford New York Toronto
Delhi Bombay Calcutta Madras Karachi
Petaling Jaya Singapore Hong Kong Tokyo
Nairobi Dar es Salaam Cape Town
Melbourne Auckland

and associated companies in
Berlin Ibadan

Oxford is a trade mark of Oxford University Press

British Library Cataloguing in Publication Data
Eighteenth-century women poets: an Oxford anthology.
1. Poetry in English, 1702–1800. Anthologies
I. Lonsdale, Roger
821.508
ISBN 0–19–282775–8

Library of Congress Cataloging in Publication Data
Eighteenth century women poets: an Oxford anthology/edited by Roger Lonsdale
p. cm.
Reprint, with corrections and additonal notes.
Includes bibliographical references.
1. English poetry—Women authors. 2. English poetry—18th century. I. Lonsdale, Roger H.
821'.50809287—dc20 PR1177.E34 1990 90–7181
ISBN 0–19–282775–8

Printed in Great Britain by Clays Ltd. Bungay, Suffolk

ACKNOWLEDGEMENTS

FOR specific information or advice I am grateful to Julia Briggs, Richard Greene, Martin Hamlyn, Terence Leach, Ann Messenger, Mary Prior, and Marguerite Stocker. It will be apparent that I have a more general debt to a number of scholars who have recently worked on women writers of the eighteenth century. It is a pleasure to acknowledge the assistance and patience of the staffs of the Bodleian and British Libraries. Although they can bear no responsibility for what has resulted, Marilyn Butler and Jerome McGann emboldened me for the task at an early stage, when I was still gathering resolution. Kim Scott Walwyn of Oxford University Press maintained a finely judged balance of encouragement and pressure in keeping me at it. My wife, who has her own busy life, listened to much about the project and cheerfully accompanied me to some far-flung graveyards.

CONTENTS

CONTENTS

CONTENTS

CONTENTS

CONTENTS

CONTENTS

CONTENTS

CONTENTS

CONTENTS

CONTENTS

CONTENTS

CONTENTS

CONTENTS

INTRODUCTION

(i)

IN the first decade of the eighteenth century two women published collections of their verse. In the 1790s more than thirty did so. Even so crude a measure may suggest that there had been an emphatic change in the literary status of women in the period. Reviewing such a collection of verse in 1798, Ralph Griffiths, for almost half a century the editor of the *Monthly Review*, felt able to celebrate

the Age of ingenious and learned Ladies; who have excelled so much in the more elegant branches of literature, that we need not to hesitate in concluding that the long agitated dispute between the two sexes is at length determined; and that it is no longer a question, whether woman *is* or is *not* inferior to man in natural ability, or less capable of excelling in mental accomplishments (New Series xxvii. 441).

Griffiths would be well aware of all the books, pamphlets, and periodical essays which had tirelessly enquired whether the mental powers of women were 'naturally' inferior or equal to, or merely different from, those of men, and debated the kind of education appropriate to their station in life. What can hardly be doubted is that the education and literary reputation of women, particularly in the middle and upper classes, had markedly improved in the course of the century and that they had come to play an increasingly significant part, both as producers and consumers, in the rapidly expanding book trade.

In retrospect Griffiths' complacency about this situation must seem ludicrously unjustified. Apart from anything else most of the verse written by women in the eighteenth century has disappeared from view: only Lady Winchilsea's 'A Nocturnal Reverie', some witty verses by Lady Mary Wortley Montagu, Mrs Greville's 'A Prayer for Indifference', and a few songs by reticent Scottish women seem to have found a place in the margins of the canon of the period's verse. Anyone admitting to an interest in eighteenth-century women poets will soon learn to live with the politely sceptical question, 'Were there any?' There were in fact dozens of women at all social levels who, with variable ambition and competence, experienced the mysterious urge to express themselves in verse and, by one means or another, found their way into print. The exact nature of their achievement, and of its literary interest, will be for the reader to assess. The purpose of the biographical headnotes is to assist such understanding by providing evidence about the social background of the writers, their educational disadvantages or opportunities, the means of publication available to them, and the reputation, if any, they enjoyed. For some readers the only relevant perspective on such literary activity will be that it all took place in the shadow of an oppressive patriarchy. Closer to the ground, the evidence, including that of the writers themselves, may seem to point in all sorts of directions, which defy easy summary and generalization, although something of the sort must be attempted.

For the first three decades of the century women poets might appear relatively isolated and vulnerable figures, typified by Lady Chudleigh (nos. 1–3) who wrote in Devonshire in the seclusion of what was evidently a joyless marriage, in moods which alternate between defiant assertion of the intellectual potential of women and a chastened religious stoicism. While Lady Chudleigh was able to publish her verse and prose in London, Octavia Walsh (no. 37) wrote so furtively for her own amusement and consolation that her relatives were unaware of her writing until her early death in 1706. Elizabeth Tollet (nos. 68–74), an intelligent and sophisticated writer, whose verse epistle to her undergraduate brother at Cambridge vicariously experiences the kind of education she herself was denied, published a collection of her verse in 1724 with such decorous anonymity that it has only recently been identified. Hetty Wright (nos. 79–82), sister of the famous Wesleys, wrote a handful of poems, mostly about the miseries of her marriage, few of which found their way into print in her lifetime.

Such figures are not, however, entirely representative. Indeed, as the century began it must have seemed that women were at last making serious inroads into the complacently dominant male literary culture. The Restoration had brought a new confidence and competence to women's verse and produced at least two admired, if very different, precedents in the virtuous and idealistic Katherine Philips, 'the matchless Orinda', whose verse had been published in the 1660s before her early death; and in Aphra Behn, a successful professional dramatist and poet in the 1670s and 1680s. Several other women poets had appeared in the 1680s—Lady Masham observed to John Locke in a letter in 1685 that publishing verse had 'grown much the Fasion of late for our sex'—and half a dozen women had had plays performed on the London stage in the 1690s. While still a teenager, Sarah Fyge Egerton (nos. 19–23) had found a publisher for a long poem in the 1680s, even if her disapproving father exiled her from London as a result. In the following decade, Elizabeth Singer Rowe (nos. 33–6) in her early twenties could anticipate the opportunities offered by the developing periodical press at a later period by sending from rural Somerset large quantities of her verse for anonymous publication in London in John Dunton's *Athenian Mercury*. From the same decade writers such as Lady Chudleigh and Elizabeth Thomas (no. 30) found encouragement in the claims of the early feminist Mary Astell for the independent dignity, intellectual self-respect, and moral autonomy of women. Something of this new confidence might seem to be expressed, as the new century began, in *The Nine Muses* (1700), a collection of verse by women on the death of John Dryden. In a poem on the same subject in the same year, Alexander Oldys visualized 'spritely Afra' among the classic English poets who welcomed Dryden to heavenly bliss.

As the moral climate changed, however, it became harder to visualize Aphra Behn in heaven, given the efficiency with which she had catered for the tastes of the licentious Restoration theatre and the irregularity of her own life. Behn could be no sort of inspiration for 'respectable' women of literary inclinations, any more than were such professional writers as Delariviere Manley and Eliza Haywood. Scandal, sometimes generated by other women, all too easily pursued those who incautiously sought literary fame or moved too freely in male literary circles: such was the fate of Sarah Fyge Egerton at the hands of Delariviere Manley (headnote to nos. 19–23) and of Martha Fowke Sansom in the pages of Eliza Haywood (headnote to nos. 59–63). Elizabeth Thomas (headnote to nos. 24–32), driven into the literary market-place only by destitution, would suffer the worse fate of humiliating immortality in Pope's *Dunciad*. As moralizers increasingly emphasized their domestic station and duties, women with intellectual or literary ambitions tended to be depicted as slatternly if not licentious. By 1718 a 'respectable', though far from stuffy, woman writer like Jane Brereton would disown the dubious precedents of Behn, Manley, and Haywood ('this motley train, | Politely lewd and wittily profane') and align herself with the 'spotless' Orinda and, of her own contemporaries, the pious Elizabeth Singer Rowe and Lady Winchilsea (no. 56).

As will be clear from the following pages, women in the lower orders of society worked as a matter of course, as servants, shopkeepers, schoolteachers, and even washerwomen. For their social superiors, even if it became acceptable later in the century to find employment as a governess or private tutor, the only serious career was marriage and the unmarried usually remained dependent on male relatives. Intellectual interests, if not guaranteeing sluttishness in a woman, might well disconcert or intimidate an unliterary suitor, which is no doubt why mothers sometimes worried more than the fathers about their bookish daughters (as in the very different cases of Laetitia Pilkington, Mary Leapor, Hester Mulso, and Anna Seward). The emphatic message of the *Spectator* would be echoed—by both men and women—for the rest of the century: 'the utmost of a Woman's Character is contained in Domestic Life; she is Blameable or Praise-worthy according as her carriage affects the House of her Father or her Husband. All she has to do in this World, is contained within the duties of a Daughter, a Sister, a Wife, and a Mother' (No. 342, 2 Apr. 1712). It would be unwise to assume that such prescriptions actually reflected how all women thought and behaved: their very frequency might suggest the opposite. Only a few years later Robert Molesworth, father of Mary Monck (nos. 50–2), deplored the fact that women were exchanging 'the Ancient good Housewi-fry of their homebred Grandmothers' and their 'Natural Sweetness and Modesty' for 'a Careless, Indecent, Masculine Air', imitation of 'the *Rakeish* Wilder sort of Gentlemen . . . and a Modish Neglect of their Husbands, Children and Families' (Mary Monck, *Poems*, 1716, sig. a6^v–a7^v).

Yet the cumulative effect of the moralists must have had its effect. Within the domestic restraints and responsibilities imposed on women, literary interests were not forbidden but inevitably had to take second place, and there were other problems and inhibitions for women. In view of the

prestige of the classics-dominated education of privileged males at school
and university, lack of self-confidence about their education was under-
standable. Exclusion from these classical mysteries would seem to entail
exclusion from the higher kinds of poetry, so obsequiously orientated
towards Greek and Latin precedent. On a humbler level, as English poetry
became more self-consciously 'correct', it was taken for granted at least
until the 1760s that most women, with their rudimentary education, would
have a precarious grasp of spelling, grammar, and metre, let alone of
decorum of diction and style: not entirely without justification, as a few lines
from Ann Dyke's *The Female Muse. A Poem on the Coronation of Her Sacred
Majesty Queen Ann* (1702) may suggest:

> The mantl'd Clouds doth now new Azur wear,
> Birds tune their Pipes to celebrate the fair;
> The sweet heavenly Harbingers all flockt to see,
> And in warbling Notes exprest their extasie . . .
> Each Beast with a suprizing Gaiety appears,
> All vaunt their Heads, and proudly toss their Ears;
> They lookt as tho' they could an Adoration claim,
> And with unheard of noises yedder forth her Name.

Ann Dyke did, let it be noted, find a publisher.

Asked by a correspondent to name 'the chief Qualifications of a good
Poet', Richard Steele replied concisely in the *Spectator*, 'To be a very well-
bred Man' (No. 314, 19 Feb. 1712). Such a definition contrived to exclude
not merely women, of course, but also the unprivileged and underbred male
population. Women of the higher classes would in fact usually have
educational, or at least self-educational, opportunities denied to all but the
most determined men of humbler birth. Given her own obscure origins, the
reputation of Constantia Grierson (no. 64) as a classicist is almost unac-
countable, but more leisured women in the period were often taught and
encouraged, if they showed any inclination, by proud fathers, helpful
brothers, occasional tutors, local clergymen or physicians, and other male
mentors. Throughout the century social considerations always complicate
issues of gender. Outright, boorish hostility to the literary aspirations of
women became relatively rare after the early decades of the century, when
Elizabeth Thomas reacted vigorously to it (nos. 26 and 28) and when
Annabella Blount was driven by her brother's contempt to destroy her verse
(no. 125). It should be noted, however, that her father had earlier encour-
aged her and that she eventually married the literary husband she wanted.
Yet Mrs Blount seems hardly to have resumed her writing and there are
other cases which suggest that the distractions and responsibilities of
marriage put a virtual end to literary ambitions. In the 1720s Judith Cowper
Madan (nos. 65–7) published verse and corresponded with Alexander
Pope, but after her marriage wrote only for her family. While there were
early cases of couples who were both writers, such as the Breretons
(nos. 56–7) and the Pilkingtons (nos. 94–5), this may only have added to the
tensions within these marriages, both of which ended in separations.

In spite of educational insecurities, the reiterated insistence on domestic, 'feminine' proprieties, and the inevitable sneers (from both sexes) at their literary ambitions, women poets could still meet encouragement and find opportunities for publication. Expecting hostility at first, Anne Finch, later the Countess of Winchilsea (nos. 4–18), was in fact applauded by male contemporaries as the new century began: her reputation was safely acquired in respectable literary circles, her verse appeared in prestigious miscellanies, and she was confident enough to publish a collection in 1713, to which she added her name later in the year. It is noticeable that in her 'Tale of the Miser and the Poet' (no. 9), Lady Winchilsea speaks not as a disadvantaged woman but on behalf of both male and female poets in a materialistic age. Given the confident and accomplished range of forms and tones in her collection, its apparent lack of influence on later women writers is surprising. Rooted in the late seventeenth century, her verse may have already seemed somewhat dated. The fact that, until the later decades of the century, women poets usually adopted styles that were being replaced by new fashions (see Mary Jones and Mary Leapor below), meant that it was all the easier to underestimate their achievements.

A contemporary praised by Lady Winchilsea in 'The Miser and the Poet' was Elizabeth Singer Rowe (nos. 33–6). Happy to forget an early collection of verse of 1696 (until Edmund Curll mischievously reprinted it in the 1730s), Rowe enjoyed the patronage and friendship of the Thynne family, especially of the Countess of Hertford and her circle, was admired by male writers and won a high reputation for the exemplary piety of her poetry, although her later fame depended rather on the religious prose works she wrote in the financial independence of her widowhood. A contrasting figure was Lady Mary Wortley Montagu (nos. 38–49), whose background made self-education relatively easy, who was acquainted from her youth with distinguished literary and political men and, by the time she was thirty, had travelled to Turkey and back. Her ambivalence about her literary ambitions is instructive. Indignant at times about the inferior education offered to most women, she was also well aware that intellectual pretensions could arouse the hostility of other women as well as men. Intelligent and talented, she considered it ill-bred to seek literary fame, so that much of her writing was published anonymously and almost accidentally. This ambivalence, the fact that no attempt was made to collect her verse until after her death, together with the fact that her erratic reputation did not appeal to a later, more prudish age, prevented Lady Mary from becoming any kind of model or inspiration to her successors. Similar inhibitions about the ill-breeding of writing professionally afflicted certain women throughout the century, the most striking case being Ann Radcliffe (no. 289). It is worth noting, however, that there were male poets, such as Thomas Gray and William Shenstone, in whom literary ambition also alternated with squeamishness about the vulgarity of the literary market-place.

(ii)

From the 1730s, for various reasons, women began to find it easier and more acceptable to publish their verse. Edward Cave's *Gentleman's Magazine* (from 1731) was the first and most influential of the numerous periodicals which were a feature of the expanding book trade, and which were soon carrying political and literary news and opinion to all parts of the country. Provincial correspondents and contributors would eventually in turn provide a significant part of the contents of the *Gentleman's Magazine*, especially in the monthly poetry pages, which gave scope to both men and women who might otherwise have found publication too complicated, expensive, or inhibiting. Condescension to 'magazine' verse in the eighteenth century is unjustified: many of the best known poets of the period appeared in the *Gentleman's Magazine* at one time or another and its literary editors were by no means undiscriminating, so that the general interest of verse in its pages is usually higher than in the average individual volume of poetry. Within a few years of its appearance, the widowed Jane Brereton (nos. 56–7) was sending from Wrexham her contributions to some lively exchanges of verse in the *Gentleman's*, and her youthful daughter Charlotte (no. 126) also contributed. Other provincial women, such as Elizabeth Teft of Lincoln (nos. 145–8), 'Ophelia' (no. 160) in Yorkshire, and Mary Whateley Darwall (nos. 166–9), the daughter of a Worcestershire farmer, could later enjoy seeing their verse in a national periodical, as would Esther Lewis Clark (nos. 153–5), whose poems were printed in the London magazines from the Bath newspaper. By the later decades of the century contributions by and publicity about Anna Seward of Lichfield (nos. 204–12) and her circle were rarely absent from the pages of the leading London periodicals.

It was also in the 1730s that it became normal for women to publish volumes of their verse by subscription. The aim of such subscriptions was often less to encourage a woman writer to embark on a precarious literary career than to reward a 'deserving' wife or mother and her family with some degree of financial security. Ambitions for her family were clearly inter-woven with any desire for literary celebrity in the elaborate subscription which accompanied the publication of the *Poems* (1734) of Mary Barber (nos. 84–90), a member of Swift's literary circle in Dublin. The tireless efforts of the distinguished 'misanthropist' on her behalf among his aristocratic and literary friends in England can be appreciated only by reading his many letters on the subject. Although her verse has some fluency and individuality, Mary Barber no doubt made herself all the more acceptable to her fashionable subscribers by emphasizing her modest literary pretensions and she was perhaps the first woman poet to make a virtue out of the original educational purposes of her poems (for her sons) and the domestic context of many of them. As Swift's efforts for Mrs Barber indicate, a successful subscription could involve considerable organization over a number of years, as names were collected through a network of literary and socially influential contacts. There was a notable subscription in the 1740s for Mary Jones of Oxford (nos. 105-9), an intelligent spinster of limited means, whose friends in the fashionable world responded generously to a well-organized campaign on behalf of her *Miscellanies in Prose and Verse* (1750). At a lower social level, there were efforts in the same decade to promote a subscription for Mary Leapor (nos. 129-44), the gifted daughter of a Northamptonshire gardener, which would have provided her with much needed financial security, had she not died at the age of twenty-four. (Her *Poems* were published posthumously by subscription for the benefit of her father.)

As the provincial book trade developed during the century, it became common for support for smaller subscriptions to be mainly local. (This anthology includes verse published at Ayr, Bath, Birmingham, Bristol, Canterbury, Coventry, Dublin, Edinburgh, Glasgow, Manchester, Newcastle, Norwich, Oxford, Portsmouth, Walsall, Winchester, and York.) Names could, however, be drawn from a much wider geographical range if distinguished supporters had been enlisted, and if the subscription were publicized in advance in newspapers and periodicals, as in the cases of Mary Whateley Darwall (nos. 166-9) and Ann Yearsley (nos. 256-9). By the end of the century some of the largest subscriptions appear to have been primarily testimonials for deserving women, as in the remarkable support for Jane Cave Winscom (nos. 244-9), as well as for the unexciting publications of Elizabeth Bentley, who obtained almost 2,000 subscribers for her *Poetical Compositions* (Norwich, 1791), and Frances Greensted, a servant, for her *Fugitive Pieces* (Maidstone, 1796). A very different case was that of Laetitia Pilkington (nos. 94-5), who survived in the 1740s by collecting subscriptions for a never-to-be-published collection of her poems, and who later realized that she could take her revenge on non-subscribers by denouncing their meanness in her *Memoirs*.

Although genteel subscribers were unlikely to support the publication of totally worthless writing, critics eventually felt driven at times to object to the mistaken benevolence which could encourage the barely talented into print. In view of the rising flood of publications by both women and undereducated men (the situation deplored by Pope in the *Dunciad*), it is clear that the high ideals of Augustanism, 'polite' taste and 'correctness', did little to inhibit many writers and their readers. At the same time there was growing interest in the phenomenon of the 'natural genius', who could versify in the most unpromising circumstances. The first notable case was Stephen Duck, the thresher-poet, rescued from rural obscurity in 1730 and later installed by Queen Caroline as the Keeper of Merlin's Cave, one of her architectural fancies in Richmond Park. While much derision accompanied the unfortunately named Duck's 'success' (he eventually committed suicide), his unexpected celebrity inspired several other humble poets, including Mary Collier, the Petersfield washerwoman (no. 113), whose *The Woman's Labour* (1739), addressed to Duck himself, was published with the aid of the local gentry. A different response to Stephen Duck came from

Catherine Cockburn, who had enjoyed some success as a dramatist early in the century and later wrote on philosophical subjects, but who had largely disappeared into the obscurity of marriage. In some 'Verses' sent anonymously from Aberdeen to the *Gentleman's Magazine* in May 1737 (p. 308), Mrs Cockburn claimed on behalf of women writers that the difficulties originally faced by Stephen Duck as an agricultural worker had been no greater

> Than those restraints which have our sex confin'd,
> While partial custom checks the soaring mind.
> Learning deny'd us, we at random tread
> Unbeaten paths, that late to knowledge lead;
> By secret steps break thro' th' obstructed way,
> Nor dare acquirements gain'd by stealth display.
> If some advent'rous genius rare arise,
> Who on exalted themes her talents tries,
> She fears to give the work (tho' prais'd) a name,
> And flies not more from infamy, than fame.

Mrs Cockburn went on to suggest that royal patronage of Duck should be extended to studious women, less to encourage more women to become writers than to help to wean them from frivolous 'feminine' amusements, and so to make them better wives and mothers.

While Mrs Cockburn's explicit comparison of women to uneducated men is unusual, the problems for the woman writer she describes are familiar: erratic education, the impropriety of seeking literary fame, the pressures of domestic respectability, and the indifference and frivolity of other women. That the poets themselves often saw other women as even more hostile to their literary ambitions than men is clear from a series of poems in which they satirically and, one would have thought, riskily visualize the reactions of their friends or subscribers to their verse (perhaps a distinctively female subgenre, related to their liking for not always flattering physical self-depiction: see nos. 59, 88, 120, 142, 146). Mary Barber (no. 90) depicted her potential subscribers in the fashionable female world as variously haughty, vain, malicious, indifferent to poetry, and convinced that women should leave poetry and wit to men, sticking to the needle rather than the pen. In the 1740s Mary Leapor (no. 135) described her search for constructive criticism of her verse from a series of unhelpful men and women. Although she paid a warm tribute to her true patron and mentor 'Artemisia', it is to the women that she attributed the most frivolous reactions (Cressida) as well as the most hostile: Parthenia believed that (Mira's) preoccupation with poetry was making her dull and slatternly, and Sophronia that it was leading her to neglect her domestic duties and into financial insecurity. Her contemporary, Esther Lewis Clark (no. 153) pictured her female acquaintance, devoted to tea-drinking, cards, and scandal, dissecting her literary aspirations: her friend Philantha has to defend her against accusations of vanity, plagiarism, and dullness, of seeking to attract men (who will only despise her) by her writing, and of brazenly corresponding with men. Although Lewis also attributed to some men the view that the pen and the needle were incompatible, her poem is addressed to a male mentor, almost certainly Dr Samuel Bowden.

Whatever the value of such testimony by the poets themselves, there was a noticeable change, in some quarters at least, in male attitudes towards women writers at the mid-century, even if the extent of what was being conceded should not be exaggerated. In 1748 Thomas Seward, father of Anna (nos. 204–12), published 'The Female Right to Literature' in Dodsley's *Collection of Poems*. Seward condemned 'The coward insults of that tyrant, man, | Self-prais'd, and grasping at despotick pow'r', who had enslaved women throughout history, and through 'Custom' still binds 'In chains of ignorance the female mind', 'her doom, | Fix'd to the toilette, the spinnet, and loom'. By now the accusations were familiar, if less so from a man, but Seward's closing commendation of the 'humble' nature of 'Athenia', his addressee, and his warnings against 'pertness', a 'self-assuming air', and 'Vanity', suggest that he was not exactly liberating women from their traditional literary diffidence. George Ballard's *Memoirs of Several Ladies of Great Britain who have been Celebrated for their Writings* (Oxford, 1752) and John Duncombe's listing of mostly post-Restoration writers in *The Feminiad* (1754; revised as *The Feminead*, 1757) helped to establish something of a canon of women authors on which later writers could draw. In 1755 George Colman and Bonnell Thornton edited *Poems by Eminent Ladies*, a substantial anthology in two volumes of verse by some eighteen women from Katherine Philips to Mary Jones, as 'a standing proof that great abilities are not confined to the men, and that genius often glows with equal warmth, and perhaps with more delicacy, in the breast of a female . . . this collection is not inferior to any miscellany compiled from the works of men'. The editors publicized the anthology in their periodical *The Connoisseur*, in a curious dream-vision involving several of the poets, which ends with the spirited Laetitia Pilkington giving the dreamer a stinging slap on the face. In case this collection should be taken as merely the creation of a female 'ghetto', it is worth noting that biographies of fifteen women had recently appeared in Robert Shiells' *Lives of the Poets* (1753).

In *The Feminiad* John Duncombe went out of his way to praise Samuel Richardson, the printer and novelist, as 'the sex's friend, | And constant patron'. In his fiction, most notably in *Clarissa* (1747–8), Richardson had given a new literary centrality to female consciousness and experience, powerfully dramatizing the moral choices and dilemmas faced by women: Anna Williams (no. 158) and, in the next generation, Hannah More (no. 217) testified to the impact of his novels. It is well known that Richardson also had a circle of women friends and correspondents, some of whom themselves became authors, and whose opinion he anxiously sought while writing his novels. Although his letters reveal him as a champion of 'female genius' against the scepticism of some of his female as well as male friends, he was equally insistent on woman's primary responsibilities: 'the great and indispensable duties of women are of the domestic kind; and . . . if a woman neglects those, or despises them, for the sake of science itself, which I call learning, she is good for nothing' (to Lady Bradshaigh, 1753). Women should cultivate their minds, not as an end in itself, but to become 'intellectual, as well as domestic, companions to men of the best sense'. Involved in the literary world in a double capacity, Richardson shrewdly sensed the increasingly important part to be played by female taste: 'The men are hastening apace, dwindling into index, into common-place, into dictionary learning. The ladies, in turn, will tell them what is in the works themselves—only taking care, as I hope, not to neglect their domestic duties' (to Lady Bradshaigh, 1751).

Richardson's circle in the 1750s to some extent overlapped with that of Samuel Johnson, who notably offered unsentimental and practical assistance to a number of women writers, especially to the blind Anna Williams (nos. 158–9) and Charlotte Lennox (nos. 149–50). Mrs Lennox's long struggle to survive as a professional author of fiction, translations, and drama, in which Johnson was a patient and loyal mentor, illustrates the problems faced by a woman who, in spite of powerful male support, seems to have failed to tread the tightrope of social respectability and propriety in a way which would commend her to the fashionable female literary establishment of the second half of the century. Johnson himself saw the increasing number of women writers as merely part of the larger phenomenon of the expanding book trade in 'the Age of Authors', in which those 'of all degrees of ability, of every kind of education, of every profession and employment' were rushing into print. In his remarks on this subject in the *Adventurer*, admiration is tempered by some apprehension at the uncertain implications of this new female boldness:

In former times, the pen, like the sword, was considered as consigned by nature to the hands of men; the ladies contented themselves with private virtues and domestic excellence; and a female writer, like a female warrior, was considered as a kind of eccentric being, that deviated, however illustriously, from her due sphere of motion, and was, therefore, rather to be gazed at with wonder, than countenanced by imitation. But as the times past are said to have seen a nation of Amazons, who drew the bow and wielded the battle-ax, formed encampments and wasted nations; the revolution of the years has now produced a generation of Amazons of the pen, who with the spirit of their predecessors have set masculine tyranny at defiance, asserted their claim to the regions of science, and seem resolved to contest the usurpations of virility. (No. 115, 11 Dec. 1753)

Among other examples, Johnson would have had in mind his friend Elizabeth Carter (nos. 110–12). By the time Mrs Cockburn published her lines about the obstructions facing women authors in 1737, the youthful Carter had already embarked on a literary career which would suggest new possibilities and triumphs for later generations. A regular contributor to the *Gentleman's Magazine* from the 1730s when she first met Johnson, she was encouraged by Edward Cave and other literary men, and by her early twenties had won a high reputation as poet, translator, and scholar. This was achieved only by remarkable singlemindedness and determination, a strong temperamental urge to independence, and an ability to maintain a reputation in the literary world of the strictest social respectability and moral rectitude. For Richardson, who printed her 'Ode to Wisdom' in *Clarissa*, she was 'an example, that women may be trusted with Latin and even Greek, and yet not think themselves above their domestic duties' (to Lady Bradshaigh, 1751). He later described her as 'ranked among our English Classics' and as superior to the doubts and inhibitions of 'the low & narrow-hearted of the one Sex or the other' (to Thomas Edwards, 25 July 1754). Her translation of Epictetus, supported by a huge subscription, not merely won her financial security but, with her collected *Poems* (1762), made her the first widely cited inspirational example for women writers with serious literary ambitions in the second half of the century. As far as her verse was concerned, she was quick to adopt the manner of the new poetry of the 1740s, stanzaic, self-consciously elevated and refined, polished in diction, and earnest in moral import. Another adept in the polished mode was Hester Mulso Chapone (no. 157), also admired by Richardson and Johnson.

The price to be paid for this poetic idiom and its new refinement of taste was that it had to exclude so much of the informality, immediacy, and humour of earlier verse by women. With the onset of 'the Age of Sensibility', such writing would soon appear unrefined and old-fashioned. Mary Jones and Mary Leapor, the most intelligent and individual female voices of the 1740s, no doubt rapidly became dated and earthbound in their reliance on couplets, the firm social context of their verse, their humour, moral shrewdness, and self-awareness. Only the naïve, the provincial, the deliberately unpretentious, or those confident of an amused private audience, would continue to write in informal or humorous modes, although, fortunately, there were many who did so. For better or worse—and the farcical portentousness of the comment would have gratified her—Mary Jones's description for the amusement of her fashionable readers in 1750 of the General's painful attack of wind (no. 109, ll. 47–56) signalled the end of an era.

(iii)

By the mid-century there was a growing consensus that women deserved an improved education, if only to fit them to be better wives and mothers, and there was increasing male sympathy for women writers, within certain limits. Changing male attitudes can in fact be traced in detail in a particular and influential quarter, which must at first have helped to reinforce the usual diffidence of women writers. The institution of systematic book-reviewing, first in Ralph Griffiths' *Monthly Review* (from 1749) and later in Smollett's *Critical Review* (from 1756), with many shorter-lived imitators, was itself a response to the ever-increasing flood of miscellaneous publications. Some interesting reactions from the *Monthly* will be considered, primarily because the anonymous reviewers can usually be identified from the editor's own marked set of the periodical. Griffiths himself seems always to have been sympathetic to women writers of merit, including long reviews in the early years of the *Monthly* of Mary Jones, Mary Leapor, and Catherine Cockburn. (Trivial publications, including most novels, were relegated to brief notice in the 'Monthly Catalogue' at the back of each number.) In the 1750s and 1760s his reviewers, however, were often patronizingly chivalrous towards women authors, especially when they were pious, distressed, or supported by reputable subscribers. Hannah More later recalled the mortification for a woman writer 'of having her sex always taken into account . . . with the qualified approbation, *that it is really extraordinary for a woman*' (*Strictures on . . . Female Education*, 1799, ii. 15).

While always inclined to such 'softer' or 'compassionate' treatment, the reviewers were increasingly aware of the importance of women as authors and readers. In one aspect this is reflected in a growing concern for delicacy and propriety, the assurances that a book contained nothing to offend an 'innocent daughter', alarm 'female delicacy', or bring blushes to virgin cheeks. If the reviewers were driven at times to defend the correctness and purity of the English language against the improprieties of women writers, they responded on the whole less harshly than they did to semi-educated males, who were often sternly advised to abandon their literary pretensions and rest content with their appropriately humble stations in life. As early as 1763 John Langhorne, for many years the chief poetry reviewer for the *Monthly*, took a stand against the growing number of 'unlettered candidates for fame' (which included women by definition), whose often loose grasp of etymology and grammar threatened linguistic propriety and purity (xxix. 74–5). On the other hand the reviewer of an educational work by Sarah Maese in 1766 concluded that she must have had male assistance, since *The School* was 'more correct than could be expected from a female pen' (xxxv. 149).

This was at a lower level than that of so inspiring an exception as Elizabeth Carter, whose translation of Epictetus convinced Owen Ruffhead in 1758 that if women 'had the same opportunity of improvement with the men, there can be no doubt that they would be equally capable of reaching any intellectual attainment' (xviii. 588). For others, the belief that some kinds of literary endeavour were simply not 'feminine' died hard. Reviewing the first volume of Catherine Macaulay's elaborate *History of England* in 1763, William Rose conceded that 'the great number of the Fair Sex, who have figured in the republic of letters' had proved that women 'have powers to keep pace with, if not to outstrip us, in the more arduous paths of literature'. Rose was not persuaded, however, that 'the soft and delicate texture of a female frame' was fitted for 'severe study', and he relied on ghastly facetiousness to make the point:

Intense thought spoils a lady's features; it banishes *le ris et les graces*, which form all the enchantment of a female face. Who ever saw Cupid hovering over a severe and studious brow? and who would not keep at awful distance from a fair one, who looks with all the gravity of a Greek professor? Besides, severe thought, it is well known, anticipates old age, makes the forehead wrinkle, and hair turn grey. . . . In truth, it is every way dangerous for the fair, for while they are wrapt in a profound reverie, they may lose—We don't know what they may lose. (xxix. 372–82)

Such a reaction might seem to justify the sentiments of an ironic poem, 'To all the Ladies oppressed with irresistible Genius', in the *Gentleman's Magazine* in 1768 (pp. 486–7), which concludes:

> Oh dread the skill of writing well,
> For fear you shou'd the men excel,
>   Who will such excellence despise;
> Since men who judge the female race,
> Think ignorance their sweetest grace,
>   And love the silly, not the wise.

Such attitudes would soon seem dated. Elizabeth Montagu's *Essay on the Writings and Genius of Shakespear* (1769), a critical defence of the great dramatist against the strictures of Voltaire, was widely acclaimed as new evidence of female intellectual capacity and placed her, according to William Cowper, 'at the head of all that is called learned' (to Lady Hesketh, 27 May 1788). Like her friend Elizabeth Carter after 1762, Mrs Montagu did not risk further publication, but they were to play a conspicuous part in the new intellectual circles of the so-called 'Bluestockings', in which men and women increasingly conversed as equals. Hester Mulso Chapone's *Letters on the Improvement of the Mind* (1773) only reinforced this new literary respectability.

By then the generation of women who had grown up in the more generous atmosphere of the mid-century were about to make female prominence in at least some fields of literary activity seem quite natural and inevitable. In context, there is a striking confidence and authority in the *Poems* (1773) of Anna Aikin Barbauld, significantly, perhaps, the product of a liberal dissenting background. There was no female precedent for the accomplishment of the blank verse in her 'Corsica', as her reviewer William Woodfall recognized, finding in it 'a smoothness and harmony, equal to that of our best poets'. Miss Aikin's verse displayed 'a justness of thought, and vigour of imagination, inferior only to the works of Milton and Shakespeare'. In spite of such admiration, and his professions of superiority 'to the popular notions which have so long been humiliating to the fair sex', Woodfall was distinctly, even irrationally, uneasy, precisely because, it would seem, her verse was not self-evidently 'feminine'. He feebly wished that she had written more about love, always a properly female subject, and regretted that she had 'trod too much in the footsteps of men', suggesting that she must have been educated by her father rather than her mother, and advising her to be content with more 'feminine beauties' (*Monthly Review*, xlviii. 133–7). Although her *Poems* immediately won her a high reputation, it may be that Mrs Barbauld (as she soon became) took such a reaction seriously. Potentially the most versatile of women poets in the period, she accepted for many years a subordinate role in an eventually painful marriage, contenting herself with writing books for children. She professed to having no interest in making the education of girls more 'serious' after the age of fifteen, when the onset of 'the passions' would prevent them from concentrating on study; and, later, in the post-Wollstonecraft era, denied that there was any 'bond of union among literary women' and refused to 'provoke a war with the other sex' (headnote to nos. 195–203).

A few months after Woodfall's article on Miss Aikin in 1773, John Langhorne introduced a favourable account of Hannah More's *Search after Happiness* with a fantasy of condescending chivalry about the male reviewer as a knight-errant, monster-slayer, and protector of the fair female author (*Monthly Review*, xlix. 202–4). More's rapid social and literary success as dramatist, poet, and essayist in the next few years rendered such gallantry as superfluous as her own rehearsal of the old anxieties of the woman writer in her pastoral drama (no. 215). The impact of these two young women writers was soon consolidated by the success of Hannah Cowley (nos. 252–4) as a dramatist from 1776 and of Fanny Burney's brilliant first novel *Evelina* in 1778 (no. 232). Mary Scott's *The Female Advocate* (1774), which reinforced the female canon outlined by Duncombe two decades earlier and protested about male condescension to women writers, was already dated, as she herself seems to have realised (headnote to no. 213). The rapidly changing situation seems, however, to have rattled Miss Scott's joint reviewers, Woodfall and Langhorne, who reacted with irrational hostility to her accusations and her predictions of future female intellectual triumphs. Their pretext was scepticism about the superficial literary education given to the products of girls' boarding-schools, but it seems to have been rather the growing self-confidence of women which disconcerted them: 'It is dreadful for a man of real knowledge and politeness to encounter one of these literary vixens. . . . The effects of real knowledge are gentleness and modesty, particularly in a sex where any thing approaching to assurance is intolerable' (*Monthly Review*, lvii. 387–90).

There were others who responded to the changing situation by reiterating that the characteristic ornament of the female sex was 'amiable sensibility', to be displayed in only a limited number of literary genres, that the mental and creative abilities of men and women were clearly differentiated, and that the rising status of women authors was introducing ominous 'innovations'. An essayist in 1777 argued that nature and custom prescribed necessary bounds to each sex, 'which the prudent and the candid will never attempt to break down'. The 'natural and moral' fragility of women meant that they would necessarily 'find their protection in their weakness, and their safety in their delicacy'. Providence had ordained the public sphere as the 'proper element' for men, not women. The female mind was capable of 'lively imaginations' and 'exquisite perceptions', but not a masculine 'strength of intellect'. Poetry by women would be characterized by 'the beautiful, the soft, the delicate'. 'There are green pastures, and pleasant vallies, where they may wander with safety to themselves, and delight to others. They may cultivate the roses of imagination, and the valuable fruits of morals and criticism'; but 'the steeps of Parnassus'—epic, tragedy, satire—'seem reserved for the bold adventurers of the other sex'. Women who had succeeded in invading male territory—Carter, Macaulay, Montagu—should be considered as exceptions, not models.

Such are the arguments and assertions not of some threatened male, but of Hannah More in her *Essays* (pp. 3–14) in 1777, at the height of her new celebrity in London. Far from wishing to lead a new generation of independent literary women to fresh triumphs, More evidently feared that her own success might only mislead impressionable young women. (In the same year, Frances Brooke, who herself enjoyed a long and successful career as dramatist and novelist, published *The Excursion*, a novel describing the dangers awaiting her heroine, a would-be author, in London, experiences which finally persuade her to return to a contented domestic life.) While everyone agreed that the education of women should continue to be improved—Hannah More believed that it still tended to delude girls into thinking 'that human life consisted of one universal holiday'—the aim was not to imbue women with ambitions of independence or literary fame, but 'to make them good daughters, good wives, good mistresses, good members of society, and good christians' (*Essays*, pp. 131–2).

Yet in the 1780s women virtually took over, as writers and readers, the territories most readily conceded to them, of popular fiction and fashionable poetry. The emergence early in the decade of Anna Seward (nos. 204–12), Helen Maria Williams (nos. 267–71), and Charlotte Smith (nos. 237–43), each of whom for a time enjoyed high reputation, consolidated the advances made by women poets in the 1770s. William Hayley, in his *Essay on Epic Poetry* (1782), p. 75, hailed Seward as the new 'leader of the lovely train' of British poetesses, whose 'potent strain' was spreading 'Poetic jealousy and envious dread' in 'spirits masculine'. (Hayley's encouragement of yet more women to turn to poetry could produce both excitement and frustration, as for Catherine Stephens: 'In vain I strive to grasp the living bay, | In vain with Hayley's verse my cottage rings', *Gentleman's Magazine*, 1790, i. 450.) Visible male competition with the new generation of women poets, provided by Hayley himself and the likes of Henry James Pye, was not as vigorous as it might have been. Gray and Goldsmith had died in the 1770s; veterans of an earlier poetic period, such as Johnson, Mason, and the Wartons, were no longer very active; and it must be remembered that, of the poets who loom retrospectively in the 1780s, Crabbe and Blake were mostly invisible still to their contemporaries, Burns was a special case as yet another 'natural genius', and Cowper's prominence also came only in the later years of the decade.

In 1789 Anna Seward named seven distinguished contemporary women poets as Barbauld, More, Williams, Piozzi, Carter, Cowley, and Smith (*Gentleman's Magazine*, i. 292), leaving it to the editor to underline the conspicuous modesty of the omission of her own name. Several at least of these writers would always be cited in any list of important living poets in the 1780s. There were, of course, many other aspirants for poetic fame who published their slim or not so slim volumes, or at least sent their verses to magazines and newspapers. (William Upton, a minor poet, boasted in 1789 that he had published verses in a newspaper under the name of 'Louisa' and had received several ardent poetic replies from male admirers.) Occasional derision of the sheer number of poetesses was inevitable, as from the anonymous author of *Modern Poets* (1791):

> See *Phoebus* trembling on th' Aonian hill,
> The clamorous *Fair* surround—*en deshabille*;
> Like flocks of geese Saint Michael's day that bless,
> Not less their *numbers*, nor their *cackling* less.
> What troops of *Druidesses* now assail,
> Their meteor-hair streams round their visage pale,
> All grim with snuff their nose, and black their length of nail!
>
> (p. 23)

In substance this was hardly more than the old dismissal of literary women as undomesticated slatterns. Closer to the mark, perhaps, was John Aikin's comment in 1796 that writing verse had become as common a polite accomplishment for young ladies as music or drawing, which he believed should be similarly confined to 'the parlour' (*Monthly Review*, New Series xx. 224). There were other signs of the impact of female taste, as authors boasted that they had avoided 'hard words' to please the ladies, publishers produced abridgements of major literary texts for their fair readers, male poets complained that satire was being emasculated by the dominant female audience for poetry, and critics feared that only the most superficial literary kinds were flourishing and that solid learning was in decline. Female taste was inevitably blamed for the vogue for sentimental fiction and poetry. Reviewing Henry Hodgson's *Effusions of the Heart and Fancy* (1779), Samuel Badcock reviled 'all those weak-stomached sentimentalists' who had 'quite overwhelmed a large part of the reading public of the *softer* sex', and who, if not resisted, would 'overwhelm the little sense which is left among us; and settle in one dull and stagnant pond of sentimental insipidity' (*Monthly Review*, lxi. 337–40).

It may perhaps be a boast of the present anthology that it underrepresents the insipidity of the fashionable poetry of this period, the many eastern pastorals, legendary tales (of which see an example by Joanna Baillie, no. 280), imitations of Ossian, laments for dead birds and small animals, and all the odes to Fancy, Sensibility, Pity, and other personifications which proliferated and which teenagers were finding it all too easy to mimic (head-note to no. 290). Less stilted and abstracted verse was still being written and has here been preferred. Some homely writers had clearly never heard about the requirements of polite taste. A talented writer in the provinces like Susanna Blamire (nos. 183–91) did not aim at publication and shared a liking for detailed observation of local rural life with Joanna Baillie (nos. 278–85), the earthiness and vigour of whose impressive first volume of verse (1790) were unfashionable and predictably ignored. Of the better known women poets of the 1780s, it may be noted that they did not, for a variety of reasons, quite consolidate their original impact. The often-invoked Carter and Barbauld had been mostly silent; Hannah Cowley remained primarily a dramatist; Hannah More and Helen Maria Williams, with diametrically opposed social and political attitudes, and Hester Thrale Piozzi (no. 255), turned increasingly to prose; and Charlotte Smith (nos. 237–43), admired especially for her anguished sonnets, was driven to support herself and her family by the steadier if hardly munificent financial rewards of fiction, as eventually were Mary Robinson (nos. 302–7) and Isabella Kelly (no. 309). Only Anna Seward seems always to have thought of herself as primarily a poet and had a lofty conception of the poetic vocation. Far from being a leader of her generation of women writers, however, she was in practice often sharply critical of her contemporaries; and her own elevated poetic ambitions were often expressed through an elaborate syntax and glittering diction which were increasingly criticized at the time as affectations and which do, indeed, detract from the undoubted intensity and individuality of which she was capable.

Yet, as the 1790s began, a striking indication of changing attitudes to women writers appeared in a paper (1791) 'On the Uses of Classical Learning' by Dr George Gregory, later printed in the *Memoirs of the Literary and Philosophical Society of Manchester*, iv. (1793), 109–30. Early in the century ignorance of the classics had been a reason for diffidence and apology on the part of women and other 'uneducated' writers, an intimidating obstacle to serious literary respectability. For Dr Gregory by 1791, the recent achievements of Anna Seward, Helen Maria Williams, Hannah Cowley and others, 'all unacquainted with the languages and compositions of the ancients', had become telling evidence that 'fastidious' attitudes to the classically uneducated were unjustified, and that the importance of the classics to literary distinction had been exaggerated.

Other evidence suggests that woman poets no longer expected hostility on grounds of gender, but were prepared for condescension on grounds of class. In the manner of Barber, Leapor, and Lewis at an earlier period, two women in the 1780s visualized the reception of their verse in the fashionable world. Jane West (no. 251), a farmer's wife who conducted her long and productive literary career from a Leicestershire village, did envisage a 'beau' gallantly professing to prefer pretty female eyes to pretty female verses, and a university don who studied only dead authors. Hostility, however, came from the aristocrat who saw a social threat in the encouragement of a lower-class writer, fearing that, if rustics became 'refined', they would also become dissatisfied with their 'humble duties' and start dictating to their betters. Elizabeth Hands, by then married to a blacksmith, published two unexpectedly derisive poems (nos. 276–7) which imagine reactions to the advertisement and publication of the poems of a servant. Given that her book was supported by a subscription among the local gentry, Hands depicts with remarkable lack of inhibition the condescension, if not contempt, she expected to greet her verse, sketching in with some deftness an upper-class world of female promiscuity and frivolity, bankrupt financiers, and debt-ridden aristocrats in which these ignorant and patronizing discussions take place. Hands took for granted that it would be the women in the company who insisted that, if female servants learnt to read more than cookery-books and works of piety, or to write more than recipes and letters to their mothers, they would start to neglect their work.

Any discussion of women writers in the eighteenth century will—or should—always find issues of gender entangled with those of class. Women of the higher classes enjoyed the possibility of better education than most men and could, as did the Countess of Hertford and Lady Mary Wortley Montagu, become the patrons of male authors. At the other end of the century, Anna Seward encouraged and 'corrected' the writings of younger male poets and patronized William Newton, the uneducated 'Derbyshire Minstrel'. Elizabeth Montagu was the patron, and for a time the employer, of James Woodhouse, the 'shoemaker poet' of the 1760s, who later reacted resentfully against her treatment of him. The most instructive and explosive entanglement of class and gender was that of Ann Yearsley of Bristol (nos. 256–9), the working-class poet of formidable personality and forceful if idiosyncratic poetic gifts, who was rescued from destitution by Hannah More and Elizabeth Montagu in 1784. Her violent quarrel with her well-meaning but condescending patrons, who had no intention of encouraging her to become a writer or of raising her more than marginally above her humble station, is a remarkable episode.

(iv)

Some evidence may by now have been provided to explain the optimistic claim by Ralph Griffiths in 1798, quoted at the opening of this introduction, that women had finally established their intellectual equality and that the long debate on the subject had been concluded. Griffiths was reviewing the *Poetic Trifles* of Elizabeth Moody (nos. 260–3), an intelligent writer of unpretentious but amusing verse, who, as Griffiths knew, was happily married to a literary husband and who subordinated her poetic interests to her domestic responsibilities (as she herself self-mockingly admitted). However heart-warming the case of Mrs Moody may have been, Griffiths was guilty of wishful thinking if he really believed the debate was over. Even as he wrote, it was rumbling on, as in the pages of the *Gentleman's Magazine* in the autumn of 1798. An article calling on women to adopt an even more inspirational moral role in society (ii. 736–9) aroused a spirited response from a writer who claimed to find men still

so jealous of their titles as lords of creation, so jealous of female rivalry in the scale of acquirements, that it has been their constant study to keep women within that contracted pale of knowledge as shall prevent their approach but at an humble distance; to check those blossoms which exhibit an appearance of ripening into independence or mental equality. The moral aristocracy of the males in this respect is as striking and as rooted as that which we have often had occasion to lament in the political world. Surely, Sir, if this be true, we cannot have much ground for exulting in the 'high rank which woman holds in society'. (ii. 945–6)

The whole debate had in fact acquired a new political dimension in the aftermath of the French Revolution with the uncompromising feminism of Mary Wollstonecraft and others. Some of the pained male reactions to these claims for moral and political freedom for women deserve brief illustration. Reviewing Maria Edgeworth's *Letters for Literary Ladies* (1795), William Enfield contrasted her praiseworthy proposals for educating women to be interesting wives and mothers with those 'high-spirited females . . . with a firm tone of philosophical pride' who had recently argued that women should be 'educated for an equal share with the men in all the labours and honours of literary and political life'. Enfield viewed with dismay the prospect of 'converting all our affectionate wives, kind mothers, and lovely daughters, into studious philosophers, or busy politicians' (*Monthly Review*, New Series xx, 1796, 24–7).

The new feminist agenda and the tone in which it was announced shattered the carefully constructed boundaries of the acceptably 'feminine'. In 1798, when Griffiths was praising Mrs Moody, Richard Polwhele published *The Unsex'd Females*, an attack, whose violence is limited only by his mediocre poetic talents, on the women writers who had abandoned 'natural' sexual modesty—in some cases leading lives of open sexual irregularity (as had Helen Maria Williams and Wollstonecraft)—supported the new democratic politics imported from France, and even demanded political equality. 'See Wollstonecraft whom no decorum checks', groaned Polwhele, adding other names more relevant to this anthology, such as Barbauld, Robinson, Smith, Williams, and Yearsley, whom he accused of democratic sympathies. Against this 'female band despising NATURE's law' and advocating 'Gallic licentiousness', especially against the 'alarming eccentricities' of Wollstonecraft, Polwhele fielded a team of writers who had always maintained the modest refinement proper to women, apparently accepting that 'it is Christianity which has given women their appropriate rank in society': Montague, Carter, Chapone, Seward, Piozzi, Burney, Radcliffe, and More. Amid all this outrage, however, Polwhele was still capable of a shrewd footnote (p. 16) on the insulting 'species of gallantry' which had once greeted the rare phenomenon of a female author: 'It implied such an inferiority of woman in the scale of intellect as was humiliating.' Now that women writers were so numerous, critics ignored what had become the clichés of female literary anxiety, 'the blushes of modest apprehension', 'the pleading eye of female diffidence that speaks of a consciousness of comparative imbecillity', 'the flimsy veil of affected timidity, that only serves to hide the smile of complacency; the glow of self-gratulation'.

Even when humorous, other male responses can be revealing about the subversion of traditional assumptions about class and gender in the 1790s. Among the forthcoming publications listed in 'Literary Prophecies for

1797' by 'Tiresias, Jun.' in the *Monthly Magazine* in February 1797 are

> Two Pindaric Odes, by a hackney coachman; a Collection of Sentimental Sonnets by a washer-woman; and an Epic Poem, in twenty books, by a printer's devil. ...
>
> A novel, by a lady, will make some noise, in which the heroine begins by committing a rape, and ends with killing her man in a duel. (iii. 92–3)

Such fear of women's new 'muscular power' was echoed in John Ferriar's review of Mary Robinson's *A Letter to the Women of England* (1799), first published under the name of Anne Frances Randall, in which he argued that 'Far from considering women as oppressed, we think that their influence is unlimited'. Ferriar professed, indeed, to be intimidated:

> We forbear any farther remarks on this vigorous and impatient writer; lest we should have occasion to exclaim, with the gentleman who was knocked down by an uncomplying mistress;
>
> 'Those frowns are cruel, but that *fist* is death!'
>
> (*Monthly Review*, New Series xxix. 477–8)

While the men fumed or flinched, it was left once more to Hannah More, in her *Strictures on the Modern System of Female Education* (1799), to exert her considerable influence (the book reached a ninth edition by 1801) against 'those petty and absurd contentions for equality which female smatterers so anxiously maintain'. The 'higher minds in each sex' desired 'co-operation and not competition'. The 'political as well as intellectual pretensions' of the feminists were exciting in the hearts of women 'an impious discontent with the post which God has assigned them in his world'. More reaffirmed the boundaries of the properly feminine in 'polite letters': 'A woman sees the world, as it were, from a little elevation in her own garden, whence she makes an exact survey of home scenes, but takes not in that wider range of distant prospects which he who stands on a loftier eminence commands' (ii. 16–30).

In the perspectives of conventional literary history and the institutionalized poetic canon these agitations may hardly seem to matter any more. What helped to consign most of the contents of this anthology to virtual oblivion was yet another literary event of 1798, the publication of the *Lyrical Ballads*, its later 'Preface', and the eventual triumph of high Romanticism. Superficially more democratic than Richard Steele's definition of the poet as 'a very well-bred Man', Wordsworth's notion of the poet may seem even more relentlessly masculine and, in the loftiness of his conception of poetic genius, even more exclusive. Throughout the 'Preface' of 1800, 'man', 'men', 'manly' always accompany his definitions of the poet and poetry: the poet, who will write in a 'manly' style, will use 'the real language of men' and is 'a man speaking to men'. In attacking the 'gaudy and inane phraseology' of fashionable poetry, Wordsworth (ostensibly attacking Thomas Gray) was in fact echoing the charge repeatedly levelled at women poets by reviewers and others in the 1780s and 1790s, that they were 'phrase-haberdashers' (John Williams, *Poetical Works*, 1789, ii. 248–50), that they were particularly attracted by the tinsel and glare of poetic language (*Monthly Review*, New Series xiii, 1794, 77–9), that they liked tinsel ornament in poetry more than male readers (*European Magazine*, xxviii, 1795, 321–2). The 'gentle reader', whose false expectations Wordsworth mocks in a poem like 'Simon Lee', was almost certainly female.

If Steele's definition of the poet in 1712 might seem effectively to exclude women from a male preserve, Wordsworth's formulations may appear calculated rather to recover that territory from the women who had recently occupied it. That is what may be enacted in the conclusion to 'Tintern Abbey', a poem variously read as preoccupied with nature, memory, poetry and, recently, politics. In the present context its most striking feature would appear to be the sublime condescension with which Wordsworth relegates his sister to a place on the foothills far below the heights of his own poetic development and moral grandeur. No more than a mirror of his immature self, Dorothy is also a representative of a generation of women poets. Oddly, Wordsworth was claiming imaginatively what, as we have seen, Hannah More would readily concede to the male poet in the following year, 'that wider range of distant prospects which he who stands on a loftier eminence commands'.

The 'revolution' announced by the *Lyrical Ballads* has always been retrospectively exaggerated and its impact was far from immediate. In the next generation John Keats was still irritated by the knowledge that readers of his poetry were likely to be female: as a friend reported, 'He says he does not want ladies to read his poetry: he writes for men' (*Letters*, ii. 163). Nevertheless, Romantic subjectivity and transcendence, the 'egotistical sublime', the confident assumption of priestly and visionary powers, quite apart from the issue of undoubted poetic genius, would effectively recover poetry for men, leaving most of the contents of the present anthology outdated or ignorable as mere 'verse'. Before the turn of the century Anna Barbauld seems to have sensed acutely what lay ahead, in her warnings to S. T. Coleridge (no. 203) in 1797. Barbauld evokes the mysteries and dangers of an 'unearthly' Romanticism, in which 'things of life, | Obvious to sight and touch'—as in her amusing 'Washing-Day' (no. 202), an exercise of the 'domestic Muse, | In slipshod measure loosely prattling on'—could have no place:

> . . . A grove extends; in tangled mazes wrought,
> And filled with strange enchantments:—dubious shapes
> Flit through dim glades, and lure the eager foot
> Of youthful ardour to eternal chase.
> Dreams hang on every leaf: unearthly forms
> Glide through the gloom; and mystic visions swim
> Before the cheated sense. Athwart the mists,
> Far into vacant space, huge shadows stretch
> And seem realities; while things of life,
> Obvious to sight and touch, all glowing round,
> Fade to the hue of shadows.

The cause of the women writers was not helped by the fact that none were included in the huge multi-volume compilations of the works of the English poets assembled by Robert Anderson (1792–5) and Alexander Chalmers (1810), which, as I have argued in an earlier anthology, have always had a remarkable influence on subsequent views of eighteenth-century verse. A partial explanation is that no living authors were included by Anderson and Chalmers and many of the best known women poets were still alive in 1810. Alexander Dyce, who attempted to remedy this situation in his *Specimens of the British Poetesses* (1825), nevertheless believed that 'the productions of women had been carefully excluded' by the earlier editors. A diligent explorer of 'the chaos of our past Poetry', Dyce had space to give only brief and, where possible, lyrical examples of his poets (including some forty from the eighteenth century) so that the cumulative effect of his representation remains slight. And, as if conscious of increasingly elevated expectations of what true poetry should be, he finally admitted to some lack of conviction about what he had assembled:

It is true that the grander inspirations of the Muse have not been often breathed into the softer frame. The magic tones which have added a new existence to the heart— the tremendous thoughts which have impressed a successive stamp on the fluctuation of ages, and which have almost changed the characters of nations,—these have not proceeded from woman; but her sensibility, her grace, have not been lost or misemployed; her genius has gradually risen with the opportunities which facilitated its ascent. (pp. iii–iv)

Ironically, no one was to express greater interest in Dyce's *Specimens* than the elderly Wordsworth, for some time an admirer of Lady Winchilsea, who also became nostalgic about the poetry of Charlotte Smith, Helen Maria Williams, and even Anna Seward which he had admired in his youth. He was aware of the limitations of Dyce's selection but his offers in the early 1830s to assist with an improved edition were not accepted.

Wordsworth's comment to Dyce in 1830 about the verse of Lady Mary Wortley Montagu, that 'She seems to have been destined for something higher than she achieved', might appear a fitting epitaph for much of the material in the present anthology. It was not merely its inaccessibility to most later readers but transformed assumptions about what poetry should be which led Elizabeth Barrett Browning in 1845 to complain about the inexplicable absence of poetic 'grandmothers' for mid-nineteenth-century women writers. Before Joanna Baillie (whose earliest volume of verse she would not have known), she could think of no 'poetess in the true sense', although she was aware of the Duchess of Newcastle in the seventeenth century and of Wordsworth's praise of Lady Winchilsea's 'eye'. Lady Mary Wortley Montagu's 'graceful *vers de société*' could hardly be described as 'poetry'. A few days later she had recalled a few exceptions, such as 'Auld Robin Gray' (no. 182), but would not concede that these were more than 'agreeable writers of verse sometimes, leaving the word poet alone': 'I look everywhere for grandmothers and see none. . . . is not the poet a different man from the cleverest versifier, and is it not well for the world to be taught the difference? The divineness of poetry is far more to me than either pride of sex or personal pride' (*Letters*, 1897, i. 229–31).

(v)

It has subsequently seemed crucial in some quarters 'for the world to be taught the difference' between true poetry and mere verse, a view in which 'verse' is not merely inferior but intolerable, and the failure to make the distinction a damaging lapse of critical discrimination. Eighteenth-century verse as a whole suffered for several generations from post-Romantic assumptions, and it is only relatively recently that, for example, a vigorous case has been made for the interest and importance of Swift's deliberately 'unpoetic' verse. In the course of the eighteenth century itself 'polite' taste had increasingly come to favour a poetry of self-conscious elevation above the facts of the mundane world, which produced much that was insipid and stilted. Throughout the century, however, there were many writers who expressed, in verse of a sociable, unpretentious, sometimes homely, sometimes idiosyncratic kind, interests and experiences which must contradict some of the generalizations made about the period. An earlier anthology, *The New Oxford Book of Eighteenth Century Verse* (1984), juxtaposed with the traditional canon of the period's verse the neglected work of many totally forgotten writers, both male and female. Its purpose was not to subvert the 'canon', nor to attack the subtlety, complexity, and imaginative power of great art. It was intended, however, as is the present anthology, to question some of the deeply ingrained preconceptions about what it was possible to feel, think, and write in the eighteenth century.

To devote a further anthology to an even wider representation of women poets of the period may run the risk of seeming to segregate them from the literary mainstream, which would be misleading. Yet, although they shared some problems of acceptability with their less privileged male contemporaries, it is not unreasonable to consider them in some aspects as a special case, given their educational insecurities and the constricted notions of the properly 'feminine' in social and literary behaviour they faced. Although their literary confidence markedly increased during the century, and even their verse reflects improved opportunities for travel and a readiness to contribute to debate on social and political matters, there had been little change in their legal or political status or in the genuine autonomy available to them. That limitation underlies the last poem in this anthology, the Duchess of Devonshire's account of her journey across the Alps (no. 323): what is not made explicit, although it animates her eagerness to return to her children, is that she was travelling back to England from the exile imposed by her promiscuous husband for her own single indiscretion.

Most of the material in this collection has not been reprinted since its original publication and will be unfamiliar to its readers. Without the usual precedents against which the anthologist's judgements and criteria can be tested, one must rely on one's own instincts and interests, which will inevitably mean prejudices and predispositions. Any anthology will in some sense misrepresent what it professes to illustrate, and others, if they had been prepared to embark on a comparable exploration, would undoubtedly have chosen differently. The misrepresentation of the verse written by women in the eighteenth century of which I am most conscious is the limited space I have devoted to their efforts in the more ambitious or morally earnest genres, their pindaric odes, paraphrases of the Scriptures, hymns, didactic blank verse treatises, long narrative poems, legendary tales, historical epics, pastorals, and florid odes to personified virtues. These are usually no worse and no better, it should be said, than the similar exercises of their male contemporaries. Most of the forgotten writers of the period, both male and female, seem more convincing in their less pretentious flights, when trusting to their own observation and experience. For women such experience was usually, by definition, relatively constricted. They must inevitably lack, Hannah More prescribed, that 'consummate knowledge of the world to which a delicate woman has no fair avenues, and which even if she could attain, she would never be supposed to have come honestly by' (*Strictures*, 1799, ii. 28–9). Early in the century, in her 'The Dream', an adaptation of Chaucer, Jane Brereton humorously admitted the embarrassments facing even the persona of a female poet. It was all very well for a man to fall asleep on a flowery bank and have a dream-vision, but for a woman this might be dangerous:

> All this, and more, full well I know it,
> Might be perform'd by a Male Poet;
> Descriptions I must lay aside,
> I slept, and dreamt at the Fire-side:
> Tho' Men in the Fields may sleep, or roam,
> Woman had best to nap at Home.

> (*Poems*, 1744, pp. 33–4)

A reviewer might well later pounce on a less cautious woman poet, who had relaxed in a too 'easy posture', as when John Langhorne mischievously italicized some lines from Elizabeth Ryves' *Poems* (1777) to reveal her in an unguarded, and ungirdled, moment:

> Where a cool spring, o'er-arch'd with trees,
> Gives freshness to the languid breeze,
> There *(with robes unzon'd) supine*
> *I'll on the velvet moss recline!*

> (*Monthly Review*, lviii. 237)

To find the strength of at least some women's verse of the period in its acceptance of a limited social and domestic role may run the risk of seeming to conspire with the forces which confined them there. The fact is that, although there were some clear exceptions, women poets, like their unfashionable male contemporaries, were often intimidated by or indifferent to the loftier poetic genres and worked most happily in less self-conscious, sociable forms: most notably, throughout the century, in the familiar verse epistle, in which generic expectations were minimal, polished diction inappropriate, and the writer would be confident of her ability to amuse a friend whose interest was guaranteed. In these and similar forms, women were often aware that they were not meeting the highest poetic demands. Mary Barber (no. 90) envisaged 'high-born Belinda' complaining of her verse:

> 'Call it not poetry,' she says:
> 'No—call it rhyming, if you please'

and Elizabeth Hands (no. 277) later gave the judicious Rector the final assessment of her writing:

> 'That "Amnon", you can't call it poetry neither,
> There's no flights of fancy, or imagery either;
> You may style it prosaic, blank verse at the best . . .'

The positive aspect of such verse, for some readers at least, will be the unaffected conversational ease with which it can describe experiences unmuffled by stylistic and generic inhibitions and obligations. In the 1770s Susanna Blamire (no. 183) explained the attractions of the familiar epistolary style: 'these trite strains | Give me no sort of thought or pains', whereas 'sublimity of style | Takes up a most prodigious while'. Yet the 'Epistle to her Friends at Gartmore', which opens with such disclaimings of ambitious literary 'performance', is an amusing, animated, and in its own way artful account of her daily life.

It would be misleading to suggest that women were capable of no more than this. There is a strong line of interesting and engaging verse running through the century, from the intelligence and versatility of the socially confident Lady Winchilsea and Lady Mary Wortley Montagu, and the spirited if subsequently despised Elizabeth Thomas, through the new, domestically secure verse of Mary Barber, the search for poise and self-knowledge in different social spheres of Mary Jones and Mary Leapor in the 1740s, to the new generation who appeared in the 1770s. If Barbauld, More, and Seward were, for better or worse, by then abreast of poetic fashion rather than lagging after it, they still had invisible contemporaries such as Blamire and Baillie, who were unrepentantly devoted to humorous and graphic observation of humble rural life. Since nothing has been included which did not seem to offer some degree of interest in manner or matter, it is arbitrary to refer to only a few of the even less familiar women represented: Hetty Wright's expressions of marital anguish (nos. 79–82), Miss W——'s startling reaction, albeit in rudimentary verse, to Swift's misogynist disgust (no. 91), Elizabeth Amherst's high-spirited verse for her family and friends (nos. 120–4), Christian Carstairs' enigmatic, and perhaps merely eccentric, utterances (nos. 173–6), Mary Savage's modest but amiable and shrewd domestic ruminations (nos. 227–30), Hands's

INTRODUCTION

unsentimental sketches of rural life and amused contempt for her 'polite' readers (nos. 273–7), Anne Batten Cristall's fresh, if uneven, evocations of pastoral neuroses (nos. 310–11), and 'Eliza''s lively and self-mocking account of her scrambling on the glaciers (no. 315). A distinguished poet recently spoke dismissively on television about poems by his contemporaries which were little more than 'home movies', implying both narrowness of vision and technical incompetence. Although 'home movies' from the eighteenth century might offer much of interest, the accusation may seem an ominous one, and I am least confident that the discriminating reader will share my interest in what is articulated in the most naïve verse I have included, such as Mary Chandler's account of an unexpected and disconcerting proposal of marriage (no. 104), the social embarrassments of the blind Priscilla Pointon (no. 180), the curiously heartless dietary advice offered anonymously to a gentleman suffering from 'Looseness of his Teeth' (no. 222), Jane Cave Winscom's unavailing search for a cure for her devastating and unaccountable monthly headaches (nos. 248–9), and Hannah Wallis's naïve piety (nos. 264–6).

Short biographical accounts of the writers included seem called for by the very obscurity of so many of them, although this has posed its own special problems. There are modern biographies of only a handful, and while there have been a few recent scholarly investigations of some lesser figures, only inadequate information is so far available about most of them. Although I have usually managed to add something to what is known about them, I have also had to start virtually from scratch in a number of cases, such as those of Mary Locke, Isabella Kelly, and Anne Batten Cristall, to name only three writers from the 1790s. I am all too well aware of the provisional nature of such accounts. Even when one can see how information might be gleaned by assiduous local research, it would take a lifetime to track down so many individuals. If this anthology is ever to reach a second edition, it will certainly contain an appendix of further biographical information. Whatever their shortcomings, the biographical notes may serve to make the point that generalizations about women writers in the eighteenth century must take account of careers and circumstances as different as those of Mary Chandler and Laetitia Pilkington, of Elizabeth Carter and Mary Robinson, of Ann Yearsley and the Duchess of Devonshire.

EDITORIAL PRINCIPLES

In general I have followed the principles adopted in my *New Oxford Book of Eighteenth Century Verse* (1984), aiming at a basically chronological arrangement in which authors are introduced by the date of publication (or of composition, if known to be significantly different) of the first poem included, but in any case not later than the date of death. I have made an exception in the case of Elizabeth Thomas (nos. 24–32): the limited evidence available indicates that much of her verse was written well before her collection of 1722, and she has accordingly been placed in the first decade of the century. No such arrangement is entirely satisfactory, especially when poets wrote over several decades. Anyone interested in the kinds of verse women were writing in the 1790s, for example, should remember that poets such as Barbauld, More, and Seward, introduced in the 1770s, were still writing two decades later. I have accepted the arbitrariness of the dates 1700–99 and have not consciously included verse written outside those limits. For reasons of space I have excluded verse written by women in America in the period.

Except for some dialect poems, texts have been modernized as tactfully as possible. Such a decision can be made only with some reservations. While there is a gain for modern readers in intelligibility and in the removal of a distancing quaintness, some price has to be paid in the loss of the historical specificity of the texts. It should be remembered, however, that spelling, punctuation, and other accidental features of texts were as often the responsibility of printers as of the writers themselves in the period; and that a general modernization of printing practices, especially affecting the initial capitalization of nouns, occurred in the mid-eighteenth century itself, as can be seen in such anthologies as Dodsley's *Collection of Poems* (1748–58) and *Poems by Eminent Ladies* (1755).

Apart from glosses, notes accompanying the texts are those of the authors themselves, which I have not always given in full. Sources for the biographical headnotes and for the texts, with concise explanatory notes, appear at the end of the volume, keyed to the numbering, not the pagination, of the poems.

MARY, LADY CHUDLEIGH (née LEE)
(1656–1710)

She was the daughter of Richard Lee of Winslade, Devon. In 1674, at the age of 17, she married George Chudleigh, the 30-year-old son of Sir George Chudleigh of Ashton in Devon to whose baronetcy he succeeded in 1691. She had two sons, the elder of whom became the 3rd baronet in 1719, and a daughter, Eliza Maria, whose early death she laments in one of her poems. Although she corresponded with Mary Astell, John Norris of Bemerton, and Elizabeth Thomas (see nos. 24–32), she evidently led a lonely life in Devon. She admired Astell's early feminist writings and addressed a poem 'To Almystrea' (an anagram of her name). Influenced by Astell's *Some Reflections on Marriage* (1700), she published *The Ladies Defence* (1701), the prefatory address to which was signed 'M—y C————', in response to *The Bride-Womans Counsellor* (1699), a sermon preached at a wedding at Sherborne by the Nonconformist John Sprint, which advocated the total subordination of women to their husbands. Her poem is a verse-debate in which Melissa argues vigorously about female education, male attitudes, and the duties of a wife with three variously prejudiced men, representative of those who, according to her preface, had 'express'd an ill-natur'd sort of Joy' at seeing women ridiculed by Sprint.

The Ladies Defence was admired by Elizabeth Thomas, who addressed a poem to her and corresponded with her for some years. As she explained to Thomas in October 1701, 'I was troubl'd to see [women] made the Jest of every vain Pretender to Wit, and expos'd by a *Scurrilous Pamphlet*, rather than a *Sermon*, to the Malicious Censures of invidious Detracters, of Men, who think *they* cannot be *obedient Wives*, without being *Slaves*, nor pay their *Husbands* that *Respect* they owe them, without sacrificing their *Reason* to their *Humour*'. She was diffident about her literary abilities and urged Thomas to 'undertake the Quarrel, and do us Justice'. She also complained that interference by the printer had rendered her preface incoherent. In a later letter, inviting Thomas to visit her in Devon, she referred to the 'rough and unpolished life' at Ashton. Her *Poems on Several Occasions* appeared in 1703, her preface explaining that they were 'the employment of my leisure hours, the innocent amusements of a solitary life'. Letters to Elizabeth Thomas in the same year confirm that 'the great Part of my Time is spent in my Closet; there I meet with nothing to disturb me, nothing to render me uneasy; I find my Books and my Thoughts to be the most agreeable Companions'. Without them, 'perhaps I should have been as unhappy as any of my Sex'. Later she stated that 'Life is what I have for many Years had no reason to be fond of, and a Grave has appeared to me the happiest and best Asylum'. *The Ladies Defence* was added without her permission to the second edition of her *Poems* (1709; later editions, 1713, 1722, 1750), as she complained in her *Essays upon Several Subjects in Verse and Prose* (1710), a collection of pious and moral writings.

She died at Ashton in 1710, 'having long laboured under the pains of a rheumatism, which had confined her to her chamber a considerable time before her death'. She left some unpublished plays and translations, and MSS of her poems have survived in the Houghton Library at Harvard and the Huntington Library. Verses in her memory were published by Elizabeth Thomas and Martha Sansom (see nos. 59–63), and short accounts of her appeared later in Ballard's *Memoirs* (1752), Shiells' *Lives of the Poets* (1753), and *Poems by Eminent Ladies* (1755).

I

from *The Ladies Defence*

'TIS hard we should be by the men despised,
Yet kept from knowing what would make us prized;
Debarred from knowledge, banished from the schools,
And with the utmost industry bred fools;
Laughed out of reason, jested out of sense,
And nothing left but native innocence;
Then told we are incapable of wit,
And only for the meanest drudgeries fit;
Made slaves to serve their luxury and pride,
And with innumerable hardships tried, 10
Till pitying heaven release us from our pain,
Kind heaven, to whom alone we dare complain.
Th' ill-natured world will no compassion show:
Such as are wretched it would still have so.
It gratifies its envy and its spite:
The most in others' miseries take delight.
While we are present, they some pity spare,
And feast us on a thin repast of air;
Look grave and sigh, when we our wrongs relate,
And in a compliment accuse our fate; 20
Blame those to whom we our misfortunes owe,
And all the signs of real friendship show,
But when we're absent, we their sport are made,
They fan the flame, and our oppressors aid;
Join with the stronger, the victorious side,
And all our sufferings, all our griefs deride.
Those generous few whom kinder thoughts inspire,
And who the happiness of all desire,
Who wish we were from barbarous usage free,
Exempt from toils and shameful slavery, 30
Yet let us, unreproved, mis-spend our hours,
And to mean purposes employ our nobler powers.
They think, if we our thoughts can but express,
And know but how to work, to dance and dress,
It is enough, as much as we should mind,
As if we were for nothing else designed,
But made, like puppets, to divert mankind.
O that my sex would all such toys despise,
And only study to be good and wise;
Inspect themselves, and every blemish find, 40
Search all the close recesses of the mind,
And leave no vice, no ruling passion there,
Nothing to raise a blush, or cause a fear;

Their memories with solid notions fill,
And let their reason dictate to their will;
Instead of novels, histories peruse,
And for their guides the wiser ancients choose;
Through all the labyrinths of learning go,
And grow more humble, as they more do know.
By doing this they will respect procure,   50
Silence the men, and lasting fame secure;
And to themselves the best companions prove,
And neither fear their malice, nor desire their love.

(1701)

2

To the Ladies

WIFE and servant are the same,
But only differ in the name:
For when that fatal knot is tied,
Which nothing, nothing can divide,
When she the word *Obey* has said,
And man by law supreme has made,
Then all that's kind is laid aside,
And nothing left but state and pride.
Fierce as an eastern prince he grows,
And all his innate rigour shows: 10
Then but to look, to laugh, or speak,
Will the nuptial contract break.
Like mutes, she signs alone must make,
And never any freedom take,
But still be governed by a nod,
And fear her husband as her god:
Him still must serve, him still obey,
And nothing act, and nothing say,
But what her haughty lord thinks fit,
Who, with the power, has all the wit.   20
Then shun, oh! shun that wretched state,
And all the fawning flatterers hate.
Value yourselves, and men despise:
You must be proud, if you'll be wise.

(1703)

3   *The Resolve*

FOR what the world admires I'll wish no more,
    Nor court that airy nothing of a name:
Such flitting shadows let the proud adore,
    Let them be suppliants for an empty fame.

If Reason rules within, and keeps the throne,
    While the inferior faculties obey,
And all her laws without reluctance own,
    Accounting none more fit, more just than they;

If Virtue my free soul unsullied keeps,
    Exempting it from passion and from stain,   10
If no black guilty thoughts disturb my sleeps,
    And no past crimes my vexed remembrance pain;

If, though I pleasure find in living here,
    I yet can look on death without surprise;
If I've a soul above the reach of fear,
    And which will nothing mean or sordid prize;

A soul, which cannot be depressed by grief,
    Nor too much raised by the sublimest joy,
Which can, when troubled, give itself relief,
    And to advantage all its thoughts employ: 20

Then am I happy in my humble state,
    Although not crowned with glory nor with bays:
A mind, that triumphs over vice and fate,
    Esteems it mean to court the world for praise.

                                                      (1703)

ANNE FINCH (née KINGSMILL), COUNTESS OF WINCHILSEA
(1661–1720)

She was born at Sydmonton near Newbury, the third child of Sir William Kingsmill
and his wife Anne Haslewood. Her father, who was descended from an old
Hampshire family and had suffered in the Civil War, died when she was only 5
months old. Her mother, who had remarried, died in 1664 and her stepfather, Sir
Thomas Ogle, in 1671. She and her sister were probably brought up by her uncle, Sir

William Haslewood. By 1683 she was Maid of Honour to Mary of Modena, wife of the Duke of York, who was shortly to become James II. Many years later she wrote of Mary's kindness to her when 'eager from the rural seat I came | Of long traced Ancestors of worthy name'. At Court she met Capt. (later Col.) Heneage Finch (1657–1726), Gentleman of the Bedchamber to the Duke of York, whom she married in May 1684. Their fortunes changed drastically after the flight of James II in 1688. Her husband was arrested while trying to follow the fallen King to France but eventually released. Thereafter the Finches retired from London and the Court and by the early 1690s had settled at Eastwell Park in Kent, the seat of Col. Finch's nephew, Charles, Earl of Winchilsea. They had no children but the marriage was evidently a contented one. Winters were spent in London and there were also visits to Tunbridge Wells and other resorts. Her husband, the former soldier and courtier, became increasingly devoted to antiquarian pursuits.

She herself had been writing verse since the 1680s. The 'Introduction' to an early MS of her verse expresses resentment of male attitudes to a woman writer, who is considered 'an intruder on the rights of man' and a 'presumptuous Creature', who should instead occupy herself with frivolous 'feminine' pursuits or 'the dull mannage, of a servile house'. Such fears turned out to be not entirely justified once her verse began to circulate and appear in various miscellanies. Four of her poems, including 'The Spleen', occupied nearly 30 pages in Charles Gildon's *New Collection of Poems on Several Occasions* (1701), where they were introduced by a long 'Epistle to Flavia' by the dramatist Nicholas Rowe, who predicted that 'Ardelia' would redeem poetry from the 'guilty Tribe' of 'wretched Bards' of the last generation: 'The Empire, which she saves, shall own her sway, | And all *Parnassus* her blest Laws obey'. She had a wide literary acquaintance. Her husband was related to the Thynne family at Longleat, where she met Elizabeth Rowe (see nos. 33–6) and the future Countess of Hertford (see nos. 77–8). Swift addressed a poem, 'Apollo Outwitted', to her in 1709 and by 1713 she had met Pope, who engaged in a somewhat enigmatic exchange of verses with her about the *Rape of the Lock*. She also addressed poems to Pope's friend, Charles Jervas the painter, and to Matthew Prior. She seems to have returned to favour at Court, where she became Lady of the Bedchamber to Queen Anne. In August 1712 her husband succeeded his nephew as Earl of Winchilsea, although as a nonjuror he did not take his seat in the House of Lords.

By then her verse had appeared in several other miscellanies, as well as in Delariviere Manley's scandalous *Secret Memoirs . . . from the New Atlantis* (1709). This may have helped to encourage her to publish her *Miscellany Poems on Several Occasions*, including an unacted tragedy, 'Aristomenes', which appeared in 1713, at first anonymously, but later in the year with her name on the title-page. (The number of reissues of the book with variant title pages in 1713 and 1714 may indicate that it did not sell well.) After a serious illness in 1715, much, though not all, of her later verse was religious. She contributed to the prefatory poems in Pope's collected *Works* in 1717 and in the same year he included several unpublished poems by her in his miscellany, *Poems on Several Occasions*. She has frequently been identified as Phoebe Clinket, the caricatured woman poet in *Three Hours After Marriage* (1717), the farce by Pope, Gay, and Arbuthnot, as has Mrs Centlivre (see nos. 54–5), but the evidence suggests that Clinket was intended as a generalized satire.

She left many unpublished poems at her death, a few of which, from MSS then in the possession of the Countess of Hertford, appeared in Thomas Birch's edition of the *General Dictionary*, Vol. x (1741). Although she featured in Ballard's *Memoirs* (1752), Shiells' *Lives of the Poets* (1753), and *Poems by Eminent Ladies* (1755), her reputation faded later in the century, when her verse was rarely reprinted. Notable among her admirers after 1800 was William Wordsworth, who praised the natural description in her 'Nocturnal Reverie' in the 'Essay, Supplementary to the Preface' in his *Poetical Works* (1815). When he compiled an anthology, 'Poems and Extracts' (pub. 1905), to present to Lady Mary Lowther in 1819, seventeen of the fifty poems he included were by Lady Winchilsea. In October 1829 he told Alexander Dyce that he was 'especially partial' to her and had 'perused her Poems frequently'. A few months later he sent Dyce detailed comments on her verse and in May 1830 wrote that 'her style in rhyme is often admirable, chaste, tender, and vigorous; and entirely free from sparkle, antithesis and . . . over-culture'. Myra Reynolds's edition of her *Poems* (Chicago, 1903) brought to light much of her MS verse but, although there have been several subsequent selections, and the important MS at Wellesley College, Massachusetts, has been edited by J. M. Ellis D'Alessandro (Florence, 1988), a new edition of her entire output is much needed.

4   from *The Spleen. A Pindaric Poem*

[*The Power of Spleen*]

O'ER me, alas! thou dost too much prevail:
  I feel thy force whilst I against thee rail;
I feel my verse decay, and my cramped numbers fail.
Through thy black jaundice I all objects see
  As dark, as terrible as thee,
My lines decried, and my employment thought
An useless folly, or presumptuous fault:
  Whilst in the Muses' paths I stray,
Whilst in their groves, and by their secret springs,
My hand delights to trace unusual things,   10
And deviates from the known and common way;
  Nor will in fading silks compose
  Faintly th' inimitable rose,
Fill up an ill-drawn bird, or paint on glass
The Sovereign's blurred and undistinguished face,
The threatening angel and the speaking ass.

Patron thou art to every gross abuse,
  The sullen husband's feigned excuse
When the ill-humour with his wife he spends,
And bears recruited wit and spirits to his friends.   20
  The son of Bacchus pleads thy power,
  As to the glass he still repairs,
  Pretends but to remove thy cares,
Snatch from thy shades one gay and smiling hour,
And drown thy kingdom in a purple shower.
When the coquette, whom every fool admires,
  Would in variety be fair,

And changing hastily the scene
From light, impertinent and vain,
Assumes a soft, a melancholy air,   30
And of her eyes rebates the wandering fires,
The careless posture, and the head reclined,
   The thoughtful and composèd face,
Proclaiming the withdrawn, the absent mind,
Allows the fop more liberty to gaze,
Who gently for the tender cause inquires.
The cause, indeed, is a defect in sense,
Yet is the spleen alleged and still the dull pretence.

   But these are thy fantastic harms,
   The tricks of thy pernicious stage,   40
Which do the weaker sort engage;
Worse are the dire effects of thy more powerful charms.
   By thee Religion, all we know
   That should enlighten here below,
   Is veiled in darkness, and perplexed
With anxious doubts, with endless scruples vexed,
And some restraint implied from each perverted text;
   Whilst *Touch not, Taste not* what is freely given
Is but thy niggard voice, disgracing bounteous heaven.
   From speech restrained, by thy deceits abused,   50
   To deserts banished or in cells reclused,
   Mistaken votaries to the Powers Divine,
   Whilst they a purer sacrifice design,
Do but the spleen obey, and worship at thy shrine.
   In vain to chase thee every art we try,
   In vain all remedies apply,
   In vain the Indian leaf infuse,
   Or the parched Eastern berry bruise;
Some pass in vain these bounds and nobler liquors use.
   Now harmony in vain we bring,   60
   Inspire the flute and touch the string.
   From harmony no help is had;
Music but soothes thee, if too sweetly sad,
And if too light, but turns thee gaily mad.

                                                      (1701)

7

5   *A Sigh*

GENTLEST air, thou breath of lovers,
    Vapours from a secret fire,
Which by thee itself discovers,
    Ere yet daring to aspire.

Softest note of whispered anguish,
    Harmony's refin'dest part,
Striking, while thou seem'st to languish,
    Full upon the listener's heart.

Safest messenger of passion,
    Stealing through a crowd of spies,   10
Which constrain the outward fashion,
    Close the lips and guard the eyes.

Shapeless sigh! we ne'er can show thee,
    Formed but to assault the ear;
Yet, ere to their cost they know thee,
    Every nymph may read thee here.

                                        (1703)

6   *Life's Progress*

HOW gaily is at first begun
    Our life's uncertain race!
Whilst yet that sprightly morning sun,
With which we just set out to run,
    Enlightens all the place.

How smiling the world's prospect lies,
    How tempting to go through!
Not Canaan to the prophet's eyes,
From Pisgah with a sweet surprise,
    Did more inviting show.   10

How promising's the book of fate,
    Till throughly understood!
Whilst partial hopes such lots create
As may the youthful fancy treat
    With all that's great and good.

How soft the first ideas prove,
    Which wander through our minds!
How full of joys, how free the love
Which does that early season move,
    As flowers the western winds!   20

Our sighs are then but vernal air,
    But April-drops our tears,
Which swiftly passing, all grows fair,
Whilst beauty compensates our care,
    And youth each vapour clears.

But oh! too soon, alas, we climb;
    Scarce feeling, we ascend
The gently rising hill of time,
From whence with grief we see that prime,
    And all its sweetness end.   30

The die now cast, our station known,
    Fond expectation past;
The thorns, which former days had sown,
To crops of late repentance grown,
    Through which we toil at last.

Whilst every care's a driving harm
    That helps to bear us down,
Which faded smiles no more can charm,
But every tear's a winter-storm,
    And every look's a frown.   40

Till with succeeding ills oppressed,
    For joys we hoped to find;
By age too rumpled and undressed,
We, gladly sinking down to rest,
    Leave following crowds behind.

                                        (1709)

7   *A Pastoral Dialogue between Two Shepherdesses*

    SILVIA pretty nymph! within this shade,
        Whilst the flocks to rest are laid,
        Whilst the world dissolves in heat,
        Take this cool and flowery seat,

And with pleasing talk awhile
Let us two the time beguile;
Though thou here no shepherd see,
To incline his humble knee,
Or with melancholy lays
Sing thy dangerous beauty's praise.   10

DORINDA Nymph! with thee I here would stay,
But have heard that, on this day,
Near those beeches, scarce in view,
All the swains some mirth pursue,
To whose meeting now I haste.
Solitude does life but waste.

SIL. Prithee, but a moment stay.

DOR. No! my chaplet would decay;
Every drooping flower would mourn,
And wrong the face they should adorn.   20

SIL. I can tell thee, though so fair,
And dressed with all that rural care,
Most of the admiring swains
Will be absent from the plains.
Gay Sylvander, in the dance
Meeting with a shrewd mischance,
To his cabin's now confined
By Mopsus, who the strain did bind;
Damon through the wood does stray,
Where his kids have lost their way;   30
Young Narcissus' ivory brow,
Rased by a malicious bough,
Keeps the girlish boy from sight,
Till time shall do his beauty right.

DOR. Where's Alexis?

SIL.   He, alas!
Lies extended on the grass;
Tears his garland, raves, despairs,
Mirth and harmony forswears;
Since he was this morning shown
That Delia must not be his own.   40

DOR. Foolish swain! such love to place—

SIL. On any but Dorinda's face.

DOR. Hasty nymph! I said not so.

Rased] Scratched

SIL. No—but I thy meaning know.
 Every shepherd thou wouldst have
 Not thy lover, but thy slave,
 To increase thy captive train,
 Never to be loved again.
 But, since all are now away,
 Prithee, but a moment stay.   50

DOR. No, the strangers from the vale
 Sure will not this meeting fail:
 Graceful one, the other fair.
 He too with the pensive air
 Told me, ere he came this way,
 He was wont to look more gay.

SIL. See! how pride thy heart inclines
 To think for thee that shepherd pines;
 When those words, that reached thy ear,
 Chloe was designed to hear;   60
 Chloe, who did near thee stand,
 And his more speaking looks command.

DOR. Now thy envy makes me smile.
 That indeed were worth his while:
 Chloe next thyself decayed,
 And no more a courted maid.

SIL. Next myself! Young nymph, forbear.
 Still the swains allow me fair,
Though not what I was that day,
 When Colon bore the prize away;   70
 When—
DOR.   Oh, hold! that tale will last
 Till all the evening sports are past;
 Till no streak of light is seen,
 Nor footstep prints the flowery green.
 What thou wert, I need not know;
 What I am, must haste to show.
 Only this I now discern,
 From the things thou'd'st have me learn,
 'That woman-kind's peculiar joys
 From past, or present, beauties arise.'   80

      (1709)

8 *Adam Posed*

COULD our first father, at his toilsome plough,
Thorns in his path, and labour on his brow,
Clothed only in a rude unpolished skin,
Could he a vain, fantastic nymph have seen,
In all her airs, in all her antic graces,
Her various fashions, and more various faces;
How had it posed that skill, which late assigned
Just appellations to each several kind,
A right idea of the sight to frame;
T' have guessed from what new element she came,   10
T' have hit the wavering form, or given this thing a name!

(1709)

9 *A Tale of the Miser and the Poet. Written about the
Year 1709*

A WIT, transported with enditing,
Unpaid, unpraised, yet ever writing,
Who, for all fights and favourite friends,
Had poems at his fingers' ends;
For new events was still providing,
Yet now, desirous to be riding,
He packed up every ode and ditty,
And in vacation left the city.
So rapt with figures and allusions,
With secret passions, sweet confusions;   10
With sentences from plays well-known,
And thousand couplets of his own,
That ev'n the chalky road looked gay,
And seemed to him the Milky Way.
But Fortune, who the ball is tossing,
And poets ever will be crossing,
Misled the steed, which ill he guided,
Where several gloomy paths divided.
The steepest in descent he followed,
Enclosed by rocks which time had hollowed,   20
Till he believed, alive and booted,
He'd reached the shades by Homer quoted.
But all that he could there discover
Was, in a pit with thorns grown over,

Posed] Puzzled

Old Mammon digging, straining, sweating,
As bags of gold he thence was getting;
Who, when reproved for such dejections
By him who lived on high reflections,
Replied: 'Brave sir, your time is ended,
And poetry no more befriended.   30
I hid this coin when Charles was swaying,
When all was riot, masking, playing;
When witty beggars were in fashion,
And learning had o'errun the nation:
But since mankind is so much wiser,
And none is valued like the miser,
I draw it hence, and now these sums
In proper soil grow up to plums*,
Which gathered once, in that rich minute,
We rule the world, and all that's in it.'   40

'But,' quoth the poet, 'can you raise,
As well as plum-trees, groves of bays?
Where you, which I would choose much rather,
May fruits of reputation gather?
Will men of quality and spirit
Regard you for intrinsic merit?
And seek you out, before your betters,
For conversation, wit, and letters?'

'Fool,' quoth the churl, who knew no breeding,
'Have these been times for such proceeding?   50
Instead of honoured and rewarded,
Are you not slighted or discarded?
What have you met with, but disgraces?
Your Prior could not keep in places,
And your Van-Brugh had found no quarter,
But for his dabbling in the mortar.
Rowe no advantages could hit on,
Till verse he left, to write *North Briton*.
Philips, who's by the *Shilling* known,
Ne'er saw a shilling of his own.   60
Meets Philomela, in the town,
Her due proportion of renown?
What preference has Ardelia seen,
T' expel, though she could write *The Spleen*?

* A *Plum* is a Cant word, signifying a Hundred Thousand Pound.

---

dejections] degradations

13

Of coach or tables can you brag,
Or better clothes than poet Rag?
Do wealthy kindred, when they meet you,
With kindness or distinction greet you?
Or have your lately-flattered heroes
Enriched you like the Roman Maroes?'   70

'No,' quoth the man of broken slumbers;
'Yet we have patrons for our numbers:
There are Maecenas's among 'em.'

Quoth Mammon, 'Pray, sir, do not wrong 'em;
But in your censures use a conscience,
Nor charge great men with thriftless nonsense;
Since they, as your own poets sing,
Now grant *no worth in anything*
But so much money as 'twill bring.
Then, never more from your endeavours   80
Expect preferment, or less favours.
But if you'll 'scape contempt, or worse,
Be sure put money in your purse;
Money! which only can relieve you
When fame and friendship will deceive you.'

'Sir,' quoth the poet humbly bowing,
And all that he had said allowing,
'Behold me and my airy fancies
Subdued like giants in romances.
I here submit to your discourses,   90
Which, since experience too enforces,
I, in that solitary pit,
Your gold withdrawn, will hide my wit:
Till time, which hastily advances,
And gives to all new turns and chances,
Again may bring it into use;
Roscommons may again produce,
New Augustean days revive,
When wit shall please, and poets thrive.
Till when, let those converse in private,   100
Who taste what others don't arrive at;
Yielding that Mammonists surpass us,
And let the Bank out-swell Parnassus.'

(1713)

10 ## from *The Petition for an Absolute Retreat*

Inscribed to the Right Honble Catherine Countess of Thanet

GIVE me, O indulgent Fate!
Give me yet, before I die,
A sweet, but absolute retreat,
'Mongst paths so lost, and trees so high,
That the world may ne'er invade,
Through such windings and such shade,
My unshaken liberty.

   No intruders thither come
Who visit but to be from home!
None who their vain moments pass   10
Only studious of their glass;
News, that charm to listening ears,
That false alarm to hopes and fears,
That common theme for every fop,
From the statesman to the shop,
In those coverts ne'er be spread,
Of who's deceased, and who's to wed,
Be no tidings thither brought;
But silent as a midnight thought,
Where the world may ne'er invade,   20
Be those windings and that shade!

   Courteous Fate! afford me there
A table spread, without my care,
With what the neighbouring fields impart,
Whose cleanliness be all its art.
When of old the calf was dressed
(Though to make an angel's feast),
In the plain, unstudied sauce
Nor truffle nor morillia was;
Nor could the mighty patriarch's board   30
One far-fetched ortolan afford.
Courteous Fate! then give me there
Only plain and wholesome fare;
Fruits indeed (would heaven bestow),
All that did in Eden grow,
All but the forbidden Tree,
Would be coveted by me;

morillia] edible fungus   ortolan] a small bird prized as a delicacy

Grapes, with juice so crowded up
As breaking through the native cup;
Figs yet growing, candied o'er   40
By the sun's attracting power;
Cherries, with the downy peach,
All within my easy reach;
Whilst, creeping near the humble ground,
Should the strawberry be found,
Springing whereso'er I strayed
Through those windings and that shade.

    For my garments: let them be
What may with the time agree;
Warm, when Phoebus does retire,   50
And is ill-supplied by fire:
But when he renews the year,
And verdant all the fields appear,
Beauty every thing resumes,
Birds have dropped their winter plumes;
When the lily full-displayed
Stands in purer white arrayed
Than that vest which heretofore
The luxurious monarch wore,
When from Salem's gates he drove   60
To the soft retreat of love,
Lebanon's all-burnished house,
And the dear Egyptian spouse:
Clothe me, Fate, though not so gay,
Clothe me light and fresh as May;
In the fountains let me view
All my habit cheap and new,
Such as, when sweet zephyrs fly,
With their motions may comply,
Gently waving to express   70
Unaffected carelessness.
No perfumes have there a part,
Borrowed from the chemist's art,
But such as rise from flowery beds,
Or the falling jasmine sheds!
'Twas the odour of the field
Esau's rural coat did yield,
That inspired his father's prayer
For blessings of the earth and air:
Of gums or powders had it smelt,   80
The supplanter, then unfelt,

Easily had been descried
For one that did in tents abide,
For some beauteous handmaid's joy,
And his mother's darling boy.
Let me then no fragrance wear,
But what the winds from gardens bear,   90
In such kind, surprising gales
As gathered from Fidentia's vales
All the flowers that in them grew;
Which, intermixing as they flew,
In wreathen garlands dropped again
On Lucullus and his men;
Who, cheered by the victorious sight,
Trebled numbers put to flight.
Let me, when I must be fine,
In such natural colours shine;   100
Wove and painted by the sun,
Whose resplendent rays to shun,
When they do too fiercely beat,
Let me find some close retreat,
Where they have no passage made
Through those windings, and that shade.

Give me there (since heaven has shown
It was not good to be alone)
A partner suited to my mind,
Solitary, pleased and kind;   110
Who, partially, may something see
Preferred to all the world in me;
Slighting, by my humble side,
Fame and splendour, wealth and pride.
When but two the earth possessed,
'Twas their happiest days, and best;
They by business, nor by wars,
They by no domestic cares,
From each other e'er were drawn,
But in some grove or flowery lawn   120
Spent the swiftly flying time,
Spent their own and nature's prime,
In love: that only passion given
To perfect man, whilst friends with heaven.
Rage, and jealousy, and hate,
Transports of his fallen state
(When by Satan's wiles betrayed),
Fly those windings, and that shade!

(1713)

17

11   *The Hog, the Sheep and Goat, Carrying to a Fair*

Who does not wish ever to judge aright,
    And, in the course of life's affairs,
To have a quick and far-extended sight,
    Though it too often multiplies his cares?
And who has greater sense, but greater sorrow shares?

This felt the swine, now carrying to the knife;
    And whilst the lamb and silent goat
In the same fatal cart lay void of strife,
    He widely stretches his foreboding throat,
Deafening the easy crew with his outrageous note.   10

The angry driver chides th' unruly beast,
    And bids him all this noise forbear;
Nor be more loud nor clamorous than the rest,
    Who with him travelled to the neighbouring fair,
And quickly should arrive and be unfettered there.

'This,' quoth the swine, 'I do believe is true,
    And see we're very near the town;
Whilst these poor fools, of short and bounded view,
    Think 'twill be well when you have set them down,
And eased one of her milk, the other of her gown.   20

'But all the dreadful butchers in a row
    To my far-searching thoughts appear,
Who know indeed we to the shambles go,
    Whilst I, whom none but Beelzebub would shear,
Nor but his dam would milk, must for my carcase fear.'

'But tell me then, will it prevent thy fate?',
    The rude, unpitying farmer cries;
'If not, the wretch who tastes his sufferings late,
    Not he, who through th' unhappy future pries,
Must of the two be held most fortunate and wise.'   30

                                            (1713)

Enquiry after Peace. A Fragment

PEACE! where art thou to be found?
Where, in all the spacious round,
May thy footsteps be pursued?
Where may thy calm seats be viewed?
On some mountain dost thou lie,
Serenely near the ambient sky,
Smiling at the clouds below,
Where rough storms and tempests grow?
Or, in some retired plain,
Undisturbed dost thou remain?   10
Where no angry whirlwinds pass,
Where no floods oppress the grass,
High above, or deep below,
Fain I thy retreat would know.
Fain I thee alone would find,
Balm to my o'er-wearied mind.
Since what here the world enjoys,
Or our passions most employs,
Peace opposes, or destroys.
Pleasure's a tumultuous thing,   20
Busy still, and still on wing;
Flying swift from place to place,
Darting from each beauteous face,
From each strongly mingled bowl,
Through th' inflamed and restless soul.
Sovereign power who fondly craves
But himself to pomp enslaves,
Stands the envy of mankind,
Peace in vain attempts to find.
Thirst of wealth no quiet knows,   30
But near the death-bed fiercer grows,
Wounding men with secret stings,
For evils it on others brings.
War who not discreetly shuns,
Thorough life the gauntlet runs:
Swords, and pikes, and waves, and flames,
Each their stroke against him aims.
Love (if such a thing there be)
Is all despair, or ecstasy.
Poetry's the feverish fit,
Th' o'erflowing of unbounded wit. *&c.*

(1713)

13 *To the Nightingale*

EXERT thy voice, sweet harbinger of spring!
  This moment is thy time to sing,
  This moment I attend to praise,
And set my numbers to thy lays.
  Free as thine shall be my song,
  As thy music, short or long.
Poets wild as thou were born,
  Pleasing best when unconfined,
  When to please is least designed,
Soothing but their cares to rest.   10
  Cares do still their thoughts molest,
  And still th' unhappy poet's breast,
Like thine, when best he sings, is placed against a thorn.

She begins. Let all be still!
  Muse, thy promise now fulfil!
Sweet, oh sweet, still sweeter yet!
Can thy words such accents fit,
Canst thou syllables refine,
Melt a sense that shall retain
Still some spirit of the brain,   20
Till with sounds like these it join?
  'Twill not be! then change thy note;
  Let division shake thy throat.
Hark! division now she tries;
Yet as far the Muse outflies.
  Cease then, prithee, cease thy tune.
  Trifler, wilt thou sing till June?
Till thy business all lies waste,
And the time of building's past!
  Thus we poets that have speech,   30
Unlike what thy forests teach,
  If a fluent vein be shown
  That's transcendent to our own,
Criticise, reform, or preach,
Or censure what we cannot reach.

                                              (1713)

division] rapid melodic passages

Reformation

A GENTLEMAN, most wretched in his lot,
A wrangling and reproving wife had got,
Who, though she curbed his pleasures and his food,
Called him 'My dear', and did it for his good,
Ills to prevent: she of all ills the worst,
So wisely froward, and so kindly cursed.
The servants too experiment her lungs,
And find they've breath to serve a thousand tongues.
Nothing went on; for her eternal clack,
Still rectifying, set all matters back;   10
Nor town, nor neighbours, nor the court could please,
But furnished matter for her sharp disease.
To distant plains at length he gets her down,
With no affairs to manage of her own,
Hoping from that unactive state to find
A calmer habit grown upon her mind:
But soon returned he hears her at his door,
As noisy and tempestuous as before;
Yet mildly asked, how she her days had spent
Amidst the quiet of a sweet content,   20
Where shepherds tend their flocks, and maids their pails,
And no harsh mistress domineers or rails.
'Not rail!', she cries—'Why I, that had no share
In their concerns, could not the trollops spare;
But told 'em they were sluts—And for the swains,
My name a terror to them still remains;
So often I reproved their slothful faults,
And with such freedom told 'em all my thoughts,
That I no more amongst them could reside.'
'Has then, alas!', the gentleman replied,   30
'One single month so much their patience tried,
Where you by day, and but at seasons due,
Could with your clamours their defects pursue?
How had they shrunk, and justly been afraid,
Had they with me one curtain-lecture heard?
Yet enter, Madam, and resume your sway:
Who can't command must silently obey.
In secret here let endless faults be found,
Till, like reformers who in states abound,
You all to ruin bring, and every part confound.'   40

(1713)

curtain-lecture] 'A reproof given by a wife to her husband in bed' (Johnson)

15   *Friendship between Ephelia and Ardelia*

> EPH. WHAT Friendship is, Ardelia, show.
> ARD. 'Tis to love as I love you.
> EPH. This account, so short (though kind),
>   Suits not my enquiring mind.
>   Therefore farther now repeat:
>   What is Friendship when complete?
> ARD. 'Tis to share all joy and grief;
>   'Tis to lend all due relief
>   From the tongue, the heart, the hand;
>   'Tis to mortgage house and land;   10
>   For a friend be sold a slave;
>   'Tis to die upon a grave,
>   If a friend therein do lie.
> EPH. This indeed, though carried high;
>   This, though more than e'er was done
>   Underneath the rolling sun,
>   This has all been said before.
>   Can Ardelia say no more?
> ARD. Words indeed no more can show:
>   *But 'tis to love, as I love you.*

(1713)

16   *A Nocturnal Reverie*

IN such a night, when every louder wind
Is to its distant cavern safe confined;
And only gentle Zephyr fans his wings,
And lonely Philomel, still waking, sings;
Or from some tree, famed for the owl's delight,
She, hollowing clear, directs the wanderer right;
In such a night, when passing clouds give place,
Or thinly veil the heaven's mysterious face;
When in some river overhung with green,
The waving moon and trembling leaves are seen;   10
When freshened grass now bears itself upright,
And makes cool banks to pleasing rest invite,
Whence springs the woodbind and the bramble-rose,
And where the sleepy cowslip sheltered grows;
Whilst now a paler hue the foxglove takes,
Yet chequers still with red the dusky brakes;
When scattered glow-worms, but in twilight fine,
Show trivial beauties, watch their hour to shine;

Whilst Salisb'ry stands the test of every light,
In perfect charms and perfect virtue bright;   20
When odours, which declined repelling day,
Through temperate air uninterrupted stray;
When darkened groves their softest shadows wear,
And falling waters we distinctly hear;
When through the gloom more venerable shows
Some ancient fabric, awful in repose,
While sunburnt hills their swarthy looks conceal,
And swelling haycocks thicken up the vale;
When the loosed horse now, as his pasture leads,
Comes slowly grazing through th' adjoining meads,   30
Whose stealing pace and lengthened shade we fear,
Till torn-up forage in his teeth we hear;
When nibbling sheep at large pursue their food,
And unmolested kine rechew the cud;
When curlews cry beneath the village walls,
And to her straggling brood the partridge calls;
Their short-lived jubilee the creatures keep,
Which but endures whilst tyrant man does sleep;
When a sedate content the spirit feels,
And no fierce light disturbs, whilst it reveals,   40
But silent musings urge the mind to seek
Something too high for syllables to speak;
Till the free soul to a compos'dness charmed,
Finding the elements of rage disarmed,
O'er all below a solemn quiet grown,
Joys in th' inferior world and thinks it like her own:
In such a night let me abroad remain,
Till morning breaks, and all's confused again:
Our cares, our toils, our clamours are renewed,
Or pleasures, seldom reached, again pursued.   50

(1713)

17   *A Ballad to Mrs Catherine Fleming in
London from Malshanger Farm in Hampshire*

FROM me, who whilom sung the town,
   This second ballad comes,
To let you know we are got down
   From hurry, smoke, and drums,
And every visitor that rolls
In restless coach from Mall to Paul's,
   With a fa-la-la-la-la-la.

And now were I to paint the seat
    (As well-bred poets use),
I should embellish our retreat,   10
    By favour of the muse:
Though to no villa we pretend,
But a plain farm at the best end,
    With a fa-la &c.

Where innocence and quiet reigns,
    And no distrust is known;
His nightly safety none maintains,
    By ways they do in Town,
Who rising loosen bolt and bar;
We draw the latch and out we are,   20
    With a fa-la &c.

For jarring sounds in London streets,
    Which still are passing by;
Where 'Cowcumbers' with 'Sand ho' meets,
    And for loud mastery vie:
The driver whistling to his team
Here wakes us from some rural dream,
    With a fa-la &c.

From rising hills through distant views,
    We see the sun decline;   30
Whilst everywhere the eye pursues
    The grazing flocks and kine:
Which home at night the farmer brings,
And not the post's but sheep's bell rings,
    With a fa-la &c.

We silver trouts and cray-fish eat,
    Just taken from the stream;
And never think our meal complete,
    Without fresh curds and cream:
And as we pass by the barn floor,   40
We choose our supper from the door,
    With a fa-la &c.

Beneath our feet the partridge springs,
    As to the woods we go;
Where birds scarce stretch their painted wings,
    So little fear they show:
But when our outspread hoops they spy,
They look when we like them should fly,
    With a fa-la &c.

Through verdant circles as we stray,   50
   To which no end we know;
As we o'erhanging boughs survey,
   And tufted grass below:
Delight into the fancy falls,
And happy days and verse recalls,
   With a fa-la &c.

Oh! why did I these shades forsake,
   And shelter of the grove;
The flowering shrub, the rustling brake,
   The solitude I love: 60
Where emperors have fixed their lot,
And greatly chose to be forgot,
   With a fa-la &c.

Then how can I from hence depart,
   Unless my pleasing friend
Should now her sweet harmonious art
   Unto these shades extend:
And, like old Orpheus' powerful song,
Draw me and all my woods along,
   With a fa-la &c.   70

So charmed like Birnam's they would rise,
   And march in goodly row,
But since it might the town surprise
   To see me travel so,
I must from soothing joys like these,
Too soon return in open chaise
   With a fa-la &c.

Meanwhile accept what I have writ,
   To shew this rural scene;
Nor look for sharp satiric wit   80
   From off the balmy plain:
The country breeds no thorny bays,
   But mirth and love and honest praise,
   With a fa-la &c.

(Wr. *c.*1719; pub. 1929)

18 *A Song on the South Sea*

OMBRE and basset laid aside,
　New games employ the fair;
And brokers all those hours divide
　Which lovers used to share.

The court, the park, the foreign song
　And harlequin's grimace,
Forlorn; amidst the city throng
　Behold each blooming face.

With Jews and Gentiles undismayed
　Young tender virgins mix,　　　　　　　　　10
Of whiskers nor of beards afraid,
　Nor all the cozening tricks.

Bright jewels, polished once to deck
　The fair one's rising breast,
Or sparkle round her ivory neck,
　Lie pawned in iron chest.

The gayer passions of the mind
　How avarice controls!
Even love does now no longer find
　A place in female souls.

(Wr. 1720; pub. 1724)

SARAH EGERTON (née FYGE, later FIELD) (1670–1723)

Born in London, she was one of the six daughters of Thomas Fyge (d. 1706), a physician descended from a land-owning family at Winslow, Buckinghamshire, and his wife Mary Beacham (d. 1704). In 1686 she published *The Female Advocate* (revised edition, 1687), a reply to Robert Gould's *Love Given O're: Or, A Satyr Against the Pride, Lust and Inconstancy, &c. of Woman* (1682). For this teenage indiscretion her father forced her to leave London and live with relatives in the country, as she complains in some of her early autobiographical poems. She eventually married an attorney, Edward Field, who had died before 1700. She may have known John Dryden, on whose death in 1700 she published an ode in *Luctus Britannici* and, as 'Mrs. S.F.', contributed to *The Nine Muses* (1700), a collection of verse by women on the late poet, edited by Mrs Manley. By 1703 the dedication to the Earl of Halifax of her *Poems on Several Occasions. Together with a Pastoral* was signed 'S.F.E.', indicating that she had remarried. (The book was reissued as *A Collection of Poems on Several*

Occasions . . . by Mrs. Sarah Fyge Egerton (1706), *The Female Advocate* being reprinted in the same year, but with the date 1707.)

Her second husband was the Revd Thomas Egerton, a second cousin, who had been Rector of Adstock, Buckinghamshire, since 1671. A wealthy widower with adult children, he was some twenty years older than she. Before and after this marriage she was apparently in love with Henry Pierce, an attorney's clerk and a friend of her first husband ('Alexis' in her poems). Evidence has recently come to light that as early as 1703 the Egertons were involved in an acrimonious divorce suit, she accusing him of cruelty, he accusing her of desertion, but the divorce seems not to have been granted. She had been friendly, but later quarrelled, with Delariviere Manley, who gave a remarkable and no doubt heightened account of the Egerton marriage in her *Secret Memoirs . . . from the New Atlantis* (1709). Manley's limited sympathy is reserved for her husband, 'an old thin raw-bon'd Priest', who is persecuted by his hysterical and violent wife ('a She-Devil incarnate'). Such is his punishment for marrying a younger wife, 'when I had Children grown up to keep my House, and administer comfortably to my Necessities'. With a good estate and income, he could keep a coach and four servants for her, but her violence had driven away his children, and 'Then she's in love with all the handsome Fellows she sees; but her Face, I believe, protects her Chastity . . . [it] is made in part like a Black-a-more, flat-nos'd, blubber-lipp'd; there is no sign of life in her Complexion, it savours all of Mortality; she looks as if she had been buried a Twelve-month'. As for her incomprehensible verse, 'Deliver me from a poetical wife. . . . She rumbles in Verses of *Atomes*, Artic and Antartic, of *Gods*, and strange things, foreign to all fashionable Understanding'. In her *Memoirs of Europe* (1710), the relentless Manley referred to her again as the 'shockingly ugly' woman who had presented the literary patron Julius Sergius (the Earl of Halifax) with 'the Labours of her Brain'. The unhappy marriage was evidently notorious: it was ridiculed again, together with her poetic ambitions, in *The Butter'd Apple-Pye* (1711), a broadsheet verse satire.

She had no children and died in February 1723 (her husband having died in 1720). She left £1 a year to the poor of Winslow, which failed to reach them because of the 'abuse' of her executor, a local mercer. In the course of some correspondence about her identity in the *Gentleman's Magazine* in 1780–1, one 'M.J.' claimed to own some 120 of her letters, but these have not come to light.

19   *The Repulse to Alcander*

WHAT is't you mean, that I am thus approached?
Dare you to hope that I may be debauched?
For your seducing words the same implies,
In begging pity, with a soft surprise,
For one who loves, and sighs, and almost dies.
In every word and action doth appear
Something I hate and blush to see or hear.
At first your love for vast respect was told,
Till your excess of manners grew too bold,
And did your base, designing thoughts unfold.   10
When a salute did seem to custom due,
With too much ardour you'd my lips pursue;

My hand, with which you played, you'd kiss and press,
Nay, every look had something of address.
Ye gods! I cried, sure he designs to woo,
For thus did amorous Phylaster do,
The youth whose passion none could disapprove,
When Hymen waited to complete his love.
But now, when sacred laws and vows confine
Me to another, what can you design?   20
At first I could not see the lewd abuse,
But framed a thousand things for your excuse.
I knew that Bacchus sometimes did inspire
A sudden transport, though not lasting fire,
For he no less than Cupid can make kind,
And force a fondness which was ne'er designed;
Or thought you'd travelled far, and it might chance
To be the foreign mode of complaisance.
Till you so oft your amorous crimes repeat,
That to permit you would make mine as great;   30
Nor stopped you here, but languishingly spake
That love which I endeavoured to mistake.
What saw you in me that could make you vain,
Or anything expect but just disdain?
I must confess I am not quite so nice
To damn all little gallantries for vice
(But I see now my charity's misplaced,
If none but sullen saints can be thought chaste):
Yet know, base man, I scorn your lewd amours,
Hate them from all, not only 'cause they're yours.   40
Oh sacred Love! let not the world profane
Thy transports, thus to sport and entertain;
The beau, with some small artifice of's own,
Can make a treat for all the wanton town.
I thought myself secure within these shades,
But your rude love my privacy invades,
Affronts my virtue, hazards my just fame:
Why should I suffer for your lawless flame?
For oft 'tis known, through vanity and pride,
Men boast those favours which they are denied;   50
Or others' malice, which can soon discern,
Perhaps may see in you some kind concern,
So scatter false suggestions of their own,
That I love too: oh, stain to my renown!
No, I'll be wise, avoid your sight in time,
And shun at once the censure and the crime.

(1703)

complaisance] politeness

28

20

To Philaster

GO, perjured youth, and court what nymph you please,
Your passion now is but a dull disease:
With worn-out sighs deceive some listening ear,
Who longs to know how 'tis and what men swear;
She'll think they're new from you, 'cause so to her.
Poor cozened fool, she ne'er can know the charms
Of being first encircled in thy arms,
When all love's joys were innocent and gay,
As fresh and blooming as the newborn day.
Your charms did then with native sweetness flow:　　　　10
The forced-kind complaisance you now bestow
Is but a false, agreeable design,
But you had innocence when you were mine,
And all your words, and smiles, and looks divine.
How proud, methinks, thy mistress does appear
In sullied clothes, which I'd no longer wear;
Her bosom too with withered flowers dressed,
Which lost their sweets in my first-chosen breast.
Perjured, imposing youth, cheat who you will,
Supply defect of truth with amorous skill:　　　　20
Yet thy address must needs insipid be,
For the first ardour of thy soul was all possessed by me.

(1703)

21

To One who said I must not Love

BID the fond mother spill her infant's blood,
The hungry epicure not think of food;
Bid the Antarctic touch the Arctic pole:
When these obey, I'll force love from my soul.
As light and heat compose the genial sun,
So love and I essentially are one:
Ere your advice, a thousand ways I tried
To ease the inherent pain, but 'twas denied,
Though I resolved, and grieved, and almost died.
Then I would needs dilate the mighty flame,　　　　10
Play the coquette, hazard my dearest fame:
The modish remedy I tried in vain,
One thought of him contracts it all again.
Wearied at last, cursed Hymen's aid I chose,
But find the fettered soul has no repose.

Now I'm a double slave to love and vows:
As if my former sufferings were too small,
I've made the guiltless torture criminal.
Ere this, I gave a loose to fond desire,
Durst smile, be kind, look, languish and admire,   20
With wishing sighs fan the transporting fire.
But now these soft allays are so like sin,
I'm forced to keep the mighty anguish in;
Check my too tender thoughts and rising sighs,
As well as eager arms and longing eyes.
My kindness to his picture I refrain,
Nor now embrace the lifeless, lovely swain.
To press the charming shade, though through a glass,
Seems a Platonic breach of Hymen's laws:
Thus nicely fond, I only stand and gaze,   30
View the dear, conquering form that forced my fate,
Till I become as motionless as that.
My sinking limbs deny their wonted aid:
Fainting, I lean against my frighted maid,
Whose cruel care restores my sense and pain,
For soon as I have life I love again,
And with the fated softness strive in vain.
Distorted Nature shakes at the control,
With strong convulsions rends my struggling soul;
Each vital string cracks with th' unequal strife,   40
Departing love racks like departing life;
Yet there the sorrow ceases with the breath,
But love each day renews th' torturing scene of death.

(1703)

22   *To Marina*

PLAGUE to thy husband, scandal to thy sex,
Whose wearying tongue does every ear perplex;
False to thy own false soul, thou dost declare
How lust and pride do reign and revel there,
Tell the world too how nicely chaste you are.
This dull, compulsive virtue's owned: for who,
With one so odious, would have aught to do?
But this misfortune you too oft condole,
Whilst loosest thoughts debauch your willing soul.
Thy best discourse is but mere ribaldry,   10
Telling how fond all that e'er see thee be,
And, loving all thyself, think'st all in love with thee.

With pious heart thou studiest vanity,
And talk'st obscene by rules of modesty.
Thus sins nick-named speak the infernal saint,
Whose shining robes are tawdry clothes and paint:
Extravagance and cheats you mark for wit,
Thou abstract of contention, fraud and spite.
If Socrates could have made choice of thee,
Thou wouldst have baffled his philosophy, 20
And turned his patience to a lunacy.
The restless waters of the raging sea
Are a serene and halcyon stream to thee:
They keep their banks and sometimes can be still,
Thou art all tempest, know'st no bounds in ill.
Pride, lust, contention reign and yet repine:
Vesuvius' noise and flame has less of hell than thine.

(1703)

The Emulation

23

SAY, tyrant Custom, why must we obey
The impositions of thy haughty sway?
From the first dawn of life unto the grave,
Poor womankind's in every state a slave,
The nurse, the mistress, parent and the swain,
For love she must, there's none escape that pain.
Then comes the last, the fatal slavery:
The husband with insulting tyranny
Can have ill manners justified by law,
For men all join to keep the wife in awe. 10
Moses, who first our freedom did rebuke,
Was married when he writ the Pentateuch.
They're wise to keep us slaves, for well they know,
If we were loose, we soon should make them so.
We yield like vanquished kings whom fetters bind,
When chance of war is to usurpers kind;
Submit in form; but they'd our thoughts control,
And lay restraints on the impassive soul.
They fear we should excel their sluggish parts,
Should we attempt the sciences and arts; 20
Pretend they were designed for them alone,
So keep us fools to raise their own renown.
Thus priests of old, their grandeur to maintain,
Cried vulgar eyes would sacred laws profane;
So kept the mysteries behind a screen:
Their homage and the name were lost had they been seen.

But in this blessèd age such freedom's given,
That every man explains the will of heaven;
And shall we women now sit tamely by,
Make no excursions in philosophy,   30
Or grace our thoughts in tuneful poetry?
We will our rights in learning's world maintain;
Wit's empire now shall know a female reign.
Come, all ye fair, the great attempt improve,
Divinely imitate the realms above:
There's ten celestial females govern wit,
And but two gods that dare pretend to it.
And shall these finite males reverse their rules?
No, we'll be wits, and then men must be fools.

(1703)

ELIZABETH THOMAS
(1675–1731)

She was the daughter of Emmanuel Thomas of the Inner Temple and his wife Elizabeth Osborne. Her father, who had married his 18-year-old bride at the age of 60, died when his daughter was 2. After a period of financial difficulty when they lived in Surrey, she and her mother returned to London to live in Great Russell Street. She educated herself by buying books and reading, and by her mid-twenties was confident enough about her poetry to show it to some distinguished literary men. In April 1699 John Norris of Bemerton thanked her for her verses addressed to him, commended her 'very pregnant Genius for *poetry*', but advised her to concentrate on 'more serious and usefull studies'. She in turn sought his advice about her self-education, telling him that she was planning to learn Latin and French. In the same year she showed her poetry to the elderly John Dryden, whose three letters to her, written a few months before his death in 1700, she more than once quoted in her later works. Dryden politely thought her verses 'too good to be a Woman's . . . the Fair Sex generally write with more Softness than Strength'. He also suggested that she adopt 'Corinna' as a pen-name. She contributed an anonymous poem in his memory to *Luctus Britannici* (1700). From 1701 she corresponded with Lady Chudleigh (see nos. 1–3), whose *The Ladies Defence* she admired. Through Norris she came to know Mary Astell, the early feminist, whom she addressed in a poem, 'To Almystrea, on her Divine Works', although she later complained that Astell had snubbed her, perhaps because she was 'too much a Williamite'.

From about 1700 she was courted by Richard Gwinnet (1675–1717), lawyer and amateur author, whom she had met in a bookshop. Although they corresponded for sixteen years, she saw him for only a week or two a year, as he insisted on deferring the marriage until he could support her suitably. During these years she received other offers, notably (with her mother's support) from a Capt. Richard Hemington. She also knew Henry Cromwell, man-about-town and minor literary figure, and through him, if only briefly, the youthful Alexander Pope. There seems no decisive evidence that she became Cromwell's mistress, although this has often been asserted: William Ayre, for example, wrote in 1745 that 'she pass'd whole Days, and often more than Days, with either Mr. *Cromwell* or Mr. *Pope*, or both'. Nevertheless, the relationship was to have damaging consequences for her personal and literary reputation. She herself still had no desire to publish her poetry, claiming in a poem that she did not wish to write for '*sordid Gain*' or '*popular Applause*', although a bookseller offered her £30 for 'a *Manuscript Folio* of my *Poems*, &c.'.

In November 1716 Richard Gwinnet, having come into his full estate, finally proposed marriage to her but, because she was nursing her mother, a dependent and very demanding invalid for many years, she was unable to accept the offer immediately. Gwinnet died a few months later in April 1717, leaving her £600, of which after some eight years of litigation with his family she was able to obtain only some £213. This problem, and the debts left by her mother at her death in 1719, led to a decade of considerable misery. She later told Cromwell that she had been 'plung'd into unforeseen, and unavoidable ruin', and had 'retreated from the world, and in manner buried myself in a dismal place, where I knew none, nor none knew me'. Hiding from her creditors, she lived 'a lingering death', without books and with only 'the Letters of my dead, or absent friends' as a financial resource. In 1722 she published her *Miscellany Poems* (reissued 1726 and 1727), many probably dating from a much earlier period, and later sold to the notorious Edmund Curll the letters she had received from Dryden, Lady Chudleigh, and John Norris, which appeared in such miscellanies as *Atterburyana* (1727) and *Whartoniana* (1727). She also sold to Curll, supposedly for ten guineas, some early letters from Pope to Henry Cromwell, given to her by Cromwell in about 1714, which Curll triumphantly published in *Miscellanea* (1727, for 1726). Although Cromwell did his best to explain her situation to Pope, she was introduced as 'Curll's Corinna' in some of the most offensive lines in *The Dunciad*. A sentence which expressed some sympathy for her misfortunes was removed from editions of the satire after 1735. Her appearance in this disagreeable context can be the only explanation of the contempt and hostility towards her of later editors and historians.

By 1727 she had been confined for debt in the Fleet Prison. William Talbot, Bishop of Durham, paid her chamber-rent while she was imprisoned, and also circulated appeals for charity on her behalf, to which various members of the nobility and clergy responded. She continued writing, although *Codrus: Or, The Dunciad Dissected* has been only uncertainly attributed to her and Curll. A letter describing Dryden's death and funeral (inaccurately, according to later scholars) appeared in *Memoirs of William Congreve* (1730), dated 15 May 1729. In the following month, under an Act of Insolvency, a warrant was issued for her release, but indigence at first prevented her from leaving prison, as is clear from a begging letter to a nobleman in April 1730, published by Malone in 1800, which describes her as 'destitute of all necessities'. In 1730 she published *The Metamorphosis of the Town: Or, A View of the Present Fashions* (5th edn., 1744), but died in her lodgings in Fleet Street on 3 February 1731. Her posthumously published correspondence with Gwinnet, *Pylades and Corinna* (2 vols., 1731–2, Vol. ii as *The Honourable Lovers*), contains the autobiography on which she was engaged at her death. Like all Curll's publications, it must be treated cautiously, particularly the account of her early years, but it remains the only detailed source of information about her. An appendix includes a case presented to the College of Physicians in 1730, describing the unpleasant after-effects of her swallowing a chicken-bone in 1711, from which she suffered to the end of her life.

24 *Epistle to Clemena. Occasioned by an Argument she had maintained against the Author*

THOUGH you my resolution still accuse,
And for misanthropy condemn the Muse,
Still finding fault with what I most commend,
And lose good humour in the name of friend:
Yet if these pettish heats you lay aside,
And by calm reason let the cause be tried,
I make no question but it would appear
You had no cause to boast, nor I to fear.

For when two bind themselves in marriage bands,
Fidelity in each, the Church commands: 10
Equal's the contract, equal are the vows,
Yet Custom different licences allows:
The man may range from his unhappy wife,
But woman's made a property for life.
To no dear friend the grief may be revealed,
No, she, poor soul, must keep her shame concealed:
And, to the height of doting folly grown,
Believe her husband's character her own.

So have I seen a lovely beauteous maid,
By duty forced, by interest betrayed,   20
Resign herself into Nefario's arms,
And make the sordid wretch sole master of her charms.
With seeming transport he the bliss receives,
With seeming gratitude rich presents gives:
The finest brillants through the town are sought,
The costliest liveries for her servants bought;
The richest tissues for herself to wear,
And nothing that she liked could purchased be too dear.
But ere the sun his annual course had run,
Or thrice three moons with borrowed lustre shone,   30
The libertine resumed his brutal life:
Oh! then how nauseous grew the name of wife.
Her conversation and her charms were stale,
Nor wit and beauty longer could prevail:
The night he turned to day, the day to night,
Yet still uneasy in Aminta's sight.

At two, perhaps, he condescends to rise,
Fetches a yawn or two, and rubs his eyes:

brillants] diamonds

34

'Run, run,' cries he, 'to Captain Hackum's straight,
And tell the rakes I for their coming wait;   40
Be sure you bring the dogs, and hark, d'ye hear,
Bid Tom the butler in my sight appear.'

The hungry bravoes to their patron run,
And wonder that his levée is so soon:
'Bless me,' says one, 'how well you look today!'
T' other replies, 'Ay, he may well look gay,
When wine and women pass his time away.
While business other mortals' peace destroys,
He gives his soul a nobler loose to joys.'
'Enough,' Nefario cries, 'sit down, my friends,   50
See where the sparkling burgundy attends.
This wine was sent from France but t' other day,
And never yet in vintner's cellar lay.'

Set in for drinking thus, they each recite
The wonderful achievements of the night.
One tells how he did Phillis serenade,
Fought with the watch, and made them run afraid;
While t' other shrugging cries, 'I changed my bed,
And was in triumph to the counter led.
But if the town does canes enough afford,   60
I'll drub that rascal where I bought my sword.'

Sated at last with fulsome lies and wine,
Nefario swears aloud, ''Tis dinner-time.'
Aminta's called, and calmly down they sit,
But she not one poor word or look can get.
'This meat's too salt, t' other's too fresh,' he cries,
And from the table in a passion flies:
Not that his cook is faulty in the least,
But 'tis the wife that palls his squeamish taste.

Well, after having ransacked park and play,   70
He with some hackney vizor sneaks away
To famed Pontack's, or noted Monsieur Locket's,
Where Mrs. Jilt as fairly picks his pockets.
Thus bubbled, in revenge he walks his round,
From loft three stories high to cellar underground;
Scours all the streets, some brother rake doth fight,
And with a broken pate concludes the night.
Or in some tavern with the gaming crew,
He drinks, and swears, and plays, till day doth night pursue.

counter] prison   hackney vizor] prostitute   bubbled] cheated

Meanwhile Aminta for his stay doth mourn,
And sends up pious vows for his return;
Fears some mishap, looks out at every noise,
And thinks each breath of wind her dear Nefario's voice.
At last the clock strikes five, and home he comes,
And kicks the spaniel servants through the rooms,
Till he the lovely pensive fair doth spy,
Nor can she 'scape the sordid tyranny:
A thousand brutish names to her he gives,
Which she poor lady patiently receives;
A thousand imprecations doth bestow,   90
And scarcely can refrain to give th' impending blow.
Till tired with rage, and overcome with wine,
Dead drunk he falls, and snoring lies supine.

Wretched Nefario no repentance shows,
But mocks those ills Aminta undergoes:
Ruined by him, with pain she draws her breath,
And still survives an evil worse than death.

Ah, friend! in these depraved, unhappy times,
When vice walks barefaced, virtues pass for crimes:
Many Nefarios must we think to find,   100
Though not so bad as this, yet villains in their kind.
Hard is that venture where our all we lose;
But harder yet an honest man to choose.

(Wr. *c.*1700?; pub. 1722)

25   *The Execration*

ENSLAVED by passions, swelled with pride,
In love with one whom all deride;
A carcase well, yet mind in pain,
Reduced to beg, but beg in vain;
To live reserved and free from blame,
And yet incur an evil fame:
Let this! this be the wretched fate
Of Rosalinda, whom I hate.

(1722)

26   *The True Effigies of a Certain Squire:*
          Inscribed to Clemena

SOME generous painter now assist my pen,
And help to draw the most despised of men:
Or else, oh Muse! do thou that charge supply,
Thou that art injured too as well as I;
Revenge thyself, with satire arm thy quill,
Display the man, yet own a justice still.

First, paint a large, two-handed, surly clown,
In silver waistcoat, stockings sliding down,
Shoes (let me see) a foot and half in length,
And stoutly armed with sparables for strength.   10
Ascend! and let a silver string appear,
Which seems to cry 'A golden watch is here';
O'er all a doily stuff, to which belongs
One pocket charged with citron peel and songs;
T' other contains, more necessary far,
A snuffbox, comb, a glass, and handkercher,
Three parts of which hangs dangling by his side,
The fourth is wisely to a button tied:
Just as it was in former days a rule
To tie young children's muckenders at school.   20
Forget not, Muse, gold buttons at the wrist,
Nor Mechlin lace to shade the clumsy fist;
Two diamond rings thy pencil next must show,
Always in sight like Prim's, the formal beau;
But if rude company their notice spare,
Then draw that hand elated to his ear,
And at one view let diamond ring and golden bob appear.
A steenkirk next, of paltry needle stuff,
Which cost eleven guineas (cheap enough).
Next draw the giant-wig of shape profuse,   30
Larger than Foppington's or Overdo's.
The greasy front pressed down with essence lies,
The spreading elf-locks cover half his eyes;
But when he coughs or bows, what clouds of powder rise!

Enough, O Muse! thou hast described him right,
Th' emetic's strong, I sicken at the sight:

Effigies] Portrait   sparables] nails   doily] woollen   muckenders] handker-
chiefs   Mechlin] i.e. from Belgium   bob] ear-ring   steenkirk] neck-
cloth   elf-locks] tangled hair

A fop is nauseating, howe'er he's dressed,
But this too fulsome is to be expressed.
Such hideous medley would thy work debase,
Where rake and clown, where ape and knave, appear with open
    face.   40

    Yet stay, proceed and paint his awkward bow,
And if thou hast forgot, I'll tell thee how:
Set one leg forward, draw his other back,
Nor let the lump a booby wallow lack;
His head bend downward, with obsequious quake,
Then quickly raise it, with a spaniel shake.
His honours thus performed, a speech begin
May show th' obliging principles within:
Thy memory to his sense I now confine,
His be the substance, but th' expression thine.   50

    'Madam,' he cries, 'Lord, how my soul is moved
To see such silly toys by you approved!
A closet stuffed with books: pray, what's your crime,
To superannuate before your time,
And make yourself look old and ugly in your prime?
Our modern pedants contradict the schools,
For learned ladies are but learned fools.
With every blockhead's whim ye load your brains,
And for a shadow take a world of pains.
What is't to you what numbers Caesar slew?   60
Or who at Marathon beat the de'il knows who?
Defend me, Fortune! from the wife I hate,
And let not bookish woman be my fate.
For when with rural sports fatigued I come,
And think to rest my wearied limbs at home,
No sooner shall I be retired to bed
Than she, for one poor word, shall break poor Priscian's head.
Perhaps you'll say in books you virtue learn,
And, by right reason, good from ill discern:
Ha, ha! believe me, virtue's but pretence   70
To cloak hypocrisy and insolence;
Let woman mind her economic care,
And let the man what he thinks fit prepare
(What he thinks fit, I say, or please to spend,
For those are fools that on their wives depend).
Nor need they musty books to pass their time,
There's twenty recreations more sublime.

    wallow] clumsy rolling movement   break poor Priscian's head] accuse (someone) o
breaking the rules of grammar

When tired with work, then let them to the play;
If fair, go visit; if a rainy day,
In cards and chat drive lazy time away.　　　　　　　80
No, hang me if I speak not as I mean:
If on my nuptial day there is not seen
Of all my spouse's books a stately pyre,
Which she herself obediently shall fire;
And oh! might Europe's learning in that blaze expire.
Now, Madam, pray, the mighty difference show:
I eat, I drink, I sleep as well as you;
I know by custom two and two is four;
My man is honest, then what need I more?
And truly speak it to my joy and praise,　　　　　　90
I never read six books in all my days.
Nor should my son; for could my wish prevail,
Blest ignorance I'd on my race entail.
Unthinking and unlearned, in plenteous ease,
My happy heir each appetite should please;
And when chance strikes the last unlucky blow,
Glutted with life, I'd have him boldly go
To try that *somewhat* or that *naught* below.'

　　How is't, my friend? Can you your spleen contain
At this ignoble wretch, this less than man?　　　　　100
Trust me, I'm weary, can repeat no more,
And own this folly worse than when 'twas acted o'er.

　　　　　　　　　　　　　　　　(1722)

27　　*A New Litany, Occasioned by an Invitation to a
Wedding*

From marrying in haste, and repenting at leisure;
Not liking the person, yet liking his treasure:
　　　　　　　　　　　　　　　　Libera nos.

From a mind so disturbed that each look does reveal it;
From abhorring one's choice, and not sense to conceal it:
　　　　　　　　　　　　　　　　Libera nos.

From a husband to govern, and buy him his wit;
From a sullen, ill-natured and whimsical cit:
　　　　　　　　　　　　　　　　Libera nos.

　　　　　　　　　　　　　　　　(1722)

cit] citizen (contemptuous)

39

28   *On Sir J—— S—— saying in a Sarcastic*
Manner, My Books would make me Mad. An Ode

UNHAPPY sex! how hard's our fate,
By Custom's tyranny confined
To foolish needlework and chat,
Or such like exercise as that,
But still denied th' improvement of our mind!
'Women!' men cry, 'alas, poor fools!
What are they but domestic tools?
On purpose made our toils to share,
And ease the husband's economic care.
To dress, to sing, to work, to play,   10
To watch our looks, our words obey,
And with their little follies drive dull thoughts away.
Thus let them humbly in subjection live;
But learning leave to man, our great prerogative.'

Most mighty sovereigns, we submit,
And own ye monarchs of the realms of Wit:
But might a slave to her superiors speak,
And without treason silence break,
She'd first implore your royal grace,
Then humbly thus expostulate the case.   20
Those who to husbands have their power resigned
Will in their house a full employment find,
And little time command to cultivate the mind.
Had we been made intuitively wise,
Like angels' vast capacities,
I would allow we need not use
Those rules experience does infuse:
But if born ignorant, though fit for more,
Can you deny we should improve our store?
Or won't you be so just to grant   30
That those perfections which we want,
And can't acquire when in a married state,
     Should be attained before?
Believe me, 'tis a truth long understood,
That those who know not why they're so, can ne'er be wise or
good.

What surer method can we take
    Than this ye seem to choose?
'Tis books ye write, and books ye use;

But yet we must a serious judgement make,
    What to elect, and what refuse.   40
Is't not by books we're taught to know
The great Creator of this world below?
The vast dimensions of this earth,
And to what minute particles poor mortals owe their birth?
  By books, th' Almighty's works we learn and prize,
  But those phenomenas, which dazzle vulgar eyes,
    We can as much despise.
  And more than this, well chosen books do show
    What unto God, and what to man we owe.
      Yet, if we enquire for a book,   50
      Beyond a novel or a play,
    Good lord! how soon th' alarm's took,
    How soon your eyes your souls betray,
      And with what spite ye look!
    How naturally ye stare and scowl,
      Like wondering birds about an owl,
And with malicious sneer these dismal accents howl:

      'Alas, poor Plato! All thy glory's past:
  What, in a female hand arrived at last!'
  'Sure,' adds another, ''tis for something worse;   60
  This itch of reading's sent her as a curse.'
  'No, no,' cries good Sir John, 'but 'tis as bad,
For if she's not already crazed, I'm sure she will be mad.'
  'Tis thus ye rail to vent your spleen,
  And think your wondrous wit is seen:
But 'tis the malice of your sex appears.
    What, suffer woman to pretend to sense!
    Oh! how this optic magnifies the offence,
      And aggravates your fears!
    But since the French in all ye ape,   70
  Why should not they your morals shape?
    Their women are as gay and fair,
Yet learned ladies are no monsters there.
    What is it from our sex ye fear,
      That thus ye curb our powers?
    D'ye apprehend a bookish war,
Or are your judgements less for raising ours?
    Come, come, the real truth confess
    (A fault acknowledged is the less),
    And own it was an avaricious soul,   80
Which would, with greedy eyes, monopolise the whole;
  And bars us learning on the selfish score,

That, conscious of our native worth,
　　Ye dread to make it more.
　　Then thanks to Heaven we're English-born and free,
And thank our gracious laws that give such liberty.

(1722)

29   from *Jill, A Pindaric Ode*

NINE times the sun his yearly course had run,
And twice nine moons with changing lustre shone,
　　Since Jill's first breath and love to me begun.
Fine was her mien, and most exact her form,
Black sparkling eyes her lovely face adorned;
Two stately dewlaps dangled o'er her breast
　　(Th' hereditary ensigns of her race);
　　Unspotted whiteness covered all the rest,
And when she barked, 'twas with majestic grace.
　　But oh! what fit expressions can I find   10
　　To show the beauties of her fairer mind!
　　So fond! so faithful! sensible and true,
　　So nobly fierce! and yet so gentle too.
　　One look or nod instructed her with ease,
　　As if her only care had been to please:
　　Such gratitude in all her actions shined,
　　Such constant love, perception so refined,
That she or was, or seemed to me, the noblest of her kind!

　　Thus long we lived, from youth together bred,
　　And at one table constantly were fed: 20
　　　Till on a fatal inauspicious day,
　　As in the sun's bright beams she basking lay,
　　Her beauteous eyes she rolled about in vain,
　　And scarcely could endure the light for pain:
　　　An atrophy her lovely form invades,
Her bones start through the skin! her skin's bright lustre fades!
　　The vital flood ebbed slowly from her heart,
　　And deadly pangs tormented every part.
　　This for the space of five long days she bore,
　　Without a sigh or one repining groan;   30
　　While I, the greater brute, her fate deplore,
　　　And teach her how to moan.
　　　At last, as I sat grieving by her side,
She fixed her fainting eyes on mine, then fetched a sigh and died.

(1722)

42

30
To Almystrea [Mary Astell], on her Divine Works

HAIL, happy virgin! of celestial race,
Adorned with wisdom, and replete with grace!
By contemplation you ascend above,
And fill your breast with true seraphic love.
And when you from that sacred mount descend,
You give us rules our morals to amend:
Those pious maxims you yourself apply,
And make the universe your family.

No more, oh Spain! thy Saint Theresa boast,
Here's one outshines her on the British coast;   10
Directs as well, and regulates her love,
But in that sphere with greater force doth move.
Whose soul, like hers, viewed its almighty end!
And to that centre all its motions tend:
Like her, she glorious monuments doth raise,
Beyond male envy! or a female praise!

Too long! indeed, has been our sex decried,
And ridiculed by men's malignant pride;
Who, fearing of a just return, forbore,
And made it criminal to teach us more.   20
That women had no souls was their pretence,
And women's spelling passed for women's sense.
When you, most generous heroine! stood forth,
And showed your sex's aptitude and worth.
Were it no more, yet you, bright maid, alone
Might for a world of vanity atone!
Redeem the coming age! and set us free
From the false brand of incapacity.

(1722)

31
The Triumvirate

OH! wondrous force of sympathy,
Where three unite in harmony;
Where master with the maid combines,
And mistress with them issue joins;
Where all unanimous agree
To club for future progeny.

Ah! may the household gods adorn
This happy infant, yet unborn,
With mother's cleanliness and air
(A stately, silly, tattered fair);   10
The mistress' form may it partake,
Her awkward mien and clumsy make,
Her broken mouth, her Judas grin,
And all the fiend which reigns within.

   But Daddy's lines! oh, let the face
Reflect, with such expressive grace!
That all who shall this infant see
May cry at sight, ''Tis very he!'

(1722)

32   *The Forsaken Wife*

METHINKS, 'tis strange you can't afford
One pitying look, one parting word;
Humanity claims this as due,
But what's humanity to you?

   Cruel man! I am not blind,
Your infidelity I find;
Your want of love my ruin shows,
My broken heart, your broken vows.
Yet maugre all your rigid hate,
I will be true in spite of fate;   10
And one preeminence I'll claim,
To be for ever still the same.

   Show me a man that dare be true,
That dares to suffer what I do;
That can for ever sigh unheard,
And ever love without regard:
I then will own your prior claim
To love, to honour, and to fame;
But till that time, my dear, adieu,
I yet superior am to you.   20

(1722)

maugre] in spite of

ELIZABETH ROWE (née SINGER)
(1674–1737)

Born in Ilchester, Somerset, she was the eldest of the three daughters of Walter Singer and his wife Elizabeth Portnell. Her father, who had been a dissenting minister and was for a time imprisoned in Ilchester, later became a prosperous clothier in Frome. He encouraged her interests in music, painting and literature and she began writing verse at the age of 12. Her poetry had led by the early 1690s to friendship with the family of Viscount Weymouth at Longleat, perhaps through the mediation of the non-juring Bishop Thomas Ken, who was known to her father and was living in retirement at Longleat. Henry Thynne, Lord Weymouth's son, taught her Italian and French and read Tasso with her, and his daughter Frances, at this time a child but later Countess of Hertford (see nos. 77–8), was to become a lifelong friend and correspondent. Anonymously, and probably unknown to her parents, she began sending verse to John Dunton's *Athenian Mercury*, particularly in 1694 and 1695, and when she was still only 22, Dunton published her *Poems On Several Occasions. Written By Philomela* (1696), many of them reprinted from the *Mercury*. The preface by Elizabeth Johnson hailed her as 'a *Champion*' for women against 'the *Tyranny* of the *Prouder Sex*', who try to 'Monopolize *Sence*' and are guilty of '*notorious* Violations on the *Liberties of Free-born* English Women'. Although a second volume, hoped for in the preface, was not forthcoming, Dunton later reprinted many of her poems in the *Athenian Oracle* (1704) and in his *Life and Errors* (1705) praised her as 'The Pindaric Lady in the West' and as 'the richest genius of her Sex'. These early poems, written, according to her biographer in 1739, 'when she was at a boarding-school in the country, or soon after leaving it', were not included in later collected editions of her works. A few, such as her spirited rejoinder 'To one that perswades me to leave the Muses', have a very different tone from the elevated piety usually associated with her ('Yet I'm so scurvily inclin'd to Rhiming, | That undesign'd my thoughts *burst out a chiming*').

In 1703 she met at Longleat the poet Matthew Prior, a colleague of Lord Weymouth at the Board of Trade and Plantations, who for several months conducted a curious correspondence with her, in the course of which he made a number of half-serious declarations of love. Her replies, which have not survived, evidently objected to his 'Familiar or Impertinent' letters, his lack of seriousness, drinking and other vices, but she took the opportunity to use his influence in getting some of her translations of Tasso into Tonson's *Poetical Miscellanies*, Vol. V (1704), in which Prior also addressed two poems to her. In the preface to his *Poems* (1709) Prior later praised her verse, 'in which the Softness of Her Sex, and the Fineness of her Genius, conspire to give Her a very distinguishing Character'. A more predictable literary friend and correspondent was the dissenter, Dr Isaac Watts, who addressed a poem to her, dated 19 July 1706, in his *Horae Lyricae* (2nd edn., 1709). During these years her poems were included in a number of miscellanies: her appearance in *Divine Hymns and Poems* (1704) is perhaps to be explained by the fact that the Revd John Bowden, minister to the dissenting community at Frome, was also a contributor.

In 1709 she met at Bath the young scholar Thomas Rowe, son of a dissenting minister and thirteen years her junior, whom she married in 1710. Having rarely left her home county hitherto, she was able during her marriage to 'bear the winter season in London', but her husband died at Hampstead of consumption in 1715, leaving her heartbroken ('Since that fatal moment, my soul has never known a joy that has been sincere. I look backward, and recal nothing but tormenting scenes of pleasures that have taken their everlasting flight; and forward, every prospect is wild and gloomy'). Thereafter, she 'indulged her unconquerable inclinations to solitude', by retiring to her father's house in Frome, 'to conceal the remainder of her life in absolute retirement'. After her father's death in 1719, she inherited substantial property in Frome and Ilchester, on the income from which she could live comfortably, although she gave half of it away to charity each year, to the point of reducing herself to 'some necessity'. She also interested herself in the education of poor children and in supporting the public school at Frome. She continued to correspond with friends but rarely left Frome, except on a few occasions at the behest of the Countess of Hertford. In the years following her husband's death, she was much occupied with the series of rapturously pious prose works for which she was to be celebrated, notably her *Friendship in Death, in Letters from the Dead to the Living* (1728), dedicated to Edward Young, and her *Letters Moral and Entertaining* (1729–32). Her *History of Joseph*, a poem in eight books on a biblical subject begun some years earlier, appeared in 1736 (reissued in 1737 with two extra books), but she disclaimed serious poetic ambitions ('I am as proud of adjusting a tulip or a butterfly in a right position on a screen, as of writing heroics'). The incorrigible Edmund Curll reprinted her 1696 collection as *Philomela* (1737), against her wishes.

She died in February 1737, having made meticulous preparations for her death and funeral, and was buried in the meeting-house at Frome in the same grave as her father. She had left a number of letters to friends to be opened after her death. Isaac Watts, who had praised her in the preface to his *Reliquiae Juveniles* (1734) for retrieving 'the Honour of Poetry . . . from the Scandal which has been cast upon it, by the abuse of Verse to loose and profane Purposes', edited her posthumous *Devout Exercises of the Heart* (1737), which he dedicated to the unnamed Countess of Hertford. Watts here expressed some reservations about Rowe's prose ('a little too rapturous, and too near a-kin to the language of the mystical writers'), and also tried to anticipate the reaction of some later readers by denying that there is any 'secret panting after a mortal love, in the language of devotion and piety'. Her *Miscellaneous Works* (2 vols., 1739), with prefatory verses by the Countess of Hertford, Elizabeth Carter (see no. 110) and others, were edited by her brother-in-law Theophilus Rowe, who also completed the memoir begun by Henry Grove. Her letters to the (unnamed) Countess of Hertford and a collection of her husband's verse appear in the second volume. Several of her works continued to be reprinted into the following century and she had been translated into French and German by the 1740s. She had many admirers during and after her lifetime. In 1753 it was said that 'The conduct and behaviour of Mrs. Rowe might put some of the present race of females to the blush, who rake the town for infamous adventures to amuse the public'. In 1756 Samuel Johnson praised her 'copiousness and luxuriance . . . her brightness of imagery, her purity of sentiments', which adapted 'the ornaments of romance in the decoration of religion'. An alternative reaction was that of the 16-year-old Fanny Burney (see no. 232), who found Mrs Rowe's *Letters from the Dead* 'so very enthusiastick, that the religion she preaches rather disgusts than charms and elevates—and so romantick, that every word betrays improbability'.

33 *A Hymn*

IN vain the dusky night retires,
    And sullen shadows fly:
In vain the morn with purple light
    Adorns the eastern sky.

In vain the gaudy rising sun
    The wide horizon gilds,
Comes glittering o'er the silver streams,
    And cheers the dewy fields.

In vain, dispensing vernal sweets,
    The morning breezes play: 10
In vain the birds with cheerful songs
    Salute the new-born day;

In vain, unless my Saviour's face
    These gloomy clouds control,
And dissipate the sullen shades
    That press my drooping soul.

O visit then Thy servant, Lord,
    With favour from on high;
Arise, my bright, immortal Sun,
    And all these shades will die.   20

When, when shall I behold Thy face,
    All radiant and serene,
Without these envious dusky clouds
    That make a veil between?

When shall that long-expected day
    Of sacred vision be,
When my impatient soul shall make
    A near approach to Thee?

                                    (1704)

34 *A Laplander's Song to his Mistress*

SHINE out, resplendent God of day,
    On my fair Orramoor;
Her charms thy most propitious ray
    And kindest looks allure.

47

In mountain, vale, or gloomy grove,
  I'd climb the tallest tree,
Could I from thence my absent love,
  My charming rover see.

I'd venture on a rising cloud,
  Aloft in yielding air;   10
From that exalted station proud,
  To view the smiling fair.

Should she in some sequestered bower
  Among the branches hide,
I'd tear off every leaf and flower,
  Till she was there descried.

From every bird I'd steal a wing
  To Orramoor to fly;
And urged by love, would swiftly spring
  Along the lightsome sky.   20

Return, and bless me with thy charms,
  While yet the sun displays
His fairest beams, and kindly warms
  Us with his vital rays.

Return before that light be gone,
  In which thou shouldst appear;
Unwelcome night is hastening on
  To darken half the year.

In vain, relentless maid, in vain
  Thou dost a youth forsake,   30
Whose love shall quickly o'er the plain
  Thy savage flight o'ertake.

Should bars of steel my passage stay,
  They could not thee secure:
I'd through enchantments find a way
  To seize my Orramoor.

                              (Wr. _c._1712?; pub. 1737)

Upon the Death of her Husband

IN what soft language shall my thoughts get free,
My dear Alexis, when I talk of thee?
Ye Muses, Graces, all ye gentle train
Of weeping loves, assist the pensive strain.
But why should I implore your moving art?
'Tis but to speak the dictates of my heart,
And all that knew the charming youth will join
Their friendly sighs and pious tears to mine:
For all that knew his merit must confess
In grief for him there can be no excess.   10
His soul was formed to act each glorious part
Of life, unstained with vanity or art;
No thought within his generous mind had birth,
But what he might have owned to heaven and earth:
Practised by him, each virtue grew more bright,
And shone with more than its own native light.
Whatever noble warmth could recommend
The just, the active, and the constant friend,
Was all his own—but oh! a dearer name,
And softer ties, my endless sorrows claim;   20
Lost in despair, distracted and forlorn,
The lover, I, and tender husband mourn.
Whate'er to such superior worth was due,
Whate'er excess the fondest passion knew,
I felt for thee, dear youth; my joys, my care,
My prayers themselves were thine, and only where
Thou wast concerned, my virtue was sincere.
Whene'er I begged for blessings on thy head,
Nothing was cold or formal that I said;
My warmest vows to heaven were made for thee,   30
And love still mingled with my piety.
O thou wast all my glory, all my pride,
Through life's uncertain paths my constant guide:
Regardless of the world, to gain thy praise
Was all that could my just ambition raise.

Why has my heart this fond engagement known,
Or why has heaven dissolved the tie so soon?
Why was the charming youth so formed to move?
Or why was all my soul so turned for love?
But virtue here a vain defence had made,   40
Where so much worth and eloquence could plead.
For he could talk—'twas ecstasy to hear,

'Twas joy, 'twas harmony to every ear:
Eternal music dwelt upon his tongue,
Soft and transporting as the muse's song.
Listening to him, my cares were charmed to rest,
And love and silent rapture filled my breast;
Unheeded the gay moments took their flight,
And time was only measured by delight.
I hear the loved, the melting accent still,   50
And still the warm, the tender transport feel:
Again I see the sprightly passions rise,
And life and pleasure kindle in his eyes.
My fancy paints him now with every grace,
But ah! the dear resemblance mocks my fond embrace;
The flattering vision takes its hasty flight,
And scenes of horror swim before my sight.
Grief and despair in all their terrors rise,
A dying lover pale and gasping lies.
Each dismal circumstance appears in view,   60
The fatal object is for ever new:
His anguish with the quickest sense I feel,
And hear this sad, this moving language still:

'My dearest wife! my last, my fondest care!
Sure heaven for thee will hear a dying prayer:
Be thou the charge of sacred providence,
When I am gone, be that thy kind defence;
Ten thousand smiling blessings crown thy head,
When I am cold, and numbered with the dead.
Think on thy vows, be to my memory just,   70
My future fame and honour are thy trust.
From all engagement here I now am free,
But that which keeps my lingering soul with thee.
How much I love, thy bleeding heart can tell,
Which does, like mine, the pangs of parting feel.
But haste to meet me on the happy plains,
Where mighty love in endless triumph reigns.'

He ceased, then gently yielded up his breath,
And fell a blooming sacrifice to death.
But oh! what words, what numbers can express,   80
What thought conceive, the height of my distress?
Why did they tear me from thy breathless clay?
I should have stayed, and wept my life away.
Yet, gentle shade, whether thou now dost rove
Through some blest vale, or ever-verdant grove,

One moment listen to my grief, and take
The softest vows that ever love can make.

   For thee all thoughts of pleasure I forego,
For thee my tears shall never cease to flow;
For thee at once I from the world retire,   90
To feed in silent shades a hopeless fire.
My bosom all thy image shall retain,
The full impression there shall still remain.
As thou hast taught my tender heart to prove
The noblest height and elegance of love,
That sacred passion I to thee confine,
  My spotless faith shall be for ever thine.

(1719)

36   *A Hymn*

YE pure inhabitants of light,
   Ye virgin minds above,
That feel the sacred violence
   And mighty force of love,

By all your boundless joys, by all
   Your love to human kind,
I charge you to instruct me where
   My absent lord to find.

I've searched the pleasant vales and plains,
   And climbed the hills around;   10
But no glad tidings of my love
   Among the swains have found.

I've oft invoked him in the shades,
   By every stream and rock;
The rocks, the streams, and echoing shades
   My vain industry mock.

I traced the city's noisy street
   And told my cares aloud;
But no intelligence could meet
   Among the thoughtless crowd.   20

I searched the temple round, for there
   He oft has blessed my sight,
And half unveiled, of his loved face
   Disclosed the heavenly light.

But with these glorious views, no more
   I feast my ravished eyes,
For veiled with interposing clouds
   My eager search he flies.

O could I in some desert land
   His sacred footsteps trace,   30
I'd with a glad devotion kneel
   And bless the happy place.

I'd follow him o'er burning sands,
   Or where perpetual snow
With horrid aspect clothes the ground,
   To find my lord I'd go.

Nor stormy seas should stay my course,
   Nor unfrequented shore,
Nor craggy Alps, nor desert wastes
   Where hungry lions roar.   40

Through ranks of interposing deaths
   To his embrace I'd fly,
And to enjoy his blissful smiles,
   Would be content to die.

                  (1737)

OCTAVIA WALSH
(1677–1706)

She was the youngest child of Joseph Walsh of Abberley Lodge, Worcestershire, and his wife Elizabeth Palmes, who had two sons and six daughters. Her father died in 1682 aged 63. Her mother, who must have been much younger, survived until 1719. Little is known about her, although her brother William (1663–1708), the early friend and mentor of Pope, enjoyed some reputation as a poet and critic. She died of smallpox in 1706 at the age of 29 and was buried in Worcester Cathedral. Her family discovered her writings after her death. The original MS of her verse in the Bodleian Library is a notebook containing drafts and copies of poems, as well as a few recipes, a note dated 22 Jan. 1705 stating that the children (not hers) returned to school that day, and a pen and wash drawing of her. Another MS, now in the Berg Collection of the New York Public Library, was no doubt prepared by her family after her death:

'The Private Entertainment of Mrs. Octavia Walsh In her Vacant Hours From the Age of Fifteen to Twenty-Nine, At which Time it pleas'd Almighty God by ye Small-pox to take her out of this World. 1706.' A note by a relative, William Bromley, states that 'The contents . . . were found among her Papers after her death, till which time none of her nearest Relations knew that she was an Author—She was pious without . . . Moroseness, Sensible without Ostentation—Beautifull without Pride . . . She died the 10th Oct. 1706'. This MS includes her prose discourses on religious subjects.

Apart from a few burlesque pieces, her verse is devotional or gloomily subjective, with some apparent references to an unhappy love-affair. Some poems are addressed to 'Urania', of whose esteem she feels unworthy. Seven examples of her pious verse were included in *Poems upon Divine and Moral Subjects . . . By Dr. Patrick . . . and other Eminent Hands* (1719), pp. 99–118 (reissued in 1734 as *A Collection of Select Original Poems and Translations*).

37 [*'At length my soul the fatal union finds'*]

AT length my soul the fatal union finds,
That with dead earth its purer nature binds;
Fettered in flesh, it seeks for soft repose,
And drags a tiresome carcase as it goes.
As an old cottage, worn by time, will bend,
And from its roof its faithful inmate send,
So my old house, disdainful of control,
Crushes and overwhelms the sickly soul.
When the quick-moving blood begins to stay,
And with less haste pursue its sanguine way,　　　　10
A heavy weight the sinking soul sustains,
And from each quarter of the camp complains.
Then sudden starts and fears the mind entrance,
And pale-faced ghosts before its fancy dance;
Impending ruin o'er its head appears,
And the whole man runs into eyes and ears.
In vain my Reason then begins to plead,
Convinced of safety, yet to fear betrayed:
As well you may by arguments assuage
The heats of those that in a fever rage.　　　　20
But, O great God! Since thou hast wisely joined
This mouldering clay to an immortal mind,
Since my great landlord makes this cot my care,
I'll strive to keep it in the best repair:
That my poor soul, unmoved by its decays,
May pay its rent in due returns of praise,
Till he sees fit his favour to recall,
And on my head let the old cottage fall.

(MS *c.*1705)

53

LADY MARY WORTLEY MONTAGU
(née PIERREPONT)
(1689–1762)

She was the eldest of the four children of Evelyn Pierrepont (who became Earl of Kingston in 1690, Marquess of Dorchester in 1706, and Duke of Kingston in 1715) and his wife Lady Mary Fielding. Her mother died when she was 13 and the children were brought up by their paternal grandmother near Salisbury. Although she later had a governess of whose 'superstitious Tales and false notions' she complained, she was able to educate herself by reading in her father's libraries at his houses at Thoresby, Nottinghamshire, and in London, began writing in her early teens, and taught herself Latin. Personal experience no doubt lay behind her warning many years later that a girl must 'conceal what Learning she attains', if she is not to arouse 'the most inveterate Hatred, of all he and she Fools'. Through her father, a leading Whig politician, she eventually met such literary figures as Addison, Steele, Congreve, and Garth. From about 1710 she was courted by Edward Wortley Montagu, a lawyer and MP for Huntingdon, also a friend of Addison and Steele, who was eleven years older than she. Although her father objected to the match on financial grounds, they met and corresponded secretly and finally eloped and married at Salisbury in August 1712. Their son Edward was born in May 1713. At this period she wrote a critique of the MS of Addison's tragedy *Cato*, the author taking into account some of her suggestions, and contributed an essay to the *Spectator* (No. 573), her first publication.

After the Hanoverian accession in 1714, her husband became a Junior Commissioner of the Treasury and they settled in London. She met and corresponded with Pope, and with his friend John Gay wrote some 'town eclogues', three of which fell into the hands of Edmund Curll, who published them without permission as *Court Poems* in 1716. 'The Small-Pox', which with two other town eclogues escaped publication until 1747, reflects her own serious illness in 1715 from the disease, from which her brother had recently died. In 1716 her husband was appointed Ambassador to Turkey and in August she accompanied him on the long journey via Hanover, Vienna, and Belgrade, reaching Constantinople in May 1717. Her letters make clear her curiosity about all aspects of Turkish life, and she also studied the Turkish language and literature. Her daughter Mary was born in 1718. She courageously had her son innoculated for smallpox, the practice she would be influential in popularizing on her return to England. Her husband's embassy, intended to mediate between Austria and Turkey, ended in failure. Their return journey began in July 1718, taking them by sea to Genoa and then across the Alps to Paris. They reached London in October.

Although her husband remained a MP, his political and diplomatic career ended at this point and he was increasingly preoccupied with business. They had a town house in Covent Garden and acquired a country residence at Twickenham, not far from Pope, with whom she had corresponded while abroad. She resumed her life in Court circles, acquiring an increasing reputation as a wit, and some of her prose and verse found its way into print, including an essay on smallpox innoculation in *The Flying-Post* in September 1722. Later in the decade she came to know the feminist Mary Astell, who unsuccessfully urged her to publish the 'Embassy Letters' she compiled at this period from the journal and letters she had written while abroad.

She met Voltaire in 1727, gave literary advice to the poet Edward Young, accepted the dedication of Richard Savage's *Miscellaneous Poems* (1726), and later acted as patron to her second cousin, Henry Fielding, at the outset of his theatrical career. The dedication of his *Love in Several Masks* (1728) effusively describes her as 'a living Confutation of those morose Schoolmen who wou'd confine Knowledge to the Male Part of the Species'.

By 1729, when he referred contemptuously to her in the *Dunciad*, her relations with Pope had seriously deteriorated, possibly because she had mockingly rejected a passionate declaration of love on his part some years earlier. A period of increasingly scurrilous literary enmity followed in lampoons and satires, to which other pamphleteers contributed. Although she never acknowledged it, it was widely assumed from the beginning that she was the co-author with Lord Hervey (Pope's 'Sporus') of *Verses Addressed to the Imitator of . . . Horace* (1733). It was at about the same period that she wrote 'Simplicity, a Comedy', adapted from Marivaux, which was not acted or printed. Later in the decade she published anonymously nine numbers of a pro-Walpole periodical, *The Nonsense of Common-Sense* (1737–8), the sixth number of which attacked male stereotypes of women which throw them 'below the Dignity of the Human Species'.

In 1736, at the age of 47, she fell passionately in love with Francesco Algarotti, a young, ambitious, and bi-sexual Italian author, for whose attentions she competed with Lord Hervey. There was little to keep her in England: her husband, who had inherited great wealth in the late 1720s, was as indifferent as he had been for most of their marriage, her daughter had recently married the Earl of Bute, and the vagaries of their incorrigible son (who had run away to sea at the age of 14) remained beyond parental control. (He later became an orientalist.) In July 1739 she set out for Venice, but her hopes of living with Algarotti (who had instead become a favourite of Prince Frederick of Prussia, later Frederick the Great) soon evaporated. With an annual income of over £1,100, she enjoyed a busy social life in Venice and was much visited by young Englishmen on the Grand Tour. Horace Walpole, who met her in Florence in 1740, reported that she freely showed her writings to friends and allowed him to copy her poems. Although she corresponded with her husband, they made no effort to meet, even during his visits to the Continent. Later she lived in Avignon (1742–6) and Brescia (1746–56), where she was swindled for several years by the unscrupulous Count Palazzi.

Throughout this period she corresponded with relatives and friends, advising her daughter in the early 1750s about female education, and often commenting on the new English books she read, especially novels (including those of Fielding and Richardson). In England her literary reputation was kept alive by Walpole's publication of her *Six Town Eclogues. With Some Poems* (1747), later reprinted in Dodsley's *Collection* (1748). At the age of 67 she moved to Venice and then Padua, but in January 1762, some months after her husband's death, returned to London, her reappearance after so long a period arousing much interest. After a few months of active social life, she died of cancer on 21 August 1762. Before her death, no doubt aware that her family would seek to prevent it, she arranged the posthumous publication of her 'Embassy Letters' in 1763, which were later frequently reprinted. The first attempt to collect her *Poetical Works*, edited by Isaac Reed, appeared in 1768.

Throughout her life she resented the fact that 'the same Studies which raise the Character of a Man should hurt that of a Woman. We are educated in the grossest ignorance, and no art omitted to stifle our natural reason.' Yet she had always professed an aristocratic disdain for publication and literary reputation. In a letter of

1753 she describes telling Lord Cornbury that 'it was not the busyness of a Man of Quality to turn Author, and that he should confine himselfe to the Applause of his Friends, and by no means venture on the press'. She nevertheless carefully collected her verse and was increasingly willing to show it to her acquaintance and let them transcribe it. What she learned about the literary world from her quarrels with Pope can hardly have encouraged her to play a more prominent role in it. The fact remains that the social status which would have enabled her to be one of the most influential women writers of the first half of the century in itself provided the inhibition which rendered such a career impossible.

38   *The Resolve*

WHILST thirst of praise, and vain desire of fame,
In every age, is every woman's aim;
With courtship pleased, of silly toasters proud;
Fond of a train, and happy in a crowd;
On each poor fool bestowing some kind glance;
Each conquest owing to some loose advance;
Whilst vain coquets affect to be pursued,
And think they're virtuous, if not grossly lewd;
Let this great maxim be my virtue's guide:
In part she is to blame, who has been tried,   10
He comes too near, that comes to be denied.

                              (Wr. 1712–13; pub. 1724)

39   from *Six Town Eclogues*

                        Saturday

                      The Small-Pox

                         FLAVIA

The wretched Flavia, on her couch reclined,
Thus breathed the anguish of a wounded mind.
A glass reversed in her right hand she bore,
For now she shunned the face she sought before.
    'How am I changed! alas! how am I grown
A frightful spectre, to myself unknown!
Where's my complexion? where the radiant bloom,
That promised happiness for years to come?
Then, with what pleasure I this face surveyed!
To look once more, my visits oft delayed!   10
Charmed with the view, a fresher red would rise,
And a new life shot sparkling from my eyes!

Ah! faithless glass, my wonted bloom restore!
Alas! I rave, that bloom is now no more!
  'The greatest good the gods on men bestow,
Ev'n youth itself, to me is useless now.
There was a time (oh! that I could forget!)
When opera-tickets poured before my feet;
And at the Ring, where brightest beauties shine,
The earliest cherries of the spring were mine.   20
Witness, O Lillie, and thou, Motteux, tell,
How much japan these eyes have made you sell.
With what contempt ye saw me oft despise
The humble offer of the raffled prize;
For at each raffle still the prize I bore,
With scorn rejected, or with triumph wore.
Now beauty's fled, and presents are no more.
  'For me the patriot has the House forsook,
And left debates to catch a passing look;
For me the soldier has soft verses writ;   30
For me the beau has aimed to be a wit.
For me the wit to nonsense was betrayed;
The gamester has for me his dun delayed,
And overseen the card I would have paid.
The bold and haughty by success made vain,
Awed by my eyes, has trembled to complain:
The bashful squire, touched with a wish unknown,
Has dared to speak with spirit not his own:
Fired by one wish, all did alike adore;
Now beauty's fled, and lovers are no more.   40
  'As round the room I turn my weeping eyes,
New unaffected scenes of sorrow rise.
Far from my sight that killing picture bear,
The face disfigure, or the canvas tear!
That picture, which with pride I used to show,
The lost resemblance but upbraids me now.
And thou, my toilette, where I oft have sat,
While hours unheeded passed in deep debate,
How curls should fall, or where a patch to place;
If blue or scarlet best became my face;   50
Now on some happier nymph your aid bestow;
On fairer heads, ye useless jewels, glow!
No borrowed lustre can my charms restore,
Beauty is fled, and dress is now no more.
  'Ye meaner beauties, I permit you shine;
Go, triumph in the hearts that once were mine;

japan] Japanese work with painted and varnished design   overseen . . . paid] under-
written her next bet

But, midst your triumphs with confusion know,
'Tis to my ruin all your charms ye owe.
Would pitying heaven restore my wonted mien,
Ye still might move unthought of and unseen: 60
But oh, how vain, how wretched is the boast
Of beauty faded, and of empire lost!
What now is left but weeping to deplore
My beauty fled, and empire now no more?

   'Ye cruel chymists, what withheld your aid?
Could no pomatums save a trembling maid?
How false and trifling is that art you boast;
No art can give me back my beauty lost!
In tears, surrounded by my friends I lay,
Masked o'er, and trembling at the light of day;   70
Mirmillo came my fortune to deplore
(A golden-headed cane well carved he bore):
"Cordials", he cried, "my spirits must restore!"
Beauty is fled, and spirit is no more!
Galen the grave, officious Squirt was there,
With fruitless grief and unavailing care:
Machaon too, the great Machaon, known
By his red cloak and his superior frown;
"And why," he cried, "this grief and this despair?
You shall again be well, again be fair;   80
Believe my oath" (with that an oath he swore);
False was his oath! my beauty is no more.

   'Cease, hapless maid, no more thy tale pursue,
Forsake mankind, and bid the world adieu.
Monarchs and beauties rule with equal sway,
All strive to serve, and glory to obey:
Alike unpitied when deposed they grow,
Men mock the idol of their former vow.

   'Adieu, ye parks—in some obscure recess,
Where gentle streams will weep at my distress,   90
Where no false friend will in my grief take part,
And mourn my ruin with a joyful heart;
There let me live in some deserted place,
There hide in shades this lost inglorious face.
Plays, operas, circles, I no more must view!
My toilette, patches, all the world, adieu!'

(Wr. 1716; pub. 1747)

40

Verses Written in the Chiosk of the British Palace, at Pera, Overlooking the City of Constantinople, Dec. 26, 1717

'GIVE me, great God!' said I, 'a little farm,
In summer shady, and in winter warm;
Where a clear spring gives birth to a cool brook,
By nature sliding down a mossy rock.
Not artfully in leaden pipes conveyed,
Nor greatly falling in a forced cascade,
Pure and unsullied winding through the shade.'
All-bounteous Heaven has added to my prayer
A softer climate and a purer air.

Our frozen isle now chilling winter binds,   10
Deformed with rains, and rough with blasting winds;
The withered woods grow white with hoary frost,
By driving storms their verdant beauty's lost;
The trembling birds their leafless covert shun,
And seek in distant climes a warmer sun:
The water-nymphs their silenced urns deplore,
Even Thames benumbed, a river now no more:
The barren meadows give no more delight,
By glistening snow made painful to the sight.

Here summer reigns with one eternal smile,   20
And double harvests bless the happy soil;
Fair fertile fields, to whom indulgent Heaven
Has every charm of every season given.
No killing cold deforms the beauteous year,
The springing flowers no coming winter fear.
But as the parent rose decays and dies,
The infant buds with brighter colours rise,
And with fresh sweets the mother's scent supplies.
Near them the violet glows with odours blessed,
And blooms in more than Tyrian purple dressed;   30
The rich jonquils their golden beams display,
And shine in glory emulating day;
These cheerful groves their living leaves retain,
The streams still murmur undefiled by rain,
And rising green adorns the fruitful plain.
The warbling kind uninterrupted sing,
Warmed with enjoyments of perpetual spring.

Here, from my window, I at once survey
The crowded city and resounding sea;

Chiosk] summer-house

59

In distant views see Asian mountains rise,   40
And lose their snowy summits in the skies;
Above those mountains high Olympus towers,
The parliamental seat of heavenly powers!
New to the sight, my ravished eyes admire
Each gilded crescent and each antique spire,
The marble mosques, beneath whose ample domes
Fierce warlike sultans sleep in peaceful tombs;
Those lofty structures, once the Christian boast,
Their names, their glories, and their beauties lost;
Those altars bright with gold, with sculpture graced,   50
By barbarous zeal of savage foes defaced;
Sophia alone her ancient sound retains,
Though unbelieving vows her shrine profanes;
Where holy saints have died in sacred cells,
Where monarchs prayed, the frantic dervish dwells.
How art thou fallen, imperial city, low!
Where are thy hopes of Roman glory now?
Where are thy palaces by prelates raised?
Where priestly pomp in purple lustre blazed,
Where Grecian artists all their skill displayed,   60
Before the happy sciences decayed;
So vast, that youthful kings might there reside,
So splendid, to content a patriarch's pride;
Convents where emperors professed of old,
The laboured pillars that their triumphs told;
Vain monuments of men that once were great,
Sunk undistinguished in one common fate.
    One little spot the small Fanar contains,
Of Greek nobility the poor remains;
Where other Helens show like powerful charms   70
As once engaged the warring world in arms;
Those names which royal ancestry can boast,
In mean mechanic arts obscurely lost;
Those eyes a second Homer might inspire,
Fixed at the loom, destroy their useless fire.
    Grieved at a view, which struck upon my mind
The short-lived vanity of humankind,
In gaudy objects I indulge my sight,
And turn where eastern pomp gives gay delight;
See the vast train in various habits dressed,   80
By the bright scimitar and sable vest
The vizier proud distinguished o'er the rest;
Six slaves in gay attire his bridle hold,
His bridle rich with gems, his stirrups gold;

His snowy steed adorned with lavish pride,
Whole troops of soldiers mounted by his side;
These toss the plumy crest, Arabian coursers guide,
With awful duty all decline their eyes,
No bellowing shouts of noisy crowds arise;
Silence, in solemn state, the march attends,   90
Till at the dread divan the slow procession ends.
    Yet not these prospects, all profusely gay—
The gilded navy that adorns the sea,
The rising city in confusion fair,
Magnificently formed, irregular,
Where woods and palaces at once surprise,
Gardens on gardens, domes on domes arise,
And endless beauties tire the wandering eyes—
So soothes my wishes, or so charms my mind,
As this retreat, secure from humankind.   100
No knave's successful craft does spleen excite,
No coxcomb's tawdry splendour shocks my sight,
No mob-alarm awakes my female fears,
No unrewarded merit asks my tears,
Nor praise my mind, nor envy hurts my ear,
Even fame itself can hardly reach me here;
Impertinence, with all her tattling train,
Fair-sounding flattery's delicious bane;
Censorious folly, noisy party rage,
The thousand tongues with which she must engage,   110
Who dare have virtue in a vicious age.

(Wr. 1717; pub. 1720)

Epitaph

41

HERE lie John Hughes and Sarah Drew.
Perhaps you'll say, what's that to you?
Believe me, friend, much may be said
On this poor couple that are dead.
On Sunday next they should have married:
But see how oddly things are carried.
On Thursday last it rained and lightened:
These tender lovers, sadly frightened,
Sheltered beneath the cocking hay,
In hopes to pass the storm away.   10
But the bold thunder found them out
(Commissioned for that end, no doubt)
And, seizing on their trembling breath,
Consigned them to the shades of death.

Who knows if 'twas not kindly done?
For had they seen the next year's sun,
A beaten wife and cuckold swain
Had jointly cursed the marriage chain.
Now they are happy in their doom,
For P[ope] has wrote upon their tomb.   20

(Wr. 1718; pub. 1763)

42   *The Lover: A Ballad*

AT length, by so much importunity pressed,
Take, Molly, at once, the inside of my breast;
This stupid indifference so often you blame
Is not owing to nature, to fear, or to shame:
I am not as cold as a virgin in lead,
Nor is Sunday's sermon so strong in my head:
I know but too well how time flies along,
That we live but few years, and yet fewer are young.

But I hate to be cheated, and never will buy
Long years of repentance for moments of joy.
Oh! was there a man (but where shall I find   10
Good sense and good nature so equally joined?)
Would value his pleasure, contribute to mine;
Not meanly would boast, nor lewdly design;
Not over severe, yet not stupidly vain,
For I would have the power, though not give the pain.

No pedant, yet learnèd; not rake-helly gay,
Or laughing, because he has nothing to say;
To all my whole sex obliging and free,
Yet never be fond of any but me;
In public, preserve the decorums are just,   20
And show in his eyes he is true to his trust;
Then rarely approach, and respectfully bow,
Yet not fulsomely pert, nor yet foppishly low.

But when the long hours of public are past,
And we meet with champagne and a chicken at last,
May every fond pleasure that hour endear;
Be banished afar both discretion and fear.
Forgetting or scorning the airs of the crowd,
He may cease to be formal, and I to be proud,
Till lost in the joy, we confess that we live,   30
And he may be rude, and yet I may forgive.

And that my delight may be solidly fixed,
Let the friend and the lover be handsomely mixed;
In whose tender bosom my soul might confide,
Whose kindness can soothe me, whose counsel could guide.
From such a dear lover, as here I describe,
No danger should fright me, no millions should bribe;
But till this astonishing creature I know,
As I long have lived chaste, I will keep myself so.   40

I never will share with the wanton coquette,
Or be caught by a vain affectation of wit.
The toasters and songsters may try all their art,
But never shall enter the pass of my heart.
I loathe the lewd rake, the dressed fopling despise:
Before such pursuers the nice virgin flies:
And as Ovid has sweetly in parables told,
We harden like trees, and like rivers are cold.

                              (Wr. *c.*1721–5; pub. 1747)

43   *Epistle* [*to Lord Bathurst*]

    HOW happy you who varied joys pursue,
    And every hour presents you something new!
    Plans, schemes, and models, all Palladio's art
    For six long months has gained upon your heart;
    Of colonnades and corridors you talk,
    The winding staircase, and the covered walk;
    Proportioned columns strike before your eye
    Corinthian beauty, Ionian majesty:
    You blend the orders with Vitruvian toil,
    And raise with wondrous joy the fancied pile.   10
       But the dull workman's slow-performing hand
    But coldly executes his lord's command;
    With dirt and mortar soon you grow displeased,
    Planting succeeds, and avenues are raised,
    Canals are cut, and mountains level made,
    Bowers of retreat, and galleries of shade.
    The shaven turf presents a living green,
    The bordering flowers in mystic knots are seen.
    With studied Art on Nature you refine—
    The spring beheld you warm in this design,   20
    But scarce the cold attacks your favourite trees,
    Your inclinations fail, and wishes freeze:
    You quit the grove, so lately so admired;
    With other views your eager hopes are fired.

Post to the city you direct your way,
Not blooming paradise would bribe your stay:
Ambition shows you power's brightest side,
'Tis meanly poor in solitude to hide:
Though certain pain attends the cares of state,
A good man owes his country to be great;   30
Should act abroad the high distinguished part,
Or show at least the purpose of his heart.
With thoughts like these, the shining Court you seek,
Full of new projects for—almost a week.
You then despise the tinsel, glittering snare;
Think vile mankind below a serious care;
Life is too short for any distant aim,
And cold the dull reward of future fame:
Be happy then, while yet you have to live,
And love is all the blessing Heaven can give.   40
Fired by new passion, you address the fair;
Survey the opera as a gay parterre:
Young Cloe's bloom had made you certain prize,
But for a sidelong glance of Celia's eyes:
Your beating heart acknowledges her power,
Your eager eyes her lovely form devour;
You feel the poison swelling in your breast,
And all your soul by fond desire possessed.
In dying sighs a long three hours is passed;
To some assembly with impatient haste,   50
With trembling hope and doubtful fear you move,
Resolved to tempt your fate, and own your love:
But there Belinda meets you on the stairs.
Easy her shape, attracting all her airs;
A smile she gives, and with a smile can wound;
Her melting voice has music in the sound,
Her every motion wears resistless grace,
Wit in her mien, and pleasure in her face:
Here while you vow eternity of love,
Cloe and Celia unregarded move.   60
   Thus on the sands of Afric's burning plains,
However deeply made, no long impress remains;
The lightest leaf can leave its figure there;
The strongest form is scattered by the air.
So yielding the warm temper of your mind,
So touched by every eye, so tossed by every wind.
O how unlike has Heaven my soul designed!
   Unseen, unheard, the throng around me move;

parterre] ornamental flowerbed

64

Not wishing praise, insensible of love:
No whispers soften, nor no beauties fire;   70
Careless I see the dance, and coldly hear the lyre.
   So numerous herds are driven o'er the rock,
No print is left of all the passing flock;
So sings the wind around the solid stone,
So vainly beat the waves with fruitless moan.
Tedious the toil, and great the workman's care,
Who dare attempt to fix impressions there.
But should some swain, more skilful than the rest,
Engrave his name on this cold marble breast,
Not rolling ages could deface that name—   80
Through all the storms of life 'tis still the same:
Though length of years with moss may shade the ground,
Deep, though unseen, remains the secret wound.

                             (Wr. *c*.1725; pub. 1748)

44   *An Answer to a Love-Letter in Verse*

Is it to me, this sad lamenting strain?
Are Heaven's choicest gifts bestowed in vain?
A plenteous fortune, and a beauteous bride,
Your love rewarded, and content your pride:
Yet leaving her—'tis me that you pursue,
Without one single charm but being new.
   How vile is man! how I detest the ways
Of artful falsehood, and designing praise!
Tasteless, an easy happiness you slight,
Ruin your joy, and mischief your delight.   10
Why should poor pug (the mimic of your kind)
Wear a rough chain, and be to box confined?
Some cup, perhaps, he breaks, or tears a fan,
While moves unpunished the destroyer, man.
Not bound by vows, and unrestrained by shame,
In sport you break the heart, and rend the fame.
Not that your art can be successful here,
Th' already plundered need no robber fear:
Nor sighs, nor charms, nor flattery can move,
Too well secured against a second love.   20
Once, and but once, that devil charmed my mind;
To reason deaf, to observation blind,
I idly hoped (what cannot love persuade?)
My fondness equalled, and my truth repaid:

44 pug] pet monkey

Slow to distrust, and willing to believe,
Long hushed my doubts, and would myself deceive;
But oh! too soon—this tale would ever last;
Sleep, sleep my wrongs, and let me think 'em past.
   For you, who mourn with counterfeited grief,
And ask so boldly like a begging thief,   30
May soon some other nymph inflict the pain
You know so well with cruel art to feign.
Though long you've sported with Dan Cupid's dart,
You may see eyes, and you may feel a heart.
   So the brisk wits, who stop the evening coach,
Laugh at the fear that follows their approach;
With idle mirth, and haughty scorn, despise
The passenger's pale cheek and staring eyes:
But seized by Justice, find a fright no jest,
And all the terror doubled in their breast.   40.

                       (Wr. 1720s; pub. 1750)

A Receipt to Cure the Vapours

45

WHY will Delia thus retire,
   And idly languish life away?
While the sighing crowd admire,
   'Tis too soon for hartshorn tea.

All those dismal looks and fretting
   Cannot Damon's life restore;
Long ago the worms have ate him,
   You can never see him more.

Once again consult your toilette,
   In the glass your face review: 10
So much weeping soon will spoil it,
   And no spring your charms renew.

I, like you, was born a woman,
   Well I know what vapours mean:
The disease, alas! is common;
   Single, we have all the spleen.

All the morals that they tell us
   Never cured the sorrow yet:
Choose, among the pretty fellows,
   One of honour, youth and wit.

45 hartshorn tea] a medicinal solution of ammonia

Prithee hear him every morning,
    At the least an hour or two;
Once again at night returning—
    I believe the dose will do.

(Wr. 1730?; pub. 1748)

46   from *Verses Addressed to the Imitator of the First
        Satire of the Second Book of Horace*

[*A Reply to Alexander Pope*]

WHEN God created thee, one would believe
He said the same as to the snake of Eve:
'To human race antipathy declare,
'Twixt them and thee be everlasting war.'
But oh! the sequel of the sentence dread,
And whilst you bruise their heel, beware your head.
    Nor think thy weakness shall be thy defence,
The female scold's protection in offence.
Sure 'tis as fair to beat who cannot fight,
As 'tis to libel those who cannot write.   10
And if thou draw'st thy pen to aid the law,
Others a cudgel, or a rod, may draw.
    If none with vengeance yet thy crimes pursue,
Or give thy manifold affronts their due;
If limbs unbroken, skin without a stain,
Unwhipped, unblanketed, unkicked, unslain,
That wretched little carcase you retain,
The reason is, not that the world wants eyes,
But thou'rt so mean, they see, and they despise:
When fretful porcupine, with rancorous will,   20
From mounted back shoots forth a harmless quill,
Cool the spectators stand; and all the while
Upon the angry little monster smile.
Thus 'tis with thee:—whilst impotently safe,
You strike unwounding, we unhurt can laugh.
'Who but must laugh, this bully when he sees,
A puny insect shivering at a breeze?'
One over-matched by every blast of wind,
Insulting and provoking all mankind.
    Is this the thing to keep mankind in awe,   30
'To make those tremble who escape the law?'
Is this the ridicule to live so long,
'The deathless satire and immortal song?'

No: like thy self-blown praise, thy scandal flies;
And, as we're told of wasps, it stings and dies.
　If none do yet return th' intended blow,
You all your safety to your dullness owe:
But whilst that armour thy poor corpse defends,
'Twill make thy readers few, as are thy friends:
Those, who thy nature loathed, yet loved thy art,　　　　40
Who liked thy head, and yet abhorred thy heart:
Chose thee to read, but never to converse,
And scorned in prose him whom they prized in verse:
Even they shall now their partial error see,
Shall shun thy writings like thy company;
And to thy books shall ope their eyes no more
Than to thy person they would do their door.
　Nor thou the justice of the world disown,
That leaves thee thus an outcast and alone;
For though in law to murder be to kill,　　　　50
In equity the murder's in the will:
Then whilst with coward-hand you stab a name,
And try at least t' assassinate our fame,
Like the first bold assassin's be thy lot,
Ne'er be thy guilt forgiven, or forgot;
But, as thou hat'st, be hated by mankind,
And with the emblem of thy crooked mind
Marked on thy back, like Cain, by God's own hand,
Wander, like him, accursèd through the land.

(1733)

47　　　　　　　　*Addressed to* ——

WITH toilsome steps I pass through life's dull road,
No packhorse half so weary of his load;
And when this dirty journey will conclude,
To what new realms is then my way pursued?
Say, then, does the unbodied spirit fly
To happier climes and to a better sky;
Or sinking, mixes with its kindred clay,
And sleeps a whole eternity away?
Or shall this form be once again renewed,
With all its frailties and its hopes endued,　　　　10
Acting once more on this detested stage
Passions of youth, infirmities of age?
　I see in Tully what the ancients thought;
And read unprejudiced what moderns taught;

But no conviction from my reading springs,
Most dubious on the most important things.
   Yet one short moment would at once explain
What all philosophy has sought in vain,
Would clear all doubt, and terminate all pain.
   Why then not hasten that decisive hour,   20
Still in my view, and ever in my power?
Why should I drag along this life I hate,
Without one thought to mitigate the weight?
Whence this mysterious bearing to exist,
When every joy is lost, and every hope dismissed?
In chains and darkness wherefore should I stay,
And mourn in prison, while I keep the key?

                      (Wr. 1736; publ. 1749)

48   *Hymn to the Moon*

            Written in July, in an Arbour

THOU silver deity of secret night,
   Direct my footsteps through the woodland shade;
Thou conscious witness of unknown delight,
   The lover's guardian, and the Muse's aid!

By thy pale beams I solitary rove,
   To thee my tender grief confide;
Serenely sweet you gild the silent grove,
   My friend, my goddess, and my guide.

E'en thee, fair queen, from the amazing height,
   The charms of young Endymion drew;   10
Veiled with the mantle of concealing night,
   With all thy greatness, and thy coldness too.

                    (Wr. by 1740; pub. 1750)

49   *Verses Written in a Garden*

    SEE how that pair of billing doves
    With open murmurs own their loves;
    And, heedless of censorious eyes,
    Pursue their unpolluted joys:
    No fears of future want molest
    The downy quiet of their nest;

No interest joined the happy pair,
Securely blest in Nature's care,
While her dear dictates they pursue:
For constancy is nature too.   10
    Can all the doctrine of our schools,
Our moral maxims, our religious rules,
Can learning, to our lives ensure
Virtue so bright, or bliss so pure?
The great Creator's happy hand
Virtue and pleasure ever blends:
In vain the Church and Court have tried
Th' united essence to divide:
Alike they find their wild mistake,
The pedant priest, and giddy rake.

(Wr. by 1740; pub. 1750)

MARY MONCK (née MOLESWORTH)
(c. 1678–1715)

She was the second daughter of Robert Molesworth of Brackenstown, near Swords, Co. Dublin, and Edlinton, near Doncaster, Yorkshire, diplomat, politician, and author, who in 1676 had married Laetitia, daughter of Richard, Lord Coote of Coloony. At about the turn of the century she married George Monk or Monck, who had entered Trinity College, Dublin, in 1690 and was Member for Philipstown in the Irish Parliament 1703–13. Her father, who became Viscount Molesworth in 1716, stated in 1721 that he had had seventeen children, of whom nine were then living. Several of them, including Mary ('Mall') Monck after her marriage, seem at times to have remained dependent on him. On 24 October 1709 he wrote from Dublin: 'I find they are all money-bound. It is well they have a father's good house to tarry in. I know not what would else become of them.' An even more serious problem for Mary was her husband's temporary derangement. On 7 July 1712 her father wrote from his Yorkshire estate that George Monck 'is now sometimes very sensible of his condition and consents to bleeding, purging &c. which he would never hear of before.' Nine days later he reported: 'We are bleeding, physicking, and dieting George Monk. He is now very sober, but by fits starts out and then 'tis always quarrelsome and withal dangerous.' Mysteriously, Molesworth later (5 October 1713) referred to 'G. Monk's disorder, or feigned disorder'.

Mary Monck eventually seems for a time to have lived apart from her husband. According to a letter by her sister Lettice, 5 October 1714, 'My sister Monk has left off housekeeping. Began last Michaelmas boarding with Mrs. Sarah Newbold—pays £25 a year for herself, £12 for the children, £10 for the servants.' She died at Bath in 1715. Her father published her *Poems* in 1716, with a dedication to the Princess of Wales, later Queen Caroline, in which he attacked modern female education (see introduction, p. xxiii). Molesworth described her verse as 'the Product of the leisure Hours of a Young Gentlewoman lately Dead, who in a Remote Country Retirement, without any Assistance but that of a good Library, and without omitting the daily

Care due to a large Family, not only perfectly acquired the several Languages here made use of, but the good Morals and Principles contain'd in those Books'. Most of her poems were found 'in her Scrittore after her Death, written with her own hand, little expecting, and as little desiring the Publick shou'd have any Opportunity of Applauding or Condemning them'. Giles Jacob in 1720 considered that her 'Poems and Translations ... shew the true Spirit and Numbers of Poetry, a Delicacy of Turns, and justness of thought and expression'.

50   *Masque of the Virtues against Love. From Guarini*

    WE the White Witches are, that free
     Enchanted hearts from slavery;
Love's dark abodes all tremble at our voice,
       And at the awful noise
    All the blind archers scud along,
     And frighted to their shady myrtles throng.
We cloud the sun that shines in Caelia's eyes,
    Hush the winds swelled by lovers' sighs,
And stop their tides of tears even when they highest rise.
    We, by our magic's guiltless power,   10
Hearts long since dead to a new life restore.

    All Love's black arts and fatal wiles,
    How he the heedless wretch beguiles,
    How in false smiles the face is dressed,
  And how false pity heaves the breast,
    Circe's spells, the Sirens' lays,
    How one transforms, the other slays,
      We open show
      To mortal view;
Come love-sick minds, see how the force of charms   20
The tyrant of his rage disarms.
Yours be the advantage all; for we
Claim naught but th' honour of the victory.

              (1716)

51   *On a Romantic Lady*

    THIS poring over your *Grand Cyrus*
    Must ruin you and will quite tire us.
    It makes you think that an affront 'tis,
    Unless your lover's an Orontes,
    And courts you with a passion frantic,
    In manner and in style romantic.

Now though I count myself no zero,
I don't pretend to be an hero,
Or a by-blow of him that thunders,
Nor are you one of the Seven Wonders,   10
But a young damsel very pretty,
And your true name is Mistress Betty.

(1716)

52   *Verses written on her Death-bed at Bath to her*
      Husband in London

THOU who dost all my worldly thoughts employ,
Thou pleasing source of all my earthly joy,
Thou tenderest husband and thou dearest friend,
To thee this first, this last adieu I send!
At length the conqueror Death asserts his right,
And will for ever veil me from thy sight;
He woos me to him with a cheerful grace,
And not one terror clouds his meagre face;
He promises a lasting rest from pain,
And shows that all life's fleeting joys are vain;   10
Th' eternal scenes of Heaven he sets in view,
And tells me that no other joys are true.
But love, fond love, would yet resist his power,
Would fain awhile defer the parting hour;
He brings thy mourning image to my eyes,
And would obstruct my journey to the skies.
But say, thou dearest, thou unwearied friend!
Say, shouldst thou grieve to see my sorrows end?
Thou know'st a painful pilgrimage I've passed;
And shouldst thou grieve that rest is come at last?   20
Rather rejoice to see me shake off life,
And die as I have lived, thy faithful wife.

(1755)

JANE HOLT (née WISEMAN)
(*fl.* 1701–17)

According to Giles Jacob, she was originally a servant in the family of William
Wright, Recorder of Oxford, to whose library she had access: 'where, having a pretty
deal of leisure Time, which she spent in Reading Novels and Plays, she began a Play,
and finish'd it after she came to *London*'. *Antiochus the Great: Or, The Fatal Relapse. A*

by-blow] natural child

72

Tragedy was performed at the New Theatre, Lincoln's Inn Fields, in 1701 and published in 1702, dedicated to John, Lord Jefferies. (It was acted again in 1711, 1712, and 1721.) She described the play as 'the first Fruits of a Muse, not yet debas'd to the Low Imployment of Scandal or Private Reflection. The Reception it met in the World, was not kind enough to make me Vain, nor yet so ill, to discourage my Proceeding.' In future, she claimed, she would have 'one of our best Poets for my Assistant', but he has not been identified, not does she seem to have written another play. Instead, she married a young vintner named Holt and, with the profits of *Antiochus*, opened a tavern in Westminster. Her *A Fairy Tale . . . With Other Poems* (1717), no doubt because of its rarity, has been ignored in brief accounts of her. It is 'Inscribed to the Honourable Mrs. W——', annotated in the Bodleian copy as 'Wilmot'.

53   *To Mr. Wren, my Valentine Six Year Old*

SINCE the good Bishop left his name,
And men and maids kept up his fame,
Since birds in honour of his day
Married and went no more astray,
No she could boast a Valentine
Lovely and innocent as mine:
He has such a charming face,
A form so faultless, such a grace,
That, with some wax or silken strings
Fasten but on a pair of wings,   10
Poets and painters would mistake
And him for very Cupid take.
Then he has wit at will, and can
Pose the wisest, learned'st man:
Artful as Cowper he can plead,
And he can bow with any reed.

Oh! whene'er you'll be as good
As, if you pleased and tried, you could;
All fretful, childish tears give o'er,
And love your book a little more;   20
Cheerful and still at dinner sit,
Renowned for manners as for wit;
And softly round the chamber creep,
When your grandpapa's asleep:
Where could be found a youth so fine
As my charming Valentine?

(1717)

SUSANNA CENTLIVRE (née FREEMAN)
(1669?–1723)

Evidence about her early life is often contradictory, but it is most likely that she was born at Whaplode, near Holbeach, Lincolnshire, the daughter of William Freeman and his wife Anne Marham. Her father, a dissenter and parliamentarian, had fled for a time to Ireland after the Restoration and died when she was 3, her mother also dying before she was 12. She was educated 'by her own Industry and Application', according to Giles Jacob, and 'was inclin'd to Poetry when very Young'. A more fanciful source relates that she ran away to become an actress before she was 16, and was befriended by Anthony Hammond, then an undergraduate at Cambridge, who dressed her in boy's clothes and supported her in the University for several months. By the age of 16 she was 'married or something like it' for about a year to a Mr Fox, nephew of Sir Stephen Fox, and later married an army officer named Carroll, who died within eighteen months.

It was under the name of Carroll that she published her first play, *The Perjured Husband* (1700), and her correspondence with Abel Boyer (as Astraea and Celadon) in his *Letters of Wit, Politicks and Morality* (1701), pp. 332–74. Some of these epistles are in verse, including one to George Farquhar. Although for a time her later plays were published anonymously, because of her publishers' fear of prejudice against women authors (as she complained in the dedication and preface to *The Platonic Lady* in 1707), she went on to enjoy considerable popular success as a dramatist, as well as wide literary acquaintance, including Nicholas Rowe, Steele, Cibber, and many others. Of her sixteen plays and three farces, some remained popular into the next century, notably *The Busy Body* (1709) and *A Bold Stroke for a Wife* (1718). It was supposedly while touring England as an actress in 1706 that she aroused the admiration of Joseph Centlivre, Yeoman of the Mouth (principal cook) to Queen Anne and later to George I, whom she married in 1707.

Throughout her career she contributed verse and prose to miscellanies and periodicals, including a poem on the death of Dryden in *The Nine Muses* (1700), prefatory verses in the *Poems* (1703) of Sarah Fyge Egerton (see nos. 19–23), a pastoral on the death of Nicholas Rowe in *Musarum Lachrymae* (1719), a number of poems in Anthony Hammond's *New Miscellany* (1720), and a series of anti-Jacobite letters in the *Weekly Journal* also in 1720. Separately published poems include one on the accession of George I in 1715 and her curious *Epistle to the King of Sweden* (1717), satirizing Jacobite hopes that Charles XII would invade Britain. Her last comedy, *The Artifice* (1722), was unsuccessful, running for only three nights. She died on 1 December 1723 at her home in Buckingham Court, Spring Gardens, London, and was buried at St Paul's, Covent Garden.

54   from *An Epistle to the King of Sweden, From a
Lady of Great Britain*

*[On Jacobite rumours that the ascetic Charles XII intended to invade
Britain]*

To thee—rude warrior, whom we once admired,
And thought thy actions spoke thee half-inspired,
While justice held the balance of thy cause,
And every language sounded thy applause;
But since ambition and revenge prevails,
Thy glories languish, and our wonder fails—
To thee a woman sends with generous care,
And warns thy rashness timely to beware.

Fame now a tale of fresher date has told,
Beyond thy mad romantic feats of old: 10
Our malcontents thy numerous squadrons boast,
Describe thy pennants waving on our coast,
And, to the fearful, cry 'Britannia's lost!'
But we, who know the genius of our isle,
At their report, and thy invasion, smile.

Are not our dames in every climate famed,
Les Belles Angloises by every nation named?
Are not our youth in foreign fields admired,
Alike by valour and by love inspired?
And shall those fair ones, who the morning pass
Consulting that dear friend to love, the glass—   20
To set the favourite, and the patch to place,
To bow, and glance it, with becoming grace
To melt the hero's heart, and charm his eyes—
Fall to thy Gothic rage a sacrifice?
No, to thy terror learn, our British youth
Are famed for honour, constancy and truth:
Each would as soon consent thy cause to aid,
As yield the fair to whom his vows are paid.
Unlike the passive females of thy land,
The arbitrators of the war we stand.   30
At flirt of fan our armèd legions fly,
And they who dare offend, must dare to die.
We know thy daring heart is nursed in blood,
Wild as the fiercest savage of the wood;
With fame like this, in northern slaughter shine,
Rough as the frozen bear, thy neighbouring sign;

favourite] curl on the temple

75

But here thy brutal force no crowns shall gain:
By love, as well as arms, our monarchs reign;
Can we our George and his loved race disown,   40
To find thy barren chastity a throne?

  No! in thy shaggy rug rude slumbers take,
And dream of conquests thou shalt never make;
At distance be thy leathern doublet worn,
Nor risk thy life to purchase certain scorn;
For now the wormwood damsels apprehend
The dismal consequences of such a friend:
Begin to tremble at the truths they hear,
And vow their champions shall for George declare;
They fear thy taste should lead young James astray,   50
And quite unman their monarch every way:
In his excuse they still would have to tell,
'Though war's his foe, he loves exceeding well;
The proof from whence he sprung is not to fight;
His surgeon proves hereditary right.'

  But if by thy example he should grow
Cold as thy rocks of ice, and hills of snow;
Should he clean linen hold in dire disgrace,
And sable crape his ivory neck enchase;
Should he, like thee, on shives of coarsest bread   60
Rudely with dirty thumbs his butter spread;
Banish the generous juice of grapes away,
And with small acid tiff his thirst allay;
Swallow lean hasty meals of tasteless roots,
And eat, and drink, and live, and reign in boots;
Should he, like thee, regardless of the fair,
Lie down to sleep, and only wake to war;
Could he in arms like gallant Brunswick shine—
Yet would his female friends his cause decline,
Nor justify a Right so slovenly Divine.   70

  Consult thy safety; send no armies forth
Beyond the confines of thy frozen north:
Since of our British fair this truth is told,
We love the chaste, but we abhor the cold:
But if thy daring folly will proceed,
Fate drives thee forward, and thy fall's decreed.

(1717)

---

rug] woollen cloak   wormwood] bitter   shives] slices   tiff] weak liquor

55 *From the Country, To Mr. [Nicholas] Rowe in Town. MDCCXVIII*

FROM a lonesome old house, near Holbeach Wash-way
(The Wash, you must know, is an arm of the sea),
A poor wanderer writes, to let your spouse know
Here's nothing can equal the charms of her Rowe.

At this distance, I hope, for the sake of my rhyme,
She'll grant me her pardon if I call you mine:
Since no other meaning the word *mine* can know
Than perfect respect for her excellent Rowe.

Here gentry, and yeomen, and farmers appear
As Christian as Jews, and as rough as a bear;   10
They tipple like swine, and they treat their wives so,
They're monsters, methinks, when compared to her Rowe.

Here Flora's fine garments unheeded are worn,
The flowers neglected the meadows adorn;
The rose's rich scent, when I smell as I go,
I think is less sweet than the voice of my Rowe.

The lark at my window her matin begins,
And constantly there still each morning she sings;
I wake, and cry 'Pretty musicianer, go,
Thy melody's naught to the verse of my Rowe.'   20

The winds catch my accents, and, striving to please,
They mournfully whisper each night through the trees:
'The longer thou stay'st thou'lt more sensible grow;
Here's nothing can charm like the wit of thy Rowe.'

Abroad as I walk through the streets and the lawns,
Where the deer frisk and play with the tender young fawns,
The brooks seem to murmur along as I go,
'Here's naught can delight like the wit of thy Rowe.'

Like the Persian each morning impatient I rise
To view the sun peeping just out of the skies;   30
Then wish that as swiftly as he I could go,
That like him each day I might visit my Rowe.

Then gaze on his beams, though he scorches my brow,
And often in raptures aloud I cry now,
'I almost adore thee because that I know
This moment thou gild'st the abode of my Rowe.'

When Phoebus forsakes me, then Cynthia's pale light
Is welcome to me, and I bless the kind night,
That in Nancy's dear arms will those pleasures bestow
She only can give to the soul of her Rowe.   40

Judicious, fair nymph, would all women like thee
Prefer wit and good sense to wealth and degree,
No ebb of our pleasures we females should know:
But ah! where's the man to compare to thy Rowe?

The Town and the Court too but few can afford:
There's Wellwood the Doctor and H——y the L—d;
To the first under heaven my life I do owe,
And thank him for saving the spouse of my Rowe.

The second, alas! I dare only declare
'Tis well he's a Lord and that I am not fair: 50
His eyes have such power—but I'll say no mo,
The Lord above bless him together with Rowe.

Oh! might I obtain but one wish I would choose,
It is that your friendship I never may lose;
And that the next age may my happiness know,
That I lived, and was known to the excellent Rowe.

(1720)

JANE BRERETON (née HUGHES)
(1685–1740)

She was the second daughter of Thomas and Ann Hughes of Bryn-Griffith, near Mould, Flintshire. After the death in about 1701 of her father, who had given her a good education, her friends encouraged her 'peculiar Genius for Poetry, which was her chief Amusement'. In 1711 she married Thomas Brereton of Brasenose College, Oxford, who had been left a considerable fortune by his father, an army officer who had fought under Marlborough. They had two sons, who died in infancy, and two daughters. Brereton pursued a literary career in London, publishing verse and two unacted plays, as well as a periodical *The Criticks* in 1718. Jane Brereton herself published *The Fifth Ode of the Fourth Book of Horace, Imitated* (1716) and *An Expostulatory Epistle to Sir Richard Steele upon the Death of Mr. Addison* (1720), which has been tentatively attributed to Elizabeth Rowe (by Foxon, *Catalogue* R273) but later appeared in Mrs Brereton's collected *Poems* (1744). All was not well, however, with this busy literary couple. Brereton turned out to have a violent temper ('his first Fit of Passion, after their Marriage, was like a Thunder-clap to her') and, while he was an indulgent father and praised her efforts at economy, he 'was so much a fine Gentleman that he soon ran out most of his Fortune'. The couple eventually separated and in about 1721 Mrs Brereton took her two daughters to live in seclusion in Wales, 'well aware what a critical Case it is to behave without the Censure of the World, when separated from an Husband'. Brereton obtained a post in the Customs at Parkgate, Chester, but, having visited his children on the previous evening, was drowned by the incoming tide at Saltney in February 1722.

For the sake of her daughters' education Mrs Brereton moved to Wrexham and was 'soon distinguish'd by the most considerable Families in and about that Town'. Much of her verse from this period was addressed to a circle of women friends. 'Writing was her darling Entertainment, and was to her a Relaxation from her Cares', although she refused to publish her poems by subscription, as a male friend proposed. She did, however, publish *Merlin: A Poem* (1735) and from 1734 began to contribute regularly to the newly established *Gentleman's Magazine* under the name of 'Melissa', particularly in a humorous verse debate (1734–6) with other contributors such as 'Fidelia' and 'Fido'. It was only after his death that she learned that her mock-antagonist 'Fido' was a neighbour in Wrexham to whom she had shown her poems before sending them to the *Magazine.* He can be identified as Thomas Beach, a wealthy Wrexham wine-merchant, the author of a poem called *Eugenio* (1737), which had been corrected by Jonathan Swift. Beach at times suffered from 'a very terrible disorder in his head' and cut his throat in May 1737. After this blow, Edward Cave, publisher of the *Gentleman's Magazine*, put her in touch with 'a young Lady of eminent Merit and learning, an Ornament to her Sex . . . so learn'd and universally admir'd', with whom she corresponded from 1738. This was Cave's protégée, the youthful Elizabeth Carter (see nos. 110–12), who mentions Mrs Brereton in a letter in June 1739. (Another correspondent of Mrs Brereton, 'Mrs. M–d–n', has been incorrectly identified as Judith Madan (see nos. 65–7), but was in fact Mrs Myddelton of Croesnewydd).

Jane Brereton died at Wrexham on 7 August 1740. Her elder daughter Lucy went to live with her uncle Thomas Hughes, a wealthy brewer in Cork. For Charlotte, who inherited her mother's literary talents, see no. 126. Presumably for the benefit of the daughters, proposals for the publication of Jane Brereton's *Poems on Several Occasions* were printed in 1741 and 1742, but the subscription moved slowly and in the end attracted only some 120 names (including that of 'Miss Carter'). The volume was published by Cave late in 1744. Charlotte probably wrote the prefatory account of her mother, which mentions her own visit to Wrexham in about 1742, when ladies of the first rank wept at the memory of their wise and entertaining friend, and the poor crowded round her in respectful gratitude for Mrs Brereton's benevolence.

56   from *Epistle to Mrs Anne Griffiths. Written from London, in 1718*

BUT should some snarling critic chance to view
These undigested lays designed for you,
The surly blade, methinks, would storm and fume:
'How dares this silly woman thus presume,
In her crude, injudicious lines, to name
Those ancient poets of immortal fame?
The women now, forsooth, are authors grown,
And write such stuff our sex would blush to own!'

That I am dull is what I own and know;
But why I mayn't be privileged to show   10
That dullness to a private friend or two
(As to the world male writers often do),
I can't conceive. Dullness alone's my fault,
Guiltless of impious jest, or obscene thought!
None e'er can say that I have loosely writ,
Nor would at that dear rate be thought a wit.
Fair modesty was once our sex's pride,
But some have thrown that bashful grace aside:
The Behns, the Manleys, head this motley train,
Politely lewd and wittily profane;   20
Their wit, their fluent style (which all must own)
Can never for their levity atone.
But Heaven still, its goodness to denote,
For every poison gives an antidote:
First, our Orinda, spotless in her fame,
As chaste in wit, rescued our sex from shame;
And now, when Heywood's soft, seducing style
Might heedless youth and innocence beguile,
Angelic wit and purest thoughts agree
In tuneful Singer, and great Winchilsea.   30
For me, who never durst to more pretend
Than to amuse myself, and please my friend:
If she approves of my unskilful lays,
I dread no critic, and desire no praise.

(Wr. 1718; pub. 1744)

57

from *To Mr Thomas Griffith, at the University of Glasgow. Written in London, 1720*

You, friend, who whilom tossed the ball,
Or made th' erected nine-pin fall,
Who at the shuffleboard were busy,
Or ran a race with little Lucy,
Are now observant of the rules
And learnèd precepts of the Schools,
Grown perfect master in dispute,
Propound, discuss, prove or confute;
In terms of art can make appear
('Gainst reasons strong that interfere)   10
A foppish coxcomb's no baboon,
Nor yet a hog a Highland loon,
Though all your logic you must use
To prove a matter so abstruse.

Sometimes, your harrassed mind t' unbend,
You chat an hour with Whiggish friend,
In pensive mood steal out unspied,
To fetch a walk by pleasant Clyde;
Or throw off your scholastic air
T' amuse yourself among the fair,   20
Where, for one Moggy you distinguish,
You vow you'd all the sex relinquish.

Sometimes you see a Highland beau
Come trading down to land called Low:
His dirk laid by, the brawny younker
By dint of argument would conquer.
By time he'll learn to make fine speeches,
To read and write—and put on breeches.

But now, methinks, I hear you say,
'Melissa still is wond'rous gay!'—   30
I strive with patience to endure
The evils which I cannot cure.
I live secluded from the town,
I know but few, by few am known;
I seldom go to park or play,
And once a fortnight drink my tea;

shuffleboard] shovelboard, 'A long board on which they play by sliding metal pieces at a mark' (Johnson)

Needle or book 'twixt thumb and finger,
Till tuneful voice of ballad-singer
Will sometimes make me throw it by,
And to the window swiftly fly.   40
From thence I hear the tattered dame,
To dirty mob, extol the fame
'Of glorious Charles of Swedeland!' . . .

    With girls and maids on evening fair
In Tuttle-fields I take the air;
Or sometimes to the Mill-bank go:
From thence I hear embroidered beau,
And belle in garden-satin dressed,
With gallantry exchange a jest,
In language as polite and neat   50
As e'er was used in Billingsgate.
Methinks my case you now deplore:
'No lady-vis'tants as of yore;
No cheerful, inoffensive chat
Of books, and wit, of this and that!
What an insipid life you lead:
'Twere better you in Wales had stayed.'

    I hate, dear Coz, to waste the day
In prating scandal, sipping tea:
The ancient custom I would choose,   60
When two good meals was all in use,
Not toper-like, from morn till night,
Indulge my sloth and appetite.
Once (and but once) your scribbling friend
On highflown lady did attend;
Some of the modish class soon came
To pay their visits to the dame;
With scandal, treason, coffee, tea,
The time passed merrily away.
Such was their malice, such their pride,   70
They Carolina's self decried!
Then masquerade, intrigue and dress,
And all the trifling, gay excess
Of equipage, rich jewels, rings,
Expensive toys, and gew-gaw things,
Were next th' elaborate themes on which,
With much redundancy of speech,

gew-gaw] trifling

The dames harangued; till, tired at last,
I to my dearer jewels haste,
Dearer to me than costly gem   80
Or laced gallant can be to them.

  When gloomy thoughts possess my head,
I pay my visits to the dead:
Naught like the Abbey pleases then,
And monuments of famous men.
This head with victor-laurel crowned,
Those brows poetic bays have bound;
The glorious warrior and the wit
Must both to death's dire stroke submit,
But here, I frankly must confess,   90
The hero does affect me less
Than sacred bard: one gains a name,
But 'tis the other stamps his fame.
E'en Marlborough, whose renown excels
The tales which ancient story tells
Of demi-gods, his name would die,
And deeds in dark oblivion lie,
But that an Addison conveys
Immortal verse to future days,
In which his acts will be read o'er,   100
Till this vast globe shall be no more.
That monument of wond'rous frame,
Raised by an emperor to his fame,
Devouring Time can waste away:
But sacred Verse will ne'er decay.

                              (wr. 1720; pub. 1744)

ANONYMOUS

58   *Cloe to Artimesa*

WHILE vulgar souls their vulgar love pursue,
And in the common way themselves undo;
Impairing health and fame, and risking life,
To be a mistress or, what's worse, a wife:
We, whom a nicer taste has raised above
The dangerous follies of such slavish love,
Despise the sex, and in our selves we find
Pleasures for their gross senses too refined.

Let brutish men, made by our weakness vain,
Boast of the easy conquest they obtain;   10
Let the poor loving wretch do all she can,
And *all* won't please th' ungrateful tyrant, Man;
We'll scorn the monster and his mistress too,
And show the world what women ought to do.

(1720)

MARTHA SANSOM (née FOWKE)
(1690–1736)

Although Johnson referred to her in his 'Life of James Thomson' in 1781 as 'a lady once too well known', she hardly features in modern reference works. She was born in 1690 at Hertingfordbury Park, Herefordshire, the home of a relative, and was the daughter of Capt. Thomas Fowke and his third wife, 'a handsome and rich widow'. After leaving the army in 1688, her father had lived in Staffordshire but, on losing his wife's jointure at her death in 1705, he returned to military service. Having finally resigned his company in Col. Lepell's Regiment of Foot in favour of his son, Ensign Thomas Fowke, in 1707, her father was murdered in 1708 (an event to which she refers more than once in her verse and prose). She had been educated by her mother as a Catholic, had learned French and began writing at an early age. After her mother's death she lived for a time with relatives and later unwillingly attended a boarding-school. According to her posthumously published autobiography, she had a steady succession of admirers from her early teens and, although she describes these relationships evasively, she evidently became the mistress of several of her suitors, probably including the Duke of Beaufort and later the Duke of Rutland. Much of her life at this period alternated between the fashionable world in London and a rural retreat at Fulham.

In 1720 she published the *Epistles of Clio and Strephon*, a verse exchange with William Bond, dramatist and miscellaneous writer, one of whose books she admired but whom she did not meet until the exchange of epistles was completed. These platonically amorous poems (which reached a third edition as *The Platonic Lovers* in 1732) had been admired, according to the dedication, by Sir Richard Steele, and were accompanied by an appreciative commentary by John Porter. A number of her shorter poems also appeared in Anthony Hammond's *New Miscellany* (1720). She soon became a prominent member of the literary circle surrounding the poet and dramatist Aaron Hill, with whom she appears to have been violently in love, if her autobiographical narrative (and the rapturous love poems it contains) are to be believed. Hill addressed her in return in both verse and prose with only slightly less ardour, and there are equally impassioned poems to her by Richard Savage and John Dyer, the poet of 'Grongar's Hill', who painted her portrait at this period. By 1726, when the Hill circle contributed substantially to the collection of *Miscellaneous Poems* edited by Richard Savage, she was well known as 'Clio', but her name appears as Mrs Sansom in the list of subscribers. She had by then married the wealthy, and much older, Arnold Sansom, probably a lawyer, whose mistress she seems to have been for several years: they may have made this move into respectability under pressure from her brother, who was now well embarked on a notable military career.

Although Giles Jacob had stated in 1720 that 'she seems to be possess'd of such a Genius, as would enable her to shew her self no less an Ornament to the *British*, than Madam *Dacier* is to the *French* nation', the literary fame of 'Clio' was shortlived. Her commendatory poem in the 2nd edition of James Thomson's *Winter* in 1726 was signed 'Mira': according to the *British Journal*, 24 September 1726, the name of Clio 'has of late been so abus'd and scandaliz'd' that Thomson's friend David Mallet, who suggested she write the verses, had persuaded her to change it to 'Mira'. This no doubt referred to the violent attack on Mrs Sansom in Eliza Haywood's *Memoirs of a Certain Island Adjacent to the Kingdom of Utopia* (1725–6). Formerly a close friend of Richard Savage, Mrs Haywood seems to have resented Martha Sansom's interference in this relationship. Her relentlessly coarse and vindictive account of Mrs Sansom as 'Gloatitia' (identified in her 'Key') accused her of incest with her father, insatiable promiscuity, prostitution, shameless infidelity to her ailing husband, to whom she had brought three illegitimate children, and the circulation of malicious scandal, 'coin'd in the hellish Mint of her own brain'. Hysterical as it may be, Mrs Haywood's attack bears an outline resemblance to Martha Sansom's autobiographical *Clio*, which she might conceivably have seen through Aaron Hill. Although *Clio* is dated October 1723, it includes a violent denunciation of 'the Scorpion Haywood' ('this female Fiend', 'this Devil', 'this Tygress'), which may have been inserted later. Although she seems to have retained the support of her literary circle—Savage contrasted 'sulph'rous Haywood' with the 'seraphic' Clio in his *The Authors of the Town* (1725)—Martha Sansom and her husband probably settled for a quieter life at this point, although as late as 16 June 1731 a contributor to *Read's Weekly Journal* reported that 'the celebrated Clio' was planning a collection of her poems (which did not appear).

She and her husband, who predeceased her, had by then retired to his native Leicestershire, where she died on 17 February 1736. She was buried in St Martin's Church, Leicester, where her epitaph referred to 'her charity, good nature, and excellent parts', as well as the poems she had written since the age of 16, 'which for their beautiful turn of thought and strength of imagination have not only met with the approbation but the admiration of the good, the learned and the witty'. Aaron Hill, to whom she had been so devoted, referred to her death in a letter dated 23 June 1736, which lacks both generosity and lucidity: 'If half of what her enemies have said of her, is true, she was a proof, that *vanity* overcomes *nature* in *women* . . . . in that amiable persuer of conquests, it prevail'd, not only against the finest reflection, but impell'd an *assum'd lightness*, over even *constitutional* modesty.' Hill died in 1750 and her autobiographical *Clio*, no doubt found among his papers, was published in 1752. The long military career of her brother Thomas Fowke extended from service in Spain in 1709 to the Battle of Prestonpans: he later became Governor of Gibraltar, was court-martialled and cashiered in 1756 in connection with the Byng affair, was reinstated by George III, and died as a Lieutenant-General in 1765.

Although later references to her have often been brief and disparaging, it would be possible to read her career as an instinctive struggle for individuality and freedom which was totally at odds with the mores of her society. In any case, whatever the biographical distractions, a pleasantly individual and unpretentious voice speaks in some of her poems.

59   from *Clio's Picture. To Anthony Hammond Esq*

[*A Self-Portrait*]

HERE let the Muse perform the painter's art,
And strike the picture of my face and heart.
Poesy is called the image of the mind,
In mine my soul and body both are joined:
Large is my forehead made, not wond'rous fair,
But room enough for all the Muses there;
Full are my eyes, and of a harmless blue,
As if no wound they made, no dart they knew;
My eyebrows, circling o'er, a shade bestow,
Veiling the dullness of the eye below;   10
Nature, so niggard to the upper part,
Fell to my lips, and gave a dash of art:
Oft have I heard her faithful lover swear
That Poetry and Love were shining there;
Even and white my teeth, but rarely shown,
In life I've little cause for smiling known;
The loss of friends fell on my tender years,
Dashed every hope, and turned my smiles to tears;
A gloomy sweetness on my features hung,
Sorrows my pen, and trembles on my tongue;   20
Slow is its speech, and with no music fraught,
Wronging the richness of my soul's best thought.

But whither is the mournful pencil strayed?
My hair, dark brown, wants not Bucelia's aid,
Flows in the wind, nor of the comb afraid,
Beneath my waist in natural rings descends,
Or pliant to the artful finger bends,
When it betides that dress and I are friends.
Easy my neck, but of no darling white,
Veiled by the lawn from the enquiring sight;   30
My shoulders full, as Nature's self informs,
Small are my fingers, nor too plump my arms.
To the nice eye no transport they afford,
But to the ear, pressing the speaking chord:
When my cares murmur with a lower breath,
Drop from my eyes, and weep themselves to death.
Again they press to wrong this artless draught,
Bribed by my fate to ruin every thought.
My feet with no ungraceful motion tread,
Though Isaac's steps are from my memory fled;   40

To decent height my stature is inclined,
Worthy the Muses and a generous mind.
To thy kind eyes Clio submits her form:
Thy verse can give it every absent charm,
Thou, in whom art, and love, and nature shines,
Immortalise my picture in thy lines.

(1720)

60   *To Cleon's Eyes*

THE love you dare but look I find:
The eyes speak best the lover's mind;
The God of Love reveals the news,
Whose dart has stamped the billet-doux;
No paper could such sweetness boast,
For half the spirit would be lost
Ere I could read that duller way,
What in a moment these convey.
Oh! let thy eyes with truth be fraught,
Mine shall repay each modest thought.   10
Thus souls employ their hours above,
Exchanging looks of deathless love;
In looking wondrous magic lies,
Oh! there is poetry in eyes:
Methinks I see a Waller shine
In every sparkling beam of thine;
Or when in nobler language dressed,
With Milton's spirit they are blessed:
Thus Adam tenderly surveyed
With guiltless looks the blushing maid,   20
Who met his eyes unskilled in art:
They were no prudes but spoke her heart.
I want not thanks, confine your tongue,
Lest words should do the passion wrong.
Sure speaking only was designed
For the dull wretches of my kind,
For scandal, or for rude disputes.
But tender lovers should be mutes:
Grief is by silence well expressed,
And silence speaks the lover best;   30
Or if kind souls must sound at all,
Slow be the words and gently fall;
As winds that whisper, and with tremblings move
The newborn blossoms of the infant grove.

(1720)

87

61   *To Lady E——— H———*

IT was not that I lost direction,
Nor is it that I want affection;
No—To be silent I submitted,
Because I found myself outwitted:
You contrive all ways to spite me,
You outlook me, and outwrite me.
Did I teach you all my graces,
All the Muse's different paces:
In heroics to be bounding
With expressions high and sounding,   10
In sweet lyrics how to amble,
Or in airy odes to ramble?
Did I not the art discover
How, in verse, to hunt a lover?
How, agreeably, to wind him,
And in pleasing fetters bind him,
So that beauty could not steal him,
Wit, nor wine, nor music heal him:
For a pen's a magic wand-a,
Governed by so fine a hand-a,   20
And the bosom, so gallanted,
May be said to be enchanted.

'Tis not face as fair as lily,
Chalky lady, looking silly,
That can hold a lover to it,
'Tis alone the Female Poet:
Still in different forms appearing,
To divert the eye and hearing,
And inspire the ravished gazer
To adore her, and to praise her;   30
Not the vapour that does lead us,
By its light o'er dewy meadows,
Makes its followers rage and fret-a
Half so much as a coquet-a.

We're a sort of midnight witches,
Men are our obedient switches:
Is it not a pretty scene-a
To behold this large machin-a,
Called the Lords of the Creation,
Ganders, drove by inclination!   40

88

Oh! I hate the wretched victors:
Fancy fain would paint their pictures:
I could hiss these hideous heroes,
Slaves before—and after, Neros.
Now my pen shall play Vandyck-a,
And, with deathless colours, strike-a.

Sighing, sending, sadly sobbing,
Leering like a thief a-robbing;
Silly, sauntering, solitary,
Lest their lying should miscarry,   50
By a bubbling stream complaining,
Staring, stamping, stars arraigning!
Languid, lolling, picking daisy,
Or a straw, like people crazy!
No dog dancing can exceed 'em,
You may drive 'em, or may lead 'em.

One of yours, of all the throng-a,
Is the favourite of my song-a:
Wit enough for all the others,
Flower and pearl of younger brothers.   60
Still in verse may he address you,
And, on every tree, confess you,
Till his penknife spare no bark-a
In his noble brother's park-a!
May every echo sigh your name,
And every puppy yelp the same,
While the flying hare pursuing,
Mourning so their master's ruin,
Who hunts *you* through every turning,
With his passion and his learning.   70

To both I wish a good success,
And this letter in the press,
Which, for wit, deserves a name-a
In the brazen book of fame-a.

(1726)

62   *The Invitation from a Country Cottage*

CLOSE to the fireside confined
By the cold fogs and piercing wind,
Blessed with my dog, and peace of mind:
The cheerful rustics all sit round,
Whose careful hands improve the ground,
After the labour of the day,
Upon the clean-swept hearth, and play.
The well-used pack of cards was found,
Grown soiled with often dealing round;
No ceremony here they use,   10
But frankly wrangle when they lose;
The hand that deals to all the rest
Returns not back to Colin's breast,
As among finer gamesters seen,
Nor is the table lined with green,
But a plain, honest, cleanly board,
Such as these humble shades afford;
No gold upon the table shines,
But chalk the homely game confines.
Some lad, more amorous than the rest,   20
Sings a sad ditty to their guest
Of some false damsel, most ingrate,
Or melancholy Bateman's fate.
Believe, it pleases me, my friend,
To see the artless tears descend:
Their eyes, that ne'er were *taught* to grieve,
Their hearts, which natural passions heave,
Show lovely Nature all undressed,
And charm my undesigning breast.
O! come, my friend, and see *one* place,   30
Where all things wear an honest face.

(1726)

63   *Song*

FOOLISH eyes, thy streams give over,
Wine, not water, binds the lover:
At the table then be shining,
Gay coquette, and all designing.
To th' addressing foplings bowing,
And thy smile or hand allowing,

Whine no more thy sacred passion,
Out of nature, out of fashion.

Let him, disappointed, find thee
False as he, nor dream to bind thee,   10
While he breaks all tender measures,
Murdering love and all its pleasures.
Shall a look or word deceive thee,
Which he once an age will give thee?
Oh! no more, no more excuse him,
Like a dull deserter use him.

(Wr. *c.*1726?; pub. 1752)

CONSTANTIA GRIERSON (née CRAWLEY)
(*c.*1705–32)

Although she was highly respected in the period for her classical learning, she has
remained a relatively obscure figure until the recent investigations of A. C. Elias. She
was born in about 1705 at Graiguenamanagh, Co. Kilkenny, of 'poor illiterate
Country People' named Crawley. Her father is said to have done his best to
encourage her reading and she herself stated that 'she had received some little
instruction from the Minister of the Parish, when she could spare Time from her
Needlework, to which she was closely kept by her Mother'. She came to Dublin at the
age of about 18, perhaps as early as 1721, to be instructed in midwifery by Dr Van
Lewen, whose daughter Laetitia (see nos. 94–5) described 'this female Philosopher'
as already 'Mistress of *Hebrew, Greek, Latin,* and *French*'. Mary Barber (see nos. 84–
90) later added history, divinity, and philosophy to Constantia's repertoire. While it
would be reasonable to question the qualifications of Pilkington and Barber as
assessors in all these fields of learning, such interest in and knowledge of languages
in a largely self-educated woman of humble background were clearly unusual. She
was also a delightful companion, according to Laetitia, who later printed the
following poem to show that her friend's muse could 'descend from its sublime
Height to the easy epistolary Stile, and suit itself to my then gay Disposition'.

Having probably worked for him already, in 1726 she became the second wife of
George Grierson, a printer of Scottish origin. She corrected the press for the
editions he published of Terence (Dublin, 1727) and Tacitus (3 vols., Dublin, 1730),
writing Latin dedications of the Terence to Richard, infant son of Lord Carteret, and
of the Tacitus to Lord Carteret himself. Her contributions to these editions were
cited in her husband's petition to the Irish House of Commons in 1729 for the
reversion of the post of King's Printer in Dublin, which he obtained in 1733. She
became a member of the Swift circle in Dublin at this time, addressing his friend Dr
Delany in *The Goddess Envy to Doctor D–l—y* (Dublin, 1730) (anonymous in Foxon,
Catalogue G 205). Swift praised her classical learning in a letter to Pope on
6 February 1730 and the Earl of Orrery inscribed his copy of the Tacitus edition (in
the Bodleian): 'This edition of Tacitus is one of the best extant: The Press was
corrected by Mrs Grierson . . . a woman of uncommon learning: and a perfect
Mistress of the Greek and Latin Tongues.' Swift also mentions her '*carmina*

Anglicana non contemnenda'. In 1734 her friend Mary Barber referred to these English poems, 'on which She set so little Value, that She neglected to leave Copies behind her but of a very few'. Barber printed five of them in her own *Poems* (1734) and Laetitia Pilkington included two more in her *Memoirs*, Vol. I (1748). A manuscript notebook containing both published and unpublished poems by her has recently come to light.

She had four children: the first, a son, was accidentally smothered in 1727; George (1728–55) succeeded his father as King's Printer in Dublin, was esteemed by Johnson, but died in Dusseldorf at the age of 27. Two daughters died in infancy in 1731 and 1733. She herself died, probably of tuberculosis, on 2 December 1732, aged about 27.

64   *To Miss Laetitia Van Lewen*

THE fleeting birds may soon in ocean swim,
And northern whales through liquid azure skim:
The Dublin ladies their intrigues forsake,
To dress and scandal an aversion take;
When you can in the lonely forest walk,
And with some serious matron gravely talk,
Of possets, poultices, and waters stilled,
And monstrous casks with mead and cyder filled;
How many hives of bees she has in store
And how much fruit her trees this summer bore;   10
Or, home returning, in the yard can stand,
And feed the chickens from your bounteous hand;
Of each one's top-knot tell, and hatching pry,
Like Tully waiting for an augury.
   When night approaches, down to table sit,
With a great crowd, choice meat, and little wit:
What horse won the last race, how mighty Tray
At the last famous hunting caught the prey;
Surely, you can't but such discourse despise:
Methinks I see displeasure in your eyes: 20
O my Laetitia, stay no longer there,
You'll soon forget that you yourself are fair;
Why will you keep from us, from all that's gay,
There in a lonely solitude to stay?—
Where not a mortal through the year you view
But bob-wigged hunters, who their game pursue
With so much ardour, they'd a cock or hare
To thee in all thy blooming charms prefer.
   You write of belles and beaux that there appear,
And gilded coaches, such as glitter here;   30
For gilded coaches, each estated clown
That gravely slumbers on the bench has one;

But beaux! they're young attorneys, sure you mean!
Who thus appear to your romantic brain.
Alas! no mortal there can talk to you,
That love, or wit, or softness ever knew—
All they can speak of's *Capias* and law,
And writs to keep the country fools in awe.
And, if to wit, or courtship they pretend,
'Tis the same way that they a cause defend;   40
In which they give of lungs a vast expense,
But little passion, thought, or eloquence:
Bad as they are, they'll soon abandon you,
And gain and clamour in the town pursue.
So haste to town, if ev'n such fools you prize;
O haste to town! and bless the longing eyes

Of your CONSTANTIA

(Wr. 1723; pub. 1748)

JUDITH MADAN (née COWPER)
(1702–81)

She was the fifth child and only daughter of Judge Spencer Cowper and his wife
Pennington Goodere, and a niece of the Lord Chancellor. She wrote verse from the
age of about 15 with some success: a poem in memory of John Hughes the dramatist
in 1720 was reprinted more than once, and a poem addressed to her brother
appeared in *The Free-Thinker* of 28 July 1721. Two ambitious early poems were
'Abelard to Eloisa', written in 1720, a response to Pope's famous poem, which
somehow found its way into William Pattison's *Poems* (1728), a misattribution
repeated later in the century. Her 'The Progress of Poetry', written in about 1721,
surveying English poets from Chaucer to Pope, was included in *The Flower-Piece*
(1731), reprinted in magazines and miscellanies, and republished as a separate poem
as late as 1783. (In the late 1720s Jane Brereton (see nos. 56–7) addressed a poem to
the author of 'The Progress of Poetry' which suggests that it had in fact first appeared
in a so far unidentified issue of the *Whitehall Evening Post*.) It will already be evident
that she was an admirer of Pope and, having addressed some lines to him in about
1720, she corresponded with him in 1722/3. Pope was apparently flattered by the
admiration of a young woman of good family, whom he seems to have met when she
was sitting for a portrait to his friend Charles Jervas, which he later managed to
'steal': he corrected the verse she showed him, encouraged her writing, addressed
some lines to her (which he later adapted to Martha Blount in his *Epistle to a Lady*),
and hoped for her friendship. It is not clear how much actual contact there was
between them and the correspondence in any case ended in November 1723, shortly
before her marriage. For a time he communicated through their common friend Mrs
Caesar but by 1733 she described herself as 'forgotten' by him. (His side of the

Capias] legal writs

correspondence was to appear as *Letters to a Lady* (1769), in which she is not identified, although she presumably approved of its publication.)

In December 1723 she married Col. Martin Madan (1700–56), from 1736 Equerry to Frederick, Prince of Wales, and MP for Wootton Bassett 1747–54. He is addressed as 'Lysander' in her verse. From 1735 the Madans lived for several years with her brother Ashley Cowper at Northill, Bedfordshire. Most of her verse was written before the age of 30, not surprisingly in view of the fact that she had nine children, of whom Maria (see nos. 177–8) also wrote poetry. From about 1749 she came under the influence of John Wesley and the Countess of Huntingdon and most of her later verse is religious. She had some reputation in her lifetime, being praised by John Duncombe in *The Feminiad* in 1754 and featuring in *Poems by Eminent Ladies* in the following year, where it is, however, erroneously stated that 'this Lady, notwithstanding her extraordinary genius, could never yet be prevailed on to commit any thing to print'. A full listing of her published and unpublished verse was given by Falconer Madan in 1933, together with an account of the Madan and Cowper families, and their literary activities, in the period. William Cowper the poet was her nephew.

65   *On her own Birthday, August 26, 1723*

THIS day beginning to a creature gave
Not apt to love, though sacred Friendship's slave.
Grandeur and pomp may catch, not fix, her eyes;
Their charms the trifler knows not how to prize.
Her little soul, to meaner prospects bound,
Prefers substantial happiness to sound.
An humble cottage, and a chrystal flood,
A silent grotto, or a leafy wood,
More strike the sense of this insipid creature
Than all the rich magnificence in nature.   10
Yet to this merit may the wretch pretend,
That Howe and Pope vouchsafe to call her friend.

(Wr. 1723; pub. 1933)

66 *An Ode Composed in Sleep**

LOVELY fairy! Charming sprite!
    Kindly listen and appear,
Whether bathed in dewdrops bright,
    Or in chrystal riv'lets clear.

Howe'er divine, the mortal youth
    Yet hopes thy gentleness to move,
With the soft energy of truth,
    And the prevailing voice of love.

(Wr. 1725; pub. 1933)

67 *To Lysander. October 3, 1726*

[*To her Husband on the First Birthday of their Son*]

THE lyre neglected, and the tuneful lay,
Whole summer suns have rolled unsung away:
Thy eyes alone can raise the stifled fire—
What cannot eyes so bright as thine inspire?
Warmed by their beams, again my voice I raise;
Love shall assist, while you command my lays.
What theme so fit to crown this fond essay
As our first hope, in thy resemblance gay?
So, to new light and grace successive born,
The rosy east precedes the breaking morn;   10
So sprightly dawns the gentle opening day,
While every meaner lustre fades away.
    Thee, lovely boy, with tender joy I view,
Less soft the genuine plum's unsullied blue;
Less sweet the violet hung with pearly rain,
When vernal showers refresh the fragrant plain.
Thy looks serene in native beauty shine,
And peace and dovelike innocence are thine.
Nature's soft pride! whose artless smiles dispense
The sparks of reason kindling into sense;   20
Whose lip, smooth rival of the vermeiled rose,
Rich in Lysander's bright resemblance glows.

* 'The above stanzas I made in a Dream, where I imagin'd My self a young Prince under the Direction and Guardianship of a Fairy: on a sudden, finding My self deserted by Her, I sung as above, so often over, that when I awak'd, finding them so perfectly imprinted on my Memory, I wrote them imediately down. 1725' (MS note)

Such was the infant promise of his charms,
So turned his graceful neck and waxen arms.
Through thy whole frame the kindred likeness speaks,
And from thine eyes in untaught language breaks.
   Ye circling hours with kindest influence roll,
And to the body fit the forming soul:
Let every grace attend the lovely care,
And faithful Nature paint Lysander there.   30

(Wr. 1726; pub. 1933)

ELIZABETH TOLLET
(1694–1754)

She was the daughter of George Tollet, Commissioner of the Navy in the reigns of
William III and Queen Anne. Early in her life she lived in his home in the Tower of
London, described in the epistle to her brother given below, later elsewhere in
London, in Stratford and West Ham. Her father, 'observing her extraordinary
genius', gave her an excellent education, encouraged by his friend Sir Isaac Newton
(whom she addressed in one of her poems). It has often been asserted that she wished
her poetry to be published only posthumously, but (as was first pointed out in my *New
Oxford Book of Eighteenth Century Verse* in 1984), a substantial collection first appeared
anonymously in 1724, when she was about 30, as *Poems on Several Occasions. With
Anne Boleyn to King Henry VIII. An Epistle* (anonymous in Foxon, *Catalogue*, p. 606).
This rare early volume, which includes poems on Congreve, Lady Mary Wortley
Montagu, and the Countess of Winchilsea, and some Latin translations of the
Psalms, seems to have been little noticed and there is only very limited evidence that
she belonged to any kind of literary circle. John Hanway addressed a poem to her on
her version of the Psalms in 1730 and Aaron Hill's 'To Mrs. T——t' in his *Works* in
1753 may have been addressed to her. She died in 1754 and was buried in West Ham
Church, where her epitaph stated that 'Religion, justice, and benevolence appeared
in all her actions; and her Poems, in various languages, are adorned with the most
extensive learning, applied to the best purposes.' Her posthumously published *Poems*
(1755), which had virtually the same full title as in 1724, made some minor omissions
and added some later verse, including lines addressed to Handel. She is said to have
left a considerable estate to her nephew George Tollet (1725–79), lawyer and
Shakespeare critic. There was an undated reissue of her *Poems*, with cancel title, in
about 1760. Some thirty of her translations of the Psalms were included in Henry
Dell's *Select Collection of the Psalms of David* (1756).

68   *To my Brother at St. John's College in Cambridge*

BLEST be the man, who first the method found
In absence to discourse, and paint a sound!
This praise old Greece to Tyrian Cadmus gives,
And still the author by th' invention lives:

Still may he live, and justly famous be,
Whose art assists me to converse with thee!
All day I pensive sit, but not alone,
And have the best companions when I've none:
I read great Tully's page, and wondering find
The heavenly doctrine of th' immortal mind;   10
An axiom first by parent Nature taught,
An inborn truth, which proves itself by thought.
But when the sun declines the task I change,
And round the walls and antique turrets range;
From hence a varied scene delights the eyes.
See! here Augusta's massive temples rise,
There meads extend, and hills support the skies;
See! there the ships, an anchored forest, ride,
And either India's wealth enrich the tide.

Thrice happy you, in Learning's other seat!   20
No noisy guards disturb your blest retreat:
Where, to your cell retired, you know to choose
The wisest author, or the sweetest muse.
Let useful toil employ the busy light,
And steal a restless portion from the night;
With thirst of knowledge wake before the day,
Prevent the sun, and chide his tardy ray,
When cheerful larks their early anthem sing,
And opening winds refreshing odours bring;
When from the hills you see the morning rise,   30
As fresh as Lansdown's cheeks, and bright as Windham's eyes.

But when you leave your books, as all must find
Some ease required, t' indulge the labouring mind,
With such companions mix, such friendships make,
As not to choose what you must soon forsake:
Mark well thy choice, let modesty and truth,
And constant industry, adorn the youth.
In books good subjects for discourse are found;
Such be thy talk when friendly tea goes round.
Mirth more than wine the drooping spirits cheers,   40
Revives our hopes, and dissipates our fears;
From Circe's cup, immeasured wine, refrain:
Start backwards and reject th' untasted bane.

Perhaps to neighbouring shades you now repair,
To look abroad and taste the scented air;

Augusta] London

97

Survey the useful labours of the swain,
The tedded grass, and sheaves of ripened grain;
The loaded trees with blushing apples graced,
Or hardy pears, which scorn the wintry blast;
Or see the sturdy hinds from harvest come,   50
To waste the setting suns in rural mirth at home.
Now on the banks of silver Cam you stray,
While through the twisted boughs the sunbeams play,
And the clear stream reflects the trembling ray.

    Think, when you tread the venerable shade,
Here Cowley sung, and tuneful Prior played.
O! would the Muse thy youthful breast inspire
With charming raptures and poetic fire!
Then thou might'st sing (who better claims thy lays?)
A tributary strain to Oxford's praise: 60
Thy humble verse from him shall fame derive,
And graced with Harley's name for ever live.
First sing the man in constant temper found,
Unmoved when Fortune smiled, undaunted when she frowned,
A mind above rewards, serenely great,
And equal to the province of the state.
Thence let thy Muse to private life descend,
Nor in the patriot's labours lose the friend.

                                                        (1724)

69   *On a Death's Head*

        ON this resemblance, where we find
        A portrait drawn for all mankind,
        Fond lover! gaze awhile, to see
        What beauty's idol charms shall be.
        Where are the balls that once could dart
        Quick lightning through the wounded heart?
        The skin, whose tint could once unite
        The glowing red, and polished white?
        The lip in brighter ruby dressed?
        The cheek with dimpled smiles impressed?   10
        The rising front, where Beauty sate
        Throned in her residence of state;
        Which, half-disclosed and half-concealed,
        The hair in flowing ringlets veiled?

                    tedded] spread out for drying

                            98

'Tis vanished all! remains alone
The eyeless scalp of naked bone;
The vacant orbits sunk within;
The jaw that offers at a grin.
Is this the object then that claims
The tribute of our youthful flames?   20
Must amorous hopes and fancied bliss,
Too dear delusions, end in this?
How high does Melancholy swell!
Which sighs can more than language tell;
Till Love can only grieve or fear:
Reflect awhile, then drop a tear
For all that's beautiful and dear.

(1724)

70   *From Virgil*

[*Aeneid III. 321–4 Adapted*]

HOW hard a fate enthrals the wretched maid
By tyrant kindred bartered and betrayed!
Whose beauty, youth and innocence are sold
For shining equipage, or heaps of gold;
Condemned to drag an odious chain for life,
A living victim and a captive wife!
More happy she, and less severe her doom,
Who falls in all the pride of early bloom,
And virgin honours dress her peaceful tomb!

(1724)

71   from *Hypatia*

WHAT cruel laws depress the female kind,
To humble cares and servile tasks confined!
In gilded toys their florid bloom to spend,
And empty glories that in age must end;
For amorous youth to spread the artful snares,
And by their triumphs to enlarge their cares.
For, once engaged in the domestic chain,
Compare the sorrows, and compute the gain;
What happiness can servitude afford?
A will resigned to an imperious lord,   10

Or slave to avarice, to beauty blind,
Or soured with spleen, or ranging unconfined.
That haughty man, unrivalled and alone,
May boast the world of science all his own:
As barb'rous tyrants, to secure their sway,
Conclude that ignorance will best obey.
Then boldly loud, and privileged to rail,
As prejudice o'er reason may prevail,
Unequal nature is accused to fail.
The theme, in keen iambics smoothly writ,   20
Which was but malice late, shall soon be wit.

   Nature in vain can womankind inspire
With brighter particles of active fire,
Which to their frame a due proportion hold,
Refined by dwelling in a purer mould,
If useless rust must fair endowments hide,
Or wit, disdaining ease, be misapplied.
'Tis then that wit, which reason should refine,
And disengage the metal from the mine,
Luxuriates, or degenerates to design.   30
Wit unemployed becomes a dangerous thing,
As waters stagnate and defile their spring.
The cultivated mind, a fertile soil,
With rich increase rewards the useful toil:
But fallow left, an hateful crop succeeds
Of tangling brambles and pernicious weeds;
'Tis endless labour then the ground to clear,
And trust the doubtful earnest of the year.

   Yet oft we hear, in height of stupid pride,
Some senseless idiot curse a lettered bride.   40

                         (1724)

72   *Winter Song*

   ASK me no more, my truth to prove,
What I would suffer for my love.
With thee I would in exile go
To regions of eternal snow,
O'er floods by solid ice confined,
Through forest bare with northern wind:
While all around my eyes I cast,
Where all is wild and all is waste.
If there the timorous stag you chase,

Or rouse to fight a fiercer race,   10
Undaunted I thy arms would bear,
And give thy hand the hunter's spear.
When the low sun withdraws his light,
And menaces an half-year's night,
The conscious moon and stars above
Shall guide me with my wandering love.
Beneath the mountain's hollow brow,
Or in its rocky cells below,
Thy rural feast I would provide,
Nor envy palaces their pride.   20
The softest moss should dress thy bed,
With savage spoils about thee spread:
While faithful love the watch should keep,
To banish danger from thy sleep.

(1755)

73   *The Rose*

BENEATH my feet when Flora cast
    Her choicest sweets of various hue,
Their charms, unheeded as I passed,
    Nor cheered my sense, nor took my view.

I chose, neglecting all the rest,
    The Provence rose too fully blown.
I lodged it in my virgin breast;
    It drooped, alas, and died too soon!

This gentle sigh, this rain of eyes,
    Thy beauty never can recall: 10
'Tis thus that all perfection flies,
    And love and life must fade and fall.

(1755)

74   *On the Prospect from Westminster Bridge, March 1750*

CAESAR! renowned in silence as in war,
Look down a while from thy maternal star:
See! to the skies what sacred domes ascend,
What ample arches o'er the river bend;

What vills above in rural prospect lie,
Beneath, a street that intercepts the eye,
Where happy Commerce glads the wealthy streams,
And floating castles ride. Is this the Thames,
The scene where brave Cassibelan of yore
Repulsed thy legions on a savage shore?   10
Britain, 'tis true, was hard to overcome,
Or by the arms, or by the arts, of Rome;
Yet we allow thee ruler of the Sphere,
And last of all resign thy Julian year.

(1755)

MARY DAVYS
(1674–1732)

She was born in Dublin, where she married the Revd Peter Davys, headmaster of the
Free School of St Patrick's. He was an early friend of Swift, who described him in
1733 as 'a man I loved very well, but marryd very indiscreetly'. After his death at the
age of 28 in 1698, 'for meer want' she left for England, eventually settling in York.
She published *The Amours of Alcippus and Leucippe* (1704), for which she received
three guineas, and *The Fugitive* (1705), based on her own experiences on arriving in
England, but seems to have been in financial difficulties: although Swift described
her as 'a rambling woman with very little taste in wit or humour', he sent her money
on a number of occasions before his return to Ireland in 1714. Her fortunes changed
when her comedy *The Northern Heiress*, set in York, was successfully performed in
London in 1716, and the proceeds probably enabled her to move to Cambridge
where she opened a coffee-house. Her later works were usually strongly supported
by Cambridge subscribers, but the list in her frequently reprinted *The Reform'd
Coquet* (1724) also includes the names of Pope, Gay, and Martha Blount, no doubt at
the prompting of Swift. In her *Works* (2 vols., 1725), to which twenty-five titled ladies
as well as Pope and Young subscribed, she replied to those who objected to a
clergyman's widow writing plays: 'a Woman left to her own Endeavours for Twenty-
seven Years together, may well be allow'd to catch at any Opportunity for that Bread,
which they that condemn her would very probably deny to give her' (i.v). Her *Works*
also include an unacted play *The Self Rival*, in the prologue to which she complains of
prejudice against women writers (i. 68).

Her last novel, *The Accomplish'd Rake* (1727), has been described as 'one of the few
mature English novels' of the period, but she did not enjoy high literary reputation in
her lifetime. *The Grub-Street Journal*, No. 80 (15 July 1731), in a satirical account of
her place in Cambridge literary life, dismissed her as the author of 'several bawdy
Novels', provoking her to reply in the next number. Swift, who had seen her in
Cambridge during his visit to England in 1727, complained about her indifference to
the fact that her sister, who was starving and had a lame child, was living on charity.
Mary Davys died in 1732, leaving her estate to Thomas Ewen, a Cambridge grocer

vills] villages

and brewer, who claimed to own several of Swift's letters to her. In 1782 it was stated that as many as thirty-six of Swift's letters to her were then in the possession of the notorious Dr W. H. Ewen of Cambridge (see *DNB*), but they have never been traced.

In a brief account of her in 1720, Giles Jacob stated that she had published a reply in verse to Susanna Centlivre's *Epistle to the King of Sweden* (1717; see no. 54). This may well have been the *Answer from the King of Sweden to the British Lady's Epistle* (anonymous in Foxon, *Catalogue* A 231), which is known only by a newspaper advertisement of 24 June 1717.

75   from *The Modern Poet*

BEHIND moth-eaten curtain, 'stead of press,
Hung up the tattered relics of his dress:
A threadbare coat, at elbows quite worn out,
Buttonless waistcoat with an old surtout;
Breeches with pockets gone, for the abuse
Of master's wit had made them of no use;
A hat some ten times dressed, much on the rust,
Was laid in box, to keep it from the dust;
On wooden peg hung piss-burned periwig,
A little out of curl, but very big;   10
In days of yore it had a noble master,
And given to set up the poetaster,
For pride has oftentimes appeared in tatters,
And strives to make us imitate our betters:
It gave him airs to strut about the town,
Flattering my lord, and railing at the Gown,
With brazen-hilted bilbo to attack
All those who dare call names behind his back;
Though certain 'tis, a poet's only weapon
Should be his pen, when people are mistaken.   20
But some, alas! have to their sorrow found
His passion, not his reason, kept its ground:
He thought it hard he should a scene run through
Of beggary, and be insulted too.
    His dress and person thus described, I come
To say a word or two on lodging-room,
The height of which already has been said:
Furniture next comes in, and first the bed,
On which coarse, dirty linen might be seen,
With store of those dear creatures (bugs) between;   30

press] cupboard   dressed] refurbished   piss-burned] stained brown
bilbo] sword

A shaggy rug, as useful as his meat,
It kept out winter's cold, and summer's heat:
Beside, that everything might live at ease,
He laid it on as refuge for the fleas.
On closet dark stood what is often useful,
Which decency forbids to call a ——,
From whence effluvia rose, which could allay
Vapours in wits, like asafoetida.
In corner of the unswept room there lay
A heap of blunted pens, as who should say,   40
'Behold the fate of all things in this world:
When we have done our best, away we're hurled;
And if our pains but little profit brought,
Our guider, not ourselves, was in the fault!'
In table-drawer whole quires most neatly writ
Lay useless by, and now for nothing fit,
Unless minced pies, or some such use inferior,
As lighting pipes, or clapping to posterior.
Two dedications he with sighs laid by,
Because his patrons did his suit deny,   50
Nor would with his necessities comply.
On chimney-piece, instead of china set,
A standish, razor, and old penknife met,
Tobacco-box, two dirty pipes, with sticks
Of scented wax, and wafers there did mix.
For want of window-curtains in his room,
Two lordly cobwebs from the spider's loom
Spread them all o'er with care, lest too much light
Should spoil the student's eyes, when set to write.
Two chairs there were, one of them had no back,   60
The other, like his verse, a foot did lack.
Thus poetry and poverty were joined,
And left the marks of both their plagues behind.
If any knocks, away in haste he runs,
Having a strange antipathy to duns;
Nor does he any see, lest they should prove
The only thing on earth he cannot love.
   The kind, good-natured mice would often come
To make him visits in his empty room;
Like modern visitors, made short their stay,   70
And like them too, untreated went away;
Because our bard's provision was but scant,
The mice and he did oft their dinners want.

---

asafoetida] gum or resin used medically   standish] inkstand   duns] debt-collectors

And now, dear readers, if this cannot win ye
Straight to turn poets, sure the devil's in ye.

(1725)

ARABELLA MORETON
(after 1690–before 1741)

For the identification of B-ll M-rt-n, to whom the poem was first attributed, see p. 539 below.

76   *The Humble Wish*

I ASK not wit, nor beauty do I crave,
Nor wealth, nor pompous titles wish to have;
But since 'tis doomed, in all degrees of life
(Whether a daughter, sister, or a wife),
That females shall the stronger males obey,
And yield perforce to their tyrannic sway;
Since this, I say, is every woman's fate,
Give me a mind to suit my slavish state.

(1726?)

FRANCES SEYMOUR (née THYNNE), COUNTESS OF HERTFORD (later DUCHESS OF SOMERSET)
(1699–1754)

Born on 10 May 1699, she was the elder daughter of the Hon. Henry Thynne, son of the 1st Viscount Weymouth, and his wife Grace Strode, daughter of Sir George Strode of Leweston, Dorset. She grew up at Longleat and, after her father's death in 1708, at Leweston, where her mother had retired. Her literary interests were developed by her reading aloud to her mother from works of history and divinity, as well as romances. From this rural upbringing she was plunged, at little more than 16, into the Court and fashionable world by her marriage in 1715 to Algernon Seymour (1684–1750), styled Earl of Hertford, who had served in the army in Flanders 1708–13, and had become Lord of the Bedchamber to the Prince of Wales. Although relations with her father-in-law, the eccentric Duke of Somerset, were strained, the marriage was a happy one. Her daughter Elizabeth, later Duchess of Northumberland, was born in 1716 and her son George, styled Viscount Beauchamp, in 1725. In 1723 she herself became prominent at Court as Lady of the Bedchamber to the Princess of Wales, later Queen Caroline.

The Countess nevertheless remained fond of rural retirement and keenly interested in literature. The Countess of Winchilsea (see nos. 4–18) was her great-aunt and addressed a poem to her. From an early age she had known Elizabeth Rowe (see nos. 33–6) and they corresponded until Rowe's death in 1737. Rowe introduced her to the poet James Thomson, who is said to have written his *Spring* while staying with the Hertfords at Marlborough Castle, Wiltshire, in the summer of 1727, and he dedicated the poem to her in 1728. Late in 1727 she intervened to help to rescue the poet Richard Savage when he was charged with murder. Through Elizabeth Rowe she also met Dr Isaac Watts in about 1725, who remained a correspondent for some twenty years. He dedicated to her his *Reliquiae Juveniles* (1734), including in it four pious poems by her (signed 'Eusebia', pp. 273–7). Later he dedicated to her his edition of Rowe's *Devout Exercises of the Heart* (1737). The Countess herself had few pretensions or ambitions as a poet, but she circulated her verse to friends such as Elizabeth Rowe, and it was no doubt inevitable that a poem such as *Inkle and Yarico* would eventually find its way into print.

Another friend and correspondent was Henrietta Knight (see nos. 151–2), who in 1736 was accused by her husband of having an affair with John Dalton, tutor to the Countess's son Lord Beauchamp. Horace Walpole later mischievously suggested that the Countess had 'chassé sur les mêmes terres' as Mrs Knight, with whom her friendship did not resume until 1742. By then the death of the Queen in 1737 had brought to an end the Countess's life at Court. She had spent much of her time when not at Court in the country, first at Marlborough Castle, later at St Leonard's Hill near Windsor, and from about 1739 at Riskins (or Richkings) near Colnbrook, formerly a seat of Pope's friend Lord Bathurst, which the Hertfords renamed Percy Lodge. Her later years were saddened by the death of her 19-year-old son from smallpox in Bologna, while on the Grand Tour. Thereafter she became increasingly religious, partly under the influence of the Countess of Huntingdon from 1747. Her husband, who had succeeded his father as Duke of Somerset in December 1748, died in February 1750. Until her own death on 7 July 1754 she lived mainly in retirement at Percy Lodge, still corresponding with her friends about literature and other subjects. Her correspondence with Mrs Knight was later published as *Select Letters between the late Duchess of Somerset, Lady Luxborough, William Shenstone and Others*, ed. Thomas Hull (2 vols., 1778), and with Lady Pomfret, whom she had known from her years at Court, as *Correspondence between Frances, Countess of Hertford, and Henrietta Louisa, Countess of Pomfret*, ed. W. Bingley (3 vols., 1805).

77   *The Story of Inkle and Yarico.*
    A most moving Tale from the Spectator [*No. 11*]

> A YOUTH there was possessed of every charm,
> Which might the coldest heart with passion warm;
> His blooming cheeks with ruddy beauty glowed,
> His hair in waving ringlets graceful flowed;
> Through all his person an attractive mien,
> Just symmetry, and elegance were seen:
> But niggard Fortune had her aid withheld,
> And poverty th' unhappy boy compelled

To distant climes to sail in search of gain,
Which might in ease his latter days maintain.　　　10
By chance, or rather the decree of Heaven,
The vessel on a barbarous coast was driven;
He, with a few unhappy striplings more,
Ventured too far upon the fatal shore:
The cruel natives thirsted for their blood,
And issued furious from a neighbouring wood.
His friends all fell by brutal rage o'erpowered,
Their flesh the horrid cannibals devoured;
Whilst he alone escaped by speedy flight,
And in a thicket lay concealed from sight!　　　20
　Now he reflects on his companions' fate,
His threatening danger, and abandoned state.
Whilst thus in fruitless grief he spent the day,
A negro virgin chanced to pass that way;
He viewed her naked beauties with surprise,
Her well-proportioned limbs and sprightly eyes!
With his complexion and gay dress amazed,
The artless nymph upon the stranger gazed;
Charmed with his features and alluring grace,
His flowing locks and his enlivened face.　　　30
His safety now became her tend'rest care,
A vaulted rock she knew and hid him there;
The choicest fruits the isle produced she sought,
And kindly to allay his hunger brought;
And when his thirst required, in search of drink,
She led him to a chrystal fountain's brink.
　Mutually charmed, by various arts they strove
To inform each other of their mutual love;
A language soon they formed, which might express
Their pleasing care and growing tenderness.　　　40
With tigers' speckled skins she decked his bed,
O'er which the gayest plumes of birds were spread;
And every morning, with the nicest care,
Adorned her well-turned neck and shining hair,
With all the glittering shells and painted flowers
That serve to deck the Indian virgins' bowers.
And when the sun descended in the sky,
And lengthening shades foretold the evening nigh,
Beneath some spreading palm's delightful shade,
Together sat the youth and lovely maid;　　　50
Or where some bubbling river gently crept,
She in her arms secured him while he slept.
When the bright moon in midnight pomp was seen,
And starlight glittered o'er the dewy green,

In some close arbour, or some fragrant grove,
He whispered vows of everlasting love.
Then, as upon the verdant turf he lay,
He oft would to th' attentive virgin say:
'Oh, could I but, my Yarico, with thee
Once more my dear, my native country see!   60
In softest silks thy limbs should be arrayed,
Like that of which the clothes I wear are made;
What different ways my grateful soul would find
To indulge thy person and divert thy mind!';
While she on the enticing accents hung
That smoothly fell from his persuasive tongue.

   One evening, from a rock's impending side,
An European vessel she descried,
And made them signs to touch upon the shore,
Then to her lover the glad tidings bore;   70
Who with his mistress to the ship descends,
And found the crew were countrymen and friends.
Reflecting now upon the time he passed,
Deep melancholy all his thoughts o'ercast:
'Was it for this,' said he, 'I crossed the main,
Only a doting virgin's heart to gain?
I needed not for such a prize to roam,
There are a thousand doting maids at home.'
While thus his disappointed mind was tossed,
The ship arrived on the Barbadian coast;   80
Immediately the planters from the town,
Who trade for goods and negro slaves, came down;
And now his mind, by sordid interest swayed,
Resolved to sell his faithful Indian maid.
Soon at his feet for mercy she implored,
And thus in moving strains her fate deplored:
   'O whither can I turn to seek redress,
When thou'rt the cruel cause of my distress?
If the remembrance of our former love,
And all thy plighted vows, want force to move;   90
Yet, for the helpless infant's sake I bear,
Listen with pity to my just despair.
Oh let me not in slavery remain,
Doomed all my life to drag a servile chain!
It cannot surely be! thy generous breast
An act so vile, so sordid must detest:
But, if thou hate me, rather let me meet
A gentler fate, and stab me at thy feet;
Then will I bless thee with my dying breath,
And sink contented in the shades of death.'   100

Not all she said could his compassion move,
Forgetful of his vows and promised love;
The weeping damsel from his knees he spurned,
And with her price pleased to the ship returned.

(1726?)

78   [*To the Countess of Pomfret: Life at Richkings*]

WE sometimes ride, and sometimes walk;
We play at chess, or laugh, or talk;
Sometimes, beside the chrystal stream,
We meditate some serious theme;
Or in the grot, beside the spring,
We hear the feathered warblers sing.
Shakespeare (perhaps) an hour diverts,
Or Scott directs to mend our hearts.
With Clarke God's attributes we explore;
And, taught by him, admire them more.   10
Gay's Pastorals sometimes delight us,
Or Tasso's grisly spectres fright us:
Sometimes we trace Armida's bowers,
And view Rinaldo chained with flowers.
Often, from thoughts sublime as these,
I sink at once—and make a cheese;
Or see my various poultry fed,
And treat my swans with scraps of bread.
Sometimes upon the smooth canal
We row the boat or spread the sail;   20
Till the bright evening-star is seen,
And dewy spangles deck the green.
   Then tolls the bell, and all unite
In prayer that God would bless the night.
From this (though I confess the change
From prayer to cards is somewhat strange)
To cards we go, till ten has struck:
And then, however bad our luck,
Our stomachs ne'er refuse to eat
Eggs, cream, fresh butter, or calves'-feet;   30
And cooling fruits, or savoury greens—
'Sparagus, peas, or kidney-beans.
Our supper past, an hour we sit,
And talk of history, Spain, or wit:

> But Scandal far is banished hence,
> Nor dares intrude with false pretence
> Of pitying looks, or holy rage
> Against the vices of the age:
> We know we all were born in sin,
> And find enough to blame within.   40

(Wr. 1740; pub. 1805)

MEHETABEL WRIGHT (née WESLEY)
(1697–1750)

Always known in her family as Hetty, she was the daughter of Samuel Wesley, Rector of Epworth and of Wroot, Lincolnshire, and his wife Susanna Annesley, and was the seventh of their nineteen surviving children, who included John and Charles Wesley, the founders of Methodism. She received the same education as her brothers and is said to have been able to read Greek by the age of 8. By her mid-twenties she was in serious conflict with her family, who were no doubt anxious for the numerous daughters to marry: this may lie behind her father's statement that he 'had been twice at the charge of setting her out handsomely', although she had returned home in each case. When she fell in love with a lawyer, however, her father opposed the match, and during 1725 she eloped on at least two occasions. By April 1725 the Wesleys had heard nothing of her for three months, but she returned during the summer, engaged in another love-affair and disappeared again on 2 August. In a letter of 12 August her father despaired of her: 'Gangrene, farewell! And mayst thou never cause me any pain hereafter.' No doubt because she was discovered to be pregnant when she reappeared, she was forced to marry William Wright of Louth at Haxey on 13 October 1725. Her husband, who was presumably attracted by a dowry, took her to Louth in November with her sister Molly as companion. Her daughter by an unnamed lover was baptized at Louth on 18 February 1726, but was buried on the following 27 December.

Hetty's behaviour continued to divide the family even after her marriage. Her brother John, recently ordained, offended his father by alluding to his harsh treatment of Hetty in a sermon preached at Wroot in August 1726. In a letter to his brother Samuel in December 1726 he stated that his father was 'inconceivably exasperated against her' and had 'disowned her long ago, and never spoke of her in my hearing but with the utmost detestation'. During a recent visit to Wroot, Hetty had indeed seemed impenitent, had greeted her mother's attempts at reconciliation with reserve and had refused to meet her father. By May 1727 she had set up a school, which was not successful, and in January 1728 the Wrights were in London, where her husband became a successful plumber and glazier in Frith Street, Soho. She did eventually resume a rather edgy correspondence with her father, replying in about 1729 to his question 'what hurt matrimony has done me', by describing just what her own marriage lacked, 'a mutual affection and desire of pleasing, something near an equality of mind and person, either earthly or heavenly wisdom, and any thing to keep love warm between a young couple'. Her bitter 'Wedlock. A Satire', which appears below, provoked 'A Full Answer' from her brother Samuel, who had earlier addressed affectionate verses to her. He told her that 'cursing wedlock is blaspheming' and urged her to 'Repent, renounce all wicked wit: | . . . So may the world your flights forget, | And God forgive, and Willy pardon'.

John Duncombe, who visited her not long before her death, described William Wright as 'a very decent respectable man, carrying on business in his own neighbourhood', and was unwilling to believe her complaints of 'the neglect and unkindness, the unfeelingness, of a worthless husband', attributing them to religious melancholy. Everything indicates, however, that Wright was her social and intellectual inferior, who preferred to spend his evenings drinking with 'low company' and soon 'broke the heart of his wife'. She also believed that the health of the family suffered from the lead-works on Wright's premises and that this had caused the early deaths of her children. The lines on her dying infant, according to Adam Clarke in 1828, were 'composed during her confinement, written down from her mouth by her husband, and sent by him to Mr. John Wesley', without punctuation and in Wright's 'barbarous orthography'. The poem was printed in October 1733 in the *Gentleman's Magazine*, where some lines on her sister, 'To the Memory of Mrs. Mary Whitelamb', also appeared in 1736. Significantly, John Wesley omitted from the text some lines printed by Clarke in 1823 from her MS, in which she referred to Mary's support during the family crisis in 1725,

> When deep immers'd in griefs beyond redress,
> And friends and kindred heightened my distress,
> And with relentless efforts made me prove
> Pain, grief, despair and *wedlock without love* . . .

By 1743, after many years of unhappiness, she had come under the religious influence of her brother John, although her husband remained unsympathetic to Methodism and she felt 'cut off from all human help or ministry'. During her serious illness in 1744, her brother John arranged for her to recuperate with the Wesleys at Bristol, where she became 'more and more convinced of [sin], especially of unprofitableness to myself and others'. She was reluctant to attend Methodist group meetings for fear of bringing 'more disgrace' upon her brother. She was described to Adam Clarke, the family historian, by one who had known her as 'an elegant woman, with great refinement of manners; and had the traces of beauty in her countenance, with the appearance of being broken-hearted'. She died on 21 March 1750. Through William and John Duncombe, who had been neighbours in Frith Street, some of her poems circulated in MS in the 1750s (Thomas Herring, Archbishop of Canterbury, was shown some in 1753). John Duncombe referred approvingly to her in *The Feminiad* in 1754, and several poems eventually found their way into print in magazines and miscellanies. It was only in the nineteenth century that historians of the Wesley family made a serious attempt to collect her verse. A long poem called 'Eupolis' has been claimed for her but was believed in the family to have been basically the work of her father.

79   *Address to her Husband*

> THE ardent lover cannot find
> A coldness in his fair unkind,
> But blaming what he cannot hate,
> He mildly chides the dear ingrate;

And though despairing of relief,
In soft complaining vents his grief.

Then what should hinder but that I,
Impatient of my wrongs, may try,
By saddest softest strains, to move
My wedded, latest, dearest love,   10
To throw his cold neglect aside,
And cheer once more his injured bride!

O thou, whom sacred rites designed
My guide, and husband ever kind,
My sovereign master, best of friends,
On whom my earthly bliss depends;
If e'er thou didst in Hetty see
Aught fair, or good, or dear to thee,
If gentle speech can ever move
The cold remains of former love,   20
Turn thee at last—my bosom ease,
Or tell me *why* I cease to please.

Is it because revolving years,
Heart-breaking sighs, and fruitless tears,
Have quite deprived this form of mine
Of all that once thou fanciedst fine?
Ah no! what once allured thy sight
Is still in its meridian height.
These eyes their usual lustre show,
When uneclipsed by flowing woe.   30
Old age and wrinkles in this face
As yet could never find a place:
A youthful grace informs these lines,
Where still the purple current shines;
Unless, by thy ungentle art,
It flies to aid my wretched heart:
Nor does this slighted bosom show
The thousand hours it spends in woe.

Or is it that, oppressed with care,
I stun with loud complaints thine ear,   40
And make thy home, for quiet meant,
The seat of noise and discontent?
Ah no! those ears were ever free
From matrimonial melody:
For though thine absence I lament
When half the lonely night is spent,

Yet when the watch or early morn
Has brought me hopes of thy return,
I oft have wiped these watchful eyes,
Concealed my cares, and curbed my sighs,   50
In spite of grief, to let thee see
I wore an endless smile for thee.

Had I not practised every art
T' oblige, divert, and cheer thy heart,
To make me pleasing in thine eyes,
And turn thy house to paradise;
I had not asked, 'Why dost thou shun
These faithful arms, and eager run
To some obscure, unclean retreat,
With fiends incarnate glad to meet,   60
The vile companions of thy mirth,
The scum and refuse of the earth;
Who, when inspired by beer, can grin
At witless oaths and jests obscene,
Till the most learned of the throng
Begins a tale of ten hours long;
While thou in raptures with stretched jaws
Crownest each joke with loud applause?'

Deprived of freedom, health, and ease,
And rivalled by such *things* as these,   70
This latest effort will I try,
Or to regain thy heart, or die.
Soft as I am, I'll make thee see
I will not brook contempt from thee!

Then quit the shuffling doubtful sense,
Nor hold me longer in suspense;
Unkind, ungrateful, as thou art,
Say, must I ne'er regain thy heart?
Must all attempts to please thee prove
Unable to regain thy love?   80

If so, by truth itself I swear,
The sad reverse I cannot bear;
No rest, no pleasure, will I see;
My whole of bliss is lost with thee!
I'll give all thoughts of patience o'er
(A gift I never lost before);
Indulge at once my rage and grief,
Mourn obstinate, disdain relief,

And call that wretch my mortal foe,
Who tries to mitigate my woe;   90
Till life, on terms severe as these,
Shall, ebbing, leave my heart at ease;
To thee thy liberty restore
To laugh when Hetty is no more.

(Wr. *c.*1730?; pub. 1823)

80   *Wedlock. A Satire*

THOU tyrant, whom I will not name,
Whom heaven and hell alike disclaim;
Abhorred and shunned, for different ends,
By angels, Jesuits, beasts and fiends!
What terms to curse thee shall I find,
Thou plague peculiar to mankind?
O may my verse excel in spite
The wiliest, wittiest imps of night!
Then lend me for a while your rage,
You maidens old and matrons sage: 10
So may my terms in railing seem
As vile and hateful as my theme.
   Eternal foe to soft desires,
Inflamer of forbidden fires,
Thou source of discord, pain and care,
Thou sure forerunner of despair,
Thou scorpion with a double face,
Thou lawful plague of human race,
Thou bane of freedom, ease and mirth,
Thou deep damnation upon earth,   20
Thou serpent which the angels fly,
Thou monster whom the beasts defy,
Whom wily Jesuits sneer at too;
And Satan (let him have his due)
Was never so confirmed a dunce
To risk damnation more than once.
That wretch, if such a wretch there be,
Who hopes for happiness from thee,
May search successfully as well
For truth in whores and ease in hell.   30

(Wr. *c.*1730; pub. 1862)

114

81   *To an Infant Expiring the Second Day*
of its Birth

TENDER softness, infant mild,
Perfect, purest, brightest child;
Transient lustre, beauteous clay,
Smiling wonder of a day:
Ere the last convulsive start
Rends thy unresisting heart;
Ere the long-enduring swoon
Weighs thy precious eyelids down;
Oh! regard a mother's moan,
Anguish deeper than thy own!   10
Fairest eyes, whose dawning light
Late with rapture blessed my sight,
Ere your orbs extinguished be,
Bend their trembling beams on me,
Drooping sweetness, verdant flower,
Blooming, withering in an hour,
Ere thy gentle breast sustains
Latest, fiercest, vital pains,
Hear a suppliant! Let me be
Partner in thy destiny!   20

(1733)

82   *An Epitaph on Herself*

DESTINED while living to sustain
An equal share of grief and pain,
All various ills of human race
Within this breast had once a place.
Without complaint she learned to bear
A living death, a long despair;
Till hard oppressed by adverse fate,
O'ercharged, she sunk beneath its weight;
And to this peaceful tomb retired,
So much esteemed, so long desired.   10
The painful mortal conflict o'er:
A broken heart can bleed no more!

(Wr. by 1750; pub. 1763)

ANONYMOUS ('A LADY')

An Epithalamium

Lo! Hymen passes through th' admiring crowds,
A saffron robe the hideous tyrant shrouds;
Behind stalks Plutus, with a tempting store;
A mimic Cupid bears the torch before:
False hopes and phantom joys, a gaudy train,
Surround his car, and dance along the plain:
Still, as he passes, witless maids and swains,
Lured by the show, put on his gilded chains.

Be wise, ye fair! and shun the tempting bait,
Nor flounce and struggle on the hook too late!   10
Too late the fatal cheat you will discover,
When you have caught the spouse, but lost the lover!
The pleasing scene shall vanish from your eye,
And gloomy discontents obscure the sky.
What though th' impatient lover's fervent kiss
May promise rapt'rous nights and endless bliss:
The hour shall be when you, become a bride,
Must hear him snore, inactive, by your side.

Mark well, ye fair! a blooming swain and maid,
While new-born flames their tender hearts invade!   20
He warm and active as the sun at noon,
She gay and genial as the wanton June;
They speak in raptures, and with transport move;
They meet, they kiss, they press, they pant, they love.
But lo! the longed-for flamen joins their hands,
And rivets on the everlasting bands;
The holy charm soon damps their warm desires
(For Hymen's torch still puts out Cupid's fires):
They grow Platonic, bodies leave off sporting,
While soul and soul go hand-in-hand in courting: 30
The vigorous lover, and the mistress gay,
Turned to a lifeless mass of mingled clay.

This sudden change in a young healthy pair
May make, perhaps, the beaus and women stare;
May puzzle court and city to detect
The mighty power, which works the sad effect.

flamen] priest

But sages, who explore each hidden cause,
Know that, by nature's necessary laws,
Two distant bodies, while they're free and loose,
May action and reaction still produce: 40
But by compulsive force together tied,
No motion can begin from either side.

This single problem may suffice to prove
The dire effect that wedlock has on love;
In order to convince the learned few,
We bring them reasons *physically* true.
But since (to make an argument more strong)
Examples must be hauled in, right or wrong,
An ancient tale, served up in modern sort,
May chance to please the fair—though 'tis but short.   50

While Hermes' son sports in the chrystal flood,
Salmacis lurks within the bordering wood;
Behind the twining boughs she stands, to view
His well-turned limbs, and pants to touch them too:
Then grown impatient, casts her robes aside,
And plunges furious through the yielding tide;
She grasps the struggling boy with eager love,
And thus directs her fatal prayer to Jove:
'Supreme of powers! oh, grant me to remain
Thus joined, for ever, to the lovely swain!'   60
Too well she's heard: the mingling sexes blend,
And the lost pair in a new monster end.

Thus many a hapless girl, through sad mistake,
Souses into the matrimonial lake,
In hope of raptures, bliss, and all the rest
Which lovers feel, possessing and possessed:
Warmed with the thought, she's tired of being alone,
Sees a brisk youth, and wishes him her own.
Her prayer is granted; by the church's doom
They're joined for ever, and one flesh become: 70
In wife and husband, girl and boy are lost,
And make one poor *Hermaphrodite* at most.

(1731)

---

physically] i.e. according to the laws of physics   Souses] plunges

MARY BARBER
(c.1690–1757)

She was the wife of Jonathan Barber, who was born in England but became a woollen-draper in Capel Street, Dublin. Of their four children, Constantine became a well-known physician and Rupert a miniature-painter. In the preface to her *Poems* (1734) she explained that she had begun writing verse 'chiefly to form the Minds of my Children', by making precepts easier to memorize, and to teach them to speak clearly. Although she also stated that 'a Woman steps out of her Province, whenever she presumes to write for the Press', she had in fact published several poems in Dublin in the 1720s. *The Widows Address* (Dublin, 1725), a verse petition on behalf of an army officer's widow, reached Lady Carteret, wife of the Lord-Lieutenant of Ireland, through Thomas Tickell, and in the same year she addressed a poem to Lord Carteret himself. Other separately published poems include *A Tale Being an Addition to Mr. Gay's Fables* (1728), appealing to the Queen to give Gay a pension. With the Carterets as her patrons she came to know Dr Delany, who by 1728 had introduced her to Swift and his circle, which soon included Constantia Grierson (see no. 64) and Laetitia Pilkington (see nos. 94–5).

In her *Memoirs* Mrs Pilkington later referred contemptuously to Mary Barber's 'dull' poems, which 'certainly would have been much worse, but that Doctor *Delany* frequently held what he called a *Senatus Consultum*, to correct these indigested Materials; at which were present sometimes the Dean, (in the Chair) but always Mrs. *Grierson*, Mr. *Pilkington*, the Doctor, and my self'. Although Swift himself, in the prefatory letter to Lord Orrery in her *Poems* (1734), praised her willingness to be 'corrected', he always considered her the most talented of the women poets in his circle. When she came to England in 1730, visiting Tunbridge Wells and Bath as well as London, Swift began an elaborate campaign to promote a subscription to a collection of her poems, writing letters of introduction for her to many aristocratic and literary friends in England and urging them to support this 'poeticall Genius'. As he told Pope, 'she was poetically given, & for a woman, had a sort of genius that way', and was 'wholly turned to Poetry'. Contrary to Swift's instructions, she irritated Pope while in England by trying to get him to 'correct' her verse: Swift, who usually thought that 'too much bashfulness' was her chief failing, concluded that there must have been 'a great Combat between her Modesty and her Ambition'. He was also agitated in 1731 when she, or a clumsy well-wisher, sent from Ireland a letter to the Queen, ostensibly signed by Swift, in support of her subscription.

In spite of these hitches, a large and impressive list of subscribers was assembled, including the names of Arbuthnot, Gay, Pope, Sir Robert Walpole, and many of the nobility. Swift himself, like the Duke of Dorset, subscribed for ten copies. Some of his women friends were sceptical about Swift's claims for Mrs Barber: Lady Elizabeth Germain subscribed for five copies, 'tho' I am of opinion we ladies are not apt to be good Poets especially if we cant spell.' One result of her residence in England was a plan of settling there permanently. In 1732 Swift tried unsuccessfully to persuade his friend John Barber (no relation), while he was Lord Mayor of London, to find her husband a post. She also had a scheme of living in Bath, where her husband would trade as a woollen-draper and she would let lodgings. By September 1732 she had returned to Ireland to fetch her family, but suffered an attack of 'gout', which seriously affected the use of her limbs. Moreover, her husband seems to have died by 1733, after which date no more is heard of him. When she returned to England in 1733, Swift was still describing her as 'the best Poetess of both Kingdoms', and his loyalty to her was no doubt strengthened when she was arrested for a time early in 1734 for bringing into England the MSS of some of his supposedly subversive poems. After her release she settled in Bath, still hoping to support herself by letting lodgings or selling Irish linen. Her son Rupert, who is known to have studied painting in Bath, may have joined her at this time.

Her *Poems on Several Occasions* were published in quarto in 1734, printed by Samuel Richardson, who was also a subscriber, and in an octavo edition in 1735 (reissued 1736). The volume included poems by her deceased friend Constantia Grierson and by her son Constantine, and one by Elizabeth Rowe (see nos. 33–6). Anne Donnellan reported to Swift in 1735 that they were 'generally greatly liked', although 'a few severe critics . . . say they are not poetic' (which was probably why Swift liked them), and that 'a few fine ladies, who are not commended in them . . . complain they are dull'. The successful subscription no doubt enabled her to remain in England for a few more years, although she was increasingly crippled by her so-called 'gout'. In 1736 she wrote from Bath to Swift, who had offered to support her if she returned to Ireland, begging the rights to the London edition of his *Complete Collection of Genteel and Ingenious Conversation*, the MS of which he duly conveyed to her through Lord Orrery in 1737 for publication in 1738. She was clearly unwell and unsettled, however. In 1737 Orrery had regretted in a letter to her that 'the Gout and Rheumatism have got possession of your hands and feet, and melancholy and langour of your heart and head', commented sceptically on her quixotic scheme of going to Georgia, and suggested that a return to Ireland might benefit her health.

A few years later she was back in Ireland, perhaps under the care of her son Constantine, a physician who had been educated at Trinity College, Dublin, and Leiden. In 1741 she wrote to Samuel Richardson from Dublin, thanking him for sending her daughter a copy of *Pamela* and suggesting that Mr B.'s second attempted rape of the virtuous heroine was 'a little too strongly painted'. In 1744 she was living in Glasnevin to the north of Dublin, not far from the Delanys and perhaps with her son Rupert, the painter, who was patronized by Mrs Delany. She was cheerful during a visit to Dèlville in 1744, Mrs Delany reported, although 'she had the gout upon her and was forced to be lifted out upon men's shoulders'. In July 1747 she wrote from Dublin to George Ballard, through an intermediary, about Constantia Grierson. She seems to have written little verse after 1734, although some lines on her sufferings from gout—for which she was treated by Dr Mead—written in London in May 1735 appeared in the *Gentleman's Magazine* in March 1737. There are also some enigmatic references in Lord Orrery's correspondence in 1752 to verses on political subjects written by 'Mother Barber' and repeated by her medical son. A substantial selection of her verse appeared in *Poems by Eminent Ladies* in 1755. (It is a sign of changing taste that only six of these twenty-eight poems were retained in the revised edition of about 1780.) She died in 1757.

84   *Written for My Son, and Spoken by Him at*
His First Putting on Breeches

WHAT is it our mammas bewitches,
To plague us little boys with breeches?
To tyrant Custom we must yield
Whilst vanquished Reason flies the field.
Our legs must suffer by ligation,
To keep the blood from circulation;
And then our feet, though young and tender,
We to the shoemaker surrender,
Who often makes our shoes so strait
Our growing feet they cramp and fret;   10
Whilst, with contrivance most profound,
Across our insteps we are bound;
Which is the cause, I make no doubt,
Why thousands suffer in the gout.
Our wiser ancestors wore brogues,
Before the surgeons bribed these rogues,
With narrow toes, and heels like pegs,
To help to make us break our legs.

  Then, ere we know to use our fists,
Our mothers closely bind our wrists;   20
And never think our clothes are neat,
Till they're so tight we cannot eat.
And, to increase our other pains,
The hat-band helps to cramp our brains.
The cravat finishes the work,
Like bowstring sent from the Grand Turk.

  Thus dress, that should prolong our date,
Is made to hasten on our fate.
Fair privilege of nobler natures,
To be more plagued than other creatures!   30
The wild inhabitants of air
Are clothed by heaven with wondrous care:
The beauteous, well-compacted feathers
Are coats of mail against all weathers;
Enamelled, to delight the eye,
Gay as the bow that decks the sky.
The beasts are clothed with beauteous skins;
The fishes armed with scales and fins,

ligation] binding

Whose lustre lends the sailor light,
When all the stars are hid in night.   40

O were our dress contrived like these,
For use, for ornament and ease!
Man only seems to sorrow born,
Naked, defenceless and forlorn.

Yet we have Reason, to supply
What nature did to man deny:
Weak viceroy! Who thy power will own,
When Custom has usurped thy throne?
In vain did I appeal to thee,
Ere I would wear his livery;   50
Who, in defiance to thy rules,
Delights to make us act like fools.
O'er human race the tyrant reigns,
And binds them in eternal chains.
We yield to his despotic sway,
The only monarch all obey.

(1731)

85   *An Unanswerable Apology for the Rich*

'ALL-bounteous Heaven,' Castalio cries,
With bended knees and lifted eyes,
'When shall I have the power to bless,
And raise up merit in distress?'

How do our hearts deceive us here!
He gets ten thousand pounds a year.
With this the pious youth is able
To build, and plant, and keep a table.
But then, the poor he must not treat:
Who asks the wretch that wants to eat?   10
Alas! to ease their woes he wishes,
But cannot live without ten dishes,
Though six would serve as well, 'tis true:
But one must live as others do.
He now feels wants unknown before,
Wants still increasing with his store.
The good Castalio must provide
Brocade, and jewels, for his bride:
Her toilet shines with plate embossed,
What sums her lace and linen cost!   20

121

The clothes that must his person grace
Shine with embroidery and lace.
The costly pride of Persian looms,
And Guido's paintings, grace his rooms.
His wealth Castalio will not waste,
But must have everything in taste.
He's an economist confessed,
But what he buys must be the best.
For common use, a set of plate;
Old China, when he dines in state;   30
A coach-and-six to take the air,
Besides a chariot and chair.
All these important calls supplied,
Calls of necessity, not pride,
His income's regularly spent,
He scarcely saves to pay his rent.
No man alive would do more good,
Or give more freely, if he could.
He grieves, whene'er the wretched sue,
But what can poor Castalio *do*?   40

Would Heaven but send ten thousand more,
He'd give—just as he did before.

(1734)

86   *The Conclusion of a Letter to the Rev. Mr C——*

'TIS time to conclude, for I make it a rule
To leave off all writing, when Con. comes from school.
He dislikes what I've written, and says I had better
To send what he calls a poetical letter.

To this I replied, 'You are out of your wits;
A letter in verse would put him in fits;
He thinks it a crime in a woman to read—
Then what would he say should your counsel succeed?
"I pity poor Barber, his wife's so romantic:
A letter in rhyme!—Why the woman is frantic!   10
This reading the poets has quite turned her head;
On my life, she should have a dark room and straw bed.
I often heard say that St. Patrick took care
No poisonous creature should live in this air:
He only regarded the body, I find,
But Plato considered who poisoned the mind.

Would they'd follow his precepts, who sit at the helm,
And drive poetasters from out of the realm!

   '"Her husband has surely a terrible life;
There's nothing I dread like a verse-writing wife: 20
Defend me, ye powers, from that fatal curse,
Which must heighten the plagues of *for better for worse*!

   '"May I have a wife that will dust her own floor,
And not the fine minx recommended by *More.
(That he was a dotard is granted, I hope,
Who died for asserting the rights of the Pope.)
If ever I marry, I'll choose me a spouse,
That shall *serve* and *obey*, as she's bound by her vows;
That shall, when I'm dressing, attend like a valet;
Then go to the kitchen, and study my palate.   30
She has wisdom enough, that keeps out of the dirt,
And can make a good pudding, and cut out a shirt.
What good's in a dame that will pore on a book?
No—give me the wife that shall save me a cook."'

   Thus far I had written—then turned to my son,
To give him advice, ere my letter was done.
'My son, should you marry, look out for a wife
That's fitted to lighten the labours of life.
Be sure, wed a woman you thoroughly know,
And shun, above all things, a *housewifely shrew*,   40
That would fly to your study, with fire in her looks,
And ask what you got by your poring on books,
Think dressing of dinner the height of all science,
And to peace and good humour bid open defiance.

   'Avoid the fine lady, whose beauty's her care;
Who sets a high price on her shape, and her air;
Who in dress, and in visits, employs the whole day,
And longs for the evening, to sit down to play.

   'Choose a woman of wisdom, as well as good breeding,
With a turn, or at least no aversion, to reading: 50
In the care of her person, exact and refined;
Yet still, let her principal care be her mind:
Who can, when her family cares give her leisure,
Without the dear cards, pass an evening with pleasure,
In forming her children to virtue and knowledge,

* See Sir Thomas More's *Advice to his Son.*

Nor trust, for that care, to a school, or a college:
By learning made humble, not thence taking airs
To despise or neglect her domestic affairs:
Nor think her less fitted for doing her duty,
By knowing its reasons, its use, and its beauty.   60

'When you gain her affection, take care to preserve it,
Lest others persuade her you do not deserve it.
Still study to heighten the joys of her life;
Nor treat her the worse for her being your wife.
If in judgement she errs, set her right, without pride:
'Tis the province of insolent fools to deride.
A husband's first praise is a Friend and Protector:
Then change not these titles for Tyrant and Hector.
Let your person be neat, unaffectedly clean,
Though alone with your wife the whole day you remain.   70
Choose books, for her study, to fashion her mind,
To emulate those who excelled of her kind.
Be religion the principal care of your life,
As you hope to be blest in your children and wife;
So you, in your marriage, shall gain its true end,
And find, in your wife, a Companion and Friend.'

(1734)

87   *Stella and Flavia*

STELLA and Flavia every hour
    Unnumbered hearts surprise:
In Stella's soul lies all her power,
    And Flavia's in her eyes.

More boundless Flavia's conquests are,
    And Stella's more confined:
All can discern a face that's fair,
    But few a lovely mind.

Stella, like Britain's monarch, reigns
    O'er cultivated lands;   10
Like Eastern tyrants, Flavia deigns
    To rule o'er barren sands.

Hector] bully

124

Then boast, fair Flavia, boast your face,
　　Your beauty's only store:
Your charms will every day decrease,
　　Each day give Stella more.

(1734)

88　　　　　*To Mrs. Frances-Arabella Kelly*

TODAY, as at my glass I stood,
To set my head-clothes and my hood,
I saw my grizzled locks with dread,
And called to mind the Gorgon's head.

　Thought I, whate'er the poets say,
Medusa's hair was only grey:
Though Ovid, who the story told,
Was too well-bred to call her old;
But, what amounted to the same,
He made her an immortal dame.　　　　　　　　　10

　Yet now, whene'er a matron sage
Hath felt the rugged hand of age,
You hear our witty coxcombs cry,
'Rot that old witch—she'll never die';
Though, had they but a little reading,
Ovid would teach them better breeding.

　I fancy now I hear you say,
'Grant heaven my locks may ne'er be grey!
Why am I told this frightful story,
To beauty a *memento mori?*'　　　　　　　　　20

　And, as along the room you pass,
Casting your eye upon the glass,
'Surely,' say you, 'this lovely face
Will never suffer such disgrace:
The bloom, that on my cheek appears,
Will never be impaired by years.
Her envy, now I plainly see,
Makes her inscribe those lines to me.
These beldames, who were born before me,
Are grieved to see the men adore me:　　　　　　30
Their snaky locks freeze up the blood;
My tresses fire the purple flood.

'Unnumbered slaves around me wait,
And from my eyes expect their fate.
I own of conquest I am vain,
Though I despise the slaves I gain.
Heaven gave me charms, and destined me
For universal tyranny.'

(1734)

89   *On seeing an Officer's Widow distracted, who*
     had been driven to Despair by a long and
     fruitless Solicitation for the Arrears of her
                      Pension

O WRETCH! hath madness cured thy dire despair?
Yes—All thy sorrows now are light as air:
No more you mourn your once loved husband's fate,
Who bravely perished for a thankless state.
For rolling years thy piety prevailed;
At length, quite sunk—thy hope, thy patience failed.
Distracted now you tread on life's last stage,
Nor feel the weight of poverty and age:
How blest in this, compared with those whose lot
Dooms them to miseries, by you forgot!   10

Now, wild as winds, you from your offspring fly,
Or fright them from you with distracted eye;
Rove through the streets; or sing, devoid of care,
With tattered garments and dishevelled hair;
By hooting boys to higher frenzy fired,
At length you sink, by cruel treatment tired,
Sink into sleep, an emblem of the dead,
A stone thy pillow, the cold earth thy bed.

O tell it not; let none the story hear,
Lest Britain's martial sons should learn to fear: 20
And when they next the hostile wall attack,
Feel the heart fail, the lifted arm grow slack;
And pausing cry—'Though death we scorn to dread,
Our orphan offspring, must they pine for bread?
See their loved mothers into prisons thrown,
And, unrelieved, in iron bondage groan?'

Britain, for this impending ruin dread;
Their woes call loud for vengeance on thy head:

Nor wonder, if disasters wait your fleets;
Nor wonder at complainings in your streets.   30
Be timely wise; arrest th' uplifted hand,
Ere pestilence or famine sweep the land.

(1734)

90   from *To a Lady, who commanded me to*
send her an Account in Verse, how I succeeded
in my Subscription

HOW I succeed, you kindly ask,
Yet set me on a grievous task,
When you oblige me to rehearse
The censures passed upon my verse.

   Though I with pleasure may relate
That many, truly good and great,
With candid eye my lines survey,
And smile upon the artless lay;
To those with grateful heart I bend—
But your commands I must attend.   10

   Servilla cries, 'I hate a wit;
Women should to their fate submit,
Should in the needle take delight;
'Tis out of character to write:
She may succeed among the men;
They tell me Swift subscribes for ten,
And some say Dorset does the same;
But she shall never have my name.
Her poetry has cost me dear;
When Lady Carteret was here,   20
The widow Gordon got my guinea;
For which I own myself a ninny.'

   Olivia loses oft at play,
So will not throw her gold away.

   Thus Sylvia, of the haughty tribe:
'She never asked me to subscribe,
Nor ever wrote a line on me,
I was no theme for poetry!
She rightly judged; I have no taste—
For women's poetry, at least.'   30

Then Fulvia made this sage reply
(And looked with self-sufficient eye):
'I oft have said, and say again,
Verses are only writ by men:
I know a woman cannot write;
I do not say this out of spite,
Nor shall be thought, by those who know me,
To envy one so much below me.'

Sabina, famed in wisdom's school,
Allows I write—but am a fool: 40
'What!—must our sons be formed by rhyme?
A fine way to employ one's time!'

Albino has no gold to waste,
Far gone in the Italian taste:
He vows he must subscribe this year
To keep dear Carestini here;
Not from a narrow party view,
He dotes on *Senesino too;
By turns their interest he'll espouse;
He's for the public good, he vows;   50
A generous ardour fires his breast;
Hail, Britain, in such patriots blest!

Says Belvidera, 'Since a wit,
Or friend or foe, alike will hit,
Deliver me from wits, I say!
Grant heaven they ne'er may cross my way!
Besides, I oft have heard it hinted
Her poems never will be printed:
Her sickness is a feint, no doubt,
To keep her book from coming out.'   60
'Of wit,' says Celia, 'I'll acquit her',
Then archly fell into a titter.

'A female bard!' Pulvillio cries;
''Tis possible she may be wise;
But I could never find it yet,
Though oft in company we met:
She talks just in the common way;
Sure wits their talents should display:
Their language surely should be bright,
Before they should pretend to write: 70

* *Two famous* Italian *singers, zealously supported by different parties.*

128

I'll ne'er subscribe for books,' says he;
''Fore Gad, it looks like pedantry.'

  High-born Belinda loves to blame;
On criticism founds her fame:
Whene'er she thinks a fault she spies,
How pleasure sparkles in her eyes!
'Call it not poetry,' she says:
'No—call it rhyming, if you please:
Her numbers might adorn a ring,
Or serve along the streets to sing: 80
'Stella and Flavia' 's well enough;
What else I saw was stupid stuff;
Nor love nor satire in the lays,
Insipid! neither pain nor please;
I promised once to patronise her,
But on reflection I was wiser:
Yet I subscribed among the rest;
I love to carry on a jest.'
Belinda thus her anger shows,
Nor tells the world from whence it flows: 90
With more success to wound my lays,
She gilds the dart with others' praise:
To her own breast I leave the fair,
Convinced I stand acquitted there.

  Amanda, your commands, you see,
Though grievous, are obeyed by me.
What my friends told me had been said,
Just as it came into my head,
No matter for the place or time,
To show your power I tag with rhyme.

                  (1734)

MISS W——

In view of the many speculations about Swift's mental state when he wrote his scatological verse, it is of interest that an unidentified woman promptly replied to his *The Lady's Dressing Room* (1732), with a poem which is, if anything, even more disgusted and disgusting, however modest its literary merits. (Although its content is unexpected, there is no evidence, internal or external, that it is not by a woman.) *The Gentleman's Study* was published anonymously in 1732. In spite of its imprint's claim that it had first appeared in London, Foxon (*Catalogue* G 123) suggests that it was published only in Dublin. The attribution to Miss W—— is found on the title-page of Samuel Shepherd's *Chloe Surpriz'd; Or, The Second Part of the Lady's Dressing-*

Room (Dublin, 1732), and also in the subtitle to his 'Thoughts upon Reading the Lady's Dressing-Room and the Gentleman's Study' (pp. 7–8), which ends: 'We may easily see, by the Spleen of what's said, | That he's an old Batchelor, she an old Maid; | Then wed them together, join her Shift to his Shirt, | And let 'em contend to excell most in dirt.'

The Gentleman's Study is not recommended to readers of a nervous disposition. Laetitia Pilkington states that her mother, 'upon reading the *Lady's Dressing-room*, instantly threw up her Dinner' and the following rejoinder might well have had the same effect.

91   *The Gentleman's Study, In Answer to* [*Swift's*]
        The Lady's Dressing-Room

SOME write of angels, some of goddess,
But I of dirty human bodies,
And lowly I employ my pen,
To write of naught but odious men;
And man I think, without a jest,
More nasty than the nastiest beast.

   In house of office, when they're bare,
And have not paper then to spare,
Their hands they'll take, half clean their bottom,
And daub the wall, O——rot 'em;   10
And in a minute, with a t—d,
They'll draw them out a beast or bird,
And write there without ink or pen:
When finger's dry, there's a—se again.
But now high time to tell my story;
But 'tis not much to all men's glory.

   A milliner, one Mrs. South,
I had the words from her own mouth,
That had a bill, which was long owing
By Strephon, for cloth, lace and sewing;   20
And on a day to's lodging goes,
In hopes of payment for the clothes,
And meeting there, and 'twas by chance,
His valet Tom, her old acquaintance,
Who, with an odd but friendly grin,
Told her his master's not within,
But bid her if she pleased to stay,
He'd treat her with a pot of tea;
So brought her to the study, while
He'd go and make the kettle boil.   30

She sat her down upon the chair,
For that was all that then was there,
And turned her eyes on every side,
Where strange confusion she espied.

There on a block a wig was set,
Whose inside did so stink with sweat;
The outside oiled with jessamine,
T' disguise the stench that was within.

And next a shirt, with gussets red,
Which Strephon slept in, when in bed;   40
But modesty forbids the rest,
It shan't be spoke, but may be guessed;
A napkin worn [up]on a head,
Enough, infection to have bred.

For there some stocks lay on the ground,
One side was yellow, t' other brown;
And velvet breeches (on her word),
The inside all bedaubed with t——d,
And just before, I'll not desist
To let you know they were be-pissed: 50
Four different stinks lay there together,
Which were sweat, turd, and piss, and leather.

There in a heap lay nasty socks,
Here tangled stockings with silver clocks,
And towels stiff with soap and hair,
Of stinking shoes there lay a pair;
A nightgown, with gold rich-brocaded,
About the neck was sadly faded.

A close-stool helped to make the fume;
Tobacco-spits about the room,   60
With phlegm and vomit on the walls;
Here powder, dirt, combs and wash-balls;
Oil-bottles, paper, pens, and wax,
Dice, pamphlets, and of cards some packs;
Pig-tail and snuff, and dirty gloves,
Some plain, some fringed, which most he loves;
A curling-iron stands upright,
False locks and oil lay down close by't;
A drabbled cloak hung on a pin,
And basin furred with piss within;   70

drabbled] muddied

131

Of pipes a heap, some whole, some broke,
Some cut-and-dry for him to smoke;
And papers that his a—se has cleaned,
And handkerchiefs with snuff all stained:
The sight and smells did make her sick,
She did not come to herself for a week.

A coat that lay upon the table,
To reach so far she scarce was able,
But drew it to her, resolved to try
What's in the pockets, by and by.   80

The first things that present her view
Were dunning-letters, not a few;
And then the next did make her wonder,
To see of tavern-bills such a number;
And a fine snuff-box there lay hid,
With bawdy picture in the lid,
And as she touched it, by the mass,
It turned, and showed a looking-glass.

The rest she found, since I'm a-telling,
Advertisements of land he's selling,   90
A syringe, and some dirty papers,
A bawdy-house screw, with box of wafers.

Then all the shelves she searched around,
Where not one book was to be found;
But gallipots all in a row,
And glistening vials, a fine show!

What one pot held she thinks was this:
Diaclom magnum cum gummis,
And spread there was with art, *secundum*
Unguentum neopolitanum;   100
Pots of pomatum, panacea,
Injections for a gonorrhea;
Of empty ones there were a score,
Of newly filled as many more.
In plenty too stood box of pills,
Nor did there lack for chirurgeon's bills,
Nor nasty rags all stiff with matter,
Nor bottle of mercurial water,

cut-and-dry] tobacco   dunning-letters] demands for payment of debts   screw]
bill(?)   wafers] seals   gallipots] earthen pots used by apothecaries

132

The use of which he does determine
To cure his itch, and kill his vermin: 110
'Oh heaven!' says she, 'what creature's man?
All stink without, and worse within!'

With that she rose and went away,
For there she could no longer stay;
And scarce she got in the bedchamber,
And thought herself there out of danger,
But quick she heard with both her ears
Strephon come swearing up the stairs;
She swiftly crept behind the screen,
In order not for to be seen.   120

Then in came Strephon, lovely sight!
Who had not slept a wink all night;
He staggers in, he swears, he blows,
With eyes like fire, and snotty nose;
A mixture glazed his cheeks and chin
Of claret, snuff, and odious phlegm;
And servant with him, to undress him,
And loving Strephon so caressed him:
'Come hither, Tom, and kiss your master;
Oons, to my groin come put a plaster.'   130

Tom dexterously his part he played,
To touch his bubo's not afraid;
Nor need he then to hesitate,
But strewed on the precipitate;
Then, in a moment, all the room
Did with the smell of ulcer fume,
And would have lasted very long,
Had not sour belches smelled as strong,
Which from her nose did soon depart,
When overcome with stink of fart,   140
And after, then came thick upon it
The odious, nauseous one of vomit,
That pourèd out from mouth and nose
Both on his bed, and floor, and clothes;
Nor was it lessened e'er a bit,
Nor overcome, by stink of s——t,
Which, in the pot and round about
The brim and sides, he squirted out;
But when poor Tom pulled off his shoes,
There was a greater stink of toes,   150

bubo] inflammation of the groin

And sure, a nasty, loathsome smell
Must come from feet as black as hell.

Then tossed in bed Tom left his Honour,
And went to call up Peggy Connor
To empty th' pot, and mop the room,
To bring up ashes and a broom,
And, after that, mostly pleasantly
To keep his master company.
The prisoner now being suffocated,
And saw the door was wide dilated,   160
She thought high time to post away,
For it was ten o'clock i' th' day;
And, ere that she got out of doors,
He turns, farts, hiccups, groans and snores.

Ladies, you'll think 'tis admirable
That this to all men's applicable;
And though they dress in silk and gold,
Could you their insides but behold,
There you fraud, lies, deceit would see,
And pride, and base impiety.   170
So let them dress the best they can,
They still are fulsome, wretched Man.

(1732)

ELIZABETH BOYD
(*fl.* 1727–45)

Scattered information about her appears in her published works. In *The Snail* (1745) she refers to her 'deceased Father having long and zealously serv'd the *Stuart* family, in a creditable Employ' (p. 15). Much earlier she had published her only novel *The Happy-Unfortunate; Or, The Female Page* (1732) to provide 'for my now ancient, indulgent Mother; whom Age, and the Charge of many Children hath render'd incapable of providing for herself' (Preface). The novel (reissued in 1737 as *The Female Page*) was dedicated to John, Duke of Argyll, who, 'when I was very young, was so condescending, as to flatter me into a Writer's Vanity'. Further dedications to Parts II and III of the novel are to the Countess of Hertford, who had read it in MS and encouraged the author, and to the Earl of Albemarle. An impressive number of the nobility appear in the list of some 300 subscribers, who 'rais'd me from the lowest Condition of Fortune, and a worse state of Health'. Her profits had presumably enabled her to carry out her plan of selling stationery goods at her house in George Court, Prince's Street, near Leicester Fields.

She had already published *Variety: A Poem . . . by Louisa* (1727) and *Verses* on the King's Birthday (1730), which were followed by eight other poems on a variety of public occasions by 1744. *Truth* (1740) contained proposals for a periodical, which did not appear until 1745 as *The Snail: Or The Lady's Lucubrations . . . by Eloisa*, when she was living in Vine Street, near St James's Church. Its appearance had been delayed by 'the Authoress's unhappy State of Health' and other 'complicated Misfortunes'. She intended to write *The Snail* by herself as 'an Amusement to the Fair Sex', but only the first number seems to have appeared. It contains attacks in both verse and prose on the Duke and Duchess of Marlborough, whom she accused of injuring the Stuart cause.

  The Humorous Miscellany (1733), in which the following poem appears, has a misleading title, since it contains some disturbing verse, including 'On an Infant's lying some Days unburied, for Want of *Money*'. *Don Sancho, Or The Student's Whim* (1739), accompanied by *Minerva's Triumph, A Masque*, is an eccentric ballad-opera, described in 1782 as follows: 'The whole plot of it is the whim of a student at one of the universities, to have the ghosts of Shakespeare and Ben Jonson raised to their view; but to what purpose it seems impossible to divine.' *Don Sancho* was never performed, although she thanked Chetwood, the prompter at Drury Lane Theatre, for having obtained it a reading there.

92   *On the Death of an Infant of five Days old, being a*
          beautiful but abortive Birth

> How frail is human life! How fleet our breath,
> Born with the symptoms of approaching death!
> What dire convulsions rend a mother's breast,
> When by a first-born son's decease distressed.
> Although an embryo, an abortive boy,
> Thy wond'rous beauties give a wond'rous joy:
> Still flattering Hope a flattering idea gives,
> And, whilst the birth can breathe, we say it lives.
> With what kind warmth the dear-loved babe was pressed:
> The darling man was with less love caressed!   10
> How dear, how innocent, the fond embrace!
> The father's form all o'er, the father's face,
> The sparkling eye, gay with a cherub smile,
> Some flying hours the mother-pangs beguile;
> The pretty mouth a Cupid's tale expressed,
> In amorous murmurs, to the full-swoll'n breast.
> If angel infancy can so endear,
> Dear angel-infants must command a tear.
> Oh! could the stern-souled sex but know the pain,
> Or the soft mother's agonies sustain,   20
> With tenderest love the obdurate heart would burn,
> And the shocked father tear for tear return.

(1733)

Woman's Hard Fate

How wretched is a woman's fate,
  No happy change her fortune knows;
Subject to man in every state,
  How can she then be free from woes?

In youth, a father's stern command
  And jealous eyes control her will;
A lordly brother watchful stands
  To keep her closer captive still.

The tyrant husband next appears,
  With awful and contracted brow;
No more a lover's form he wears: 10
  Her slave's become her sovereign now.

If from this fatal bondage free,
  And not by marriage-chains confined,
But, blessed with single life, can see
  A parent fond, a brother kind;

Yet love usurps her tender breast,
  And paints a phoenix to her eyes:
Some darling youth disturbs her rest,
  And painful sighs in secret rise.   20

Oh cruel powers, since you've designed
  That man, vain man, should bear the sway,
To a slave's fetters add a slavish mind,
  That I may cheerfully your will obey.

(1733)

LAETITIA PILKINGTON (née VAN LEWEN)
(c. 1708?–50)

She was the second of the three children of Dr John Van Lewen, a physician and obstetrician of Dutch descent who had settled in Dublin, and his wife (née Meade), a descendant of the Earls of Kilmallock. Although she claimed to have been born in 1712, the correct date must have been several years earlier. Her mother at first discouraged her reading, 'regarding more the Beauty of my Face, than the Improvement of my Mind', but her father was more indulgent and from an early age she loved and wrote poetry. On 31 May 1725 she married Matthew Pilkington (c.1701–74), a poor but ambitious clergyman and poet. Through her friend Constantia Grierson (see no. 64) she came to know Dr Patrick Delany, who by 1730 had introduced the Pilkingtons to Swift and his circle, including Mary Barber (see nos. 84–90). She later gave a valuable and in some ways unique account of Swift's domestic life in his later years in her *Memoirs*. Swift referred in October 1730 to Pilkington as 'a little poetical parson, who has a littler young poetical wife', and did his best to further his career, correcting his *Poems on Several Occasions* (Dublin, 1730) and revising the London edition of 1731. In that year he agreed to be godfather to the Pilkingtons' son, who survived, however, only a few days. When his friend John Barber became Lord Mayor of London in 1732/3, Swift obtained for Pilkington the appointment as his Chaplain, planning at the same time to use him as the agent for London editions of his works. Having equipped Pilkington with letters of introduction to some important English friends, Swift was angry to receive a complaint from Pope that the young poet was 'a most forward, shallow, conceited Fellow', and a later warning from Bolingbroke against such incautious recommendations, since 'the fellow wants morals & as I hear Decency sometimes'.

Several months later, in the company of Mary Barber, Mrs Pilkington followed her husband to London, leaving her three children with her parents, only to discover that he was involved with an actress and was prepared for her to have an affair with his friend James Worsdale the painter. Late in 1733 she returned alone to Dublin: the fact that, as she admits, prudish women were already casting aspersions on her own behaviour suggests that more may have happened in London than she was prepared to reveal. After her husband's return to Ireland, their relations rapidly deteriorated. By 1738 Swift was sadly disillusioned about his former protégés: 'he proved the falsest Rogue, and she the most profligate whore in either Kingdom. She was taken in the fact by her own Husband.' Early in 1738 Pilkington had obtained a divorce in the Spiritual Court on the grounds of her adultery with a Mr Adair. Her own account of the crucial incident in the middle of the night has not convinced all her readers:

I own my self very indiscreet in permitting any Man to be at an unseasonable Hour in my Bedchamber; but Lovers of Learning will, I am sure, pardon me, as I solemnly declare, it was the attractive Charms of a new Book, which the Gentleman would not lend me, but consented to stay till I read it through, that was the sole Motive of my detaining him.

After such damage to her reputation, she removed to London, leaving her children (the youngest had been born after their separation) with her husband. Because Pilkington provided only part of the maintenance he had promised, she was in a precarious financial position. Although she published *The Statues; Or, The Trial of Constancy. A Tale for the Ladies* (1739), an allegorical poem about male infidelity for which Dodsley gave her 5 guineas, and *An Excursory View on the Present State of Men and Things. A Satire* (1739; anonymous in Foxon, *Catalogue* E 601, but claimed in her *Memoirs*), she was unable to support herself by orthodox literary activity. Throughout her London years, when she usually used her mother's maiden name of Meade, she collected subscriptions for an edition of her poems which was never to appear, as well as making direct appeals to the charity of the aristocracy and clergy, sometimes by means of an all-purpose panegyrical poem. For a time she lived with, and was probably the mistress of, James Worsdale, for whom she wrote songs and, as she claims, three ballad-operas, which he passed off as his own work. Her wide male acquaintance, especially the gentlemen at White's Chocolate House who feature in many anecdotes in her *Memoirs*, may suggest that she had other ways of supplementing her income. (In 1753 Robert Shiells wrote of this period: 'Her virtue seems now to have been in a declining state; at least, her behaviour was such, that a man must have extraordinary faith, who can think her innocent.')

After coming close to suicide, she was imprisoned for nine weeks in 1742 in the Marshalsea for debt, but was released through the efforts of the ageing Colley Cibber. Another sympathetic friend and correspondent during the 1740s was Samuel Richardson the novelist. She and Cibber were early readers of *Clarissa* before its publication and in June 1745 protested at the fate Richardson was planning for his heroine: 'Spare her virgin purity, dear Sir! Spare it! Consider, if this wounds both Mr. Cibber and me (who neither of us set up for immaculate chastity), what must it do with those who possess that inestimable treasure?' In the summer of 1743, assisted by Cibber, Richardson, and the Duke of Marlborough, she had opened a pamphlet- and print-shop in St James's St, where she also advertised that she would write letters and petitions to order. Various tribulations followed, including the closing of the shop after a burglary and the reappearance of her impoverished son, who had been at sea and whom Richardson helped to clothe, and of her pregnant unmarried daughter. After nine years in London, Dr Delany and others helped her to clear her debts and return to Dublin in 1747, where she published the first volume of her *Memoirs* (1748) which she had started writing in London on the suggestion of Cibber. Its success was due not merely to her anecdotes of Swift, but to the vigour with which she defended herself against the accusations of her husband and other scandalous rumours, and to the severity with which she attacked those who had refused to assist her in the past. An even more self-assured second volume appeared in 1749 and a posthumous third was edited by her son, John Carteret Pilkington, in 1754. Entertaining and highly idiosyncratic, the *Memoirs* have aroused very different reactions. Of her contemporaries, John Cleland was sympathetic, convinced that she would have made 'an irreproachable wife, had she not been married to such a villain . . . to do that sex Justice, most of their errors are originally owing to our treatment of them'. Richardson, with whom she had corresponded as recently as May 1749, classed her in 1750 with other women authors of scandalous memoirs, as 'a Set of Wretches, wishing to perpetuate their Infamy'.

She is said to have written 'The Turkish Court; or, The London 'Prentice. A Burlesque Satirical Piece', performed at the Little Theatre in Capel St, Dublin, but never published. She died on 29 August 1750 and was buried in St Anne's Church, Dawson St, Dublin. Her husband, who was to disown and denounce his children in his will, remarried within a few days. He later published a well-known *Dictionary of Painters* (1770) and enjoyed a respectability so different from his first wife's devastating portrait of him that the *DNB* mistakenly insisted that they were two distinct Matthew Pilkingtons. For what it is worth, a note by Isaac Reed the antiquarian in his copy of her *Memoirs* (in the Bodleian) may be recorded: Reed states that he had been told by Ralph Griffiths, publisher of the London edition of the *Memoirs*, that John Carteret Pilkington confessed to him to having had an incestuous relationship with his mother.

94   *Memory, a Poem*

IN what recesses of the brain
Does this amazing power remain,
By which all knowledge we attain?

What art thou, Memory? What tongue can tell,
What curious artist trace thy hidden cell,
Wherein ten thousand different objects dwell?

Surprising storehouse! in whose narrow womb
All things, the past, the present, and to come,
Find ample space, and large and mighty room.

O falsely deemed the foe of sacred wit!
Thou, who the nurse and guardian art of it,
Laying it up till season due and fit.

Then proud the wond'rous treasure to produce,
As understanding points it, to conduce
Either to entertainment, or to use.

Nor love nor holy friendship, without thee,
Could ever of the least duration be;
Nor gratitude, nor truth, nor piety.

Where thou art not, the cheerless human mind
Is one vast void, all darksome, sad and blind;
No trace of anything remains behind.

The sacred stores of learning all are thine;
'Tis only thou record'st the faithful line;
'Tis thou mak'st human-kind almost divine.

And when at length we quit this mortal scene,
Thou still shalt with our tender friends remain,
And time and death shall strike at thee in vain.

Lord, let me so this wond'rous gift employ,
It may a fountain be of endless joy,
Which time, or accident, may ne'er destroy.

Still let my faithful Memory impart,
And deep engrave it on my grateful heart,
How just, and good, and excellent Thou art.

(Wr. *c*.1733; pub. 1748)

95 *Sorrow*

WHILE sunk in deepest solitude and woe,
My streaming eyes with ceaseless sorrow flow;
While anguish wears the sleepless night away,
And fresher grief awaits returning day;
Encompassed round with ruin, want, and shame,
Undone in fortune, blasted in my fame;
Lost to the soft endearing ties of life,
And tender names of daughter, mother, wife—
Can no recess from calumny be found?
And yet can fate inflict a deeper wound!   10

    As one who in a dreadful tempest tossed,
If thrown by chance upon some desert coast,
Calmly a while surveys the fatal shore,
And hopes that fortune can inflict no more;
Till some fell serpent make the wretch his prey,
Who 'scaped in vain the dangers of the sea;
So I, who hardly 'scaped domestic rage,
Born with eternal sorrows to engage,
Now feel the poisonous force of slanderous tongues,
Who daily wound me with envenomed wrongs.   20

    Shed then a ray divine, all-gracious Heaven,
Pardon the soul that sues to be forgiven,
Though cruel humankind relentless prove
And least resemble thee in acts of love;
Though friends who should administer relief
Add pain to woe and misery to grief,
And oft! too oft with hypocritic air
Condemn those faults in which they deeply share.
Yet thou who dost our various frailties know,
And see'st each spring from whence our actions flow,   30
Shalt, while for mercy to thy throne I fly,
Regard the lifted hand and streaming eye.

    Thou didst the jarring elements compose
Whence this harmonious universe arose;
O speak the tempest of the soul to peace,
Bid the tumultuous war of passion cease;
Receive me to thy kind paternal care,
And guard me from the horrors of despair.
And since no more I boast a mother's name,
Nor in my children can a portion claim,   40

The helpless babes to thy protection take,
Nor punish for their hapless mother's sake:

Thus the poor bird, when frighted from her nest
With agonizing love and grief distressed,
Still fondly hovers o'er the much-loved place,
Though strengthless to protect her tender race;
In piercing notes she movingly complains,
And tells the unattending woods her pains.

And thou, once my soul's fondest dearest part,
Who schemed my ruin with such cruel art, 50
From human laws no longer seek to find
A power to loose that knot which God has joined;
The props of life are rudely pulled away,
And the frail building falling to decay;
My death shall give thee thy desired release,
And lay me down in everlasting peace.

(Wr. *c.*1737; pub. 1748)

JEAN ADAMS
(1710–65)

She was the daughter of a shipmaster in Crawfordsdyke, Renfrewshire. Orphaned at an early age, she worked as maid and governess for the Revd Mr Turner of Greenock, and educated herself by reading in his library. Her *Miscellany Poems* were published at Glasgow in 1734, with a preface by Archibald Crawford and a list of 154 subscribers, mostly local clergy, gentry, and tradesmen. (On the title-page her first name appears as Jane, but as Jean in the signature to the dedication.) According to Cromek in 1810, her poems were collected and edited for her by a Mr Drummond of Greenock. He also relates that a 'large bale' of copies were exported to Boston, where they remained unsold. Later she taught at a school for girls, where she is said to have fainted away with emotion when reading *Othello* to her pupils. According to another anecdote, she admired Richardson's *Clarissa* (1747–8) so much that she walked to London in six weeks to meet the author (a story unconfirmed by any evidence at Richardson's end). In her later years she became a hawker and by 1760, when she accepted some old clothes from a former pupil, was destitute. She died on 3 April 1765, a day after being admitted to the parish workhouse of Glasgow as 'a poor woman, a stranger in distress:—for some time she has been wandering about; she came from Greenock'.

The well-known song, 'There's nae luck aboot the house', was claimed for her after her death, but the version now familiar seems to have been at least rewritten by W. J. Mickle: it is unlikely that the problem of authorship can be resolved.

96   *A Dream, or the Type of the Rising Sun*

LOOSED from its bonds my spirit fled away,
And left behind its moving tent of clay.
Aloft it soars through fields of painted air,
Which Fancy's pencil could not paint too fair.
I looked, and saw the God of Day arise;
With graceful steps he travels up the skies:
By just degrees at length he reached the line.
I saw the utmost limits of him shine:
While moon and stars before his chariot fly,
He in the floating mirror fixed his eye.   10

  'Here fix, my eye, come to the porch, my ear:
Sit still, my thought, that I the sound may hear.'
They all obeyed, when lo, I heard a cry,
'Come out and meet the ruler of the sky.'

  Implicit Nature all together ran,
Their numerous voices seemed a single man.
How from my heart the flame leaped to my eye,
While through the clear perspective I descry
Pure Nature's unconsulted harmony.

  'I am his bed,' cried out the torrid clime,   20
'He fixed my periods,' cried revolving Time;
'He is my husband,' cried the quickening shower,
'He's my physician,' cried the drooping flower.
I heard the little insect world all cry,
'He gave me life, and force, and wings to fly.'

  The vine cried out, 'He nursed me when a plant,
Ev'n to this hour he gives me what I want;
His virtue brought the moisture to my crop,
He formed the blossoms on my trembling top;
He made my clusters ready for the press,   30
And shall not I express my thankfulness?'

  'He cut my channels,' cried exulting flood,
'I owe him all my beauties,' cried the wood.
'He gave me light and heat,' said smiling flame,
'I am his shadow,' cried exalted Fame.
'I am his darling,' cried unfeignèd Truth,
'And so am I,' replied the wingèd youth;
'In all his actions thou may'st see me move.'
'Nay, I have all his soul,' cried divine Love.

  Dumb Echo cried, 'He taught me to repeat;   40
None else could e'er teach me to imitate.'
'I am his cup,' cried pure unmixèd Grief;
Said heavenly Joy, 'I fly to his relief.'

'I am his sword,' cried uncorrupted Hate;
'I quake before him,' cried relentless Fate.
   This harmony was noble and divine:
All joyed to see their benefactor shine.
The feathered choir clapped all their wings for joy,
Whose notes made up a perfect harmony.
Now russet garments on the fields are spread,   50
And now palm branches in his way are laid.
All Nature seemed to wanton in her prime;
Pure pleasure seemed to turn the wheel of Time.

   Forward I went, and saw society,
The pleasure-garden of the deity;
In which almighty Jove took such delight,
He walked around her walls both day and night.
At his own cost he built the threefold wall
So high, that thieves could never miss to fall.
The wall of Duty seemèd to my eye   60
For altitude above the starry sky.
Rich curious carvings were upon the stone;
A fair foundation it was laid upon:
I saw inscribèd conscious Fortitude.

   The glorious hedge of Honour next I saw,
One of the fairest rules in Nature's law:
The hedge of Honour was of holy thorn,
Its natural fruit was high heroic scorn.
I thought him mad, who would attempt to climb
Where every thorn must fix its points in him.   70

   The hedge of Int'rest was but very low,
Yet to the eye it had a glaring show;
Its worth was less than anything I saw,
But I observed it keepèd most in awe.

                        (1734)

97   *On the Phoenix*

   COME, Phoenix, come, if such a bird there be,
   Point me out the happy tree,
   Whose boughs can boast they bear the nest
   Wherein thou lov'st to rest:
   O lead me to the envied place,
   Which thou dost with thy presence grace.

   Arabia boasts she is the spot of earth
   Wherein thou first got birth.

Dost thou never change thy clime
In so vast a space of time?   10
What entertainment hast thou there,
That is not any other where?
Come westward, noble bird, and see
What homage we will pay to thee.

But hark! I hear Arabia's sons reply:
'We enjoy tranquillity
In a more enlarged extent
Than any other continent;
We possess a richer soil,
With less labour and less toil,   20
   Than any men below,
And live at greater distance from a foe.

'Our stately trees all kinds of spices bear,
Our fountains gratify the ear,
Each leaf in consort joins to please
With the soft whispers of the evening breeze.
Here doth Phoebus make his bed,
'Tis by him she's hither led:
Why should not we the honour have
To her a residence to give?   30

'To our blest land did Nature send the fire
In which her mother did expire:
Five hundred years she lived a chaste exile,
Then died upon the funeral pile;
Out of her fragrant ashes came
This exalted bird of fame;
To Phoebus' burning rays she owes her life;
In his chaste arms her mother died, ere she was made a wife.'

Such fables oft are told of thee,
Yet I confess thou seems to me   40
A bird begot by Poetry.
Thousands have beheld thee on
The fabled mountain Helicon:
   'Tis there thou loves to dwell.
Nay, I myself have seen thee there,
But never any other where,
   Except at Pindar's well.

(1734)

98　　　　　　　　　*To the Muse*

COME hither to the hedge, and see
The Walks that are assigned to thee:
All the bounds of Virtue shine,
All the plain of Wisdom's thine,
All the flowers of harmless Wit
Thou mayest pull, if thou think'st fit,
In the fair field of History.
All the plants of Piety
Thou mayest freely thence transplant:
But have a care of whining Cant.　　　　　　　10

(1734)

ANONYMOUS ('THE AMOROUS LADY')

The poems are found in a series published between November 1733 and March 1735 in the *Barbados Gazette*, the first West Indian newspaper, established by Samuel Keimer, a London printer who emigrated to Philadelphia in 1723 (where Benjamin Franklin became his foreman) and moved to Barbados in 1731. The *Gazette* appeared bi-weekly between 1731 and 1738 and Keimer later reprinted selections from it in London as *Caribbeana* (2 vols., 1741).

Although other women contributed to the *Gazette*, the highly emotional poems from this pen are distinctive. The editor usually referred to her as 'the amorous lady', and the evidence suggests that they were written in England. According to the preface to *Caribbeana*, they were addressed 'to a Gentleman of *Barbados*, by a Lady then living here [i.e. in England] (since deceased) and whom to name would be an additional Credit to the Work'. She had published poems elsewhere which had been 'admired by the best Judges'. Introducing the first of her poems on 28 November 1733, the editor stated that they 'were wrote about Twelve Years ago' by a lady 'who made a considerable Figure in the *Beau Monde* at Home'. On 7 February 1734 he explained that the MSS of 'the amorous fair one' had been received through a third party, on the understanding that names would be concealed. The editor enjoyed encouraging speculation among his readers about the identity of the 'Damon' who excited such passion, but revealed only that by 1734 he had lived in Barbados for at least seven years.

Some of the poems travelled rapidly back to London, appearing in periodicals within a few months of their publication in Barbados, though never with any indication of their origins. The first of the following poems, written, according to the editor, when 'the lovely young Minx' was only nineteen, appeared in the *Gentleman's Magazine* (1734, p. 327), two months after its appearance in the *Barbados Gazette*. 'A Letter to my Love' was reprinted in the *London Magazine* in November 1734 and more than half a century later reappeared without explanation in the *European Magazine* in November 1788.

99   *On being Charged with Writing Incorrectly*

I'M incorrect: the learnèd say
That I write well, but not their way.
For this to every star I bend:
From their dull method heaven defend,
Who labour up the hill of fame,
And pant and struggle for a name!
My free-born thoughts I'll not confine,
Though all Parnassus could be mine.
No, let my genius have its way,
My genius I will still obey: 10
Nor with their stupid rules control
The sacred pulse that beats within my soul.
I from my very heart despise
These mighty dull, these mighty wise,
Who were the slaves of Busby's nod,
And learned their methods from his rod.
Shall bright Apollo drudge at school,
And whimper till he grows a fool?
Apollo, to the learned coy,
In nouns and verbs finds little joy.   20
The tuneful Sisters still he leads
To silver streams, and flowery meads.
He glories in an artless breast,
And loves the goddess Nature best.
Let Dennis haunt me with his spite;
Let me read Dennis every night,
Or any punishment sustain,
To 'scape the labour of the brain.
Let the dull think, or let 'em mend
The trifling errors they pretend;   30
Writing's my pleasure, which my Muse
Would not for all their glory lose:
With transport I the pen employ,
And every line reveals my joy.
No pangs of thought I undergo,
My words descend, my numbers flow;
Though disallowed, my friend, I swear
I would not think, I would not care,
If I a pleasure can impart,
Or to my own, or thy dear heart,   40
If I thy gentle passions move,
'Tis all I ask of fame or love.

This to the very learnèd say,
If they are angry—why, they may:
I from my very soul despise
These mighty dull, these mighty wise.

(1734)

100   *A Letter to my Love.—All alone,*
           past 12, in the Dumps

OH! weep with me the changing scene,
Torn from thy arms, devoured with spleen.
Instead of those dear eyes, I look
Upon the fire, or else a book:
But oh! how dull must either be
To eyes that have been studying thee!
Unless the poet does express
Something that strikes my tenderness,
I throw the leaves neglected by,
And in my chair supinely lie;   10
Or to the pen and ink I haste,
And there a world of paper waste.
All I can write, though love is here,
Does much unlike my soul appear.
Angry, the scrawling side I turn,
I write and blot, and write and burn.
Then to the bottle I repair,
The poets tell us ease is there:
But I thy absent hand repine,
Whose sweetness used to zest the wine;   20
Wine in this sullen moment fails;
I burn my pen, I bite my nails,
Rail at my stars, nay, I accuse
Even my lover, and my Muse.
'Why did he let me go?', I cry.
—And, now I think on't, tell me why.
You might have kind excuses made
To one so willing to have stayed:
The night was rainy, and the wind
To all thy softest wishes kind.   30
For thee and love methought it blew,
As if my parting pains it knew,
As if it was a lover too.
I'm safely shaded from its power,
But I regard its rage no more:

147

Now let it tempest as it please,
Or move the groves, or fright the seas,
It cannot now alarm my rest,
Unless it reach thy dearer breast.
Oh! hasten to me; let my arms   40
Protect thee from the wintry storms.
I tremble lest the cold should dare
To pierce thee—let my image, there,
Defend it, if it has a charm,
From these and every other harm.
I want thy bosom to repose
My beating heart, oppressed with woes;
I want thy voice my soul to cheer,
Thy voice is music to my ear;
I want thy dear loved hand to press   50
My neck, with silent tenderness;
I want thy eyes to make me bright,
And charm this sullen hour of night.
This hour, when pallid ghosts appear,
Oh! could it bring thy shadow here,
I every substance would resign
To clasp thy aerial breast to mine;
Or if, my love, that could not be,
I would turn air to mix with thee.

(1734)

101   *To my Love*

WHEN, in my fond embraces fast confined,
   My trembling arms my agonies expressed,
No tear in sad society was joined
   To cheer me, pale and speechless on thy breast;
Scarce had I life from thy dear sight to part,
So fixed my eyes, so full my breaking heart.

Fain would my lips have sighed 'Adieu! Adieu!',
   But rising sorrow would not give them leave;
My words, like traitors, they forsook me too;
   My sighs themselves had scarcely power to heave;   10
My arms alone with grasping could impart
The agony that filled my breaking heart.

As I a thousand, thousand times embraced,
　Hoping by every one to make thee kind,
In vain my weeping eyes thy features traced
　(And features speak the passions of the mind):
Still wert thou unconcerned; nor didst impart
One sigh of thine to those that swell'st my heart.

While I was grieved to such a kind excess,
　Oh! how untimely must thy prudence be,　　　　　　20
To bid me *meet, with artful tenderness,*
　The arms that were no friends to love or thee.
Beware how you instruct me in that part,
Lest I give him the true, and thee the faithless heart.

Bid the rude North be gentle to the spring,
　Or kiss the new-born flowers with tender care;
To reconcilements all aversions bring;
　But oh! to me thy dull advice forbear:
No faithless maxims to my breast impart,
To change the nature of my breaking heart.　　　　　　30

(1735)

ANNE INGRAM (née HOWARD, later DOUGLAS), VISCOUNTESS IRWIN
(*c.* 1696–1764)

She was the second daughter of Charles Howard, Earl of Carlisle, and his wife, Lady Anne Capell, daughter of the Earl of Essex. Her early life was spent at Castle Howard in Yorkshire, where Lady Mary Wortley Montagu (whose father was a close friend of the Earl) stayed with the three Howard sisters in 1714. In 1717 she married Richard Ingram, 5th Viscount Irwin (or Irvine). After financial losses in the South Sea Bubble in 1720, he accepted appointment as Governor of Barbados but died of smallpox in 1721 before taking it up. It was to the widowed Lady Irwin that Lady Mary Wortley Montagu addressed the poem, 'Why will Delia thus retire' (see no. 45), to which Lady Irwin wrote a reply (printed in *Additions to the Works of Alexander Pope* (1776), i. 170). Of Lady Mary, who had been attacking 'constancy' as 'inconsistent with reason and nature', she said at the time that 'her principles are as corrupt as her wit is entertaining, and I never heard a woman, let her practice be never so scandalous, maintain such arguments'. Many years later, Lady Mary recalled that, 'giving way to the vanity and false pretentions of Lady Irwin, [I] allways liv'd well with her. It was possible to laugh at her, but impossible to be angry with her. I never saw any Malice in her Composition.'

Lady Irwin wrote regularly to her father at Castle Howard on political and literary matters. She travelled to the Low Countries in 1730 and in 1732 published a descriptive poem, *Castle Howard* (anonymous in Foxon, *Catalogue* C 61). In the 1730s she read Pope's poems attentively as they appeared. Her restrained reply to his *On the Characters of Women* (published in February 1735) was well known later in the century, although reference works have not cited a printed text earlier than 1773. Perhaps first printed in a newspaper, it appeared in the *Gentleman's Magazine* in December 1736 and the *London Magazine* in January 1737. Both periodicals later reprinted it (in 1771 and 1759 respectively) and it also appeared in Ashley Cowper's *Norfolk Poetical Miscellany* (1744) and the *New Foundling Hospital for Wit*, Vol. vi (1773).

In 1736 Lady Irwin was appointed Lady of the Bedchamber to the Princess of Wales and travelled to Holland to escort the Princess to England. Her letters frequently report events in the troubled Court in these years. In 1737, 'contrary to the opinion and advice of every relative and friend she has', she married Col William Douglas, who died at Kew in 1748. Some verses by her ('a Lady of Quality') on the accession of George III were printed in the *Gentleman's Magazine* (1761), p. 89. She had no children and died on 2 December 1764. Horace Walpole reported that 'Poor Lady Irwin had a party at cards on Friday and died on Sunday morning'.

102   from *An Epistle to Mr. Pope. Occasioned by his Characters of Women*

> A FEMALE mind like a rude fallow lies;
> No seed is sown, but weeds spontaneous rise.
> As well might we expect, in winter, spring,
> As land untilled a fruitful crop should bring;
> As well might we expect Peruvian ore
> We should possess, yet dig not for the store:
> Culture improves all fruits, all sorts we find,
> Wit, judgement, sense—fruits of the human mind.
>   Ask the rich merchant, conversant in trade,
> How nature operates in the growing blade;   10
> Ask the philosopher the price of stocks,
> Ask the gay courtier how to manage flocks;
> Inquire the dogmas of the learned schools
> (From Aristotle down to Newton's rules)
> Of the rough soldier, bred to boisterous war,
> Or one still rougher, a true British tar:
> They'll all reply, unpractised in such laws,
> Th' effect they know, though ignorant of the cause.
> The sailor may perhaps have equal parts
> With him bred up to sciences and arts;   20
> And he who at the helm or stern is seen
> Philosopher or hero might have been.
> The whole in application is comprised,
> Reason's not reason, if not exercised;
> Use, not possession, real good affords;
> No miser's rich that dares not touch his hoards.

Can female youth, left to weak woman's care,
Misled by Custom (Folly's fruitful heir);
Told that their charms a monarch may enslave,
That beauty like the gods can kill or save;   30
Taught the arcanas, the mysterious arts,
By ambush dress to catch unwary hearts;
If wealthy born, taught to lisp French and dance,
Their morals left (Lucretius-like) to chance;
Strangers to reason and reflection made,
Left to their passions, and by them betrayed;
Untaught the noble end of glorious truth,
Bred to deceive even from their earliest youth;
Unused to books, nor virtue taught to prize;
Whose mind, a savage waste, unpeopled lies;   40
Which to supply, trifles fill up the void,
And idly busy, to no end employed:
Can these, from such a school, more virtue show,
Or tempting vice treat like a common foe?
Can they resist, when soothing pleasure woos;
Preserve their virtue, when their fame they lose?
Can they on other themes converse or write
Than what they hear all day, and dream all night? . . .
Would you, who can instruct as well as please,
Bestow some moments of your darling ease   50
To rescue woman from this Gothic state,
New passions raise, their minds anew create:
Then for the Spartan virtue we might hope,
For who stands unconvinced by generous Pope?
Then would the British fair perpetual bloom,
And vie in fame with ancient Greece and Rome.

(1736)

MARY CHANDLER
(1687–1745)

She was born at Malmesbury, Wiltshire, the eldest daughter of Henry Chandler, a
dissenting minister who later moved to Bath, and his wife, formerly a Miss Bridgman
of Marlborough. Her deformity ruled out marriage, and family circumstances
obliged her to set up a milliner's shop in Bath, probably by the time she was 20.
Successful in business and fully occupied in the fashionable Bath season, she still
found time for self-education by reading and writing. Her wide acquaintance among
those 'of reputation and fortune', some of whom invited her to visit their country
houses, makes clear that she was treated as more than a tradeswoman. Her friends

included Elizabeth Rowe and the Countess of Hertford, whom she visited at Marlborough, and her verses refer to other titled acquaintance.

In 1733 she published anonymously *A Description of Bath*, a history and survey in verse of Bath and its environs, in which she refers to the crooked spine which had doomed her to spinsterhood, and mentions that Dr William Oliver, who had also given her medical advice, had helped to 'smooth her Verse' and 'improve the Thought'. She added her name to the 2nd edition (1734), dedicated to the Princess Amelia, and some miscellaneous poems to the 3rd edition (1736). The *Description* was popular with visitors to Bath and reached an 8th edition by 1767. It was also often cited by writers on Bath. The 2nd to 7th (1755) editions were printed by Samuel Richardson for his brother-in-law, James Leake of Bath, whose bookshop she describes in her poem. Richardson quoted her lines in praise of Ralph Allen and his house at Prior Park near Bath in his revision of Defoe's *Tour of Great Britain* (1738), ii. 247–8. To the 6th edition (1744) she added the poem given below, which describes an unexpected proposal of marriage from a rich country gentleman who admired her verse.

The dedication to her *Description of Bath* explains that she preferred to be thought of as an honest tradeswoman than as a writer, but she was proud to relate that she had been complimented on her poem by Alexander Pope, who visited her when in Bath, probably on the suggestion of their common friend Dr Oliver. In her later years she planned 'a large poem on the Being and Attributes of God', fragments of which were found at her death. She was an industrious and courageous woman, who had decided early in life 'That as her person would not recommend her, she must endeavour to cultivate her mind, to make herself agreeable'. Often in poor health, she became in later years a vegetarian, persevering with this 'mortifying diet' as a matter of principle as well as for medical reasons. She retired after thirty-five years in business and died on 11 September 1745. A poem on her death, addressed to her two surviving sisters, appears in Jacob Axford's *Poems on Various Subjects* (Bath, 1764), pp. 28–31. Mary Scott (see no. 213) praised her in *The Female Advocate* (1774), pp. 18–19.

103   *My Own Epitaph*

> HERE lies a true maid, deformed and old,
> Who, that she never was handsome, need never be told;
> Though she ne'er had a lover, much friendship had met,
> And thought all mankind quite out of her debt.
> She ne'er could forgive, for she ne'er had resented;
> As she ne'er had denied, so she never repented.
> She loved the whole species, but some had distinguished;
> But time and much thought had all passion extinguished.
> Though not fond of her station, content with her lot;
> A favour received she had never forgot.   10
> She rejoiced in the good that her neighbours possessed,
> And piety, purity, truth she professed.
> She lived in much peace, but ne'er courted pleasure;
> Her book and her pen had her moments of leisure;

Pleased with life, fond of health, yet fearless of death,
Believing she lost not her soul with her breath.

(1736)

104   *A True Tale*
        To Mrs. J——s. Written at her Request

WHY, Madam, must I tell this idle tale?
You want to laugh. Then do so, if you will.
Thus take it, as it was, the best I can;
And laugh at me, but not my little man:
For he was very good, and clean, and civil,
And, though his taste was odd, you own not evil.
You know one loves an apple, one an onion;
One man's a Papist, one is a Socinian:
We differ in our taste, as in opinion.
Not often reason guides us; more, caprice,   10
Or accident, or fancy: so in this.
His person pleased, and honest was his fame;
'Tis true there was no music in his name,
But, had I changed for *A* the letter *U*,
It would sound grand, and musically too,
And would have made a figure. At my shop
I saw him first, and thought he'd eat me up.
I stared, and wondered who this man could be,
So full of complaisance, and all to me:
But when he'd bought his gloves, and said his say,   20
He made his civil scrape, and went away.
I never dreamed I e'er should see him more,
Glad when he turned his back, and shut the door.
But when his wond'rous message he declared,
I never in my life was half so scared!
Fourscore long miles, to buy a crooked wife!
Old too! I thought the oddest thing in life;
And said, 'Sir, you're in jest, and very free;
But, pray, how came you, Sir, to think of me?'
This civil answer I'll suppose was true: 30
'That he had both our happiness in view.
He sought me as one formed to make a friend,
To help life glide more smoothly near its end,
To aid his virtue, and direct his purse,
For he was much too well to want a nurse.'

104 scrape] bow

He made no high-flown compliment but this:
'He thought to've found my person more amiss.
No fortune hoped; and,' which is stranger yet,
'Expected to have bought me off in debt!
And offered me my *Wish*, which he had read,   40
For 'twas my *Wish* that put me in his head.'
Far distant from my thoughts a husband, when
Those simple lines dropped, honest, from my pen!

   Much more, he spake, but I have half forgot:
I went to bed, but could not sleep a jot.
A thing so unexpected, and so new!
Of so great consequence—So generous too!
I own it made me pause for half that night:
Then waked, and soon recovered from my fright;
Resolved, and put an end to the affair: 50
So great a change, thus late, I could not bear;
And answered thus: 'No, good Sir, for my life,
I cannot now obey, nor be a wife.
At fifty-four, when hoary age has shed
Its winter's snow, and whitened o'er my head,
Love is a language foreign to my tongue:
I could have learned it once, when I was young,
But now quite other things my wish employs:
Peace, liberty, and sun, to gild my days.
I dare not put to sea so near my home,   60
Nor want a gale to waft me to my tomb.
The smoke of Hymen's lamp may cloud the skies,
And adverse winds from different quarters rise.
I want no heaps of gold; I hate all dress,
And equipage. The cow provides my mess.
'Tis true, a chariot's a convenient thing;
But then perhaps, Sir, you may hold the string.
I'd rather walk alone my own slow pace,
Than drive with six, unless I choose the place.
Imprisoned in a coach, I should repine: 70
The chaise I hire, I drive and call it mine.
And, when I will, I ramble, or retire
To my own room, own bed, my garden, fire;
Take up my book, or trifle with my pen;
And, when I'm weary, lay them down again:
No questions asked; no master in the spleen—
I would not change my state to be a queen.

mess] meal

Your great estate would nothing add to me,
But care, and toil, and loss of liberty.
Your offer does me honour, I confess;   80
And, in your next, I wish you more success.'

And thus this whole affair begins and ends:
We met as lovers, and we parted friends.

(1744)

MARY JONES
(d. 1778)

She was the daughter of Oliver Jones of St Aldate's, Oxford. Her mother belonged to the Penn family of South Newington, near Banbury (of whose history she gives an amusing account in a letter in August 1734). She learned both French and Italian from a master and was translating from Italian by the age of 16. For most of her life she lived in Oxford with her brother, the Revd Oliver Jones (*c.*1706–75), Chanter of Christ Church Cathedral, later Senior Chaplain of Christ Church. (Because of a misprint in Boswell's *Life of Johnson*, his name has often been given as River Jones.) Her knowledge of languages may have led to a period as a governess or tutor, but there may be some other explanation for her close friendship by the early 1730s with an aristocratic circle which included the Lovelace, Clayton, and Bowyer families, who were interrelated by marriage. Many of her letters and poems were addressed from 1732 to Martha Lovelace, daughter of John, 4th Baron Lovelace of Hurley, who had just been appointed Governor of New York when he died in 1709. Martha Lovelace became a Maid of Honour to Queen Caroline in 1732 and in June 1739 married Lord Henry Beauclerk, later becoming Housekeeper of Windsor Castle (1756). Another close friend, a relative of the Lovelaces, was Charlot Clayton, daughter of Lieut.-General Jasper Clayton, who died at Dettingden in 1743. From the 1730s Mary Jones regularly visited Miss Lovelace at Windsor Castle and, after her marriage, at New Lodge in Windsor Forest, as well as the Clayton family at Fern Hill, also in Windsor Forest. She was aware of the contrast between her own circumstances and those of her friends, describing herself in 1734 as 'a Traveller or Pilgrim, wandering about from House to House, in order to partake of the Bene-volence of such good People as you are'. Admitting that her maternal grandfather 'was the first of his particular Branch that ever set up for a Gentleman', she declared that 'Our real Worth must depend upon Our Selves'.

Later in the century she would probably have found more scope for her literary talents. As it was, she concealed her writing from her friends in Oxford, including her brother, who had pedantic views about grammar and critical rules. When Joseph Spence showed her Mary Barber's *Poems* in 1735, she wished that women would do more to 'Exercise . . . our Heads', but knew that 'Custom, and . . . the Lords over us' conspired to discourage them. Nevertheless, some of her verse found its way into print. In April 1742 she found that her ballad *The Lass of the Hill* was on sale in the streets of London and was 'the Fashion of the Town'. At about the same time she wrote a poem in memory of Lord Aubrey Beauclerk, brother of Lord Henry

Beauclerk, who had died at Cartagena in 1741 (anonymous in Foxon, *Catalogue* T 393) and, at his widow's request, wrote the prose-inscription on his monument in Westminster Abbey, to accompany verses by Edward Young, whom she consulted about the commission in 1744. Aware of the intelligence and wit of her prose and verse, her friends, notably Lady Bowyer, began to plan the publication by subscription of her *Miscellanies* early in the 1740s. By 1748 she herself had come to believe that her 'scatter'd Leaves' were 'at length destin'd for the Press'. The subscription in the fashionable world had been highly organized, for a list of some 1,400 names, headed by the Princess Royal, accompanied her *Miscellanies in Prose and Verse* (Oxford, 1750). Its respectable purpose had been to raise money to support 'a relation, grown old and helpless thro' a series of misfortunes', perhaps her mother, who died shortly before the book appeared. Commercial publication followed only when the subscribers' copies had been delivered and it was not generally advertised until early 1752, accompanied by a minor publicity campaign. In December 1751 a poem addressed to her by 'J. P——s' appeared in the *London Magazine*, which ran a series of excerpts from her volume during 1752.

In March 1752 Ralph Griffiths gave the *Miscellanies* a prominent article in the *Monthly Review*, describing Mary Jones as the best woman writer since Katherine Philips in the seventeenth century. An intensely grateful letter from her, dated 1 June 1752, to the anonymous reviewer of her 'imperfect Performances' has survived. Later she corresponded directly with Griffiths, who eventually paid her the unusual compliment of inviting her to become one of his reviewers. Modestly declining this invitation on 16 March 1761, she explained: 'All I ever did in ye poetic Fields was spontaneous, or by mere accident—I sought not ye Numbers, but ye Birds sung, & ye Numbers *came*. That season, however, is over & I find myself much more inclin'd to read now, than to write.' She was well known by then in Oxford literary circles. In a letter to Charlotte Lennox on 16 December 1754 she mentions having met Samuel Johnson in Oxford in the previous summer and in a letter of 21 June 1757 Johnson himself threatened to complain to Miss Jones that Thomas Warton had not written to him. In a letter to Boswell of 15 April 1786, later quoted in the *Life of Johnson*, Warton mentioned that Mary Jones 'was often of our parties' in Oxford: 'She was a very ingenious poetess . . . and, on the whole, was a most sensible, agreeable, and amiable woman.' He recalled that Johnson used to call her 'the Chantress' (alluding to her brother's post as Chanter of the Cathedral) and would quote Milton's *Il Penseroso* to her: 'Thee, Chantress, oft the woods among | I woo'.

Her death was reported on 10 February 1778 in *Jackson's Oxford Journal*, which on 17 March 1778 also announced the sale of her house, next to the Wheatsheaf and Anchor in St Aldate's (which she always called 'St. Toll's'). One source stated later that at her death she was 'Post-mistress of Oxford', perhaps a sinecure obtained for her after the death of her brother in 1775. Although a substantial selection of her verse had appeared in *Poems by Eminent Ladies* (1755), i. 253–312, her writing, which reflects her admiration for Pope, would eventually have come to seem old-fashioned. Neglected as she remains, her prose and verse show her to have been one of the most intelligent and amusing women writers of her period.

105   *An Epistle to Lady Bowyer*

HOW much of paper's soiled! what floods of ink!
And yet how few, how very few can think!

The knack of writing is an easy trade;
But to think well requires—at least a head.
Once in an age, one genius may arise,
With wit well cultured, and with learning wise.
Like some tall oak, behold his branches shoot!
No tender scions springing at the root.
Whilst lofty Pope erects his laurelled head,
No lays like mine can live beneath his shade.   10
Nothing but weeds, and moss, and shrubs are found.
Cut, cut them down, why cumber they the ground?

   And yet you'd have me write!—For what? for whom?
To curl a favourite in a dressing-room?
To mend a candle when the snuff's too short?
Or save rappee for chamber-maids at court?
Glorious ambition! noble thirst of fame!—
No, but you'd have me write—to get a name.
Alas! I'd live unknown, unenvied too;
'Tis more than Pope with all his wit can do;   20
'Tis more than you with wit and beauty joined,
A pleasing form, and a discerning mind.
The world and I are no such cordial friends;
I have my purpose, they their various ends.
I say my prayers, and lead a sober life,
Nor laugh at Cornus, or at Cornus' wife.
What's fame to me, who pray, and pay my rent?
If my friends know me honest, I'm content.

   Well, but the joy to see my works in print!
Myself too pictured in a mezzotint!   30
The preface done, the dedication framed,
With lies enough to make a lord ashamed!
Thus I step forth, an Auth'ress in some sort;
My patron's name? 'O choose some lord at court.
One that has money which he does not use,
One you may flatter much, that is, abuse.
For if you're nice, and cannot change your note,
Regardless of the trimmed, or untrimmed coat,
Believe me, friend, you'll ne'er be worth a groat.'

   Well then, to cut this mighty matter short,   40
I've neither friend nor interest at Court.
Quite from St. James's to thy stairs, Whitehall,
I hardly know a creature, great or small,

rappee] a kind of snuff   nice] fastidious

Except one Maid of Honour*, worth them all.
I have no business there—Let those attend
The courtly levee, or the courtly friend,
Who more than fate allows them dare to spend;
Or those whose avarice, with much, craves more,
The pensioned beggar, or the titled poor.
These are the thriving breed, the tiny great!   50
Slaves! wretched slaves! the journeymen of state.
Philosophers! who calmly bear disgrace,
Patriots who sell their country for a place.
Shall I for these disturb my brains with rhyme?
For these, like Bavius creep, or Glencus climb?
Shall I go late to rest, and early rise,
To be the very creature I despise?
With face unmoved, my poem in my hand,
Cringe to the porter, with the footman stand?
Perhaps my lady's maid, if not too proud,   60
Will stoop, you'll say, to wink me from the crowd.
Will entertain me, till his lordship's dressed,
With what my lady eats, and how she rests:
How much she gave for such a Birthday-gown,
And how she tramped to every shop in town.

 Sick at the news, impatient for my lord,
I'm forced to hear, nay smile at every word.
Tom raps at last—'His lordship begs to know
Your name? your business?'—'Sir, I'm not a foe:
I come to charm his lordship's listening ears   70
With verses, soft as music of the spheres.'
'Verses!—Alas! his lordship seldom reads:
Pedants indeed with learning stuff their heads;
But my good lord, as all the world can tell,
Reads not ev'n tradesmen's bills, and scorns to spell.
But trust your lays with me—some things I've read,
Was born a poet, though no poet bred:
And if I find they'll bear my nicer view,
I'll recommend your poetry—and you.'

 Shocked at his civil impudence, I start,   80
Pocket my poem, and in haste depart;
Resolved no more to offer up my wit,
Where footmen in the seat of critics sit.

* *Honourable Miss* Lovelace.

Is there a Lord* whose great unspotted soul,
Not places, pensions, ribbons can control;
Unlaced, unpowdered, almost unobserved,
Eats not on silver while his train are starved;
Who, though to nobles or to kings allied,
Dares walk on foot, while slaves in coaches ride;
With merit humble, and with greatness free,   90
Has bowed to Freeman, and has dined with me;
Who, bred in foreign courts, and early known,
Has yet to learn the cunning of his own;
To titles born, yet heir to no estate,
And harder still, too honest to be great;
If such an one there be, well-bred, polite,
To him I'll dedicate, for him I'll write.

Peace to the rest—I can be no man's slave;
I ask for nothing, though I nothing have.
By fortune humbled, yet not sunk so low   100
To shame a friend, or fear to meet a foe.
Meanness, in ribbons or in rags, I hate;
And have not learned to flatter ev'n the great.
Few friends I ask, and those who love me well;
What more remains, these artless lines shall tell.

Of honest parents, not of great, I came;
Not known to fortune, quite unknown to fame.
Frugal and plain, at no man's cost I eat,
Nor knew a baker's or a butcher's debt.
O be their precepts ever in my eye!   110
For one has learned to live, and one to die.
Long may her widowed age by heaven be lent
Among my blessings! and I'm well content.
I ask no more, but in some calm retreat
To sleep in quiet, and in quiet eat.
No noisy slaves attending round my room;
My viands wholesome, and my waiters dumb.
No orphans cheated, and no widow's curse,
No household lord, for better or for worse.
No monstrous sums to tempt my soul to sin,   120
But just enough to keep me plain and clean.
And if sometimes, to smooth the rugged way,
Charlot should smile, or you approve my lay,
Enough for me—I cannot put my trust
In lords; smile lies, eat toads, or lick the dust.

* *Right Hon.* Nevil *Lord* Lovelace, *who died soon after in the 28th year of his age.*

eat toads] toady, flatter

Fortune her favours much too dear may hold:
An honest heart is worth its weight in gold.

(Wr. *c*.1736; pub. 1750)

106   *The Lass of the Hill*

AT the brow of a hill a fair shepherdess dwelt,
Who the pangs of ambition or love ne'er had felt;
A few sober maxims still ran in her head,
That 'twas better to earn ere she ate her brown bread;
That to rise with the lark was conducive to health,
And to folks in a cottage contentment was wealth.

Young Roger that lived in the valley below,
Who at church and at market was reckoned a beau,
Would oftentimes try o'er her heart to prevail,
And rest on his pitchfork to tell her his tale;   10
Till his winning behaviour so wrought on her heart,
That, quite artless herself, she suspected no art.

He flattered, protested, he kneeled and implored,
And would lie with the grandeur and air of a lord;
Her eyes he commended with language well dressed,
And enlarged on the tortures he felt in his breast:
With his sighs and his tears he so softened her mind,
That, in downright compassion, to love she inclined.

But as soon as he'd melted the ice of her breast,
The heat of his passion that moment decreased;   20
And now he goes flaunting all over the vale,
And boasts of his conquest to Richard and Hal;
Though he sees her but seldom, he's always in haste,
And whenever he mentions her, makes her his jest.

All the day she goes sighing, and hanging her head,
And her thoughts are so pestered, she scarce earns her bread;
The whole village cries 'shame!' when a-milking she goes,
That so little affection is showed to the cows:
But she heeds not their railing, e'en let 'em rail on,
And a fig for the cows, now her sweetheart is gone.   30

Take heed, ye young virgins of Britain's fair isle,
How you venture your hearts for a look or a smile;

For young Cupid is artful, and virgins are frail,
And you'll find a false Roger in every vale,
Who to court you, and tempt you, will try all their skill;
But remember the lass at the brow of the hill.

(1742)

107   *Stella's Epitaph*
(Which the Author hopes will live as long as she
does)

HERE rests poor Stella's restless part:
A riddle! but I loved her heart.
Through life she rushed, a headlong wave,
And never slept, but in her grave.
Some wit, I think, and worth she had:
No saint indeed, nor yet quite mad;
But laughed, built castles, rhymed and sung,
'Was everything, but nothing long.'
Some honest truths she would let fall;
But much too wise to tell you all.   10
From thought to thought incessant hurled,
Her scheme was but—to rule the world.
At morn she won it with her eyes,
At night, when beauty sickening sighs,
Like the mad Macedonian cried,
'What, no more worlds, ye gods!'—and died.

(1750)

108   *Soliloquy on an Empty Purse*

ALAS, my Purse! how lean and low!
My silken Purse! what art thou now!
Once I beheld—but stocks will fall—
When both thy ends had wherewithal.
When I within thy slender fence
My fortune placed, and confidence;
A poet's fortune!—not immense:
Yet, mixed with keys, and coins among,
Chinked to the melody of song.

Canst thou forget, when, high in air,   10
I saw thee fluttering at a fair?

And took thee, destined to be sold,
My lawful Purse, to have and hold?
Yet used so oft to disembogue,
No prudence could thy fate prorogue.
Like wax thy silver melted down,
Touch but the brass, and lo! 'twas gone:
And gold would never with thee stay,
For gold had wings, and flew away.

   Alas, my Purse! yet still be proud, 20
For see the Virtues round thee crowd!
See, in the room of paultry wealth,
Calm Temperance rise, the nurse of health;
And Self-Denial, slim and spare,
And Fortitude, with look severe;
And Abstinence, to leanness prone,
And Patience, worn to skin and bone:
Prudence and Foresight on thee wait,
And Poverty lies here in state!
Hopeless her spirits to recruit, 30
For every Virtue is a mute.

   Well then, my Purse, thy sabbaths keep;
Now thou art empty, I shall sleep.
No silver sounds shall thee molest,
Nor golden dreams disturb my breast.
Safe shall I walk with thee along,
Amidst temptations thick and strong;
Catched by the eye, no more shall stop
At Wildey's toys, or Pinchbeck's shop;
Nor cheapening Payne's ungodly books, 40
Be drawn aside by pastry-cooks:
But fearless now we both may go
Where Ludgate's mercers bow so low;
Beholding all with equal eye,
Nor moved at—'Madam, what d'ye buy?'

   Away, far hence each worldly care!
Nor dun nor pick-purse shalt thou fear,
Nor flatterer base annoy my ear.
Snug shalt thou travel through the mob,
For who a poet's purse will rob? 50
And softly sweet in garret high
Will I thy virtues magnify;

disembogue] discharge, empty

Outsoaring flatterers' stinking breath,
And gently rhyming rats to death.

(1750)

109   *Epistle from Fern Hill*

CHARLOT, who my controller is chief,
And dearly loves a little mischief,
Whene'er I talk of packing up,
To all my measures puts a stop;
And though I plunge from bad to worse,
Grown duller than her own dull horse,
Yet out of complaisance exceeding,
Or pure perverseness, called good-breeding,
Will never let me have my way
In anything I do or say.   10

At table, if I ask for veal,
In complaisance she gives me quail.
'I like your beer: 'tis brisk and fine'—
'O no; John, give Miss Jones some wine.'
And though from two to four you stuff,
She never thinks you're sick enough;
In vain your hunger's cured, and thirst,
If you'd oblige her, you must burst.

Whether in pity, or in ire,
Sometimes I'm seated next the fire;   20
So very close, I pant for breath,
In pure good manners scorched to death.
Content I feel her kindness kill,
I only beg to make my will;
But still in all I do or say,
This nuisance Breeding's in the way;
O'er which to step I'm much too lazy,
And too obliging to be easy.

Oft do I cry, 'I'm almost undone
To see our friends in Brooke Street, London.'   30
As seriously the nymph invites
Her slave to stay till moon-shine nights.
Lo! from her lips what language breaks,
What sweet persuasions when she speaks!
Her words so soft! her sense so strong!
I only wish—to slit her tongue.

But this, you'll say, 's to make a clutter,
Forsooth! about one's bread and butter.
Why, be it so; yet I'll aver
That I'm as great a plague to her;   40
For well-bred folks are ne'er so civil,
As when they wish you at the devil.
So, Charlot, for our mutual ease,
Let's e'en shake hands, and part in peace;
To keep me here is but to tease ye,
To let me go would be to ease ye.

As when (to speak in phrase more humble)
The General's guts begin to grumble,
Whate'er the cause that inward stirs,
Or pork, or pease, or wind, or worse;   50
He wisely thinks the more 'tis pent,
The more 'twill struggle for a vent:
So only begs you'll hold your nose,
And gently lifting up his clothes,
Away th' imprisoned vapour flies,
And mounts a zephyr to the skies.

So I (with reverence be it spoken)
Of such a guest am no bad token;
In Charlot's chamber ever rumbling,
Her pamphlets and her papers tumbling,   60
Displacing all the things she places,
And, as is usual in such cases,
Making her cut most sad wry faces.
Yet, spite of all this rebel rout,
She's too well-bred to let me out,
For fear you squeamish nymphs at court
(Virgins of not the best report)
Should on the tale malicious dwell,
When me you see, or of me tell.

O Charlot! when alone we sit,   70
Laughing at all our own (no) wit,
You wisely with your cat at play,
I reading Swift, and spilling tea;
How would it please my ravished ear
To hear you from your easy chair,
With look serene, and brow uncurled,
Cry out, 'A—— for all the world!'
But you, a slave to too much breeding,
And I, a fool with too much reading,

Follow the hive, as bees their drone,   80
Without one purpose of our own;
Till tired with blundering and mistaking,
We die sad fools of others' making.

Stand it recorded on yon post,
That both are fools then to our cost!
The question's only, which is most?
I, that I never yet have shown
One steady purpose of my own;
Or you, with both your blue eyes waking,
Run blundering on, by choice mistaking?—   90
Alas! we both might sleep contented,
Our errors purged, our faults repented;
Could you, unmoved, a squeamish look meet,
Or I forget our friend in Brooke Street.

(1750)

ELIZABETH CARTER
(1717–1806)

She was born at Deal, the eldest daughter of the Revd Nicholas Carter, Perpetual Curate of Deal Chapel and a preacher at Canterbury Cathedral, and his wife Margaret Swayne. Her father gave her the same education as her brothers and she became proficient in classical and modern languages. The intensity of her self-imposed early studies was often taken to explain her lifelong headaches, nearsightedness, and addiction to snuff (to keep her awake). Her mother died when she was about 10. Her father was friendly with Edward Cave, proprietor of the newly founded *Gentleman's Magazine*, to which she began contributing regularly in 1734. (Her letters to Cave from this period are in the British Library.) Cave published her immature *Poems upon Particular Occasions* (1738), her translation of Crousaz's *Examination of Mr. Pope's Essay on Man* (1738), and her translation from Italian of Algarotti's *Sir Isaac Newton's Philosophy Explain'd, for the Use of the Ladies* (1739). At the age of 22, the *History of the Works of the Learned* could describe her as worthy 'to be rank'd with the *Cornelia's*, *Sulpicia's*, and *Hypatia's* of the Antients, and the *Schurmans* and *Daciers* of the Moderns' (i. 392–3). Through the *Gentleman's Magazine* she met Samuel Johnson, who became a lifelong friend, and the scholar Thomas Birch, who saw much of her in London in 1738/9, may have written the tribute quoted above, and seems to have hoped to marry her. She may already have resolved against marriage: her father had advised her in 1738 to live quietly if she intended to remain single, since living expensively in the world 'is reasonable upon the prospect of getting an husband, but not otherwise'. A few years later, when under pressure from her father to marry, she rejected a suitor because he had 'published some verses, which, though not absolutely indecent, yet seemed to show too light and licentious a turn of mind'.

By now a correspondent of the Countess of Hertford, admired a few years later by the poet William Collins, she continued to study assiduously, describing in 1746 her arrangement with the local sexton that he should wake her between 4 and 5 a.m. by pulling a thread in the garden attached to a bell by her bed. Her 'Ode to Wisdom' was by then circulating in MS and was printed by Samuel Richardson in his *Clarissa* in 1747 without knowing the identity of its author (for which he later apologized). She contributed two essays to Johnson's *Rambler* (Nos. 44 and 100) and four of her poems were included in Dodsley's *Collection* in 1758. Since 1749 she had been working on her major project, a translation of Epictetus from the Greek, encouraged and assisted by her friend Thomas Secker, Bishop of Oxford, which she completed by 1756. In that year she found time to prepare her stepbrother Henry for entrance to Cambridge, 'perhaps the only instance of a student at Cambridge' who had been educated by a woman, as her nephew and biographer later suggested. Proposals for *All the Works of Epictetus* were circulated in 1757 and the large quarto volume, printed by Samuel Richardson, was published in 1758, with a list of subscribers which brought her almost £1000. No longer dependent on her father, she spent several months each winter in London in lodgings, her disinclination to stay with friends again making clear her wish for independence. After her stepmother's death, she bought a house in Deal, part of which she rented to her father, who died in 1774.

A new circle of friends, including William Pulteney, Earl of Bath, Lord Lyttelton, and Mrs Montagu, persuaded her to collect her *Poems on Several Occasions* in 1762 (4th edition by 1789), her last serious publication. Lyttelton provided some prefatory verses for the book, and Bath is said to have written the dedication to himself, to save her from the 'meanness' of flattery. In 1763 she travelled on the Continent with him and Mrs Montagu, as she did again with members of the Pulteney family in 1782. She was financially comfortable, especially after the Pulteneys and Mrs Montagu both settled on her annuities of £100. Her literary ambitions seem now to have been satisfied, although after the death of her friend and correspondent, Catherine Talbot, she helped with the posthumous publication of some of her writings (1770–2). She was a familiar figure in literary circles in the later decades of the century, particularly those of Mrs Montagu, Mrs Vesey, and Mrs Hunter, and was friendly with younger writers such as Hannah More and Joanna Baillie. By no means humorless, she was not amused when William Hayley dedicated his *Essay on Old Maids* (1785) to her. She refused to countenance the authors of works injurious to religion or virtue, or having 'the least tendency towards levelling and democratic principles', and was predictably hostile to the French Revolution. Although she had an 'extreme partiality for writers of her own sex', believing that the mental powers of women were underrated, she 'highly disapproved' of the writings of Charlotte Smith and detested Mary Wollstonecraft's 'wild theory' about the rights of women. The Queen asked to be introduced to her in 1791 and more than one member of the Royal Family visited her in old age. She died in Clarges St, London, in 1806 at the age of 88.

Early in her career, Elizabeth Carter did much to make the woman writer 'respectable', taking advantage of the new opportunities offered by the periodical press, dealing confidently from an early age with publishers and literary men, and dedicating herself to impressive scholarship, without arousing the mockery or hostility usually directed at women who wrote professionally or at 'learned ladies'. For these reasons she was often cited and hailed with some awe as an exemplary figure for women. Having won high literary reputation and financial security by the 1760s, she did not thereafter develop this inspirational role. Her elegant and decorous, if relatively small, output of verse was highly influential (it was inevitable that a fantasy in the *Gentleman's Magazine* in 1766 about handing the government of

Britain over to women should nominate her as Poet Laureate), but its effect was mostly inhibiting. An obituary praised the 'Sublime simplicity of sentiment, melodious sweetness of expression, and morality the most amiable' in her poems, but her nephew and biographer granted her 'ease, correctness, and elegance' rather than 'fire or strength'. She herself stated that 'she never wrote a line without considering whether it was possible that it would do mischief', a remarkable constraint on creativity. She is perhaps doomed to be best remembered for Johnson's intended compliment, that 'My old friend, Mrs. Carter, could make a pudding as well as translate Epictetus.'

110   *On the Death of Mrs. [Elizabeth] Rowe*

    ACCEPT, much honoured shade! the artless lays
The Muse a tribute to thy memory pays.
The sad relation of thy loss to hear,
What friend to virtue can refrain a tear?
A loss to no one private breast confined,
But claims the general sorrow of mankind.

    Since here, alas, thy longer life's denied,
Farewell, our sex's ornament and pride!
Born with a genius fitted to excel,
And blessed with sense t' apply that genius well.   10
Long did romance o'er female wits prevail,
Th' intriguing novel and the wanton tale.
What different subjects in thy pages shine!
How chaste the style, how generous the design!
Thy better purpose was, with lenient art,
To charm the fancy, and amend the heart;
From trifling follies to withdraw the mind,
To relish pleasures of a nobler kind.
No lawless freedoms e'er profaned thy lays,
To virtue sacred and thy maker's praise.   20
This still shall last, when every meaner theme
In death must quit the memory like a dream.
In the bright regions of unfading joy,
This forms the happy spirit's blest employ:
To God each raptured seraph tunes his tongue,
The inexhausted subject of their song;
Where human minds the same glad concert raise,
And spend their blest eternity in praise.

                                (1737)

111 *A Dialogue*

Says Body to Mind, ' 'Tis amazing to see,
We're so nearly related yet never agree,
But lead a most wrangling strange sort of a life,
As great plagues to each other as husband and wife.
The fault's all your own, who, with flagrant oppression,
Encroach every day on my lawful possession.
The best room in my house you have seized for your own,
And turned the whole tenement quite upside down,
While you hourly call in a disorderly crew
Of vagabond rogues, who have nothing to do   10
But to run in and out, hurry-scurry, and keep
Such a horrible uproar, I can't get to sleep.
There's my kitchen sometimes is as empty as sound,
I call for my servants, not one's to be found:
They all are sent out on your ladyship's errand,
To fetch some more riotous guests in, I warrant!
And since things are growing, I see, worse and worse,
I'm determined to force you to alter your course.'

    Poor Mind, who heard all with extreme moderation,
Thought it now time to speak, and make her allegation: 20
' 'Tis I that, methinks, have most cause to complain,
Who am cramped and confined like a slave in a chain.
I did but step out, on some weighty affairs,
To visit, last night, my good friends in the stars,
When, before I was got half as high as the moon,
You despatched Pain and Languor to hurry me down;
Vi & Armis they seized me, in midst of my flight,
And shut me in caverns as dark as the night.'

    ' 'Twas no more,' replied Body, 'than what you deserved;
While you rambled abroad, I at home was half starved: 30
And, unless I had closely confined you in hold,
You had left me to perish with hunger and cold.'

    'I've a friend,' answers Mind, 'who, though slow, is yet sure,
And will rid me at last of your insolent power:
Will knock down your walls, the whole fabric demolish,
And at once your strong holds and my slavery abolish:
And while in the dust your dull ruins decay,
I'll snap off my chains and fly freely away.'

                                                         (1741)

Vi & Armis] by force of arms

Ode to Wisdom

THE solitary bird of night
Through the pale shades now wings his flight,
   And quits the time-shook tower;
Where, sheltered from the blaze of day,
In philosophic gloom he lay,
   Beneath his ivy bower.

With joy I hear the solemn sound,
Which midnight echoes waft around,
   And sighing gales repeat.
Favourite of Pallas! I attend,   10
And, faithful to thy summons, bend
   At Wisdom's awful seat.

She loves the cool, the silent eve,
Where no false shows of life deceive,
   Beneath the lunar ray.
Here Folly drops each vain disguise,
Nor sport her gaily-coloured dyes,
   As in the beam of day.

O Pallas! queen of every art
That glads the sense, or mends the heart,   20
   Blest source of purer joys:
In every form of beauty bright,
That captivates the mental sight
   With pleasure and surprise:

At thy unspotted shrine I bow:
Attend thy modest suppliant's vow,
   That breathes no wild desires:
But, taught by thy unerring rules
To shun the fruitless wish of fools,
   To nobler views aspires.   30

Not Fortune's gem, Ambition's plume,
Nor Cytherea's fading bloom,
   Be objects of my prayer:
Let Avarice, Vanity, and Pride,
Those envied glittering toys, divide
   The dull rewards of care.

To me thy better gifts impart,
Each moral beauty of the heart,
  By studious thought refined;
For Wealth, the smiles of glad content,
For Power, its amplest, best extent,
  An empire o'er the mind.

When Fortune drops her gay parade,
When Pleasure's transient roses fade,
  And wither in the tomb,
Unchanged is thy immortal prize;
Thy ever-verdant laurels rise
  In undecaying bloom.

By thee protected, I defy
The coxcomb's sneer, the stupid lie
  Of ignorance and spite:
Alike condemn the leaden fool,
And all the pointed ridicule
  Of undiscerning wit.

From envy, hurry, noise and strife,
The dull impertinence of life,
  In thy retreat I rest:
Pursue thee to the peaceful groves,
Where Plato's sacred spirit roves,
  In all thy graces dressed.

He bade Illissus' tuneful stream
Convey thy philosophic theme
  Of Perfect, Fair and Good:
Attentive Athens caught the sound,
And all her listening sons around
  In awful silence stood:

Reclaimed, her wild licentious youth
Confessed the potent voice of Truth,
  And felt its just control.
The passions ceased their loud alarms,
And Virtue's soft persuasive charms
  O'er all their senses stole.

Thy breath inspires the Poet's song,
The Patriot's free, unbiased tongue,
  The Hero's generous strife;
Thine are Retirement's silent joys,
And all the sweet endearing ties
  Of still, domestic life.

No more to fabled names confined,
To Thee! supreme all-perfect Mind,　　　　　　　　80
　　My thoughts direct their flight:
Wisdom's thy gift, and all her force
From thee derived, unchanging source
　　Of intellectual light.

O send her sure, her steady ray
To regulate my doubtful way,
　　Through life's perplexing road:
The mists of error to control,
And through its gloom direct my soul
　　To happiness and good.　　　　　　　　　　90

Beneath her clear discerning eye
The visionary shadows fly
　　Of Folly's painted show:
She sees, through every fair disguise,
That all but Virtue's solid joys
　　Is vanity and woe.

　　　　　　　　　　　　(1747)

MARY COLLIER
(1690?–c. 1762)

Information about her derives largely from the 'Remarks of the Author's Life, drawn by herself', prefixed to her *Poems on Several Occasions* (Winchester, 1762). She was born near Midhurst, Sussex, of 'poor, but honest Parents', in about 1690. (A poem on the marriage of George III in 1761 describes her as then in her 72nd year, which is at odds with a recent identification of her as the Mary Collyer of Heyshott, Sussex, who was baptized in 1679, the daughter of Robert and Mary Collyer. Heyshott is, however, close to Midhurst.) Her parents taught her to read but, because of her mother's early death, she did not attend school and was eventually 'set to such labour as the Country afforded'. After her father's death in the 1720s, she moved to Petersfield in Hampshire, 'where my chief Employment was, Washing, Brewing and such labour, still devoting what leisure time I had to Books', when she could buy or borrow them. After the appearance of Stephen Duck's *Poems on Several Occasions* (1730), she composed a reply to his criticism of the idleness of rural women in 'The Thresher's Labour', 'to vindicate the injured Sex', and perhaps also with some hope of attracting aristocratic patronage of the kind enjoyed by Duck. While nursing for a local family, she repeated some of her verses, news of her unexpected talent spread, and she was advised to publish her poems. (Her remark that 'I had learn'd to write to assist my memory', which meant that her verses could be transcribed for the printer, suggests that she had at first relied entirely on memory.)

The Woman's Labour: An Epistle to Mr. Stephen Duck was published in London in

1739, the title-page describing her as 'Now a WASHER-WOMAN, at *Petersfield* in *Hampshire*'. A prefatory 'Advertisement' signed 'M.B.' explains that 'her Friends are of Opinion that the Novelty of a *Washer-Woman*'s turning Poetess, will procure her some Readers', and suggests that other working women would be better occupied with verse than 'tossing Scandal to and fro'. It is also frankly admitted that the author, 'whose Life is toilsome, and her Wages inconsiderable', had had in mind 'the View of her putting a small sum of Money in her Pocket, as well as the Reader's Entertainment'. She must have encountered the scepticism which often greeted uneducated women poets, since the 3rd edition of 1740 contains a statement by nine residents of Petersfield, dated 21 September 1739, testifying to the authenticity of her verses. In 1762 she claimed that she had made little profit from *The Woman's Labour*: it had been published 'at my own charge, I lost nothing, neither did I gain much, others run away with the profit'.

She continued working as a washerwoman until the age of 63, then ran a farmhouse at Alton until she was about 70, when 'the infirmities of Age' forced her to retire 'to a Garret (The Poor Poets Fate)' in Alton, 'where I am endeavouring to pass the Relict of my days in Piety, Purity, Peace, and an Old Maid'. Her *Poems on Several Occasions* (Winchester, 1762) was well supported by local subscribers and included some additions to her works, such as an 'Elegy upon Stephen Duck' (to whom she was more sympathetic after his 'success' story ended in suicide), 'An Epistolary Answer To an Exciseman, Who doubted her being the Author of the Washerwoman's Labour', and the poem on George III's marriage in 1761. A later undated edition at Petersfield speculated that, 'had her genius been cultivated, she would have ranked with the greatest poets of the kingdom'.

113   from *The Woman's Labour. An Epistle to Mr Stephen Duck*

[*The Washerwoman*]

> WHEN bright Orion glitters in the skies
> In winter nights, then early we must rise;
> The weather ne'er so bad, wind, rain or snow,
> Our work appointed, we must rise and go,
> While you on easy beds may lie and sleep,
> Till light does through your chamber-windows peep.
> When to the house we come where we should go,
> How to get in, alas! we do not know:
> The maid quite tired with work the day before,
> O'ercome with sleep; we standing at the door,   10
> Oppressed with cold, and often call in vain,
> Ere to our work we can admittance gain.
> But when from wind and weather we get in,
> Briskly with courage we our work begin;
> Heaps of fine linen we before us view,
> Whereon to lay our strength and patience too;

Cambrics and muslins, which our ladies wear,
Laces and edgings, costly, fine and rare,
Which must be washed with utmost skill and care;
With holland shirts, ruffles and fringes too,   20
Fashions which our forefathers never knew.
For several hours here we work and slave,
Before we can one glimpse of daylight have;
We labour hard before the morning's past,
Because we fear the time runs on too fast.

  At length bright Sol illuminates the skies,
And summons drowsy mortals to arise;
Then comes our mistress to us without fail,
And in her hand, perhaps, a mug of ale
To cheer our hearts, and also to inform   30
Herself what work is done that very morn;
Lays her commands upon us, that we mind
Her linen well, nor leave the dirt behind.
Not this alone, but also to take care
We don't her cambrics nor her ruffles tear;
And these most strictly does of us require,
To save her soap and sparing be of fire;
Tells us her charge is great, nay furthermore,
Her clothes are fewer than the time before.
Now we drive on, resolved our strength to try,   40
And what we can we do most willingly;
Until with heat and work, 'tis often known,
Not only sweat but blood runs trickling down
Our wrists and fingers: still our work demands
The constant action of our labouring hands.

  Now night comes on, from whence you have relief,
But that, alas! does but increase our grief.
With heavy hearts we often view the sun,
Fearing he'll set before our work is done;
For, either in the morning or at night,   50
We piece the summer's day with candlelight.
Though we all day with care our work attend,
Such is our fate, we know not when 'twill end.
When evening's come, you homeward take your way;
We, till our work is done, are forced to stay,
And, after all our toil and labour past,
Sixpence or eightpence pays us off at last;
For all our pains no prospect can we see
Attend us, but old age and poverty.

                                       (1739)

SARAH DIXON*
(1672–1765)

Her *Poems on Several Occasions* were published anonymously at Canterbury in 1740: she is identified by inscriptions in the British Library and Bodleian copies, the latter describing her as a widow of Canterbury. The British Library copy has additional poems transcribed on the endpages from MSS then owned by her niece Mrs Eliza Bunce ('late De Langle'), widow of the Revd John Bunce (d. 1786), Vicar of St Stephen's near Canterbury. At her request Bunce had corrected Mrs Dixon's verse for publication. The earliest of these additional poems is dated 1716; another, dated August 1739, was addressed to Mr and Mrs Bunce on the death of their 4-year-old daughter; and a third, 'The Expedition to Swinfield Minnis', was written in 1745 in expectation of a French invasion. Pasted on the flyleaf is a long poem, 'On the Ruins of St. Austin's, Canterbury', from the *Kentish Gazette* of 9 July 1774, written when she was 73. It was reprinted anonymously in the *Gentleman's Magazine* (1780), 241–2.

Her 1740 volume includes 'On the Death of My Dear Brother, Late of University College, Oxford, Who Dy'd Young' (pp. 169–70). The inscription in the British Library copy may suggest that her own maiden name was De Langle, and there are several subscribers of that name to her volume, but no De Langle appears to have been admitted to University College at this period. Most of her 500 or so subscribers were local, but the list includes Elizabeth Carter, Edward Cave, and Alexander Pope (whose views on women are praised in one of her poems, p. 54), as well as members of the nobility. Her 'Preface' describes her poems as 'innocent Folly', 'the Employment . . . of a Youth of much Leisure . . . in a Country Solitude'. But 'To the Muse' (pp. 121–5) suggests that, in spite of her attempts to abandon it for 'the trifling, gigling Crowd', poetry was important to her: 'Through every change of Life and Fortune, *Thou*, | My constant Solace, to this instant *Now*.'

114   *Verses left on a Lady's Toilet*

WHEN Celia frowns, I vow and swear
She makes both friends and foes despair:
I hate to think that things so vain
As heedless maids and dirty men,
A dish ill-cooked, a glass unwashed,
A petticoat wrong cut and slashed,
Should make good humour, wit, and sense
Give way to their impertinence.
Rather let me with sops in ale,
In nut-brown bowl, myself regale;   10
In Scottish plod, or Irish frieze,

* See p. 539 below.

slashed] i.e. so as to expose a different coloured lining or undergarment   plod]
plaid   frieze] coarse woollen cloth

Let me be dressed, if toys like these,
So foreign to substantial joy,
Can Celia's peace of mind destroy.

(1740)

115   *To Strephon*

WHEN you and I shall to our earth return,
And the world thinks each quiet in their urn;
When life's gay scene no more shall cheat the eye
With flattering prospects of uncertain joy;
When truth and falsehood shall unveiled appear,
And gold, which rules below, no influence shall bear:
Then tell me, Strephon, where our souls shall move,
And how our tale shall be received above.
Of broken vows, a long account for you;
For me—the sin of loving aught below.   10
Ah, Strephon! why was I ordained by fate
To please a swain, so fickle and ingrate?
Why, from the airy, witty and the fair,
Was I the choice of one so insincere?
And why, my constant heart, art thou the same?
Why not extinguished the disastrous flame?
Fond heart! False Strephon!—but the conflict's o'er;
You can betray, nor I believe, no more.
Forgive us, Heaven! though never, never here
We meet again, may we be angels there: 20
There may my faithful passion find reward;
Your guilt be pardoned, and my prayers be heard.

(1740)

116   *The Slattern*

SALINA sauntering in a shade,
    Her shoes were slipped, her gown untied,
A single pinner on her head;
    And thus the easy trollop cried:

'Thus disengaged from all the crew,
    Which on a lady's rising wait,
I can without constraint pursue
    The pleasure of this soft retreat.'

She oft had heard that poets chose
 To be retired from noise and rout;   10
And fancied she could now compose,
 If she could find a subject out.

By chance she had one pocket on;
 Therein a pencil neatly made:
She pulled it out, and sat her down,
 And thought she'd more than half her trade.

The back-side of a *billet doux*
 Was ready to receive her notions:
The first thing she resolved to do,
 To put in rhyme her morn devotions.   20

She then began with the sublime;
 But found the theme so much above her,
She passed it till another time,
 And chose to poetise her lover.

The great dispute, which name to use
 Of Damon, Pythias, or Endymion,
Did, by the way, so damp her muse,
 That soon she altered her opinion.

'Aid me, Melpomene!', she cries,
 'The weakness of my sex to sing;   30
While I lament their vanities,
 Do thou thy choicest numbers bring.

'Bless me! how trifling is the lass
 Spends ever half the day in dressing;
It makes me hate a looking-glass,
 And loathe a toilet past expressing.'

No farther had the nymph the power;
 Abrupt she threw the paper by;
Quo' she, ' 'Tis an unlucky hour;
 Walk one turn more, and then I'll try.   40

'Help, Thalia! comic strains to sing;
 Apollo, pray attend it';
Just then her petticoat broke a string,
 And forced her home to mend it.

(1740)

117 *The Returned Heart*

IT must be mine! no other heart could prove
Constant so long, yet so ill-used in love.
How bruised and scarified! how deep the wound!
Senseless, of life no symptom to be found!
Can it be this, that left me young and gay?
Just in the gaudy bloom it fled away:
Unhappy rover! what couldst thou pretend?
Where tyrants reign, can innocence defend?
I'll vow thou art so altered, I scarce know
Thou art the thing, which Strephon sighed for so: 10
Look how it trembles! and fresh drops declare
It is the same, and he the murderer.
    Thus lawless conquerors our town restore,
With the sad marks of their inhuman power;
No art, nor time, such ravage can repair;
No superstructure can these ruins bear.

                                          (1740)

118 *Cloe to Aminta. On the Loss of her Lover*

CLOE Tell, dear Aminta, now 'tis over,
    How came you to lose your lover?
AMIN. Tell me first how I obtained him.
CLOE O, 'twas youth and beauty gained him.
AMIN. My youth and beauty still remain;
    Yet, you see, I have lost the swain.
    Ah! my girl, the thing's too certain;
    The pangs he felt were for my fortune.
    Why—five and forty—thousand—pound
    Had given the Great Mogul a wound!   10
    The mighty Czar, had he been living,
    Had thought the present worth receiving.
    But that delightful South Sea scheme—
    That charming, warming, golden dream,
    Which made so many fools and knaves,
    And left so many well-bred slaves—
    Fell to the depths from whence it came,
    And quenched at once his towering flame.

                                          (1740)

119   *Lines Occasioned by the Burning of Some Letters*

NOT all pale Hecate's direful charms,
When hell's invoked to rise in swarms,
When graves are ransacked, mandrakes torn,
And rue and baleful nightshade torn,
Could give that torturing, racking pain
These magic lines did once obtain;
There's not a letter in the whole,
But what conspired to wound the soul.

But now! the dread enchantment's o'er;
The spell is broke, they plague no more.   10
'Twas only paper daubed with art:
Could such a trifle gain a heart,
Obstruct the peace of early life,
And set the passions all at strife,
Admit no cure, till time erased
The fond ideas fancy placed?

Combustible I'm sure you are;
Arise, ye flames! assist me, air!
Waft the vain atoms to the wind,
Disperse the fraud, and purge mankind.   20
The fatal relics thus removed,
Does Celia look like one who loved,
Who durst her future peace repose
On vows, and oaths, and toys like those?

Fallacious deity! to thee
The guilt, and the simplicity,
Who thought such cobweb-arts could bind,
To all eternity, the mind.
When honour's fled, thy flames expire,
And end in smoke like common fire.   30

Thus the entangled bird, set free,
Finds treble joy in liberty.
Her little heart may throb and beat,
Nor soon the danger past forget,
Dread to forsake the safeguard wood,
And shun awhile the chrystal flood;
But with the next returning spring,
Retire to shades—you'll hear her sing.

(1740)

178

ELIZABETH FRANCES AMHERST (later THOMAS)

(*c.* 1716–79)

She was the daughter of Jeffrey Amherst (1677–1750) of Riverhead, near Sevenoaks, Kent, and his wife Elizabeth Kerrill. Her sister Margaret died in 1734 at the age of 18. Of her seven brothers, John became a Vice-Admiral, William a Lieutenant-General, and Jeffrey, the most distinguished, became Lord Amherst in 1776 and a Field-Marshal in 1796. His great achievement was the 'conquest' of Canada, notably the taking of Montreal in 1760, when he was Commander-in-Chief of the British forces in North America. On his return to England he replaced the family mansion at Riverhead with his new seat of Montreal. Elizabeth's sprightly verse, which survives in a Bodleian manuscript, 'The Whims of E.A. afterwards Mrs. Thomas', and is mostly unpublished, was written for the amusement of family and friends, and alludes to local events and places. Some of it may have been written after her marriage to the Revd John Thomas of Welford, Gloucestershire, who in 1748 became Rector of Notgrove, near Northleach, in the Cotswolds.

After her marriage she continued an intense interest in collecting fossils, which had started at Riverhead and which she described as 'a sort of Wild Passion'. Between 1757 and 1760 she corresponded on the subject with the naturalist Emanuel Mendes da Costa (1717–91), author of *A Natural History of Fossils* (1757), and supplied him with examples of her discoveries in local stone-quarries and elsewhere. Apparently without children of their own, the Thomases had by 1758 adopted the youngest son of her brother-in-law, 'a beautiful healthy child of 9 months old; he is now just beginning to talk and walk alone, and will be crying for his Ma every day (or I shall fancy so) till I return'. This letter refers to a visit to London to see her military brothers, of whom she was intensely proud, before their departure for America.

The appearance of some of her verse in more than one Bodleian manuscript indicates that it had some circulation, and a few of her poems found their way into print in the 1760s. In September 1761 she sent William Shenstone an anonymous poem about his gardens at The Leasowes; it was published a few months later in the *London Magazine* as 'To William Shenstone, Esq; the Production of half an hour's Leisure' by 'Cotswouldia'. It was reprinted in his posthumous *Works* (1764) as 'Verses received by the post, from a lady unknown', and again in Moses Mendez' *Collection of Poems* (1767), pp. 115–16. In 1762 she published at Gloucester *A Dramatic Pastoral. By a Lady* on the occasion of George III's coronation, in support of a collection 'for portioning young women of virtuous character'. In 1767 the *Gentleman's Magazine* printed the prose inscription on an obelisk erected at Sir Jeffrey Amherst's new mansion of Montreal to commemorate a reunion there of the three military brothers. Mrs Thomas provided the accompanying verses, 'Written on the Walls of the Root-House' (p. 602), which are also found in her MS poems. She left Notgrove after the death of her husband in 1770, and died at Newbold, Warwickshire, in May 1779.

120   *A Prize Riddle on Herself when 24*

I'M a strange composition as e'er was in nature,
Being wondrously studious and yet a great prater.
Retirement and quiet I love beyond measure,
Yet always am ready for parties of pleasure.
I can cry till I laugh, or laugh till I cry,
Yet few have a temper more equal than I.
    My shape is but clumsy, I see it and know it,
Yet always am dancing and skipping to show it.
My visage is round, just the shape of a bowl,
With a great pair of grey eyes resembling an owl.   10
My nose and my mouth are none of the least,
Though one serves me to smell and the other to taste.
    What I gain in these features makes up for no chin,
But here's my misfortune, my smile's a broad grin.
My temper is rather addicted to satire,
And yet, without vanity, fraught with good nature.
My friends I can laugh at, but most at myself.
I've no inclination for titles or pelf;
And this I can vouch for, believe me or nay,
To my friend's my own interest does always give sway.   20
    I really am cleanly, but yet my discourse,
If you're squeamish, may make you as sick as a horse.
Without any voice, I can sing you a song,
And though I grow old, I shall always be young.
I put on assurance, though nat'rally shy,
And most people love me, though none can tell why.
I'm not yet disposed of: come bid for a blessing,
For those who first guess me shall have me for guessing.

                                        (MS 1740)

121   *A Song for the Single Table on New Year's Day*

    YE single folks all, that adorn this gay table,
Come join in a chorus as loud as you're able:
Let the married ones know, by your mirth and your song,
That for us every New Year comes smiling along.
                                Derry down &c.

Sweet Liberty's ours, to the wise ever dear,
And while it is ours we have nothing to fear:
No wives ever-scolding, our hearts to dismay,
Nor husbands to thank us 'cause wiser than they.
                              Derry down &c.   10

No brats that are squalling for victuals at home,
No grave curtain-lectures when thither we come;
No faults to be found with our persons or minds,
For who in himself imperfections e'er finds?
                              Derry down &c.

Can ambition desire more absolute sway
Than to be our own masters for good and for aye?
Be this then your maxim, and follow it still,
Those only are happy who have their own will.
                              Derry down &c.   20

But happiness only is known by compare,
As foils set off diamonds. Lo! our foil is there*.
Ah! Hymen, the looks of thy victims explain
The comfort of dragging an old rusty chain.
                              Derry down &c.

                              (MS c.1740–50)

122   *The Welford Wedding*

        SUSAN and Charlotte and Letty and all
Jump and skip and caper and brawl,
        Frisk in the drawing-room, romp in the hall,
Susan and Charlotte and Letty and all.
        Hark! the fiddle each gay spirit moves;
See, the beaux have all drawn on their gloves.
                Mr. Archer will dance,
                And Jack Hobland will prance,
                And Jack Shirley'll advance,
                If my Lady approves.   10
Chorus: Susan and Charlotte and Letty and all &c.

---

* The Married Table.

---

curtain-lectures] i.e. from nagging wives (see no. 14 above)

'Make Parson Strother stand up for a post!'
Poor fat wretch, his breath will be lost:
Do but consider what sweat it will cost,
If we make Parson Strother stand up for a post,
Black's his coat, and all grey his huge wig,
D'ye think he can move to cotillon or jig?
  No, no, he will pout,
   And he'll dance like a lout,
   And he'll put us all out   20
   With his carcase so big.
Cho. Susan and Charlotte &c.

'Sweet Lady Bustle, come, you're to call next.'
No, you're out, I'm sure you'll be vexed.
Good Mr. Parson, pray stick to your text,
For indeed Lady Bustle is not to call next.
Smart Jack Hobland shall dance an allemand;
So lightly he foots it, by none he's outdone.
  Besides, the 'Bath Gate'
   I have called for, and wait,   30
   But the man's dunny pate
   Makes him play it all wrong.
Cho. Susan and Charlotte &c.

Oh, could we but foot it to dear Warner's harp,
Tinkle cum tinkle, and sweet flat and sharp;
At our turnings and windings sour critics might curse,
If we could but foot it to dear Warner's harp.
 Oh, my stars! all the couples are out!
 See, pray see, what confusion and rout.
  Mrs. Abdy, come here,   40
   Sister Charlotte turn there,
   Mr. Shirley don't stare,
   But mind what you're about.
Cho. Susan and Charlotte &c.

Oh, my dear Charlotte, our dance we give o'er:
The supper-bell rings, and we can call no more;
And Shepherd stands bowing and holding the door,
So you see, my dear Charlotte, we can dance no more.
 See, the servants in grand cavalcade,
 Fruits-compost and sweet crust colonnade.   50

---

dunny pate] thick skull

See, some carry rusk in,
And turkey al-buskin,
And chickens al-gruskin
In order are laid.
Cho. Susan and Charlotte &c.

Dear Lady Mary, don't kill us with treats,
Patés de veau and transmogrified meats;
Of fish, soup and ven'son the fat Parson eats,
Till indeed, Lady Mary, you'll kill us with treats.
  Mark how clear the choice burgundy flows;   60
  Brisk champagne sparkles under one's nose.
      The toasts of the day
      Make us all blithe and gay.
      Hark to mirth, hark away,
      Ne'er think of repose.
Cho. Susan and Charlotte &c.

Health, love and joy to the sweet smiling bride:
Bless her, kind heaven, with all bliss beside.
May the hours all laughing serene round her glide,
And give health and joy to the sweet smiling bride.   70
Guard dear Charlotte too, safe from all harms,
While time moving gently improves all her charms.
      May prudence direct her,
      Till some kind protector,
      Like Hobland or Hector,
      Shall fly to her arms.
Susan and Charlotte and Letty and all
Jump and skip and caper and brawl,
Frisk in the drawing-room, romp in the hall,
Susan and Charlotte and Letty and all.   80

(MS *c.*1740–50)

123   *From a Young Woman to an Old Officer who Courted her*

DEAR Colonel, name the day,
Let your love no longer stay   with a fal la la.
  The battles you have won
Have my tender heart undone   with a fal la la.

Oh! think no more of wars
You'll get nothing there but scars   with a fal la la.
　　But fly into my arms
As a shelter from all harms   with a fal la la.

　　Though you have got the gout,
Yet your heart is very stout   with a fal la la—　　　　　　10
　　You can sit in elbow-chair,
I can nurse you with great care   with a fal la la.

　　I can patch your old red clothes,
I can darn your old yarn hose   with a fal la la.
　　Still listening with delight,
While you brag of former fight   with a fal la la.

　　And when you chance to die,
As in dust we all must lie   with a fal la la—
　　It shall be my special care
My loss quickly to repair   with a fal la la.　　　　　　　20

(MS *c.* 1740–50)

124　　　　*Verses designed to be Sent to Mr. Adams*

*On his having read a French author, who supposed that the fallen angels abide in
brute beasts, and his inferring from thence that Jocky, Dicky and Cornet (a dog, a
canary-bird and a cat belonging to three of his friends) are possessed with evil
spirits*

INDEED, good Sir, you're quite mistaken,
If you've for evil spirits taken
My faithful Jock, or Dick or Cornet,
For let me tell you, Sir, they scorn it.
My Jocky I'll first vindicate,
Then on the others I'll debate.
My dog is honest and sincere,
I never saw him fawn and sneer;
He's faithful, kind, and never did
Love me the worse when I have chid;　　　　　　　　　10
He'd follow me though I were poor
And begged my bread from door to door.
If I caress him, he is pleased;
If I neglect him, I'm ne'er teased.
In any danger he's assistance:
With teeth and claws he'd make resistance.
Then tell me, pray, with all this merit,
Can Jocky have an evil spirit?

Poor Cornet is a quiet creature:
One reads his mind in every feature; 20
He ne'er makes mischief in the house,
Nor quarrels e'er but with a mouse,
But sits and purrs beside the fire,
For his ambition soars not higher.
Then how submissive does he stand
At meals, to watch Miss Jenny's hand;
With scraps of cheese or crusts of bread
Thinks his attendance nobly paid.
Should he a secret overhear,
That he'll divulge you need not fear; 30
In short, the creature is so civil,
You cannot think his spirit evil.

Against Miss Betty's dicky-bird
I cannot let you say a word,
When I reflect that he is come,
From all his friends and native home,
To a cold climate 'cross the seas,
And prisoner kept in little ease;
Yet far from mourning his sad fate, 40
He never shows the least regret,
But daily tires his lungs and throat
To sing Miss Betty some sweet note;
And what's surprising, ne'er did he
Attempt to gain his liberty.

Thus far I vindicate my friends:
If you're convinced, I've gained my ends.
Men oft may err, and books deceive,
But sure experience you'll believe.
That this I vouch, take on my credit:
Had it been false, I'd ne'er have said it. 50
If these are evil spirits, then
What spirits, pray, possess you men?

(MS *c.*1740–50)

ANNABELLA BLOUNT (née GUISE)
(*fl.* 1700–41)

She was the elder daughter of Sir John Guise of Rendcomb, Gloucestershire, and his wife, Elizabeth Grubham Howe, who had married by about 1674. After the death in 1695 of her father, who had encouraged her interest in literature and languages, and the marriage of her younger sister, she settled in London with her mother. As is clear from the following verses, as well as from his own autobiography, her brother, the second Sir John Guise, actively discouraged her literary interests. Describing Annabella as 'a woman of great witt which I think did her no more good than the other [sister]'s beauty', Guise believed that it was to please 'her bookish humour', and from a wish to learn to read Greek and Latin authors in the original, that, against the advice of all her friends, she married Edward Blount, a man of twice her age, in about 1700. Blount was not merely a Catholic but 'without land or money': 'His person was very disagreeable, but his conversation insinuating', and he had 'the reputation of a wit and a critick'. In spite of Guise's scepticism, Blount's qualities were sufficient to make him later a valued friend and correspondent of Alexander Pope. His elder brother, Sir Walter Blount, eventually gave him the maternal estate of Blagdon in Torbay, Devonshire. Sir John Guise recorded that his sister, who had at first shown 'a great aversion' to 'the popish religion', after thirteen or fourteen years of marriage 'turned papist and that way became more entirely united' to her husband and his family.

Because of the penalties imposed on Catholics after 1715, Blount took his wife and daughters to Bruges in 1717, but had returned by 1721. In that year Pope wrote to him after a visit to Rendcomb, imaginatively evoking the scenes of Mrs Blount's childhood; later he spoke of envying the Blounts 'for loving one another so well' and described their home at Torbay as 'a Paradise'. In turn the Blounts and their daughters visited the poet at Twickenham. Two of the daughters were soon married: Elizabeth to Hugh Clifford, later Lord Clifford of Chudleigh, and Mary to Edward Howard, later Duke of Norfolk. After her husband's death in 1727, Mrs Blount took her two other daughters to Antwerp, where Henrietta married Peter Proli, a merchant, and after his death, Philip Howard, younger brother of her sister's husband, the Duke of Norfolk. Anne became an Ursuline nun and Superioress of her Convent.

In August 1741 Lady Clifford, accompanied by Henrietta, Countess of Pomfret, visited her mother, who must have been about 60. Mrs Blount was living outside Antwerp in a small moated house with a drawbridge, which was raised at night. According to Lady Pomfret, she had 'retired (with three or four servants) to prepare for the next world, and calls herself the *Solitaire*'. Although her children and friends had tried in vain to persuade her out of this retirement, she liked visitors and 'talked with such vivacity and variety of wit, that you would imagine she was still in the midst of the beau monde'. She told Lady Pomfret that she had burned most of her poetry, the 'follies of her youth', but added: 'Since you will have something of mine, I'll shew you how I was cured of poetry', and gave her the following lines, which were sent in a letter of 5 August 1741 to the Countess of Hertford.

125   *[A Cure for Poetry]*

I SOUGHT instruction from my dawning years,
My father to my playfellows preferred;
Whate'er he spoke with deep attention heard:
He laid those grounds that nothing can remove,
Care of my honour, and my country's love.
Whate'er he taught I eagerly would learn;
And, while to please him was my whole concern,

His chase I followed o'er his spacious down,
Joyed with his grace, and trembling at his frown.
   Early I tasted the Castalian spring;   10
My almost infant muse had tried her wing:
A father fondly looked on all I writ;
Winkle himself had voted me a wit:
Old Guiret, charmed with all that I had done,
Declared my verses tasted of the sun.
Already fired with sacred love of praise,
I longed for fame, and hungered after bays.
Cypress I scorned; the Muses were my care;
And Phoebus heard my late and early prayer:
He heard indeed and, standing by my bed,   20
Assumed my brother's friendly form, and said:
   'Why wilt thou, Nan, so ill employ thy wit
In manly works, for ladies' hands unfit?
Of all thy sex that sought the poet's fame,
Is there one character thou dost not blame?
And wilt thou vainly misemploy thy days
In what ne'er was the virtuous woman's praise?
Turn thou thy sense to housewife's wiser cares,
Mind well thy needlework, and say thy prayers:
Secure, in this advice that I have given,   30
Of peace on earth, and endless peace in heaven.'
   He said, and vanished in a flash of light;
My opened mind began to judge aright;
Muse, rhymes and verse in mixed confusion fled,
I burned the trifling products of my head.
Where poets stood before, receipt-books stand,
Silk, thread and worsted are my next demand,
And chairs and stools increase beneath my labouring hand.
Yet would I learn what ancient bards have taught,
But wisdom now, not wit, in Horace sought.   40
Apollo, pleased I thus obeyed his voice,
(Himself my Cupid) made my marriage choice.
No vulgar genius did his care commend,
He gave me Blount*, his favourite and his friend;
To draw whose character exceeds my art,
I bear it deep engraven in my heart;
Yet this one print drawn out, I'll dare to say
Phoebus himself can scarce the whole display.

---

* Edward Blount, Esq. of Blagdon, in Devonshire.

receipt-] recipe-

Though the least blot his piercing wit could know,
He would not sharply censure ev'n his foe;   50
Yet what was bad he never would commend,
But silent hide the errors of his friend.
   His fair example, and endearing art,
Improved my judgement, and reformed my heart.

(Wr. by 1741; pub. 1805)

CHARLOTTE BRERETON
(b. *c.*1720)

She was the younger daughter of Thomas and Jane Brereton (see nos. 56–7), who separated shortly after her birth, her father dying in 1722. She and her sister were brought up by their mother in Wrexham. Like her mother she wrote verse for the *Gentleman's Magazine*: she contributed under the name of 'Carolina' between 1736, when she was only 16 ('To a sprightly, beautiful Boy, in his third Year' and 'On the death of a young Gentleman', pp. 545–6), and 1742, when she published the following poem. Her identity is established by the reappearance of two of 'Carolina' 's poems on the death of her mother in the prefatory material to Jane Brereton's *Poems on Several Occasions* (1744), which also includes a poem addressed to Miss Charlotte Brereton. Her poem on the anniversary of her mother's death (*Gentleman's Magazine* (1741), 438) describes Jane Brereton admiringly as 'replete with learning's store', and adds: 'Life's journey now all comfortless I run, | Thou, my true guide, and *best* protection gone!' The following poem indicates that for a time she found an occupation as governess in an aristocratic Scottish family. The identity of her employers is made easier by their support of the subscription for her mother's *Poems*. Alexander Stewart of Galloway House, near Garlieston, Wigtownshire, was styled Lord Garlies (line 31) before becoming Earl of Galloway in 1746. His wife (line 32) was Catherine Cochrane, daughter of the Earl of Dundonald, and the Countess of Strathmore (line 30) was her widowed elder sister, Susan Cochrane. The several Misses Stewart who are also listed as subscribers may well be the 'infantry' described in the poem. The friend addressed in the poem was no doubt the Miss Travers who appears as yet another subscriber. In the memoirs of her mother in 1744 (p. ix), Charlotte was said by then to be living in Stratford, Essex. Since nothing has come to light about her later career, it is possible that she married.

126   *To Miss A*[*nn*]*a M*[*ari*]*a Tra*[*ver*]*s. An Epistle from Scotland*

   I RISE about eight, if the morning is warm,
   So you'll think early rising will do me no harm;
   My morning array is thrown on in a trice,
   In which did you see me, you'd say I'm not nice:

An hour in good reading delightfully flies,
For as I grow older, I ought to grow wise.
The infantry next are called out of bed,
Are dressed, get their breakfast, their prayers duly said,
And then, now you'll smile, with a matron-like look,
I bid each young pupil sit down to her book,   10
While I change my ribband or cap to be ready,
When summoned below by my lord and my lady.
Now in order I march with my dear charming train,
Of whom there's great danger I soon shall grow vain,
Since I ne'er heard of beauty or goddess had more
Than three Graces attending, but I have got four!
The coffee, tea, chocolate spread o'er the table,
We eat, sip and talk as long as we're able;
For those who plain bread and butter can't eat,
There's orange, and jelly, and honey so sweet.   20
When this scene is over, to battle we go,
And give the poor shuttlecock many a blow,
Till, tired of the sport, to the garden repair,
There ramble about and breathe the fresh air.
Around us no gay rural landscapes arise,
All the prospect is sea, rocks, mountains and skies;
Then back we return, at which time, I confess,
One eighth of an hour I employ on my dress.
What's next to be done? Why, to dinner we sit,
Where Lady S[tra]th[mo]re entertains with her wit;   30
Lord G[ar]l[ie]s with humour and frankness is seen,
And my lady appears like beauty's fair queen.
When the glass is gone round, with success to the Fleet,
The young ladies and Caroline make their retreat,
To study their reading and handle their pen,
Till the tea-table summons invites us again.
The rest of the evening is passed in chit-chat,
In admiring the *Mag.*, a song, and all that;
Or if gaily disposed, we dance a Scotch reel*,
In which how you'd stare at each nimble heel.   40
To end this account, there's no more to be said,
But 'the goose to the fire, and the children to bed'.
And then, if alone, perhaps I find leisure,
By writing to you, to give myself pleasure.
When the night is far spent, I creep to my nest,
Which puts me in mind that you should have rest

* A Scotch Dance, extremely quick, only by three Persons.

_____

infantry] infants

From this dull rhyming stuff, which I beg you'll excuse;
As likewise my having but one piece of news,
That wild Ch——ly is grown so prudent and tame,
You hardly would know me except by my name,   50
And that still I continue, with affection so fervent,
Your friend most sincere, and true humble servant.

(1742)

FRANCES GREVILLE (née MACARTNEY)
(c.1724–89)

She was the third of the four daughters of James and Catherine Coote Macartney of Longford, Ireland. As early as November 1741 Horace Walpole referred to her as companion to the Duchess of Richmond and he praised her as 'Fanny' in his poem on fashionable women of the day, *The Beauties* (1746). The first of her poems given below, not printed until 1784, suggests the high spirits of the Macartney circle in the 1740s. It is apparently addressed to Margaret (Peggy) Eleanor Banks (d. 1793), a 'celebrated beauty', according to Walpole: 'one of the favourite toasts of George II's reign, of all the superior gaieties of which she had her share'. She later married the Hon. Henry Greville (1717–84), mentioned in the poem. In 1748 Frances Macartney eloped with Fulke Greville (1717–c.1805) of Wilbury House in Wiltshire, a man of fashion, a music-lover, and a gambler. It is usually assumed that she contributed to her husband's *Maxims, Characters, and Reflections* (1756; later edns., 1757, 1768), in which she herself is characterized as 'Flora': 'Flora has something original and peculiar about her, a charm which is not easily defined; to know her and to love her is the same thing, but you cannot know her by description. Her person is rather touching than majestic, her features more expressive than regular, and her manner pleases rather because it is restrained, than because it is conformable to any that custom has established' (pp. 50–2).

Shortly afterwards, she wrote her 'Prayer for Indifference', the most celebrated poem by a woman in the period. Apparently first printed in incomplete texts in the *Edinburgh Chronicle* in 1759 and the *London Magazine* in 1761, it had circulated previously in manuscript: Thomas Percy mentioned it in a letter in the autumn of 1758, at about the time that William Shenstone transcribed it into his 'Miscellany'. It was often reprinted in miscellanies and magazines from the 1760s onwards, sometimes with replies which stressed the positive aspects of 'sensibility', such as Lady Carlisle's 'The Fairy's Answer'. Mrs Greville otherwise published little. Her husband, on the edge of financial ruin, became Envoy to Bavaria 1764–70, and she herself travelled in England and on the Continent in the 1760s and 1770s, often with her only daughter Frances-Anne, later, as Lady Crewe, a famous Whig hostess. In 1781 R. B. Sheridan dedicated *The School for Scandal* to her daughter and *The Critic* to Mrs Greville herself, referring to her as the author of the 'most elegant productions of judgement and fancy'.

Fanny Burney described her in later years as having a reputation for being 'pedantic, sarcastic, and supercilious': 'she affrighted the timid, who shrunk into silence; and braved the bold, to whom she allowed no quarter'. The 'feminine delicacy' of her features contrasted with her mental powers: 'Her understanding was truly masculine; not from being harsh or rough, but from depth, soundness, and capacity'. Fanny Burney mentioned her habit in company of 'lounging completely at her ease . . . with her head alone upright', and praised her good humour and kindness to intimate friends. She died at Hampton Court Green in 1789.

127   *Miss F[an]ny M[acar]t[ne]y to Miss P[egg]y
B[ank]s*

THE night in soft slumbers rolled gently away,
Nor did Peggy once dream what would happen next day;
When eager she rose, impatient to dress,
Well pleased her gay friends with her presence to bless;
But alas! on a sudden her schemes were o'erthrown,
Though her prayers were just said, and her cloak ready on:
For behold, who should enter, oh, grief beyond measure!
But——*, that total destroyer of pleasure,
With look so demure, and face dull and wise,
Brim-full of sage counsel and sober advice.   10
Thus the fair she accosted: 'Pray, whither so early?
Well may your poor friends say they see you but rarely;
Your mad comrades possess you so wholly of late,
That I and my maxims are quite out of date;
What, lost to all sense and discretion?', she cried;
'Are prudence and decency quite thrown aside?
For, if I mistake not, from ten till near four,
A gentleman's chariot was seen at your door;
This progress is great for so young a beginner;
From Peggy the saint you're turned Peggy the sinner.   20
Your conduct at church, and the way you behave,
Escape not the censures and frowns of the grave.
That same Mr. G[re]n[vil]le the world talks so loud of,
And the Duchess† and Countess‡ that you are so proud of,
And eke the three sisters§—well, mark the event;
God send that you may'nt these friendships repent!
The first, a fine lady, so great and so high;
The second, the grave, is by all reckoned sly;
And as for the third, oh! Peggy, beware,
And of that giddy girl¶ I beseech you take care.'   30
With this caution the matron her sermon just ended,
While the fair one with patience uncommon attended.

---

* Her Aunt.   † Duchess of Richmond.   ‡ Lady Albemarle.
§ Three Miss M[acar]tn[e]ys.   ¶ The author herself.

Thus then are our parties and pastimes destroyed,
'Cause she grudged us the bliss souls like hers ne'er enjoyed?
And the dame, full of envy, with specious pretext,
While she preached upon scandal, made prudence her text.
Advisers like these, oh, my friend! ever dread,
Nor be by such troublesome neighbours misled.
Should this dull formal stuff o'er my Peggy prevail,
Ere her beauty, wit, youth, and her good humour fail?   40
No, consult *my sweet mistress**; in her book read one chapter,
You'll despise the vain lectures of prudes ever after;
Be sure she'll soon teach you, whate'er they can say,
That a heart formed as yours is can ne'er go astray.
Meanwhile, on the matrons let's take some compassion,
Nor forbid them t' indulge their last, favourite passion;
We'll laugh, let them talk and abuse at their leisure:
Their province is railing, but ours is pleasure.

(Wr. *c*.1745; pub. 1784)

128   *A Prayer for Indifference*

OFT I've implored the gods in vain,
    And prayed till I've been weary;
For once I'll try my wish to gain
    Of Oberon, the fairy.

Sweet airy being, wanton sprite,
    That liv'st in woods unseen,
And oft by Cynthia's silver light
    Trip'st gaily o'er the green;

If e'er thy pitying heart was moved,
    As ancient stories tell,   10
And for th' Athenian maid, who loved,
    Thou sought'st a wondrous spell,

Oh! deign once more t' exert thy power;
    Haply some herb or tree,
Sovereign as juice from western flower,
    Conceals a balm for me.

I ask no kind return in love,
    No tempting charm to please;
Far from the heart such gifts remove,
    That sighs for peace and ease.   20

* A cant word for inclination.

Nor ease nor peace that heart can know,
  That, like the needle true,
Turns at the touch of joy or woe,
  But, turning, trembles too.

Far as distress the soul can wound,
  'Tis pain in each degree;
Bliss goes but to a certain bound,
  Beyond is agony.

Take then this treacherous sense of mine,
  Which dooms me still to smart;   30
Which pleasure can to pain refine,
  To pain new pangs impart.

Oh! haste to shed the sovereign balm,
  My shattered nerves new-string;
And for my guest, serenely calm,
  The nymph Indifference bring.

At her approach, see Hope, see Fear,
  See Expectation fly,
With Disappointment in the rear,
  That blasts the promised joy.   40

The tears, which pity taught to flow,
  My eyes shall then disown;
The heart, that throbbed at others' woe,
  Shall then scarce feel its own.

The wounds, which now each moment bleed,
  Each moment then shall close,
And peaceful days shall still succeed
  To nights of sweet repose.

Oh, fairy elf, but grant me this,
  This one kind comfort send,   50
And so may never-fading bliss
  Thy flowery paths attend!

So may the glow-worm's glimmering light
  Thy tiny footsteps lead
To some new region of delight,
  Unknown to mortal tread;

And be thy acorn goblets filled
  With heaven's ambrosial dew,
From sweetest, freshest flowers distilled,
  That shed fresh sweets for you.   60

And what of life remains for me
  I'll pass in sober ease,
Half-pleased, contented will I be,
  Contented, half to please.

         (1759)

MARY LEAPOR
(1722–46)

She was the daughter of Philip and Anne Leapor, and was born at Marston St Lawrence, Northamptonshire, where her father was a gardener on the estate of Sir John Blencowe. In about 1726, perhaps on the death of Blencowe, her father moved to Brackley to keep a nursery garden and work for the local gentry. She learned to read at an early age, and to write by the time she was 10 or 11, but her mother discouraged her early attempts at poetry. After Anne Leapor's death in about 1742, she kept house for her father, but spent her leisure in writing or reading, her neighbours fearing that she would 'overstudy herself, and be mopish'. An account written some forty years later states that she was also 'some time cook-maid in a gentleman's family in the neighbourhood', probably, at Weston Hall, a few miles north of Brackley, and there are predictable anecdotes of her writing verse 'while the jack was standing still, and the meat scorching'. Her employer, according to the same writer, described her as having been 'extremely swarthy, and quite emaciated, with a long crane-neck, and a short body, much resembling, in shape, a bass-viol'.

    Her verse circulated locally and eventually attracted the attention of Bridget Fremantle ('Artemisia'), the daughter of a former Rector of Hinton, who was impressed by Leapor's writing and character. Far from condescending to her, Fremantle felt honoured by the friendship of one of 'such true Greatness of Soul' and found it impossible to think of her as 'a mean Person'. Given that she was 'engag'd in her Father's Affairs, and the Business of his House, in which she had nobody to assist her', she was now writing verse with extraordinary speed. A letter of this period reveals her sense of precariousness: if her father were to die, she would be 'left naked and defenceless, without Friend, and without Dependence; with a weak and indolent Body to provide for its own Subsistence; and a restless Mind, rack'd with unprofitable Invention'. Her only ambition was 'a Competency', which would give her time for her writing and a modest social life. Miss Fremantle, assisted by a local gentleman, began to organize a subscription for her, and her play and samples of her verse were sent to London for advice. Such plans made Leapor uneasy, especially when she was asked to provide specimens of her work, since her poems were 'only a Parcel of chequer'd Thoughts, scarce tolerable when together', and making a 'sad Figure' in isolation. She was also alarmed at the prospect of having to write a dedication to some titled lady.

    Although her play was not accepted in London, the plan of publishing her poems would presumably have gone ahead, had she not died of measles on 12 November 1746, after being in poor health for some time. She was buried at Brackley. Her dying wish had been that her poems should be published for the benefit of her father. Proposals for the volume were circulated, dated 1 January 1747 (a later suggestion that they were drawn up by Garrick is unconfirmed), one of her poems was printed in the *London Magazine* in January 1747, and her *Poems upon Several Occasions* was published in April 1748, with a list of some 600 subscribers, including Miss Fremantle and several members of the Blencowe family, the Countess of Hertford, Mary Delany, and Stephen Duck. The cautious address 'To the Reader' emphasized her modesty, cheerfulness, and contentment in the humble station assigned her by Providence. Copies may not have been available to non-subscribers for some time, as it was not until November 1749 that Ralph Griffiths, the editor, gave the book a prominent if non-committal article in the *Monthly Review*.

At this point Samuel Richardson became interested in Leapor, and by December 1750 had seen the account of her by Bridget Fremantle quoted above. He had shown it to the poet Christopher Smart and asked him to write an epitaph for her gravestone. Although Smart had published her 'Colinetta' in *The Midwife* of 16 November 1750, he did not fulfil his promise to print more of her verse, and was probably not the author of the epitaph printed in the new volume of her *Poems*, which Richardson edited (and printed) with Isaac Hawkins Browne in March 1751. The subscribers now numbered only some 300, explaining the relative rarity of this second volume, but included the Earl of Chesterfield, Richard Owen Cambridge, Colley Cibber, William and John Duncombe, Thomas Edwards, Miss Highmore, Mrs Montagu, and William Pitt. Several of these names indicate that the main support of the subscription came from within the Richardson circle. The volume contained the memoir by Bridget Fremantle and the letters by Leapor which have been quoted above. Ralph Griffiths again gave the volume a long notice in the *Monthly Review* in June 1751, several poems were reprinted in the *London Magazine*, John Duncombe praised her in *The Feminiad* (1754), and a substantial selection of her verse appeared in *Poems by Eminent Ladies* (1755), ii. 17–134. In spite of scattered appearances in later miscellanies, her poems, influenced as they were by her favourite author Pope, would eventually have come to seem old-fashioned. Only recently has interest in a writer whom Duncombe in 1784 rightly called 'a most extraordinary, uncultivated genius' revived.

129   *The Headache. To Aurelia*

AURELIA, when your zeal makes known
Each woman's failing but your own,
How charming Silvia's teeth decay,
And Celia's hair is turning grey;
Yet Celia gay has sparkling eyes,
But (to your comfort) is not wise:
Methinks you take a world of pains
To tell us Celia has no brains.

Now you wise folk, who make such a pother
About the wit of one another, 10
With pleasure would your brains resign,
Did all your noddles ache like mine.

Not cuckolds half my anguish know,
When budding horns begin to grow;
Nor battered skull of wrestling Dick,
Who late was drubbed at single-stick;
Not wretches that in fevers fry,
Not Sappho when her cap's awry,
E'er felt such torturing pangs as I;
Nor forehead of Sir Jeffrey Strife, 20
When smiling Cynthio kissed his wife.

Not lovesick Marcia's languid eyes,
Who for her simpering Corin dies,
So sleepy look or dimly shine,
As these dejected eyes of mine:
Not Claudia's brow such wrinkles made
At sight of Cynthia's new brocade.

Just so, Aurelia, you complain
Of vapours, rheums, and gouty pain;
Yet I am patient, so should you, 30
For cramps and headaches are our due:
We suffer justly for our crimes,
For scandal you, and I for rhymes;
Yet we (as hardened wretches do)
Still the enchanting vice pursue;
Our reformation ne'er begin,
But fondly hug the darling sin.

Yet there's a mighty difference too
Between the fate of me and you; 40
Though you with tottering age shall bow,
And wrinkles scar your lovely brow,
Your busy tongue may still proclaim
The faults of every sinful dame:
You still may prattle nor give o'er,
When wretched I must sin no more.
The sprightly Nine must leave me then,
This trembling hand resign its pen:
No matron ever sweetly sung,
Apollo only courts the young.

Then who would not (Aurelia, pray)   50
Enjoy his favours while they may?
Nor cramps nor headaches shall prevail:
I'll still write on, and you shall rail.

                                        (Wr. by 1746; pub. 1748)

130   *Strephon to Celia. A Modern Love-Letter*

MADAM,
          I hope you'll think it's true
I deeply am in love with you,
When I assure you t' other day,
As I was musing on my way,
At thought of you I tumbled down
Directly in a deadly swoon:
And though 'tis true I'm something better,
Yet I can hardly spell my letter:
And as the latter you may view,
I hope you'll think the former true.   10
You need not wonder at my flame,
For you are not a mortal dame:
I saw you dropping from the skies;
And let dull idiots swear your eyes
With love their glowing breast inspire,
I tell you they are flames of fire,
That scorch my forehead to a cinder,
And burn my very heart to tinder.
Your breast so mighty cold, I trow,
Is made of nothing else but snow: 20
Your hands (no wonder they have charms)
Are made of ivory like your arms.
Your cheeks, that look as if they bled,
Are nothing else but roses red.
Your lips are coral very bright,
Your teeth—though numbers out of spite
May say they're bones—yet 'twill appear
They're rows of pearl exceeding dear.

   Now, madam, as the chat goes round,
I hear you have ten thousand pound: 30
But that as I a trifle hold,
Give me your person, dem your gold;
Yet for your own sake 'tis secured,
I hope—your houses too insured;

                          197

I'd have you take a special care,
And of false mortgages beware;
You've wealth enough 'tis true, but yet
You want a friend to manage it.
Now such a friend you soon might have,
By fixing on your humble slave;   40
Not that I mind a stately house,
Or value money of a louse;
But your five hundred pounds a year,
I would secure it for my dear:
Then smile upon your slave, that lies
Half murdered by your radiant eyes;
Or else this very moment dies—

STREPHON

(Wr. by 1746; pub. 1748)

131   *Soto. A Character*

IN Soto's bosom you may find
The glimmering of a worthy mind:
'Tis but a faint and feeble ray,
Imperfect as the dawning day;
Yet were the jarring passions tuned,
And the wild branches nicely pruned,
The soil from thorns and thistles clear,
Some latent virtue might appear.
I' th' morning catch him (early though,
Your bird will else be flown, I trow),   10
Ere he has reached the boozing-can,
You'll find the stamp of reasoning man:
Then see the wretch whom none can rule,
Ere night, a madman and a fool;
The witty Soto then you'll find
Just level with the brutal kind.
With crimson face and winking eyes,
That look like woodcocks, mighty wise;
See streams a current down his chin,
From soft tobacco lodged within;   20
Be pleased to steal a glance or two,
But one may serve to make you—.

He fain would walk, but cannot stand,
And see, a palsy in his hand;

And though his throat has swallowed down
Two gallons of October brown,
His greedy guts impatient roar,
And seem to call aloud for more.
More they shall have: but hark, within
Is heard a rude and lawless din;   30
Wind, ale and phlegm their powers wage,
And hiccups call them to engage;
And now, ah now! incessant flows
The frothy tide from mouth and nose:
No more is seen the covered ground,
But a huge river floating round.
Down drops the youth, his giddy head
Falls easy on the liquid bed:
So swam Achilles fierce and brave
On angry Xanthus' swelling wave,   40
And 'scaped with being wet to th' skin,
For Pallas held him up by th' chin;
So Bacchus saves, by mighty charms,
His helpless devotee from harms;
And Soto sleeps till break of day,
Then shakes his ears and walks away.

(Wr. by 1746; pub. 1748)

132   *Proserpine's Ragout*

As once grave Pluto drove his royal wheels
O'er the large confines of the Stygian fields:
With kingly port he sat, and by his side
Rode his fair captive, now his awful bride;
But from the lakes a sulphurous mist invades,
And strikes the fainting empress of the shades.
The trembling queen is seized with sickly yawns,
With griping colics, and with feverish qualms.
'Back to the palace!' was the general cry:
Before the lash her sable coursers fly: 10
There rests the dame, and sought her royal bed,
Where the soft pillows raised her drooping head:
Restoring lenitives were sought in vain
To cool her vitals and assuage her pain.
On nothing would the peevish matron feed:
Then useful Mercury was called with speed,

October brown] ale   132 Ragout] highly seasoned French stew

And sent on earth some curious dish to frame
Of light digestion for the sickly dame.
To earth he posted, where he quickly found
Proper ingredients on our fertile ground.   20
Here first he seized, as nonsubstantial foods,
The courtier's friendship and the zeal of prudes,
The sighs of widowers, and blends with those
The vows of lovers and the brains of beaux,
The miser's charity, the drunkard's cares,
The wealth of poets, and the tears of heirs,
Philander's patience, when his lord denies,
The frowns of Celia, when her heart complies:
Then with a breath along the air he drives
The love of husbands and the charms of wives;   30
Where trifles dwell sagacious Hermes knew:
The wingèd youth to lordly senates flew,
From thence debates and long harangues to cull,
And steeped them softly in a statesman's skull.
And now the frothy dish began to seem
A proper viand for his sickly queen.
To crown the rest, he met by lucky chance
The wit of England, and the truth of France.

(Wr. by 1746; pub. 1748)

133   *Mira to Octavia*

FAIR one, to you this monitor I send;
Octavia, pardon your officious friend:
You think your conduct merits only praise,
But outlawed poets censure whom they please.
Thus we begin—your servant has been told
That you (despising settlements and gold)
Determine Florio, witty, young and gay,
To have and hold for ever and for aye;
And view that person as your mortal foe,
Who dares object against your charming beau;   10
But now, to furnish metre for my song,
Let us suppose Octavia may be wrong:
'Tis true you're lovely; yet the learned aver
That even beauties like the rest may err.

I know, to shun you hold it as a rule
The arrant coxcomb and the stupid fool:

Not such is Florio, he has wit—'tis true,
Enough, Octavia, to impose on you:
Yet such a wit you'll, by experience, find
Worse than a fool that's complaisant and kind: 20
It only serves to gild his vices o'er,
And teach his malice how to wound the more.

    I need not tell you, most ingenious fair,
That hungry mortals are not fed with air,
But solid food: and this voracious clay
Asks drink and victuals more than once a day:
Now could your Florio by his wit inspire
The chilly hearth to blaze with lasting fire;
Or when his children round the table throng,
By an allusion or a sprightly song   30
Adorn the board, i' th' twinkling of an eye,
With a hot pasty or a warden-pie,
There might be reason on Octavia's side,
And not a sage could blame the prudent bride.

    Yet (or some authors often deal in lies)
Lovers may live on nuts and blackberries;
For roving knights bewildered in their way,
Who in black forests half a season stray,
Unless they find provision on the trees,
Must sup on grass and breakfast on the breeze.   40
But as you've been long used to nicer fare,
Your constitution would but hardly bear
Such food as this: and therefore I advise
That you'd consider (for you're mighty wise)
If sober Dusterandus would not make
A better husband than your darling rake.
Grave Dusterandus: he whose steadfast mind
Is yet untainted, though not much refined;
Whose soul ne'er roves beyond his native fields,
Nor asks for joys but what his pasture yields;   50
On life's dull cares with patience can attend,
A gentle master and a constant friend;
Who in soft quiet spends the guiltless days,
His servants' blessing and his neighbours' praise.
Say, would you, in his happy mansion, reign,
Toast of the village and the rural plain;
With honest friends your cheerful days beguile,
While peace and plenty on your table smile:

warden-pie] i.e. made of pears

Or, cold and hungry, writhe your tired jaws,
And dine with Florio upon hips and haws?   60
In truth I think there's little room to pause.

  In spite of all romantic poets sing,
This gold, my dearest, is an useful thing:
Not that I'd have you hoard the precious store,
For not a wretch is like the miser poor:
Enjoy your fortune with a cheerful mind,
And let the blessing spread amongst the kind;
But if there's none but Florio that will do,
Write ballads both, and you may thrive—Adieu.

(Wr. by 1746; pub. 1748)

134   *Man the Monarch*

  AMAZED we read of Nature's early throes,
How the fair heavens and ponderous earth arose;
How blooming trees unplanted first began;
And beasts submissive to their tyrant, man:
To man, invested with despotic sway,
While his mute brethren tremble and obey;
Till heaven beheld him insolently vain,
And checked the limits of his haughty reign.
Then from their lord the rude deserters fly,
And, grinning back, his fruitless rage defy;   10
Pards, tigers, wolves to gloomy shades retire,
And mountain-goats in purer gales respire.
To humble valleys, where soft flowers blow,
And fattening streams in chrystal mazes flow,
Full of new life, the untamed coursers run,
And roll and wanton in the cheerful sun;
Round their gay hearts in dancing spirits rise,
And rouse the lightnings in their rolling eyes:
To craggy rocks destructive serpents glide,
Whose mossy crannies hide their speckled pride;   20
And monstrous whales on foamy billows ride.
Then joyful birds ascend their native sky:
But where! ah, where shall helpless woman fly?

  Here smiling Nature brought her choicest stores,
And roseate beauty on her favourite pours:
Pleased with her labour, the officious dame
Withheld no grace would deck the rising frame.

Then viewed her work, and viewed and smiled again,
And kindly whispered, 'Daughter, live and reign.'
But now the matron mourns her latest care,   30
And sees the sorrows of her darling fair;
Beholds a wretch, whom she designed a queen,
And weeps that e'er she formed the weak machine.
In vain she boasts her lip of scarlet dyes,
Cheeks like the morning, and far-beaming eyes;
Her neck refulgent, fair and feeble arms—
A set of useless and neglected charms.
She suffers hardship with afflictive moans:
Small tasks of labour suit her slender bones.
Beneath a load her weary shoulders yield,   40
Nor can her fingers grasp the sounding shield;
She sees and trembles at approaching harms,
And fear and grief destroy her fading charms.
Then her pale lips no pearly teeth disclose,
And time's rude sickle cuts the yielding rose.
Thus wretched woman's shortlived merit dies:
In vain to Wisdom's sacred help she flies,
Or sparkling Wit but lends a feeble aid:
'Tis all delirium from a wrinkled maid.

A tattling dame, no matter where or who—   50
Me it concerns not, and it need not you—
Once told this story to the listening Muse,
Which we, as now it serves our turn, shall use.

When our grandsire* named the feathered kind,
Pondering their natures in his careful mind,
'Twas then, if on our author we rely,
He viewed his consort with an envious eye;
Greedy of power, he hugged the tottering throne,
Pleased with the homage, and would reign alone;
And, better to secure his doubtful rule,   60
Rolled his wise eyeballs, and pronounced her *fool*.
The regal blood to distant ages runs:
Sires, brothers, husbands, and commanding sons,
The sceptre claim; and every cottage brings
A long succession of domestic kings.

(Wr. by 1746; pub. 1751)

* Mrs Leapor frequently writes the Words *Sire, Fire, Spire, Hour*, &c. each as if two Syllables.

135 ## from *An Epistle to Artemisia*

['*The Patrons of my early Song*']

ONCE Delpho read—sage Delpho, learned and wise,
O'er the scrawled paper cast his judging eyes,
Whose lifted brows confessed a critic's pride,
While his broad thumb moved nimbly down the side.
His form was like some oracle profound:
The listening audience formed a circle round.
But Mira, fixing her presuming eyes
On the stern image, thus impatient cries:
'Sir, will they prosper?—Speak your judgement, pray.'
Replies the statue—'Why, perhaps they may.'   10
For further answers we in vain implore:
The charm was over, and it spoke no more.

Cressida comes, the next unbidden guest:
Small was her top-knot, and her judgement less;
A decent virgin, blessed with idle time,
Now jingles bobbins, and now ponders rhyme:
Not ponders—reads; not reads—but looks 'em o'er
To little purpose, like a thousand more.

'Your servant, Molly.'
                                        'I am yours the same.'
'I pay this visit, Molly, to your fame: 20
'Twas that that brought me here, or let me die.'
'My fame's obliged: and truly so am I.'
'Then fetch me something, for I must not stay
Above four hours.'
                          'But you'll drink some tea?'
We sip and read; we laugh and chat between.
'The air is pleasant, and the fields are green.
Well, Molly, sure, there never was thy fellow.
But don't my ruffles look exceeding yellow?
My apron's dirty—Mira, well, I vow
That thought of yours was very pretty now.   30
I've read the like, though I forget the place:
But, Mrs. Mira, how d'ye like my lace?'

Afflicted Mira, with a languid eye,
Now views the clock, and now the western sky:

'The sun grows lower: will you please to walk?'
'No; read some more.'
                              'But I had rather talk.'
'Perhaps you're tired.'
                              'Truly, that may be.'
'Or think me weak.'
                              'Why, Cressy, thoughts are free.'
At last we part, with congees at the door:
'I'd thank you, Mira; but my thanks are poor.   40
I wish, alas! but wishes are in vain.
I like your garden; and I'll come again.
Dear, how I wish!—I do, or let me die,
That we lived near.'
                              Thinks Mira, 'So don't I.'

    This nymph, perhaps, as some had done before,
Found the cold welcome, and returned no more.

    Then Vido next to Mira's cot appears,
And with some praise salutes her listening ears;
Whose maxim was, with truth not to offend,
And, right or wrong, his business to commend.   50
'Look here,' cries Mira, 'pray peruse this song:
Even I, its parent, see there's something wrong.'
'But you mistake: 'tis excellent indeed.'
'Then I'll correct it.'
                              'No, there is no need.'
'Pray, Vido, look on these. Methinks they smell
Too much of Grub Street: that myself can tell.'
'Not so, indeed; they're easy and polite.'
'And can you bear 'em?'
                              'I could read till night.'
But Mira, though too partial to the bays,
And, like her brethren, not averse to praise,   60
Had learned this lesson: praise, if planted wrong,
Is more destructive than a spiteful tongue.

    Comes Codrus next, with talents to offend,
A simple tutor, and a saucy friend,
Who poured thick sonnets like a troubled spring,
And such as Butler's wide-mouthed mortals sing:
In shocking rhymes a nymph's perfections tells,
Like the harsh ting-tong of some village-bells.
Then a rude quarrel sings through either ear,
And Mira's levee once again is clear.   70

congees] farewells

205

Now the dull Muses took their usual rest;
The babes* slept soundly in their tiny chest.
Not so their parent: fortune still would send
Some proud director, or ill-meaning friend:
At least we thought their sour meanings ill,
Whose lectures strove to cross a stubborn will.

Parthenia cries, 'Why, Mira, you are dull,
And ever musing, till you crack your skull;
Still poking o'er your what-d'ye-call—your Muse:
But prithee, Mira, when dost clean thy shoes?'   80

Then comes Sophronia, like a barbarous Turk:
'You thoughtless baggage, when d'ye mind your work?
Still o'er a table leans your bending neck:
Your head will grow preposterous, like a peck.
Go, ply your needle: you might earn your bread:
Or who must feed you when your father's dead?'
She sobbing answers, 'Sure, I need not come
To you for lectures: I have store at home.
What can I do?'
                    —'Not scribble.'
                                    —'But I will.'
'Then get thee packing—and be awkward still.'   90

Thus wrapped in sorrow, wretched Mira lay,
Till Artemisia swept the gloom away:
The laughing Muse, by her example led,
Shakes her glad wings, and quits the drowsy bed.

(Wr. by 1746; pub. 1751)

136   *Advice to Sophronia*

WHEN youth and charms have ta'en their wanton flight,
And transient beauty bids the fair good-night;
When once her sparkling eyes shall dimly roll,
Then let the matron dress her lofty soul;
Quit affectation, partner of her youth,
For goodness, prudence, purity and truth.
These virtues will her lasting peace prepare,
And give a sanction to her silver hair.

* Her Poems.

peck] a scythe (dialect) or peck measure

These precepts let the fond Sophronia prove,
Nor vainly dress her blinking eyes with love.   10
Can roses flourish on a leafless thorn,
Or dewy woodbines grace a wintry morn?
The weeping Cupids languish in your eye;
On your brown cheek the sickly beauties die.
Time's rugged hand has stroked your visage o'er;
The gay vermilion stains your lip no more.
None can with justice now your shape admire;
The drooping lilies on your breast expire.
Then, dear Sophronia, leave thy foolish whims:
Discard your lover with your favourite sins.   20
Consult your glass; then prune your wanton mind,
Nor furnish laughter for succeeding time.
'Tis not your own; 'tis gold's all-conquering charms
Invite Myrtillo to your shrivelled arms:
And shall Sophronia, whose once-lovely eyes
Beheld those triumphs which her heart despised,
Who looked on merit with a haughty frown,
At five-and-fifty take a beardless clown?
Ye pitying Fates, this withered damsel save,
And bear her safely to her virgin grave.

(Wr. by 1746; pub. 1751)

137   *An Essay on Woman*

WOMAN, a pleasing but a short-lived flower,
Too soft for business and too weak for power:
A wife in bondage, or neglected maid;
Despised, if ugly; if she's fair, betrayed.
'Tis wealth alone inspires every grace,
And calls the raptures to her plenteous face.
What numbers for those charming features pine,
If blooming acres round her temples twine!
Her lip the strawberry, and her eyes more bright
Than sparkling Venus in a frosty night;   10
Pale lilies fade and, when the fair appears,
Snow turns a negro and dissolves in tears,
And, where the charmer treads her magic toe,
On English ground Arabian odours grow;
Till mighty Hymen lifts his sceptred rod,
And sinks her glories with a fatal nod,
Dissolves her triumphs, sweeps her charms away,
And turns the goddess to her native clay.

But, Artemisia, let your servant sing
What small advantage wealth and beauties bring.　20
Who would be wise, that knew Pamphilia's fate?
Or who be fair, and joined to Sylvia's mate?
Sylvia, whose cheeks are fresh as early day,
As evening mild, and sweet as spicy May:
And yet that face her partial husband tires,
And those bright eyes, that all the world admires.
Pamphilia's wit who does not strive to shun,
Like death's infection or a dog-day's sun?
The damsels view her with malignant eyes,
The men are vexed to find a nymph so wise:　30
And wisdom only serves to make her know
The keen sensation of superior woe.
The secret whisper and the listening ear,
The scornful eyebrow and the hated sneer,
The giddy censures of her babbling kind,
With thousand ills that grate a gentle mind,
By her are tasted in the first degree,
Though overlooked by Simplicus and me.
Does thirst of gold a virgin's heart inspire,
Instilled by nature or a careful sire?　40
Then let her quit extravagance and play,
The brisk companion and expensive tea,
To feast with Cordia in her filthy sty
On stewed potatoes or on mouldy pie;
Whose eager eyes stare ghastly at the poor,
And fright the beggars from her hated door;
In greasy clouts she wraps her smoky chin,
And holds that pride's a never-pardoned sin.

If this be wealth, no matter where it falls;
But save, ye Muses, save your Mira's walls:　50
Still give me pleasing indolence and ease,
A fire to warm me and a friend to please.

Since, whether sunk in avarice or pride,
A wanton virgin or a starving bride,
Or wondering crowds attend her charming tongue,
Or, deemed an idiot, ever speaks the wrong;
Though nature armed us for the growing ill
With fraudful cunning and a headstrong will;
Yet, with ten thousand follies to her charge,
Unhappy woman's but a slave at large.　60

(Wr. by 1746; pub. 1751)

138 *The Epistle of Deborah Dough*

DEARLY beloved Cousin, these
Are sent to thank you for your cheese;
The price of oats is greatly fell:
I hope your children all are well
(Likewise the calf you take delight in),
As I am at this present writing.
But I've no news to send you now;
Only I've lost my brindled cow,
And that has greatly sunk my dairy.
But I forgot our neighbour Mary;   10
Our neighbour Mary—who, they say,
Sits scribble-scribble all the day,
And making—what—I can't remember;
But sure 'tis something like December;
A frosty morning—let me see—
O! now I have it to a T:
She throws away her precious time
In scrawling nothing else but rhyme;
Of which, they say, she's mighty proud,
And lifts her nose above the crowd;   20
Though my young daughter Cicely
Is taller by a foot than she,
And better learned (as people say);
Can knit a stocking in a day;
Can make a pudding, plump and rare;
And boil her bacon to an hair;
Will coddle apples nice and green,
And fry her pancakes—like a queen.

But there's a man, that keeps a dairy,
Will clip the wings of neighbour Mary: 30
Things wonderful they talk of him,
But I've a notion 'tis a whim.
Howe'er, 'tis certain he can make
Your rhymes as thick as plums in cake;
Nay more, they say that from the pot
He'll take his porridge, scalding hot,
And drink 'em down;—and yet they tell ye
Those porridge shall not burn his belly;
A cheesecake o'er his head he'll throw,
And when 'tis on the stones below,   40
It shan't be found so much as quaking,
Provided 'tis of his wife's making.

From this some people would infer
That this good man's a conjuror:
But I believe it is a lie;
I never thought him so, not I,
Though Win'fred Hobble who, you know,
Is plagued with corns on every toe,
Sticks on his verse with fastening spittle,
And says it helps her feet a little.
Old Frances too his paper tears,   50
And tucks it close behind his ears;
And (as she told me t'other day)
It charmed her toothache quite away.

   Now as thou'rt better learned than me,
Dear Cos', I leave it all to thee
To judge about this puzzling man,
And ponder wisely—for you can.

   Now Cousin, I must let you know
That, while my name is Deborah Dough,   60
I shall be always glad to see ye,
And what I have, I'll freely gi' ye.

   'Tis one o'clock, as I'm a sinner;
The boys are all come home to dinner,
And I must bid you now farewell.
I pray remember me to Nell;
And for your friend I'd have you know
Your loving Cousin,

DEBORAH DOUGH

(Wr. by 1746; pub. 1751)

139   ## from *Crumble Hall*

[*In the Kitchen*]

O'ER the warm kettles, and the savoury steams,
Grave Colinettus of his oxen dreams:
Then, starting, anxious for his new-mown hay,
Runs headlong out to view the doubtful day.
But dinner calls with more prevailing charms,
And surly Gruffo in his awkward arms
Bears the tall jug, and turns a glaring eye,
As though he feared some insurrection nigh
From the fierce crew, that gaping stand a-dry.

conjuror] magician

O'er-stuffed with beef, with cabbage much too full,　10
And dumpling too (fit emblem of his skull!),
With mouth wide open, but with closing eyes,
Unwieldy Roger on the table lies.
His able lungs discharge a rattling sound:
Prince barks, Spot howls, and the tall roofs rebound.
Him Ursula views; and, with dejected eyes,
'Ah! Roger, ah!', the mournful maiden cries,
'Is wretched Ursula then your care no more,
That, while I sigh, thus you can sleep and snore?
Ingrateful Roger! wilt thou leave me now?　20
For you these furrows mark my fading brow;
For you my pigs resign their morning due;
My hungry chickens lose their meat for you;
And was it not, ah! was it not for thee,
No goodly pottage would be dressed by me.
For thee these hands wind up the whirling jack,
Or place the spit across the sloping rack.
I baste the mutton with a cheerful heart,
Because I know my Roger will have part.'

Thus she—but now the dish-kettle began　30
To boil and blubber with the foaming bran.
The greasy apron round her hips she ties,
And to each plate the scalding clout applies:
The purging bath each glowing dish refines,
And once again the polished pewter shines.

(Wr. by 1746; pub. 1751)

140　*Upon her Play being returned to her, stained
with Claret*

WELCOME, dear wanderer, once more!
　　Thrice welcome to thy native cell!
Within this peaceful humble door
　　Let thou and I contented dwell!

But say, O whither hast thou ranged?
　　Why dost thou blush a crimson hue?
Thy fair complexion's greatly changed:
　　Why, I can scarce believe 'tis you.

Then tell, my son, O tell me, where
   Didst thou contract this sottish dye?   10
You kept ill company, I fear,
   When distant from your parent's eye.

Was it for this, O graceless child!
   Was it for this you learned to spell?
Thy face and credit both are spoiled:
   Go drown thyself in yonder well.

I wonder how thy time was spent:
   No news, alas, hast thou to bring?
Hast thou not climbed the Monument?
   Nor seen the lions, nor the King?   20

But now I'll keep you here secure:
   No more you view the smoky sky;
The Court was never made, I'm sure,
   For idiots like thee and I.

             (Wr. by 1746; pub. 1751)

141   *The Visit*

   WITH walking sick, with curtseys lame,
And frighted by the scolding dame,
Poor Mira once again is seen
Within the bounds of Goslin-Green.
   O Artemisia! dear to me
As to the lawyer golden fee;
Whose name dwells pleasant on my tongue,
And first and last shall grace my song;
Receive within your friendly door
A wretch that vows to rove no more.   10
In some close corner let me hide,
Remote from compliments and pride;
Where morals grave, or sonnets gay,
Delude the guiltless, cheerful day;
Where we a sprightly theme may find,
Besides enquiring where's the wind,
Or whispering who and who's together,
And criticising on the weather;
Where careless creatures, such as I,
May 'scape the penetrating eye   20
Of students in physiognomy;

Who read your want of wit or grace
Not from your manners, but your face;
Whose tongues are for a week supplied
From one poor mouth that's stretched too wide;
Who greatly blame a freckled hand,
A skinny arm, full shoulders; and,
Without a microscope, can spy
A nose that's placed an inch awry.
In vain to gloomy shades you flee,   30
Like mice, in darkness they can see;
In vain to glaring lights you run,
Their eyes can face a mid-day sun:
You'll find no safety in retreat,
Like sharks they never mince their meat;
Their dreadful jaws they open throw,
And, if they catch you, down you go.

(Wr. by 1746; pub. 1751).

142   from *Mira's Picture. A Pastoral*

CORYDON. PHILLARIO

[*A Portrait of the Artist*]

PHIL. But who is she that walks from yonder hill,
    With studious brows, and nightcap dishabille?
    That looks a stranger to the beams of day,
    And counts her steps, and mutters all the way?
CORY. 'Tis Mira, daughter to a friend of mine;
    'Tis she that makes your what-d'ye-call—your rhyme.
    I own the girl is something out o' th' way:
    But how d'ye like her, good Phillario, say?
PHIL. Like her!—I'd rather beg the friendly rains
    To sweep the nuisance from thy loaded plains;   10
    That——
CORY. ——Hold, Phillario! She's a neighbour's child:
    'Tis true, her linen may be something soiled.
PHIL. Her linen, Corydon!—Herself, you mean.
    Are such the dryads of thy smiling plain?
    Why I could swear it, if it were no sin,
    That yon lean rook can show a fairer skin.
CORY. What though some freckles in her face appear?
    That's only owing to the time o' th' year.
    Her eyes are dim, you'll say. Why, that is true:
    I've heard the reason, and I'll tell it you.   20

213

By a rush-candle (as her father says)
She sits whole evenings, reading wicked plays.
PHIL. She read!—She'd better milk her brindled cows:
I wish the candle does not singe her brows,
So like a dry furze-faggot, and beside,
Not quite so even as a mouse's hide.
CORY. Come, come; you view her with malicious eyes:
Her shape——
PHIL. ——Where mountains upon mountains rise!
And, as they feared some treachery at hand,
Behind her ears her listening shoulders stand.   30
CORY. But she has teeth——
PHIL.——Considering how they grow,
'Tis no great matter if she has or no:
They look decayed with posset and with plums,
And seem prepared to quit her swelling gums.
CORY. No more, my friend! for see the sun grows high,
And I must send the weeders to my rye:
Those spurious plants must from the soil be torn,
Lest the rude brambles overtop the corn.

(Wr. by 1746; pub. 1751)

143   *Mira's Will*

IMPRIMIS—My departed shade I trust
To heaven—My body to the silent dust;
My name to public censure I submit,
To be disposed of as the world thinks fit;
My vice and folly let oblivion close,
The world already is o'erstocked with those;
My wit I give, as misers give their store,
To those who think they had enough before.
Bestow my patience to compose the lives
Of slighted virgins and neglected wives;   10
To modish lovers I resign my truth,
My cool reflection to unthinking youth;
And some good-nature give ('tis my desire)
To surly husbands, as their needs require;
And first discharge my funeral—and then
To the small poets I bequeath my pen.

posset] hot milk curdled with ale or wine

Let a small sprig (true emblem of my rhyme)
Of blasted laurel on my hearse recline;
Let some grave wight, that struggles for renown
By chanting dirges through a market-town,   20
With gentle step precede the solemn train;
A broken flute upon his arm shall lean.
Six comic poets may the corse surround,
And all free-holders, if they can be found:
Then follow next the melancholy throng,
As shrewd instructors, who themselves are wrong:
The virtuoso, rich in sun-dried weeds,
The politician, whom no mortal heeds,
The silent lawyer, chambered all the day,
And the stern soldier that receives no pay.   30
But stay—the mourners should be first our care:
Let the freed 'prentice lead the miser's heir;
Let the young relict wipe her mournful eye,
And widowed husbands o'er their garlic cry.

All this let my executors fulfil,
And rest assured that this is Mira's will,
Who was, when she these legacies designed,
In body healthy, and composed in mind.

(Wr. by 1746; pub. 1748)

144   *An Epistle to a Lady*

IN vain, dear Madam, yes, in vain you strive,
Alas! to make your luckless Mira thrive,
For Tycho and Copernicus agree,
No golden planet bent its rays on me.

'Tis twenty winters, if it is no more,
To speak the truth it may be twenty-four:
As many springs their 'pointed space have run,
Since Mira's eyes first opened on the sun.
'Twas when the flocks on slabby hillocks lie,
And the cold Fishes rule the watry sky: 10
But though these eyes the learnèd page explore,
And turn the ponderous volumes o'er and o'er,
I find no comfort from their systems flow,
But am dejected more as more I know.

144 slabby] damp, muddy

Hope shines a while, but like a vapour flies
(The fate of all the curious and the wise),
For, ah! cold Saturn triumphed on that day,
And frowning Sol denied his golden ray.

You see I'm learnèd, and I show't the more,   20
That none may wonder when they find me poor.
Yet Mira dreams, as slumbering poets may,
And rolls in treasures till the breaking day,
While books and pictures in bright order rise,
And painted parlours swim before her eyes:
Till the shrill clock impertinently rings,
And the soft visions move their shining wings:
Then Mira wakes—her pictures are no more,
And through her fingers slides the vanished ore.
Convinced too soon, her eye unwilling falls
On the blue curtains and the dusty walls: 30
She wakes, alas! to business and to woes,
To sweep her kitchen, and to mend her clothes.

But see pale Sickness with her languid eyes,
At whose appearance all delusion flies:
The world recedes, its vanities decline,
Clorinda's features seem as faint as mine;
Gay robes no more the aching sight admires,
Wit grates the ear, and melting music tires.
Its wonted pleasures with each sense decay,
Books please no more, and paintings fade away,   40
The sliding joys in misty vapours end:
Yet let me still, ah! let me grasp a friend:
And when each joy, when each loved object flies,
Be you the last that leaves my closing eyes.

But how will this dismantled soul appear,
When stripped of all it lately held so dear,
Forced from its prison of expiring clay,
Afraid and shivering at the doubtful way?

Yet did these eyes a dying parent see,
Loosed from all cares except a thought for me,   50
Without a tear resign her shortening breath,
And dauntless meet the lingering stroke of death.
Then at th' Almighty's sentence shall I mourn,
'Of dust thou art, to dust shalt thou return'?
Or shall I wish to stretch the line of fate,
That the dull years may bear a longer date,

To share the follies of succeeding times
With more vexations and with deeper crimes?
Ah no—though heaven brings near the final day,
For such a life I will not, dare not pray;   60
But let the tear for future mercy flow,
And fall resigned beneath the mighty blow.
Nor I alone—for through the spacious ball,
With me will numbers of all ages fall:
And the same day that Mira yields her breath,
Thousands may enter through the gates of death.

(Wr. by 1746; pub. 1748)

ELIZABETH TEFT
(*fl.* 1741–7)

Little is known of 'Elizabeth Teft of Lincoln', except that she published *Orinthia's Miscellanies* in London in 1747. She professed diffidence about publication, but in one poem (pp. 7–8) imagines a male friend assuring her that allowance would be made for her 'want of learning', that 'Some will indulge you for your Sex's Sake', and that 'Illit'rate Duck' was an encouraging precedent. She had in fact already in September 1741 contributed anonymously to the *Gentleman's Magazine* 'Orinthia's Plea to the Gentlemen of Fortune', which she reprinted, with associated verse, in 1747. The poem humorously begged the 'generous Great' to help make her fortune by buying lottery-tickets for her. The *Magazine* took this suggestion seriously, requested her address and, in October and November 1741, announced that 'J. Hazard', 'Loveworth', and a syndicate of other gentlemen had purchased tickets for her. In July 1742, replying to 'The Batchelor's Address' in the previous month, she announced that she had had no luck in the lottery, 'mourns her humble state, | And rests content to be unfortunate' (pp. 328, 384).

  She was presumably a relative of the only Teft to appear in the admissions registers of Oxford or Cambridge: John Teft of Tealby, Lincs., who entered Magdalene College, Cambridge in 1716 aged 20, and was ordained a deacon at Lincoln in 1720 and a priest in 1724. Local historians in Lincoln who have kindly searched the records there have not so far been able to produce further information about her.

145   *On Learning. Desired by a Gentleman*

WELL, Ignorance, the cause is yet unknown
Why thou'rt confined unto my sex alone.
Why are not girls, as boys, sent forth when young
To learn the Latin, Greek and Hebrew tongue?

ball] globe, world

I the first founders of great Rome would know,
Their funeral piles, their mounting eagles too,
Would trace through Greece, through Athens and old Troy;
For potent wonders give a reason why;
Search out the nature of all things below,
From what great causes dire effects do flow;   10
In conference with deathless Homer be,
And Virgil's thoughts, and Milton's poetry;
Study the actions of the bravest men,
Copy their worth, and shine as bright as them.
Good, great and brave, these are such envied charms,
Me, hero-like, a martial spirit warms.
And yet, methinks, I would not be a man.
No, not to put imperial purple on:
I'd rather be the foolish thing I am.
Our sex against you justly may exclaim,   20
To link our knowledge to so short a chain.
Cowards, you fear, had we full lengths to run,
We should eclipse your starlight with our sun.
We in their native dress our thoughts impart,
Yours decked with learning, and adorned with art.
Every error generously excuse:
Consider, Sir, a simple virgin's muse.

(1747)

146   *On Viewing Herself in a Glass*

WAS Nature angry when she formed my clay?
Or, urged by haste to finish, could not stay?
Or dressed with all her store some perfect she,
So lavish there, she'd none to spare for me?
I oft converse with those she's deemed to grace
With air and shape, fine mien, and charming face:
When self-surveyed, the glass hears this reply:
'Dear! what a strange, unpolished thing am I!'
Not that I think it hard, or once upbraid;
Conscious I am that transient charms will fade.   10
Not but, ye fair, your beauty gives delight:
'Tis pleasing, wond'rous pleasing to the sight.
Since here defective, Heaven, be so kind
With never-fading charms to dress my mind!

(1747)

147 *On Snuff-Taking*

CUSTOM, in this small article I find
What strong ascendance thou hast o'er the mind.
My friend's advice the first inducements were:
'Take it,' said she, 'it will your spirits cheer.'
All resolute the offered drug to take,
But in the trial sickened with my hate.
By repetition I was brought to bear,
Then rather liked, now love it too, too dear.
Be careful, oh, my soul! how thou let'st in
The baneful poison of repeated sin;   10
Never be intimate with any crime,
Lest Custom makes it amiable in time.

(1747)

148 *To a Gentleman who disordered a Lady's*
Handkerchief, and immediately cut his Thumb

YOUR punishment is just, you must confess,
'Cause you the rules of chastity transgress.
Good heaven saw, and did the sight detest,
An impious hand upon a virgin's breast.
To expiate the fault that hand had done,
Blood runs in torrents from your wounded thumb;
Let this deter you from an act so rude,
Lest serpents sting you, when you next intrude.

(1747)

CHARLOTTE LENNOX (née RAMSAY)
(1729?–1804)

Confusion has been caused by her statements to the Royal Literary Fund at the end
of her life that she was born in 1720 and that her father had been Governor of New
York, both perhaps intended to enhance her claims on the Fund's benevolence. She
was the daughter of James Ramsay, an army officer, who was sent to Gibraltar in
1727, where she may have been born in about 1729. By the late 1730s he was Captain
of an Independent Company of Foot in New York Province, where she spent some
years of her childhood in the Albany area, which is described in her first and last
novels, *Harriot Stuart* (1750) and *Euphemia* (1790). Her father died in about 1743

148 Handkerchief] i.e. neck-covering

and, aged about 15, she came to England, leaving behind her mother. An aunt with whom she had planned to live turned out to be senile, but she was patronized by the Countess of Rockingham and her sister Lady Isabella Finch, to whom she dedicated her *Poems on Several Occasions. Written by a Young Lady* (1747). In October 1747 she married Alexander Lennox, a Scotsman said to have been employed by William Strahan, the eminent printer, but he was indigent and unreliable, and she had in effect to support herself, and later her children, by her own efforts. Between 1748 and 1750 she took unsuccessfully to the stage, Horace Walpole describing her in September 1748 as 'a poetess, and a deplorable actress'. Thereafter she lived by her pen.

She soon acquired some important male supporters in the literary world and between 1749 and 1751 there is evidence of an organized campaign to promote a new volume of her verse in the *Gentleman's Magazine* (reprints of her earlier poems, poems addressed to her, a new ode on the Princess of Wales' birthday), but, like all similar efforts in later years, the subscription came to nothing. One key to her problems as a writer is apparently her capacity for offending influential literary women and an increasingly decorous female readership. Her 'Art of Coquetry' offended Elizabeth Carter, who was 'much scandalised' by its 'doctrine'. Her first novel, *Harriot Stuart* (1750), greeted by a famous all-night party organized by her friend Samuel Johnson, contained a tactless satiric portrait of her patroness Lady Isabella Finch (readily identified by Lady Mary Wortley Montagu when she read the novel in 1752).

Samuel Richardson met her through Johnson (with whom he thought her a great favourite) and the two men pressurized a reluctant Andrew Millar to publish her one popular novel, *The Female Quixote* (1752). It was much admired, notably in the *Covent-Garden Journal* of 24 March 1752 by Henry Fielding, who later referred to her in his *Journal of a Voyage to Lisbon* (1754) as 'shamefully distress'd'. Other male friends at this period were the Earl of Orrery and Giuseppe Baretti, the Italian author, but a renewed attempt to launch the subscription edition of her poems in 1752 evidently failed once more, and for much of the 1750s she lived by undertaking a series of arduous translations of French works, although she also published *Shakespear Illustrated* (3 vols., 1752–3), a collection of source materials in which Johnson took much interest, and *Henrietta* (1758), another novel. As he remained until his death, Johnson was a remarkably loyal friend, often 'at her elbow' in these years, supplying dedications and other contributions to her books, and doing his best to further her career by advice and publicity.

While editing *The Ladies Monthly* (11 nos., 1760–1), she referred in a letter to the Duchess of Newcastle of October 1760 to a recent illness, and to her 'present slavery to the Booksellers, whom I have the mortification to see adding to their heaps by my labours, which scarce produce me a scanty and precarious subsistence'. Later in the decade the Duchess obtained a post in the Customs and an apartment in Somerset House for her husband, where for a time they lived with their two children, Harriot (b. 1765) and George (b. 1771). But there are repeated references to her 'great distress', from which she must have known only a successful subscription or a theatrical success, rather than the translations and fiction she continued to publish, would effectively relieve her. *The Sisters*, a play adapted from her novel *Henrietta*, for which Goldsmith provided an epilogue, received only a single performance at Covent Garden in 1769. In 1774 she failed to interest Garrick in a translation of Racine's *Bajazet*, but he did produce her *Old City Manners*, an adaptation of *Eastwood Hoe* by Jonson, Marston, and Chapman, at Drury Lane in 1775, and it ran long enough to earn her a benefit night.

Plans in 1773 for a subscription edition of *The Female Quixote*, to be illustrated by Sir Joshua Reynolds, and in 1775 for an edition of her *Original Works*, for which Johnson as usual wrote the proposals, both came to nothing. The repeated failures of her subscription schemes seem in part to have been due to her indecorous manners and habits. Fanny Burney reports Mrs Thrale saying of Mrs Lennox in 1778 that 'tho' her books are generally approved, nobody likes her'. Laetitia-Matilda Hawkins later described the 'want of all order and method, all decorum of appearance, and regularity of proceeding' in her household, and told a story of a 'low female servant' taking her to court because of the 'ill words and hard blows' she had received from her mistress. The Lennox papers which came to light in 1965 contain letters from John Murray, the bookseller, declining to solicit Lady Gower to patronize *The Sisters* in 1769, and from Lady Bute refusing the dedication of *Old City Manners* in 1775. That she may have been too insistent and tactless in her demands for patronage is suggested by a letter from Johnson in the same year about her latest subscription scheme, warning her not to demand too much from her fashionable acquaintance, nor to expect Reynolds to solicit his aristocratic sitters on her behalf, and, revealingly, assuring her that disapproval of her character was unlikely to harm her subscription, since her 'manners as far as the publick needs to know are very elegant and ladylike', the point presumably being precisely that they were not. A curious undated note among her papers, offered as a 'hint from a friend', advised her that several ladies who had recently met her had been offended by her personal uncleanliness. Even Johnson, who could call her 'Dearest Partlet', visit her cottage in Marylebone to eat apple-dumplings, and tolerate the noise made by her small son, had at times to point out her shortcomings and rebuke her for writing hurtful letters to her friends.

Things did not improve in the 1780s. Johnson, her mentor for over thirty years, died in 1784, not long after the death of her daughter at the age of about 18. Her son George, after signs of precocious literary talent, was, she said, later driven to 'desperation by a most unnatural father' and then deserted in 'dreadful circumstances'. The astonishment which greeted Boswell's revelation in 1791 that Johnson had thought her abilities superior to those of Carter, More, and Burney may have been small compensation for her growing problems. She separated from her husband in 1792 (he died in 1797) and in the following year William Beloe and others obtained grants for her from the newly founded Royal Literary Fund to enable her to send her son George to relatives in America. By then she had published her last novel *Euphemia* (1790) and was planning a subscription edition of her *Shakespear Illustrated*, for which Boswell had agreed to write the proposals. Subscriptions were received but the edition did not appear, to the indignation of the fashionable ladies who had collected names for her. Thereafter, she published no more. (*The History of Sir George Warrington* (1797), in which the hero goes mad after reading Paine's *Rights of Man*, was falsely attributed to her on the title-page.) On 20 January 1802 Lady Chambers wrote to the Royal Literary Fund, describing Mrs Lennox's 'great distress for the common necessaries of life', after which a series of regular payments were made to her. She died in Dean's Yard, Westminster, on 4 January 1804 at the age of about 75.

149   *A Song*

> WHAT torments must the virgin prove
> That feels the pangs of hopeless love.
> What endless cares must rack the breast
> That is by sure despair possessed.
>
> When love in tender bosoms reigns,
> With all its soft, its pleasing pains,
> Why should it be a crime to own
> The fatal flame we cannot shun?
>
> The soul by nature formed sincere
> A slavish forced disguise must wear,   10
> Lest the unthinking world reprove
> The heart that glows with generous love.
>
> But oh! in vain the sigh's repressed,
> That gently heaves the pensive breast,
> The glowing blush, the falling tear,
> The conscious wish, and silent fear.
>
> Ye soft betrayers, aid my flame,
> And give my new desires a name;
> Some power my gentle griefs redress,
> Reveal, or make my passion less.   20

                                    (1747)

150   from *The Art of Coquetry*

> FIRST form your artful looks with studious care,
> From mild to grave, from tender to severe.
> Oft on the careless youth your glances dart,
> A tender meaning let each glance impart.
> Whene'er he meets your looks, with modest pride
> And soft confusion turn your eyes aside,
> Let a soft sigh steal out, as if by chance,
> Then cautious turn, and steal another glance.
> Caught by these arts, with pride and hope elate,
> The destined victim rushes on his fate: 10
> Pleased, his imagined victory pursues,
> And the kind maid with soft attention views,
> Contemplates now her shape, her air, her face,
> And thinks each feature wears an added grace;

Till gratitude, which first his bosom proves,
By slow degrees sublimed, at length he loves.
'Tis harder still to fix than gain a heart;
What's won by beauty must be kept by art.
Too kind a treatment the blest lover cloys,
And oft despair the growing flame destroys: 20
Sometimes with smiles receive him, sometimes tears,
And wisely balance both his hopes and fears.
Perhaps he mourns his ill-requited pains,
Condemns your sway, and strives to break his chains;
Behaves as if he now your scorn defied,
And thinks at least he shall alarm your pride:
But with indifference view the seeming change,
And let your eyes to seek new conquests range;
While his torn breast with jealous fury burns,
He hopes, despairs, adores and hates by turns;   30
With anguish now repents the weak deceit,
And powerful passion bears him to your feet.

(1747)

HENRIETTA KNIGHT (née ST JOHN), LADY LUXBOROUGH
(1699–1756)

She was the only daughter of Henry, Viscount St John and his wife Angelica
Magdalene Pillesoy. She was half-sister to Henry St John, Viscount Bolingbroke,
whom she visited during his exile in France after 1714. In 1727 she married
Bolingbroke's friend Robert Knight of Barrells, Warwickshire, who became Baron
Luxborough in 1745. His father had been Cashier to the South Sea Company and
had absconded to France after the crash of 1720. She reluctantly spent much time
after her marriage in France, keeping house for her father-in-law and his invalid
wife. She had a son and two daughters, but in 1736 was accused of adultery with John
Dalton, clergyman and poet, who was then tutor to the son of her close friend the
Countess of Hertford (see nos. 77–8). (Verses to each other by Mrs Knight, Lady
Hertford, and Dalton are preserved in the Countess's Commonplace Book.) Horace
Walpole later described Mrs Knight as 'a high-coloured lusty black woman', who
'fell in love with Parson Dalton for his poetry, and they rhymed together till they
chimed'. A legal separation from her husband followed and she was forbidden to see
her children, to correspond with Lady Hertford, to live outside England or within
twenty miles of London. She was allowed to live at Barrells at Wootton Wawen, the
delapidated family residence, where by one account she had an illegitimate daughter.
    Lord Bolingbroke, who believed in her misconduct with Dalton, eventually
secured some alleviation of these conditions in 1742. She resumed correspondence
with Lady Hertford, who was surprised by a visit in 1743 from Mrs Knight, 'who has
been so long a prisoner, and I am convinced upon a false accusation'. She thought

that her friend's misfortunes had been caused by her 'light and giddy' behaviour and was disappointed to find that 'she is the same person she was ten, nay twenty, years ago, her dress as French, her manner as thoughtless'. At Barrells Mrs Knight occupied herself with building and gardening, converting a dairy into a library and erecting a summerhouse containing busts of Pope, Dryden, Milton, Shakespeare, Newton, Locke, and Bolingbroke. From 1739 she corresponded with the poet William Shenstone, some fifteen miles away at The Leasowes, about gardening and literature. Shenstone increasingly used her as an audience for his verse, and was in turn responsible for the appearance of four of her poems in Dodsley's *Collection* in 1755, disconcerting her by arranging this without her permission. Having become Lady Luxborough in 1745, she died in 1756. Her *Letters to William Shenstone* were published in 1775 and more were included in Thomas Hull's *Select Letters between the late Duchess of Somerset, Lady Luxborough, William Shenstone and Others* (2 vols., 1778). Walpole commented on the first collection that 'she does not write ill, or, as I expected, affectedly, like a woman', but 'She had no spirit, no wit, knew no events; she idolizes poor Shenstone, who was scarce above her, and flatters him, to be flattered'.

151 *Written to a near Neighbour in a tempestuous Night*
1748

> YOU bid my muse not cease to sing,
>   You bid my ink not cease to flow;
> Then say it ever shall be spring,
>   And boisterous winds shall never blow:
> When you such miracles can prove,
> I'll sing of friendship, or of love.
>
> But now, alone, by storms oppressed,
>   Which harshly in my ears resound;
> No cheerful voice with witty jest,
>   No jocund pipe, to still the sound;   10
> Untrained beside in verse-like art,
> How shall my pen express my heart?
>
> In vain I call th' harmonious Nine,
>   In vain implore Apollo's aid;
> Obdurate, they refuse a line,
>   While spleen and care my rest invade.
> Say, shall we Morpheus next implore,
> And try if dreams befriend us more?
>
> Wisely at least he'll stop my pen,
>   And with his poppies crown my brow: 20
> Better by far in lonesome den
>   To sleep unheard-of—than to glow

With treacherous wildfire of the brain,
Th' intoxicated poet's bane.

(Wr. 1748; pub. 1755)

152   *The Bullfinch in Town*

HARK to the blackbird's pleasing note,
    Sweet usher of the vocal throng!
Nature directs his warbling note,
    And all that hear admire the song.

Yon bullfinch, with unvaried tone,
    Of cadence harsh, and accent shrill,
Has brighter plumage to atone
    For want of harmony and skill.

Yet, discontent with nature's boon,
    Like man, to mimic art he flies;
On opera-pinions hoping soon
    Unrivalled he shall mount the skies.

And while, to please some courtly fair,
    He one dull tune with labour learns,
A well-gilt cage remote from air,
    And faded plumes, is all he earns!

Go, hapless captive! still repeat
    The sounds which nature never taught;
Go, listening fair! and call them sweet,
    Because you know them dearly bought.   20

Unenvied both! go hear and sing
    Your studied music o'er and o'er;
Whilst I attend th' inviting spring,
    In fields where birds unfettered soar.

(1755)

ESTHER LEWIS (later CLARK)
(*fl.* 1747–89)

The daughter of the Revd Mr Lewis of Holt in Wiltshire, she was contributing poetry
to the *Bath Journal* under the name of 'Sylvia' by 1749. She became friendly with Dr
Samuel Bowden, a physician at Frome, who seems to have attended her when she

had smallpox and who was also a prolific contributor of verse to the *Bath Journal*. Their poems were reprinted from time to time in the London periodicals, including Bowden's 'To a Young Lady at Holt on her late Ingenious Poems' in the *Gentleman's Magazine* (1749), 179. Bowden was a tireless champion of the 'celebrated *Sylvia* of Holt' and included some of her verses in his own *Poems on Various Subjects* (Bath, 1754). The first of her poems given below, probably addressed to Bowden, shows that she had a defiant sense of herself as a writer, but her views on marriage were basically conservative. Her 'Advice to a Young Lady lately married', originally in the *Bath Journal* in 1752, was often reprinted in periodicals in the following decades and is also found in commonplace-books of the period. The third poem is addressed to Sarah Fielding, the novelist and sister of Henry Fielding, whom she had probably met at Bath, where Miss Fielding later settled. In about 1760 Esther Lewis married Robert Clark of Tetbury. She had been married for nearly thirty years when she collected her *Poems Moral and Entertaining* (Bath, 1789) for the benefit of charities in Bath and Gloucester and of Sunday Schools in Tetbury.

153 *A Mirror for Detractors. Addressed to a Friend*

THIS wit was with experience bought
(And that's the best of wit, 'tis thought),
That when a woman dares indite,
And seek in print the public sight,
All tongues are presently in motion
About her person, mind, and portion;
And every blemish, every fault,
Unseen before, to light is brought.
Nay, generously they take the trouble
Those blemishes and faults to double.   10

Whene'er you chance her name to hear,
With a contemptuous, smiling sneer,
A prude exclaims, 'O, she's a wit!'
And I've observed that epithet
Means self-conceit, ill-nature, pride,
And fifty hateful things beside.

The men are mighty apt to say,
'This silly girl has lost her way;
No doubt she thinks we must admire
And such a rhyming wit desire;   20
But here her folly does appear,
We never choose a learned fair,
Nor like to see a woman try
With our superior parts to vie.
She ought to mind domestic cares,
The sex were made for such affairs.

She'd better take in hand the needle,
And not pretend to rhyme and riddle.
Shall women thus usurp the pen?
That weapon nature made for men.
Presumptuous thing! how did she dare
This implement from us to tear?

'In short, if women are allowed
(Women by nature vain and proud)
Thus boldly on the press to seize,
And say in print whate'er they please,
They'll soon their lawful lords despise,
And think themselves as Sybils wise.'

Thus far the men their wit display;
Let's hear now what the women say.

Now we'll suppose a tattling set
Of females o'er tea-table met,
While from its time-consuming streams
Arise a hundred idle themes,
Of fans, of flounces, flies, and faces,
Of lap-dogs, lovers, lawns and laces.
At length this well-known foe to fame
In luckless hour brings forth my name;
Then all exclaim with great good-nature,
'O Lord! that witty, rhyming creature!'
Alternate then their parts sustain:
'Pray, don't you think she's mighty vain?',
Says one; 'No doubt,' another cries;
'Vain, Lord, of what?', a third replies;
'What though suppose the thing can rhyme,
And on the changing numbers chime,
No merit lies in that, 'tis plain,
And others, if they were as vain,
I make no doubt could write as well,
Would they but try, perhaps excel.'

Then thus Philantha, in whose breast
Good-nature is a constant guest:
'I own I've heard before, with pain,
Some people call her proud and vain;
I know her well, yet ne'er could see
This mighty pride and vanity.'

'You, Madam, are, I find, her friend;
But I can never apprehend
She ever yet a poem penned.
They're all another's works, no doubt,   70
With which she makes this mighty rout.'

'That's very like, but, Miss, suppose
She does the tedious stuff compose,
Yet for my part, though some may praise,
And stick the creature out with bays,
I can see nothing in the scrawls,
That for such vast encomiums calls.
'Tis true, in length if merit lies,
From all she'll bear away the prize.

'This for her poems may be said,   80
They're mighty good to lull the head;
For nothing there piquant you'll find,
To raise a laugh, or rouse the mind.
No doctor's opiate can exceed 'em,
Whene'er I want a nap I read 'em.'

Philantha then—' 'Tis so well known
That all those poems are her own,
I wonder anyone can doubt it,
Or have a single thought about it,
And oft I've heard the lines commended;   90
Then all allow they're well intended.'

'That may perhaps be true enough;
But who's the better for her stuff?
I see no difference in the times,
The world's not mended by her rhymes.
She to the men, I apprehend,
Intends herself to recommend
By scribbling verses, but she'll find
They don't so much regard the mind;
For though they're civil to her face,   100
'Tis all a farce, and mere grimace;
Her back once turned, I've heard 'em swear
They hated wisdom in the fair.

'Then she's so nice and so refined
About the morals, and the mind,
That really, Madam, I'm afraid
This rhyming wit will die a maid;

And if she weds, it is high time,
I think she's almost past her prime.
Why, with the men, as I've been told,   110
She'll paper-conversation hold.'

    'Madam, that's fact, I long have known it,
Without a blush I've heard her own it.'

    'Good Lord! some women are so bold,
I vow I blush to hear it told;
I hate censoriousness, but when
Girls freely correspond with men,
I can't forbear to speak my mind,
Although to scandal ne'er inclined.
Well, I protest I never yet   120
To any man a letter writ;
It may be innocent, 'tis true,
But 'tis a thing I ne'er could do.'

    'Well,' cried Philantha, 'I protest
I almost think you are in jest,
For really, Miss, I cannot see
In this the breach of modesty;
With men we chat away our time,
And none regard it as a crime;
And where's the difference, if we write: 130
'Tis but our words in black and white.
I think we may, without offence,
Converse by pen with men of sense.'

    'Well, let us say no more about her,
But entertain ourselves without her;
No harm I meant, nor none I wish;
Miss, won't you drink another dish?'
'Not one drop more, I thank you, Madam.'
'Here, take away the tea-things, Adam.
And bring the cards, and since we're met,   140
Pray let us make at whist a set.'

    Thus tea and scandal, cards and fashion,
Destroy the time of half the nation.

    But, Sir, methinks 'tis very hard
From pen and ink to be debarred:
Are simple women only fit
To dress, to darn, to flower, or knit,
To mind the distaff, or the spit?

Why are the needle and the pen
Thought incompatible by men?   150
May we not sometimes use the quill,
And yet be careful housewives still?
Why is it thought in us a crime
To utter common sense in rhyme?
Why must each rhymer be a wit?
Why marked with that loathed epithet?
For envy, hatred, scorn, or fear
To wit, you know, is often near.
Good-natured wit, polite, refined,
Which seeks to please, not pain the mind, 160
How rare to find! for O, how few
Have true and generous wit like you!
Your mind in different mould was cast,
To raise a character, not blast;
Pleased to encourage what I write,
And smile upon my humble flight.

       (Wr. 1748; pub. 1754)

154 *Advice to a Young Lady lately married*

DEAR Peggy, since the single state
You've left, and chose yourself a mate;
Since metamorphosed to a wife,
And bliss or woe's ensured for life,
A friendly muse the way would show
To gain the bliss, and miss the woe.
But first of all, I must suppose
You've with mature reflection chose;
And this premised, I think you may
Here find to married bliss the way.   10

 Small is the province of a wife,
And narrow is her sphere in life;
Within that sphere to move aright
Should be her principal delight;
To guide the house with prudent care,
And properly to spend and spare;
To make her husband bless the day
He gave his liberty away;
To form the tender infant mind:
These are the tasks to wives assigned; 20
Then never think domestic care
Beneath the notice of the fair;

But matters every day inspect,
That naught be wasted by neglect.
Be frugal plenty round you seen,
And always keep the golden mean.

Be always clean, but seldom fine,
Let decent neatness round you shine;
If once fair decency be fled,
Love soon deserts the genial bed.   30

Not nice your house, though neat and clean;
In all things there's a proper mean.
Some of our sex mistake in this,
Too anxious some, some too remiss.

The early days of wedded life
Are oft o'ercast by childish strife;
Then be it your peculiar care
To keep that season bright and fair;
For then's the time by gentle art
To fix your empire in his heart.   40
With kind, obliging carriage strive
To keep the lamp of love alive;
For should it through neglect expire,
No art again can light the fire.

To charm his reason dress your mind,
Till love shall be with friendship joined;
Raised on that basis, 'twill endure,
From time and death itself secure.

Be sure you ne'er for power contend,
Nor try by tears to gain your end;   50
Sometimes the tears which cloud your eyes
From pride and obstinacy rise.
Heaven gave to man superior sway,
Then heaven and him at once obey.
Let sullen frowns your brow ne'er cloud;
Be always cheerful, never loud;
Let trifles never discompose
Your features, temper, or repose.

Abroad for happiness ne'er roam;
True happiness resides at home;   60
Still make your partner easy there
(Man finds abroad sufficient care).

If everything at home be right,
He'll always enter with delight;
Your converse he'll prefer to all
Those cheats the world does pleasure call;
With cheerful chat his cares beguile,
And always meet him with a smile.

   Should passion e'er his soul deform,
Serenely meet the bursting storm;   70
Never in wordy war engage,
Nor ever meet his rage with rage.
With all our sex's softening art
Recall lost reason to his heart;
Thus calm the tempest in his breast,
And sweetly soothe his soul to rest.

   Be sure you ne'er arraign his sense;
Few husbands pardon that offence;
'Twill discord raise, disgust it breeds,
And hatred certainly succeeds.   80
Then shun, O shun that fatal shelf,
Still think him wiser than yourself;
And if you otherwise would b'lieve,
Ne'er let him such a thought perceive.

   When cares invade your partner's heart,
Bear you a sympathising part,
And kindly claim your share of pain,
And half his troubles still sustain;
From morn to noon, from noon to night,
To see him pleased your chief delight.   90

   But now, methinks, I hear you cry,
'Shall she pretend, O vanity!
To lay down rules for wedded life,
Who never was herself a wife?'

   I own you've ample cause to chide,
And blushing throw the pen aside.

(1752)

155   from *A Letter to a Lady* [Sarah Fielding]
                      in London

YOU midst gay crowds reside, I, hid in shades,
Rove by the mazy stream through flowery meads;
Ah! flowery, did I say? alas! no more
Those meads with spangled robes are covered o'er;
Their leafy honours from the groves are torn,
And down the winding stream impetuous borne:
The painted birds forsake the naked wood,
And seek in hospitable yards their food;
The purling rills, that o'er the pebbles mourned,
Are now to deep and rapid currents turned;   10
Soft Philomela now no more complains,
Nor tells her woeful tale in pensive strains;
An universal change around appears,
The dreary face of winter nature wears.

    Exalted now on iron stilts I move,
Through dirt, with cane supported, fearless rove,
Till rooted deep upon the yielding plain,
A breathing monument awhile remain,
To warn each wandering she my fate to shun,
Nor such defiling, dirty hazards run.   20

    At length returning to my humble cell,
Closed in with dirt, at home contented dwell;
Now think, work, read, then write a line or two,
Talk, hear, then take a pinch, and think on you;
For still the snuff-box shines with golden grace,
Nor does one scratch its polished charms deface;
Still well replenished with ambrosial dust,
Breathing rich odours fresh as at the first,
Though many a pinch each day the nose regales,
And well supplies the loss of fragrant vales.   30

    Thus time, beneath whose mighty, ponderous weight
So many wretches groan, I still find light.
Such generously upon their friends bestow
A heavy thing they know not where to throw;
But lest you of this tribe should think me one,
I'm sure 'tis best in prudence to have done,

Nor rob you of your better managed time,
Nor tire your patience with my tedious rhyme;
And am, with every compliment which due is,
Your most obedient servant, ESTHER LEWIS.   40

(Wr. *c.*1758; pub. 1789)

CATHERINE JEMMAT (née YEO)
(*fl.* 1750–66)

She was born in Exeter, the daughter of Capt. John Yeo, who later moved to Plymouth. Her mother died when she was 5 and, within a few weeks, her father married 'a giggling girl of nineteen', by whom he had five further children. With her father often away at sea, and neglected by her stepmother, she was for a time educated with her sister at a boarding-school. Temperamentally rebellious, she had (by her own account) a stream of admirers, including naval officers, and may have damaged her reputation more seriously than her *Memoirs* admit. Eventually—'not for love indeed, but to avoid the persecutions of a too rigid father, whose behaviour was insupportable'—she impulsively married an apparently prosperous Plymouth silk-mercer named Jemmat, by whom she had a daughter. He turned out to be a violent, debt-ridden drunkard, who within three years was bankrupt. At this point, according to her *Memoirs*, she was 'thrown upon the wide world for support'.

Apart from the fact that her father died on 9 November 1756 'as a rear admiral on half pay', little verifiable information about her has survived. By 1760 she was circulating proposals for her *Memoirs*, which would contain 'a Variety of affecting and entertaining Occurrences', while adhering 'strictly to the Rules prescribed by that great Mistress TRUTH'. She had been driven reluctantly into authorship by 'a mighty disagreeable Companion . . . Misfortune'. On 14 July 1760 she sent a copy of her proposals to the Duke of Newcastle, begging him 'to assist in raiseing her above some distresses, which have for a long time past pressed heavy upon her and from which this Method is her only resource'. She enclosed a list of aristocratic and military subscribers who had already promised their half-guineas, including 'a great many Captns. of the Navy'. In the dedication of her *Memoirs* (2 vols., 1762; later editions, 1765, 1771) to the Duke of York, she described herself as 'the daughter of an English admiral, labouring under the misconceived prejudice of friends, and the still worse misrepresentations of designing enemies'.

Her *Memoirs*, in which no dates are given, appear to cover her life only to the later 1740s. Her later book, *Miscellanies in Prose and Verse* (1766), contains several poems referring to events and persons in Dublin, implying that she lived there in the early 1750s. On the other hand, her admission to her subscribers in 1766 that, to fill her quarto volume, she had included poems by 'a friend or two, and even some which perhaps have made their appearance in public before', may cast doubt on her authorship of any particular poem. 'The Rural Lass' had appeared in the *Gentleman's Magazine* in 1750, and other poems already printed, such as 'Fanny Careless' in the *Gentleman's Magazine* (1754), p. 479, and 'Question on the Art of Writing' in Dodsley's *Collection*, vi (1758), 196, were conceivably the work of other hands.

What seems clear is that by the 1760s she was dependent on a number of aristocratic patrons, to whose benevolence the destitute daughter of an English admiral would make a strong appeal. A poem in her *Memoirs*, addressed to 'a very beneficent Nobleman', begs 'A slender annual pittance'. At the same time, it seems that her reputation had been damaged in some irretrievable way. It is noticeable that twenty-three of the subscribers to her *Memoirs* sheltered in the unusual anonymity of asterisks. A prose essay, 'In Vindication of the Female Sex', in *Miscellanies* (1766) suggests an explanation. It protests at the 'perpetual odium' attaching to a woman guilty of 'a young and inconsiderate attachment to the practice of debauchery', while male reputation is unaffected by 'the most lewd and debauched actions' (pp. 101–8).

Other mysteries surround her. The recent death of 'Mrs. Jemmatt, daughter of the late Admiral Yeo, who published her own memoirs, some-time since' was reported in the *London Magazine*, 35 (Nov. 1766), 599. In the Bodleian copy of her *Miscellanies*, the date has been altered by pen to 1768, and some sixty names added by hand to the original subscribers' list. Similar emendations and additions appear in other copies. In 1771 the *Miscellanies* were reprinted with an entirely new list of subscribers. Unless her death had been misreported, someone, perhaps her daughter, had continued to obtain additional subscriptions to 'new' editions of Catherine Jemmat's works. More hard evidence about her career is much needed.

156   *The Rural Lass*

MY father and mother (what ails 'em?)
    Pretend I'm too young to be wed;
They expect, but in troth I shall fail 'em,
    That I finish my chairs and my bed.

Provided our minds are but cheery,
    Wooden chairs wonnot argue a glove,
Any bed will hold me and my deary,
    The main chance in wedlock is love.

My father, when asked if he'd lend us
    An horse to the parson to ride,   10
In a wheel-barrow offered to send us,
    And John for the footman beside.

Would we never had asked him, for, whip it!
    To the church though two miles and a half,
Twice as far 'twere a pleasure to trip it;
    But then how the people would laugh!

The neighbours are nettled most sadly,
    'Was e'er such a forward bold thing!
Sure never girl acted so madly!'
    Through the parish these backbitings ring.   20

Yet I will be married tomorrow,
    And charming young Harry's the man;
My brother's blind nag we can borrow,
    And he may prevent us that can.

Not waiting for parents' consenting,
    My brother took Nell of the Green,
Yet both, far enough from repenting,
    Now live like a king and a queen.

Pray when will your gay things of London
    Produce such a strapper as Nell's?   30
There wives by their husbands are undone,
    As Saturday's newspaper tells.

Poll Barnley said, over and over,
    I soon should be left in the lurch;
For Harry, she knows, was a rover,
    And never would venture to church.

And I know the sorrows that wound her;
    He courted her once, he confessed:
With another too great when he found her,
    He bid her take him she liked best.   40

But all that are like her, or would be,
    May learn from my Harry and me,
If maids would be maids while they should be,
    How faithful their sweethearts would be.

My mother says clothing and feeding
    Will soon make me sick of a brat:
But though I prove sick in my breeding,
    I care not a farthing for that.

For if I'm not hugely mistaken,
    We can live by the sweat of our brow,   50
Stick a hog, once a year, for fat bacon,
    And all the year round keep a cow.

I value no dainties a button,
    Coarse food will our stomachs allay;
If we cannot get veal, beef and mutton,
    A chine and a pudding we may.

A fig for your richest brocading;
　　In linsey there's nothing that's base;
Your finery soon sets a-fading,
　　My dowlas will last beyond lace.　　　　　　　　　60

I envy not wealth to the miser,
　　Nor would I be plagued with his store:
To eat all and wear all is wiser;
　　Enough must be better than more.

So nothing shall tempt me from Harry,
　　His heart is as true as the sun:
Eve with Adam was ordered to marry;
　　This world it should end as begun.

(1750)

HESTER MULSO (later CHAPONE)
(1727–1801)

She was born at Twywell, Northamptonshire, the daughter of Thomas Mulso, a gentleman-farmer, and his wife (née Thomas). Her brothers, Thomas, John, and Edward, all became clergymen. After the early death of her mother, who had discouraged her early literary efforts, she became her father's housekeeper, but found time to educate herself in French and Latin, as well as music and drawing. Her earliest dated poem, 'To Peace. Written during the late Rebellion. 1745', was written when she was 18. While visiting an aunt in Canterbury in 1749, she met Elizabeth Carter and William and John Duncombe. She sent an ode 'To Health' to Miss Carter in November 1751 and later addressed to her the 'Ode' which was prefixed to her *Epictetus* in 1758. By 1750 she had also become a member of the circle of Samuel Richardson's admirers in London, and was friendly with Thomas Edwards (with whom she exchanged complimentary poems) and Susanna Highmore, to whom 'To Stella' was addressed. In 1750–1 she wrote a series of long letters, arising from *Clarissa*, on the subject of parental authority, of which she approved. She also knew Samuel Johnson and wrote for him some letters included in *Rambler*, No. 10, contributing later to *The Adventurer* (1753), Nos. 77–9. Richardson, who once called her a 'little spitfire', suspected in 1753 that Johnson was 'in love with her'. Certainly, Johnson paid her the unusual compliment of quoting 'To Stella' in his *Dictionary* in 1755 (under 'Quatrain') and was said to have stated that 'he never before had any opinion of female poetry'.

Frances Reynolds, sister of Sir Joshua, later related that Johnson became irritated by her admiration of Richardson and neglect of himself. Johnson in turn told Mrs Thrale that her friendship with Richardson ended because of her fondness for hearing her verses read in public, but it is likely that relations cooled when she became engaged to John Chapone, an attorney, who was also in the Richardson

dowlas] coarse linen

circle. She eventually married Chapone in December 1760, but he died in the following September. Thereafter Mrs Chapone lived in London on a small income, often visiting relatives and friends. Her reputation was enhanced by the publication of her *Letters on the Improvement of the Mind* (2 vols., 1773), originally written for a niece and dedicated to Mrs Montagu. Dealing with such topics as 'Government of the Temper', 'Economy', and 'Politeness and Accomplishments', the *Letters* were frequently reprinted into the following century. Her *Miscellanies in Verse and Prose* (1775) collected her previously published miscellaneous writing. Well known in literary circles in the later decades of the century, Mrs Chapone is often mentioned in letters and diaries of the period. (Fanny Burney and others describe her as being remarkably ugly in old age.) She died in 1801. Her *Works* were collected in 4 volumes in 1807, with 2 further volumes of *Posthumous Works*, also in 1807. Some of her MS verse is in the Forster Collection in the Victoria and Albert Museum.

157   *To Stella*

No more, my Stella, to the sighing shades
    Of blasted hope and luckless love complain;
But join the sports of Dian's careless maids,
    And laughing Liberty's triumphant train.

And see, with these is holy Friendship found,
    With chrystal bosom open to the sight;
Her gentle hand shall close the recent wound,
    And fill the vacant heart with calm delight.

Nor Prudence slow, that ever comes too late,
    Nor stern-browed Duty, check her generous flame;   10
On all her footsteps Peace and Honour wait,
    And Slander's ready tongue reveres her name.

Say, Stella, what is Love, whose tyrant power
    Robs Virtue of content and Youth of joy?
What nymph or goddess in a fatal hour
    Gave to the world this mischief-making boy?

By lying bards in forms so various shown,
    Decked with false charms or armed with terrors vain,
Who shall his real properties make known,
    Declare his nature, and his birth explain?   20

Some say, of Idleness and Pleasure bred,
    The smiling babe on beds of roses lay,
There, with sweet honey-dews by Fancy fed,
    His blooming beauties opened to the day.

His wanton head with fading chaplets bound,
  Dancing he leads his silly vot'ries on
To precipices deep o'er faithless ground,
  Then laughing flies, nor hears their fruitless moan.

Some say from Etna's burning entrails torn,
  More fierce than tigers on the Libyan plain,   30
Begot in tempests, and in thunders born,
  Love wildly rages like the foaming main.

With darts and flames some arm his feeble hands,
  His infant brow with regal honours crown;
Whilst vanquished Reason, bound with silken bands,
  Meanly submissive, falls below his throne.

Each fabling poet sure alike mistakes
  The gentle power that reigns o'er tender hearts!
Soft Love no tempest hurls, nor thunder shakes,
  Nor lifts the flaming torch, nor poisoned darts.   40

Heaven-born, the brightest seraph of the sky,
  For Eden's bower he left his blissful seat,
When Adam's blameless suit was heard on high,
  And beauteous Eve first cheered his lone retreat.

At Love's approach all earth rejoiced, each hill,
  Each grove that learned it from the whispering gale;
Joyous the birds their liveliest chorus fill,
  And richer fragrance breathes in every vale.

Well pleased in Paradise awhile he roves,
  With Innocence and Friendship, hand in hand;   50
Till Sin found entrance in the withering groves,
  And frighted Innocence forsook the land.

But Love, still faithful to the guilty pair,
  With them was driven amidst a world of woes,
Where oft he mourns his lost companion dear,
  And trembling flies before his rigid foes.

Honour, in burnished steel completely clad,
  And hoary Wisdom, oft against him arm;
Suspicion pale, and Disappointment sad,
  Vain Hopes and frantic Fears his heart alarm.   60

Fly then, dear Stella, fly th' unequal strife,
  Since Fate forbids that Peace should dwell with Love!
Friendship's calm joys shall glad thy future life,
  And Virtue lead to endless bliss above.

(Wr. *c.*1751; pub. 1775)

ANNA WILLIAMS
(1706–83)

She was born at Rosemarket near Milford Haven, Pembrokeshire, the daughter of Zachariah Williams (1673?–1755), physician and inventor. Convinced that he had discovered the means of ascertaining longitude at sea (for which a reward of £20,000 had been offered in 1714), Williams came to London with his daughter in the 1720s, but his hopes were disappointed. In 1729 he was nominated by Sir Robert Walpole for admission as a pensioner to the Charterhouse. His daughter, who was supporting herself by her needle, visited him there, and came to know the scientist Stephen Grey, assisting him with his electrical experiments. In a note to a poem on Grey's death in 1736, she later claimed 'to have been the first to observe and notify the emission of the electrical spark from a human body' (*Miscellanies*, pp. 42–3). Although by about 1740 her sight was deteriorating because of a double cataract, she published a translation from the French of a *Life of the Emperor Julian* (1746). In 1748 her bedridden father was expelled from the Charterhouse, partly on the grounds that his daughter, on whom he was totally dependent, had been living there with him for two years, against the rules.

    Samuel Johnson interested himself in the plight of Williams and his daughter, organizing a subscription for her projected *Essays in Verse and Prose* as early as 1750 and addressing the public on her behalf: 'When a Writer of my sex solicits the regard of the publick, some apology seems always to be expected. . . . Censure may surely be content to spare the compositions of a woman, written for amusement, and published for necessity.' Left totally blind after an operation in 1752, she moved into Johnson's house soon after the death of his wife, and continued to live with him for long periods until her own death some thirty years later. Having introduced her to Samuel Richardson in 1753 (when she wrote the verses to the novelist printed below), Johnson tried unsuccessfully in 1754 to interest him in her plan of compiling (with the aid of an amanuensis) a dictionary of some kind, which would cover chemistry and 'many other arts with which Ladies are seldom acquainted' and to which Johnson would have helped to give 'method'. Of Miss Williams herself he stated that 'a being more pure from any thing vicious I have never known'. Having helped her father write numerous letters to officials pleading his case, he compiled an account of Williams's 'discoveries' about the longitude in 1755, but Williams died a few months later. In 1756 Johnson took much trouble to publicize a benefit performance by Garrick of Aaron Hill's *Merope*, which raised £200 for her. On this sum, on annual allowances from Elizabeth Montagu and others, and on the subscriptions to her intended book, Miss Williams managed to survive. Over the years there were spasmodic efforts to publish the volume, but, whether because of Johnson's dilatoriness or his lack of confidence about the contents, her *Miscellanies in Prose and Verse* did not appear until 1766, bolstered by contributions from Mrs Thrale, Percy, Johnson himself, and others. The book raised some £300 for her.

Anna Williams is a familiar figure in the pages of James Boswell, who was fascinated by 'the intimacy in which she had long lived with Johnson, by which she was well acquainted with his habits, and knew how to lead him on to talk'. Johnson's high opinion of her, and his sensitive concern for her feelings, are always apparent, in spite of her well-known peevishness in old age. After her death at his house in Bolt Court in September 1783, he told Charles Burney that she would be 'much missed, for her acquisitions were many, and her curiosity universal'.

158   *Verses to Mr. Richardson, on his History of*
        Sir Charles Grandison

LONG the loose wits of a degenerate age
Had filled with ribaldry the venal page,
Scorned all restraints of virtue or of shame,
And raised the titled prostitute to fame:
Their idle novels, thus the public pest,
Effused their bane, and poisoned every breast.
 Thou, zealous friend of long insulted truth,
Didst first appear the guardian of our youth;
'Twas thine a juster lesson to impart,
To move the passions, and to mend the heart.   10
Bright *Pamela*, in native beauty dressed,
Then burst upon the world, a welcome guest;
Each fair one read, with emulation fired,
All joyed to imitate what all admired.
 Nor here, great mind, thy moral labours end:
Through life's wide round successive works extend,
From tale to tale the mighty plan pursue,
And raise new scenes before the unwearied view.
 Here, blessed with mind, with fortune, and with face,
The virgin falls, but falls without disgrace;   20
Touched with the woes her suffering virtue felt,
The generous kindle, and the tender melt.
In distant times, when *Jones* and *Booth* are lost,
Britannia her *Clarissa*'s name shall boast.
 Yet take from grateful worlds the present wreath,
Nor owe thy garland to the hand of death;
Even now not rocks nor waves thy fame can bound,
The Rhine's rude banks *Clarissa*'s worth resound;
And Tuscan bards her mournful tale relate,
In groves where Virgil sung of Dido's fate.   30
 As where the Alps in awful grandeur rise,
And mix their hoary summits with the skies,

All Nature's power exhausted in the past
We think, but still the greatest is the last:
Thus every mind *Clarissa*'s tomes revered,
Great work of art, till *Grandison* appeared.
The firm and kind, the daring and polite,
To form one character, in one unite;
So highly finished, and so well designed,
It charms with every grace of every mind.   40
In *Byron* all the softer beauties shine,
But heavenly *Clementina*'s worth be mine;
At her distress each maid shall drop a tear,
Each pious maid her firm resolve revere,
Deplore her woes, and emulate her soul,
And learn from her their passions to control.

   Thus, in each character new beauties shine,
And fresh instruction flows in every line.

   Thou sweet preceptor of the rising age,
Let still another work thy thoughts engage;   50
Proceed to teach, thy labours ne'er can tire,
Thou still must write, and we must still admire.

   O long may bounteous Nature bid thee live,
Good to bestow, and honour to receive;
And when at fate's mild call, replete with praise,
Thou goest to join the great of ancient days,
Thy dust shall emblematic shades embower,
The hero's laurel, and the maiden's flower.

(1753)

159   *The Nunnery*

WHAT wond'rous projects formed the fickle fair?
How stately rose the castle built in air,
When maids, their charms from lovers' eyes to screen,
Made a rash vow no longer to be seen?
Whose pen shall dare to tell what secret cause
Incited nymphs to spurn great Hymen's laws,
Or show how soon the fatal covenant failed,
And mirth, and flattery, and show prevailed?

   Of maids a beauteous bevy late disdained
In matrimonial fetters to be chained;
All banish man with one consenting voice,   10
Some think by force, but more agree by choice.

But how this bold rebellion to maintain?
A thousand stratagems fill every brain;
Through different ways their resolutions tend,
But all unite in the same fatal end.

Round the tea-table many a time they sat,
Th' important scheme at leisure to debate;
Till one prolific head above the rest,
With serious mien, th' assembled fair addressed: 20

'How blessed the nymphs in cloistered walks immured,
From all the follies of the world secured;
With what contempt its empty pomp they view,
And with its pleasures bid its cares adieu;
Whatever joys they see, they envy none,
Because no state is equal to their own.
Triumphant votaries! whose hearts possess
Unshaken peace and genuine happiness.
This bliss shall no good Protestant obtain?
Shall only Papists break the nuptial chain?   30
Forbid it, stars! Let English wit contrive
At equal ease and liberty to live.
If you, my sisters, this advice approve,
My scheme our ills will cure, our fears remove.

'Each fleeting will more durably to bind,
Let all our fortunes in one stock be joined;
Then, where some gloomy grove or lonely plain
Hears the faint murmurs of the distant main,
Let modest art a pleasing mansion build,
With thirty willing votaries to be filled;   40
But volunteers alone let choice admit;
One crossed in love is but a hypocrite.
One only male our vestal floor shall tread,
A priest with ardent heart and hoary head,
Of blameless manners, and of learning tried,
To read good lessons, and good books provide.
Hereafter on the hours we will agree,
For prayer, for work, for reading and for tea.'

Thus spoke the fair: the project all commend,
And all their wishes to the Nunnery bend.   50
The Chaplain named, and articles begun,
Full half the work appeared already done.
Whene'er they met, they spoke of future joys,
And the Nuns' Castle all their thoughts employs.

But when the various statutes were surveyed,
And nicely read by each judicious maid,
What sudden changes in their looks appear!
Some are too mild, and some are too severe.
Dorinda cried, 'Are visits then a crime?
And shall we see no friends at any time?'   60
'Shall dancing be allowed,' Sempronia said,
'And yet no partner ever to be had?'
'Must no man enter here?', brisk Lucia cried;
'Then burn the plan,' fair Thestylis replied;
'Let fellows rather style me wife than nun.'
And thus the Castle sunk ere yet begun.

(1766)

ANONYMOUS ('OPHELIA')

'Ophelia', with some initial diffidence, began sending poems from Yorkshire to the
Gentleman's Magazine in January 1751, and did so fairly regularly until the end of
1752. Thereafter she seems to have sent only three further poems, in 1754, 1756,
and 1759. Snaith is some ten miles south of Selby in Yorkshire. The fact that Maria
Cowper (see nos. 177–8), a known poet, moved with her husband to Newland Park
near Snaith in 1751 might seem a clue to her identity. In April 1752, however,
'Ophelia' contributed a poem, dated 24 February 1752, on the death of her father:
Maria Cowper's father, Col. Madan, did not die until 1756.

Quite different from 'Ophelia' 's other verse, 'Snaith Marsh' is unusual for the
period in its use of dialect and its treatment of enclosure. In 1757 it was reprinted in
The Muse in a Moral Humour. A quite distinct 'Yorkshire Pastoral' had appeared
earlier in the *London Magazine*, 11 (1742), 41.

160   *Snaith Marsh. A Yorkshire Pastoral*

YOUNG Robin of the plain, erst blithest blade
That e'er with sickle keen the fields disrayed,
Who whistling drove the smoking team along,
Or trimmed the thorny fence, with rustic song,
Through every season busy still, and gay,
He ploughed, he sowed; he made and stacked the hay.
Not dreary winter reached to Robin's breast:
He threshed, he winnowed, and he cracked his jest.
But now not spring's return with joys he sees,
Nor flowery plain he heeds, nor budding trees,   10
Nor linnet warbling from the dewy brakes,
Nor early lark who towering circles takes,

160 *The following glosses accompany the original text*: erst] an old word signifying time past

Nor tuneful thrushes from the hedge that sing,
Nor the shrill blackbird's welcome to the spring.
Against a gate he leans in rueful plight,
And eyes the plain that late was Snaith Marsh hight.
  'Ah! wae is me,' thus doleful 'gan he mourn;
'Ah! wae the time when ever I was born,
But far more waeful still that luckless day,
Which with the commons gave Snaith Marsh away;   20
Snaith Marsh, our whole town's pride, the poor man's bread,
Where, though no rent he paid, his cattle fed,
Fed on the sweetest grass which here rife grew,
Common to all, nor fence nor landmark knew,
Whose flowery turf no crooked share had razed,
Nor wide-destroying scythe its green effaced.
But now, ah! now, it stoops, sad seet I ween,
In mony a row, with rails suspended 'tween.
  'Wae warth the day when, 'ticed sure by Old Nick,
All to grow rich at once, like neighbour Dick,   30
To town I hied and, on a luckless fair,
For cattle here to graze, wared all my gear,
And boldly ventured at one cast to buy
A deft fine breeding mear, and newted whye,
Ten ewes, a tup, and more, a flock of geese,
All which I thought would here so fast increase,
That, though they'd cost me all my worldly store,
I rekenned soon to gain as mickle more;
But now Snaith Marsh's taid and all my gain blown o'er.
  'My goodly stock, ere yet they tasted food,   40
By cross-grained hinds were driv'n from their abode,
Though, lest bad neighbours might have owed me spite,
I forehand taid a house to give me right,
With bonny Susan where I hoped to dwell;
But now I prove that proverb on my sell,
Which says, that one grief brings another on:
Too sure, alas, and mine will ne'er have done.
For Susan, whom I thought my sweetheart true,
Whenas my crosses came, 'gan look askue;
And what, than all beside, my heart most pains,   50
For landed Roger now my love disdains,
Roger, not to be named with me, I trow,
More than muckmidden vile with barley mow;

wae] woe	rife] plentiful	seet] sight	ween] think or conceive	Wae
warth] a phrase	wared] laid out	gear] riches	deft] lively or nimble	
mear] mare	newted whye] new calv'd young cow		tup] a ram	taid]
took	sell] self	muckmidden] dunghill		

But Roger has a house in yonder lane,
And my sad loss proves every way his gain.
Yet wilt thou, Susan, wilt thou, selfish lass,
For sake of sordid wealth thy love debase?
No, do not think content is in mich store,
But be to Robin kind, as heretofore,
And we'll in love be blessed, though Snaith Marsh be no more. 60
    'Alas! will Roger e'er his sleep forgo,
Afore larks sing, or early cock 'gins crow,
As I've for thee, ungrateful maiden, done,
To help thee milking, ere day-wark begun,
And when thy well stript kye would yield no more,
Still on my head the reeking kit I bore.
And, oh! bethink thee then what lovesome talk
We've held together ganging down the balk,
Maundering at time which would na' for us stay,
But now, I ween, mais no such haste away. 70
Yet oh! return eftsoon and ease my woe,
And to some distant parish let us go.
And there again them leetsome days restore,
Where unassailed by meety folk in power,
Our cattle yet may feed, though Snaith Marsh be no more.
    'But wae is me, I wot I fand am grown,
Forgetting Susan is already gone,
And Roger aims ere Lady Day to wed:
The banns last Sunday in the church were bid.
But let me, let me first i' the churchyard lig, 80
For soon I there must go, my grief's so big.
All others in their loss some comfort find:
Though Ned's like me reduced, yet Jenny's kind;
And though his fleece no more our parson takes,
And roast goose, dainty food, his table lacks,
Yet he, for tithes ill-paid, gets better land,
While I am every way o' th' losing hand:
My adlings wared, and yet my rent to pay,
My geese, like Susan's faith, flown far away,
My cattle, like their master, lank and poor, 90
My heart with hopeless love to pieces tore:
And all these sorrows came, syne Snaith Marsh was no more.'

(1754)

kye] cow   kit] pail   balk] a land in the field for foot paths and carriages
Maundering] finding fault   na] not   mais] makes   eftsoon] an old word for
very soon   leetsome] lightsome or very cheerful   meety folk] mighty men
fand] foolish or stupid   aims] intends   lig] be laid   adlings] earnings

CLARA REEVE
(1729–1807)

Born at Ipswich, she was the eldest daughter of the Revd William Reeve, Rector of Freston and Kerton, Suffolk, and perpetual curate of St Nicholas, Ipswich. Her mother, Hannah Smythies, was the daughter of George I's jeweller and goldsmith. She had seven brothers and sisters, one brother becoming a Vice-Admiral, another a clergyman, and a third a teacher. After the death in 1755 of her father, who had encouraged her education, she lived with her mother and sisters in Colchester and later Ipswich. Some of her poems date from the 1750s but her literary ambitions developed seriously only as she approached the age of 40. In her *Original Poems on Several Occasions* (1769) by 'C.R.' she included a resentful 'Prologue to a Play that Never was Acted. Which Remains Unacknowledged, and Unanswered, In the Hands of a Certain M[anage]r' (pp. 39–40). She also included 'Ruth: An Oratorio' (pp. 85–107), a libretto which, as she explains with irritation in her 'Address to the Reader' (pp. xxi–xxiv), had been written in 1768 for a fickle young composer (identifiable as Samuel Arnold), who had commissioned and set a different text before she had completed it. Her volume was dedicated to the Hon. Mrs Stratford, wife of the Hon. Edward Stratford, in gratitude for their 'esteem and protection'. Members of the aristocracy appear in her long list of subscribers, but most of the names are from East Anglia. Interestingly, she admits that she had once believed that 'my sex was an insuperable objection' to 'pretensions to literary merit', but that she was aware of the changed attitude to women writers, who were now esteemed and rewarded by the public (p. xi).

Although her verse had little or no reputation in her lifetime, she was later well known as a novelist. After translating Barclay's *Argenis* from Latin as *The Phoenix* (1772), she published *The Champion of Virtue. A Gothic Story* (1777), better known as *The Old English Baron* (from 1778). The 1780 edition was dedicated to Mrs Bridgen, Samuel Richardson's only surviving daughter, who had helped to revise it. In 1785 her *Progress of Romance*, a discussion of contemporary fiction, angered Anna Seward of Lichfield (see nos. 204–12), who in January 1786 protested in the *Gentleman's Magazine* at Reeve's judgement that *Pamela* was Richardson's most original novel. Reeve replied indignantly to this 'malevolence' in February, stating that she had 'lived many years in intimate friendship with a daughter of Mr. Richardson, the only one now living', whom she had consulted about her discussion of his novels. Seward dismissed this reply as 'weak and artful' in letters to Mary Scott in March, and probably wrote the further rejoinder to Reeve by 'A Constant Reader' in the *Magazine* in April.

Her other works include *The Two Mentors* (2 vols., 1783), *The Exiles* (3 vols., 1788), *The School for Widows* (3 vols., 1791), *Plans of Education* (1792), *Memoirs of Sir Roger de Clarendon* (3 vols., 1793), and *Destination: or, Memoirs of a Private Family* (3 vols., 1799). She died at Ipswich in 1807. According to a rather pompous obituary, 'her works discover her to have cultivated useful knowledge with considerable success; and to have applied that knowledge less frivolously than is frequently the case with female Authors'.

161 from *To my Friend Mrs. ——. On her holding an Argument in Favour of the Natural Equality of both the Sexes. Written in the Year MDCCLVI*

THE sacred Heliconian spring,
Of which old poets sweetly sing
(Though modern writers only flout it,
Alleging they can do without it),
Produces very strange effects
On the weak brains of our soft sex;
Works worse vagaries in the fancy
Than Holland's gin or royal Nancy.
In short, to what you will compare it,
Few women's heads have strength to bear it.   10
See some, with strong and lively fancies,
Write essays, novels and romances.
Others, by serious cares and pains,
With politics o'erset their brains.
Children, some call themselves, of Phoebus,
By virtue of a pun or rebus;
Some much affect the strain satiric,
And others all for panegyric.
In all and each of these you find
Strong markings of the female mind,   20
Still superficial, light and various;
Loose, unconnected, and precarious:
Life and vivacity I grant,
But weight and energy they want;
That strength that fills the manly page,
And bids it live to future age. . . .
     As some among the men we find
Effeminate in form and mind,
Some women masculine are seen
In mind, behaviour, and in mien: 30
For Nature seldom kindly mixes
The qualities of both the sexes.
These instances are sometimes quoted,
As owls are shown but to be hooted.
Dare now to ope your eyes, and see
These truths exemplified in me.
What though, while yet an infant young,
The numbers trembled on my tongue;

Nancy] probably 'Nants' or 'Nantz', brandy from Nantes   rebus] riddle

As youth advanced, I dared aspire,
And trembling struck the heavenly lyre;   40
What by my talents have I gained?
By those I love to be disdained,
By some despised, by others feared,
Envied by fools, by witlings jeered.
See what success my labours crowned,
By birds and beasts alike disowned.
Those talents, that were once my pride,
I find it requisite to hide;
For what in man is most respected,
In woman's form shall be rejected.   50

(Wr. 1756; pub. 1769)

162   *A Character*

A QUAKER'S stiffness, with a tradesman's grin;
A Jesuit's conscience, with an open mien;
A sailor's breeding, with a courtier's art;
A zealot's fury, with an atheist's heart;
These are thy honours!—Not thy wild expense,
Fed and supported by the public pence,
Poured forth in awkward, splendid, motley treats,
Where dirt with cleanness, want with fullness meets;
Devoured by hungry parsons, sots, and fools,
All well-picked, servile, suppliant, fawning fools;   10
Who with dull flatt'ry, and admiring eyes,
Applaud thy bawdy, blasphemy, and lies.

(1769)

163   *A New Cantata*

Recitative

FROM out the crowd of vanity and noise,
Composed of giggling girls and wanton boys,
Clodio withdrew his Laura and, apart,
Thus spoke the dictates of an anxious heart:

Air

Would you wish to keep your lover,
    Lay these wanton airs aside;
Do not all your charms discover,
    Let discretion be your guide.

When the object is deserving,
  And your heart declares for one,   10
All your charms for him reserving,
  Show the rest he reigns alone.

Smiles and looks, to all imparted,
  Have no value, no regard;
But to be by all deserted
  Is the vain coquette's reward.

Recitative

Laura, who scarce her passion could constrain,
Laughed at his lesson—paused—and laughed again;
Contempt and scorn sat obvious on her face,
Pointed each glance, yet heightened every grace;   20
Provokingly she smiled, and 'Stay,' she cried,
'And hear my answer to thy spleen and pride!'

Air

When men like you pretend to preach,
And dare their musty morals teach,
'Tis fit their wisdom we defy,
And thus in equal strains reply:

Did men of fashion live by rule,
And act by laws from wisdom's school,
We'd take the sober air with ease:
From you we learn the ways to please.   30

When all that's serious you despise,
And laugh to scorn the grave and wise;
We learn the secret to subdue,
And captivate such fops as you.

'Tis levity's your pride and boast,
And wanton airs attract you most;
And she that would successful prove,
Must act the character you love.

(1769)

ANONYMOUS ('A LADY')

There are no clues as to the identity of the author of this unsympathetic portrait of a surely well-meaning enthusiast. Its subject resembles the activities of John Rhudde, Minister of St Peter's, Portesham, Dorset, who published an eccentric poem, *The Ribband: Verses, Addressed to Three Young Ladies* (Sherborne, 1774). It included an advertisement, apparently circulated as early as 1748, for one of his subsidiary interests: 'The Portesham Parish Minister's [Giving, Lending, Selling] Library, Prose and Verse, Considered, In General, As a Means of Promoting Moral and Christian Knowledge'. Part of his plan was 'The Expulsion of Bad Books: Prophane Novels; Obscene Plays; Wanton Songs, etc.'. If bought, the books were available at cost price and could be paid for in small instalments. There is nothing to connect Rhudde with the present poem, although the parallel throws a little light on a minor development in book-distribution in the period.

164   *The Domestic Philosopher*

> HUGE glaring maps the walls surround,
>   His furniture and taste;
> Nor less the labouring shelves abound
>   With books in order placed:
>
> Like bold militia troops, who scorn
>   To break their rank or file;
> Yet, coward-like, their backs they turn,
>   Like ******** on Belleisle.
>
> Here ponderous folios grace the board,
>   There sturdy quartos stand;   10
> And squat octavos, at his word,
>   Salute the master's hand.
>
> The minor twelves (subaltern tribes!)
>   Possess the loftier line:
> While with the name, that each inscribes,
>   The lettered labels shine.
>
> In both he takes no small delight:
>   While, o'er his native soil,
> From north to south he wings his flight,
>   Without expence or toil;   20

But chief he gluts his ravished eyes,
    Which o'er his volumes gaze:
Their garb he views with fond surprise,
    Their numbers with amaze!

'Well—what a sight!', the sage exclaims;
    'My hand the work has done:
Here's books! here's order! and here's names!
    And these—are all my own!'

Now throngs of visitants attend,
    And at the prospect stare;   30
Acquaintance here and strangers blend:
    You'd take it for a fair,

Or public sale—where various books,
    And various pamphlets vie;
Address your pocket or your looks,
    As courting you to buy.

But nothing less—they're not for bread:
    They're bought to lend abroad.
Syphon would fain have science spread,
    For science—is his God!   40

'Come, sir, pray take your choice, and you,
    Oblige me if you can:
Here's Latin, Greek, and Hebrew too,
    If you're a learned man.

'But you, ma'am, here's an English one;
    And, if you have a friend
That you would serve—'tis easy done:
    I bought 'em all to lend.

'It is my talent to dispense
    Such valuable things: 50
I value manners more than sense,
    And honour more than kings.

'Ay—there now—that's the life of one,
    You have it in your hand;
That book's incomparably done:
    'Tis *Louis*, sir, *le Grand*!

'I s'pose you know by whom 'tis wrote:
  'Twas written by Voltaire,
A lively head as ever thought,
  Were verity his care.   60

'However, he's a charming hand;
  There's nothing he can't do:
His lies so clean, and at command,
  I scarce can wish 'em true.

'Well—pray—will no one help themselves
  To what stands here in view;
Here's folios, quartos, eights, and twelves:
  Come, pray now, ladies, do.

'You mind—I've nothing for my pains,
  The cost is all my own;   70
Your kind acceptance is my gains,
  And your applause my crown.'

Thus Syphon wastes the livelong day,
  How learnedly employed!
While the sly moments steal away,
  Unfelt and unenjoyed.

But this is Syphon's constant course,
  His calling and his pride:
The model of a parish horse,
  That all the parish ride!   80

(1758)

MARY LATTER
(1722?–77)

Although she herself implied that she was born in about 1725 (*Miscellaneous Works*, Reading, 1759, p. 48), she was probably, as Betty Rizzo has suggested, the Mary Latter christened at Frilsham, Berkshire, in 1722, the daughter of George and Mary Latter. She would therefore have been 18 and not 15 when she published a rhyming advertisement in the *Reading Mercury* of 17 November 1740, disowning some verses about the ladies of Reading. By then her father, an attorney, had died and she and her mother had a milliner's shop in Butcher Row, Reading. After her mother's death in 1748, the business failed and she seems eventually to have been imprisoned for debt, an experience reflected in her 'Soliliquies on Temporal Indigence'. In her *Miscellaneous Works* she describes herself as living 'not very far from the *Market-Place*, where I continue immersed in Business and in *Debt*, wishing Jupiter to rain me a Shower of Gold; sometimes madly hoping to gain a Competency; sometimes justly fearing Dungeons and Distress!' (p. 80). The book was dedicated to Mrs Penelope Loveday of Caversham, but sections are separately dedicated to Mrs Forrest and the Hon. Mrs Poyntz. Evidence of a somewhat combative temperament, as in her 'Essay [on] the *Unpoliteness* of the People of *no* Fashion' to their social inferiors, suggests that she may have brought some of her problems on herself.

From 1759 her hopes were invested in a tragedy she was writing. A friend showed it to John Rich, manager of Covent Garden Theatre, who visited her in Reading, gave her five guineas and encouraged her. Later she lived in his house in London for ten weeks to improve her practical knowledge of the theatre. In her *Miscellaneous Poetical Essay* (1761) she states that Rich had obtained 100 subscribers for her, perhaps as a way of giving her a further £25. (The *Essay* refers to her rural childhood, the misery to which 'legal Fraud' had reduced her in 'This thorn-abounding Wilderness of Woe', and the benevolence of an anonymous clergyman.) In September 1761, after giving her £10 to pay off her latest debts, Rich again invited her to London, where she worked on an adaptation of a French farce and other works. Her hopes collapsed with Rich's death in November 1761, his successors disclaiming any previous commitment to perform her tragedy. In 'Stage-Craft, An Essay', prefixed to her *The Siege of Jerusalem, By Titus Vespasian; A Tragedy* (1763), she described her relations with Rich and denounced the new managers at length, reinforced by a contribution by R. Cole of Reading (who had already sent a poem about her to the *Gentleman's Magazine* in 1761). She refers resentfully to the 'Slavery . . . of *Writing for Bread*', particularly for 'those whom Fate (perhaps to complete their Curse) confines within the Circle of the Petticoat', since some men are offended 'When a *Woman* has Assurance enough to shew the World her Thoughts'. Yet again she mentions her 'incredible Misfortunes in Life (occasioned by a Complication of Injustice and Inhumanity)'.

She also published *A Lyric Ode, On the Birth of . . . the Prince of Wales* (1763), *Liberty and Interest: A Burlesque Poem on the Present Times* (1764), and *Pro & Con; Or, The Opinionists; An Ancient Fragment* (1771), an eccentric prose work which a reviewer considered 'deranged'. Her tragedy is said to have been performed unsuccessfully at Reading in 1768, but on 26 March 1774 she submitted a revised version to Garrick, who replied on 5 April that he believed it 'would fail of Success in the Representation'. In a remarkable rejoinder of 12 June 1774, provoked by the 'withering blast of refusal', she claimed that the play had received 'universal approbation' from 'an incredible number among the impartial and judicious' throughout the country, and offered to send a list of 'the nobility, gentry, &c. on whose interest I chiefly depend'. If it were to be performed, she would 'have more than two hundred letters to write—some to go as far as Russia'. Garrick merely endorsed the letter 'fine and conceited'.

In spite of all her efforts she never enjoyed a serious literary reputation, reviewers usually considering that her sex and circumstances exempted her from criticism. She died at Reading in 1777.

from *Soliloquies on Temporal Indigence*

(i)
Soliloquy V

WITH tearful eye, how frequent have I seen
The paltry tester drawn (as't were by force!),
And with a sullen, magisterial air
Flung, brutish, on the ground: while the pale wretch
(Less abject than the swine whose husks he craves),
Perhaps with sickness pained, and want oppressed,
Can scarcely stoop to glean the trifling prize.
Is this, O Heaven, the mercy thou shalt crown?
Is such the charity thou shalt regard
To endless ages with eternal smile?   10
Ah, no!—'tis virtue blackened into vice,
By insult poisoned, and by pride undone!

(ii)
Soliloquy VI

STRANGERS to meek compassion's tender touch,
Th' obdurate Many, sullen or severe,
Or silent frown, or surly turn aside,
Or angrily reject the suppliant's prayer
With scoffing insolence, in terms like these:
'Begone with your impertinence, begone;
And trouble us no more. Go, tell your tale
To fools, who credit such dissembling cant:
We're not disposed to have our ears abused
With sham pretences, and unreal tears.'   10
O poisoned darts, unutterably keen,
Piercing with agony the tortured heart:
O vinegar and gall to festering wounds,
Increasing smart, severer for severe!

(iii)
Soliloquy XVI
(*With particular Reference to Mrs. ——r and Co.*)

NOW calumnies arise, and black Reproach
Triumphant croaks aloud, and joyful claps
Her raven wing! Insinuations vile
And slanderous spring from pestilential breath,

tester] sixpence

And tongues thrice dipped in hell. Contagion foul
Steams from th' infernal furnace, hot and fierce,
And spreads th' infectious influence o'er his fame!
Then each unworthy, ignominious fool,
Each female basilisk with forky sting,
And outward-seeming, heart-unmeaning tear   10
(Offspring most loathsome of Hypocrisy,
That vile, detested, double-damning sin:
Confusion and perdition overwhelm
And blast them, execrable, into ruin!),
Chin-deep in malice shoot their bitter darts
Of mockery and derision: adding, sly,
Th' invidious wink, the mean, contemptuous leer,
And flouting grin, 'emphatically scornful'.
Nor less th' insidious knave, supremely dull!
Mixture of monkey, crocodile and mole,   20
Yet stupid as the ostrich, ass and owl;
In high redundance of Typhonic rage,
With harsh stentorian tone, disdainful, flings
Unmerited reflections, vehement, long,
Nonsensical and noisy. Vain, he struts
With domineering insolence replete,
And, lordly, tramples on distress in anguish.

(1759)

MARY WHATELEY (later DARWALL)
(1738–1825)

She was born in February 1738 at Beoley, Worcestershire, the youngest of the nine
children of William Whateley, a substantial farmer who 'occupies his own estate',
and his wife Mary. In spite of a limited education she loved literature and during
1759, at the age of 21, contributed a number of poems to the *Gentleman's Magazine*
(pp. 282, 334, 483, 538) under the pseudonym of 'Harriet Airey', not all of which she
would later reprint. The first two, in June 1759, replied to verses in earlier numbers
of the periodical, and her lines 'To Mr. Copywell' excited a response in July (p. 334)
from the poet William Woty ('Jeremy Copywell'), who invited her to send her address
to Robin's Coffee House, Shire Lane, Temple Bar, so that he could communicate
directly with her. Whatever her family might have thought of these transactions, the
farmer's daughter in rural Worcestershire no doubt enjoyed arousing such interest in
London literary men.

During 1761 there began what appears to have been an organized campaign to
further the publication of her poetry by subscription. By then she was acting as
housekeeper to her brother, an attorney in Walsall, Staffordshire. In September

Typhonic] tempestuous

1761 William Shenstone the poet received 'a large Collection of Poetry' in MS, 'by a Miss Wheatley of Walsall': 'many of the pieces written in an excellent and truly classical style; simple, sentimental, harmonious, and more correct than I almost ever saw written by a lady'. Lord Dartmouth was said to be acting as patron of the subscription. In December 1761 an account of her appeared in the *Gentleman's Magazine* (pp. 635–6) in a letter by Dr J. Wall of Worcester, which described her as having had the education of 'the meanest of menial servants, barely learning to read and write; and her whole life has been employed in the common drudgery of a mean farm-house'. Her reading, he reported, had been confined to Shakespeare, the *Spectator*, and *Gentleman's Magazine*, and a few novels. Dr Wall in fact revised this first account in the *Magazine* in February 1762 (p. 84), presenting her as a much more respectable figure and less of a 'natural genius', claiming that, in spite of her limited education, she had written some 'very extraordinary' poems, 'not unworthy of the best of our poets'. Modest and disinterested, she had been persuaded to agree to the opening of the subscription. A similar account, with samples of her verse, appeared in the *London Magazine* in 1762 (pp. 46, 81).

Her *Original Poems on Several Occasions*, published by Dodsley in 1764, were dedicated to Lady Wrottesley at Perton. Among the 600 subscribers were Elizabeth Carter, Erasmus Darwin, Mary Delany, and the Revd Thomas Seward (father of Anna), as well as the Revd Mr Loggin, Vicar of Beoley, and his daughter Elizabeth, who, to judge from the poems addressed to her, was a close friend. The early encouragement of the Revd Mr Welchman of Tanworth is acknowledged in another poem (pp. 90–4), which admits her lack of a 'Learn'd Education', explains that she began writing verse when depressed with 'pale Care, and melancholy Gloom', pays tribute to her parents, and rejoices that she lacks the beauty which might have 'tempted the Seducer's Wiles'. The volume contained prefatory lines by John Langhorne, the poet and reviewer, who, like Shenstone, must have been shown the poems before publication, and who duly praised them in the *Monthly Review*. (She had addressed a poem to him, pp. 114–17.) The collection was reprinted at Dublin in 1764.

Among the subscribers, and addressed in a poem (pp. 100–1), was the Revd John Darwall, Vicar of Walsall, who also wrote verse. She married him on 4 Nov. 1766 and her domestic responsibilities—he was a widower with five small children and by 1776 she had had six children of her own, one dying in infancy—no doubt seriously affected her literary ambitions. After her husband's death in 1789, however, she published by subscription a new collection of *Poems on Several Occasions* (2 vols., Walsall, 1794), the dedication to which is dated from Newtown, Montgomeryshire, where she evidently lived for a time. Some lines addressed to her by Dr Luke Booker of Dudley (i. 1–4) remark that 'Erst, unarraign'd, tyrannic man confin'd | In chains of ignorance the female mind', but that 'Lib'ral Thought' has now illumined 'hapless woman's dark Egyptian night'. Some of the verse was contributed by two young friends (ii. 128–58): one was conceivably her daughter Elizabeth, who later published *The Storm, With Other Poems* (1810), which contains a poem addressed to her by her mother. Mary Darwall died at Walsall on 5 December 1825, aged 87.

166 *Ode to Truth*

DESCEND, fair Truth, celestial maid, descend,
And with thy lustre radiate the dark cloud,
    Which deep envelopes half
    The sapient sons of men.
At thy approach shall the infernal train,
Which now oppress the human breast, depart,
    And, in primeval night,
    Their fiendlike forms conceal.
There dark Distrust and Incredulity,
Parents of Care, shall fly, when thou resum'st   10
    Thy godlike reign in man's
    Deserted, cheerless breast.
Through thy transparent veil, the only charm
I have to boast, let all the world survey
    My guileless heart, and trace
    Each action to its spring.
If consciousness of cursed hypocrisy,
Or fraud unmanly, which my soul disdains,
    Produce one guilty pang,
    Let anguish be my lot.   20
But let me bless the providential hand,
Which kindly formed me female, and denied
Superior genius and superior pride;
Mistaken pride, which all desert confines
To man, and in his breast each virtue shrines,
Though learning's ample field he rules alone,
Nor fears a female near his awful throne:
Unsatiated with empire so immense,
He'd fain divest our sex of common sense.

                                            (1759)

167 *The Power of Destiny*

SURE some malignant star diffused its ray,
When first my eyes beheld the beams of day;
Whose baleful influence made me dip in ink,
And write in rhyme before I knew to think.
Had Fate, propitious to my wish, assigned
Me, wayward girl, of man's superior kind,
This strong propensity had marred each scheme,
And prudence yielded to a golden dream.

Perhaps I'd then been bred a learned divine,
With Greek and Hebrew in this head of mine;   10
With musty classics stuffed, dry grammar rules,
And all the specious lumber of the schools:
Yet, had an itch for scribbling filled my brain,
This care and cost had been bestowed in vain.
  Or had I, studious of the healing art,
Been taught with care to act old Galen's part,
Perused Hippocrates's laboured page,
And thumbed with reverence each time-honoured sage;
Yet when, from college rules and orders free,
My pen had once regained its liberty,   20
Thoughtless of gain, and warm with fancied fire,
I certainly had quitted Mead and Floyer,
For Milton, Shakespeare, Dryden, Pope and Young,
And left Sanctorius for an idle song;
Strother, Boerhaave, and Celsus had given way
To a smart satire or a roundelay:
For who, bemused, and in a rhyming strain,
Could mark the various fibres of the brain?
Leave all the dear ideas fancy forms,
To learn the strange effect of snails and worms?   30
Try with what qualities each drug is fraught,
And praise the virtues of some nauseous draught?
  Had I been bred at Gray's or Lincoln's Inn,
'Mid lawsuits, empty quibbles, doubts and din,
Attended duly at the wrangling hall,
And learned to baffle, bluster, bounce and bawl:
Yet with impatience in the long vacation,
I should have left this profitable station;
Have quitted Salkeld and the lawyer's gown,
And all the gay amusements of the town;   40
Have fled in raptures to the peaceful grange,
And left Coke, Carthew, Nelson, Wood and Strange,
Hughes, Hale and Hawkins, Bacon, King and Cay,
For Swift, Hill, Congreve, Cowley, Garth and Gay;
And in some cot, retired from crowd and noise,
Have sought serene delights and rural joys;
Mused by a fountain, slept beneath a tree,
And, 'stead of drafts, composed—an elegy.
Inspired by Silvia's eyes, or Daphne's air,
Or Cynthia's rosy cheeks, and curling hair,   50
My most exalted wish, and only aim,
Had been to eternise the favourite dame:
Her charms in softest numbers to express,
And paint my passion in the liveliest dress.

In short, whatever my employ had been,
It soon had yielded to this darling sin:
And naught but Russel's land, or Gideon's purse,
Had saved the poet from—the poet's curse.

(1764)

168   *The Vanity of External Accomplishments*

YE smarts and belles, whose airs and arts confess
Th' important study of your lives is dress;
Who gaily a polite contempt display
For all the learned, the wise, or good can say;
Forgive an artless maid who boldly tries
To vindicate the notions you despise.
  Who would not sigh for that enchanting air,
Which speaks Belinda fairest of the fair,
Which men of sense admire, and beaus adore,
Did one charm last when beauty blooms no more?   10
When those resistless eyes no longer shine,
And the fresh roses in those cheeks decline;
When age contracts those gay, enlivening airs,
And that fair forehead crowns with hoary hairs;
What then must fix the friend? or what sustain
The long-collected load of years and pain?
Will the light air, the practised smile avail,
When love and triumph with her face must fail?
For peace or pleasure can she hope, from skill
In dear detraction, and adored quadrille?   20
  Why then is Delia by the world admired?
Her talk is trifling, and her tongue untired.
For sense or nonsense—'tis no matter which—
Her ruby lips give sanction to her speech.
Yet fluttering Delia would be counted wise;
But, should you ask where Delia's judgement lies,
You'll find her wisdom centred in her eyes.
  But gentle Silvia loves the languid air;
Faint voice and dying smiles describe the fair.
The lucid orb cast upward seems to prove   30
The virgin meditates on things above;
Yet Silvia's life proves this a vain pretence,
And seeming thought but hides defect of sense:
She seeks with these soft languors to disarm
The guarded breast, and reinforce each charm.
  From the same motive, though by different ways,
The bold Camilla seeks the palm of praise.

With manly stride Camilla spurns the ground,
Or on the prancing steed pursues the hound;
Through brakes, down precipices, lo! she speeds,   40
Dares the rough torrent, bounds along the meads:
For what?—the gentle fair will blush to hear—
With her own hand to kill the trembling deer.

  Satire on men superfluous would be:
What they approve by our own sex we see.
Since woman's happiness depends on man,
'Tis easy to conclude where first began
This group of follies, that o'erspread the earth:
From our wise Lords they first received their birth;
These our fond females, bent to please mankind,   50
Enlarged, exalted, softened and refined.

  But who would waste their bloom, and not engage
One friend to soothe the wintry storms of age?
Let me, ye powers! inspired by Reason's laws,
Though coxcombs censure, gain my own applause;
In useful learning, as in years, advance;
Improve my mind and leave my form to chance:
Good sense and virtue gild the darkest scene,
And bloom as bright at sixty as sixteen.

  Though Silvia's softness, Delia's sprightly grace,   60
Belinda's air, nor Arabella's face,
Conspire to make me lovely, health supplies
These cheeks with colour, and with strength these eyes:
These eyes, untaught to languish or to roll,
Convey instruction to th' inquiring soul.

  O! Nature, never let thy bounty cease!
Still grant me health, and poetry, and peace.
Let me enjoy my visionary scene,
Stranger to envy, flattery, pride, or spleen;
So my last breath shall praise thee when I die,   70
And my life vanish in a tuneful sigh.

                    (1764)

169   *On the Author's Husband Desiring her to Write*
Some Verses

      VERSES, my love! As soon could I
      Without a wing or feather fly;
      My head, with other matters fraught,
      No more attempts poetic thought:—
      Yet, as I hold your sovereign sway,
      In spite of genius I obey.

Ye Muses, aid me to explore
The shadowy grots, and mountains hoar,
Where ye your tuneful influence shed,—
And twine with bays your poet's head.   10

Erato hears my invocation,—
My bosom glows with inspiration,—
Instant the fairy scenes appear,
Pierian sounds salute my ear:—
Connubial Love! enchanting theme!
Sweet subject of my muse-rapt dream,
To thee I consecrate my lays,
And thus my heart pours forth thy praise:

Blessed state! by gracious heaven designed
    To soothe our passions into peace,   20
To twine in union sweet the kindred mind,
Th' endearing ties of social life to bind
    In chains so strong, yet soft, they but with life can cease.

The mutual interest all reserve disclaiming,
The scheme of pleasure each for other framing,
The kindling transports of parental love,
Which the sweet smiles of innocence can move,
Are thine alone, O Hymen! to bestow,
Which hearts that do not feel them cannot know:—
    —But hark!—my darling infant cries,   30
    And each poetic fancy flies.

(Wr. *c.* 1780; pub. 1794)

ALISON COCKBURN (née RUTHERFORD)
(1713–94)

She was the youngest daughter of Robert Rutherford of Fairnilee, Selkirkshire, and
his second wife, Alison Ker, who had three sons and three daughters. After her
mother's death when she was 10, her eldest sister encouraged her literary interests
and her father taught her arithmetic. Later she boarded with a private teacher and
learned French, needlework, and dancing. In 1731, aged 17, she married Patrick
Cockburn, an advocate who seems not to have practised at the bar, but was later
commissioner in charge of the estates of the Duke of Hamilton. Their son Adam
(1732–80) became an army officer. After her husband's death in 1753 she lived
mostly in Edinburgh and was prominent in literary circles there, entertaining David
Hume (to whom she wrote some lively letters), John Home, Lord Monboddo and,
later, Robert Burns. Walter Scott compared her appearance to that of Queen

Elizabeth and her rank in Edinburgh society to that of 'French women of talents' in Paris.

Although she wrote verse throughout her life, little of it was published. As she stated in 1775, 'I am very certain that no woman ought to write anything but from the heart to the heart; never for the public eye, without male correction', and later, 'As for printing, never fear. I hate print.' Her one popular success, 'The Flowers of the Forest', first published in *The Blackbird* (Edinburgh, 1765), was an attempt to set words to the old Scottish air which also inspired Jane Elliot (see no. 171), an acquaintance of Mrs Cockburn. By 1786 it had appeared in at least seventeen songbooks and miscellanies. According to Scott, it referred to events in Ettrick Forest in Selkirkshire, 'when there was a great deal of distress & misfortune come upon the Forest by seven Lairds becoming ruined in one year'. She was distantly related to Scott, whose literary precocity at the age of five ('the most extraordinary genius of a boy I ever saw') she described in a letter in November 1777. In his *Minstrelsy of the Scottish Border* (1802) Scott stated that in old age she 'retained a play of imagination, and an activity of intellect' which were 'almost preternatural at her period of life'. Her surviving letters from her later years justify such admiration, in spite of her declining health. In 1792 she wrote, 'I am deaf, blind, and lame, but content, because I know God made and knows best how to take down his own work'; and, in the following year, 'When my maidens come to carry me from my bed to my chair or *vice versa*, I sing to them all the way to cheer the weariness of attendance'. She died on 22 November 1794.

170   *The Flowers of the Forest*

I'VE seen the smiling of Fortune beguiling,
I've felt all its favours and found its decay;
Sweet was its blessing, kind its caressing,
But now it is fled, fled far, far away.
I've seen the Forest adorned the foremost,
With flowers of the fairest, most pleasant and gay;
Sae bonny was their blooming, their scents the air perfuming,
But now they are withered and wade all away.

I've seen the morning with gold the hills adorning,
In loud tempest storming before middle day.   10
I've seen Tweed's silver stream, shining in the sunny beam,
Grow drumly and dark as it rolled on its way.
O fickle Fortune, why this cruel sporting?
Why thus torment us poor sons of day?
Nae mair your smiles can cheer me, nae mair your frowns can
    fear me,
For the flowers of the Forest are a' wade away.

                                  (Wr. *c.*1764; pub. 1765)

        wade] weeded   drumly] turbid, discoloured

JANE ELLIOT
(1727–1805)

Born at Minto House, Teviotdale, she was the third daughter of Sir Gilbert Elliot, 2nd baronet of Minto, and his wife Helen Stewart of Allanbank. She is said to have behaved with unusual resourcefulness in helping her father to escape from a party of Jacobites during the rising of 1745/6. Other anecdotes have traditionally dated her one famous composition in about 1755, when her brother Gilbert, politician, author, and later the 3rd baronet, challenged her during a coach journey to write a ballad on the battle of Flodden, which she had drafted before the end of the journey. Whatever part her brother may have played, she herself in 1801 dated the poem several years later in 1763 or 1764, in answer to Walter Scott's enquiries about its composition: 'I was travelling on the turnpike road down Gala water. The solitary desolate appearance of the Country made me think of the battle of Flodden & the *Flowers of the Forest* then a very fashionable tune, occurring to my imagination at the same time produced the enclosed stanzas.' Lines 1 and 4 were the only original words she had heard sung to the old tune, for which Alison Cockburn (see no. 170) also wrote words at about the same time.

Usually said to have been first published in 1776, the song in fact appeared in David Herd's *The Ancient and Modern Scots Songs, Heroic Ballads, &c.* (Edinburgh, 1769), pp. 338–9, as 'Flowdenhill: or, Flowers of the Forest'. In Herd's enlarged edition of this collection (2 vols., Edinburgh, 1776, i. 45–9) the song was conflated with Alison Cockburn's lines in a longer poem about Flodden, most of which Scott later suggested Herd had written himself. Elliot's song was, however, reprinted in several miscellanies and was apparently first attributed to her by James Currie in his edition of Burns's *Works* in 1800. In 1801 Scott asked Dr Thomas Somerville, who had told him 'long ago' of her authorship, for further information. Somerville obtained from Jane Elliot 'an exact copy' of the song and the account of its composition quoted above, but with a request that 'her name may not be mentioned'. Scott complied (while thinking such anonymity 'somewhat prudish') when he printed the song in his *Minstrelsy of the Scottish Border* (2 vols., Kelso, 1802), ii. 156–9, attributing it to 'a lady of family in Roxburghshire'. Scott described the song, inspired by 'the fatal battle of Flodden (in the calamities accompanying which the inhabitants of Etricke Forest suffered a distinguished share)', as 'a strain of elegiac simplicity and tenderness which has seldom been equalled'.

After her father's death in 1766 Jane Elliot had lived with her mother and sisters mainly in Edinburgh, 'where she mingled a good deal in the better sort of society'. She was remembered in old age as 'a remarkably agreeable old maiden lady, with a prodigious fund of Scottish anecdote, but did not appear to have ever been handsome'. She died in 1805.

The Flowers of the Forest

I'VE heard them lilting, at the ewe milking,
   Lasses a' lilting, before dawn of day;
But now they are moaning, on ilka green loaning;
   The flowers of the forest are a' wede awae.

At bughts in the morning, nae blithe lads are scorning;
   Lasses are lonely, and dowie and wae;
Nae daffing, nae gabbing, but sighing and sabbing;
   Ilk ane lifts her leglin, and hies her awae.

At har'st at the shearing, nae youths now are jearing;
   Bandsters are runkled, and lyart or gray;   10
At fair, or at preaching, nae wooing, nae fleeching;
   The flowers of the forest are a' wede awae.

At e'en in the gloaming, nae younkers are roaming,
   'Bout stacks, with the lasses at bogle to play;
But ilk maid sits dreary, lamenting her deary—
   The flowers of the forest are weded awae.

Dool and wae for the order, sent our lads to the border!
   The English, for ance, by guile wan the day;
The flowers of the forest, that fought aye the foremost,
   The prime of our land are cauld in the clay.   20

We'll hae nae mair lilting at the ewe milking;
   Women and bairns are heartless and wae:
Sighing and moaning, on ilka green loaning—
   The flowers of the forest are a' wede away.

(Wr. c.1764; pub. 1769)

LADY DOROTHEA DUBOIS (née ANNESLEY)
(1728–74)

Born in Ireland, she was the eldest daughter of Richard Annesley, Lord Altham,
from 1737 Earl of Anglesey, and Ann Simpson of Dublin. In about 1740 he
repudiated this marriage, declared his three daughters illegitimate, and married (or

loaning] uncultivated ground near a farm used for milking   wede] weeded
bughts] sheepfolds   dowie] dreary   daffing] making merry   leglin] milk-
pail   har'st] harvest   bandsters] binders   runkled] wrinkled   lyart]
grizzled   fleeching] beseeching   bogle] (game of) ghost(s)   Dool] dole, grief

lived with) Juliana Donovan, the daughter of a Wexford merchant, whom he definitely married in 1752. He refused to pay the maintenance awarded by the Ecclesiastical Court after a legal action by Dorothea's mother. His defence was that his marriage to Ann Simpson had been rendered invalid by the fact of an earlier marriage in 1715 to Ann Prust, from whom he had separated by 1719. In about 1752 Dorothea secretly married a young French musician named Dubois and by 1760 had six children. In that year she made an unsuccessful visit to Ireland to persuade her father to acknowledge his marriage to her mother. The Earl had supposedly made a will leaving her five shillings as a natural daughter. At his death in 1761 his son Arthur by his wife Juliana inherited his property.

Complex legal battles over the Annesley estates continued from the 1740s to the 1770s and were not simplified by the fact that from about 1742 one James Annesley was claiming to be the true heir. 'Lady' Dorothea, as she always claimed to be, began to write in the 1760s to support her family and to advance her claim to her legal rights. Her *Poems on Several Occasions* (Dublin, 1764) include 'A True Tale', an autobiographical poem about her father's desertion of the family, and there are other poems on the same subject. The volume was dedicated to George III and published by subscription. After the death of her mother in 1765, she repeated her claims in *The Case of Ann Countess of Anglesey . . . and of her Three Surviving Daughters* (1766). A single-sheet *Advertisement*, dated 9 April 1767, in which she calls herself the 'Eldest Lawful Daughter of Richard late Earl of Anglesey', was a response to Arthur Annesley's attempts to raise a mortgage on his father's estates. Her *Theodora* (2 vols., 1770) is a novel on the same subject. She also published *The Divorce* (1771), a musical entertainment for Marylebone Gardens, and *The Lady's Polite Secretary, Or, New Female Letter-Writer* (also 1771: variously dated in reference works, but see *Gentleman's Magazine* (1771), 605). 'The Haunted Grove', acted at Dublin in 1772, was apparently not published. All her efforts brought her no legal benefit and she died impoverished in Dublin in 1774 'of an apopleptic fit'.

172   *Song*

> A SCHOLAR first my love implored,
> And then an empty titled lord;
> The pedant talked in lofty strains;
> Alas! his lordship wanted brains:
> I listened not to one or t' other,
> But straight referred them to my mother.
>
> A poet next my love assailed,
> A lawyer hoped to have prevailed;
> The bard too much approved himself;
> The lawyer thirsted after pelf: 10
> I listened not to one or t' other,
> But still referred them to my mother.
>
> An officer my heart would storm,
> A miser sought me too, in form;

But Mars was over-free and bold;
The miser's heart was in his gold:
I listened not to one or t' other,
Referring still unto my mother.

And after them, some twenty more
Successless were, as those before;   20
When Damon, lovely Damon came,
Our hearts straight felt a mutual flame:
I vowed I'd have him, and no other,
Without referring to my mother.

(1764)

CHRISTIAN CARSTAIRS
(*fl.* 1763–86)

She was the daughter of James Bruce Carstairs of Kinross in Fife (d. 1768) and is said to have become a governess. What little is known of her derives almost entirely from her anonymous *Original Poems. By A Lady* (Edinburgh, 1786), most copies of which are signed 'Christian Carstairs' at the end. Dedicated to Miss Ann Henderson and with a small list of subscribers, the volume collects eight separate parts (with individual title-pages in some copies), which may have been circulated privately over a period of years. The earliest poem dates from 1763. One refers to her brother's death in action, 'near to Patna in Bengal', on 1 July 1763. Others have such dates as 'Burntisland Castle, August 1764', 'Kinross-House, September 9, 1768', and 'Otterstone, 1772'. A presentation copy to the Antiquarian Society of Scotland is in the National Library in Edinburgh.

Her other publication, mentioned in *Original Poems*, was *The Hubble-Shue* [*c.*1780], an inconsequential farce of obscure purpose. The antiquarian James Maidment reprinted it at Edinburgh in 1834 (with the subtitle, 'A Mystification'), in an edition of thirty copies. His ironic 'Introductory Notice' is the source for the statement that she had been a governess. A long MS note in the British Library copy of *Original Poems*, by someone who 'was afterwards slightly acquainted with her', describes its contents as 'neither prose nor verse, rhyme nor reason', and suggests that the author 'seems to have lost her senses': 'the ravings of a disordered imagination are not fit subjects for criticism'.

She was conceivably the Mrs Grizel Carstairs, daughter of the late James Bruce Carstairs of Kinross, who died in New Street, Edinburgh, on 20 December 1794.

173 *[On Loch Leven]*

Kinross, 1767

SCARCE a breeze on the lake, with four oars to our boat;
    The landscape no pencil could paint!
I thought of her fate, the midst of this scene,
    When a boar puts us all in a fright.
Confusion and terror, my heart beat my breast,
    Neither castle nor bower could I see;
The beautiful Queen* who once made her escape
    Was scarcely so frighted as me.
The house—and the trees—the town and the spire;
    The hills—and the cottages round;   10
The water—the wind—and the flight of the birds;
    Did only my senses confound.
No thought was distinct—or but lost in myself;
    I prayed—and our fate did deplore;
When Serff†, that good saint, from his peaceful retreat
    Came quickly, and brought us to shore.

(Wr. 1767; pub. 1786)

174 *Addressed to a Beech Tree, on observing that some of
its Leaves were tinged by the Smoke of a Fire that
had been kindled under it*

WHAT taints thy shade—or doth the year decay?
Yet soon again—thy tender leaf revives.
I too, in silence, to the grave go down;
But hope inspires—that still a sweeter spring

                                   Awaits new joys;
Sweeter than even these fields;
Where oft the Muse in plaintive notes
Invites the coming year,
Or mourns the time delayed.

Otterstone, 1772

(Wr. 1772; pub. 1786)

* Queen Mary.   †St Serff's Island in Loch-Leven.

175   *Nightingale*

O! COULD my sweet plaint lull to rest,
Soften one sigh—as thou dreamst,
I'd sit the whole night on thy tree,
And sing, — — sing, — —
                    With the thorn at my breast.

                                                    (1786)

176   *A Song*

FAREWELL my Betty, and farewell my Annie,
And farewell my Ammie, and farewell my friends.
                                                    &c.

Farewell to these plains and to innocent freedom,
Believe me, my heart was akin to these scenes;
                                                    &c.

In each cheerful moment I meant you a pleasure,
And ne'er gave offence, but it gave me more pain.
                                                    &c.

Through the lang muir I'll think of my Willie,
And through the lang muir I'll think o' him again.
Through the lang muir I'll think o' my Willie,
And through the lang muir I'll think o't again.   10

                                                    (1786)

MARIA FRANCES CECILIA COWPER (née MADAN)
(1726–97)

She was the eldest daughter of Col. Martin Madan and his wife Judith Cowper (see nos. 65–7). In childhood she had weak eyesight and in about 1736 and again in 1740 was sent to a Mrs King, a female oculist of Gravesend, from whom she learned to read and write. She also attended a school at Wells, learned French, acted in Racine's *Athalie*, and longed to become an actress. Her interest in languages and literature was encouraged by both her parents. (She considered her mother 'a woman of the most exalted understanding and taste in the world'.) In the 1740s she and her sister Penelope were notable 'beauties' in London society. As early as 1743 her cousin William Cowper (1721?–69) of Lincoln's Inn, and a Major in the

Hertfordshire militia, had proposed to her, but her mother was uneasy about the marriage of first cousins, as well as doubting his ability to support his wife. They eventually married in August 1749, living first at Hertingfordbury Park and, from late 1751, at Newland Park, near Snaith, West Yorkshire. They had four sons and three daughters: the infant addressed in the following poem was Charles (1765–1820), who became a lawyer.

As is clear from her correspondence with her mother, she became deeply religious and from 1766 she also wrote many letters on devotional subjects to her cousin, William Cowper the poet, whose belated fame in the 1780s delighted her ('That worthy Creature so many years buried in shades, is now the *conversation* as well as *admiration* of the highest Ranks of people!'). After her husband's death in 1769 she lived in York and from 1772 in London. William Cowper helped her to revise her religious verse for publication as *Original Poems on Various Occasions* (1792; later editions, 1797, 1810). The *English Review* disliked 'the deep tincture of methodism which pervades the whole', but the *Evangelical Magazine* was predictably more sympathetic. She died at Paddington, London, on 15 October 1797.

177   *On Viewing her Sleeping Infant (C[harles] C[owpe]r)*
       Written at the Park, Hertfordshire, in 1767

I HAVE seen the rosebud blow,
And in the jocund sunbeam glow,
Sportive lambs on airy mound,
Skipping o'er the velvet ground;
And the sprightly-footed morn,
When every hedge and every thorn
Was decked in spring's apparel gay,
All the pride of opening May:
Yet—nor rosebud early blowing,
In the jocund sunbeam glowing,   10
Nor the sportive lambs that bound
O'er the sweet enamelled ground,
Nor the sprightly-footed morn,
When brilliants hang on every thorn—
These not half thy charms display:
Thou art fairer still than they,
Still more innocent, more gay!

   Mild thou art as evening showers,
Stealing on ambrosial flowers;
Or the silver-shining moon   20
Riding near her highest noon.
Who, to view thy peaceful form,
Heeds the winter-blowing storm?

Thy smiles the calm of heaven bestow,
And soothe the bitterest sense of woe!
As bees, that suck the honeyed store
From silvery dews, on blushing flower,
So on thy cheek's more lovely bloom
I scent the rose's quick perfume.
Thine ivory extended arms,   30
To hold the heart—what powerful charms!
    Come, soft babe! with every grace
Glowing in thy matchless face—
Come, unconscious innocence!
Every winning charm dispense—
All thy little arts—thine own—
For thou the world hast never known!
And yet thou canst, a thousand ways,
A mother's partial fondness raise!
And all her anxious soul detain   40
With many a link of pleasing chain;
Leading captive at thy will,
Following thy little fancies still.
Though nature yet thy tongue restrains,
Nor canst thou lisp thy joys or pains!
Yet every gracious meaning lies
Within the covert of thine eyes:
Wit, and the early dawn of sense,
Live in their silent eloquence.
    May every future day impart   50
New virtues to adorn thy heart;
May gracious heaven profusely shed
Its choicest blessings o'er thy head!
Blessed, and a blessing, mayst thou prove,
Till crowned with endless joys above!

                                        (MS 1767)

178   *The World Not Our Rest, &c.*

VAIN are those joys that erring man provides,
    Vain the pursuit of sublunary things!
Wisdom the sandy edifice derides,
    Scoffs at the fading pageantry of kings.
Sooner some witless trifler shall essay
    To carve the image on the quivering flame,
Than wrest contentment from a single day
    Given to the world, to pleasure, wealth, or fame.

The noontide of Lorenzo's joy is o'er,
 And youth's intoxicating smiles are gone;   10
The world's fantastic scenes delight no more;
 Loud-laughing mirth, and wit and jest are flown.
Yet these are trivial losses, and he feels
 A thousand woes than these far more intense;
With soul-distracting pangs of guilt he reels,
 While threatening Death demands his victim hence.

Quick o'er his lonely couch pale Sickness throws
 The trembling horrors of some dire disease:
To injured Heaven he pours his impious vows;
 But vows, nor prayers, his frighted soul appease. 20
Alas, Lorenzo! what avail thee now
 The gifts of Fortune, or the phantom Power,
Those idols, deaf and dumb, that ne'er bestow
 One solid comfort in the trying hour?

As soon the traveller on his darksome way,
 Benumbed with winds and chilling frost, shall gain
New warmth and vigour from the feeble ray
 Of meteors gliding through th' ethereal plain.
To what new system shall Lorenzo fly?
 Shall 'moral rectitude' his soul secure?   30
What 'deed' the force of quickening grace supply?
 Or 'conscious virtue' make the sinner pure?

Say, can the tinkling of the neighbouring stream
 The riches of the Gospel truths convey?
Or can the glow-worm, with her languid beam,
 Unfold the glories of immortal day?
As soon shall these the wondrous task perform,
 To wounded minds the healing balm impart,
As Man—vain, impotent, self-righteous worm—
 With aught but faith console his aching heart. 40

         (1792)

PRISCILLA POINTON (later PICKERING)
(c. 1740–1801)

She was born in Lichfield in about 1740 and at the age of 12 lost her sight after 'a violent headache'. She had little education and was 'frequently at the greatest loss for an amanuensis, held under the strictest subjection by an aged parent, who having long ago bid adieu to the polite world, and, as it were, shut herself up in a convent, will seldom admit any authors but the primitive Fathers'. A subscription to her *Poems on Several Occasions* was advertised in the *Birmingham Gazette* on 12 September 1768 and the volume was published at Birmingham in 1770, with a preface (quoted above) by John Jones of Kidderminster, who had addressed her in his own *Poems on Several Subjects* [1768], pp. 65–8. Her name was given as Pointon on her title-page in 1770, but it should be noted that relatives in the subscribers' list have the spelling 'Poynton'. A reference in the volume (p. 5) suggests that she became blind in about 1752 and would therefore have been born in about 1740. Of the long list of her subscribers, running to some fifty pages, she herself wrote in her 'Epistle to a Friend' (pp. 90–1):

> Fifteen hundred and upwards the list does adorn,
> Lords, Ladies, Knights, 'Squires, and scores nobly born;
> Divinity, Physic, and Law, it is true,
> Nay, the milit'ry Smarts have my int'rest in view,
> And Tradesmen of spirit, the number not few ...

Lichfield subscribers included the Revd Thomas Seward and Lucy Porter, Samuel Johnson's stepdaughter.

The subscribers' list and several of her poems indicate that she had relatives in Chester, whom she visited frequently, and it was there (as references in her poem on the subject make clear) that she married a Mr I. Pickering in 1788, said to have been a saddler. Her husband had died, however, after an illness of five months, by 1794, when 'her desolate situation, and her irremediable calamity' prompted another subscription to a further collection of her *Poems*, published at Birmingham and edited by Joseph Weston of Solihull. Weston described the problem of editing an MS which had so often been shown to potential subscribers as to be mutilated and partly illegible. Poems by Weston himself and by John Morfitt were included in the strangely organized volume, the third section of which contains some of her poems as rewritten (because partly illegible?) by Weston. Although she wrote a poem 'To Miss Seward, On being honour'd with hearing her read her *Louisa*, at the Palace, Litchfield' (pp. 16–18) and another 'On Her *Louisa*' (pp. 18–20), there appear to be no references to her in Anna Seward's *Letters*. Her death was noted in the *Birmingham Gazette* on 15 June 1801.

179   from *To the Critics*

[*On her Blindness*]

I NEVER tasted the Pierian spring,
Of which great Pope does with such rapture sing.
For, since deprived from infancy of sight,
How should my muse in lofty numbers write?
Milton and Homer both, you say, were blind,
And where on earth can we their equals find?
But were they blind like me in infant state?
Or did they taste like me tenebrous fate?
No—long they lived great nature to explore,
Their minds enriching with poetic store.   10

Then in compassion say, ye critics, say
You'll cheer my soul with one reviving ray;
Nor frown indignant on my night-struck strain,
But for amusement bid me write again;
Yet friendly tell me, though I'm not sublimed,
My thoughts are rude, my numbers unrefined;
Since liberal pity all the wise commend,
Be then for once an *helpless* woman's friend!

(1794)

180   *Address to a Bachelor on a Delicate Occasion*

YOU bid me write, Sir, I comply,
Since I my grave airs can't deny.
But say, how can my Muse declare
The situation of the fair,
That full six hours had sat, or more,
And never once been out of door?
Tea, wine, and punch, Sir, to be free,
Excellent diuretics be:
I made it so appear, it's true,
When at your house, last night, with you: 10
Blushing, I own, to you I said,
'I should be glad you'd call a maid.'
'The girls,' you answered, 'are from home,
Nor can I guess when they'll return.'
Then in contempt you came to me,
And sneering cried, 'Dear Miss, make free;
Let me conduct you—don't be nice—
Or if a basin is your choice,
To fetch you one I'll instant fly.'
I blushed, but could not make reply;   20
Confused to find myself the joke,
I silent sat till Trueworth spoke:
'To go with me, Miss, don't refuse,
Your loss the freedom will excuse.'
To him my hand reluctant gave,
And out he led me very grave;
Whilst you and Chatfree laughed aloud,
As if to dash a maid seemed proud.
But I the silly jest despise,
Since well I know each man that's wise   30

180 loss] i.e. blindness

All affectation does disdain,
Since it in prudes and coxcombs reign:
So I repent not what I've done:
Adieu—enjoy your empty fun.

(1770)

181   from *Letter to a Sister, Giving an Account of the
Author's Wedding-Day*

IN a post-coach and four, with postillions as fine
As e'er drove a Countess, that day I did shine.
In the morn did Aurora her influence display,
And Cynthia at night seemed to vie with the day.
Good Barnes and his consort, gay Caelia beside,
And my husband's step-mother attended the bride;
And know the groom's man was a person of fame,
A youth of large fortune—and Patten his name.

At Shotwig I chose to be married, my dear
(A small country church, and to Saughall quite near);   10
For myself I had flattered, in that rural scene
No other spectators around me would reign,
Excepting fair Flora, and the feathered train.
But trust me, when we to the village drew near,
The nymphs and the swains all in ranks did appear,
To see us fine folks; for sure, fine we must be,
When powdered, and dressed, à la mode de Paris!
In pink, blue and white, to the skies trimmed, you know,
With our white gloves and ribbons we made a great show;
And well might the lads and the lasses all stare,   20
For such belles and such beaux are at Shotwig most rare.
Had you seen but my niece, when for bridesmaid she stood,
You'd have thought she was Venus, just sprung from the flood.

The knot being tied, with the Vicar we went,
And an hour or two we most agreeably spent,
In regaling our palates with plum-cake and wine;
Then drove to Parkgate, where at four we did dine
On fish, lamb, and ducks, puddings, tarts, whips, my dear,
Drinking red wine and white, jaded spirits to cheer.
At seven we ordered in coffee and tea;   30
We sipped; paid our bill; and drove rapid away
To the Two Mills, my friend, where again we did call
Ourselves to refresh, men and horses and all.

At tea we returned to our house, with due pride,
In a post-coach and four, and a post-chaise beside;
And, had but Maria joined this bridal train,
My transports to paint all attempts would be vain.
Yet I hope, when convenient, to see me you'll come;
For good wives, you well know, must go seldom from home.
Methinks, I by this hear you cry, with a sneer,   40
'Lord bless me! what wonders one may live to hear!
That thus my gay sister should suddenly change!'
Get married, Maria—you'll not think it strange;
The old maxim you'll find to hold good, I am sure,
That 'Home still is home, be it ever so poor';
But, if it's a good one, what can we wish more?

(Wr. *c.*1788; pub. 1794)

LADY ANNE LINDSAY (later BARNARD)
(1750–1825)

She was the eldest child of James Lindsay, 5th Earl of Balcarres, and his wife Anne Dalrymple. Her father spent many years attempting to restore the family fortunes, much reduced by the Jacobite Rebellion. She was brought up in Fife with visits in winter to Edinburgh where her mother and sisters settled after her father's death in 1768. She came to know the Edinburgh intelligentsia of the period, such as David Hume, Henry Mackenzie, Lord Monboddo and others, and in November 1773 met Samuel Johnson at the end of his tour of Scotland, and recorded his conversation. In 1770 her sister, Lady Margaret Lindsay, left for England to marry Alexander Fordyce of Roehampton, a wealthy banker. It was at this point that Lady Anne wrote the only poem for which she is remembered: 'I was melancholy, and endeavoured to amuse myself by attempting a few poetical trifles.' She took the name of Robin Gray from 'the old herd at Balcarres', and she wrote the poem to replace the 'improper words' of an old Scottish air ('The Bridegroom greets when the Sun gangs down'). Although she was pleased by the popularity of her version, 'such was *my dread* of being suspected of writing *anything*, perceiving the shyness it created in those who could write *nothing*, that I carefully kept my own secret'. Her account of its composition, printed by Scott in 1825, also mentions a controversy as to its authenticity as a 'very ancient' composition and the offer of a reward by newspapers for a solution to the question. It was popular 'from the highest to the lowest', while 'I hugged my self in my obscurity'. She later wrote an inferior continuation, not included below.

    A few years later she moved to London to live with her sister, Lady Margaret, whose husband had not, as is sometimes said, recently died, but had gone spectacularly bankrupt and fled for a time to France, leaving debts of £150,000 and ruining many others. (Mrs Thrale and Horace Walpole were both scandalized that the Fordyces were eventually given a government pension.) Their home in Berkeley Square became a salon frequented by Pitt, Burke, Sheridan, Windham, Dundas and others, and for many years she was friendly with the Prince of Wales. In 1793, when in her early forties, she 'stood the world's smile' and married Andrew Barnard, son of

Bishop Thomas Barnard, the friend of Johnson. Her husband, a half-pay officer, was younger and poorer than she, but through her influence he was appointed Colonial Secretary to Lord Macartney, the new Governor of the Cape of Good Hope, and they accompanied him there in 1797. Her letters from the Cape between 1797 and 1802 give a unique account of the colony at this period. After their return to England the Barnards lived in Wimbledon until 1806, when her husband went back to the Cape for a limited period, but died there of a fever in May 1807. Although she had outlived most of her earlier literary and political acquaintance, she remained prominent in London society for another decade. It was after Walter Scott attributed 'Auld Robin Gray' to her in *The Pirate*, ch. 26, in 1821, that she wrote to him, admitting her authorship for the first time outside her family, and giving the account of its composition quoted above, which he published in his edition of the poem in 1825. She died on 6 May 1825.

182   *Auld Robin Gray*

WHEN the sheep are in the fauld, when the cows come hame,
When a' the weary world to quiet rest are gane,
The woes of my heart fa' in showers frae my ee,
Unkenned by my gudeman, who soundly sleeps by me.

Young Jamie loo'd me weel, and sought me for his bride;
But saving ae crown-piece, he'd naething else beside.
To make the crown a pound, my Jamie gaed to sea;
And the crown and the pound, oh! they were baith for me!

Before he had been gane a twelvemonth and a day,
My father brak his arm, our cow was stown away;   10
My mither she fell sick—my Jamie was at sea—
And auld Robin Gray, oh! he came a-courting me.

My father cou'dna work, my mother cou'dna spin;
I toiled day and night, but their bread I cou'dna win;
And Rob maintained them baith, and, wi' tears in his ee,
Said, 'Jenny, oh! for their sakes, will you marry me?'

My heart it said na, and I looked for Jamie back;
But hard blew the winds, and his ship was a wrack:
His ship it was a wrack! Why didna Jenny dee!
Or, wherefore am I spared to cry out, Woe is me!   20

My father argued sair—my mother didna speak,
But she looked in my face till my heart was like to break:
They gied him my hand, but my heart was in the sea;
And so auld Robin Gray, he was gudeman to me.

Unkenned] unknown

277

I hadna been his wife, a week but only four,
When mournfu' as I sat on the stane at my door,
I saw my Jamie's ghaist—I cou'dna think it he,
Till he said, 'I'm come hame, my love, to marry thee!'

O sair, sair did we greet, and mickle say of a';
Ae kiss we took, nae mair—I bad him gang awa.   30
I wish that I were dead, but I'm no like to dee;
For O, I am but young to cry out, Woe is me!

I gang like a ghaist, and I carena much to spin;
I darena think o' Jamie, for that wad be a sin.
But I will do my best a gude wife aye to be,
For auld Robin Gray, oh! he is sae kind to me.

(Wr. 1771; pub. 1776)

SUSANNA BLAMIRE
(1747–94)

She was the youngest of the four children of William Blamire, a yeoman farmer at
The Oaks near Dalston, six miles from Carlisle, and his wife Isabella Simpson. Her
mother died when she was 7 and, when her father remarried in 1755 (he died three
years later), she, her sister Sarah, and her two brothers went to live with their
widowed aunt, Mary Simpson (1702–85) on her substantial farm at Thackwood,
near Stokedalewath. She was educated at the village school at Raughton Head a mile
away and showed an early aptitude for reading and writing, although her earliest
surviving poem dates from 1766. In 1767 her sister Sarah married Lieut.-Col.
Graham (or Graeme) of the 42nd Highland Regiment, and Susanna stayed with
them at Gartmore in the Highlands, as well as accompanying them to London and
Ireland. She also visited an aunt, Mrs Fell, the wife of a curate at Chilingham in the
Border Country, where she became friendly with the family of the Earl of
Tankerville. According to family tradition, she and Lord Ossulton, the Earl's son,
were attracted to each other, but this unsuitable match was prevented by sending him
abroad. When Col. Graham died in 1773, his widow returned to live at Thackwood.
    Susanna 'had a graceful form, somewhat above the middle size, and a coun-
tenance—though slightly marked with smallpox—beaming with good nature; her
dark eyes sparkled with animation, and won every heart at the first introduction'. She
drew, played the guitar and flageolet, enjoyed dancing and, without any plan of
publication, wrote verse, although her aunt and eldest brother William, a naval
surgeon before his return to Thackwood, discouraged this last activity. At the end of
'Stoklewath' she mentions her local reputation as a medical adviser, describing
herself as one who is 'fam'd for joke, | For physic, too, some little is renown'd, | With
every salve that loves to heal the wound; | The pulse she feels with true mysterious air
. . .'. Only two of her lively and intelligent letters have survived, probably written in
her twenties. Prosperous local families usually spent the winter in Carlisle, where she
met Catherine Gilpin of Scaleby Castle, who also wrote verse, and for a time they

shared lodgings and occasionally wrote poems together. A number of poems indicate that her health had started to deteriorate by the mid-1780s: she mentions this in, for example, her lines 'On the dangerous illness of my friend Mrs. L.' (March 1788), which is also evidence of her friendship with the family of Edmund Law, Bishop of Carlisle. She died in Carlisle in 1794, attended by her brother William, and was buried, by her own request, at Raughton Head Chapel. She left most of her property to her sister Sarah Graham, who died in 1798.

Some of her songs had begun to find their way into print in the 1780s as anonymous single sheets, which were reprinted in magazines and such collections as *Calliope, or the Musical Miscellany* (1788) and Johnson's *Scots Musical Museum*, Vol. iii (1790). A few later appeared in Robert Anderson's *Ballads* (Wigtown, 1808). Her memory was kept alive through the enthusiasm of Patrick Maxwell of Edinburgh and Dr Henry Lonsdale of Carlisle, who met in 1836 and began systematically collecting her verse and tracing her relatives. Advertisements in the *Carlisle Journal* and other enquiries brought to light MS collections in the possession of her niece, Jane Christian Blamire, and of Susanna Brown of Newcastle, daughter of Susanna's half-sister Bridget Brown, and elsewhere. Lonsdale later described the MSS as often written on the backs of old letters or recipes, usually in the form of corrected drafts and rarely ('Stoklewath' was an exception) in fair copy. These efforts led to *The Poetical Works of Miss Susanna Blamire, 'The Muse of Cumberland'* (Edinburgh, 1842), with preface, memoir, and notes by Maxwell, and the collection of materials and factual information attributed to Lonsdale, who added some further information about her in his *Worthies of Cumberland*, iv (1873), 41–107. Maxwell considered her 'unquestionably the best female writer of her age' and believed she would have been recognized as such if she had chosen to publish in her lifetime, but her poems have never been reprinted as a whole since 1842 and remain little known.

183   *Epistle to her Friends at Gartmore*

MY Gartmore friends a blessing on ye,
And all that's good still light upon ye!
Will you allow this hobbling rhyme
To tell you how I pass my time?
'Tis true I write in shortened measure,
Because I scrawl but at my leisure;
For why?—sublimity of style
Takes up a most prodigious while;
To count with fingers six or seven,
And mind that syllables are even,—   10
To make the proper accent fall,
La! 'tis the very deuce of all:
Alternate verse, too, makes me think
How to get t'other line to clink;
And then your odes with two lines rhyming,
An intermitting sort of chiming,
Just like the bells on birthdays ringing,
Or like your friend S. Blamire's singing,

Which only pleases those whose ears
Ne'er heard the music of the spheres.   20
As for this measure, these trite strains
Give me no sort of thought or pains;
If that the first line ends with head,
Why then the rhyme to that is bed;
And so on through the whole essay,
For careless ease makes out my say;
And if you'll let me tell you how
I pass my time, I'll tell you now.
    First, then, I've brought me up my tea,—
A medicine which I'd ordered me;   30
It's from the coast of Labrador,
Sir Hugh, the gallant Commodore,
Brought it to me for my rheumatics,—
O girls! these aches play me sad tricks;—
And e'en in London had you found me,
You'd found a yard of flannel round me.
At eight I rise—a decent time!
But aunt would say 'tis oftener nine.
I come down stairs, the cocoa ready,—
For you must know I'm turned fine lady,   40
And fancy tea gives me a pain
Where 'tis not decent to complain.
When breakfast's done, I take a walk
Where English girls their secrets talk;
But as for you, ye're modest maids,
And shun the house to walk i' the shades;
Often my circuit's round the garden,
In which there's no flower worth a farthing.
I sit me down and work a while,
But here, I think, I see you smile;   50
At work! quoth you;—but little's done,
Thou lik'st too well a bit of fun.
At twelve, I dress my head so smart,
Were there a man—he'd lose his heart;
My hair is turned the lovelist brown,
There's no such hair in London town!
Nor do I use one grain of powder,
Either the violet or the other;
Nature adopts me for her child,—
Fair is her fruit when not run wild.   60
    At one, the cloth is constant laid
By little Fan, our pretty maid.
Round her such native beauty glows,
You'd take her cheek to be some rose

Just spreading forth its blossom sweet,
Where red and white in union meet;
She's prettier much than her young lady,
But that, you know, full easily may be.
'Well, Fanny, do you wish to go
To the dance there in the town below?'   70
'Yes;—but I dare not ask my mistress.'
'O! I'll relieve you from that distress!'
I ask for her,—away she goes,
And shines a belle among the beaus.
Now, my good friends, by this you see
Rustics have balls as well as we;
And really as to different stations,
Or comforts in the various nations,
They're more upon an equal par
Than we imagine them by far.   80
They love and hate—have just the same
Feeling of pleasure and of pain;
Only our kind of education
Gives ours a greater elevation.
I oft have listened to the chat
Of country folks 'bout who knows what!
And yet their wit, though unrefined,
Seems the pure product of the mind.
    You'd laugh to see the honest wives
Telling me how their household thrives;   90
For, you must know, I'm famed for skill
In the nice compound of a pill.
'Miss Sukey, here's a little lass,
She's not sae weel as what she was;
The peer peer bairn does oft complain,—
A'd tell ye where, but I think shame.'
'Nay, speak, good woman,—mind not me;
The child is not quite well I see.'
'Nea;' she says, 'her belly aches,
And Jwohnie got her some worm-cakes;   100
They did nea good—though purged her well,—
What is the matter we can't tell;
She sadly whets her teeth at neet,
And a' the day does nought but freet;
It's outher worms, or wind, or water,
Something you know mun be the matter.'
'My little woman, come to me;
Her tongue is very white I see;
Come, wrap her little head up warm,
And give her this,—'twill do no harm;   110

'Twill give a gentle stool, or so.'
'Is it a purge?' 'No, Peggy, no;
Only an easy gentle lotion,
To give her once a-day a motion;
For 'pothecaries late have found
Diseases rise from being bound,
'Gainst which they've physic in their shop,
And many a drug, and useless slop;
This here will purify your blood,
And this will do your stomach good;   120
This is for vapours when splenetic,
And here's a cure for the sciatic;
But let her take what I have given,
'Twill help to keep your child from heaven.'
'Lord grant it may! and if it do,
Long as I live I'll pray for you.'
   After I've dined, maybe I read,
Or write to favourites 'cross the Tweed;
Then work till tea, then walk again,
If it does neither snow nor rain.   130
If e'er my spirits want a flow,
Up stairs I run to my bureau,
And get your letters—read them over
With all the fondness of a lover;
This never fails to give me pleasure,
For these are Friendship's hoarded treasure,
And never fail to make me gay;
How oft I bless the happy day
Which made us friends and keeps us so,
Though now almost five years ago!   140
Trust me, my dear, I would not part
With the share, I hope, I've in your heart,
For any thing that wealth could give;
Without a friend, O who would live!
My favourite motto runs—'He's poor
Who has a world and nothing more;
Exchange it for a friend, 'tis gain,
A better thing you then obtain.'
   But stop, my journal's nearly done;
Through the whole day 'tis almost run.   150
I think I'd sipped my tea nigh up,
O! yes, I'm sure I drank my cup;
I work till supper, after that
I play or sing, maybe we chat;

stool] evacuation of the bowels   bound] constipated

At ten we always go to bed,
And thus my life I've calmly led
Since my return;—as Prior says
In some of his satiric lays,
'I eat, and drink, and sleep,—what then?
I eat, and drink, and sleep again;   160
Thus idly lolls my time away,
And just does nothing all the day!'

(Wr. *c.* 1772; pub. 1842)

184   from *Stoklewath; or, The Cumbrian Village*

FROM where dark clouds of curling smoke arise,
And the tall column mounts into the skies;
Where the grim arches of the forge appear,
Whose fluted pillars prop the thickening air;
Where domes of peers and humble roofs are found
Alike to spread their mingled vapours round;
From denser air and busy towns I run,
To catch a glimpse of the unclouded sun;
Foe to the toils which wealth and pomp create,
And all the hard-wrought tinsel of the great.   10

.   .   .   .   .   .

Adown the stream where woods begin to throw
Their verdant arms around the rocks below,
A rustic bridge across the tide is thrown,
Where briars and woodbine hide the hoary stone;
A simple arch salutes th' admiring eye,
And the mill's clack the tumbling waves supply.
But lest society some loss should share,
And nearest neighbours lack their neighbour's fare,
The tottering step-stones cross the stream are laid,
O'er which trips lightly many a busy maid,   20
And many a matron; when one failing cow
Bids no big cheese within the cheese-vat grow,
Their wealthier neighbour then, her bowls to swell,
Will gladly take what they as gladly sell.
The morning toils are now completely o'er,
The bowls well scalded, and well swept the floor.
The daughter at the needle plies the seam,
While the good mother hastens to the stream:
There the long webs, that wintry moons began,
Lie stretched and beaming in the summer's sun;   30

And lest he scorch them in his fervid hours,
She scoops along the nice conducted showers;
Till like the snow, that tips the mountain's height,
The brown's dull shade gives place to purest white;
While her sweet child knee-deep is wading seen,
Picking bright stones, or tumbling on the green.
  But now the sun's bright whirling wheels appear
On the broad front of noon, in full career.
A sign more welcome hangs not in the air,
For now the sister's call the brothers hear;   40
Dinner's the word, and every cave around
Devours the voice, and feasts upon the sound.
' 'Tis dinner, father!' all the brothers cry,
Throw down the spade, and heave the pickaxe by;
' 'Tis dinner, father!' Home they panting go,
While the tired parent still pants on more slow.
Now the fried rasher meets them on the way,
And savoury pancakes welcome steams convey.
Their pace they mend, till at the pump they stand,
Deluge the face and purify the hand,   50
And then to dinner. There the women wait,
And the tired father fills his chair of state;
Smoking potatoes meet their thankful eyes,
And Hunger wafts the grateful sacrifice;
To her libations of sweet milk are poured,
And Peace and Plenty watch around the board.
  Now, till the sun has somewhat sunk in height,
Yet long before he dips his wheels in night,
The nut-brown labourers their senses steep
In the soft dews of renovating sleep;   60
The worthy sire to the soft bed repairs,
The sons beneath the shade forget their cares.
The clock strikes two, it beats upon the ear,
And soon the parent's anxious voice they hear:
'Come, come, my lads, you must not sleep all day!'
They rub their eyes, start up, then stalk away.

              .   .   .   .

  From noon till morn rests female toil; save come
The evening hours when lowing cows draw home.
Now the good neighbour walks her friend to see,
And knits an hour, and drink a dish of tea.   70
She comes unlooked for—wheat-bread is to seek,
The baker has none, got no yeast last week;
And little Peggy thinks herself ill sped,
Though she has got a great piece gingerbread.

Home she returns, but disappointment's trace
Darkens her eye, and lengthens all her face;
She whispers lowly in her sister's ear,
Scarce can restrain the glistening, swelling tear.
The mother marks, and to the milk-house goes,   80
Blithe Peggy smiles, she well the errand knows;
There from the bowl, where cream so coolly swims,
The future butter generously skims,
And, flour commixing, forms a rural bread
That for the wheaten loaf oft stands in stead;
Cup after cup sends steaming circles round,
And oft the weak tea's in the full pot drowned;
It matters not, for while their news they tell
The mind's content, and all things move on well.

   The sun has now his saffron robe put on,
Stepped from his chariot that with rubies shone;   90
The glittering monarch gains the western gate,
And for a moment shines in regal state;
His streaming mantle floats along the sky,
While he glides softly from the gazing eye;
From saffron tinge to yellow soon it flew,
Sea-green the next, and then to darkest blue.

   Now different cares employ the village train,
The rich in cattle press the milky vein;
When, lo! a voice sends direful notes around,
And sharp vexation mingles in the sound;   100
'Tis little Peggy, she the pail would fill,
And on old Hawky try her early skill.
She stroked and clapped her, but she'd not allow;
The well-known hand best pleased the knowing cow;
Though cabbage leaves before her band was cast,
Hawky refused the coaxing rich repast;
And when the little hand unapt she found,
She kicked, and whelmed her on the slippery ground.

   Along yon hedge now mouldering and decayed,
In gathered heaps you see the fragments laid;   110
Piled up with care to swell the nightly blaze,
And in the widow's hut a fire to raise.
See where she comes with her blue apron full,
Crowned with some scattered locks of dingy wool.
In years she seems, and on her well-patched clothes
Want much has added to her other woes.
There is a poor-house; but some little pride
Forbids her there her humbled head to hide;
O'er former scenes of better days she runs,
And everything like degradation shuns!   120

Now hooded Eve slow-gliding comes in view,
Busied in threading pearls of diamond dew;
Waking the flowers that early close the eye,
And giving drops to those that else would die.
And what is man but such a tender flower,
That buds, blooms, fades and dies within the hour?
　Where round yon cottage the rosemary grows,
And turncap lilies flaunt beside the rose,
Two aged females turn the weary wheel,
And, as they turn, their slumbering thoughts reveal: 　　130
'How long is't, think ye, since th' old style was lost?
Poor England may remember't to her cost!
E'er since that time the weather has grown cold'
(For Jane forgets that she is now grown old).
'I know when I lived servant at Woodmile,
So scorching hot the weather was in April,
The cows would startle, and by ten o'clock
My master used his horses to unyoke;
Tis not so now; the sun has lost its power;
The very apples now-a-days are sour! 　　140
Could not the Parson tell the reason why
There are such changes both in earth and sky?'
　' 'Tis not these only,' Margaret replied,
'For many a change besides have I espied.
Look at the girls!—they all dress now-a-days
Like them fine folk mob act them nonsense plays!
No more the decent mob surrounds the face,
Bordered with edging, or bit good bone-lace;
Gauze flappets soon—that will not last a day—
We'll see them flaunting whilst they're making hay! 　　150
All things are changed, the world's turned upside down,
And every servant wears a cotton gown,
Bit flimsy things, that have no strength to wear,
And will like any blotting-paper tear!
I made my Nelly a half-worsted gown,
She slighting told me 't would not do in town!
This pride! this pride! it sure must have a fall,
And bring some heavy judgement on us all!
They're grown so bold too, and their lads allow,
When courting them, to skulk behind a cow, 　　160
Till all's in bed. My John, when courting me,
Used after supper to come manfully;

---

old style] i.e. the calendar before its adjustment to the Gregorian Calendar (New Style) in
1752, with the loss of eleven days　　　mob] mob-cap fastening under the chin

For oft he used to say he knew no place
Where honesty need fear to show its face.
No more it need! My master used to cry,
He feared but two things—to turn thief, and lie.'

(Wr. *c.*1780; pub. 1842)

185 *Written on a Gloomy Day, in Sickness*
Thackwood, 4th June, 1786

THE gloomy lowering of the sky,
 The milky softness of the air,
The hum of many a busy fly,
 Are things the cheerful well can spare;
But, to the pensive, thoughtful mind,
 Those kindred glooms are truly dear,
When in dark shades such wood-notes wind
 As woo and win Reflection's ear;—
The birds that warble overhead,
 The bees that visit every flower,   10
The stream that murmurs o'er its bed
 All aid the melancholy hour.
Added to this, the wasting frame,
 Through which life's pulses slowly beat,
Would fain persuade that naught's the same
 As when health glowed with genial heat.
Where are the spirits, light as air,
 That self-amused, would carol loud?
Would find out pleasure everywhere,
 And all her paths with garlands strowed? 20
Nature's the same: the Spring returns,
 The leaf again adorns the tree;
How tasteless this to her who mourns—
 To her who droops and fades like me!
No emblem for myself I find,
 Save what some dying plant bestows—
Save where its drooping head I bind,
 And mark how strong the likeness grows.
No more sweet Eve with drops distilled
 Shall melt o'er thee in tender grief; 30
Nor bid Aurora's cup be filled
 With balmy dew from yonder leaf.

What, though some seasons more had rolled
  Their golden suns to glad thine eye!
Yet as a flower of mortal mould
  'Twas still thy lot—to bloom and die.

(Wr. 1786; pub. 1842)

186   *I've Gotten a Rock, I've Gotten a Reel*

I'VE gotten a rock, I've gotten a reel,
I've gotten a wee bit spinning-wheel;
An' by the whirling rim I've found
How the weary, weary warl goes round.
'Tis roun' an' roun' the spokes they go,
Now ane is up, an' ane is low;
'Tis by ups and downs in Fortune's wheel,
That mony ane gets a rock to reel.

I've seen a lassie barefoot gae,
Look dashed an' blate, wi' nought to say;   10
But as the wheel turned round again,
She chirped an' talked, nor seemed the same:
Sae fine she goes, sae far aglee,
That folks she kenned she canna see;
An' fleeching chiels around her thrang,
Till she miskens her a' day lang.

There's Jock, when the bit lass was poor,
Ne'er trudged o'er the lang mossy moor,
Though now to the knees he wades, I trow,
Through winter's weet an' winter's snow: 20
An' Pate declared the ither morn
She was like a lily amang the corn;
Though ance he swore her dazzling een
Were bits o' glass that blacked had been.

Now, lassies, I hae found it out,
What men make a' this phrase about;
For when they praise your blinking ee,
'Tis certain that your gowd they see:
An' when they talk o' roses bland,
They think o' the roses o' your land;   30

186 rock] distaff   blate] bashful   aglee] awry   kenned] knew
fleeching chiels] flattering lads   ee] eyes   gowd] gold

But should dame Fortune turn her wheel,
They'd aff in a dance of a threesome reel.

(Wr. *c*.1790; pub. 1842)

187   *When Home We Return*

WHEN home we return, after youth has been spending,
And many a slow year has been wasting and ending,
We often seem lost in the once well-known places,
And sigh to find age has so furrowed dear faces;
For the rose that has faded the eye still keeps mourning,
And weeps every change that it sees on returning.

Should we miss but a tree where we used to be playing,
Or find the wood cut where we sauntered a-Maying,—
If the yew-seat's away, or the ivy's a-wanting,
We hate the fine lawn and the new-fashioned planting.   10
Each thing called improvement seems blackened with crimes,
If it tears up one record of blissful old times.

When many a spring had called forth the sweet flowers,
And many an autumn had painted the bowers,
I came to the place where life had its beginning,
Taking root with the groves that around me were springing;
When I found them all gone, 'twas like dear friends departed,
And I walked where they used to be, half broken-hearted!

When distant, one bower my fancy still haunted,
'Twas hung round with woodbine my Jessy had planted;   20
I ran to the spot, where a weak flower remaining
Could just nod its head to approve my complaining.
A tear for a dewdrop I hid in its fringes,
And sighed then to think what one's pleasures unhinges!

But, ah! what is that to the friends oft estranging,
Their manners still more than their looks daily changing;
Where the heart used to *warm* to find *civil* behaviour,
Make us wish we had stayed from our country for ever,
With the sweet days of youth in our fancies still glowing,
And the love of old friends with old Time ever growing!

(Wr. *c*.1790; pub. 1842)

188 *The Siller Croun*

'AND ye shall walk in silk attire,
  And siller hae to spare,
Gin ye'll consent to be his bride,
  Nor think o' Donald mair.'
O wha wad buy a silken goun
  Wi' a poor broken heart!
Or what's to me a siller croun,
  Gin frae my love I part!

The mind wha's every wish is pure
  Far dearer is to me;   10
And ere I'm forced to break my faith
  I'll lay me doun an' dee!
For I hae pledged my virgin troth
  Brave Donald's fate to share;
And he has gi'en to me his heart,
  Wi' a' its virtues rare.

His gentle manners wan my heart,
  He gratefu' took the gift;
Could I but think to seek it back
  It wad be waur than theft!   20
For langest life can ne'er repay
  The love he bears to me;
And ere I'm forced to break my troth
  I'll lay me doun an' dee.

(1790)

189 *Wey, Ned, Man!*

The subject of this song was actually overheard

'WEY, Ned, man! thou luiks sae down-hearted,
  Yen wad swear aw thy kindred were dead;
For sixpence, thy Jean and thee's parted,—
  What then, man, ne'er bodder thy head!
There's lasses enow, I'll uphod te,
  And tou may be suin as weel matched;
Tou knows there's still fish i' the river
  As guid as has ever been catched.'

'Nay, Joe! tou kens nought o' the matter,
  Sae let's hae nae mair o' thy jeer;   10
Auld England's gown's worn till a tatter,
  And they'll nit new don her, I fear.
True liberty never can flourish,
  Till man in his reets is a king,—
Till we tek a tithe pig frae the bishop,
  As he's duin frae us, is the thing.'

'What, Ned! and is this aw that ails thee?
  Mess, lad! tou deserves maist to hang!
What! tek a bit lan frae its owner!—
  Is this then thy fine *Reets o' Man?*   20
Tou ploughs, and tou sows, and tou reaps, man,
  Tou cums, and tou gangs, where tou will;
Nowther king, lword, nor bishop, dar touch thee,
  Sae lang as tou dis fwok nae ill!'

'How can tou say sae, Joe! tou kens, now,
  If hares were as plenty as hops,
I durstn't fell yen for my life, man,
  Nor tek't out o' auld Cwoley's chops:
While girt fwok they ride down my hedges,
  And spang o'er my fields o' new wheat,   30
Nought but ill words I get for my damage;—
  Can ony man tell me *that's reet?*'

'Why, there I mun own the shoe pinches,
  Just there to find faut is nae shame;
Ne'er ak! there's nae hard laws in England,
  Except this bit thing about game:
Man, were we aw equal at mwornin,
  We couldn't remain sae till neet;
Some arms are far stranger than others,
  And some heads will tek in mair leet.   40

'Tou couldn't mend laws an' tou wad, man;
  'Tis for other-guess noddles than thine;
Lord help te! sud beggars yence rule us,
  They'd tek off baith thy cwoat an' mine.
What is't then but law that stands by us,
  While we stand by country and king?
And as to being parfet and parfet,
  I tell thee, there is nae sec thing.'

                              (Wr. 1792; pub. 1842)

190 *Auld Robin Forbes*

AND auld Robin Forbes hes gien tem a dance,
I pat on my speckets to see them aw prance;
I thout o' the days when I was but fifteen,
And skipped wi' the best upon Forbes's green.
Of aw things that is I think thout is meast queer,
It brings that that's by-past and sets it down here;
I see Willy as plain as I dui this bit leace,
When he tuik his cwoat lappet and deeghted his feace.

The lasses aw wondered what Willy cud see
In yen that was dark and hard-featured leyke me;   10
And they wondered ay mair when they talked o' my wit,
And slily telt Willy that cudn't be it:
But Willy he laughed, and he meade me his weyfe,
And whea was mair happy thro' aw his lang leyfe?
It's e'en my great comfort, now Willy is geane,
That he offen said—nea pleace was leyke his awn heame!

I mind when I carried my wark to yon steyle
Where Willy was deykin, the time to beguile,
He wad fling me a daisy to put i' my breast,
And I hammered my noddle to mek out a jest.   20
But merry or grave, Willy often wad tell
There was nin o' the leave that was leyke my awn sel;
And he spak what he thout, for I'd hardly a plack
When we married, and nobbet ae gown to my back.

When the clock had struck eight I expected him heame,
And wheyles went to meet him as far as Dumleane;
Of aw hours it telt *eight* was dearest to me,
But now when it streykes there's a tear i' my ee.
O Willy! dear Willy! it never can be
That age, time, or death, can divide thee and me!   30
For that spot on earth that's aye dearest to me,
Is the turf that has covered my Willy frae me!

(Wr. by 1794; pub. 1842)

speckets] spectacles   deeghted] dighted, cleaned   deykin] dyking, digging a
ditch   leave] lave, rest   plack] small coin

191 *O Jenny Dear*

'O JENNY dear, lay by your pride,
    Or else I plainly see
Your wrinkles ye'll be fain to hide,
    May-be at sixty-three.
But, take my word, 'tis then o'er late
    To gain a wayward man;
A maiden auld her hooks may bait,
    But catch us gin you can!'

'An unco prize forsooth ye are!
    For, when the bait is tane,   10
Ye fill our hearts sae fu' o' care,
    We wish them ours again.
To witch our faith, ye tell a tale
    O' love that ne'er will end;
Nae hinnyed words wi' me prevail,
    For men will never mend.'

'But, Jenny, look at aunty Kate,
    Wha is a maiden auld,
I's warrant she repented late
    When wooers' hearts grew cauld.   20
An ape to lead's a silly thing
    When ye step down below,
Or here to sit wi' chittering wing
    Like birdies i' the snow.'

'That's better than to sit at hame
    Wi' saut tears i' my ee;
An ape I think's a harmless thing
    To sic a thing as ye.
Good men are changed frae wooers sair,
    And naething do but slight;   30
A wife becomes a drudge o' care,
    And never's in the right.

'There's bonny Tibby o' the glen,
    And Anny o' the hill,
Their beauty crazèd baith their men,
    And might delight them still;

hinnyed] honeyed   An ape to lead ... below] to lead apes in hell, to die an old maid   chittering] shivering

But now they watch their lordies' frowns,
  Their sauls they daurna own;
'Tis tyranny that wedlock crowns,
  And woman's joys are flown.'   40

(Wr. by 1794; pub. 1842)

ANNE PENNY (née HUGHES, formerly CHRISTIAN)
(1731–84)

She was the daughter of the Revd Owen Hughes of Bangor, Caernarvonshire. In 1746, aged about 15, she married Capt. Thomas Christian (1716–51), a naval officer who had acquired an estate in Oxfordshire with the proceeds of the capture of a Spanish galleon. Their son became Rear-Admiral Sir Hugh Cloberry Christian (1747–98). After her husband's death she published *Cambridge. A Poem* (1756), dedicated to the Duchess of Hamilton, describing herself as 'the unfriended Muse'. She later married Peter Penné or Penny, who is said to have overcome her 'strong resolutions against a second marriage' by his extreme good nature. According to one source he was a naval officer who had lost a leg and gained a small pension, which may not contradict another statement that he was of French origin and became a customs officer in Oxfordshire. She is said to have been 'much esteemed' by Samuel Johnson, to whom she dedicated her *Anningait and Ajutt, A Greenland Tale* (1761), versified from the *Rambler*, Nos. 186–7. She translated Gessner's *Select Poems* (1762) and in 1771 published her *Poems, With a Dramatic Entertainment* by subscription. The volume is dated from Bloomsbury Square, London, and dedicated to Jonas Hanway (1712–86), the philanthropist, who in 1756 had founded the Marine Society, for which the following songs were later written. *A Pastoral Elegy on the Death of Lord Lyttelton* [1775?] is also attributed to her. Her second husband died in 1779, leaving her in great distress. Her friends organized a second subscription for a new edition of her *Poems* in 1780, in which twelve poems were omitted and seventeen added. Her 300 or so subscribers include Horace Walpole, to whom she addressed some flattering lines (pp. 127–8). She died in 1784, described in some verses to her memory by Hanway as 'one who had long tried affliction's rod'.

192 *Odes Sung in Commemoration of the Marine Society*

*On occasion of their Anniversary Dinner at the Crown and
Anchor Tavern in the Strand, the 22d Day of February, 1773*

(i)

*Sung by a Choir of Boys marching round the Room, at the Head of
the Society's Poor Boys*

SOCIAL Virtue's liberal plan
Cheers the helpless race of man:
O'er the poor's defenceless head,
See! her healing wings are spread!

Plants from Britain's earth behold
(Britain, parent of the bold),
Snatched from Vice's horrid train,
Chilling penury and pain!

Raised by Virtue's powerful arm,
See! their throbbing bosoms warm!   10
Certain pledge how well they'll prove
What they owe to Social Love.

Hail! thou blessing all divine!
Still, O still through Albion shine;
Whilst thy golden chain's unbroke,
Her foes shall bend beneath her yoke.

(ii)

Sung at Table by the same Choir

SEE these happy youths, now made
Bulwarks of our wealth and trade.
From this glorious source will flow
Vigorous strength, to quell each foe.

May such noble plans sustain
GEORGE's empire on the main!
May rich Commerce, England's pride,
Still adorn her swelling tide!

While ye guardians of our isle,
Favoured by his gracious smile,   10

Band of patriot-brothers, tie
The knot of social amity;

Virtue hails the great design,
She owns the impulse quite divine;
Bids her patriot King approve
The golden band of Social Love!

(Wr. 1773; pub. 1780)

ANONYMOUS ('A LADY')

193   *The Self-Examination*

WHY throbs my heart when he appears?
    From whence this tender sigh?
Why are my eyes dissolved in tears,
    When he's no longer nigh?

Where are my wonted pleasures fled?
    Nor books nor lyre can please;
That lies untouched, and these unread:
    All occupations tease.

One loved idea still employs
    All hopes and all desires!   10
Walks are insipid, music's noise,
    And conversation tires.

But when Philander speaks, 'tis then
    I all attention pay;
And fondly wish the power to pen
    Whate'er he deigns to say!

O with what skill I strive to hide
    The joy my bosom feels!
When he, oft seated by my side,   20
    To me his thoughts reveals.

Wit, sense, and genius then conspire
    Each faculty to seize!
And while I fondly thus admire,
    I lose the power to please.

A pause ensues, his eyes still speak,
    As waiting a reply:
My words in faltering accents break,
    Or on my lips they die.

Oh were Philander once to bear
    In all my woes a part;   30
And softly whisper in my ear
    The secret of his heart!

What pleasure through each sense would glide!
    What transport should I feel!
O say, my heart, thus sweetly tried,
    Couldst thou thy joys conceal?

                      (1773)

194   *The Visit*

BY absence, and unkind neglect,
    Fond passion almost cured,
No greater ills did I expect
    Than those I had endured.

Time's lenient hand a cordial brought
    To ease my love-sick breast;
Which softly soothed each anxious thought,
    And lulled my cares to rest.

When lo! before my dazzled sight   10
    The swain in smiles appears:
My beating heart felt new delight!
    Far flew its wonted fears!

The moments gaily glided on;
    He never charmed me more:
Love was the subject he begun,
    And well expressed its power.

With curious search, he meant to learn
    What I resolved to hide;   20
A tender heart he might discern,
    In spite of all my pride.

But its emotions so concealed,
　　The flame it long had known,
By no unguarded word revealed,
　　By no fond look was shown.

In friendly guise, I gently leant
　　On his unkind neglect,
My thoughts on all his words intent,
　　Some gleam of hope expect.

What pleasures round my bosom steal,
　　When, with a gentle smile,　　　　　　30
'The truth from thee I'll not conceal,'
　　He cried, and paused awhile.

Delusive wish was on the wing,
　　With phantoms fair to cheat;
Inviting views from fancy spring,
　　And aid the soft deceit.

But ah! what hideous forms succeed,
　　To chill my panting heart!
My doom I felt at once decreed!　　　　　40
　　Swift flew the killing dart:

When from Philander's lips I heard
　　A nymph divinely fair
Employed each thought, her smiles reward
　　With joy each tender care.

Then dwelling on the dire event,
　　He poured forth all his mind:
Expressed, in full, his fond content,
　　And when the fair was kind.

Ah! why to me the sickening tale,　　　　50
　　And all thy joys reveal?
Did generous sentiments prevail,
　　With candour thus to deal?

Was my fond passion known to thee,
　　In spite of all my care?
And thy intent to set me free,
　　To cure me by despair?

What motives could thy purpose guide
  To this destructive theme?
The fatal secret to confide,
  And wound me with esteem!   60

O Love! whose power so few resist!
  Why cruelly delight
To lead us to the summit wished,
  Then cast us from its height!

Like tyrants fell, on mischief bent,
  Thy treacherous arts bestow
Short intervals of sweet content;
  But lasting hours of woe!

(1773)

ANNA LAETITIA BARBAULD (née AIKIN)
(1743–1825)

The elder child of Dr John Aikin and his wife Jane Jennings, she was born at Kibworth, Leicestershire, where her father kept a school for boys. Her brother John (1747–1822) became a physician and voluminous author. She herself later attributed her diffidence in polite society to her rural childhood and the fact that she grew up surrounded by boys. In 1758 her father became a tutor at the new Warrington Academy for Dissenters, a notable centre of liberal intellectual life, where she spent the next fifteen years. She was encouraged to write verse by Dr Joseph Priestley, a tutor at Warrington, later famous for his scientific, theological, and political writings. Her brother included some of her shorter poems in his *Essay on Song-Writing* (Warrington, 1772) and encouraged her to publish her *Poems* (1773), which immediately won her a high reputation. In the same year she published with her brother *Miscellaneous Pieces in Prose*.

  In 1774 she married Rochemont Barbauld, a clergyman of French descent, who had been educated at Warrington Academy. They settled at Palgrave, Sussex, where Barbauld had charge of a dissenting congregation and opened a school for boys, in which his wife taught a class of the younger pupils and kept the accounts. Without children of their own, they adopted her nephew, Charles Rochemont Aikin, later a physician and chemist. In these years she published *Devotional Pieces* (1775) and her popular and much-reprinted *Lessons for Children* (1778) and *Hymns in Prose for Children* (1781). During visits to London she made a large literary acquaintance, including Elizabeth Montagu, Hester Chapone, and Hannah More: she later compared the experience of reading Boswell's *Life of Johnson* in 1791 to meeting all one's friends at Ranelagh. Although the school at Palgrave prospered and had some notable pupils, the strain on her husband's unstable temperament was probably already apparent and it was closed in 1785. After travelling on the Continent for a year, the Barbaulds settled in Hampstead, where her husband officiated at a small chapel and she was increasingly preoccupied with literary work.

ANNA LAETITIA BARBAULD

After the French Revolution she published prose pamphlets on political subjects, including *An Address to the Opposers of the Repeal of the Corporation and Test Acts* (1790), which includes praise of the Dissenting Academies as opposed to the ancient universities; *Civic Sermons to the People* (1792), on democratic government and popular education; and *Sins of the Government, Sins of the Nation* (1793), against the war with France. As early as 1791 Horace Walpole violently denounced her political writings in a letter to Hannah More. Much of the verse she had written since 1773 had remained unpublished, but in 1791 her brother John appealed to her in his own *Poems* to return to poetry, and her *Epistle to William Wilberforce* (1791) was one of several attacks in verse on the slave trade by women in these years. She later contributed some of her best and most amusing verse to the *Monthly Magazine*, of which her brother was the literary editor from 1796. She also wrote fourteen of the ninety-nine numbers of his *Evenings at Home* (6 vols., 1792–5) and edited Akenside (1794) and Collins (1797) for a series of eighteenth-century poets her brother was publishing.

In 1802 the Barbaulds moved to Stoke Newington, where John Aikin now lived, her husband becoming minister of a chapel at Newington Green. His mental health deteriorated and he became so dangerously violent towards his wife that he had to be placed under restraint. After escaping from his keeper, he was found drowned in 1808. Mrs Barbauld remained highly productive in these years, editing Samuel Richardson's *Letters* (6 vols., 1804) and *The British Novelists* (50 vols., 1810), as well as reviewing fiction for the *Monthly Review* (1809–15). Her literary acquaintance by now included Joanna Baillie, Maria and Richard Lovell Edgeworth, Scott, Wordsworth, Southey, Coleridge, and Samuel Rogers. Her last works of significance were *The Female Speaker* (1811), an anthology for girls, and *Eighteen Hundred and Eleven* (1811), a poem so harshly reviewed by J. W. Croker in the *Quarterly Review* in June 1812 as virtually to end her public career as a writer. She died at Stoke Newington in 1825, in which year her niece, Lucy Aikin, edited her *Works* in 2 volumes.

Given her liberal political opinions and her high reputation as a poet and writer for children, Mrs Barbauld's views on women writers and female education are of interest. In 1774 Elizabeth Montagu, an admirer of her verse and prose, proposed that she should become principal of an academy for women, to set new standards in female education. Miss Aikin (as she still was) replied that she saw no point in producing *femmes savantes* rather than 'good wives or agreeable companions'. A father or brother would be the best teacher for girls, who, by the age of 15, when 'the empire of the passions is coming on', would in any case be capable of learning little. Having 'stepped out of the bounds of female reserve in becoming an author', she evidently had no wish to be thought of primarily as a writer. Thirty years later, in 1804, she wrote a number of letters to Maria and Richard Lovell Edgeworth which make clear that she had little sense of a tradition of women's writing, felt no common cause with other literary women ('There is no bond of union among literary women'), and believed that it would be pointless to 'provoke a war with the other sex'.

Note. Bibliographies of Mrs Barbauld's writings usually begin with *Corsica. An Ode* (1768), but James Boswell, who is praised in it and reviewed it, believed this stanzaic poem to be by Edward Burnaby Greene. In a letter of 13 June 1769 Joseph Priestley urged Anna Aikin to send her own poem on Corsica to Boswell: 'Its being written by a *lady* . . . will be a circumstance very much in their [i.e. the 'noble islanders' in their struggle for liberty] favour, and that of the poem'. But Priestley seems to have introduced her poem (in blank verse) to Boswell for the first time on 9 April 1772, when he read it to him in the London Coffeehouse, and it was evidently first published in her *Poems* (1773).

195   from *Corsica*

[*On General Paoli and the Corsican Struggle for Liberty*]

WHEN the storm thickens, when the combat burns,
And pain and death, in every horrid shape
That can appal the feeble, prowl around,
Then Virtue triumphs; then her towering form
Dilates with kindling majesty; her mien
Breathes a diviner spirit, and enlarged
Each spreading feature, with an ampler port
And bolder tone, exulting rides the storm,
And joys amid the tempest: then she reaps
Her golden harvest; fruits of nobler growth   10
And higher relish than meridian suns
Can ever ripen; fair, heroic deeds,
And godlike action. 'Tis not meats and drinks,
And balmy airs, and vernal suns, and showers
That feed and ripen minds; 'tis toil and danger;
And wrestling with the stubborn gripe of fate;
And war, and sharp distress, and paths obscure
And dubious. The bold swimmer joys not so
To feel the proud waves under him, and beat
With strong repelling arm the billowy surge;   20
The generous courser does not so exult
To toss his floating mane against the wind,
And neigh amidst the thunder of the war,
As Virtue to oppose her swelling breast
Like a firm shield against the darts of Fate.
And when her sons in that rough school have learned
To smile at danger, then the hand that raised
Shall hush the storm, and lead the shining train
Of peaceful years in bright procession on.
Then shall the shepherd's pipe, the muse's lyre,   30
On Cyrnus' shores be heard: her grateful sons
With loud acclaim and hymns of cordial praise
Shall hail their high deliverers; every name
To Virtue dear be from oblivion snatched,
And placed among the stars: but chiefly thine,
Thine, Paoli, with sweetest sound shall dwell
On their applauding lips; thy sacred name,
Endeared to long posterity, some muse,
More worthy of the theme, shall consecrate

Cyrnus] Corsica

To after ages, and applauding worlds   40
Shall bless the godlike man who saved his country.

*   *   *   *   *   *   *   *   *   *   *   *

So vainly wished, so fondly hoped the Muse:
Too fondly hoped: the iron fates prevail,
And Cyrnus is no more. Her generous sons,
Less vanquished than o'erwhelmed, by numbers crushed,
Admired, unaided fell. So strives the moon
In dubious battle with the gathering clouds,
And strikes a splendour through them; till at length
Storms rolled on storms involve the face of heaven
And quench her struggling fires. Forgive the zeal   50
That, too presumptuous, whispered better things
And read the book of destiny amiss.
Not with the purple colouring of success
Is virtue best adorned: th' attempt is praise.
There yet remains a freedom, nobler far
Than kings or senates can destroy or give;
Beyond the proud oppressor's cruel grasp
Seated secure; uninjured; undestroyed;
Worthy of gods: the freedom of the mind.

(Wr. 1769; pub. 1773)

196   *The Mouse's Petition to Doctor Priestley Found
in the Trap where he had been confined all Night*

OH! hear a pensive captive's prayer,
For liberty that sighs;
And never let thine heart be shut
Against the prisoner's cries.

For here forlorn and sad I sit,
Within the wiry grate;
And tremble at th' approaching morn,
Which brings impending fate.

If e'er thy breast with freedom glowed,
And spurned a tyrant's chain,   10
Let not thy strong oppressive force
A free-born mouse detain.

Oh! do not stain with guiltless blood
Thy hospitable hearth;
Nor triumph that thy wiles betrayed
A prize so little worth.

The scattered gleanings of a feast
My scanty meals supply;
But if thine unrelenting heart
That slender boon deny,   20

The cheerful light, the vital air,
Are blessings widely given;
Let nature's commoners enjoy
The common gifts of heaven.

The well-taught philosophic mind
To all compassion gives;
Casts round the world an equal eye,
And feels for all that lives.

If mind, as ancient sages taught,
A never-dying flame,   30
Still shifts through matter's varying forms,
In every form the same,

Beware, lest in the worm you crush
A brother's soul you find;
And tremble lest thy luckless hand
Dislodge a kindred mind.

Or, if this transient gleam of day
Be *all* of life we share,
Let pity plead within thy breast
That little *all* to spare.   40

So may thy hospitable board
With health and peace be crowned;
And every charm of heartfelt ease
Beneath thy roof be found.

So, when unseen destruction lurks,
Which mice like men may share,
May some kind angel clear thy path,
And break the hidden snare.

(1773)

197 *Tomorrow*

SEE where the falling day
In silence steals away,
Behind the western hills withdrawn:
Her fires are quenched, her beauty fled,
While blushes all her face o'erspread,
As conscious she had ill fulfilled
The promise of the dawn.

Another morning soon shall rise,
Another day salute our eyes,
As smiling and as fair as she,   10
And make as many promises:
But do not thou
The tale believe,
They're sisters all,
And all deceive.

(Wr. *c.*1780; pub. 1802)

198 *On the Expected General Rising of the French*
Nation in 1792

RISE, mighty nation, in thy strength,
And deal thy dreadful vengeance round;
Let thy great spirit, roused at length,
Strike hordes of despots to the ground!

Devoted land! thy mangled breast
Eager the royal vultures tear;
By friends betrayed, by foes oppressed—
And Virtue struggles with Despair.

The tocsin sounds! arise, arise!   10
Stern o'er each breast let Country reign;
Nor virgin's plighted hand, nor sighs,
Must now the ardent youth detain:

Nor must the hind who tills thy soil
The ripened vintage stay to press,
Till Rapture crown the flowing bowl,
And Freedom boast of full success.

Briareus-like extend thy hands,
That every hand may crush a foe;
In millions pour thy generous bands,
And end a warfare by a blow!   20

Then wash with sad repentant tears
Each deed that clouds thy glory's page;
Each frenzied start impelled by fears,
Each transient burst of headlong rage:

Then fold in thy relenting arms
Thy wretched outcasts where they roam;
From pining want and war's alarms,
O call the child of misery home!

Then build the tomb—O not alone
Of him who bled in Freedom's cause;   30
With equal eye the martyr own
Of faith revered and ancient laws.

Then be thy tide of glory stayed;
Then be thy conquering banners furled;
Obey the laws thyself hast made,
And rise the model of the world!

(Wr. 1792; pub. 1825)

199   *The Rights of Woman*

YES, injured Woman! rise, assert thy right!
Woman! too long degraded, scorned, oppressed;
O born to rule in partial Law's despite,
Resume thy native empire o'er the breast!

Go forth arrayed in panoply divine,
That angel pureness which admits no stain;
Go, bid proud Man his boasted rule resign
And kiss the golden sceptre of thy reign.

Go, gird thyself with grace, collect thy store
Of bright artillery glancing from afar;   10
Soft melting tones thy thundering cannon's roar,
Blushes and fears thy magazine of war.

Thy rights are empire; urge no meaner claim,—
Felt, not defined, and if debated, lost;
Like sacred mysteries, which withheld from fame,
Shunning discussion, are revered the most.

Try all that wit and art suggest to bend
Of thy imperial foe the stubborn knee;
Make treacherous Man thy subject, not thy friend;
Thou mayst command, but never canst be free.   20

Awe the licentious and restrain the rude;
Soften the sullen, clear the cloudy brow:
Be, more than princes' gifts, thy favours sued;—
She hazards all, who will the least allow.

But hope not, courted idol of mankind,
On this proud eminence secure to stay;
Subduing and subdued, thou soon shalt find
Thy coldness soften, and thy pride give way.

Then, then, abandon each ambitious thought;
Conquest or rule thy heart shall feebly move,   30
In Nature's school, by her soft maxims taught
That separate rights are lost in mutual love.

(Wr. *c.*1795; pub. 1825)

200   *To the Poor*

CHILD of distress, who meet'st the bitter scorn
Of fellow-men to happier prospects born,
Doomed Art and Nature's various stores to see
Flow in full cups of joy—and not for thee;
Who seest the rich, to heaven and fate resigned,
Bear *thy* afflictions with a patient mind;
Whose bursting heart disdains unjust control,
Who feel'st oppression's iron in thy soul,
Who dragg'st the load of faint and feeble years,
Whose bread is anguish, and whose water tears;   10
Bear, bear thy wrongs—fulfil thy destined hour,
Bend thy meek neck beneath the foot of Power;
But when thou feel'st the great deliverer nigh,
And thy freed spirit mounting seeks the sky,
Let no vain fears thy parting hour molest,
No whispered terrors shake thy quiet breast:

Think not their threats can work thy future woe,
Nor deem the Lord above like lords below;—
Safe in the bosom of that love repose
By whom the sun gives light, the ocean flows;   20
Prepare to meet a Father undismayed,
Nor fear the God whom priests and kings have made.*

(Wr. 1795; pub. 1825)

201   *To a Little Invisible Being who is Expected Soon
to Become Visible*

GERM of new life, whose powers expanding slow
For many a moon their full perfection wait—
Haste, precious pledge of happy love, to go
Auspicious borne through life's mysterious gate.

What powers lie folded in thy curious frame—
Senses from objects locked, and mind from thought!
How little canst thou guess thy lofty claim
To grasp at all the worlds the Almighty wrought!

And see, the genial season's warmth to share,
Fresh younglings shoot, and opening roses glow!   10
Swarms of new life exulting fill the air—
Haste, infant bud of being, haste to blow!

For thee the nurse prepares her lulling songs,
The eager matrons count the lingering day;
But far the most thy anxious parent longs
On thy soft cheek a mother's kiss to lay.

She only asks to lay her burden down,
That her glad arms that burden may resume;
And nature's sharpest pangs her wishes crown,
That free thee living from thy living tomb.   20

She longs to fold to her maternal breast
Part of herself, yet to herself unknown;
To see and to salute the stranger guest,
Fed with her life through many a tedious moon.

---

* These lines, written in 1795, were described by Mrs B., on sending them to a friend, as 'inspired by indignation on hearing sermons in which the poor are addressed in a manner which evidently shows the design of making religion an engine of government'. [1825]

Come, reap thy rich inheritance of love!
Bask in the fondness of a Mother's eye!
Nor wit nor eloquence her heart shall move
Like the first accents of thy feeble cry.

Haste, little captive, burst thy prison doors!
Launch on the living world, and spring to light!   30
Nature for thee displays her various stores,
Opens her thousand inlets of delight.

If charmèd verse or muttered prayers had power
With favouring spells to speed thee on thy way,
Anxious I'd bid my beads each passing hour,
Till thy wished smile thy mother's pangs o'erpay.

(Wr. c.1795; pub. 1825)

202   *Washing-Day*

THE Muses are turned gossips; they have lost
The buskined step, and clear high-sounding phrase,
Language of gods. Come then, domestic Muse,
In slipshod measure loosely prattling on
Of farm or orchard, pleasant curds and cream,
Or drowning flies, or shoe lost in the mire
By little whimpering boy, with rueful face;
Come, Muse, and sing the dreaded Washing-Day.
Ye who beneath the yoke of wedlock bend,
With bowèd soul, full well ye ken the day   10
Which week, smooth sliding after week, brings on
Too soon;—for to that day nor peace belongs
Nor comfort;—ere the first grey streak of dawn,
The red-armed washers come and chase repose.
Nor pleasant smile, nor quaint device of mirth,
E'er visited that day: the very cat,
From the wet kitchen scared, and reeking hearth,
Visits the parlour,—an unwonted guest.
The silent breakfast-meal is soon dispatched;
Uninterrupted, save by anxious looks   20
Cast at the lowering sky, if sky should lower.
From that last evil, O preserve us, heavens!
For should the skies pour down, adieu to all
Remains of quiet: then expect to hear
Of sad disasters—dirt and gravel stains
Hard to efface, and loaded lines at once

Snapped short—and linen-horse by dog thrown down,
And all the petty miseries of life.
Saints have been calm while stretched upon the rack,
And Guatimozin smiled on burning coals;   30
But never yet did housewife notable
Greet with a smile a rainy washing-day.
—But grant the welkin fair, require not thou
Who call'st thyself perchance the master there,
Or study swept, or nicely dusted coat,
Or usual 'tendance;—ask not, indiscreet,
Thy stockings mended, though the yawning rents
Gape wide as Erebus; nor hope to find
Some snug recess impervious: shouldst thou try
The 'customed garden walks, thine eye shall rue   40
The budding fragrance of thy tender shrubs,
Myrtle or rose, all crushed beneath the weight
Of coarse-checked apron—with impatient hand
Twitched off when showers impend: or crossing lines
Shall mar thy musings, as the wet cold sheet
Flaps in thy face abrupt. Woe to the friend
Whose evil stars have urged him forth to claim
On such a day the hospitable rites!
Looks, blank at best, and stinted courtesy,
Shall he receive. Vainly he feeds his hopes   50
With dinner of roast chicken, savoury pie,
Or tart or pudding:—pudding he nor tart
That day shall eat; nor, though the husband try,
Mending what can't be helped, to kindle mirth
From cheer deficient, shall his consort's brow
Clear up propitious:—the unlucky guest
In silence dines, and early slinks away.
I well remember, when a child, the awe
This day struck into me; for then the maids,
I scarce knew why, looked cross, and drove me from them: 60
Nor soft caress could I obtain, nor hope
Usual indulgencies; jelly or creams,
Relic of costly suppers, and set by
For me their petted one; or buttered toast,
When butter was forbid; or thrilling tale
Of ghost, or witch, or murder—so I went
And sheltered me beside the parlour fire:
There my dear grandmother, eldest of forms,
Tended the little ones, and watched from harm,
Anxiously fond, though oft her spectacles   70
With elfin cunning hid, and oft the pins
Drawn from her ravelled stocking, might have soured

One less indulgent.—
At intervals my mother's voice was heard,
Urging dispatch: briskly the work went on,
All hands employed to wash, to rinse, to wring,
To fold, and starch, and clap, and iron, and plait.
Then would I sit me down, and ponder much
Why washings were. Sometimes through hollow bowl
Of pipe amused we blew, and sent aloft   80
The floating bubbles; little dreaming then
To see, Montgolfier, thy silken ball
Ride buoyant through the clouds—so near approach
The sports of children and the toils of men.
Earth, air, and sky, and ocean, hath its bubbles,
And verse is one of them—this most of all.

(1797)

203   *To Mr. [S. T.] C[olerid]ge*

MIDWAY the hill of science, after steep
And rugged paths that tire the unpractised feet,
A grove extends; in tangled mazes wrought,
And filled with strange enchantment:—dubious shapes
Flit through dim glades, and lure the eager foot
Of youthful ardour to eternal chase.
Dreams hang on every leaf: unearthly forms
Glide through the gloom; and mystic visions swim
Before the cheated sense. Athwart the mists,
Far into vacant space, huge shadows stretch   10
And seem realities; while things of life,
Obvious to sight and touch, all glowing round,
Fade to the hue of shadows.—Scruples here,
With filmy net, most like the autumnal webs
Of floating gossamer, arrest the foot
Of generous enterprise; and palsy hope
And fair ambition with the chilling touch
Of sickly hesitation and blank fear.
Nor seldom Indolence these lawns among
Fixes her turf-built seat; and wears the garb   20
Of deep philosophy, and museful sits
In dreamy twilight of the vacant mind,
Soothed by the whispering shade; for soothing soft
The shades; and vistas lengthening into air,
With moonbeam rainbows tinted.—Here each mind
Of finer mould, acute and delicate,

In its high progress to eternal truth
Rests for a space, in fairy bowers entranced;
And loves the softened light and tender gloom;
And, pampered with most unsubstantial food,   30
Looks down indignant on the grosser world,
And matter's cumbrous shapings. Youth beloved
Of Science—of the Muse beloved,—not here,
Not in the maze of metaphysic lore,
Build thou thy place of resting! lightly tread
The dangerous ground, on noble aims intent;
And be this Circe of the studious cell
Enjoyed, but still subservient. Active scenes
Shall soon with healthful spirit brace thy mind;
And fair exertion, for bright fame sustained,   40
For friends, for country, chase each spleen-fed fog
That blots the wide creation.—
Now heaven conduct thee with a parent's love!

(Wr. 1797; pub. 1799)

ANNA SEWARD
(1742–1809)

She was the elder daughter of Thomas Seward (1708–90), Rector of Eyam, Derbyshire, and his wife Elizabeth Hunter, whose father had taught Samuel Johnson at Lichfield School. A brother and two sisters died in infancy. In 1750 her father became Canon of Lichfield Cathedral, living from 1754 in the Bishop's Palace, where his daughter remained until her death. Later described by Boswell as 'a genteel well-bred dignified clergyman', who 'had lived much in the great world', Seward had contributed to Dodsley's *Collection* (1748), including 'The Female Right to Literature', and had edited the *Works* of Beaumont and Fletcher (10 vols., 1750). He encouraged her literary education and early verse, as did Dr Erasmus Darwin, then a Lichfield physician, 'but my mother threw cold water on the rising fires', and her father also supposedly later resented his daughter's superior poetic talents. From an early age she was deeply attached to Honora Sneyd, adopted as a child by the Sewards, and was emotionally disturbed as if by a bereavement when Honora married Richard Lovell Edgeworth in 1773. By then her younger sister Sarah had died (1764) and her own attachments to a number of young men had been terminated partly out of obedience to her father.

Her literary ambitions developed only in her mid-30s. She contributed 'A Rural Coronation' to F. N. C. Mundy's *Needwood Forest* (1776) and was also stimulated by Anna Miller's poetry sessions at Bath-Easton. In spite of her increasing responsibility for her ailing father after her mother's death in 1780, she rapidly established her reputation as a poet with her *Elegy on Captain Cook* (1780; at first rumoured to be the work of Darwin) and her *Monody on the Unfortunate Major André* (1781), an early admirer of Honora Sneyd, who had been executed as a spy in the American War. (Her violent denunciation of 'remorseless Washington' in this poem led him to send

an emissary to her some years later, defending his limited part in André's fate.)
These poems, with her *Poem to the Memory of Lady Miller* (1782) and her *Louisa, A Poetical Novel* (1784), a popular if not critical success, won her the friendship and admiration of William Hayley, with whom she exchanged visits in 1781–2. For a time Hayley and Seward were considered the outstanding new poets of the 1780s, although their public expressions of mutual admiration were already being mocked, and reviewers were soon objecting to the affectations of her poetic style.

With her increasingly dependent father on the edge of senility (see 'Eyam'), she was able to visit London only occasionally, but her literary presence in the metropolis was felt through her frequent contributions of both verse and prose to periodicals, especially the *Gentleman's Magazine*. Poems by or to her, reviews of her works with counterblasts from her or members of her circle, and other contributions are so pervasive in the 1780s and early 1790s as to defy brief summary. For example, her conviction that Johnson was receiving uncritical adulation after his death led to a series of letters signed 'Benvolio' in the *Gentleman's Magazine* in 1786, and the publication of Boswell's *Life* led to another long-running controversy in 1793–4, in which Boswell is thought to have come out better. A lengthy correspondence with Joseph Weston and others about the relative merits of Dryden and Pope ran in the same periodical from 1788 to 1791; and there is clear evidence of changing attitudes to women writers in the polite reception given to her free paraphrases of Horace's *Odes* (she knew neither Greek nor Latin) which appeared in the *Magazine* from 1785 until the early 1790s. Many poets, both men and women, addressed her flatteringly in verse, she patronized and 'corrected' the verse of younger writers such as H. F. Cary, Thomas Lister, and Thomas Park, and assisted the uneducated William Newton, the 'Derbyshire minstrel' (for Newton, in particular, see *Letters*, 1811, i. 290–4, 317–20, 325–6, iv. 134; and *Gent. Mag.*, 1785, 169–70, 212–14).

After her father's death in 1790, she continued to live in the Bishop's Palace in Lichfield on a comfortable income of £400 p.a., finding some emotional satisfaction in a secret devotion to John Saville, a singer at the Cathedral, whose death in 1803 was a severe blow. At first an enthusiast for the French Revolution (her sonnet on France in the *Gentleman's Magazine* in August 1789 was one of the earliest poetic reactions), she was appalled by its later developments and in February 1793 denounced the continuing enthusiasm of her friend Helen Maria Williams (see nos. 267–71). In 1795 she visited Lady Eleanor Butler and Sarah Ponsonby, the celebrated 'Ladies of Llangollen', and described the visit in the title-poem of her *Llangollen Vale, With Other Poems* (1796). Her *Original Sonnets* (1799) included poems previously published in periodicals: others, to which dates in the early 1770s were attached, would have been highly unusual on stylistic grounds in that decade, and may be reworkings in the increasingly popular sonnet form of earlier poems. Her last notable publication was her *Memoir of Dr. Darwin* (1804), which portrays the intellectual life of Lichfield in the period, at the centre of which she had been for several decades.

As her health deteriorated, she made careful plans for posthumous editions of her poetry and letters, bargaining shrewdly over the sale of the copyright and involving her correspondent Walter Scott in these arrangements. Scott edited her *Poetical Works* (3 vols., Edinburgh, 1810), a year after her death in 1809, but declined involvement in the edition of her *Letters* (6 vols., Edinburgh, 1811), perhaps aware that she had revised them extensively for publication. Although they remain reveal-ing in many ways, they cannot, as has been said, 'be implicitly trusted for facts or contemporary opinions and not even for a strict chronology of the period'. As the letters confirm, she was an avid and wide-ranging reader and at times a trenchant critic. Ridiculed for her hostility to Johnson and for her apparently uncritical admiration for such poets as Hayley (whom she rated the equal of Dryden) and T. S. Whalley, she had an unusually lofty sense of the importance of literature and of poetry in particular. For that reason alone, if for no other, she could be more severe than male readers on her female contemporaries: she quarrelled in print with Clara Reeve (see nos. 161–3) and Helen Maria Williams (see nos. 267–71), had reservations about Hannah More's affected erudition and unharmonious versification, was contemptuous of Charlotte Smith (see nos. 237–43) and did not hesitate to send her acquaintance Mrs Piozzi (see no. 255) a letter deploring her stylistic 'vulgarisms' in her *Observations and Reflections* (1789). From her headquarters in Lichfield Close, she projected herself for many years as perhaps the most prominent and formidable woman writer of the later century. Before her death her verse was being increasingly criticized for affectation, prolixity, and obscurity. Mary Russell Mitford later wrote: 'Sometimes affected, sometimes *fade*, sometimes pedantic, and sometimes tinselly, none of her works were ever simple, graceful, or natural.' Wordsworth, however, preferred her verses, 'with all their faults' of floridity and elaboration, to those of Mrs Barbauld (to Dyce, 10 May 1830). Although her verse has usually proved unappealing to later generations, Anna Seward was rarely insipid in the fashionable manner of the time and, in spite of her fondness for tortuous syntax, her poetic voice can have intensity and individuality.

204   *Sonnet. To Honora Sneyd*

HONORA, should that cruel time arrive
    When 'gainst my truth thou should'st my errors poise,
    Scorning remembrance of our vanished joys;
    When for the love-warm looks in which I live,
But cold respect must greet me, that shall give
    No tender glance, no kind regretful sighs;
    When thou shalt pass me with averted eyes,
    Feigning thou see'st me not, to sting, and grieve,
And sicken my sad heart, I could not bear
    Such dire eclipse of thy soul-cheering rays;   10
    I could not learn my struggling heart to tear
From thy loved form, that through my memory strays;
    Nor in the pale horizon of Despair
    Endure the wintry and the darkened days.

                    (Wr. April 1773; pub. 1799)

205   *Sonnet. Ingratitude*

INGRATITUDE, how deadly is the smart
    Thou giv'st, inhabiting the form we love!
    How light compared all other sorrows prove!
    Thou shed'st a night of woe—from whence depart

The gentle beams of patience, that the heart
  Midst lesser ills illume. Thy victims rove,
  Unquiet as the ghost that haunts the grove
  Where murder spilt the life-blood. O! thy dart
Kills more than life—ev'n all that makes it dear;
  Till we 'the sensible of pain' would change   10
  For frenzy, that defies the bitter tear;
Or wish in kindred callousness to range
  Where moon-eyed Idiocy, with fallen lip,
  Drags the loose knee and intermitting step.

(Wr. July 1773; pub. 1789)

206   *Verses Inviting Stella to Tea on the Public Fast-Day [During the American War], February, MDCCLXXXI*

DEAR Stella, midst the pious sorrow
Our Monarch bids us feel tomorrow,
The ah's! and oh's! supremely trist,
The abstinence from beef and whist,
Wisely ordained to please the Lord,
And force him whet our edgeless sword,
Till, skipping o'er th' Atlantic rill,
We cut provincial throats at will;
Midst all the penitence we feel
For merry sins—midst all the zeal   10
For vengeance on the saucy foe,
Who lays our boasted legions low,
I wish, when sullen evening comes,
To gild for me its falling glooms,
You would, without cold pause, agree
Beneath these walls to sip your tea.
From the chaste, fragrant Indian weed
Our sins no pampering juices feed;
And though the Hours, with contrite faces,
May banish the ungodly aces,   20
And take of food a sparing bit,
They'll gluttonise on Stella's wit.

  'Tea,' cries a Patriot, 'on *that* day!
'Twere good you flung the drug away!
Remembering 'twas the cruel source
Of sad distrust, and long divorce,
'Twixt nations which, combined, had hurled
Their conquering javelin round the world.

314

'O Indian shrub! thy fragrant flowers
To England's weal had deadly powers,   30
When Tyranny, with impious hand,
To venom turned its essence bland;
To venom subtle, fierce and fell,
As drenched the dart of Isdabel.

'Have we forgot that cursed libation,
That cost the lives of half the nation?
When Boston, with indignant thought,
Saw poison in the perfumed draught,
And caused her troubled Bay to be
But one vast bowl of bitter tea*;   40
While Até, chiefly-bidden guest,
Came sternly to the fatal feast,
And mingled with th' envenomed flood
Brothers', parents', children's blood:
Dire as the banquet Atreus served,
When his own sons Thyestes carved,
And Phoebus, shrinking from the sight,
Drew o'er his orb the pall of night.

'Tomorrow then, at least, refrain,
Nor quaff thy gasping country's bane!   50
For, O! reflect, poetic daughter,
'Twas vanquished Britain's laurel-water!'†

(Wr. 1781; pub. 1791)

207   *Sonnet. December Morning*

I LOVE to rise ere gleams the tardy light,
    Winter's pale dawn;—and as warm fires illume,
    And cheerful tapers shine around the room,
    Through misty windows bend my musing sight
Where, round the dusky lawn, the mansions white,
    With shutters closed, peer faintly through the gloom,
    That slow recedes; while yon grey spires assume,
    Rising from their dark pile, an added height

* Alluding to the ships' cargoes of tea which the Colonists, on finding it taxed, threw into the Bay of Boston [in 1773]; upon which hostilities between them and the Mother Country commenced.
† Alluding to the then recent murder of Sir Theodosius Boughton, by laurel-water.
* This Sonnet was written in an Apartment of the West Front of the Bishop's Palace at Lichfield, inhabited by the Author from her thirteenth year. It looks upon the Cathedral-Area, a green Lawn encircled by Prebendal Houses, which are white from being rough-cast.

By indistinctness given.—Then to decree
   The grateful thoughts to God, ere they unfold   10
   To Friendship, or the Muse, or seek with glee
Wisdom's rich page!—O, hours! more worth than gold,
   By whose blest use we lengthen life, and, free
   From drear decays of age, outlive the old!

(Wr. 19 Dec. 1782; pub. 1799)

208   *Sonnet. To Colebrooke Dale*

THY Genius, Colebrooke, faithless to his charge
   Amid thy woods and vales, thy rocks and streams,
   Formed for the train that haunt poetic dreams,
   Naiads and nymphs,—now hears the toiling barge
And the swart Cyclops' ever-changing forge
   Din in thy dells;—permits the dark-red gleams,
   From umbered fires on all thy hills, the beams,
   Solar and pure, to shroud with columns large
Of black sulphureous smoke, that spread their veils
   Like funeral crape upon the sylvan robe   10
   Of thy romantic rocks, pollute thy gales,
And stain thy glassy floods;—while o'er the globe
   To spread thy stores metallic, this rude yell
   Drowns the wild woodland song, and breaks the Poet's spell.

(Wr. c.1787; pub. 1799)

209   *Eyam**

FOR one short week I leave, with anxious heart,
Source of my filial cares, the Full of Days;
Lured by the promise of harmonic Art
To breathe her Handel's soul-exalting lays.
Pensive I trace the Derwent's amber wave,
Foaming through sylvan banks, or view it lave
The soft romantic valleys, high o'er-peered
By hills and rocks, in savage grandeur reared.

---

* This Poem was written August 1788, on a journey through Derbyshire, to a music-meeting at Sheffield. The Author's Father was Rector of EYAM, an extensive Village, that runs along a mountainous terrace, in one of the highest parts of the Peak. She was born there, and there passed the first seven years of her life. . . .

---

208 umbered] dark brown

Not two short miles from thee,—can I refrain
Thy haunts, my native Eyam, long unseen?   10
Thou, and thy loved inhabitants, again
Shall meet my transient gaze.—Thy rocky screen,
Thy airy cliffs I mount; and seek thy shade,
Thy roofs, that brow the steep, romantic glade;
But, while on me the eyes of friendship glow,
Swell my pained sighs, my tears spontaneous flow.

In scenes paternal, not beheld through years,
Nor viewed till now but by a father's side,
Well might the tender tributary tears
From keen regrets of duteous fondness glide.   20
Its pastor to this human flock no more
Shall the long flight of future days restore;
Distant he droops—and that once gladdening eye
Now languid gleams, e'en when his friends are nigh.

Through this known walk, where weedy gravel lies
Rough and unsightly, by the long coarse grass
Of the once smooth and vivid green, with sighs
To the deserted rectory I pass;
Stray through the darkened chamber's naked bound,
Where childhood's earliest, liveliest bliss I found.   30
How changed since erst, the lightsome walls beneath,
The social joys did their warm comforts breathe!

Ere yet I go, who may return no more,
That sacred pile, mid yonder shadowy trees,
Let me revisit.—Ancient massy door,
Thou gratest hoarse! My vital spirits freeze,
Passing the vacant pulpit to the space
Where humble rails the decent altar grace;
And where my infant sister's ashes sleep,
Whose loss I left the childish sport to weep.   40

Now the low beams, with paper garlands* hung
In memory of some village youth or maid,
Draw the soft tear from thrilled remembrance sprung;
How oft my childhood marked that tribute paid;
The gloves suspended by the garland's side,
White as its snowy flowers, with ribbands tied:
Dear village! long these wreaths funereal spread,
Simple memorials of thy early dead!

* The ancient custom of hanging a garland of white roses made of writing-paper, and a pair of
white gloves over the pew of the unmarried Villagers, who die in the flower of their age. . . .

But O! thou blank and silent pulpit! thou
That with a father's precepts, just and bland,   50
Didst win my ear, as reason's strengthening glow
Showed their full value, now thou seem'st to stand
Before my sad, suffused and trembling gaze,
The dreariest relic of departed days;
Of eloquence paternal, nervous, clear,
Dim apparition thou!—and bitter in my tear.

(Wr. 1788; pub. 1792)

210   *Sonnet. To the Poppy*

WHILE summer roses all their glory yield
   To crown the votary of love and joy,
   Misfortune's victim hails, with many a sigh,
   Thee, scarlet Poppy of the pathless field,
Gaudy, yet wild and lone; no leaf to shield
   Thy flaccid vest that, as the gale blows high,
   Flaps, and alternate folds around thy head.
So stands in the long grass a love-crazed maid,
Smiling aghast; while stream to every wind
   Her garish ribbons, smeared with dust and rain;   10
   But brain-sick visions cheat her tortured mind,
And bring false peace. Thus, lulling grief and pain,
   Kind dreams oblivious from thy juice proceed,
   Thou flimsy, showy, melancholy weed.

(Wr. c.1789; pub. 1799)

211   *Sonnet*

FROM a rived tree, that stands beside the grave
   Of the self-slaughtered, to the misty moon
   Calls the complaining owl in night's pale noon;
   And from a hut, far on the hill, to rave
Is heard the ban-dog. With loud wave
   The roused and turbid river surges down,
   Swoll'n with the mountain-rains, and dimly shown
   Appals the sense.—Yet see! from yonder cave,
Her shelter in the recent stormy showers,
   With anxious brow, a fond-expecting maid   10
   Steals towards the flood!—Alas!—for now appears

211 rived] split   ban-dog] mastiff

Her lover's vacant boat!—the broken oars
Roll down the tide!—What images invade!
Aghast she stands, the statue of her fears!

(Wr. *c.*1790; pub. 1799)

212   *An Old Cat's Dying Soliloquy*

YEARS saw me still Acasto's mansion grace,
The gentlest, fondest of the tabby race;
Before him frisking through the garden glade,
Or at his feet in quiet slumber laid;
Praised for my glossy back of zebra streak,
And wreaths of jet encircling round my neck;
Soft paws that ne'er extend the clawing nail,
The snowy whisker and the sinuous tail;
Now feeble age each glazing eyeball dims,
And pain has stiffened these once supple limbs;   10
Fate of eight lives the forfeit gasp obtains,
And e'en the ninth creeps languid through my veins.
    Much sure of good the future has in store,
When on my master's hearth I bask no more,
In those blest climes, where fishes oft forsake
The winding river and the glassy lake;
There, as our silent-footed race behold
The crimson spots and fins of lucid gold,
Venturing without the shielding waves to play,
They gasp on shelving banks, our easy prey: 20
While birds unwinged hop careless o'er the ground,
And the plump mouse incessant trots around,
Near wells of cream that mortals never skim,
Warm marum creeping round their shallow brim;
Where green valerian tufts, luxuriant spread,
Cleanse the sleek hide and form the fragrant bed.*
    Yet, stern dispenser of the final blow,
Before thou lay'st an aged grimalkin low,
Bend to her last request a gracious ear,
Some days, some few short days, to linger here;   30
So to the guardian of his tabby's weal
Shall softest purrs these tender truths reveal:
    'Ne'er shall thy now expiring puss forget
To thy kind care her long-enduring debt,
Nor shall the joys that painless realms decree
Efface the comforts once bestowed by thee;

---

* The affection of cats for marum and valerian is well known. They will beat the stems down, mat them with their feet, and then roll upon them.

To countless mice thy chicken-bones preferred,
Thy toast to golden fish and wingless bird;
O'er marum borders and valerian bed
Thy Selima shall bend her moping head,   40
Sigh that no more she climbs, with grateful glee,
Thy downy sofa and thy cradling knee;
Nay, e'en at founts of cream shall sullen swear,
Since thou, her more loved master, art not there.'

(1792)

MARY SCOTT (later TAYLOR)
(1752?–93)

She was the daughter of a linen-merchant at Milborne Port, Somerset. Little is known of her early life before the publication of *The Female Advocate* (1774), apart from the poor health she had suffered. At the end of her poem she pays tribute to a male friend, with 'The gentlest manners, and the kindest heart', who had 'Enjoin'd me still to court the Muse's smile, | The tiresome hours of languor to beguile'. An MS note in the Huntington Library copy of the poem identifies this early mentor as 'Pultney, a well known physician who lives at Blandford', identifiable as Richard Pulteney (1730–1801), a physician who in 1764 settled in Blandford, Dorset, some thirteen miles from Milborne Port, and published on botanical subjects. The poem also speaks warmly of other personal friends, William Steele, a timber merchant and lay baptist preacher of Broughton, Hampshire, and his daughter Anna Steele, author of *Poems on Subjects Chiefly Devotional* by 'Theodosia' (1760).

The Female Advocate (which was reissued in 1775) is an annotated survey of British women writers, intended as a supplement to John Duncombe's *The Feminiad* (1754). Scott goes back to the Renaissance and also discusses more than twenty eighteenth-century writers. Although, as her 'Preface' explains, years of ill-health 'have impaired every faculty of my mind', she wrote with 'fervent zeal' about male illiberality towards women: 'have they not prohibited us from cultivating an acquaintance with the sciences? Do they not regard the woman who suffers her faculties to rust in a state of listless indolence, with a more favourable eye, than her who engages in a dispassionate search after truth?' (p. vi). She admitted, however, that the situation was changing, 'and of late, Female Authors have appeared with honour, in almost every walk of literature. Several have started up since the writing of this little piece' (p. vii). She may also have been the Miss Scott whose 'Dunotter Castle' and 'Verses, On a Day of Prayer, for Success in War' later appeared in *Poems by the Most Eminent Ladies* [1780?], ii. 171–7.

In *The Female Advocate* she praised Canon Thomas Seward of Lichfield as an early champion of women writers, and this may explain her friendship (mainly by correspondence) with his daughter Anna, from whose letters most of what is known of Mary Scott's later years derives. By about 1774 she had met John Taylor, a student and later a tutor at the Daventry Academy for Unitarians (perhaps through her brother Russell Scott, who became a Unitarian minister in Portsmouth). Her mother evidently opposed the match and she and Taylor must have agreed not to marry while her mother was alive. In June 1783 she published 'Verses addressed to Miss Seward, on the publication of her Monody on Major André' in the *Gentleman's Magazine*, which makes clear the importance of her friend's 'sympathetic kindness', 'Whilst thro' the labyrinth of life I stray'. Her ill health continued: in 1786 she had trouble with her eyes and was suffering from 'visible dejection'. Responsibility for her parents ended with the deaths of her mother, who had long been an invalid, in 1787 and of her father early in 1788. Plans for marriage to John Taylor followed rapidly, although Anna Seward, praising his 'fine understanding and strict piety', observed that 'his temper had severe trials in the sacrifices you made of his happiness to the surely unreasonable opposition of a parent'. They married in May 1788, at about the time she published ('for the Benefit of the General Hospital at Bath') *The Messiah*, a long poem on a subject which Anna Seward thought 'not the happiest for poetry' and which the *Monthly Review* considered faintly heretical.

Taylor had become Minister of the Chapel at Ilminster, Somerset, where they lived in a house once inhabited by Elizabeth Rowe (see nos. 33–6). A daughter and son were born in 1789 and 1791, but her poor health made pregnancy and childbirth considerable ordeals. Her despondency was only increased by her husband's 'changing systems', a switch from Calvinism to Quakerism. By July 1792 he could allow 'no test of truth but inward feeling and imaginary inspiration' and, having formerly been 'a warm admirer of the elegant arts', was now equating 'genius for them' with vice. Anna Seward's letter to Mary Taylor of 10 September 1793 refers to the 'corrosive pains of mind' caused by her husband's 'veering piety, and consequent inquietude'; but, if the letter is correctly dated, it would receive no reply, since Mary Taylor had died on 5 June 1793, at the age of 41, in St James's Square, Bristol, 'about three weeks previous to her expected delivery' of a third child. Her son John Edward Taylor (1791–1844) was educated in Manchester at the school to which his father had moved from Ilminster. After a notable career in politics and education, he established the *Manchester Guardian* in 1821, and remained its editor until his death.

213   from *The Female Advocate*

[*Women of the Future*]

MAN, seated high on Learning's awful throne,
Thinks the fair realms of knowledge his alone;
But you, ye fair, his Salic Law disclaim:
Supreme in science shall the tyrant reign,
When every talent all-indulgent heaven
In lavish bounty to your share hath given?
  With joy ineffable the Muse surveys
The orient beams of more resplendent days:
As on she raptured looks to future years,
What a bright throng to Fancy's view appears!   10
To them see Genius her best gifts impart,
And Science raise a throne in every heart!
One turns the moral, one th' historic page;
Another glows with all a Shakespeare's rage!

Salic Law] i.e. that excludes women from a dynastic succession

With matchless Newton now one soars on high,
Lost in the boundless wonders of the sky;
Another now, of curious mind, reveals
What treasures in her bowels Earth conceals;
Nature's minuter works attract her eyes;
Their laws, their powers, her deep research descries,   20
From sense abstracted, some, with arduous flight,
Explore the realms of intellectual light;
With unremitting study seek to find
How mind on matter, matter acts on mind:
Alike in nature, arts, and manners read,
In every path of knowledge, see they tread!
Whilst men, convinced of Female Talents, pay
To Female Worth the tributary lay.

(1774)

ANONYMOUS ('A FEMALE HAND')

Her *Literary Amusements* (2 vols., 1782) consists mainly of short fiction and prose essays such as 'Thoughts on the Advantages of improving the Mind in the Female Sex', an essay on 'The Marriage State', and a letter 'ridiculing Masculine Amusements for Ladies'. The earliest poem is dated 1757. The opening 'History of Mr. Allen' is a no doubt fictitious account of the discovery of the MS of the book, in the manner of Mackenzie's *The Man of Feeling* (1771). Samuel Badcock, in the *Monthly Review*, 66 (1782), 476, dismissed the work as fit only for the illiterate.

214   *To my Niece, A.M. With a new Pair of Shoes on her
first going alone. Written Dec. 22, 1774*

WHEN little girls begin to walk,
Their next attempt should be to talk.
Then why thus, Nancy, why thus long
Do you persist to hold your tongue?
Full sixteen months gone o'er your head,
And not a word by you been said!
Oh! let it never once be told
That silence reigned in girl so old!
But let us hear, by Christmas day,
Your speech at last hath found its way: 10
In lisping accents sweetly prattle
Of fine new shoes, of doll, and rattle,
And prove to all your friends around
Your sex's province you have found.

(Wr. 1774; pub. 1782)

HANNAH MORE
(1745–1833)

She was the fourth of the five daughters of Jacob More (d. 1783), Master of the Free School of Fishponds, Stapleton, near Bristol, and his wife Mary Grace, a farmer's daughter. From an early age the daughters were prepared by their father to support themselves as teachers and in 1758 the three eldest opened a boarding school in Bristol by subscription. Hannah was a precocious child with a gift for languages, including Latin, who was taught first by her father (with some misgivings about female pedants) and later by masters at her sisters' school, including the Revd James Newton of Bristol Baptist Academy. Eventually she taught and lived at the successful school, which removed to larger premises in 1762. From about 1767 she was engaged to Edward Turner of Belmont, near Bristol, twenty years her senior, who repeatedly postponed the marriage, and finally broke the engagement, giving her an annuity of £200 and £1,000 at his death.

With some measure of financial independence, she was able to indulge her literary ambitions, no doubt encouraged by a meeting with the poet and reviewer John Langhorne in 1773. Her first publication was *The Search after Happiness: A Pastoral Drama* (Bristol, 1773), written, according to the preface, when she was 18, and already popular in boarding-schools. It was promptly praised by Langhorne in the *Monthly Review*. In 1774 her tragedy *The Inflexible Captive* was published at Bristol and acted at Bath and Exeter in 1775, with a prologue by Langhorne and an epilogue by Garrick, who was present at the first night. She had met Garrick during a visit to London with two of her sisters in 1774, when she had been armed with a letter of introduction from Dr James Stonhouse, a Bristol physician and family friend. Stonhouse described Hannah, who had sent Garrick a copy of her tragedy in advance, as 'a young Woman of an amazing Genius, & remarkable Humility', who would be conveniently living in lodgings 'just by you', and he also enclosed a copy of an admiring letter she had written about Garrick's acting. Not surprisingly after such an introduction, she soon met Garrick, and before long Edmund Burke, Samuel Johnson, and Sir Joshua Reynolds (perhaps through her Bristol friend Mrs Gwatkin, to whom *The Search after Happiness* is dedicated, and whose son later married one of Reynolds's nieces). Johnson, who playfully rebuked her for flattery in some well-known passages in Boswell's *Life*, was fond of her, and later described her as the most 'powerful versifatrix in the English language'. Garrick, who nicknamed her 'Madam Nine' (referring to the Nine Muses), became particularly friendly with her, and in 1776 she lived for several months with the great actor and his wife. (Her *Ode to Dagon*, Garrick's dog, was published in 1777.) She also became well known in the literary circles of Mrs Montagu, Mrs Chapone, and Mrs Boscawen, and was friendly with Elizabeth Carter, Horace Walpole, and the Burneys. In a curious numerical assessment of her acquaintance in 1778, Mrs Thrale gave Hannah More maximum marks for 'Worth of Heart', 'Useful Knowledge', and 'Ornamental Knowledge', but none for 'Person Mien & Manner', a mere 7 out of 20 for 'Conversation Powers', and only 10 for 'Good Humour'.

In 1776 she published *Sir Eldred of the Bower and The Bleeding Rock: Two Legendary Tales* (favourably reviewed by Langhorne), of which a second edition, revised by Johnson, appeared in 1778. She is said to have received 40 guineas for these poems, but the stage remained more profitable. Her tragedy *Percy*, with a prologue and epilogue by Garrick who had revised it with her during 1776–7, was produced at

Covent Garden in December 1777, had a run of twenty-two nights (bringing her some £600) and sold 4,000 copies in two weeks. Another tragedy, *The Fatal Falsehood*, which also benefited from Garrick's advice, was produced in May 1779 with less success. It was this play which led to an abusive quarrel with Hannah Cowley (see nos. 252–4). Although she remained a close friend of Mrs Garrick, David Garrick's death in January 1779 in effect ended her career in the theatre, to which in later years she became hostile, regretting that she had ever written for the stage.

Other publications were already reflecting her didactic and educational interests: *Essays on Various Subjects. Principally Designed for Young Ladies* (1777) and *Sacred Dramas, Chiefly Intended for Young Persons, to which is added, Sensibility, A Poem* (1782) both enjoyed many later editions. *Florio: A Tale for Fine Gentlemen and Fine Ladies: and The Bas Bleu; Or, Conversation: Two Poems* (1786), dedicated respectively to Horace Walpole and Mrs Vesey, had been read and praised by Johnson before his death in 1784. *Bas Bleu* celebrates the 'Bluestocking' circles of Mrs Montagu and Mrs Boscawen, contrasting true conversation with the stiff and sterile gatherings described in the extract given below. Apart from *Bishop Bonner's Ghost* (1789), a short satire published by Walpole at Strawberry Hill, her writings thereafter became steadily more didactic and pious, partly under the influence of some eminent clergymen and such new friends as William Wilberforce. Her ill-fated attempt at patronage of the uneducated Ann Yearsley in 1784 is described below (see nos. 256–9).

In the late 1780s she built a cottage at Cowslip Green, Wrington, in Somerset, some ten miles from Bristol. During the winters she often lived with her sisters, who had retired to Bath, and also paid annual visits to London. A sequence of serious works now appeared: *Slavery, A Poem* (1788), *Thoughts on the Importance of the Manners of the Great to General Society* (1788; 8th edn. by 1792), *An Estimate of the Religion of the Fashionable World* (1791; 5th edn. by 1793), and *Strictures on the Modern System of Female Education* (1799), in which she made the controversial judgement that a woman who had lapsed from strict morality should be excluded from polite society. (In October 1799 Mrs Thrale-Piozzi was told that the boys at Westminster School had 'burned her [i.e. Hannah More] in Effigy for writing against the Dissipation of Youth'.) Many other moral, religious, and political works followed down to the 1820s, including her only novel, *Coelebs in Search of a Wife* (1809). From 1789 she and her sisters had been active in promoting Sunday Schools in their neighbourhood, but she saw dangers in over-educating the lower classes and making them unhappy with their humble station in life, perhaps remembering her painful experience with Ann Yearsley.

She was disturbed by the social tensions which followed the French Revolution, countering them first in *Village Politics, by Will Chip* (1792). This was followed by her forty-nine contributions (signed 'Z') to the Cheap Repository Tracts which she wrote with her sisters and friends for mass distribution as broadsides by committees all over the country, three a month appearing over a period of some three years. Her use of simple diction and verse forms to appeal to uneducated readers can make her didactic conservatism not entirely predictable in its effects. (It is of some interest that she was sympathetic to the *Lyrical Ballads*, telling Joseph Cottle that 'Your young friend Wordsworth surpasses all your other young friends'.)

In 1802 she moved a short distance to a larger house at Barley Wood near Wrington, where she was joined by her sisters. In later years she was known to, and sometimes reviled by, the new literary generation of Coleridge, Southey, De Quincey, and even Thomas Macaulay. Describing a visit to her in 1814 with

Coleridge, Cottle referred to Barley Wood as 'the seat of piety, cheerfulness, literature, and hospitality', which had 'more visits from bishops, nobles, and persons of distinction, than, perhaps, any private family in the kingdom'. In 1828 she moved to Clifton, where she died in 1833 at the age of 88, leaving £30,000 to some seventy charities.

215   from *Epilogue to The Search after Happiness: A Pastoral Drama*

Spoken by two young Ladies

SECOND LADY   Child! we must quit these visionary scenes,
   And end our follies when we end our teens;
   These bagatelles we must relinquish now,
   And good matronic gentlewomen grow:
   Fancy no more on airy wings shall rise,
   We now must scold the maids, and make the pies;
   Verse is a folly—we must get above it,
   And yet I know not how it is—I love it.
   Though we should still the rhyming trade pursue,
   The men will shun us—and the women too: 10
   The men, poor souls! of scholars are afraid,
   We should not, did they govern, learn to read,
   At least, in no abstruser volume look
   Than the learned records—of a cookery-book;
   The ladies too their well-meant censure give:
   'What!—does she write? A slattern, as I live.
   I wish she'd leave her books, and mend her clothes.
   I thank my stars I know not verse from prose;
   How well so'er these learned ladies write,
   They seldom act the virtues they recite;   20
   No useful qualities adorn their lives,
   They make sad mothers, and still sadder wives.'

FIRST LADY   I grant this satire just in former days,
   When Sapphos and Corinnas tuned their lays,
   But in our chaster times 'tis no offence,
   When female virtue joins with female sense;
   When moral Carter breathes the strain divine,
   And Aikin's life flows faultless as her line;
   When all-accomplished Montagu can spread
   Fresh-gathered laurels round her Shakespeare's head;   30
   When wit and worth in polished Brooke unite,
   And fair Macaulay claims a Livy's right.

Thus far, to clear her from the sin of rhyme,
Our author bade me trespass on your time,
To show that, if she dares aspire to letters,
She only sins in common with her betters;
She bids me add—though Learning's cause I plead,
One virtuous sentiment, one generous deed,
Affords more genuine transport to the heart
Than genius, wit, or science can impart;   40
For these shall flourish, fearless of decay,
When wit shall fail, and science fade away.

(1774)

216   *Inscription in a Beautiful Retreat called*
                        Fairy Bower

AIRY spirits, you who love
Cooling bower or shady grove,
Streams that murmur as they flow,
Zephyrs bland that softly blow;

Babbling Echo, or the tale
Of the lovelorn nightingale,
Hither, airy spirits, come,
This is your peculiar home.

If you love a verdant glade,
If you love a noontide shade,   10
Hither, sylphs and fairies, fly,
Unobserved of earthly eye.

Come, and wander every night
By the moonbeam's glimmering light,
And again at early day
Brush the silver dews away.

Mark where first the daisies blow,
Where the bluest violets grow,
Where the sweetest linnet sings,
Where the earliest cowslip springs;   20

Where the largest acorn lies,
Precious in a fairy's eyes;
Sylphs, though unconfined to place,
Love to fill an acorn's space.

Come, and mark within what bush
Builds the blackbird or the thrush:
Great his joy who first espies,
Greater his, who spares the prize.

Come, and watch the hallowed bower,
Chase the insect from the flower;   30
Little offices like these
Gentle souls and fairies please.

Mortals! formed of grosser clay,
From our haunts keep far away,
Or, if you should dare appear,
See that you from vice are clear.

Folly's minion, Fashion's fool,
Mad Ambition's restless tool,
Slave of passion, slave of power,
Fly, ah! fly this tranquil bower!   40

Son of Avarice, soul of frost,
Wretch of Heaven abhorred the most,
Learn to pity others' wants,
Or avoid these hallowed haunts.

Eye, unconscious of a tear,
When Affliction's train appear,
Heart, that never heaved a sigh
For another, come not nigh.

But ye darling sons of Heaven,
Giving freely what was given,   50
Who, like Providence, dispense
Blessings of benevolence;

You who wipe the tearful eye,
You who stop the rising sigh,
You who well have understood
The luxury of doing good;

Come, ye happy virtuous few,
Open is my bower to you;
You the mossy banks may press,
You each guardian fay shall bless.   60

(1774)

217   from *Sensibility: A Poetical Epistle*

SWEET Sensibility! thou soothing power,
Who shedd'st thy blessings on the natal hour,
Like fairy favours! Art can never seize,
Nor affectation catch, thy power to please:
Thy subtle essence still eludes the chains
Of Definition, and defeats her pains.
Sweet Sensibility! thou keen delight!
Thou hasty moral! sudden sense of right!
Thou untaught goddess! Virtue's precious seed!
Thou sweet precursor of the generous deed!   10
Beauty's quick relish! Reason's radiant morn,
Which dawns soft light before Reflection's born!
To those who know thee not, no words can paint,
And those who know thee, know all words are faint!
'Tis not to mourn because a sparrow dies;
To rave in artificial ecstasies:
'Tis not to melt in tender Otway's fires;
'Tis not to faint when injured Shore expires:
'Tis not because the ready eye o'erflows
At Clementina's or Clarissa's woes.   20

Forgive, O Richardson! nor think I mean,
With cold contempt, to blast thy peerless scene:
If some faint love of virtue glow in me,
Pure spirit! I first caught that flame from thee.

While soft Compassion silently relieves,
Loquacious Feeling hints how much she gives;
Laments how oft her wounded heart has bled,
And boasts of many a tear she never shed.

As words are but th' external marks, to tell
The fair ideas in the mind that dwell;   30
And only are of things, the outward sign,
And not the things themselves they but define;
So exclamations, tender tones, fond tears,
And all the graceful drapery Pity wears,
These are not Pity's self, they but express
Her inward sufferings by their pictured dress;
And these fair marks, reluctant I relate,
These lovely symbols may be counterfeit.
Celestial Pity! why must I deplore
Thy sacred image stamped on basest ore?   40

There are, who fill with brilliant plaints the page,
If a poor linnet meets the gunner's rage:
There are, who for a dying fawn display
The tenderest anguish in the sweetest lay;
Who for a wounded animal deplore,
As if friend, parent, country were no more;
Who boast quick rapture trembling in their eye,
If from the spider's snare they save a fly;
Whose well-sung sorrows every breast inflame,
And break all hearts but his from whom they came: 50
Yet, scorning life's *dull* duties to attend,
Will persecute a wife, or wrong a friend;
Alive to every woe by *fiction* dressed,
The innocent he wronged, the wretch distressed,
May plead in vain; their sufferings come not near,
Or he relieves them cheaply with a tear.

(1782)

218   from *The Bas Bleu: Or, Conversation*

[*Cold Ceremony*]

WHERE the dire Circle keeps its station,
Each common phrase is an oration;
And cracking fans, and whispering misses,
Compose their Conversation blisses.
The matron marks the goodly show,
While the tall daughter eyes the beau—
The frigid beau!—Ah! luckless fair,
'Tis not for you that studied air;
Ah! not for you that sidelong glance,
And all that charming nonchalance;   10
Ah! not for you the three long hours
He worshipped the 'cosmetic powers';
That finished head which breathes perfume,
And kills the nerves of half the room;
And all the murders meant to lie
In that large, languishing, grey eye.
Desist;—less wild th' attempt would be
To warm the snows of Rhodope:
Too cold to feel, too proud to feign,
For him you're wise and fair in vain.   20
    Chill shade of that affected Peer,
Who dreaded Mirth! come safely here;

For here no vulgar joy effaces
Thy rage for polish, ton, and graces.
Cold Ceremony's leaden hand
Waves o'er the room her poppy wand.
Arrives the stranger: every guest
Conspires to torture the distressed;   30
At once they rise—so have I seen—
You guess the simile I mean,
Take what comparison you please,
The crowded streets, the swarming bees,
The pebbles on the shores that lie,
The stars, which form the galaxy;
This serves t' embellish what is said,
And shows, besides, that one has read;—
At once they rise—th' astonished guest
Back in a corner slinks, distressed;   40
Scared at the many bowing round,
And shocked at her own voice's sound,
Forgot the thing she meant to say,
Her words, half-uttered, die away;
In sweet oblivion down she sinks,
And of her ten appointments thinks:
While her loud neighbour on the right
Boasts what she has to do tonight;
So very much, you'd swear her pride is
To match the labours of Alcides;   50
'Tis true, in hyperbolic measure,
She nobly calls her labours *pleasure*;
In this, unlike Alcmena's son,
She never means they should be done;
Her fancy of no limits dreams,
No! *ne plus ultra* bounds her schemes;
Fired at th' idea, out she flounces,
And a new martyr John announces.

(1786)

219   ### from *Slavery, A Poem*

PERISH th' illiberal thought which would debase
The native genius of the sable race!
Perish the proud philosophy, which sought
To rob them of the powers of equal thought!
Does then th' immortal principle within
Change with the casual colour of the skin?
Does matter govern spirit? or is mind
Degraded by the form to which 'tis joined?

No: they have heads to think, and hearts to feel,
And souls to act with firm, though erring, zeal;   10
For they have keen affections, kind desires,
Love strong as death, and active patriot fires;
All the rude energy, the fervid flame,
Of high-souled passion, and ingenuous shame:
Strong but luxuriant virtues boldly shoot
From the wild vigour of a savage root.
    Nor weak their sense of honour's proud control,
For pride is virtue in a pagan soul;
A sense of worth, a conscience of desert,
A high, unbroken haughtiness of heart: 20
That self-same stuff which erst proud empires swayed,
Of which the conquerors of the world were made.
Capricious fate of man! that very pride
In Afric scourged, in Rome was deified. . . .

    And thou, White Savage! whether lust of gold,
Or lust of conquest, rule thee uncontrolled!
Hero, or robber!—by whatever name
Thou plead thy impious claim to wealth or fame;
Whether inferior mischiefs be thy boast,
A petty tyrant rifling Gambia's coast: 30
Or bolder carnage track thy crimson way,
Kings dispossessed, and provinces thy prey;
Panting to tame wide earth's remotest bound,
All Cortez murdered, all Columbus found;
O'er plundered realms to reign, detested lord,
Make millions wretched, and thyself abhorred;—
In Reason's eye, in Wisdom's fair account,
Your sum of glory boasts a like amount;
The means may differ, but the end's the same:
Conquest is pillage with a nobler name.   40
Who makes the sum of human blessings less,
Or sinks the stock of general happiness,
No solid fame shall grace, no true renown
His life shall blazon, or his memory crown.

                                       (1788)

220   *Patient Joe, or The Newcastle Collier*

HAVE you heard of a collier of honest renown,
Who dwelt on the borders of Newcastle Town?
His name it was Joseph—you better may know,
If I tell you he always was called Patient Joe.

Whatever betided he thought it was right,
And Providence still he kept ever in sight;
To those who love God, let things turn as they would,
He was certain that all worked together for good.

He praised his Creator whatever befell;
How thankful was Joseph when matters went well! 10
How sincere were his carols of praise for good health,
And how grateful for any increase in his wealth!

In trouble he bowed him to God's holy will;
How contented was Joseph when matters went ill!
When rich and when poor he alike understood
That all things together were working for good.

If the land was afflicted with war, he declared
'Twas a needful correction for sins which *he* shared;
And when merciful Heaven bid slaughter to cease,
How thankful was Joe for the blessing of peace! 20

When taxes ran high, and provisions were dear,
Still Joseph declared he had nothing to fear;
It was but a trial he well understood
From Him who made all work together for good.

Though his wife was but sickly, his gettings but small,
A mind so submissive prepared him for all;
He lived on his gains, were they greater or less,
And the Giver he ceased not each moment to bless.

When another child came he received him with joy,
And Providence blessed who had sent him the boy; 30
But when the child died—said poor Joe, 'I'm content,
For God had a right to recall what he lent.'

It was Joseph's ill-fortune to work in a pit
With some who believed that profaneness was wit;
When disasters befell him much pleasure they showed,
And laughed and said—'Joseph, will this work for good?'

But ever when these would profanely advance
That *this* happened by luck, and *that* happened by chance,
Still Joseph insisted no chance could be found,
Not a sparrow by accident falls to the ground. 40

Among his companions who worked in the pit,
And made him the butt of their profligate wit,
Was idle Tim Jenkins, who drank and who gamed,
Who mocked at his Bible, and was not ashamed.

One day at the pit his old comrades he found,
And they chatted, preparing to go under ground;
Tim Jenkins as usual was turning to jest
Joe's notion—that all things which happened were best.

As Joe on the ground had unthinkingly laid
His provision for dinner of bacon and bread,   50
A dog on the watch seized the bread and the meat,
And off with his prey ran with footsteps so fleet.

Now to see the delight that Tim Jenkins expressed!
'Is the loss of thy dinner too, Joe, for the best?'
'No doubt on't,' said Joe, 'but as I must eat,
'Tis my duty to try to recover my meat.'

So saying he followed the dog a long round,
While Tim, laughing and swearing, went down under ground.
Poor Joe soon returned, though his bacon was lost,
For the dog a good dinner had made at his cost.   60

When Joseph came back, he expected a sneer,
But the face of each collier spoke horror and fear;
'What a narrow escape hast thou had,' they all said,
'The pit is fall'n in, and Tim Jenkins is dead!'

How sincere was the gratitude Joseph expressed!
How warm the compassion which glowed in his breast!
Thus events great and small, if aright understood,
Will be found to be working together for good.

'When my meat,' Joseph cried, 'was just now stol'n away,
And I had no prospect of eating today,   70
How could it appear to a short-sighted sinner,
That my life would be saved by the loss of my dinner?'

(1795)

221   from *The Gin-Shop; or, A Peep into Prison*

COME, neighbour, take a walk with me
    Through many a London street,
And see the cause of penury
    In hundreds we shall meet.

We shall not need to travel far—
    Behold that great man's door;
He well discerns that idle crew
    From the deserving poor.

He will relieve with liberal hand
    The child of honest thrift;   10
But where long scores at Gin-Shops stand
    He will withhold his gift.

Behold that shivering female there,
    Who plies her woeful trade!
'Tis ten to one you'll find that Gin
    That hopeless wretch has made.

Look down these steps, and view below
    Yon cellar under ground;
There every want and every woe,
    And every sin is found.   20

Those little wretches, trembling there
    With hunger and with cold,
Were by their parents' love of Gin
    To sin and misery sold . . .

To prison dire misfortune oft
    The guiltless debtor brings;
Yet oftener far it will be found
    From Gin the misery springs.

See the pale manufacturer there,
    How lank and lean he lies!   30
How haggard is his sickly cheek!
    How dim his hollow eyes!

He plied the loom with good success,
    His wages still were high;
Twice what the village-labourer gains
    His master did supply.

No book-debts kept him from his cash,
   All paid as soon as due;
His wages on the Saturday
   To fail he never knew.   40

How amply had his gains sufficed,
   On wife and children spent!
But all must for his pleasures go;
   All to the Gin-Shop went.

See that apprentice, young in years,
   But hackneyed long in sin;
What made him rob his master's till?
   Alas! 'twas love of Gin.

That serving-man—I knew him once,
   So jaunty, spruce and smart!   50
Why did he steal, then pawn the plate?
   'Twas Gin ensnared his heart.

But hark! what dismal sound is that?
   'Tis Saint Sepulchre's bell!
It tolls, alas! for human guilt,
   Some malefactor's knell.

O! woeful sound, O! what could cause
   Such punishment and sin?
Hark! hear his words, he owns the cause—
   Bad Company and Gin.   60

And when the future lot is fixed
   Of darkness, fire and chains,
How can the drunkard hope to 'scape
   Those everlasting pains?

For if the murderer's doomed to woe,
   As holy writ declares,
The drunkard with Self-murderers
   That dreadful portion shares.

(1795)

ANONYMOUS

222 *On a Gentleman's complaining to a Lady that he could not eat Meat, owing to the Looseness of his Teeth*

YOU told me, Sir, your teeth were loose,
And soon would be unfit for use;
And, if I rightly recollect,
My answer was to this effect:
  That Nature meant they should be so,
As I imagined you must know:
'For what our stomachs cannot bear
Ought never to be placèd there;
As, even in youth, physicians own
That meat unchewed is worse than none,   10
So meat unchewed will never do
With such old gentlemen as you.'

  'What! not eat meat!', you made reply,
'Why, Madam, I should starve and die;
For what besides, I should be glad
To know, is daily to be had?
Or, if it could, what can men eat
So wholesome or so good as meat?'

  'Of many things, good Sir,' I say,
'As you shall hear another day,   20
When I for you a list will make
Of proper food for you to take,
And better much for you to eat
Than game, or fowl, or other meat.'

  So now, that I may keep my word,
I send you what to me's occurred.

  First then, use milk, which you may boil,
And eat for dinner for a while;
Then, for a change, new milk quite cold,
With bread that's neither new nor old;   30
Sometimes a pudding, made of flour
And water, not boiled half an hour—
I see you look so very sad
That you some seasoning may add,
Or, if you please, some sugar take,
Though that may make your loose teeth ache.

When tired, as you may be, of these,
I give you leave to eat some peas,
With greens, and every wholesome root
The gardener's art can furnish out.   40
Plain soups, or boiled or stewed, I hold
Not much amiss for young or old;
But such as aldermen would choose
'Twere death for aged men to use.
    Eggs for a meal may sometimes please,
But sparingly regale on these:
And, would you follow my advice,
Of nothing eat so much as rice;
For though by doctors, wondrous wise!
'Tis held unfriendly to the eyes,   50
Yet many doubt their wisdom's skill,
And you have naught to fear of ill,
For long you cannot hope to see—
(At least it so appears to me).
Then you eat rice, and never mind
Though one year sooner you go blind:
Your wife and little ones, no doubt,
Will gladly lead you all about;
Or, if they should, perchance, refuse,
You then a dog and string may use.   60

    'If nothing more I am to have,
You soon will send me to my grave.'
    Have patience, Sir, and give me leave
To take a little time to breathe.

    Now then, I say that I could wish
That twice a week you'd eat of fish;
As fish is held nutritious food,
And so by Catholics allowed.
    Yet one thing more—and then you will
Of eatables have had your fill—   70
And that is, fruit of every sort
That with your pocket will comport,
From apples-John to apples-pine,
And the rich product of the vine,
With cherries red, and cherries black,
And strawberries, a numerous pack;
With nectarines, apricots and peaches,
And what besides within your reach is,

apples-John] apples said to be ripe after two years, when withered   apples-pine]
pineapples

Excepting nuts, for nuts won't do
For such an aged man as you.   80
     Thus you'll have food enough, I think,
So now let me prescribe you drink.
     As I, good Sir, have little doubt
But you have bile, or cramp, or gout,
So I, who life in study pass,
Unused to circulate the glass,
No sort of wine can recommend
To anyone I call my friend;
Nor beer nor ale, for these, I'm sure,
No *gentleman* can *now* endure: 90
But rum or brandy, well diluted
With water that is soft reputed;
And, to repel the gout's attack,
Take now and then a little 'rack.
     With proper regimen and these,
You may, I think, rub on with ease,
Till you have tired the friends about ye,
And they are glad at heart to rout ye;
Then, not to plague or them or you,
Oblige them with a Last Adieu.   100

     My list for you thus at an end,
Excuse the freedom of a friend
In recommending what I love,
And what, by use, you'd soon approve:
But if you never mean to try,
Then you must be to blame, not I,
If pains approach, and death draws nigh.
For't nothing will avail the Muse
The powers of poetry to use,
If obstinate as old you prove,   110
And slight the dictates of her love;
Then make the most of what is writ,
For here is *quantum sufficit*.

                                                        (1775)

ANONYMOUS ('A LADY')

A copy in the Bodleian Library of *Poems by a Lady* (1781), a quarto volume of 204
pages, is inscribed: 'To Henry Harford Esqr. the following Poems are affectionately
presented by the Author.' Henry Harford, whose book-plate is in this copy, was
conceivably the charismatic Henry in the following poem, who makes other

rack] arrack, a spirit made from coconut   *quantum sufficit*] as much as suffices

338

appearances in the volume. He was the illegitimate son of the libertine Lord
Baltimore, who was acquitted after a notorious trial for rape in 1768. On Baltimore's
death in Naples in 1771 without legitimate children, the title became extinct, but in
his will he left an annuity to Mrs Hester Wheeland, mother of Henry Harford and his
sister, and his considerable estate to be held in trust for the children until they
reached the age of 21. Baltimore also bequeathed to Henry Harford, who was still a
schoolboy, the proprietorship of the State of Maryland owned by his ancestors.
Harford entered Exeter College, Oxford, on 4 May 1776, at the age of 18, not long
after his (if it is his) glamorous appearance in St James's Park. He is said to have been
granted £90,000 by Pitt in compensation for the loss of his Maryland revenues after
the war with America. He died in 1805.

Little else can be gleaned about the author, who refers to herself as 'Elvira'. Some
lines dated 1778 refer to the death of her father seven years earlier, and she addresses
poems to her friends Mrs Bevel, Mrs Severn, and Mrs Plestow.

223　*On meeting —— ——, Esq. in St. James's Park,
on the 22d of March, 1776*

ONE day in March, I ranged a verdant plain,
Where sweets salute you from each well-dressed swain;
Where tower-capped heads with lace and ribbon vie,
Like ancient Babel's tower, to reach the sky!
Where Yemen's* scents from snowy 'kerchiefs breathe,
And gales of fragrance passing coxcombs leave;
Where belles parade in hopes to be admired,
And beaux too, with the same ambition fired.
Through this gay mead one morn I vainly roved,
Nor had my heart the sweets of fondness proved:　　　　　　　10
Thought Venus' son possessed no power to wound,
Nor dreaded love, from fops who there abound.
I wandered long—at length a youth I spied,
'Is't human! or an angel's form!' I cried—
Unnumbered loves and graces round him played,
And won the heart of each admiring maid.
So much his form does other forms excel,
As were an angel to descend in hell,
The fiends with envy would the guest admire;
Thus men with admiration and with envy fire:　　　　　　　20
Women with nobler flame the youth approve,
Admiring, view his charms, and fondly love!
For all that gazed on beauteous Henry's eyes
Yielded their hearts the willing sacrifice.
I like the rest, with thoughtless rashness, run;
Nor, warned by them, the dangerous angel shun.

* Yemen, the most fragrant Vale in Arabia.

I gazed—Insensibility's no more my boast:
For in that look—my heart, my soul, I lost!
And finding every virtue, every grace,
That heaven has giv'n to the whole human race,   30
United in this lovely charming youth,
I've plighted to him my eternal truth;
His every smile can captivate a heart:
Learn then, ye fair, to shun the fatal dart.
Elvira has obtained the glorious prize!
Haste, haste away, nor trust your longing eyes:
For, charming as he is, the gazer dies!

(Wr. 1776; pub. 1781)

LADY SOPHIA BURRELL (née RAYMOND, later CLAY) (1750?–1802)

She was the elder daughter of Sir Charles Raymond, a wealthy banker of Valentine House, Barking, Essex, and his wife Sarah Webster. In 1773 she married (with a fortune of £100,000) William Burrell (1732–96), advocate, Director of the South Sea Company 1763–75, MP for Haslemere 1768–74, and from 1774 Commissioner of the Excise. They had five sons and two daughters. In 1788 her father's baronetcy reverted to her husband. Her father's will divided his estate, estimated at £200,000, between his two daughters independent of their husbands. She wrote verse throughout her married life, perhaps as an amusement when her husband was absorbed in his antiquarian researches for an unpublished 'History of Sussex' (12 volumes of materials for which are in the British Library). After he suffered a stroke in 1787, they retired to Deepdene, near Dorking, in Surrey. Her *Poems* (2 vols., 1793) illustrate the taste in the period for ballads, versifications of Ossian, and poems deriving from Goethe's *Werther*, as well as for druids, ruins, sensibility, mice, redbreasts and other creatures as subject-matter, but she also wrote some sprightly verse to friends. She later published *The Thymbriad* from Xenophon's *Cyropaedia* and a poem based on Fénélon's *Telemachus* (both 1794) and in 1800 two tragedies, *Maximian* (from Corneille) and *Theodora*, neither of which was performed. Her husband died in 1796 and in the following year she married the Revd William Clay. They lived in West Cowes, Isle of Wight, where she died on 20 June 1802, aged about 52.

224   from *Verses to a Lady, on her saying she preferred Commonalty to an Irish Peerage. May 20th, 1776*

THE clock strikes five—the watchman goes
To take his portion of repose;
The morning dawns—the idle sleep,
The pilfering tribe to cellars creep;

The beggar wanders from his shed,
The careful housemaid leaves her bed:
Blest Saturday again is come,
And citizens are free to roam.

Rich Mr. Bug, when Betty calls,
Prepares to leave his smoky walls—   10
The barber enters with his wig,
A bob in shape, but full and big:
In haste fair Madam Bug comes down,
With ruffles starched, and satin gown,
As brisk and busy as a bee,
Though full of fat and dignity;
Into a one-horse chaise they pop,
And bid the foreman mind the shop;
Within the boot the porters cram
Some beef for roasting, and a ham,   20
With divers savoury things beside,
Which Ma'am was careful to provide.

The party amble through the streets—
Bug nods to every friend he meets,
And then with consequential leer
Looks great, and simpers on his dear;
While prating Jacky sits between,
'As fine a child as e'er was seen'.

Thus as they jog in pride elate,
Th' apprentice, envious of their state,   30
Beholds the chaise with wishful eyes,
And at his master's fortune sighs;
To rise into the same condition
Is both his hope and his ambition,
The highest point at which he aims,
The sole reward his labour claims.

Meantime, pursuing their career,
Bug passes by a wild young Peer,
Who with self-consequence elate,
Gloried in honours, wealth, and state,   40
And from his phaeton looked down
On Bug, with a sarcastic frown;
Then thus bethought him: 'Oh, ambition!
Thou art annexed to each condition:

phaeton] light four-wheeled open carriage

341

See how that fellow Bug aspires
To leave his shop, and vie with squires!
How different 'tis with him and me,
His *forte* is cash—mine dignity.
When such comparisons I draw,
I'm happy in my own éclat;   50
Nor would I change my situation
For any other in the nation—
Except an Earldom chanced to lay
Unoccupied, and in my way.'
He passed—the cit with arch grimace
Began to sneer, and laugh apace,
Then thus addressed the female Bug
(Beginning with a graceful shrug):

'Behold that macaroni Lord!
So gay in clothes—profuse in board,   60
His fine apparel marks the fool,
And points him out for ridicule;
Proud as a peacock he appears,
Though to his tradesmen he arrears;
I know that his estate is dipped,
His name disgraced, his woodlands stripped,
To dress that carcase, and support
An idle puppy of the court,
A useless bawler in the House,
Whose brains would hardly serve a louse.   70
His pocket and his skull are brothers,
They thrive by borrowing from others;
I thank my stars, with heart sincere,
I was not born to be a Peer;
Make *me* an Alderman, kind fate!
And let these glory in their state.'

Thus through this life opinions go!
The word is, *chacun à son goût*.

(Wr. 1776; pub. 1793)

macaroni] dandyish, foppish   arrears] is in debt   dipped] mortgaged

225   *The Picture of a Fine Gentleman*

SEE Florio in his *vis-à-vis*—
No comet shines more bright than he;
The spectacle attracts the eye,
And captive fair ones round him die;
Or if, exalted in his seat,
On phaeton he shakes the street,
Trembling with wonder, we behold
A Macaroni grown so bold;
He lashes on his prancing steeds,
And looks disdainful o'er our heads;   10
But should he to the Opera come,
Elate with pride in beauty's bloom,
There guard your hearts, ye tender misses!
For Florio there the sex bewitches.

He comes in all the pomp of dress,
And lovely spite of haughtiness;
A *broche* is on his jabot placed,
His finger with a diamond graced,
And to complete the finished Beau,
A giant buckle hides his shoe;   20
A muff as vast as Ajax' shield,
Behold this modern Paris wield;
A sword is dangling at his side,
Of tempered steel, but never tried;
A feather, white as Celia's breast,
Adorns his *chapeau bras*; his vest,
Enriched with spangles, foils, and lace,
Is deemed the finest in the place.

A golden snuff-box he displays,
Takes snuff, and talks in foreign phrase;   30
Looks at his watch, whose brilliant chain
A hundred trinkets does sustain,
Games, swears, and acts the man of *ton*,
By self-importance only known;
Makes love, and rhymes, *coquets*, and sings,
Whilst with his praise th' assembly rings.
But could we follow Florio home,
And view him in his dressing-room,

vis-à-vis] a light carriage for two persons face to face   *broche*] jewel   jabot] shirt-
frill   *chapeau bras*] a small three-cornered flat silk hat   *ton*] fashion

Without the aid of powerful art,
How would the pretty misses start,   40
To see him void of the disguise,
Which fashionable dress supplies!
Florio no longer could be ' nown
The gay Lothario of the town;
But all your sex would spurn the creature,
Nor recollect a single feature
Of him who, not an hour before,
Each was ambitious to adore.

(1793)

226   *The School for Satire*

HOW oft we see the female sex
Themselves with jealous fancies vex!
With envy, which they cannot smother,
They tell the failings of each other;
Or if a dear, provoking creature
Has not one blemish in her nature,
A mole, an eyelash can supply
The means for female industry.
(A spider clinging to a thread
Can soon the web of mischief spread.)   10

Black-eyed Narissa cries, ' 'Tis true
That Celestina's eyes are blue!
But can we find expression there?—
Besides, the fool has flaxen hair.'

I see *brown* Amarilla sneer,
Because Polyxena is *fair*,
'Tis mighty easy, she avers,
To wear a skin as white as hers;—
But, for her part, she'd rather be
From artificial fairness free.   20

Cynthia, whose teeth Dumergue has made,
Follows the same censorious trade;
Cries, 'What d'ye mean by Flavia's youth?
You see that she has lost a tooth!'
Tall Lucy rails at little Dy,
Who only measures four feet high;

Fat Bell detests her cousin Prue,
Since she so thin and airy grew;
And snub-nosed Chloe hates a woman
Whose nose but borders on the Roman.   30

Doris the saucy, free and rude,
Rails at Myrtilla for a prude;
And Galatea says, with spite,
Dorinda's eyebrows are too light,
When it is known to half the town
That Galatea makes her own.

Ah why, ye fair! this cruel rage?
Do ye not all adorn the stage?
Decreed to charm in different ways,
Do ye not all create a blaze?   40
And, after all that has been said,
Ye can but sparkle, bloom, and fade.

Then be contented with your lot,
Nor covet charms your friends have got;
And learn that candour and good-nature
Act like a charm on every feature,
Restoring to Medusa's face
Composure, harmony and grace.

                                        (1793)

MARY SAVAGE
(*fl.* 1763–77)

In the prefatory 'Letter to Miss E.B.', the friend whom she also addressed in verse, Mrs Savage states that her *Poems on Various Subjects and Occasions* (2 vols., 1777) were

written by a Woman, who at the Time she amused her self in Planning 'em, never intended them for publick Inspection—who unblest with a learned Education, has no School Rules to boast—a stranger even to the Grammar of her native Language—of a Disposition rather inclined to gaiety—'till the cares of the world and some years experience wean'd her from Company and Diversions; and a necessity of staying at home gave Opportunity to blot over many a harmless sheet of Paper; both in Verse and Prose; rather than interrupt others with a set of thoughts that to them might be out of Season—and I could farther inform them, (because *every one loves to hear private Anecdotes of those who Write.*) that I have the care of a large Family which really finds me full employment—and without being in Trade may properly be called a Woman of Business—which I can safely say I never yet neglected for the sake of writing any thing I have yet produced—and what no one else could inform them—I confess I have so much the Spirit of Contradiction, that I much doubt, had it been my Lot, to pass a Life of Leisure, whether I should have the Inclination for Writing that I now find, when perhaps, I am not five Minutes alone, from Morn. to Night—and to prevent all Criticism on my Writings of every kind, I confess that I believe them full of faults: Which, had I abilities to amend I certainly should have set about long ago—but were those Alterations to be made by a Person of real knowledge in the Art of Writing, they must I suppose destroy one half to save the other—and then they would be no longer my works (i, pp. ii–v).

The only clue to her identity is the poem addressed to her son at Eton, who was probably George Savage (1750–1816), born in London, the son of William and Mary Savage. He attended Eton 1758–69, became a Fellow of King's College, Cambridge and an assistant at Eton, and held livings at Kingston and St Mary Aldermary. (There was one other boy with this surname at Eton at this period, whose father was William Savage of Guildford.) A William Savage died at Brentford in 1772: it would be merely speculation to suggest that he was her husband and that she collected her miscellaneous poems a few years later to help to support herself. But, given that her son was now in his late twenties, it is not easy to see why she still had the 'care of a large Family', unless she had many younger children or had found employment as a housekeeper. Mrs Savage explained that only one of her poems had been previously published (i, p. vii): 'Oeconomy', which, after he had accidentally seen it, Dr John Hawkesworth asked permission to print in the *Gentleman's Magazine* (November 1763), pp. 558–9, of which he was the literary editor.

227   *Letter to Miss E.B. at Bath*

To doggerel now I turn my pen:
A time may come (but lord knows when)
That I may try to think again.
At present in my brain there floats
A thousand parti-coloured motes;
From which, if time would but permit,
I might sift out some sparks of wit;
And many a line in verse and prose
Are lost, whilst half-asleep I doze.
My *pineal gland could you but view,   10
You'd scarce believe your eyes see true:
There's such a jumble; good and bad,
All sorts of thoughts, may there be had;
Like broker's shop, where we may find
Goods that belonged to half mankind;
Which, should the master dare produce,
Are little worth, and out of use;
And joy would sparkle in his face,
Could he put better in their place.
Thus oft, from shop of brain, I try   20
To throw the dirt and rubbish by;
But still they gain their former state,
Or leave a vacuum in the pate.

And plagued I am, against my mind,
With thoughts, by far too much refined,

* See the Spectator No. 275, the Dissection of a Beau's Head.

That preach a doctrine, out of fashion,
Of tender love and inclination;
Which fancy, ere our youth is past,
Vainly concludes will always last;
In words and gestures still the same,   30
As when they both were nymph and swain.

   Then skims across my rambling head
Thoughts of the absent and the dead;
Of what's to eat, and what's to drink;
Of children's welfare then I think;
Next, wonder if you've —— read;
Then wish to get by twelve to bed;
Declare no more at home I'll stay;
Was Garrick here, I'd to the play:
'Then why not go to church?' they'd say;   40
I don't pretend myself to know,
But sure religion is but show.
What the good saint did erst declare,
That we should always be at prayer,
Was never meant that we should be
For ever on our bended knee:
And though I have not time to read,
Or say at church my mother creed,
A sigh sincere may wing its way,
Though round the room the cat's at play.   50

   Thus far as sample I produce,
To show my head's of little use;
Till, roused to a more active scene,
I throw aside this waking dream;
And laying idle schemes apart,
Set hand to plough with all my heart;
And only snatch an hour to prove
I still am yours, in friendly love;
And wish sincerely you may find
Your pleasure and your health still joined: 60
And if you come to town to stay,
Desire you'll pass with me one day;
And pray don't fail to write a line
In answer to this scrawl of mine,
Which (stranger to your dwelling-place)
I mean shall bar of Pump Room grace.

   Oh! should it fail to reach your hand,
And there a public victim stand,

What food for laughter I should be,
To those who nothing know of me;   70
But let that prove as it may hap;
I'm now inclined to take a nap;
Adieu, my friend—in every state,
May ease and plenty be thy fate,

       Is the sincere wish of yours &c.

          (1777)

228   from *Letter to Miss E.B. on Marriage*

  MANKIND should hope, in wedlock's state,
A friend to find as well as mate:
And ere the charm of person fails,
Enquire what merit there remains,
That may, by help of their wise pate,
Be taught through life to bless the state;
And oft they'd find, by their own fire,
What they in others so admire.
But as 'tis law that each good wife
Should true submission show for life,   10
What's right at home they often slight,
What's right abroad shines very bright.

  Each female would have regal power,
But every male wants something more;
And that same balsam to the mind,
Which both would in compliance find,
Is, to this very time and hour,
Miscalled by them the want of power.
Then right of privilege they claim,
For every fair to vow a flame,   20
Which we are bound, with partial eye,
To find of true platonic dye;
For they've so fixed the certain rule,
How far with ladies they may fool,
That 'tis impossible they can
Go wrong—though not a man
Among them all would patience find,
If lady-wife should be inclined
To praise each swain, whose face or wit
Might chance her sprightly mind to hit.   30

  Then there's a something in the mind,
That is not only just—but kind;

That's fixed to neither taste nor sense,
Nor to be taught by eloquence;
But yet is that which gives a grace
To every feature of the face;
And is the surest chance for ease:
I mean a strong desire to please.
But own I must (though 'tis with shame)
Both parties are in this to blame;   40
They take great pains to come together,
Then squabble for a straw or feather;
And oft I fear a spark of pride
Prevails too much on either side.

   Then hear, my girl—if 'tis your lot
To marry, be not this forgot:
That neither sex must think to find
Perfection in the human kind;
Each has a fool's cap—and a bell—
And, what is worse, can't always tell   50
(While they have got it on their head)
How far astray they may be led.
Let it be then your mutual care,
That never both at once may wear
This fatal mark of reason's loss,
That whirlwind-like the soul does toss.
Obtain this point, and friendship's power
Will rise and bless each future hour.

                (1777)

229   *To a School-Boy at Eton. Yes and No*

MY dearest Boy,
             Since time begun,
Since earth was earth, and sun was sun;
Since thought by words was brought to light,
And answer mild set passion right:
The hardest task assigned to man
(Deny it, lordlings, if ye can),
In two short words has been confined
(I beg you'll keep them in your mind,
For much upon their use depends,
To make us still continue friends).   10
I mean the use of No and Yea:
They are but simple words, you'll say,

'For surely, ma'am, 'tis long ago,
Since first I learned both Yes and No.'
I learned them too, when I was young,
But still they blunder on my tongue;
And though unlike as day to night,
'Tis ten to one I use them right;
For Yes will run, when No should drudge,
Or Yes won't stir, and No will trudge;   20
And sure if they'll dispute with me,
They won't (as yet) with you agree.

    But that you may a little guard
Against their blows, when they come hard,
We'll state a few familiar cases,
To take the mask from both their faces.

    If you an apple-tree should spy,
With fruit delicious hanging high,
Secure from sight and out of bounds,
Where no preposter comes his rounds,   30
And chums at hand to lend a lift,
To have a taste you might make shift,
And Yes would then, with all its force,
As sure be first as headstrong horse:
But should by chance the fact be known,
Or pain in stomach cause a groan,
And make your worship cry out 'Oh!',
Then how you'll wish you had said No.

    In winter's morn, if ice abound,
Or white with snow appears the ground,   40
Or heavy rain from clouds descend,
Or stormy winds the branches rend;
Should you submit to wicked No,
And lay in bed, whilst others go
With cautious steps and well-conned book,
To watch the Doctor's mystic look;
When next you're called, and found to fail,
You'll grieve that Yes did not prevail.

    Returned to school, with cash in hand,
Full near your elbow Yes will stand: 50
In tempting shape of top and whip,
Or hoop to drive, or rope to skip;

preposter] prefect, monitor

350

Ere long as swift as lightning run
For hackney tit, or boat, or gun.
Perhaps some buck, with lively face,
More full of spirit than of grace,
With gay deportment may advance
A scheme at cards, to try your chance:
Or else advise a cheerful glass,
A few years hence, perhaps a lass;   60
Unmarked the cash will glide away,
And naught but empty pockets stay.
Then, if a friend distressed should come,
And ask your help—what says my son?
'A trifling Yes has ruled my day;
I naught for thee but sighs can pay.'

    'Tis fit that pleasure have a share—
Always to labour, who can bear?—
But prior claims in life you'll find,
When social duties touch your mind;   70
And time's slow hand shall point the way,
Where to object, and when obey:
A task too hard for me to teach;
Should I proceed, you'd say I preach.

    A few words more, and I am off:
At prudence fools will often scoff;
If you a parent's look attend,
Or fear in play to hurt a friend,
And won't your only farthing lend,
You'll be the jest of every wight,   80
Whose passions are his rule of right.
But let the laugh go ever so,
Be virtue's friend, and vice's foe,
And never blush at proper No.

(1777)

230   *The Disaster*

THE Author had informed her Friend, that among other amusements she had
diverted her self with taming two Sparrows—in answer to which her Friend sent
the following paragraph in her next letter—

    'What a whimsical account do you give of the advocations that take up your time;
among which taming of Sparrows seems to be one part—if you can bring them to
draw your chariot, I beseech you to direct their flight our way—with what pleasure

hackney tit] small hired horse   wight] person

shall I see them fluttering their little wings and gently descending for you to alight
at our door—'

By sparrows drawn, there's now no chance
To see your car-borne friend advance.
A dire disaster—hang the cat:
Far better had she killed a rat.
Supinely seated in my chair,
And building castles in the air,
Contriving how to form the traces,
And where to fix the springs and braces,
To make my car secure and tight,
And guide the little flutterers right;   10
A buzzing fly sports round my head,
And straight the airy castle fled.

My son, with arm of mighty force,
Soon stopped the fly's progressive course:
The trembling insect fast he held,
With joy elate his bosom swelled,
And thus he spoke to Dick and Phill,
'I give this victim to your will.'
Then oped the cage, that each might vie
To seize the half-expiring fly;   20
With wings outspread, to try their chance
The little chirpers soon advance:
With tail erect, and back raised high,
The cat appeared—her sparkling eye
Was green as is the emerald's dye:
With outstretched paw, and lofty bound,
She gave poor Dick a fatal wound.

Oh, dire mishap! oh, fell despair!
His fleeting breath was lost in air.
Struck with the sight, fixed pale and dumb   30
(Like coward when he hears a drum),
The youth remained—but kindled rage
Glows on my cheeks—and war I wage;
While puss, exulting o'er the prey,
Essays in vain to break away,
With hand of force I gripped her throat
(Her life was then not worth a groat):
'Unfeeling wretch, declare I say,
Deep mischief brooding, where you lay;

car-] carriage-

Unloose thy hold, release the corse,   40
Nor tear those limbs with brutal force;
'Twas impious theft that prompts the deed,
But impious theft shall ne'er succeed;
Nor shalt thou bear the prize away;
Grimalkin, hold—I charge thee, stay.
Life now no longer swells his breast,
Yet safe entombed my bird shall rest.

   'But, caitiff vile, live thou disgraced,
Nor ever more of sparrow taste;
Thy share of toast and cream shall fail,   50
Nor e'er in mirth pursue thy tail.
No tender mouse shall grace thy dish,
Nor shalt thou ever taste of fish;
At dreary eve of winter's day,
Warm by the fire each cat shall lay,
Whilst thou, shut out, shall mew in vain,
Exposed to storms of wind and rain;
Through pools of wet be forced to tramp,
Thy limbs benumbed with painful cramp.'

   With trembling nerves and glaring eye,   60
She heard my threats without reply.

   First in my hand I held her still,
To show I had the power to kill;
Then raised her high to strike the blow,
And lay the sprawling victim low;
But rage subsides—to give her pain
Would not bring back poor Dick again.
'Grimalkin, go—thy life I spare,
But never more my friendship share.'

   His mate, poor Phill, in silence mourns,   70
And pensive to the cage returns.
While I lament the fatal day
That snatched my flattering hopes away.
For never yet in one-horse chair
Did god or goddess mount in air;
And shall a mortal dare to fly,
With single sparrow, through the sky?
No—rather let me wait my doom,
And in my husband's chariot come.

                                        (1777)

ANNE WILSON
(*fl.* 1778)

Nothing is known about the author of *Teisa* (Newcastle, 1778), an elaborate topographical survey in verse (1615 lines) of the course of the River Tees. Although at the end of the poem Father Teisus promises this 'northern female Bard' that her celebration of the river will preserve her own fame from oblivion, the pamphlet is very rare. A short autobiographical passage (p. 20) refers to her 'humble lot', laments 'That in a hir'd-house all my days are spent', refers to 'Lycidas', a deceased friend (admirer or husband?), and wishes for a 'blest retreat' in which she could 'quiet pass the few remaining years'. There seems nothing to link her with the Mrs Ann Wilson who published *Jephthah's Daughter. A Dramatic Poem* in London in 1783, although the two works do share an occasionally uncertain grasp of metre and grammar.

231   from *Teisa: A Descriptive Poem of the River Tees,*
        Its Towns and Antiquities

[*In Praise of Drainage*]

YONDER behold a little purling rill,
Sweet flowing down the green, enamelled hill:
This aqueduct proceeds from Morrit's drains,
And well compensates his ingenious pains.
The rotten ground, which trembled as we trod,
Is now released from the exuberant load
Of chilly waters, that the grass deprive
Of its nutritious particles, and drive,
With moist, diluting qualities, away
The salts impregnating the foodful hay.   10
Where the dejected sheep all bleating stood,
Benumbed with chilly damps, and starved for food,
Behold firm land appear, with wholesome grass;
The cattle's looks proclaim it as we pass;
Death, which so oft in tainted rots appeared,
Is by the farmer now no longer feared.

   This plan would each landholder but pursue,
England a paradise we then might view:
Not then would her own sons, like exiles, seek
More lands to till beyond the foaming deep.   20
Lovers of agriculture all might here
Employment find throughout the circling year,
Since convenient are all seasons found
To drain off waters from the spongy ground.

The model of the drains prepare to sing,
O Sylvan Muse! Find out the hidden spring
Where bubbling waters rise, then with a spade
Let a broad trench, three feet in depth, be made;
Observe that with descent your conduit run,
Whether to the rising or the setting sun;   30
Let it in breadth about a foot extend,
And with a wall you must its sides defend;
This wall in height at least must be a foot,
And over the canal be sure to put
Large shelvy stones—the wall will them sustain;
With ling or straw then cover it again;
And careful stop each little hole or chink,
Lest through these the mouldering earth should sink,
Which oft the water's rapid course impedes.
But when th' earth is fixed, there no longer needs   40
Aught, save the stones, to bear it off the rills,
Which now the springing water quickly fills;
Every lesser duct must have its course
Into a larger one, which adds its force
To drive redundant fluids off the land,
Which, like a deluge, once were used to stand:
When this is done, it only now remains
With their own earth to cover up the drains. . . .

                                                        (1778)

FRANCES BURNEY (later D'ARBLAY)
(1752–1840)

She was born at King's Lynn, the second daughter of Charles Burney and his first
wife, Esther Sleepe. Her father, a musician, had been forced by ill health to leave
London and had taken a post as church-organist at King's Lynn. Her mother died in
1762, two years after the family—there were by now six children—had returned to
London, where her father became a successful music-teacher. In 1767 he married
Elizabeth Allen, a widow with three children of her own. The diary Fanny began
keeping in 1768 gives a vivid account of life in the crowded Burney household and of
its musical and literary visitors, especially after her father published accounts of his
travels on the Continent (in 1770 and 1772) in search of materials for his *History of
Music* (4 vols., 1776–89). She won her own celebrity with the publication of *Evelina*
(3 vols., 1778), although at first only her brothers and sisters knew the secret of its
authorship; her father, to whom she addressed the following prefatory lines, did not
learn it for several months. Friendship with Mrs Thrale, Johnson, Reynolds, Burke,
and many others soon followed and her high reputation as a novelist was confirmed
by *Cecilia* (5 vols., 1782). To please her much-loved father, who was intensely proud
of the appointment, she reluctantly accepted the post of Second Keeper of the Robes

to Queen Charlotte in 1786, but was unhappy at Court and resigned on the grounds of ill health in 1791, with a pension of £100 a year. Two years later she married Alexandre d'Arblay, a French general who had left France after the Revolution. They settled near Mickleham in Surrey and had one child, Alexander, born in 1795. She published *Camilla* (5 vols., 1796) by subscription and supposedly made over £3,000 from it, although it was less admired than her two earlier novels. Between 1802 and 1812 she lived in France with her husband, finally settling in England for good in 1815. In the previous year, in which her father died, she published her last novel, *The Wanderer* (5 vols.). Her last major publication was her *Memoirs* of her father (3 vols., 1832). She wrote little verse but a number of plays, of which only *Edwy and Elgiva* (1795) was performed, and that for one night only. She died in London in 1840 at the age of 87. Her *Diary and Letters* (7 vols., 1842–6) have often been reprinted and re-edited.

232   *To [Charles Burney]*

Oh author of my being!—far more dear
    To me than light, than nourishment, or rest,
Hygieia's blessings, Rapture's burning tear,
    Or the life-blood that mantles in my breast!

If in my heart the love of Virtue glows,
    'Twas planted there by an unerring rule;
From thy example the pure flame arose,
    Thy life, my precept—thy good works, my school.

Could my weak powers thy numerous virtues trace,
    By filial love each fear should be repressed;   10
The blush of Incapacity I'd chase,
    And stand, recorder of thy worth, confessed:

But since my niggard stars that gift refuse,
    Concealment is the only boon I claim;
Obscure be still the unsuccessful Muse,
    Who cannot raise, but would not sink, your fame.

Oh! of my life at once the source and joy!
    If e'er thy eyes these feeble lines survey,
Let not their folly their intent destroy;
    Accept the tribute—but forget the lay.   20

(1778)

ANN MURRY
(*c*.1755–after 1816)

Born in London in about 1755, she was the daughter of a wine-merchant, 'who gave her an excellent education, which she highly improved by her own application'. She earned a living as a private tutor and was best known for her *Mentoria: Or, The Young Lady's Instructor, in Familiar Conversations* (1778), in which one of the plates is a map drawn by the author. Her dedication to the Princess Royal, who had approved the work before publication, is dated from Tottenham High Cross. These dialogues on a variety of improving subjects were written 'for the use of her pupils', and were a task, her preface admits, 'perhaps above her years and abilities'. In spite of this modesty, *Mentoria* was frequently reprinted and had reached a 12th edition by 1823. She later published a *Sequel to Mentoria* (1782), *A Concise History of the Kingdoms of Israel and Judah* (2 vols., 1783) for 'Young Minds', *Mentorian Lectures, on Sacred and Moral Subjects* (1809), and an *Abridgement of the History of France* (1815?).

An impressive list of subscribers, including the Duchess of Bedford, other titled women, and David Garrick, appears in her *Poems on Various Subjects* (1779). She refers in a note to the 'two young Ladies of fashion' for whom she wrote *Mentoria*, and to Mr and Mrs V—— (a Mrs Vaughan was a subscriber) to whom she was indebted for many favours (pp. 80–1 n.) Apart from the three 'Town Eclogues', her poems are conventional or pious. The 'Eclogues' were particularly praised by reviewers. The other two are 'The Card Party', which mimics the chatter of the cardplayers, and 'City Splendor', a dialogue between a newly elected Lord Mayor of London and his wife.

233   *The Tête à Tête, Or Fashionable Pair. An Eclogue*

[SIR CHARLES MODISH and LADY MODISH]

SIR C. My dear! this morning we will take a ride,
      And call on Lord Rupee, and Lady Pride.

LADY M. With all my heart; and bring them home to dine:
      I like the scheme, the weather is so fine.
      Sir Charles! now read the news: pray, who is dead?
      And see if Lady Jane is brought to bed.

SIR C. The last new tragedy is well received;
      And Harrison, I see, is clear reprieved;
      Good Captain Bluster has obtained a Flag:
      I hope he will promote Lieutenant Brag!   10
      Where is my chocolate? The toast is cold.
      Lord Squander's pictures are, I find, just sold.

357

LADY M. Indeed, I feared his fortune was deranged;
    Of late his countenance was vastly changed;
    Like a barometer, the face explains
    The fall and rise of our uncertain gains.

SIR C. He was good-natured, and a well-bred man,
    Yet seemed surrounded with a dangerous clan.
    Tomorrow I'm resolved to go to town,
    To settle that affair with Captain Brown.   20

LADY M. And leave me quite alone in this dull place!
    Whilst you are gone, to see no human face!
    This dreary season gaiety best suits;
    'Tis hard to spend my time with rustic brutes.

SIR C. No cause but business e'er could make me leave
    Your Ladyship, whose absence I shall grieve;
    But really, our expenses are so great,
    To keep up the parade of useless state,
    'Tis needful for to live a rural life,
    Though with my inclination oft at strife.   30
    My steward plagues me with his loud complaint,
    Enough to tire the patience of a saint,
    With such a catalogue of human ills,
    Repairs, subscriptions, and long tradesmen's bills;
    The land-tax is so high, the stocks so low,
    And for my credit, 'tis, alas—so so!
    Though hard my lot, I must avoid a worse,
    And e'en consent to put m' estate to nurse.

LADY M. How cruel is my fate! how great the fall!
    So large my fortune, yet my jointure small.   40
    Then my precedence is, alas! so low,
    That even citizens before me go:
    A Lady-Mayoress e'en as good as me,
    Though her weak husband may retail bohea.

SIR C. Nay, pray my Lady! cease to be so loud,
    Nor of your consequence be yet so proud;
    The fortune which you boast was basely won,
    And by your father's gains Lord George undone.
    Women of highest rank so thoughtless live,
    They naught but sorrow and vexation give;   50
    In dissipated scenes they spend their time,
    Infants in sense, thought oft in years past prime.

before me go] i.e. at ceremonies and social occasions   bohea] tea

LADY M. In vain, Sir Charles! you strive my heart to vex;
   I will revere and vindicate my sex.
   Deign but to ask where female grace is seen,
   I thus reply—in our benignant Queen!
   In her, the mother and the wife we find,
   Blended with majesty, and sense refined:
   Blest with a Monarch's love, a nation's praise,
   Her worth transcendent shall adorn my lays;   60
   Not Faction's venom can her power disown,
   Or Slander tarnish her illustrious throne.
   From Royal George a bright example take,
   As good an husband and a father make,
   And strive like him no ordinance to break.

SIR C. Your Ladyship, with wond'rous skill and might,
   Brings strong conviction for to act aright:
   Be thou what Charlotte is, and then my heart
   Sure cannot fail to act a George's part.

LADY M. Pray now, Sir Charles! explain your present view,   70
   And for the children what will you pursue?

SIR C. As for the girls, I'll send them all to France,
   Where they will learn to chatter French, and dance:
   But if you like it better, or as well,
   I'll have at home a modern Mad'moiselle.
   The boys I mean to thrive by trade or law;
   And bring them up with due respect and awe.
   Charles, who I think is something like an ass,
   May do, perhaps, at Bombay or Madras.

LADY M. In Britain bred, in Britain freely born,   80
   A foreign education hence I scorn.
   Will foreign teachers English minds expand,
   And point the beauties of our native land?
   Will they not strive to alienate the heart,
   And gain new proselytes with laboured art?
   Will they not deem it heresy to teach
   Minds that have fled from Superstition's reach?
   Knowledge so gained is purchased much too dear;
   Such measures I oppose, with heart sincere.
   The boys, I trust, by industry will rise,   90
   And all be happy, fortunate, or wise;
   As for poor Charles, I can't endure the plan,
   Though rich as Croesus, or as Kouli Khan;
   I hate a Nabob's great and ill-got wealth,

Nabob] one who has returned from India with a large fortune

Bought at th' expense of peace and precious health;
If they return with treasures vast of gold,
Conscience upbraids them, nor e'er quits her hold;
The poisoned dagger, and the tainted bowl,
Are ever present to the guilty soul:
Remember Harpax, thy unhappy friend,   100
How splendid was his life!—how sad his end!

SIR C. You think too closely, weigh each point and grain,
Which ill accords with more substantial gain.
As for myself, a Patriot I will turn,
Yet for my private good with ardour burn;
Oppose the Minister in all his views,
And make my fortune in the way I choose.

LADY M. Fictitious Patriots are a fixed disgrace,
And found too oft but statesmen out of place;
Like Reynard in the fable, gasp for power,   110
And only yelp because the grapes are sour.
For Liberty they roar like idle boys,
Which they misuse as children do their toys.
Licentious freedom is the gift they ask,
Which wears, sweet Liberty! thy pleasing mask.

SIR C. But list! I think I hear the children's noise:
How I am plagued with chattering girls and boys!

LADY M. To you, I must confess, their infant sounds
Are not so pleasing as your dice and hounds.
Sir Charles, I wonder you dislike their talk;   120
Their opening reason you oppress and balk.

SIR C. The nursery's best suited to their plays,
I hate the fuss of all their childish ways;
At meals especially I will be quiet,
And where they are, there is perpetual riot.

LADY M. Alas! you hate the matrimonial life,
Domestic joys, and e'en your faithful wife;
Your children are a burthen, and your home
A cheerless place, and melancholy dome.

SIR C. I never will forgo the joys of life   130
To please the haughty or capricious wife.

dome] building, house

360

The man who lets a thoughtless woman rule
Must needs be deemed a most egregious fool.
My future prospects I resign to chance,
And for the present will retire to France;
The remedy you'll gain in legal course:
A separate stipend, or a kind divorce.

(1779)

ANN THOMAS
(*fl.* 1784–95)

On the title-page of her *Poems on Various Subjects* (Plymouth, 1784), she is described
as 'An Officer's Widow of the Royal Navy'. She lived at Millbrook, near Plymouth, in
Cornwall. The volume is dedicated to Lady Eliot of Port-Eliot, whose husband,
Lord Eliot, was a powerful political figure in Cornwall and a friend of Johnson and
Reynolds. A line in a poem about Shetland—'The humble Muse sprung from thy
rocky shore'—suggests that she grew up there. Her respectable list of subscribers
and her own modesty disarmed William Enfield in the *Monthly Review* in 1785. When
she published *Adolphus de Biron, A Novel. Founded on the French Revolution* (2 vols.,
Plymouth, 1795), a firm celebration of the British constitution, she was still living at
Millbrook. Dedicated again to Lady Eliot, the novel once more had many aristocratic
and naval subscribers. Perhaps having noted Enfield's earlier reaction, she claimed
to approach the public with 'Diffidence and Awe', acknowledged 'Encouragement
and Protection' beyond her merits, and told her reviewers that 'it is with pleasure that
I have often observed your generous Allowances for the Errors of a female Pen'.

234   *To Laura, On the French Fleet parading before*
      Plymouth in August 1779

OUR ears were stunned with noisy drum,
That beats to arms—the foe is come!
The combined fleets plain did appear,
The van, the centre, and the rear;
You cannot think what horrid rout,
And how the people ran about.
For fear my spirits should grow damp,
I thought I'd go and view the Camp;
And Laura, if you had been there,
You'd had no thought of dread or fear;   10
The good old Fraser marched along,
Like Hector brave—Achilles strong;
His Royal First Battalion too
Looked as brave soldiers ought to do;

And Highlanders you there might see
With legs quite bare up to their knee;
They looked as we are often told
Brave Roman warriors did of old;
Each County band in armour bright
Seemed well disposed the foe to fight.   20

So when I'd seen the martial plain,
Contented I went home again;
All through the streets the wagons creak,
They jumble—and the dishes break;
'Twill take some time sure to repair
The loss sustained in china-ware;
Yet that's a loss we may regain,
When India ships come home again.
But as for me I thought I'd stay,
And see the fortune of the day;   30
For, Laura, very well you know
I need not fear the plundering foe;
I had no money—had no plate,
Nor title-deeds for an estate,
So at the last I could but pack,
And take my fortune on my back.

But when the foe had made this rout,
They took one ship—and so went out;
A mighty victory sure was won:
An hundred ships have captured one.   40
And now we are from danger free,
And all the folks are in high glee,
I wonder you so long can stay.
We'd such amusements every day;
The people from the country tramp
To see the manners of the Camp,
And when of that they'd had a view,
Then they consult our conjurer too;
Poor man—indeed he cannot see,
But reads the stars like ABC;   50
He tells them all what will betide,
And when each lass shall be a bride;
And when the destined youth appears,
Describes the very coat he wears;
He'd tell her too, if he may prove
An object worthy of her love:
When these important things they know,
Then home again contented go.

conjurer] fortune-teller

Laura, if you should longer stay,
I think I'll come some holiday;   60
And Jenny call a thousand sluts,
Unless she gives me store of nuts;
And when I come, I hope her hoard
Good red-streaked apples will afford.
Laura, I think it's time to end:
I'll only say I am thy friend.

(Wr. 1779; pub. 1784)

ANNE HUNTER (née HOME)
(1742–1821)

She was the eldest daughter of Robert Home, surgeon of Burgoyne's Regiment of Light Horse, later of Greenlaw Castle, Berwickshire, and his wife Mary Hutchison. Her father is said to have been forced into his profession by lack of financial support from relatives who opposed his early and imprudent marriage. Her first publication was a song ('Adieu ye streams that softly glide') to the air 'The Flowers of the Forest' for which Jane Elliot and Alison Cockburn also provided words (see nos. 170–1). It appeared in *The Lark* and *The Charmer* (both published at Edinburgh in 1765) and in later songbooks. In July 1771, after a long engagement, she married John Hunter (1728–93), the distinguished surgeon of Jermyn Street, London. Her brother became a pupil of her husband in 1772 and was himself later a famous surgeon as Sir Everard Home (1756–1832). She had four children in the first five years of marriage, only two of which survived childhood. She later became well known in fashionable literary society in London, her enjoyment of which was not shared by her taciturn and obsessively hard-working husband. Her friends included Elizabeth Carter, Mary Delany, Elizabeth Montagu, Horace Walpole, and Hester Thrale (Piozzi), who recorded her 'North American Death Song' in her journal in April 1782 with the comment, 'I had no Notion she could write so well'.

As Robert Nares wrote after her death, 'she never assumed, or in the least affected, the character of a poetess; but with modesty delivered her productions in manuscript to a favoured few'. Inevitably some found their way into print in miscellanies and magazines. In the 1790s she became friendly with Haydn during his visits to England and anonymously provided the words for his *Six Original Canzonettas* (1794), which he dedicated to her, for his *Second Set of Canzonettas* (1795) in which some were selected from other poets, and for two separately published songs, 'The Spirit's Song' and 'O Tuneful Voice'. In 1793, after quarrelling with colleagues at St George's Hospital, her husband died of a heart attack, leaving a complicated will which forced her to leave her home. For some years she and her two children lived on the sale of other parts of his estate, with the help of a pension from the Queen and with the support of her husband's friend Dr Maxwell Garthshore. In 1799 Parliament voted to purchase the Hunterian Museum for £15,000 and established it in the Royal College of Surgeons, and she lived comfortably thereafter. She collected her *Poems* in 1802 (further edition 1803), dedicating them to her son Capt. John Banks Hunter. In 1804 she published *The Sports of the Genii*, written in 1797, inspired by the drawings of Susan Macdonald, who had died in 1803 at the age of 21. *A New Ballad, Entitled and Called The Times* (1804?), an anonymous single sheet, has also been attributed to her. Her daughter, who had married General Sir James Campbell, was a widow by the time of her mother's death in London in 1821.

235   *North American Death Song*

Written for, and adapted to, An Original Indian Air

THE sun sets in night, and the stars shun the day,
But glory remains when their lights fade away:
Begin, you tormentors! your threats are in vain,
For the son of Alknomook will never complain.

Remember the arrows he shot from his bow,
Remember your chiefs, by his hatchet laid low:
Why so slow? do you wait till I shrink from the pain?
No; the son of Alknomook shall never complain.

Remember the wood, where in ambush we lay,
And the scalps which we bore from your nation away: 10
Now the flame rises fast; you exult in my pain;
But the son of Alknomook can never complain.

I go to the land where my father is gone,
His ghost shall rejoice in the fame of his son:
Death comes like a friend to relieve me from pain;
And thy son, O Alknomook, has scorned to complain.

(Wr. by 1782; pub. 1802)

236   *A Pastoral Song*

MY mother bids me bind my hair
    With bands of rosy hue,
Tie up my sleeves with ribbons rare,
    And lace my bodice blue.

'For why,' she cries, 'sit still and weep,
    While others dance and play?'
Alas! I scarce can go or creep,
    While Lubin is away.

'Tis sad to think the days are gone,
    When those we love were near;   10
I sit upon this mossy stone,
    And sigh, when none can hear.

And while I spin my flaxen thread,
    And sing my simple lay,
The village seems asleep, or dead,
    Now Lubin is away.

(1794)

CHARLOTTE SMITH (née TURNER)
(1749–1806)

Born in London, she was the elder daughter of Nicholas Turner of Stoke House, Surrey, and Bignor Park, Sussex, and his wife Anna Towers. After her mother's death when she was 3, she and her sister (who, as Catherine Ann Dorset, later wrote children's books) were brought up by an aunt and educated at schools in Chichester and Kensington. Her father encouraged her first attempts at poetry, some of which she is said to have sent to the *Lady's Magazine* in the early 1760s. After her father's second marriage in 1764, he and her aunt arranged that she herself should marry in February 1765 (when she was 15) Benjamin Smith, the 21-year-old son of Richard Smith, a wealthy West Indian merchant and director of the East India Company. For a time the couple lived uncomfortably with his parents in London but, after her mother-in-law's death and Richard Smith's remarriage, they moved with their numerous children to Lys Farm, Hampshire. In 1776 Richard Smith died, leaving considerable property to his grandchildren, but litigation over the terms of the will and his West Indian estates was to plague her for the rest of her life. Meanwhile her husband's extravagance and misuse of the trust established by his father led eventually to Benjamin Smith's imprisonment in the King's Bench for seven months from December 1783, some of which she shared with him. He was released when his brother-in-law, John Robinson, MP, agreed to act as trustee for his affairs, and Lys Farm was sold.

In 1792 she recalled that she had 'first struck the chords of the melancholy lyre . . . never intended for publication' in 'the Beech Woods of Hampshire': 'It was unaffected sorrow drew them forth: I wrote mournfully because I was unhappy.' She contributed some sonnets to the *European Magazine* in 1782 and in May 1784 published her *Elegiac Sonnets, and Other Essays*, shortly before her husband's release. The pamphlet was dedicated to the poet William Hayley, a neighbour of the Turner family in Sussex, who assisted her with its publication. (It seems to have been printed in Chichester, but published with the London imprint of J. Dodsley.) Her poetry soon won her a considerable reputation, to be explained by her distinctive blend of natural description with an intense but mysterious melancholy in the increasingly fashionable sonnet form. The financial and marital problems behind her habitual gloom were not at first explained, and reviewers tended to be both sympathetic to, and worried by, her melancholy. A contributor to the *Gentleman's Magazine* in 1786 considered her sonnets superior to those of Shakespeare and Milton, while earnestly hoping that 'the misfortunes she so often hints at, are all imaginary'. Anna Seward (see nos. 204–12) found this judgement preposterous, dismissing Mrs Smith's sonnets as 'pretty tuneful centos from our various poets, without anything original': 'and these hedge-flowers to be preferred, by a critical dictator, to the roses and amaranths of the two first poets the world has produced!!!—It makes one sick.' These remarks in a letter of July 1786 were echoed in an anonymous letter in the *General Evening Post* of 7–10 October 1786, which criticized both Smith and Hannah Cowley (see nos. 252–4) and was no doubt written by Seward herself (who is mentioned approvingly).

For a period in the mid-1780s after Benjamin Smith's release from prison, the family rented a house near Dieppe, probably to avoid his creditors. Here she translated Prévost's *Manon Lescaut* (1785), which had to be withdrawn after hostile comment, and *The Romance of Real Life* (1787), based on famous French trials. Her death was reported in a long obituary in the *Gentleman's Magazine* (July 1786), which made scathing accusations about the conduct of her father, brother, and husband, but the *Magazine* later reassured its readers about her health. On their return to England, the Smiths, with their nine children (two had died in infancy, a third in childhood) settled for a time near Midhurst in Sussex. By 1788, however, she had decided on a permanent separation from her bad-tempered, debt-ridden, and unfaithful husband, who moved to Scotland, while continuing to make regular financial claims on her. Between 1788 and 1793 she lived in Brighton.

Her high reputation as a poet is reflected in the list of over 800 subscribers, many from the nobility and the literary world, in the expanded 5th edition of her *Elegiac Sonnets* (1789). She was widely considered an exemplary writer of sonnets, as is implied in W. L. Bowles' heated denial of a reviewer's suggestion that he had imitated her, in his own *Sonnets* (2nd edition, 1789); in Coleridge's discussion in 1796 of her importance in re-establishing the form in England; and in the tributes of many other poets, including Burns and Wordsworth, who in December 1802 read over her sonnets before writing some of his own. By 1793 her poetry was being read enthusiastically by expatriates in China. Yet she could not support herself and her nine children by poetry and soon embarked on the publication of a long series of popular novels and educational works, which began with *Emmeline* (4 vols., 1788), *Ethelinde* (5 vols., 1789), *Celestina* (4 vols., 1791), *Desmond* (3 vols., 1792), and *The Old Manor House* (4 vols., 1793). Basically sentimental, her novels also include satirical episodes and poetry, not all her own (see Henrietta O'Neill, nos. 293–4), and sometimes have an autobiographical basis.

Until the friendship cooled in 1794, William Hayley continued to help her. Visiting Hayley at Eartham in August 1792, William Cowper the poet found that she and George Romney, the painter, were also guests. He reported that she spent four hours each morning writing what was to become *The Old Manor House*, which she read to the company in the evenings. He later referred to her as 'Chain'd to her desk like a slave to his oar, with no other means of subsistence for herself and her numerous children, with a broken constitution'. A few months later he heard that she had had her goods seized by her landlord and had been locked out of her lodgings. Her financial problems, her repeated demands for advances from her publishers and her struggles to launch her sons on military or legal careers are fully illustrated in letters from this period which came to light in 1952. By now she was complaining in public about the conduct of the trustees of her father-in-law's estate, as in the preface to her expanded *Elegiac Sonnets* (6th edition, 1792). The 'Honourable Men' had still not obtained for her children what 'their grandfather designed for them' and were treating her applications to them with 'scorn and insult': hence the usual 'despondence' of her poetry and her frequent appearances as an author, although 'I am well aware that for a woman—"The Post of Honor is a Private Station" '.

For a time she had high hopes of the French Revolution. In November 1791 Wordsworth, on his way to France, called on her in Brighton to obtain a letter of introduction to Helen Maria Williams (see nos. 267–71): over fifty years later he spoke of her as still associated in his mind with the Revolution. In the preface to *Desmond*, the most political of her novels, she defended her right to deal with such matters in fiction, but one result, according to Cowper, was an unfounded rumour that the 'democratic party' was using her as a paid agent. *The Emigrants* (1793), her most elaborate poem, which she dedicated to Cowper, acknowledges the growing hostility to supporters of the Revolution, and marks a reluctant change in her views. She herself described it as 'not a party book but a conciliatory book'. A second volume of her *Elegiac Sonnets* appeared in 1797. After many other publications, various removals, continuing anxieties about her children (a newly married daughter died in 1795), and some years of deteriorating health, she died at Tilford near Farnham in Surrey in 1806, some eight months after the death of her husband in Berwick gaol, and a few weeks after that of her son George from malaria in Surinam. A posthumous collection, *Beachy Head; With Other Poems*, was published in 1807.

237   *Sonnet Written at the Close of Spring*

THE garlands fade that Spring so lately wove,
   Each simple flower, which she had nursed in dew,
Anemonies, that spangled every grove,
   The primrose wan, and harebell mildly blue.
No more shall violets linger in the dell,
   Or purple orchis variegate the plain,
Till Spring again shall call forth every bell,
   And dress with humid hands her wreaths again.—
Ah! poor humanity! so frail, so fair,
   Are the fond visions of thy early day,   10
Till tyrant passion, and corrosive care,
   Bid all thy fairy colours fade away!
Another May new buds and flowers shall bring;
Ah? why has happiness—no second Spring?

                                              (1782)

238   *Sonnet Written in the Church Yard at*
                     Middleton in Sussex

PRESSED by the moon, mute arbitress of tides,
   While the loud equinox its power combines,
   The sea no more its swelling surge confines,
But o'er the shrinking land sublimely rides.

The wild blast, rising from the western cave,
    Drives the huge billows from their heaving bed,
    Tears from their grassy tombs the village dead,
And breaks the silent sabbath of the grave!
With shells and sea-weed mingled, on the shore
    Lo! their bones whiten in the frequent wave;   10
    But vain to them the winds and waters rave;
They hear the warring elements no more:
While I am doomed—by life's long storm oppressed,
To gaze with envy on their gloomy rest.

(1789)

239   *Thirty-Eight. To Mrs. H——y*

IN early youth's unclouded scene,
The brilliant morning of eighteen,
With health and sprightly joy elate,
We gazed on youth's enchanting spring,
Nor thought how quickly time would bring
The mournful period—*thirty-eight*!

Then the starch maid, or matron sage,
Already of the sober age,
We viewed with mingled scorn and hate;
In whose sharp words, or sharper face,   10
With thoughtless mirth, we loved to trace
The sad effects of—*thirty-eight*!

Till, saddening, sickening at the view,
We learned to dread what time might do;
And then preferred a prayer to Fate
To end our days ere that arrived,
When (power and pleasure long survived)
We meet neglect, and—*thirty-eight*!

But Time, in spite of wishes, flies;
And Fate our simple prayer denies,   20
And bids us Death's own hour await!
The auburn locks are mixed with grey,
The transient roses fade away,
But Reason comes at—*thirty-eight*!

Her voice the anguish contradicts
That dying vanity inflicts;
Her hand new pleasures can create,
For us she opens to the view
Prospect less bright—but far more true,
And bids us smile at—*thirty-eight*! 30

No more shall Scandal's breath destroy
The social converse we enjoy
With bard or critic, *tête à tête*—
O'er youth's bright blooms her blight shall pour,
But spare th' improving, friendly hour
Which Science gives at—*thirty-eight*!

Stripped of their gaudy hues by Truth,
We view the glittering toys of youth,
And blush to think how poor the bait
For which to public scenes we ran, 40
And scorned of sober sense the plan
Which gives content at—*thirty-eight*!

O may her blessings now arise,
Like stars that mildly light the skies,
When the sun's ardent rays abate!
And in the luxuries of mind—
In friendship, science—may we find
Increasing joys at—*thirty-eight*!

Though Time's inexorable sway
Has torn the myrtle bands away, 50
For other wreaths—'tis not too late:
The amaranth's purple glow survives,
And still Minerva's olive thrives
On the calm brow of—*thirty eight*!

With eye more steady, we engage
To contemplate approaching age,
And life more justly estimate;
With firmer souls and stronger powers,
With reason, faith, and friendship ours,
We'll not regret the stealing hours 60
That lead from *thirty-* e'en to *forty-eight*!

(1791)

369

240   from *The Emigrants: A Poem*

[Disillusion with the French Revolution]

So many years have passed,
Since, on my native hills, I learned to gaze
On these delightful landscapes; and those years
Have taught me so much sorrow, that my soul
Feels not the joy reviving Nature brings;
But, in dark retrospect, dejected dwells
On human follies, and on human woes.—
What is the promise of the infant year,
The lively verdure, or the bursting blooms,
To those, who shrink from horrors such as War   10
Spreads o'er the affrighted world? With swimming eye,
Back on the past they throw their mournful looks,
And see the Temple, which they fondly hoped
Reason would raise to Liberty, destroyed
By ruffian hands; while, on the ruined mass,
Flushed with hot blood, the Fiend of Discord sits
In savage triumph; mocking every plea
Of policy and justice, as she shows
The headless corse of one, whose only crime
Was being born a Monarch—Mercy turns,   20
From spectacle so dire, her swollen eyes;
And Liberty, with calm, unruffled brow
Magnanimous, as conscious of her strength
In Reason's panoply, scorns to distain
Her righteous cause with carnage, and resigns
To Fraud and Anarchy the infuriate crowd.—
   What is the promise of the infant year
To those, who (while the poor but peaceful hind
Pens, unmolested, the increasing flock
Of his rich master in this sea-fenced isle)   30
Survey, in neighbouring countries, scenes that make
The sick heart shudder; and the man, who thinks,
Blush for his species? *There* the trumpet's voice
Drowns the soft warbling of the woodland choir;
And violets, lurking in their turfy beds
Beneath the flowering thorn, are stained with blood.
There fall, at once, the spoiler and the spoiled;
While War, wide-ravaging, annihilates
The hope of cultivation; gives to Fiends,
The meagre, ghastly Fiends of Want and Woe,   40
The blasted land—There, taunting in the van

Of vengeance-breathing armies, Insult stalks;
And, in the ranks, 'Famine, and Sword, and Fire,
Crouch for employment.'

(1793)

241   *Fragment Descriptive of the Miseries of War*

To a wild mountain, whose bare summit hides
Its broken eminence in clouds; whose steeps
Are dark with woods; where the receding rocks
Are worn with torrents of dissolving snow;
A wretched woman, pale and breathless, flies,
And, gazing round her, listens to the sound
Of hostile footsteps:—No! they die away—
Nor noise remains, but of the cataract,
Or surly breeze of night, that mutters low
Among the thickets, where she trembling seeks   10
A temporary shelter—clasping close
To her quick-throbbing heart her sleeping child,
All she could rescue of the innocent group
That yesterday surrounded her.—Escaped
Almost by miracle!—Fear, frantic Fear,
Winged her weak feet; yet, half repenting now
Her headlong haste, she wishes she had stayed
To die with those affrighted Fancy paints
The lawless soldiers' victims.—Hark! again
The driving tempest bears the cry of Death;   20
And with deep, sudden thunder, the dread sound
Of cannon vibrates on the tremulous earth;
While, bursting in the air, the murderous bomb
Glares o'er her mansion.—Where the splinters fall
Like scattered comets, its destructive path
Is marked by wreaths of flame!—Then, overwhelmed
Beneath accumulated horror, sinks
The desolate mourner!

                *   *   *   *   *   *

The feudal Chief, whose Gothic battlements
Frown on the plain beneath, returning home   30
From distant lands, alone and in disguise,
Gains at the fall of night his castle walls,
But at the silent gate no porter sits
To wait his lord's admittance!—In the courts

All is drear stillness!—Guessing but too well
The fatal truth, he shudders as he goes
Through the mute hall; where, by the blunted light
That the dim moon through painted casement lends,
He sees that devastation has been there;
Then, while each hideous image to his mind   40
Rises terrific, o'er a bleeding corse
Stumbling he falls; another intercepts
His staggering feet.—All, all who used to rush
With joy to meet him, all his family
Lie murdered in his way!—And the day dawns
On a wild raving Maniac, whom a fate
So sudden and calamitous has robbed
Of reason; and who round his vacant walls
Screams unregarded, and reproaches Heaven!

(1793; revised, 1797)

242 *Sonnet. On being Cautioned against Walking on an Headland Overlooking the Sea, because it was Frequented by a Lunatic*

Is there a solitary wretch who hies
   To the tall cliff, with starting pace or slow,
And, measuring, views with wild and hollow eyes
   Its distance from the waves that chide below;
Who, as the sea-born gale with frequent sighs
   Chills his cold bed upon the mountain turf,
With hoarse, half-uttered lamentation, lies
   Murmuring responses to the dashing surf?
In moody sadness, on the giddy brink,
   I see him more with envy than with fear;   10
He has no *nice felicities* that shrink
   From giant horrors; wildly wandering here,
He seems (uncursed with reason) not to know
The depth or the duration of his woe.

(1797)

243 *Sonnet. The Sea View*

The upland shepherd, as reclined he lies
   On the soft turf that clothes the mountain brow,
Marks the bright sea-line mingling with the skies;
   Or, from his course celestial sinking slow,

The summer-sun, in purple radiance low,
Blaze on the western waters; the wide scene,
  Magnificent and tranquil, seems to spread
Even o'er the rustic's breast a joy serene,
  When, like dark plague-spots by the Demons shed,
Charged deep with death, upon the waves far seen,   10
  Move the war-freighted ships; and fierce and red,
  Flash their destructive fires.—The mangled dead
And dying victims then pollute the flood.
Ah! thus man spoils Heaven's glorious works with Blood!

(1797)

JANE CAVE (later WINSCOM)
(*c.*1754–1813)

What is known about her derives largely from editions of her verse. She was born in about 1754, probably in Wales, since one of her poems refers to the death of her mother, Mrs Cave of Brecon, in 1777. Her father was still alive aged 81 in 1794: she praised his fervent piety in a humble station and there is some evidence of Methodist sympathies in her own early verse. How she supported herself is unclear, but it was perhaps as a servant or teacher. By November 1779 she had been for some time in Bath and was leaving for Winchester, going 'To a strange place, unknowing and unknown'. By the time her *Poems on Various Subjects, Entertaining, Elegiac, and Religious* appeared at Winchester in 1783, she had acquired a remarkable list of some 2,000 subscribers, mostly from large towns in the south and west of England, including nearly 500 from Oxford alone. Such a subscription must have been highly organized as some kind of testimonial to her: the fact that Dr Joseph Warton, headmaster of Winchester College, appeared in her list suggests that she may have had some connection with the school. Whatever her employment, it was demanding: in 'The Author's Plea' she describes her early love of poetry, but also her tantalizing dealings with the Muses, whose visitations were usually interrupted by the 'number-less impediments' of her duties.

By 1786, when a 2nd edition of her *Poems* appeared at Bristol, she had married a Mr Winscom, an Excise officer in that city. A slightly expanded edition of the *Poems* was published at Shrewsbury in 1789, and there were further additions in the 4th edition at Bristol in 1794. One poem, addressed to the citizens of Exeter, describes how in 1791 she had rescued a friendless woman from the debtors' prison by raising money for her locally. Her own problems were now medical. Several poems refer to the excruciating headaches which had long been afflicting her for several days each month: all recommended cures, including seabathing, had proved useless. The second poem on the subject given below (no. 249) first appeared in a Bristol newspaper on 25 May 1793, as a public appeal for medical advice. Little is known of her thereafter, although it is clear from her publications that she had at least two sons. She died at Newport, Monmouthshire, in January 1813 at the age of 58. An obituary, referring to an unexplained incident two years earlier, described her as 'a woman of extraordinary genius and vigour of intellect, possessing great firmness and presence of mind in the most imminent danger, as her miraculous escape from a watery grave, about two years since, evinced. She was an authoress of no mean talents; and her domestic character, both as wife and mother, was exemplary.'

244 *A Poem for Children. On Cruelty to the Irrational Creation*

OH! what a cruel wicked thing
For me, who am a little King,
To give my hapless subjects pain,
And make them groan beneath my reign.

Were I a chafer, and could fly,
Ah! should I not with anguish cry,
Should naughty children take a pin,
And run me through to make me spin?

Were I a bird took from my nest,
Should I not think myself oppressed,   10
If tossed about in wanton play,
Till, maimed and faint, I die away?

Now, and when I'm a bigger boy,
Let cruelty my heart annoy,
Because it is a dreadful evil,
That only fits me for the Devil.

If I *must* aught of life deprive,
The quickest way I will contrive
To stop the trembling victim's breath,
And give it *little* pain in death.   20

I'll not torment a dog or cat,
A toad, a viper, or a rat:
They're formed by an Almighty hand,
And sprang to life at his command.

A bull, a horse, yea, every creature,
Of the most mild or savage nature,
Were kindly given for my use,
But never meant for my abuse.

Good men, Thy holy word attests,
Are kind and tender to their beasts: 30
May I be merciful and kind,
That I with Thee may mercy find.

(1783)

chafer] cockchafer, beetle

245 *Written by Desire of a Lady, on an Angry, Petulant*
Kitchen-Maid

GOOD Mistress Dishclout, what's the matter?
Why here the spoon—and there the platter?
What demon causes all this lowering,
Black as the pot you oft are scouring?
Hot as the fire you daily light,
Your speech with low invectives blight,
While rage impregnates every vein,
And dyes the face one crimson stain.
  Sure, someone has a word misplaced,
Or looked not equal to your taste;   10
Or, is this just the time you've chose
Your great acquirements to disclose,
Display the graces of your tongue,
Show with what eloquence 'tis hung,
As 'dog, rogue, scoundrel, scrub', what not,
And twenty more I've quite forgot;
Which prove to a demonstration
You've had a liberal education?
Such titles must enchant the ear,
And make the bounteous donor dear;   20
But while these bounties are dispensing,
I wish I'd learned the art of fencing,
Lest, while at John you aim to throw,
My nob should chance to catch the blow;
Then I should get a broken pate,
And marks of violence I hate.
  Good Mistress Dishclout, condescend
To hear the counsel of a friend:
When next you are disposed to brawl,
Pray let the scullery hear it all,   30
And learn to know your fittest place
Is with the dishes and the grease;
And, when you are inclined to battle,
Engage the skimmer, spit, or kettle,
Or any other kitchen guest,
Which you in wisdom might think best.

(1783)

246   *An Elegy on a Maiden Name*

ADIEU, dear name which birth and nature gave—
Lo! at the altar I've interred dear CAVE;
For there it fell, expired, and found a grave.

  Forgive, dear spouse, this ill-timed tear or two,
They are not meant in disrespect to you;
I hope the name which you have lately given
Was kindly meant and sent to me by heaven.
But ah! the loss of CAVE I must deplore,
For that dear name the tend'rest mother bore.
With that she passed full forty years of life,   10
Adorned th' important character of wife:
Then meet for bliss from earth to heaven retired,
With holy zeal and true devotion fired.

  In me what blessed my father may you find,
A wife domestic, virtuous, meek and kind.
What blessed my mother may I meet in you,
A friend and husband—faithful, wise, and true.

  Then be our voyage prosperous or adverse,
No keen upbraiding shall our tongues rehearse;
But mutually we'll brave against the storm,   20
Remembering still for helpmates we were born.
Then let rough torrents roar or skies look dark,
If love commands the helm which guides our bark,
No shipwreck will we fear, but to the end
Each find in each a just, unshaken friend.

                                                     (1786)

247   *Written a Few Hours before the Birth of a Child*

MY God, prepare me for that hour
    When most thy aid I want;
Uphold me by thy mighty power,
    Nor let my spirits faint.

I ask not life, I ask not ease,
    But patience to submit
To what shall best thy goodness please,
    Then come what thou seest fit.

Come pain, or agony, or death,
   If such the will divine;   10
With joy shall I give up my breath,
   If resignation's mine.

One wish to name I'd humbly dare,
   If death thy pleasure be;
O may the harmless babe I bear
   Haply expire with me.

                    (1786)

248   *Written the First Morning of the Author's
       Bathing at Teignmouth, For the Head-Ache*

WHILST on the beach I stood, my courage fainted,
And busy thought a thousand horrors painted!
Stranger to each, and each to me was strange,
With none a kind 'Good-morrow' could exchange;
With pensive mind, whilst tears my cheeks bedewed,
Fierce Boreas, and a nymph immerged I viewed;
Langour and pain her timid looks express,
As by the women carried in to dress.
'Ah, me!', I cried, 'to plunge into the main
Should I presume, this weak afflicted brain   10
Will grow deranged, and I shall die with pain!'
But some kind fair*, impressed with sympathy,
Consoled my grief, and bade my sorrows flee;
Of whom, to practise what themselves had taught,
One plunged into the sea, with courage fraught;
Near thrice twice-told she dipped quite undismayed,
And then ascends to dress, nor asks for aid.
I chid my fears—my cowardice was nipped,
And next below the wave my head was dipped:
A strange sensation—in a second o'er,   20
And I quite braced, much happier than before;
When I bathe next, I'll have two dippings more.

O Neptune! should thy waves propitious prove,
And once this grievous malady remove,
Which long has baffled each physician's art,
Moved by the impulse of a grateful heart,

---

* Three LADIES who had been accustomed to bathe.

I'll chant thy virtues—sue the tuneful Nine,
And mighty Jove, to lend his aid divine
To fill me with devout poetic fire,
While I to Neptune tune the grateful lyre!   30

(1794)

249   from *The Head-Ache, Or An Ode to Health*

AH! why from *me* art thou for ever flown?
Why deaf to every agonising groan?
Not *one* short month for *ten* revolving years,
But pain within my frame its sceptre rears!
In each successive month full *twelve* long days
And tedious nights my sun withdraws his rays!
Leaves me in silent anguish on my bed,
Afflicting all the members in the head;
Through every particle the torture flies,
But centres in the temples, brain, and eyes;   10
The efforts of the hands and feet are vain,
While bows the head with agonising pain;
While heaves the breast th' unutterable sigh,
And the big tear drops from the languid eye.
For ah! my children want a mother's care,
A husband too should due assistance share;
Myself, for action formed, would fain through life
Be found th' assiduous, valuable wife;
But now, behold, I live unfit for aught;
Inactive half my days except in thought,   20
And this so vague while torture clogs my hours,
I sigh, 'Oh, 'twill derange my mental powers,
Or by its dire excess dissolve my sight,
And thus entomb me in perpetual night!'

Ye sage physicians, where's your wonted skill?
In vain, the blisters, boluses and pill;
Great Neptune's swelling waves in vain I tried,
My malady its utmost power defied;
In vain, the British and Cephalic Snuff,
All patent medicines are empty stuff;   30
The lancet, leech, and cupping swell the train
Of useless efforts, which but give me pain;
Each art and application vain has proved,
For ah! my sad complaint is not removed.

(1794)

249 boluses] large pills   Cephalic Snuff] a remedy for headaches

378

JANE WEST (née ILIFFE)*
(1758–1852)

According to her autobiographical letter of 28 June 1800 to Thomas Percy, she was born on 30 April 1758 in London, in what later became the St Paul's Coffeehouse. When she was about 11, her father moved to Desborough in Northamptonshire, near Market Harborough. Entirely self-educated, she began writing poetry at the age of 13, when she versified seven chapters of the book of Acts, followed by 'an astronomic poem', and, at 16, wrote an epic on 'the glories of Caractacus': 'The catalogue of my compositions previous to my attaining 20 would be formidable. Thousands of lines flowed in very easy measure; I scorned correction, and never blotted.' She married Thomas West, a yeoman farmer at neighbouring Little Bowden in Leicestershire where his ancestors had been clergymen for some generations. She was later anxious to correct reports that she was in a 'low situation': 'her worthy husband farms . . . his own estate, and she superintends the management of her household with the most exemplary economy', the *Gentleman's Magazine* was informed in 1802. She had three sons.

Her first publication has been listed as *Miscellaneous Poems, Translations, and Imitations* (1780), an evident confusion with a volume of that title published at Northampton by a Benjamin West. Her earliest and least interesting collection was *Miscellaneous Poetry: Written at an Early Period of Life* (1786), dedicated to Lady Charlotte Wentworth, which includes an elegy on 'a Great Mortality' at Little Bowden when she was 18. Her 'Advertisement' explains that poetry could be only a relaxation to one 'so fully engrossed by the essential duties of domestic life', and her 'Elegy to a Friend' (pp. 1–4) expresses her fear of publication, although she was confident that her writing would not injure 'Religion and Morality'. Always self-deprecating, Jane West was also very persistent. The preface to her *Miscellaneous Poems, and a Tragedy* (York, 1791) refers again to the 'disadvantages of a confined education' and her indispensable family duties, but she had by then acquired a large list of subscribers, many from Northamptonshire and Yorkshire, but others from Oxford and Cambridge, and including the names of Thomas Percy, Henry James Pye (about to become Poet Laureate), and Anna Seward, who wrote warmly of Mrs West's poetry in two letters to Christopher Smyth of Christ Church, Oxford, in 1792. (Mrs West was gratified to see them in print when Anna Seward's *Letters* were published in 1811.) Seward would have noticed that Mrs West had praised her, together with Elizabeth Carter, Charlotte Smith, and Sarah Trimmer, in a series of poems on women writers (pp. 92–9).

During the 1790s her verse and fiction included *The Advantages of Education, or The History of Maria Williams* (2 vols., 1793), *A Gossip's Story, and a Legendary Tale* (2 vols., 1796), *An Elegy on the Death of Edmund Burke* (1797), and *A Tale of the Times* (3 vols., 1799), culminating in her *Poems and Plays* (4 vols., 1799–1805). Her more ambitious verse, some of which had appeared in periodicals, is fashionably florid, but she was always capable of a more appealing informal mode. By the age of 40, still living in seclusion at Little Bowden, Mrs West came to feel that she deserved greater recognition and remuneration, and some sort of campaign on her behalf began. In the *Gentleman's Magazine* in 1799, 'X.Y.' described her as exemplary both in 'the pure morality and forcible arguments' of her writings and in 'the exercise of the duties of a wife, a mother, and a daughter'. According to 'X.Y.', 'a highly respected prelate' had recommended her novels to the Queen, who had acquired several copies

* See p. 539 below.

of one of them. Friends to religion and virtue must wish that a woman, 'who, unfriended, and personally unknown to the great, has made so resolute a stand against the prevailing torrent of licentious manners', would be rewarded by the public, particularly when 'women of corrupt manners and vitiated principles have risen to affluence by their nefarious attempts on the virtue of their sex'. Her plays had been denied performance, at a time when the theatres offered false German morality and 'the tinsel of sentiments'.

A few months later, on 19 May 1800, Mrs West wrote to Thomas Percy, Bishop of Dromore (whose wife came from Desborough), asking for his support, since her 'retired situation, and few connexions' had limited both her reputation and the 'emoluments' necessary to support 'a rising family'. In the following month she explained that in some of her poetry she had been helped by Christopher Smyth of Northampton, 'an elegant scholar', particularly when alluding to authors she knew only through 'the mist of a translation'. Of herself, she said, 'My needle always claims the pre-eminence of my pen. I hate the name of "rhyming slattern".' Percy duly recommended her work to such friends as Robert Anderson and Robert Nares. He himself reviewed her popular *Letters to a Young Man* (3 vols., 1801), corrected by Smyth and dedicated to Percy, in the *British Critic* in September–November 1801, and Nares gave *The Infidel Father* (3 vols., 1802) a prominent article in the same journal in April 1803. It may have been with the same purpose of gaining greater prominence that she sent poetry to the *Gentleman's Magazine* in 1800 (pp. 99–100), including a sonnet on dreaming of her dead mother, and further material by or about her followed down to 1802.

Her other letters to Percy date from 1810–11, not long before his death and when he was already blind. She visited him at Dromore for a month in the autumn of 1810 and, writing to thank him, hoped that he would think of her 'not as what I am, but as what I might have been', if allowed to be more than 'the oddity of a writing housewife'. Percy replied to her request for advice about her latest novel and later wrote attacking Anna Seward's *Letters* (1811) for their egotism and malignity, Mrs West in turn defending the 'sweetness of sublimity' in Seward's verse. Although her literary acquaintance was limited, especially after Percy's death, she continued to produce fiction, educational works, and some verse, her last publication being *Ringrove, Or, Old-Fashioned Notions* (2 vols., 1827), when she was nearly 70. In her obituary of her husband, who died in January 1823, she mentioned his depression and irritability in his later years, due to 'water on the chest', agricultural failures, and the death of his youngest son, Edward. She died in 1852 at Little Bowden, where she had lived throughout her married life.

250   from *To a Friend on her Marriage, 1784*

> MARRIED, poor soul! your empire's over;
> Adieu the duteous kneeling lover;
> Farewell, eternally farewell,
> The glory of the stately belle;
> The plumèd head, the trailing gown,
> The crowded ball, the busy town,
> For one short month are yours, and then
> Must never be resumed again;

No more attentive Strephon flies,
Awed by the lightning of your eyes;   10
No longer, 'Madam, hear my vows,'
But 'Mend this ragged wristband, spouse;
I mean to call upon a friend,
Do you your household cares attend.'
'Mayn't I go too, my dear?'—'Oh, Lord!
What, married women go abroad!
Your horse is lame, the roads are rough,
Besides, at home you've work enough.'
Off goes the husband, brisk and airy;
The wife in a profound quandary,   20
Whilst he of wit or scandal chatters,
Remains mumchance, and darns old tatters.
    I almost think the nuptial hour
Possessed of talismanic power;
For in a little time, how strange,
We grow enamoured of the change.
Our tables and our chairs, in fact,
Possess perfections which attract,
Till, like the snail, we gladly bear
The constant weight of household care;   30
The things are trifles which we leave,
For trifles none but triflers grieve.
Like insects of the summer sky,
Were we but born to sport and die,
Then might we spread our gilded plumes,
And court the flower that sweetest blooms;
But heaven, which gave us nobler powers,
With ample duties filled our hours;
These shrink from solitary life
To grace the faithful active wife;   40
Her breast each social virtue warms,
Her mind each useful science charms;
Pleased, when she walks abroad, to hear
The orphan's thanks, the poor man's prayer;
Whene'er she makes the social call,
Her neighbour meets her in the hall,
And cries, 'I'm glad to see you come,
You really grow too fond of home':
That home, well ordered, proves her merit,
She is its animating spirit.   50
Each servant, at the task assigned,
Proclaims a regulating mind.

mumchance] silent

381

Pleased she surveys her infant charge,
Beholds the mental powers enlarge,
And as the young ideas rise,
Directs their issues to the skies.
Thus whilst performing Martha's part,
To serve the master of her heart,
How sweet the thought, that he approves,
Silent esteems, and deeply loves!   60
   Joy then, my Sally, since I see
The path of wedlock trod by thee;
Thy virtues shall secure the palm,
Hymeneal friendship's placid calm,
And show to a too polished nation
Example worthy imitation.

(Wr. 1784; pub. 1799)

251   *To the Hon. Mrs. C[ockayn]e*

C———e, whom providence hath placed
In the rich realms of polished taste,
Where judgement penetrates to find
The treasures of the unwrought mind,
Where conversation's ardent spirit
Refines from dross the ore of merit,
Where emulation aids the flame
And stamps the sterling bust of fame:
Can you, accustomed to behold
The purest intellectual gold,   10
Where genius sheds its living rays,
Bright as the sunny diamond's blaze,
Like idle virtuoso deign
To pick up pebbles from the plain?
Pleased, if the worthless flints pretend
Fantastic characters to blend;
These in your cabinet insert,
And real excellence desert?
   Just the comparison will be,
If you suppose the pebble me.   20
My verse, inelegant and crude,
Confused in sense, in diction rude,
You, not content with praising, spout
To friends of fashion at a rout.

251 rout] fashionable evening party

You said the author was a charmer,
Self-taught, and married to a farmer;
Who wrote all kind of verse with ease,
Made pies and puddings, frocks and cheese.
Her situation, though obscure,
Was not contemptible or poor.   30
Her conversation spoke a mind
Studious to please, but unrefined.
So warm an interest you expressed,
It was not possible to jest.
The company, amazed, perplexed,
Wondering what whim would seize you next,
Perhaps expecting you would praise
The muse of Quarles, or Sternhold's lays,
Stammered, as due to complaisance,
The civil speech of nonchalance.   40
But at the instant you withdrew,
The conversation turned on you.
The sonnet might perhaps have merit.
You had recited it with spirit.
Your manner was so full of grace,
They could not judge in such a case.
But give each character its due,
You seemed a little partial too.
All, to commend your taste, agreed—
But friendship would the best mislead.   50
A warm enthusiastic heart
Would soon be wrought upon by art.
The Poem—though, indeed, no wonder
Th' uneducated Muse should blunder—
Had here and there a small defect,
But 'twere invidious to object.
One thought alliteration fine,
And liked it every other line.
Another, might she be so free,
Would substitute a *that* for *the*.   60
A third said, 'Judges will perceive
Crown has a harsher sound than *wreath*.'
A witty beau observed, the nation
Had verse enough for exportation,
Wished ladies would such arts despise,
And trust their conquests to their eyes.
For, on his honour, if the whim
Should spread, they'd be too wise for him.
A man of rank grew warm, and swore
The times were bad enough before.   70

He offered to bet ten to one
The nation would be soon undone:
For honour, spirit, courage, worth,
Were all appendages on birth;
And if the rustics grew refined,
Who would the humble duties mind?
They might, from scribbling odes and letters,
Proceed to dictate to their betters.
A fellow of a college said
He studied nothing but the dead;   80
For men of sense have ne'er denied
That learning with the ancients died.
A lady, of distinguished taste,
Much stress on well-bred authors placed.
Though she could never time bestow
On trash inelegant and low;
Yet science was her darling passion,
And she read everything in fashion.
With her a lovely nymph agreed,
That people should with caution read: 90
And really, if she must confess,
That what with visiting and dress,
Music, her ever-dear delight,
And cards, the business of the night,
Her leisure was so very small,
She could not say she read at all.
    Oh! that the great ones would confine
Such treatment to such verse as mine,
Adapted but to entertain
A partial friend or simple swain.   100
Yet, with a votary's ardent zeal,
The sorrows of the Muse I feel.
While Painting for her sons can claim
At once emolument and fame;
While Music, when she strikes the chord,
Confers distinction and reward;
Contemptuous scorn, or cold regard,
Awaits the heaven-illumined Bard.
No more shall wealth, with fostering care,
Fair Poesy's frail blossoms rear.   110
No more shall favour's influence bland
Bid the luxuriant growth expand.
No more shall candid judgement deign
That wild luxuriance to restrain.
No more shall chiefs, in arms renowned,
Sue by the Muses to be crowned.

Neglected, while the wintry storm
Tears the fine fibres of its form,
As if disdaining to complain
Of patronage, implored in vain,   120
It withering droops its lovely head,
And sinks upon its native bed;
Mourned only by the liberal few—
I mean the counterparts of YOU.

(1791)

HANNAH COWLEY (née PARKHOUSE)
(1743–1809)

She was the daughter of Philip Parkhouse of Tiverton, Devon, who was originally
intended for the Church but became a bookseller, 'a man of great Talents and
Probity, and a thorough scholar'. Her mother was said to have been a relative of John
Gay. She obviously felt affectionately towards her father, who was still alive in 1780
when she dedicated her *Maid of Aragon* to him. At the age of about 25 she married
Thomas Cowley, a clerk in the Stamp Office, and moved to London. It seems likely
that she turned to writing because of financial problems, although, according to an
anecdote, she did so merely to prove that she could produce a play as good as one she
and her husband had just seen. She is said to have written *The Runaway* in two weeks
and later claimed that it was produced by 'mere accident' and was her 'first literary
attempt of any kind'. By August 1774 Garrick had read it and was consulting Richard
Cumberland, describing its author as clever, modest and 'distress'd'. In September
he mentioned her charm and desire for criticism. Garrick himself probably revised
the comedy, which was acted with great success at Drury Lane in February 1776.
She is said to have received 800 guineas for *The Runaway*, which, she stated in 1779,
had 'opened a new prospect of advantage to my Family, which I have since pursued
with alacrity'. She was probably the most productive woman dramatist of the later
eighteenth century and twelve more of her comedies, farces, and tragedies had been
acted by 1795. Some were still being performed well into the next century, notably
The Belle's Stratagem (1780), dedicated to the Queen and often performed before the
Royal Family, for which she is said to have received 1,200 guineas.

Her career did not run entirely smoothly. She and her husband, who at first
superintended productions of her plays, were evidently sensitive to affront. In May
1777 she complained to Garrick about his servants' rudeness when her husband
called at his house. In the summer of 1779 she was involved in an indecorous public
quarrel with Hannah More, whom she accused of plagiarizing her tragedy *Albina*.
Such behaviour would not readily win acceptance in polite literary society. In her
preface to *Albina* (1779), having denounced Harris and Sheridan for their expensive
delay in performing her play, she thanked the 'candid and liberal' George Colman,
who had finally produced it at the Haymarket. Colman, however, under the cloak of
anonymity offered by the *Monthly Review*, described her in 1780 as irritable, insolent,
and vain. Mrs Piozzi remarked in her journal in 1788: 'That Mrs Cowley seems an
active Woman, whom nobody likes, yet all are forced to esteem. . . . She and I never
met; I fancy her Vulgar & ill behav'd; for no one speaks ill of her, yet She is never in

385

polite Circles.' (A few days later she said of an admired epilogue by Mrs Cowley that 'one might write such Stuff in one's Sleep'.) In turn, Mrs Cowley herself had little taste for literary society. After her death it was said of her that she 'never seemed to hold Literature in much esteem. Her Conversation was never literary. She was no storer up of her Letters. She disliked literary Correspondence', and preferred reading travel-books to plays or poems.

For reasons which have not been explained, her husband joined the East India Company as a soldier and left for India in 1783. There is no hint of marital discord in the dedication 'To the Author's Husband in India' of her comedy *More Vows Than One* (1784). She later dedicated *The Fate of Sparta* (1788) to her brother-in-law John Cowley, a London merchant. Also in 1788 she visited France to superintend the education of her daughters, one of whom died in 1790 aged 17, the other marrying the Revd David Brown in Calcutta in 1796. Her last play, *The Town Before You* (1795), was dedicated to Mrs Frushard of Calcutta, leading, perhaps unnecessarily, to suggestions that she herself had visited India.

Her fame as a poet was relatively short-lived. Having published *The Maid of Aragon: A Tale* (1780) and *The Scottish Village, or Pitcairne Green* (1786), she acquired much publicity, and later ridicule, by her contributions as 'Anna Matilda' to *The World* (between 10 July 1787 and 26 May 1788), to which Robert Merry as 'Della Crusca' replied. This led to the florid 'Della-Cruscan' collections of verse, such as *The Poetry of Anna Matilda* (1788), *The Poetry of the World* (1788), and *The British Album* (1790), later to be effectively derided by William Gifford in *The Baviad* (1791) and *The Maeviad* (1795). She later contributed 'Edwina', a tale set in the Lake District, to William Hutchinson's *History of Cumberland* (Carlisle, 1794) and published *The Siege of Acre. An Epic Poem* (1801). In 1795 she had bidden farewell to the stage with *The Town Before You* ('What mother can now lead her daughters to the great National School, THE THEATRE, in the confidence of their receiving either polish or improvement?', p. xi). Her husband died in India in June 1797, where he had long suffered from 'the country disorder': attempting to visit his daughter in Calcutta, 'he expired in his budgerow [a sort of barge used on the Ganges], near Dinapore, on his passage from Chunar, in the East Indies'. In about 1801 Mrs Cowley retired to Tiverton, where she is said to have disliked card-parties and fashionable evening entertainments, but, one morning a week, 'established a singular custom, of throwing open her house . . . for ladies only, and was on those occasions attended by a crowd'. Her collected *Works*, with a short memoir, were published in 3 volumes in 1813.

252   *An Elegiac Ballad*

WHERE is my lover and my friend?
    Surely he will not linger long:
He early used to seek my cot,
    And cheer me with his dulcet song.

Where is my lover and my friend?
    Sadder the pensive twilight grows:
Its latest gleams are now no more,
    The screech-owl flaps, the north wind blows.

Where is my lover and my friend?
  Hark! the hoarse thunder growls around;   10
Nearer and nearer are its peals,
  The livid lightnings skim the ground.

Where is my lover and my friend?
  The storm is past, the sky is clear:
I'll leave the cot, and trace the path
  Which each dear evening brings him here.

Where is my lover and my friend?
  My eye darts o'er the mead, the vale,
He is not there!—What caused his stay?
  I'll chide, nor listen to his tale.   20

Where is my lover and my friend?
  Perhaps he loiters through the grove:
I'll thither bend my eager steps—
  Guide them, kind Fortune, to my love.

There is my lover and my friend!
  I know his dear, his graceful form:
Yon lofty oak supports his head—
  Its foliage kept him from the storm.

O speak, my lover and my friend!
  See! anxious through the night I came;   30
I scorn the babbling neighbours' talk,
  Nor heed their comments or their blame.

O gracious God! my hair upheaves!
  Thou didst the blasting lightning send!
I sink—O neighbour, dig the grave—
  I join my lover and my friend.

(1784)

253   *Departed Youth*

WHAT though the rosebuds from my cheek
Have faded all! which once so sleek
Spoke youth, and joy, and careless thought.
By guilt, or fear, or shame uncaught,
My soul, uninjured, still hath youth,
Its lively sense attests the truth!

Oh! I can wander yet, and taste
The beauties of the flowery waste,
The nightingale's deep swell can feel
Till to the eye a tear doth steal;   10
Rapt! gaze upon the gem-decked night,
Or mark the clear moon's gradual flight,
Whilst the bright river's rippled wave
Repeats the quivering beams she gave.
   Nor yet does Painting strive in vain
To waken from its canvas plain
The lofty passions of the mind,
Or hint the sentiment refined:
To the sweet magic yet I bow,
As when youth decked my polished brow.   20
The chisel's lightest touch to trace
Through the pure form, or softened grace,
Is lent me still; I still admire,
And kindle at the Poet's fire—
   Why Time! since these are left me still,
Of lesser thefts e'en take thy fill.
Yes, take all lustre from my eye,
And let the blithe carnation fly,
My tresses sprinkle o'er with snow,
That boasted once their auburn glow,   30
Break the slim form that was adored
By him so loved, my wedded lord;
But leave me, whilst all these you steal,
The mind to taste, the nerve to feel!

(Wr. *c.*1797; pub. 1813)

254   *Blank Verse. Written on the Sea Shore*

DELICIOUS morning! how thy gentle beams
Glide through the veil of blue, which the mild air
Spreads out o'er all the isle. The silver waves
Spring to thy soft caress, whilst on the shore,
As the blithe reapers bring the produce down,
Rich Ceres heaps her light-bound yellow sheaves.
   Soft press the zephyrs on the huddled ears,
Whilst smiling infant gleaners prattle on
And gather strength in gathering future bread.
The skylark mounts, and fills the air aloft   10
With all the music that melodious nature
For its clear pipe composed. The seaman's note,

Gliding o'er watery plains, its bass immingles,
And the pleased listener owns the concert sweet!
   Beneath my roving eye blithe Ramsgate spreads
Her haunts alluring. There, awakening beauties
Ponder the victims of the last night's ball,
And smile at thought of recollected wounds
They gave insidious midst the lively dance:
Or future wily stratagems prepare,   20
Arrange the robe, th' attractive feather place
In newer point of view.—Ah! little think
Incautious gazers that the floating down,
That waves so graceful o'er Sabrina's brow,
Heads a keen arrow levelled at the heart!
   I turn from scenes domestic, feast my thought
Again upon the view the placid ocean
In beauteous breadth expands around the dome.
Ah! 'tis all rapture! Whether glides the eye
O'er smooth acclivities with harvest swelling,   30
Or rests upon the white receding sails,
Which on th' horizon's utmost verge appear
But flitting butterflies escaped from shore,
Where'er my view doth glance, my mind is filled
With all the sweet sensations of the Muse:
All, all around is bliss—the bliss of Taste!

(Wr. c.1800; pub. 1813)

HESTER LYNCH PIOZZI (née SALUSBURY, formerly THRALE)
(1741–1821)

She was born at Bodwell Hall, near Pwllheli, Caernarvonshire, the only child of John Salusbury and his cousin, Hester Maria Cotton. In 1749 her impoverished father accepted a post in the colony at Nova Scotia, and she and her mother lived with relatives, especially with her uncle and aunt at Offley Park, Herefordshire, until her father's final return to England in 1753. She was largely self-educated, but her aunt encouraged her interest in languages and she later learned Latin from a tutor, Dr Arthur Collier. She wrote verse from an early age and contributed to the *St James's Chronicle* in 1762 and 1763. Her father died suddenly in December 1762. After a carefully negotiated marriage settlement, she unwillingly married in October 1763 Henry Thrale of Streatham, the son of a wealthy brewer, a respectable but unaffectionate personality, later MP for Southwark 1765–80. Occupied for many years with childbearing—of her twelve children born between 1764 and 1778 only four survived infancy—she retained a strong interest in literature, and Streatham Park eventually became the centre of a notable literary and intellectual circle, including

Burke, the Burneys, Garrick, Goldsmith, Reynolds, and Samuel Johnson, who stayed with the Thrales for periods from as early as 1765. These and many other acquaintances, male and female, feature in the lively and detailed journal she began keeping in these years, first published in full in 1942 as *Thraliana*. She continued writing verse (there are more than 170 poems in *Thraliana*) and contributed 'The Three Warnings' to Anna Williams's *Miscellanies* (1766; see nos. 158–9). It was only after her husband's death in 1781, however, that her career as an author began with any seriousness.

Although there had been problems with the family brewery, it was eventually sold to Barclay's for £135,000. Financially independent at last, she ignored strong opposition from her daughters and friends (notably Johnson, a few months before his death, and most of the female intelligentsia), and married Gabriel Piozzi, an Italian musician, in July 1784. They immediately set off for Italy, where she contributed verse to *The Florence Miscellany* (Florence, 1785) and compiled her *Anecdotes of the Late Samuel Johnson* (1786). After their return to England in 1787, she edited Johnson's *Letters* (2 vols., 1788) and published *Observations and Reflections Made in the Course of a Journey through France, Italy, and Germany* (2 vols., 1789), *British Synonymy* (2 vols., 1794), and *Retrospection* (2 vols., 1801). Other works from these years survive in MS. In 1795 the Piozzis moved to Wales, living at Brynbella, near Denbigh, and spending the winters in London or Bath. Piozzi died in 1809 and his widow at Clifton in 1821. Her close friendship with Johnson and the existence of her huge journal have led to the unusually detailed documentation of her life and acquaintance, although her letters have yet to be collected.

The following poem was written in Italy in the autumn of 1785, in a setting she evoked when she published it in 1789:

The haughty mountain St. Juliano lifting its brown head over our house on one side, the extensive plain stretched out before us on the other; a gravel walk neatly planted by the side of a peaceful river, which winds through a valley richly cultivated with olive yards and vines; and sprinkled, though rarely, with dwellings, either magnificent or pleasing: this lovely prospect, bounded only by the sea, makes a variety incessant as the changes of the sky; exhibiting early tranquillity, and evening splendour by turns.

255   *An Ode to Society*

[*Written at the Bagni di Pisa, in the Appenines*]

SOCIETY, gregarious dame!
Who knows thy favoured haunts to name?
Whether at Paris you prepare
The supper and the chat to share;
Where, fixed in artificial row,
Laughter displays his teeth of snow;
Grimace with raillery rejoices,
And song of many-mingled voices;
Till young Coquetry's artful wile
Some foreign novice shall beguile,   10
Who, home returned, still prates of thee,
Light, flippant, French Society.

Or whether, with your zone unbound,
You ramble gaudy Venice round,
Resolved th' inviting sweets to prove
Of wanton mirth and willing love,
Where gently roll th' obedient seas,
Sacred to luxury and ease.
In coffee-house or casino gay,
Till the too quick return of day,   20
Th' enchanted votary who sighs
For sentiments without disguise,
Clear, unaffected, fond and free,
In Venice finds Society.

Or if, to wiser Britain led,
Your vagrant feet desire to tread,
With measured step and anxious care,
The precincts pure of Portman Square;
While wit with elegance combined,
And polished manners, there you'll find,   30
The taste correct and fertile mind;
Remember Vigilance lurks near,
And Silence with unnoticed sneer,
Who watches but to tell again
Your foibles with tomorrow's pen,
Till tittering Malice smiles to see
Your wonder—grave Society!

Far from your busy, crowded court,
Tranquillity makes her resort,
Where, mid cold Staffa's columns rude,   40
Resides majestic Solitude;
Or where, in some sad Brachman's cell,
Meek Innocence delights to dwell,
Weeping with inexperienced eye
The fate of a departed fly;
Or in Hetruria's heights sublime,
Where Science' self might fear to climb,
But that she seeks a smile from thee,
And wooes thy praise, Society.

Thence let me view the plains below,   50
From rough St. Julian's rugged brow;
Hear the loud torrents swift descending,
Or watch the beauteous rainbow bending,

zone] belt, girdle   Brachman] Brahmin

Till heaven regains its favourite hue,
Aether divine! celestial blue!
Then bosomed high in myrtle bower,
View lettered Pisa's pendent tower;
The sea's wide scene, the port's loud throng
Of rude and gentle, right and wrong—
A motley group! which yet agree   60
To call themselves Society.

Oh thou! still sought by Wealth and Fame,
Dispenser of applause or blame!
While Slander, ever at thy side,
With Flattery can thy smiles divide:
Far from thy haunts oh! let me stray,
But grant *one friend* to cheer my way,
Whose converse bland, whose music's art,
May soothe my soul—and heal my heart;
Let soft Content our steps pursue,   70
And bliss eternal bound our view—
Power I'll resign, and pomp, and glee,
Thy best-loved sweets—Society.

(Wr. 1785; pub. 1789)

ANN YEARSLEY (née CROMARTIE)
(1752–1806)

Born in 1752, she was the daughter of humble parents who lived on Clifton Hill, Bristol. Her mother, Ann Cromartie, sold milk from door to door, as did her daughter later. She had little education, although her brother taught her to read and her mother borrowed books for her. In June 1774 she married John Yearsley, a labourer, with her brother William as witness. Hannah More later described him as 'honest and sober' and he was said elsewhere to be 'of no vice, but very little capacity'; but in private, in August 1784, More stated that she had been 'sacrificed for *money* ... to a silly man whom she did not like; the Husband had an Estate of near *Six Pounds* a year, and the marriage was thought too advantageous to be refused'. In six years they had six children (one of whom died) and in the severe winter of 1783–4 the family had to be rescued from starvation by a Mr Vaughan, although her mother died in March 1784.

Somehow during these years she had managed to read and write poetry, as Hannah More (see nos. 215–21) learned a few months later through her cook, from whom Yearsley was in the habit of collecting pig-swill. As More reported to Elizabeth Montagu in August 1784, 'tho' she never allowed herself to look into a book till her work was done and her children asleep, yet in those moments she found that reading and writing cou'd allay hunger and subdue calamity'. More was impressed by the uneducated poet, rightly considering her verse 'extraordinary for a milker of Cows, and a feeder of Hogs, who has never even *seen* a Dictionary', and was also attracted by the role of patron: Bristol had, after all, been the birthplace of Thomas Chatterton, the neglected genius whose posthumous fame was a recent phenomenon. With the help of Elizabeth Montagu, More began organizing the publication of Yearsley's poems by subscription. Although she was convinced of the danger of taking the milkwoman 'out of her station' and that she should not be made '*idle* or *useless*', she also, with winter approaching, 'hired her a *little* Maid, to help her feed her pigs, and nurse the little ones, while she herself sells her Milk'. An unsigned account of her (prompted, if not written, by Hannah More) appeared in the *Gentleman's Magazine* in December 1784, and she was announced again as a 'literary phenomenon' in the *London Chronicle* of 4–6 January 1785, with a list of the distinguished subscribers already collected. Some of her poems were also published in periodicals in the next few months. By June 1785 when her *Poems on Several Occasions* were published, over a thousand subscribers had been obtained, including seven duchesses and sixteen countesses, a number of bishops, as well as Reynolds, Walpole, Burney, the Blue-stockings, and many other prominent names. The volume was prefaced by a letter from More to Elizabeth Montagu, dated November 1784, giving a detailed account of Yearsley's background, reading, and character.

Still determined that Yearsley should not be tempted into a career as an author, More now planned that she should open a school. Having persuaded the Yearsleys to agree that she and Mrs Montagu should act as trustees of the subscription money (partly 'lest her Husband shou'd spent it'), More invested £350 in June 1785 to produce an annual income of £18, and advanced Yearsley £20 for food and furniture. Within a month, she was horrified by Yearsley's 'blackest ingratitude' in claiming that More was defrauding her: 'I cou'd weep over our fallen human Nature. . . . I hear she wears very fine Gauze Bonnets, long lappets, gold Pins etc. Is such a Woman to be trusted with her poor Children's money?' By September 1785 More was admitting that 'The Peace of my life is absolutely broken by her revenge'. Yearsley, whose true strength of character was now becoming apparent, was in fact objecting to a scheme which was intended to make her and her children lifelong dependants on Hannah More, and she eventually stated her case in an indignant 'Autobiographical Narrative' added to the 4th edition of her *Poems* in 1786. Her ingratitude shocked the fashionable world, which sadly concluded that such 'assuming' behaviour was that of which 'those who have been raised from very low stations are sometimes guilty'.

Horace Walpole, perhaps sensitive about his supposed neglect of Chatterton, had supported the subscription, assuming that, once she had received her money, she would 'hum no more ditties', and enjoying the thought that she wrote no worse than Anne Seward ('I am sick of all these sweet singers'). His letters to Hannah More on the subject were sympathetic: he was now 'sick of mendicant poetesses', astonished by Yearsley's 'superlative' ingratitude to More, who had 'washed and combed her trumpery verses and taught them to dance in tune'. He concluded that 'parish Sapphos' should be kept at their own social level. More herself was to remain baffled by Yearsley's 'unaccountable depravity' and 'deep malice' in her public attacks on her patron. Anna Seward understood much better Yearsley's 'gloomy and jealous dignity of spirit', which resented dependence on More. (Seward thought that, like Chatterton, she might eventually commit suicide.) Having been told by More at their final interview that she was 'a savage', that she 'had a reprobate mind, and was a bad woman', Yearsley by 1786 had a new patron in Frederick Augustus Hervey, Bishop of Derry and Earl of Bristol. He gave her £50 to publish the 4th edition of her *Poems*, and she dedicated two of her later works to him. Her 'Autobiographical Narrative' was reprinted in her *Poems on Various Subjects* (1787), a new collection which, in view of rumours that only More's revision of her verse had made it tolerable, was emphatically advertised as her own unaided work ('Nature's unclipt wing of poetic fancy'). The quarrel with More was never to be healed, although the original subscription money was eventually released to her through various intermediaries.

Yearsley continued to publish, encouraged by favourable critical comment on her poetic boldness and her fierce self-respect. Her *Poem on the Inhumanity of the Slave Trade* (1788), which has been seen as competing with Hannah More's poem on the same subject, extended her sense of injustice from the personal to the international sphere. Some of her verse appeared in Bristol newspapers, and other publications concerned local subjects, such as her *Stanzas of Woe* (1790), which boldly denounced Levi Eames, a former Mayor of Bristol, who had been caught playing on his property; and the related prose pamphlet *The Dispute: Letter to the Public from the Milkwoman*, ridiculing a threat by Eames' supporters to withdraw their subscriptions, when she wrote an ode for a benefit at the Magdalen Hospital. More substantial were *Earl Goodwin* (1791), a historical tragedy which had been performed at Bristol in 1789, and *The Royal Captives* (4 vols., 1795), a novel based on the story of the Man in the Iron Mask, for which she is said to have received £200. *The Rural Lyre* (1796), her last and rarest collection of verse, had a frontispiece by her son William, whom she had apprenticed to an engraver in 1790, and a much reduced subscription list.

By 1793 she had opened a circulating library at Bristol Hot Wells, when she was evidently helped by Ralph Griffiths, editor of the *Monthly Review*, Dr Thomas Beddoes, and Joseph Cottle, then a young bookseller in Bristol. He remembered her as 'a very extraordinary individual'. Her natural abilities were eminent, with 'an unusually sound masculine understanding', and she 'altogether evinced, even in her countenance, unequivocal marks of genius'. Although her health was now deteriorating, as late as September 1799 Robert Southey was hoping to obtain a poem from 'poor Mrs. Yearsley' for the *Annual Anthology* he was editing. By then she was depressed by the deaths of two of her sons, and it may have been after her husband's death in 1803 that she finally retired to Melksham in Wiltshire, probably because a third son John was a clothier at Trowbridge a few miles away. Here she spent her last years 'in a state of almost total seclusion', seen only when taking 'her solitary walk in the evening'. She died at Melksham on 8 May 1806 and was buried at Clifton.

'Lactilla', the 'poetical milkwoman of Bristol', has seemed to many a self-evidently preposterous phenomenon. As the *Monthly Review* enquired in 1791, 'when milk-women write tragedies, is it possible to refrain from a little vulgar wonderment?', and a similar reaction might be expected to the fact that in *The Rural Lyre* she published several hundred lines about Brutus, the mythological founder of Britain, about whom Pope had been planning to write an epic in his last years. Those who can hardly have read her verse have dismissed her as conventional or derivative, or, absurdly, as belonging to 'Hayley's school' (*DNB*). In fact, her early reading of Milton and, especially, Edward Young, whose 'ardour and boldness in his Imagination' she admired, explain, without explaining away, the idiosyncratic energy and extravagance of which her verse is capable, with flashes of imagination and originality illuminating her most obscure or turgid passages. (It should be noted, however, that in some poems in her last volume (see no. 259) she was evidently experimenting with a barer, more economical style.) Yet it is hard to separate impressions of her verse from those of her fiercely independent and combative personality. Hannah More paid insufficient attention to a statement about her sufferings by Yearsley at one of their first meetings: 'I'm afraid my mind is rather *hardened* than *subdued*.' Anna Seward, who admired her 'depth and strength of thought', was shrewder about the complexity of her character: 'Ah Yearsley! thou hast a proud and jealous spirit, of the Johnsonian cast. It will be difficult to oblige thee, without cancelling the obligation by the manner of conferring it.'

256 *On Mrs. Montagu*

WHY boast, O arrogant, imperious man,
Perfection so exclusive! are thy powers
Nearer approaching Deity? canst thou solve
Questions which high Infinity propounds,
Soar nobler flights, or dare immortal deeds,
Unknown to woman, if she greatly dares
To use the powers assigned her? Active strength,
The boast of animals, is clearly thine;
By this upheld, thou think'st the lesson rare
That female virtues teach; and poor the height   10
Which female wit obtains. The theme unfolds
Its ample maze, for Montagu befriends
The puzzled thought, and, blazing in the eye
Of boldest opposition, straight presents
The soul's best energies, her keenest powers,
Clear, vigorous, enlightened; with firm wing
Swift she o'ertakes *his* Muse, which spread afar
Its brightest glories in the days of yore;
Lo! where she, mounting, spurns the steadfast earth,
And, sailing on the cloud of science, bears   20
The banner of Perfection.—
Ask Gallia's mimic sons how strong her powers,
Whom, flushed with plunder from her Shakespeare's page,
She swift detects amid their dark retreats
(Horrid as Cacus in their thievish dens);
Regains the trophies, bears in triumph back
The pilfered glories to a wondering world.
So Stella boasts, from her the tale I learned;
With pride she told it, I with rapture heard.

O, Montagu! forgive me, if I sing   30
Thy wisdom tempered with the milder ray
Of soft humanity, and kindness bland:
So wide its influence, that the bright beams
Reach the low vale where mists of ignorance lodge,
Strike on the innate spark which lay immersed,
Thick-clogged, and almost quenched in total night—
On me it fell, and cheered my joyless heart.

Unwelcome is the first bright dawn of light
To the dark soul; impatient, she rejects,
And fain would push the heavenly stranger back;   40
She loathes the cranny which admits the day;
Confused, afraid of the intruding guest;
Disturbed, unwilling to receive the beam,
Which to herself her native darkness shows.

The effort rude to quench the cheering flame
Was mine, and e'en on Stella could I gaze
With sullen envy, and admiring pride,
Till, doubly roused by Montagu, the pair
Conspire to clear my dull, imprisoned sense,
And chase the mists which dimmed my visual beam.   50

Oft as I trod my native wilds alone,
Strong gusts of thought would rise, but rise to die;
The portals of the swelling soul ne'er oped
By liberal converse, rude ideas strove
Awhile for vent, but found it not, and died.
Thus rust the Mind's best powers. Yon starry orbs,
Majestic ocean, flowery vales, gay groves,
Eye-wasting lawns, and heaven-attempting hills,
Which bound th' horizon, and which curb the view;
All those, with beauteous imagery, awaked   60
My ravished soul to ecstasy untaught,
To all the transport the rapt sense can bear;
But all expired, for want of powers to speak;
All perished in the mind as soon as born,
Erased more quick than cyphers on the shore,
O'er which the cruel waves, unheedful, roll.

Such timid rapture as young *Edwin seized,
When his lone footsteps on the Sage obtrude,
Whose noble precept charmed his wondering
Such rapture filled ‡Lactilla's vacant soul,   70
When the bright Moralist, in softness dressed,
Opes all the glories of the mental world,
Deigns to direct the infant thought, to prune
The budding sentiment, uprear the stalk
Of feeble fancy, bid idea live,
Woo the abstracted spirit from its cares,
And gently guide her to the scenes of peace.
Mine was that balm, and mine the grateful heart,
Which breathes its thanks in rough, but timid strains.

(1785)

* See the Minstrel [by James Beattie, 1771–4, II. x ff.]   ‡The Author.

257   from *Remonstrance in the Platonic Shade,*
             Flourishing on an Height

THESE feeble sounds
Give not my soul's rich meaning; or my thought
Rises too boldly o'er the human line
Of alphabets (misused). Why should I wish
For words to form a picture for the world
Too rare? O world! what hast thou in thy sounds
So dear as silent memory when she leads
The shade of the departed? Ask despair
What renovation is, when friendship bends
To kiss her tears away; but ask her eyes;   10
The pleasing anguish dwells not on her tongue.
Will friendship stay, when love and virtue fly?
Sooner Leviathan shall pierce the skies,
Roll 'mid the burning chamber of the sun,
And hate the chrystal caverns in the deep!
'Folly' could ne'er o'ertake me. Oft I verge,
When warmed by fancy, to the farthest bound
My sense of words can bear; but at the extreme
Condemn the sense that chastity throws off.—
'Folly!' Good heaven! have I not climbed an height   20
So frightful, e'en from comfort so remote,
That had my judgement reeled, my foot forgot
Its strenuous print, my inexperienced eye
The wondrous point in view; or my firm soul,
Made early stubborn, her exalted pride,
Though of external poor; the stagnant lake
Of Vice beneath, than Cocytus more foul,
Had oped its wave to swallow me, and hide
My frame for ever. This I saw: the year
Ne'er riped the corn, or strewed the yellow leaf,   30
But some too feeble maid, who in the morn
Ascended with me, lost her hold and fell,
Leaving the glorious plaudit of the wise
To rough laborious spirits. I attained
With wretchedness this summit; hence, look down
On the lapsed ages, towers, and sleeping kings,
Whose heads repose 'mid monarchies engulfed,
With temples, oracles, long-whispering fanes,
Through which the mystic meaning awed the crowd,
And stooped the public spirit to its lore: 40
There lie vast amphitheatres, to behold
How beasts of prey could tear the human heart,

Rich with some loved impression.—O forbear,
My muse! turn from the vision, lest thou wake
Emotion, and compare that heart with mine—
There gentle Petrarch sleeps; mild victim long
To that serene despair, which once imbibed
The soul grows fond of, and withdraws, to give
Her tints of sympathy, ideal grace,
Languishing sentiment, and faithful tear,   50
To the wild woodland: there she feels enlarged,
And far from noise, looks calmly o'er the grave.
Petrarch! hadst thou not lived, what mind had dared
To own that flame, kindled so near the throne
Of God, it makes men like him? From this height
I see the bleating lamb trot o'er the turf
That covers long-descended kingdoms: hear
The tiger roar, where tyrants scourged mankind;
On roofs of buried palaces remark
The mole rearing her fabric; learn the hymn   60
Sweet Philomel sings to the warrior's shade—
Far o'er the plain, beneath the midnight moon.

                                        (1796)

258   from *To Mira, On the Care of her Infant*

MIRA, as thy dear Edward's senses grow,
Be sure they all will seek this point—*to know*:
Woo to enquiry—strictures long avoid;
By force the thirst of weakly sense is cloyed:
Silent attend the frown, the gaze, the smile,
To grasp far objects the incessant toil;
So play life's springs with energy, and try
The unceasing thirst of knowledge to supply.
    I saw the beauteous Caleb t' other day
Stretch forth his little hand to touch a spray,   10
Whilst on the grass his drowsy nurse inhaled
The sweets of Nature as her sweets exhaled:
But, ere the infant reached the playful leaf,
She pulled him back—His eyes o'erflowed with grief;
He checked his tears—Her fiercer passions strove,
She looked a vulture cowering o'er a dove!
'I'll teach you, brat!' The pretty trembler sighed—
When, with a cruel shake, she hoarsely cried—
'Your mother spoils you—every thing you see
You covet. It shall ne'er be so with me!   20

Here, eat this cake, sit still, and don't you rise—
Why don't you pluck the sun down from the skies?
I'll spoil your sport—Come, laugh me in the face—
And henceforth learn to keep your proper place.
You rule me in the house!—To hush your noise
I, like a spaniel, must run for toys:
But here, Sir, let the trees alone, nor cry—
Pluck if you dare—Who's master? you, or I?'
    O brutal force, to check th' enquiring mind,
When it would pleasure in a rosebud find!   30

(1796)

259   *Familiar Poem from Nisa to Fulvia of the Vale*

ARGUMENT

NISA of the Sabine race, having been informed by Marl, a goatherd, that old
Fulvia, who lived harmlessly by selling poultry, was a sybil, or witch, writes to
the dame on a subject that seems to have interested her. Fearing, however, to
reveal too much, she merely inquires if Fulvia can cure the mind, and artfully
breaks off:

Fulvia, our Consul bids me thank thee: why
My thanks to thee are due, I know not.—Dawn
Had scarcely borrowed from the wakeful sun
One hour of light, when hooting to our door
The camel-drivers came. Their crookèd horns
They blew, to waken Tellus. Gentle sleep
Had on our lowly pillow laid his head;
His breath, sweet as the newmown herbage, flew
In fragrant gales auspicious to the east.
Down his fair bosom drooped his golden hair   10
In heavy ringlets; these I softly moved,
To steal one parting kiss, ere the rude horn
Should from my wish abash me. Blest is he
Who drives no camels! Hapless lot! Ah! when
Will Ceres* come, and bid the swain repose
Some minutes after sunrise? The loud laugh,
From men who tarried with their market-ware,
Came high to shame him. He arose, unclasped
Our latticed casement, breathed one soft adieu,
Descended, and renewed his daily toil,   20
Befriended by my prayer. I slept too long.

* Supposed here to be the Goddess of Plenty.

My duty, soon as Tellus went, had been
Fulfilled, had I arose and took my reel.
   Fulvia, old churlish Marl, who sometimes milks
His goats beside the Tarpeian mount, that night
When thunder shook the Capitol†, and woods
In one sad murmur hailed that scathing fire
Which Jove sends down to warn us, cried aloud,
'Hey! Fulvia! midnight hag!' We marvelled much.
The hind went on: 'My cabin will come down,   30
Flat, smooth to the turf! She has already scathed
My beechen bower. Ah me! what safer chance
Waits my she-goat, behind the fatal rock
Whence we plunge quick the guilty?—Yes, my kids,
Bad omen! both this morn mistook their dams.
My chickens, too, lingered around their grain,
Nor did their bills rebound. All Fulvia's work!
Fulvia, sweet Nisa, mirks the blessed sun
With mists, that many swear rise from the sea.
Aye, aye! I know!—Nisa, I ween mischance   40
Will come to thee and me; yea, all who dwell
Within a stone's-throw of the beldam's cell.'
   We chided surly Marl for this. 'Away!',
He cried—'Dolts feel no lack of wisdom. Now,
The hag is somewhere circling round her spell,
Pinching our trembling blades; or, on the turf,
Sprinkling her juice of aconite. Dark yews
She clips, o'erhanging sacred dust; collects
Night-dew; draws mimic mandrakes from their sleep;
And dries the forehead of the early foal,   50
To strew against the north wind, as it blows
Directly to my cabin. I ne'er met
That woman first at morning, when to the hills
I hied with my young kids, but foul mischance
Struck me or mine. Nisa, do thou beware,
Nor meet her; or, if meeting, ne'er offend.'
   Art thou thus wise, dear Fulvia? Dar'st thou coop
The furies in a ring? unclose their lips
On the dread secrets of Tartarean realms?
What! teach the sun to woo the waves on high?   60
To shape centaurs, and gorgon-headed men,
Around the horizon, whilst the shepherd strains
Fancy to their wild measurement? I guess,

† A temple on the same mount. The whole has since been named Capitolium.

reel] i.e. for spinning   mirks] darkens   aconite] poison

If Phoebus, at thy bidding, dress his skies
With exhalations in the evening hour,
Thou wilt, when I implore, arrest the moon;
When brazen in her belt she draws up woe
From the deep breast t' o'erwhelm the gentle thought,
And tremulate the wise and virtuous mind.
Should this dread power be thine, if thou art grown   70
A favourite with the gods, O Fulvia, try
In mercy to compose the troubled soul
Of one brave Roman ...
                              Here I purposed much;
Yet have I not, in this epistle, penned
Great information.—Tellus is arrived
Weary and faint; his aged camel fell
Near the hill-side. He looks so pensive!—Well,
I am so apt to check myself—In haste
I wrote; am grown uncheerful. When
We pay our holy rites to Juno, come: 80
Thou shalt our priestess be; all who lack wealth
Should not lack piety. To Fulvia health.

(1796)

ELIZABETH MOODY (née GREENLY)
(d. 1814)

Her maiden name is revealed by the elegy on her brother Edward Greenly of Clifton
in her *Poetic Trifles* (1798), in the preface to which she stated that she had been
'educated' in poetry by Edward Lovibond (1724–75) of Hampton, Middlesex.
Described as 'a very accomplished Lady in that neighbourhood', she was the Miss
G——— to whom Lovibond addressed several poems and who contributed some
prefatory lines on his death to the posthumous edition of his *Poems on Several
Occasions* (1785). She married Christopher Lake Moody (1753–1815), a clergyman
who lived at Surbiton Farm and later at Turnham Green, where he was a neighbour
of Ralph Griffiths, to whose *Monthly Review* he contributed regularly from 1787 until
shortly before his death. (Two knowledgeable references in his articles to Lovibond's
MSS suggest that he and/or his wife could have edited Lovibond's *Poems* in 1785,
which had been entrusted by the poet's brother, Anthony Lovibond Collins, to an
anonymous editor.) The fact that her earliest poem is dated 1760 suggests that she
was older than her husband. In the 1780s she published some anonymous miscel-
laneous verse: *The Temptation, Or, Satan in the Country* (1781); 'Dr. Johnson's Ghost'
in the *General Evening Post* in March 1786; and 'The Rose', addressed to Dr Joseph
Priestley, in the *Gentleman's Magazine* in March 1788. She later contributed 'Anna's
Complaint; Or, The Miseries of War. Written in the Isle of Thanet, 1794' to George
Miller's *War a System of Madness and Irreligion* (1796). These poems and many others
were collected in her *Poetic Trifles* in 1798, which includes verses addressed to
Erasmus Darwin, Mrs Trimmer, and John Opie the painter.

Between 1789 and 1808 she also contributed occasionally to the *Monthly Review*, usually dealing with fiction, which, as she stated in 1790, she believed had been dominated by women in the later decades of the century. She seems to have been the first woman reviewer used on anything approaching a regular basis by Ralph Griffiths. Four of her letters to him (1791–4) are found with her husband's genial correspondence with Griffiths, including a poem satirizing Fulke Greville, husband of Frances Greville (see nos. 127–8). A pained note of 13 April 1791 expresses disappointment that Griffiths had not printed her review of Mrs Inchbald's *A Simple Story*: a loyal covering letter from her husband protested that Griffiths had 'rejected one of the best articles I ever read on a Novel', but amicable relations were soon restored. (For some reason, Griffiths had decided to review it himself.) She died at Turnham Green Terrace in 1814, 'at an advanced period of life, but young to the last in her faculties, brilliant as they were.—Blessed with genius by Nature, she took up at an early age a passion for taste in literature, for poetical ingenuity, for wit, and for the charm of style, whether in verse or in prose; a passion which formed the innocent happiness of her life, and sustained itself against the weight of years.' This obituary, perhaps written by her husband (who died a year later), rightly praised her light verse, as well as her private letters to numerous correspondents.

260   *Dr. Johnson's Ghost*

[*On Boswell's Journal of a Tour to the Hebrides*]

'TWAS at the solemn hour of night,
  When men and spirits meet,
That Johnson, huge majestic sprite,
  Repaired to Boswell's feet.

His face was like the full-orbed moon
  Wrapped in a threatening cloud,
That bodes the tempest bursting soon,
  And winds that bluster loud.

Terrific was his angry look,
  His pendent eyebrows frowned;   10
Thrice in his hand he waved a book,
  Then dashed it on the ground.

'Behold,' he cried, 'perfidious man,
  This object of my rage:
Bethink thee of the sordid plan
  That formed this venal page.

'Was it to make this base record
  That you my friendship sought;
Thus to retain each vagrant word,
  Each undigested thought?   20

'Dar'st thou pretend that, meaning praise,
    Thou seek'st to raise my name,
When all thy babbling pen betrays
    But gives me churlish fame?

'Do readers in these annals trace
    The man that's wise and good?
No!—rather one of savage race,
    Illiberal, fierce and rude.

'A traveller, whose discontent
    No kindness can appease;   30
Who finds for spleen perpetual vent
    In all he hears and sees.

'One whose ingratitude displays
    The most ungracious guest;
Who hospitality repays
    With bitter, biting jest.

'Ah! would, as o'er the hills we sped,
    And climbed the sterile rocks,
Some vengeful stone had struck thee dead,
    Or steeple, spared by Knox!   40

'Thy adulation now I see,
    And all its schemes unfold:
Thy avarice, Boswell, cherished me
    To turn me into gold.

'So keepers guard the beasts they show,
    And for their wants provide;
Attend their steps where'er they go,
    And travel by their side.

'O! were it not that, deep and low,
    Beyond thy reach I'm laid,   50
Rapacious Boswell had ere now
    Johnson a mummy made.'

He ceased, and stalked from Boswell's sight
    With fierce indignant mien,
Scornful as Ajax' sullen sprite
    By sage Ulysses seen.

Dead paleness Boswell's cheek o'erspread,
  His limbs with horror shook;
With trembling haste he left his bed,
  And burnt his fatal book.   60

And thrice he called on Johnson's name.
  Forgiveness to implore!
Then thrice repeated—'injured fame!'
  And word—wrote never more.

(1786)

261   *To a Gentleman Who Invited Me to Go*
              A-Fishing

FOR vacant hours of man's destructive leisure
Were sports invented of the barbarous kind;
But tempt not me to share thy cruel pleasure—
No sports are guiltless to the feeling mind.

And thou, who know'st the charms of lettered taste,
Whose treasured memory classic stores commands,
Shalt thou thy valuable moments waste,
Sauntering by streams with fish-rods in thy hands?

Shall I, who cultivate the Muse's lays,
And pay my homage at Apollo's shrine,   10
Shall I to torpid angling give my days,
And change poetic wreaths for fishing-line?

Sit like a statue by the placid lake,
My mind suspended on a gudgeon's fate;
Transported if the silly fish I take,
Chagrined and weary, if it shuns the bait?

(1798)

262   *The Housewife's Prayer, On the Morning*
Preceding A Fete

To Economy

GODDESS adored! who gained my early love,
And formed my mind thy precepts to improve;
Taught me to practice each penurious rule,
And made my heart a pupil of thy school;
Taught me that waste is an atrocious sin,
And bade me cull from dust the scattered pin:
Remembering this thy maxim to revere,
'One pin a day collects a groat a year'.
Thou value stamp'st on every rag I wear,
And show'st that patchwork makes an elbow-chair;   10
Bid'st me respect the dyer's useful trade,
That gives new being to my old brocade,
Restores my Persian to its pristine hue,
Or makes my faded red celestial blue.
Source of my health thy indurating power,
Inspired by thee I brave the threatening shower;
Nor seek defence against the winter's wind,
But scorn the cloak with costly ermine lined.
Let the blue current stagnate in my veins,
And age come on with all his rheums and pains;   20
Nor hood nor bonnet will I deign to wear,
Nor aught that Nature will consent to spare;
In these privations still adoring thee,
All-*saving* Power, divine Economy!
This night impart thy parsimonious grace
To all that wasteful tribe, the vassal race;
Vouchsafe protection to each sacred hoard,
And grant no lavish hand profane my board.
Infuse thy spirit in the chosen fair,
Ordained the tea and coffee to prepare;   30
May she distribute both with frugal hand,
And patient let the brewing teapot stand!
May blundering John his careless steps control,
And heed the frailty of the china bowl!
Cakes, lemonade, orgeat, do thou defend!
And guard, O Goddess, guard each candle's end!

(1798)

groat] a coin of small denomination   Persian] i.e. silk   indurating] hardening
vassal race] servants   orgeat] a cooling drink made from almonds and orange-flower water

263   *Sappho Burns her Books and Cultivates the Culinary Arts*

[*On Miss R.P.'s Saying she would find Love only if she did so*]

COMPANIONS of my favourite hours,
By winter's fire, in summer's bowers,
That wont to chase my bosom's care,
And plant your pleasing visions there!
Guarini, Dante, honoured names,
Ah, doomed to feel devouring flames!
Alas, my Petrarch's gentle loves!
My Tasso's rich enchanted groves!
My Ariosto's fairy dreams,
And all my loved Italian themes!   10
I saw you on the pile expire,
Weeping I saw the invading fire;
There fixed remained my aching sight,
Till the last ray of parting light
The last pale flame consumed away,
And all dissolved your relics lay.

Goddess of Culinary Art,
Now take possession of my heart!
Teach me more winning arts to try,
To salt the ham, to mix the pie;   20
To make the paste both light and thin,
To smooth it with a rolling-pin;
With taper skewer to print it round,
Lest ruder touch the surface wound.
Then teach thy votary how to make
That fair rotundo—a plum-cake;
To shake the compound sweets together,
To bake it light as any feather,
That, when complete, its form may show
A rising hillock topped with snow;   30
And how to make the cheesecake, say,
To beat the eggs and turn the whey;
To strain my jelly fair and clear,
That here no *misty fog* appear;
But plain to view each form may rise
That in its glassy bosom lies.

rotundo] a circular building

Now fancy soars to future times,
When all extinct are Sappho's rhymes;
When none but cooks applaud her name,
And naught but recipes her fame.   40
When sweetest numbers she'll despise,
When Pope shall sing beneath *minced-pies*,
And Eloise in her *tin* shall mourn
Disastrous fate and love forlorn;
Achilles too, that godlike man,
Shall bluster in the *patty-pan*;
And many a once-loved Grecian chief
Shall guard from flames the roasting beef.

Then, when this transformation's made,
And Sappho's vestments speak her trade;   50
When girt in towels she is seen,
With cuffs to keep the elbows clean:
Then, Sorceress, she'll call on thee!
Accomplish then thy fair decree!
If, like your sisters of the heath,
Whose mystic sound betrayed Macbeth,
Fallacious charms your arts dispense,
To cheat her with ambiguous sense;
Severest torments may you prove!–
Severest—disappointed love.   60

(1798)

HANNAH WALLIS
(*fl.* 1787)

She is known only by *The Female's Meditations; Or, Common Occurrences Spiritualised, in Verse* (1787), which could be obtained from the author at 3 Duke Street, Grosvenor Square, London, as well as from trade booksellers. From her verse it can be deduced that she grew up in a village in Essex, presumably Bromfield or Broomfield a few miles north of Chelmsford. She was elderly by 1787, and refers to the deaths of her father, who collapsed in Chelmsford Market, mother, sister, and brother. One poem, 'The emptiness of Praise', recalls her youthful embarrassment when a 'row of Swains' praised her own and her sister's beauty, but there are no indications that she had been married. In March 1789 the *Monthly Review* merely quoted four lines from her book as evidence that this 'poor Methodist' would 'never write tolerable verse'. But some readers at least may find that her blend of naïve reminiscence and simple piety has a certain homely immediacy. Although she herself admitted in 'The Conclusion' that I think that my Poems may be called the "Wet

patty-pan] a pan for baking small pies

Eye," | For as I repeat them my hearers oft cry', her melancholy is to some extent countered by her Christian faith and the simplicity of her diction and stanzaic forms.

264   *To Mrs. ——, on the Death of her Husband*

THE day invited me to walk,
    Prudence, at home to stay;
God's Providence called me to work,
    His Word, to watch and pray.

I called to mind a pleasant walk,
    And those I there did see;
And since those friends are absent now,
    'Twould be no joy to me.

Here Sally did with Tommy walk,
    Young Jenny was with me;   10
We cast our eyes on Welling's farm,
    And Primrose Hill would see.

I do remember on our way
    We through a field did pass,
Where quantities of grasshoppers
    Were jumping in the grass.

Here Sally much affrighted was,
    And often out did cry;
But Tommy led her safely through—
    On him she did rely.   20

We soon ascended Primrose Hill,
    And did those buildings view,
Which sure have stood in ancient times,
    And many that were new.

Did Moses view the promised land,
    But never entered there?
But we were going to return;
    Our dwelling it was near.

Here Sally on her spouse did lean,
    And viewed the landscape o'er,   30
But all her joys are turned to pain,
    Because he's now no more.

No more? Oh, yes! he lives above:
   Remember he did say,
'In Heaven I shall then rejoice,
   When here a corpse I lay.'

Does he rejoice in Jesus, then?
   Behold, he lives anew,
And would not quit his Saviour's arms,
   No, Sally, not for you.   40

Oh! bow your head in silence then,
   Say, 'Lord, thy will be done.'
Turn all your love and grace, I pray,
   From father unto son.

Does he not need your utmost care,
   To cultivate his mind?
This opening flower beautify,
   That you may comfort find.

                      (1787)

265   *The Female's Lamentations; or The Village in Mourning*

ONCE more I visited the place
   Where first I drew my breath;
But oh! what desolation made
   By that grim monster Death!

There hardly was a building here,
   But some kind friend was gone;
And former joys are turned to pain,
   When this is thought upon.

I went and viewed that empty house
   Where my late brother dwelt;   10
A wife and offspring he has left:
   Oh! the keen grief I felt!

And walking on, I cast a look
   Upon that empty Hall*;
Those friends that once lived there are dead:
   'Tis all in vain to call.

* Bromfield-Hall, in Essex.

409

And did I see that mansion, where
　　His Honour† once did dwell?
Ye poor, that did receive his gifts,
　　'Tis vain your wants to tell.　　　　　　　　20

For now he slumbers in the dust,
　　Regardless of your cry:
Each empty room bespeaks your loss,
　　Those gardens ruined lie.

Oh! where is now the pleasure which
　　Once sparkled in each face?
The widow's heart sure sung for joy:
　　How cheerful was that place!

The mother here her garments showed,
　　The father told the son;　　　　　　　　30
His Honour did their schooling pay:
　　What good his spouse has done!

But now the village seems to mourn,
　　And that remark is just:
'Oh! put no confidence in man,
　　Do not in princes trust.'

I only had to cross the Green,
　　Where once my parents lived;
The owner of that dwelling now
　　Did me refreshment give.　　　　　　　　40

I in the garden saw the trees
　　My own dear brother bought;
And though they live, yet he is dead:
　　How mournful was the thought!

Here is the orchard, where I, with
　　My sister, oft did walk;
With pleasure we the grass did tread,
　　Or sit us down to talk.

'Twas all in vain to look around,
　　Alas! she was not there;　　　　　　　　50
Oh! Death has hid her from my sight,
　　She does not charm my ear.

† The late Hon. EDWARD HATTON, Esq.

I went and viewed that room once more,
   Where my dear parent lay,
When Death with solemn tidings came
   To take her life away.

Here did I see her jaw-bone fall,
   And then her eye-strings break;
And just before, I thought she strove
   These words to me to speak: 60

'Oh, Hannah! put your trust in God';
   And could she then foresee
The train of troubles that did come
   Upon unhappy me?

What could a dying mother say
   More to a daughter dear,
Than bid her put her trust in God,
   A friend that's ever near?

Again I was in that doleful room,   70
   When thus to me 'twas said:
'Your father you'll alive not see'—
   I cried, 'What! is he dead?';

As if in frenzy, scarce believed
   What they to me did say;
But oh! indeed, he dropped down dead*,
   'Twas on a market day.

Why do I wound my heart afresh?
   These sorrows are too keen:
Then stop, my Muse, and turn, my thoughts,
   Unto a pleasing theme.   80

For all that ever died in Christ
   Shall meet him in the air;
So grand, so sweet, so fine a sight!
   I hope I shall be there.

Oh! talk not of a Birth-day Night,
   Nor Coronation Day;
Compared, they lose their beauties all,
   When Saints shall come away:

* The Author's Father dropt down Dead in Chelmsford-Market, Essex.

Birth-day Night] celebration of a royal birthday

With palms of victory in their hands,
  And crowns upon each head;   90
And loud hosannas will proclaim
  His praise, that once was dead.

Rejoice, ye Saints, he lives anew.
  Your Judge is now your King;
Sweet hallelujahs all will cry,
  And endless praises sing.

                              (1787)

266   *To a Sick Friend*

DEAR girl, you're growing very thin,
  Your roses too are fled;
You say you are low-spirited,
  And death you seem to dread.

Why do you dread this cruel foe?
  He's only so through sin:
Be careful to examine oft
  The state your soul is in.

Is it the terror of the law
  Does on your spirits prey?   10
I know you strictly was brought up
  In a religious way.

But as you did in Adam fall,
  So must a sinner be;
My dear, you must be born again—
  Look in God's Word, and see.

If you've experienced such a change,
  You'll love the Saviour dear;
Then happier you will be in death,
  Than longer living here.   20

                              (1787)

HELEN MARIA WILLIAMS
(1761?–1827)

She was the daughter of Charles Williams, an army officer of Welsh descent, and his wife Helen Hay (of Scottish ancestry), and was born in London, probably in 1761, although she later gave her date of birth as 1769. After her father's death in 1769, her family moved to Berwick-upon-Tweed, where she was educated by her mother. In 1781 she came to London, where her mother and sister later joined her, and, with the help of Dr Andrew Kippis, dissenting minister and author, who was a family friend, published her *Edwin and Eltruda, A Legendary Tale* (1782). In a prefatory 'Advertisement', Kippis gave a brief account of her, explaining that, when she wrote the poem, she was unaware of Edmund Cartwright's *Armine and Elvira* (1771) and Percy's *Hermit of Warkworth* (1771), which had made such legendary tales fashionable. Writing of her poem in the *Monthly Review*, Cartwright himself doubted that it was her own unaided work and described the difficulty of distinguishing 'natural' simplicity from mere 'silliness' in such tales, but in general the poem was well received and was later included in Thomas Evans's *Old Ballads, Historical and Narrative* in 1784. Her wide literary acquaintance soon included Fanny Burney, William Hayley, Samuel Johnson, Elizabeth Montagu, Anna Seward, and the Wartons, and later Hester Piozzi, Samuel Rogers, and Charlotte Smith.

She went on to publish an *Ode on the Peace* (1783) and *Peru* (1784), dedicated to Mrs Montagu, an ambitious historical poem on European exploitation of South America, which Cartwright described in a review as 'masterly', and which inspired Anna Seward to address a sonnet to her 'Poetic sister'. A successful subscription brought her considerable profit, as did the even larger subscription of more than 1,500 names, organized by the lawyer George Hardinge, to her collected *Poems* (2 vols., 1786), which she dedicated to the Queen. She included her first verse epistle to Dr John Moore, physician, former friend of Smollett, and novelist, through whom she entered into correspondence with Robert Burns. In 1788 she published her *Poem [on] the Slave Bill*, a subject which inspired poems by Hannah More and Ann Yearsley in the same year.

By the end of the decade she was prominent in dissenting and radical circles, and was one of the warmest of English enthusiasts for the French Revolution, as she made clear in the lines on 'The Bastille' in her novel *Julia* (2 vols., 1790). After visiting France, she published *Letters Written in France in the Summer of 1790* (1790), describing the celebrations of the anniversary of the fall of the Bastille as 'the most sublime spectacle which, perhaps, was ever represented on the theatre of this earth' (p. 2). Having published an expanded edition of her *Poems* (1791), she returned to France in July 1791, announcing her departure in her *Farewell to England*. Later in the year Wordsworth, who had addressed his first published poem to her in 1787, obtained a letter of introduction to her from Charlotte Smith (see nos. 237–43) on his way to France, but failed to meet her. She finally settled in France in 1792 and thereafter seems to have lived abroad continuously. Most of her output in the 1790s was in prose, notably her further volumes of *Letters from France* (1792–6). She was known to many prominent figures in post-revolutionary France, and was friendly with Thomas Paine and Mary Wollstonecraft in Paris, but was imprisoned by Robespierre in October 1793. In prison she translated St Pierre's *Paul and Virginia* (1796), in which she included six sonnets. On her release she began a long relationship with John Harford Stone, Unitarian and revolutionary, who had left his wife for her, and in 1794 travelled in Switzerland for six months, an experience described in her *Tour in Switzerland* (2 vols., 1798), which contains verse inspired by the Alps.

By now she had offended most of her English friends. In 1793 Boswell deleted the epithet 'amiable' he had used of her in the *Life of Johnson*, because of her support for 'the savage Anarchy, with which France had been visited'. Anna Seward felt obliged to publish a letter to her in the *Gentleman's Magazine* in February 1793: 'Fly, dear Helen, that land of carnage! from the pernicious influence of the equalizing system, which, instead of diffusing universal love, content, and happiness, lifts every man's hand against his brother.' Mrs Piozzi confided to her journal that her friend was 'sacrificing her Reputation to her Spirit of Politics', and by 1795 that she had 'totally lost her Character—as a *Woman*' by living with Stone, and that her 'Friends are all ashamed of *her*'. Her Gallic enthusiasm in the 1790s inevitably aroused many other scathing condemnations, and later historians have also noted the inaccuracy of the lively record of French events in her *Letters*. In the Napoleonic period she published translations and further prose works on France, and later her *Poems on Various Subjects* (1823). She was naturalized in France in 1817, but lived for some years in Amsterdam with her niece, whose husband, Athanase Coquerel, was pastor to a French protestant congregation. She died in Paris in 1827.

267   *Sonnet on Reading the Poem upon the Mountain*
Daisy, by Mr. Burns

WHILE soon the 'garden's flaunting flowers' decay,
And, scattered on the earth, neglected lie,
The mountain daisy, cherished by the ray
A poet drew from heaven, shall never die.
Ah! like that lovely flower the poet rose,
'Mid penury's bare soil and bitter gale!
He felt each storm that on the mountain blows,
Nor ever knew the shelter of the vale.
By Genius in her native vigour nursed,
On Nature with impassioned look he gazed,   10
Then through the cloud of adverse fortune burst
Indignant, and in light unborrowed blazed.
Scotia! from rude affliction shield thy bard;
His heaven-taught numbers Fate herself will guard.

(Wr. by 1787; pub. 1791)

268   *Sonnet to Hope*

OH, ever skilled to wear the form we love!
To bid the shapes of fear and grief depart,
Come, gentle Hope! with one gay smile remove
The lasting sadness of an aching heart.

Thy voice, benign enchantress! let me hear;
    Say that for me some pleasures yet shall bloom,
That fancy's radiance, friendship's precious tear,
    Shall soften, or shall chase, misfortune's gloom.
But come not glowing in the dazzling ray
Which once with dear illusions charmed my eye;   10
Oh, strew no more, sweet flatterer! on my way
The flowers I fondly thought too bright to die.
Visions less fair will soothe my pensive breast,
That asks not happiness, but longs for rest!

(1790)

269   *Elegy on a Young Thrush, which Escaped from
    the Writer's Hand, and Falling down the Area
    of a House, could not be Found*

MISTAKEN bird, ah whither hast thou strayed?
    My friendly grasp why eager to elude?
This hand was on thy pinion lightly laid,
    And feared to hurt thee by a touch too rude.

Is there no foresight in a thrush's breast,
    That thou down yonder gulf from me wouldst go?
That gloomy area lurking cats infest,
    And there the dog may rove, alike thy foe.

I would with lavish crumbs my bird have fed,
    And brought a chrystal cup to wet thy bill;   10
I would have made of moss and down thy bed,
    Soft, though not fashioned with a thrush's skill.

Soon as thy strengthened wing could mount the sky,
    My willing hand had set my captive free;
Ah, not for her who loves the Muse to buy
    A selfish pleasure, bought with pain to thee!

The vital air, and liberty, and light
    Had all been thine; and love, and rapturous song,
And sweet parental joys, in rapid flight,
    Had led the circle of thy life along.   20

269 Area] the sunken court giving access to the basement of a house

Securely to my window hadst thou flown,
　　And ever thy accustomed morsel found;
Nor should thy trusting breast the wants have known
　　Which other thrushes know when winter frowned.

Framed with the wisdom nature lent to thee,
　　Thy house of straw had braved the tempest's rage,
And thou through many a spring hadst lived to see
　　The utmost limit of a thrush's age.

Ill-fated bird!—and does the thrush's race,
　　Like Man's, mistake the path that leads to bliss?　　　　30
Or, when his eye that tranquil path can trace,
　　The good he well discerns through folly miss?

(Wr. *c.*1791; pub. 1823)

270　　*To Dr. Moore, in Answer to a Poetical Epistle*
　　　　Written by Him in Wales

[*On the French Revolution*]

WHILE in long exile far from you I roam,
To soothe my heart with images of home,
For me, my friend, with rich poetic grace
The landscapes of my native isle you trace;
Her cultured meadows, and her lavish shades,
Her winding rivers, and her verdant glades;
Far as where, frowning on the flood below,
The rough Welsh mountain lifts its craggy brow;
Where nature throws aside her softer charms,
And with sublimer views the bosom warms.　　　　10

Meanwhile my steps have strayed where Autumn yields
A purple harvest on the sunny fields;
Where, bending with their luscious weight, recline
The loaded branches of the clustering vine;
There, on the Loire's sweet banks, a joyful band
Culled the rich produce of the fruitful land;
The youthful peasant and the village maid,
And feeble age and childhood lent their aid.
The labours of the morning done, they haste
Where the light dinner in the field is placed;　　　　20

Around the soup of herbs a circle make,
And all from one vast dish at once partake:
The vintage-baskets serve, reversed, for chairs,
And the gay meal is crowned with tuneless airs;
For each in turn must sing with all his might,
And some their carols pour in nature's spite.

Delightful land! ah, now with general voice
Thy village sons and daughters may rejoice;
Thy happy peasant, now no more—a slave
Forbade to taste one good that nature gave—   30
Views with the anguish of indignant pain
The bounteous harvest spread for him in vain.
Oppression's cruel hand shall dare no more
To seize with iron grip his scanty store,
And from his famished infants wring those spoils,
The hard-earned produce of his useful toils;
For now on Gallia's plains the peasant knows
Those equal rights impartial heaven bestows.
He now, by freedom's ray illumined, taught
Some self-respect, some energy of thought,   40
Discerns the blessings that to all belong,
And lives to guard his humble shed from wrong.

Auspicious Liberty! in vain thy foes
Deride thy ardour, and thy force oppose;
In vain refuse to mark thy spreading light,
While, like the mole, they hide their heads in night,
Or hope their eloquence with taper-ray
Can dim the blaze of philosophic day;
Those reasoners who pretend that each abuse,
Sanctioned by precedent, has some blest use!   50
Does then some chemic power to time belong,
Extracting by some process right from wrong?
Must feudal governments for ever last,
Those Gothic piles, the works of ages past?
Nor may obtrusive reason boldly scan,
Far less reform, the rude, mishapen plan?
The winding labyrinths, the hostile towers,
Whence danger threatens, and where horror lowers;
The jealous drawbridge, and the moat profound,
The lonely dungeon in the caverned ground;   60
The sullen dome above those central caves,
Where lives one despot and a host of slaves?—
Ah, Freedom, on this renovated shore
That fabric frights the moral world no more!

Shook to its basis by thy powerful spell,
Its triple walls in massy fragments fell;
While, rising from the hideous wreck, appears
The temple thy firm arm sublimely rears;
Of fair proportions, and of simple grace,
A mansion worthy of the human race.   70
For me, the witness of those scenes, whose birth
Forms a new era in the storied earth,
Oft, while with glowing breast those scenes I view,
They lead, ah friend beloved, my thoughts to you!
Ah, still each fine emotion they impart
With your idea mingles in my heart;
You, whose warm bosom, whose expanded mind,
Have shared this glorious triumph of mankind;
You, whom I oft have heard, with generous zeal,
With all that truth can urge or pity feel,   80
Refute the pompous argument, that tried
The common cause of millions to deride;
With reason's force the plausive sophist hit,
Or dart on folly the bright flash of wit;
Too swift, my friend, the moments winged their flight,
That gave at once instruction and delight;
That ever from your ample stores of thought
To my small stock some new accession brought.
How oft remembrance, while this bosom bleeds,
My pensive fancy to your dwelling leads;   90
Where, round your cheerful hearth, I weeping trace
The social circle, and my vacant place!—
When, to that dwelling friendship's tie endears,
When shall I hasten with the 'joy of tears'?
That joy whose keen sensation swells to pain,
And strives to utter what it feels, in vain.

(1792)

271   *On the Death of the Rev. Dr. Kippis*

PLACED midst the tempest, whose conflicting waves
The buoyant form of Gallic Freedom braves,
I from its swelling surge unheedful turn,
While o'er the grave where Kippis rests I mourn.
Friend of my life, by every tie endeared,
By me lamented, as by me revered!
Whene'er remembrance would the past renew,
His image mingles with the pensive view;

Him through life's lengthening scene I mark with pride,
My earliest teacher, and my latest guide.   10
First, in the house of prayer, his voice impressed
Celestial precepts on my infant breast;
'The hope that rests above' my childhood taught,
And lifted first to God my ductile thought.
And, when the heaven-born Muse's cherished art
Shed its fresh pleasures on my glowing heart;
Flashed o'er my soul one spark of purer light,
New worlds unfolding to my raptured sight;
When first with timid hand I touched the lyre,
And felt the youthful poet's proud desire,   20
His liberal comment fanned the dawning flame,
His plaudit soothed me with a poet's name;
Led by his counsels to the public shrine,
He bade the trembling hope to please be mine;
What he forgave, the critic eye forgives,
And, for a while, the verse he sanctioned lives.

When on that spot where Gallic Freedom rose,
And where she mourned her unexampled woes,
Scourge of his nature, and its worst disgrace,
Curse of his age, and murderer of his race,   30
Th' ignoble Tyrant of his Country stood,
And bathed his scaffolds in the patriot's blood;
Destined the patriot's fate in all to share,
To feel his triumphs, and his pangs to bear;
To shun th' uplifted axe, condemned to roam
A weeping exile from my cherished home*;
When Malice poured her dark insatiate lie,
Called it, though death to stay, a crime to fly;
And, while the falsehood served her hateful ends,
Congenial audience found in hollow friends;   40
Who to the tale 'assent with civil leer,
And, without sneering, teach the rest to sneer';
His friendship o'er me spread that guardian shield,
Which his severest virtue best could wield;
Repelled by him, relentless Slander found
Her dart bereft of half its power to wound.

Alas! no more to him the task belongs
To soothe my sorrows, or redress my wrongs;
No more his lettered aid, enlightened sage!
Shall mark the errors of my careless page;   50
Shall hide from public view the faulty line,
And bid the merit he bestows be mine.

---

* Miss W. took refuge in Switzerland during the tyranny of Robespierre.

Ah! while with fond regret my feeble verse
Would pour its tribute o'er his hallowed hearse,
For him his Country twines her civic palm,
And Learning's tears his honoured name embalm;
His were the lavish stores her force sublime,
Through every passing age, has snatched from Time;
His the historian's wreath, the critic's art,
A rigid judgement, but a feeling heart;   60
His the warm purpose for the general weal,
The Christian's meekness and the Christian's zeal;
And his the moral worth to which is given
Earth's purest homage, and the meed of heaven.

(1796)

HELEN LEIGH
(*fl.* 1788)

She is known only by her *Miscellaneous Poems* (Manchester, 1788). She lived in
Middlewich, near Manchester (title-page), and was 'the Wife of a Country Curate,
and Mother of seven Children' (preface). The large subscribers' list contains mostly
local names, including Thomas Wills of Swettenham, to whom the volume is
dedicated. Many of her poems are fables, ballads, and tales, one of them, 'A
Specimen of Modern Female Education', being about a spoiled child.

272   *The Natural Child*

LET not the title of my verse offend,
    Nor let the prude contract her rigid brow;
That helpless Innocence demands a friend,
    Virtue herself will cheerfully allow:

And should my pencil prove too weak to paint
    The ills attendant on the babe ere born,
Whose parents swerved from Virtue's mild restraint,
    Forgive th' attempt, nor treat the muse with scorn.

Yon rural farm, where Mirth was wont to dwell,
    Of Melancholy now appears the seat;   10
Solemn and silent as the hermit's cell—
    Say what, my muse, has caused a change so great?

This hapless morn, an infant first saw light,
  Whose innocence a better fate might claim
Than to be shunned as hateful to the sight,
  And banished soon as it receives a name.

No joy attends its entrance into life,
  No smile upon its mother's face appears.
She cannot smile, alas! she is no wife,
  But vents the sorrow of her heart in tears.   20

No father flies to clasp it to his breast,
  And bless the power that gave it to his arms;
To see his form, in miniature, expressed,
  Or trace, with ecstasy, its mother's charms.

Unhappy babe! thy father is thy foe!
  Oft shall he wish thee numbered with the dead;
His crime entails on thee a load of woe,
  And sorrow heaps on thy devoted head.

Torn from its mother's breast, by shame or pride—
  No matter which—to hireling hands assigned;   30
A parent's tenderness when thus denied,
  Can it be thought its nurse is over-kind?

Too many like this infant we may see,
  Exposed, abandoned, helpless and forlorn;
Till death, misfortune's friend, has set them free
  From a rude world, which gave them naught but scorn.

Too many mothers—horrid to relate!
  Soon as their infants breathe the vital air,
Deaf to their plaintive cries, their helpless state,
  Led on by shame, and driven by despair,   40

Fell murderers become—Here cease, my pen,
  And leave these wretched victims of despair;
But ah! what punishments await the men,
  Who, in such depths of misery, plunge the fair?

(1788)

ELIZABETH HANDS
(*fl.* 1789)

She was for many years a valued servant in the family of Mr Huddesford of Allesly and his daughter, but by 1785 had married a blacksmith at Bourton, a few miles south-west of Rugby. Although she described herself in 1789 as 'born in obscurity, and never emerging beyond the lower stations of life', she had in fact published verse under the name of 'Daphne' in the *Coventry Mercury* some years earlier. Her main poem, 'The Death of Amnon', came to the attention of Philip Bracebridge Homer, a minor poet and assistant master at Rugby School, who showed it to Dr Thomas James, his headmaster, and 'other Criticks at Rugby'. The unanimous opinion was that it deserved publication and a successful subscription was opened in the neighbourhood. A letter promoting the subscription from the Revd Henry Homer, Rector of Birdingbury and father of P. B. Homer, is dated 4 November 1788. Homer feared that the subject of her main poem would 'not be a popular one, but the manner in wch She has decorated it will in my opinion get over the prejudices wch it may have to struggle with'. *The Death of Amnon. A Poem. With An Appendix; Containing Pastorals, and Other Poetical Pieces* appeared at Coventry in 1789. Henry Homer's nervousness no doubt arose from the fact that the title-poem deals in five cantos with the subject of incestuous rape, albeit in a biblical context. It is clear from the poems below that the author herself expected the subject to disconcert her social superiors. Among her supplementary poems, some ironic sketches of rural life and the two poems about reactions to her poetical pretensions are more effective than some insipid pastorals.

Richard Gough, who reviewed the book in the *Gentleman's Magazine* (June 1790), p. 540, had some knowledge of her, perhaps through P. B. Homer. He referred to her husband's occupation and hoped that, while her poetical talents were unlikely to rescue her from oblivion, the successful subscription would 'make the remainder of her life comfortable to herself and family'. Gough mentions the poet (surely P. B. Homer) who was 'particularly attentive to female merit' and who had been the main promoter of the subscription, which had attracted 1,200 names at 5 shillings each. Homer, if it was he, had also stated that 'there is no woman's poetry in this age, from whom he has received so much entertainment' as from 'The Death of Amnon'. George Ogle, in the *Monthly Review* in November 1790, merely sidestepped the issue by citing her own self-deprecating lines on the possible reception of her verse. The volume was dedicated to Bertie Greatheed of Guy's Cliffe, near Warwick, the dramatist. Her subscribers included Anna Seward and several members of the Hands families of Napton and Stoneleigh near Coventry.

273   *Lob's Courtship*

As Lob among his cows one day
Was filling of their cribs with hay;
As he to the crib the hay did carry,
It came into his head to marry;

422

Says he, 'There's little merry Nell,
I think I like her very well;
But she, perhaps, at me will scoff;
Besides, she lives a great way off.'
He mused a while, then judged it better
The courtship to begin by letter;   10
So he a bit of paper found,
'Twas neither long, nor square, nor round;
It was the best that he could find,
And on it thus he wrote his mind:

'Dear Nelly, I make bold to send
My love to you, and am your friend;
I think you are a pretty maid,
And wonder much that you don't wed;
If you can like a country man,
I'll come and see you, if I can,   20
When roads are good, and weather fine,
But first I hope you'll send a line.'

Then he in haste this letter sent,
Also two apples did present,
Which Nell received, and read the letter
(But she liked the apples better);
When read, she into the fire threw it,
And never sent an answer to it.

When spring drew on, the cuckoo sung,
The roads were dry, and days were long,   30
The cows were all turned out to grass,
Then Lob set out to see his lass;
He oiled his shoes, and combed his hair,
As if a-going to a fair:
He was a very clever clown,
His frock was of the fustian brown,
His stick was bended like a bow,
His handkerchief too made a show,
His hat stood like the pot-lid round,
So on he went, and Nell he found: 40

'What, Nelly! how dost do?', says he.
'Come, will you go along with me
O'er yonder stile, a little way
Along that close; Nell, what dost say?'

'Me go with you o'er yonder stile?',
Says Nell; 'indeed, I can't a-while.'
So she stepped in, and shut the door,
And he shabbed off, and said no more.

(1789)

frock] tunic, overall   shabbed] sneaked

423

274 *On an Unsociable Family*

O WHAT a strange parcel of creatures are we,
Scarce ever to quarrel, or even agree;
We all are alone, though at home altogether,
Except to the fire constrained by the weather;
Then one says, ''Tis cold', which we all of us know,
And with unanimity answer, ''Tis so':
With shrugs and with shivers all look at the fire,
And shuffle ourselves and our chairs a bit nigher;
Then quickly, preceded by silence profound,
A yawn epidemical catches around: 10
Like social companions we never fall out,
Nor ever care what one another's about;
To comfort each other is never our plan,
For to please ourselves, truly, is more than we can.

(1789)

275 *Written, originally extempore, on seeing a Mad
Heifer run through the Village where the Author
lives*

WHEN summer smiled, and birds on every spray
In joyous warblings tuned their vocal lay,
Nature on all sides showed a lovely scene,
And people's minds were, like the air, serene;
Sudden from th' herd we saw an heifer stray,
And to our peaceful village bend her way.
She spurns the ground with madness as she flies,
And clouds of dust, like autumn mists, arise;
Then bellows loud: the villagers, alarmed,
Come rushing forth, with various weapons armed;   10
Some run with pieces of old broken rakes,
And some from hedges pluck the rotten stakes;
Here one in haste, with hand-staff of his flail,
And there another comes with half a rail;
Whips, without lashes, sturdy ploughboys bring,
While clods of dirt and pebbles others fling.
Voices tumultuous rend the listening ear:
'Stop her', one cries; another, 'Turn her there':

But furiously she rushes by them all,
And some huzza, and some to cursing fall.   20
A mother snatched her infant off the road,
Close to the spot of ground where next she trod;
Camilla, walking, trembled and turned pale:
See o'er her gentle heart what fears prevail!
At last the beast, unable to withstand
Such force united, leaped into a pond:
The water quickly cooled her maddened rage;
No more she'll fright our village, I presage.

(1789)

276   *A Poem, On the Supposition of an
Advertisement appearing in a Morning Paper, of
the Publication of a Volume of Poems, by a
Servant-Maid*

THE tea-kettle bubbled, the tea things were set,
The candles were lighted, the ladies were met;
The how d'ye's were over, and entering bustle,
The company seated, and silks ceased to rustle:
The great Mrs. Consequence opened her fan,
And thus the discourse in an instant began
(All affected reserve and formality scorning):
'I suppose you all saw in the paper this morning
A volume of *Poems* advertised—'tis said
They're produced by the pen of a poor servant-maid.'   10
'A servant write verses!' says Madam Du Bloom:
'Pray what is the subject—a Mop, or a Broom?'
'He, he, he,' says Miss Flounce: 'I suppose we shall see
An Ode on a Dishclout—what else can it be?'
Says Miss Coquettilla, 'Why, ladies, so tart?
Perhaps Tom the footman has fired her heart;
And she'll tell us how charming he looks in new clothes,
And how nimble his hand moves in brushing the shoes;
Or how, the last time that he went to May Fair,
He bought her some sweethearts of gingerbread ware.'   20
'For my part I think,' says old Lady Marr-joy,
'A servant might find herself other employ:
Was she mine I'd employ her as long as 'twas light,
And send her to bed without candle at night.'
'Why so?', says Miss Rhymer, displeased: 'I protest
'Tis pity a genius should be so depressed!'

'What ideas can such low-bred creatures conceive?',
Says Mrs. Noworthy, and laughed in her sleeve.
Says old Miss Prudella, 'If servants can tell
How to write to their mothers, to say they are well, 30
And read of a Sunday *The Duty of Man*,
Which is more I believe than one half of them can;
I think 'tis much *properer* they should rest there,
Than be reaching at things so much out of their sphere.'
Says old Mrs. Candour, 'I've now got a maid
That's the plague of my life—a young gossiping jade;
There's no end of the people that after her come,
And whenever I'm out, she is never at home;
I'd rather ten times she would sit down and write,
Than gossip all over the town every night.' 40
'Some whimsical trollop most like,' says Miss Prim,
'Has been scribbling of nonsense, just out of a whim,
And, conscious it neither is witty or pretty,
Conceals her true name, and ascribes it to Betty.'
'I once had a servant myself,' says Miss Pines,
'That wrote on a wedding some very good lines.'
Says Mrs. Domestic, 'And when they were done,
I can't see for my part what use they were *on*;
Had she wrote a receipt, to've instructed you how
To warm a cold breast of veal, like a ragout, 50
Or to make cowslip wine, that would pass for Champagne,
It might have been useful, again and again.'
On the sofa was old Lady Pedigree placed;
She owned that for poetry she had no taste,
That the study of heraldry was more in fashion,
And boasted she knew all the crests in the nation.
Says Mrs. Routella, 'Tom, take out the urn,
And stir up the fire, you see it don't burn.'
    The tea things removed, and the tea-table gone,
The card-tables brought, and the cards laid thereon, 60
The ladies, ambitious for each others' crown,
Like courtiers contending for honours, sat down.

                                              (1789)

in her sleeve] to herself   Betty] a generic name for a lady's maid

277 *A Poem, On the Supposition of the Book having been Published and Read*

THE dinner was over, the tablecloth gone,
The bottles of wine and the glasses brought on,
The gentlemen filled up the sparkling glasses,
To drink to their king, to their country and lasses:
The ladies a glass or two only required,
To the drawing-room then in due order retired,
The gentlemen likewise that chose to drink tea;
And, after discussing the news of the day,
What wife was suspected, what daughter eloped,
What thief was detected, that 'twas to be hoped   10
The rascals would all be convicted, and roped;
What chambermaid kissed when her lady was out;
Who won, and who lost, the last night at the rout;
What lord gone to France, and what tradesman unpaid,
And who and who danced at the last masquerade;
What banker stopped payment with evil intention,
And twenty more things much too tedious to mention:
Miss Rhymer says, 'Mrs. Routella, ma'am, pray
Have you seen the new book (that we talked of that day
At your house, you remember) of *Poems*, 'twas said   20
Produced by the pen of a poor servant-maid?'
    The company, silent, the answer expected;
Says Mrs. Routella, when she'd recollected:
'Why, ma'am, I have bought it for Charlotte; the child
Is so fond of a book, I'm afraid it is spoiled:
I thought to have read it myself, but forgat it;
In short, I have never had time to look at it.
Perhaps I may look it o'er some other day;
Is there anything in it worth reading, I pray?
For your nice attention there's nothing can 'scape.'   30
She answered, 'There's one piece, whose subject's a Rape.'
'A Rape!', interrupted the Captain Bonair;
'A delicate theme for a female, I swear';
Then smirked at the ladies, they simpered all round,
Touched their lips with their fans—Mrs. Consequence frowned.
The simper subsided, for she, with her nods,
Awes these lower assemblies, as Jove awes the gods.
She smiled on Miss Rhymer, and bade her proceed—
Says she, 'There are various subjects indeed:
With some little pleasure I read all the rest,   40
But the "Murder of Amnon"'s the longest and best.'

rout] fashionable evening party

'Of Amnon, of Amnon, Miss Rhymer, who's he?
His name,' says Miss Gaiety, ''s quite new to me.'—
''Tis a Scripture tale, ma'am—he's the son of King David,'
Says a reverend old Rector. Quoth madam, 'I have it;
A Scripture tale?—ay—I remember it—true;
Pray, is it i' th' Old Testament or the New?
If I thought I could readily find it, I'd borrow
My housekeeper's Bible, and read it tomorrow.'
''Tis in Samuel, ma'am,' says the Rector:—Miss Gaiety   50
Bowed, and the Reverend blushed for the laity.
   'You've read it, I find,' says Miss Harriot Anderson;
'Pray, sir, is it anything like *Sir Charles Grandison*?'
'How you talk,' says Miss Belle, 'how should such a girl write
A novel, or anything else that's polite?
You'll know better in time, Miss.'—She was but fifteen:
Her mamma was confused—with a little chagrin,
Says, 'Where's your attention, child? did not you hear
Miss Rhymer say that it was poems, my dear?'
Says Sir Timothy Turtle, 'My daughters ne'er look   60
In anything else but a cookery-book:
The properest study for women designed.'
Says Mrs. Domestic, 'I'm quite of your mind.'
'Your haricots, ma'am, are the best I e'er eat,'
Says the Knight; 'may I venture to beg a receipt?'
''Tis much at your service,' says madam, and bowed,
Then fluttered her fan, of the compliment proud.
Says Lady Jane Rational, 'The bill of fare
Is th' utmost extent of my cookery care:
Most servants can cook for the palate, I find,   70
But very few of them can cook for the mind.'
   'Who,' says Lady Pedigree, 'can this girl be?
Perhaps she's descended from some family—'.
'Of family, doubtless,' says Captain Bonair;
'She's descended from Adam, I'd venture to swear.'
Her Ladyship drew herself up in her chair,
And, twitching her fan-sticks, affected a sneer.
'I know something of her,' says Mrs. Devoir;
'She lived with my friend, Jacky Faddle, Esq.
'Tis some time ago, though; her mistress said then   80
The girl was excessively fond of a pen;
I saw her, but never conversed with her, *though*:
One can't make acquaintance with servants, you know.'
''Tis pity the girl was not bred in high life,'
Says Mr. Fribello.—'Yes,—then,' says his wife,
'She doubtless might have wrote something worth notice.'
''Tis pity,' says one—says another, 'and so 'tis.'

'O law!', says young Seagram, 'I've seen the book, now
I remember; there's something about a mad cow.'
'A mad cow!—ha, ha, ha, ha,' returned half the room;   90
'What can y' expect better?', says Madam Du Bloom.
   They look at each other—a general pause—
And Miss Coquettilla adjusted her gauze.
The Rector reclined himself back in his chair,
And opened his snuff-box with indolent air:
'This book,' says he (snift, snift), 'has, in the beginning,'
(The ladies give audience to hear his opinion),
'Some pieces, I think, that are pretty correct:
A style elevated you cannot expect;
To some of her equals they may be a treasure,   100
And country lasses may read 'em with pleasure.
That "Amnon", you can't call it poetry neither,
There's no flights of fancy, or imagery either;
You may style it prosaic, blank verse at the best;
Some pointed reflections, indeed, are expressed;
The narrative lines are exceedingly poor:
Her Jonadab is a ——'. The drawing-room door
Was opened, the gentlemen came from below,
And gave the discourse a definitive blow.

(1789)

JOANNA BAILLIE
(1762–1851)

She was the younger daughter of James Baillie, a presbyterian clergyman of Both-
well, Lanarkshire, and his wife Dorothea Hunter. From the age of 10 she was
educated at a boarding-school in Glasgow. In 1775 her father was appointed
Professor of Divinity in the University of Glasgow, but he died in 1778. His widow
and daughters lived at Long Calderwood, near Hamilton, Lanarkshire, presumably
the community described in her early verse. Her mother's brothers were the famous
surgeons William and John Hunter (see Anne Hunter, nos. 235–6). At his death in
1783 Dr William Hunter left the use of his house and Museum in Great Windmill
St., London, to his nephew Matthew Baillie, Joanna's brother, physician and
anatomist. In the following year Mrs Baillie and her daughters joined Matthew in
London and lived with him until his marriage in 1791, after which they eventually
settled in Hampstead. Her mother died in 1806, but the two sisters lived together
until Joanna's death.

   She had probably written songs and ballads early in her life. In 1790 she published
a volume of poems, some of which she reprinted fifty years later in her *Fugitive Verses*
(1840), explaining that the original book was 'not noticed by the public, or circulated
in any considerable degree', although one reviewer had praised its 'true unsophisti-
cated representations of nature'. This untraced anonymous publication has accord-
ingly often been listed among her works as *Fugitive Verses* (1790). It was first

identified in 1984 in my *New Oxford Book of Eighteenth Century Verse*, its actual title being *Poems; Wherein it is Attempted to Describe Certain Views of Nature and of Rustic Manners* (1790), published by Joseph Johnson. The one favourable notice it received was by William Enfield in the *Monthly Review* in November 1791. In 1840 she explained that the appearance of a few pieces from the book in an anthology by Mrs Barbauld had encouraged her to publish revised selections from it. Her revisions were in fact more extensive than she suggested, as she tended to refine away some of the earthy, at times clumsy, concreteness of the originals, as well as some 'Scotch expressions', and she also made some pious additions: for example, to 'A Winter Day' some lines about 'family worship', which she now apologised for having left unmentioned in 1790.

Her interest in contrasting psychological states—as in the elaborate series of 'Addresses to the Night' by 'A Fearful Mind', 'A Discontented Mind', 'A Sorrowful Mind', and 'A Joyful Mind' in *Poems* (1790)—anticipates the verse dramas which were to win her a high reputation a few years later: the *Series of Plays, in which it is attempted to Delineate the Stronger Passions of the Mind* (3 vols., 1798–1812). The first volume aroused much interest and speculation about the author, widely assumed to be a man. Mrs Barbauld had known the retiring Miss Baillie, a member of her husband's congregation at Hampstead, for some time before learning about her literary talents. Her authorship was acknowledged after 1800, in which year her *De Monfort* was performed. Although her numerous plays were often criticized for theatrical implausibility, she had an unrivalled reputation as a woman dramatist in the period, and a very wide literary acquaintance, including Mrs Barbauld, Maria Edgeworth, Samuel Rogers, William Wordsworth, and Walter Scott, who once called her 'the best dramatic writer since the days of Shakespeare and Massinger'. Francis Jeffrey, in contrast, was a relentless critic of her plays in the *Edinburgh Review* from 1803. Vols. I and II of her *Series of Plays* were translated into German in 1806. She continued writing and publishing for some fifty years after her first book, living in Hampstead until her death in 1851 at the age of 88. Her elder sister Agnes died in 1861 at the age of 100.

278   from *A Winter Day*

[*Morning*]

THE cock, warm roosting midst his feathered dames,
Now lifts his beak and snuffs the morning air,
Stretches his neck and claps his heavy wings,
Gives three hoarse crows and, glad his task is done,
Low-chuckling turns himself upon the roost,
Then nestles down again amongst his mates.
The labouring hind, who, on his bed of straw
Beneath his home-made coverings, coarse but warm,
Locked in the kindly arms of her who spun them,
Dreams of the gain that next year's crop should bring;   10
Or at some fair disposing of his wool,
Or by some lucky and unlooked-for bargain,

Fills his skin purse with heaps of tempting gold,
Now wakes from sleep at the unwelcome call,
And finds himself but just the same poor man
As when he went to rest.——
He hears the blast against his window beat,
And wishes to himself he were a lord,
That he might lie abed.——
He rubs his eyes, and stretches out his arms;   20
'Heigh ho! heigh ho!', he drawls with gaping mouth,
Then most unwillingly creeps out of bed,
And without looking-glass puts on his clothes.
With rueful face he blows the smothered fire,
And lights his candle at the reddening coal;
First sees that all be right amongst his cattle,
Then hies him to the barn with heavy tread,
Printing his footsteps on the new-fall'n snow.
From out the heap of corn he pulls his sheaves,
Dislodging the poor redbreast from his shelter,   30
Where all the livelong night he slept secure;
But now affrighted, with uncertain flight
He flutters round the walls, to seek some hole
At which he may escape out to the frost.
And now the flail, high whirling o'er his head,
Descends with force upon the jumping sheaf,
Whilst every rugged wall and neighbouring cot
Re-echoes back the noise of his [   ] strokes.

The family cares call next upon the wife
To quit her mean but comfortable bed.   40
And first she stirs the fire and blows the flame,
Then from her heap of sticks, for winter stored,
An armful brings; loud-crackling as they burn,
Thick fly the red sparks upward to the roof,
While slowly mounts the smoke in wreathy clouds.
On goes the seething pot with morning cheer,
For which some little wishful hearts await,
Who, peeping from the bed-clothes, spy well pleased
The cheery light that blazes on the wall,
And bawl for leave to rise.——   50
Their busy mother knows not where to turn,
Her morning work comes now so thick upon her.
One she must help to tie his little coat,
Unpin his cap, and seek another's shoe.
When all is o'er, out to the door they run,
With new-combed sleeky hair, and glistening cheeks,
Each with some little project in his head.

One on the ice must try his new-soled shoes;
To view his well-set trap another hies,
In hopes to find some poor unwary bird   60
(No worthless prize) entangled in his snare;
Whilst one, less active, with round rosy face,
Spreads out his purple fingers to the fire,
And peeps, most wishfully, into the pot.

(1790)

279   from *A Summer Day*

[*Evening*]

NOW weary labourers perceive, well pleased,
The shadows lengthen, and th' oppressive day
With all its toil fast wearing to an end.
The sun, far in the west, with sidelong beam
Plays on the yellow head of the round haycock,
And fields are chequered with fantastic shapes,
Or tree, or shrub, or gate, or rugged stone,
All lengthened out in antic disproportion
Upon the darkened grass.——
They finish out their long and toilsome task,   10
Then, gathering up their rakes and scattered coats,
With the less cumbrous fragments of their feast,
Return right gladly to their peaceful homes.

The village, lone and silent through the day,
Receiving from the fields its merry bands,
Sends forth its evening sound, confused but cheerful;
Whilst dogs and children, eager housewives' tongues,
And true-love ditties, in no plaintive strain
By shrill-voiced maid at open window sung;
The lowing of the home-returning kine,   20
The herd's low droning trump, and tinkling bell
Tied to the collar of his favourite sheep,
Make no contemptible variety
To ears not over-nice.——
With careless lounging gait, the sauntering youth
Upon his sweetheart's open window leans,
And, as she turns about her buzzing wheel,
Diverts her with his jokes and harmless taunts.
Close by the cottage-door, with placid mien,
The old man sits upon his seat of turf,   30
His staff with crookèd head laid by his side,

Which oft the younger race in wanton sport,
Gambolling round him, slyly steal away,
And, straddling o'er it, show their horsemanship
By raising round the clouds of summer sand,
While still he smiles, yet chides them for the trick.
His silver locks upon his shoulders spread,
And not ungraceful is his stoop of age.
No stranger passes him without regard;
And every neighbour stops to wish him well,   40
And ask him his opinion of the weather.
They fret not at the length of his discourse,
But listen with respect to his remarks
Upon the various seasons he remembers;
For well he knows the many divers signs
Which do foretell high winds, or rain, or drought,
Or aught that may affect the rising crop.
The silken-clad, who courtly breeding boast,
Their own discourse still sweetest to their ears,
May grumble at the old man's lengthened story,   50
But here it is not so.——

From every chimney mounts the curling smoke,
Muddy and grey, of the new evening fire;
On every window smokes the family supper,
Set out to cool by the attentive housewife,
While cheerful groups at every door convened
Bawl 'cross the narrow lane the parish news,
And oft the bursting laugh disturbs the air.
But see who comes to set them all agag!
The weary-footed pedlar with his pack.   60
How stiff he bends beneath his bulky load!
Covered with dust, slipshod, and out at elbows;
His greasy hat sits backward on his head;
His thin straight hair divided on his brow
Hangs lank on either side his glistening cheeks,
And woebegone yet vacant is his face.
His box he opens and displays his ware.
Full many a varied row of precious stones
Cast forth their dazzling lustre to the light.
To the desiring maiden's wishful eye   70
The ruby necklace shows its tempting blaze;
The china buttons, stamped with love-device,
Attract the notice of the gaping youth;
Whilst streaming garters, fastened to a pole,

agag] agape

433

Aloft in air their gaudy stripes display,
And from afar the distant stragglers lure.
The children leave their play and round him flock;
E'en sober aged grand-dame quits her seat,
Where by the door she twines her lengthened threads,
Her spindle stops, and lays her distaff by,   80
Then joins with step sedate the curious throng.
She praises much the fashions of her youth,
And scorns each gaudy nonsense of the day;
Yet not ill-pleased the glossy ribband views,
Uprolled, and changing hues with every fold,
New measured out to deck her daughter's head.

   Now red but languid, the last weakly beams
Of the departing sun across the lawn
Deep gild the top of the long sweepy ridge,
And shed a scattered brightness, bright but cheerless,   90
Between the openings of the rifted hills;
Which, like the farewell looks of some dear friend,
That speak him kind, yet sadden as they smile,
But only serve to deepen the low vale,
And make the shadows of the night more gloomy.
The varied noises of the cheerful village
By slow degrees now faintly die away,
And more distinct each feeble sound is heard
That gently steals adown the river's bed,
Or through the wood comes with the ruffling breeze.   100
The white mist rises from the swampy glens,
And from the dappled skirting of the heavens
Looks out the evening star.——
The lover skulking in the neighbouring copse
(Whose half-seen form shown through the thickened air,
Large and majestic, makes the traveller start,
And spreads the story of the haunted grove),
Curses the owl, whose loud ill-omened scream,
With ceaseless spite, robes from his watchful ear
The well-known footsteps of his darling maid;   110
And, fretful, chases from his face the night-fly,
Who, buzzing round his head, doth often skim,
With fluttering wing, across his glowing cheek:
For all but him in deep and balmy sleep
Forget the toil of the oppressive day;
Shut is the door of every scattered cot,
And silence dwells within.

                                        (1790)

434

280   *Night Scenes of Other Times* (Part II)

[The Ghost of Edward]

'Loud roars the wind that shakes this wall,
    It is no common blast:
Deep hollow sounds pass through my hall:
    O would the night were past!

'Methinks the demons of the air
    Upon the turrets growl,
While down the empty winding stair
    Their deepening murmurs roll.

'The glimmering fire cheers not the gloom,   10
    How blue its weakly ray!
And, like a taper in a tomb,
    But spreads the more dismay.

'Athwart its melancholy light
    The lengthened shadow falls;
My grandsires, to my troubled sight,
    Lower on me from these walls.

'Methinks yon angry warrior's head
    Doth in its casement frown,
And darts a look, as if it said,   20
    "Where hast thou laid my son?"

'But will these fancies never cease?
    O would the night were run!
My troubled soul can find no peace
    But with the morning sun.

'Vain hope! the guilty never rest:
    Dismay is always near;
There is a midnight in the breast
    No morn shall ever cheer.

'The weary hind is now at rest,
    Though lowly is his head;   30
How sweetly lies the guiltless breast
    Upon the hardest bed!

435

'The beggar, in his wretched haunt,
    May now a monarch be;
Forget his woe, forget his want,
    For all can sleep but me.

'I've dared whate'er the boldest can,
    Then why this childish dread?
I never feared a living man,
    And shall I fear the dead?   40

'No; whistling storms may shake my tower,
    And passing spirits scream:
Their shadowy arms are void of power,
    And but a gloomy dream.

'But lo! a form advancing slow
    Across my dusky hall!
Art thou a friend?—art thou a foe?
    O answer to my call!'

Still nearer to the glimmering light
    The towering figure strode,   50
Till full, and horrid to the sight,
    The murthered Edward stood.

His hand a broken dagger swayed,
    Like Time's dark threatening dart,
And pointed to the rugged blade
    That quivered in his heart.

The blood still trickled from his head,
    And clotted was his hair,
That on his manly shoulders spread;
    His mangled breast was bare.   60

His face was like the muddy sky
    Before the coming snow;
And dark and dreadful was his eye,
    And cloudy was his brow.

Pale Conrad shrunk, but grasped his sword;
    Fear thrilled in every vein;
His quivering lip half-spoke its word;
    He paused, and shrunk again.

'Pale bloody spectre, at this hour
   Why dost thou haunt the night?   70
Has the deep gloomy vault no power
   To keep thee from my sight?

'Why dost thou glare? Why dost thou wave
   That fatal cursèd knife?
The deed is done, and from the grave
   Who can recall to life?

'Why rolls thine eye beneath thy brow,
   Dark as the midnight storm?
What dost thou want? O let me know,
   But hide thy dreadful form.   80

'I'd give the life's blood from my heart
   To wash my crime away:
If thou'rt a spirit, O depart,
   Nor haunt a wretch of clay!

'Say, dost thou with the blessèd dwell?—
   Return and blessèd be!
Or com'st thou from the lowest hell?—
   I am more cursed than thee.'

The form advanced with solemn step,
   As though it meant to speak;   90
And thrice it moved its muttering lip,
   But silence did not break.

Then sternly stalked with heavy pace,
   Which shook the trembling wall,
And frowning turned its angry face,
   And vanished from the hall.

With fixèd eyes, pale Conrad stood,
   That from their sockets swell;
Back on his heart ran the cold blood,
   He shuddered as he fell.   100

Night fled, and through the windows 'gan
   The early light to play;
But on a more unhappy man
   Ne'er shone the dawning day.

The gladsome sun all nature cheers,
　　But cannot charm his cares;
Still dwells his mind with gloomy fears,
　　And murthered Edward glares.

(1790)

281　　　　　　　*A Reverie*

BESIDE a spreading elm, from whose high boughs
Like knotted tufts the crow's light dwelling shows,
Where screened from northern blasts, and winter-proof,
Snug stands the parson's barn with thatchèd roof;
At chaff-strewed door where, in the morning ray,
The gilded motes in mazy circles play,
And sleepy Comrade in the sun is laid,
More grateful to the cur than neighbouring shade;
In snowy shirt unbraced, brown Robin stood,
And leant upon his flail in thoughtful mood:　　　　10
His full round cheek where deeper flushes glow,
The dewy drops which glisten on his brow;
His dark cropped pate that erst at church or fair,
So smooth and silky, showed his morning's care,
Which, all uncouth in matted locks combined,
Now, ends erect, defies the ruffling wind;
His neck-band loose, and hosen rumpled low,
A careful lad, nor slack at labour, show.
Nor scraping chickens chirping 'mongst the straw,
Nor croaking rook o'erhead, nor chattering daw;　　20
Loud-breathing cow amongst the rampy weeds,
Nor grunting sow that in the furrow feeds;
Nor sudden breeze that shakes the quaking leaves,
And lightly rustles through the scattered sheaves;
Nor floating straw that skims athwart his nose,
The deeply-musing youth may discompose.
For Nelly fair, the blithest village maid,
Whose tuneful voice beneath the hedgerow-shade,
At early milking, o'er the meadows borne,
E'er cheered the ploughman's toil at rising morn:　　30
The neatest maid that e'er, in linen gown,
Bore cream and butter to the market town:
The tightest lass, that, with untutored air,
E'er footed alehouse floor at wake or fair,
Since Easter last had Robin's heart possessed,

281 rampy] juicy

And many a time disturbed his nightly rest.
Full oft, returning from the loosened plough,
He slacked his pace, and knit his thoughtful brow;
And oft, ere half his thresher's task was o'er,
Would muse, with arms across, at cooling door:⁣   40
His mind thus bent, with downcast eyes he stood,
And leant upon his flail in thoughtful mood.
His soul o'er many a soft remembrance ran,
And, muttering to himself, the youth began:

   'Ah! happy is the man whose early lot
Hath made him master of a furnished cot;
Who trains the vine that round his window grows,
And after setting sun his garden hoes;
Whose wattled pales his own enclosure shield,
Who toils not daily in another's field.   50
Where'er he goes, to church or market-town,
With more respect he and his dog are known;
A brisker face he wears at wake or fair,
Nor views with longing eyes the pedlar's ware,
But buys at will or ribbands, gloves or beads,
And willing maidens to the alehouse leads;
And, oh! secure from toils which cumber life,
He makes the maid he loves an easy wife.
Ah, Nelly! canst thou, with contented mind,
Become the helpmate of a labouring hind,   60
And share his lot, whate'er the chances be,
Who hath no dower but love to fix on thee?
Yes, gayest maid may meekest matron prove,
And things of little note may 'token love.
When from the church thou cam'st at eventide
And I and red-haired Susan by thy side,
I pulled the blossoms from the bending tree,
And some to Susan gave, and some to thee;
Thine were the best, and well thy smiling eye
The difference marked, and guessed the reason why.   70
When on a holiday we rambling strayed,
And passed old Hodge's cottage in the glade;
Neat was the garden dressed, sweet hummed the bee,
I wished both cot and Nelly made for me;
And well methought thy very eyes revealed
The self-same wish within thy breast concealed.
When artful, once, I sought my love to tell,
And spoke to thee of one who loved thee well,
You saw the cheat, and jeering homeward hied,
Yet secret pleasure in thy looks I spied.   80

Ah, gayest maid may meekest matron prove,
And smaller signs than these have 'tokened love.'

Now, at a distance, on the neighbouring plain,
With creaking wheels slow comes the heavy wain:
High on its towering load a maid appears,
And Nelly's voice sounds shrill in Robin's ears.
Quick from his hand he throws the cumbrous flail,
And leaps with lightsome limbs the enclosing pale.
O'er field and fence he scours, and furrow wide,
With wakened Comrade barking by his side;   90
Whilst tracks of trodden grain, and sidelong hay,
And broken hedge-flowers sweet, mark his impetuous way.

(1790)

282   from *An Address to the Muses*

YE are the spirits who preside
In earth and air and ocean wide;
In hissing flood and crackling fire;
In horror dread and tumult dire;
In stilly calm and stormy wind,
And rule the answering changes in the human mind.

High on the tempest-beaten hill,
Your misty shapes ye shift at will;
The wild fantastic clouds ye form;
Your voice is in the midnight storm,   10
Whilst in the dark and lonely hour,
Oft starts the boldest heart, and owns your secret power.

From you, when growling storms are past,
And lightning ceases on the waste,
And when the scene of blood is o'er,
And groans of death are heard no more,
Still holds the mind each parted form,
Like after-echoing of th' o'erpassed storm.

When closing glooms o'erspread the day,
And what we love has passed away,   20
Ye kindly bid each pleasing scene
Within the bosom still remain,
Like moons who do their watches run
With the reflected brightness of the parted sun.

The shining day, and nightly shade,
The cheerful plain and gloomy glade,
The homeward flocks, and shepherd's play,
The busy hamlet's closing day,
Full many a breast with pleasures swell,
Who ne'er shall have the gift of words to tell.   30

Oft when the moon looks from on high,
And black around the shadows lie;
And bright the sparkling waters gleam,
And rushes rustle by the stream,
Shrill sounds and fairy forms are known
By simple 'nighted swains, who wander late alone.

Ye kindle up the inward glow,
Ye strengthen every outward show;
Ye overleap the strongest bar,
And join what Nature sunders far: 40
And visit oft, in fancies wild,
The breast of learned sage, and simple child.

From him who wears a monarch's crown
To the unlettered artless clown,
All in some strange and lonely hour
Have felt, unsought, your secret power,
And loved your roving fancies well:
You add but to the bard the art to tell.

Ye mighty spirits of the song,
To whom the poet's prayers belong,   50
My lowly bosom to inspire,
And kindle with your sacred fire,
Your wild obscuring heights to brave,
Is boon, alas! too great for me to crave.

But O, such sense of matter bring!
As they who feel and never sing
Wear on their hearts; it will avail
With simple words to tell my tale;
And still contented will I be,
Though greater inspirations never fall to me.   60

(1790)

283   *A Mother to her Waking Infant*

Now in thy dazzling half-oped eye,
Thy curlèd nose and lip awry,
Thy up-hoist arms and noddling head,
And little chin with chrystal spread,
Poor helpless thing! what do I see,
    That I should sing of thee?

From thy poor tongue no accents come,
Which can but rub thy toothless gum;
Small understanding boasts thy face,
Thy shapeless limbs nor step nor grace;   10
A few short words thy feats may tell,
    And yet I love thee well.

When sudden wakes the bitter shriek,
And redder swells thy little cheek;
When rattled keys thy woes beguile,
And through the wet eye gleams the smile,
Still for thy weakly self is spent
    Thy little silly plaint.

But when thy friends are in distress,
Thou'lt laugh and chuckle ne'er the less;   20
Nor e'en with sympathy be smitten,
Though all are sad but thee and kitten;
Yet little varlet that thou art,
    Thou twitchest at the heart.

Thy rosy cheek so soft and warm;
Thy pinky hand and dimpled arm;
Thy silken locks that scantly peep,
With gold-tipped ends, where circles deep
Around thy neck in harmless grace
So soft and sleekly hold their place,   30
Might harder hearts with kindness fill,
    And gain our right good will.

Each passing clown bestows his blessing,
Thy mouth is worn with old wives' kissing:
E'en lighter looks the gloomy eye
Of surly sense, when thou art by;
And yet I think whoe'er they be,
    They love thee not like me.

dazzling] dazed   noddling] nodding

Perhaps when time shall add a few
Short years to thee, thou'lt love me too.   40
Then wilt thou through life's weary way
Become my sure and cheering stay:
Wilt care for me, and be my hold,
   When I am weak and old.

Thou'lt listen to my lengthened tale,
And pity me when I am frail—
But see, the sweepy spinning fly
Upon the window takes thine eye.
Go to thy little senseless play—
   Thou dost not heed my lay.   50

(1790)

284   *A Child to his Sick Grandfather*

GRAND-DAD, they say you're old and frail,
Your stockèd legs begin to fail:
Your knobbèd stick (that was my horse)
Can scarce support your bended corse;
While back to wall you lean so sad,
   I'm vexed to see you, dad.

You used to smile and stroke my head,
And tell me how good children did;
But now, I wot not how it be,
You take me seldom on your knee;   10
Yet ne'ertheless I am right glad
   To sit beside you, dad.

How lank and thin your beard hangs down!
Scant are the white hairs on your crown;
How wan and hollow are your cheeks!
Your brow is rough with crossing breaks;
But yet, for all his strength is fled,
   I love my own old dad.

The housewives round their potions brew,
And gossips come to ask for you: 20
And for your weal each neighbour cares,
And good men kneel, and say their pray'rs:
And ev'rybody looks so sad,
   When you are ailing, dad.

443

You will not die, and leave us then?
Rouse up and be our dad again.
When you are quiet and laid in bed,
We'll doff our shoes and softly tread:
And when you wake we'll aye be near,
   To fill old dad his cheer.   30

When through the house you shift your stand,
I'll lead you kindly by the hand;
When dinner's set, I'll with you bide,
And aye be serving by your side;
And when the weary fire burns blue,
   I'll sit and talk with you.

I have a tale both long and good,
About a partlet and her brood;
And cunning greedy fox that stole,
By dead of midnight, through a hole,
Which slyly to the hen-roost led—   40
   You love a story, dad?

And then I have a wond'rous tale
Of men all clad in coats of mail,
With glitt'ring swords—you nod, I think?
Your fixèd eyes begin to wink;
Down on your bosom sinks your head;
   You do not hear me, dad.

                (1790)

285   *The Horse and his Rider*

BRACED in the sinewy vigour of thy breed,
In pride of generous strength, thou stately steed,
Thy broad chest to the battle's front is given,
Thy mane fair floating to the winds of heaven.
Thy champing hoofs the flinty pebbles break;
Graceful the rising of thine archèd neck.
White-churning foam thy chafèd bits enlock;
And from thy nostril bursts the curling smoke.
Thy kindling eyeballs brave the glaring south,
And dreadful is the thunder of thy mouth;   10
Whilst low to earth thy curving haunches bend,
Thy sweepy tail involved in clouds of sand;
Erect in air thou rear'st thy front of pride,
And ring'st the plated harness on thy side.

But lo! what creature, godly to the sight,
Dares thus bestride thee, chafing in thy might,
Of portly stature and determined mien,
Whose dark eye dwells beneath a brow serene,
And forward looks unmoved to fields of death,
And, smiling, gently strokes thee in thy wrath,   20
Whose brandished falchion dreaded gleams afar?
It is a British soldier, armed for war!

(1790)

REBEKAH CARMICHAEL (later HAY)
(*fl.* 1790–1806)

From her *Poems* (Edinburgh, 1790), to which Burns subscribed, it is apparent that
she had been orphaned at an early age. She later married, but was left destitute on the
early death of her husband. Her son David Ramsay Hay (*c.* 1798–1866) was educated
by David Ramsay, an Edinburgh banker, after whom he was named. (He later had
some reputation as a decorative artist and author, and was involved in the decoration
of Sir Walter Scott's library at Abbotsford.) In a letter of 1806 to the Edinburgh
bookseller and publisher, Archibald Constable, she begged a small loan: 'what I have
suffered in my illness and still suffer from want of suport [*sic*] is more than I can
describe.' The letter also sends Constable a 'small composition', presumably some
extempore lines on the recent funeral of Sir William Forbes, the Edinburgh banker
and author, which were printed on a single sheet.

286   *The Tooth*

O LOOK not, lady, with disdain!
    Nor fill our hearts with ruth;
You still may charm some humble swain,
    Although you've lost a tooth!

Thy beaming eyes are black as jet,
    And pretty is thy mouth;
No angel ever smiled so sweet,
    Before you lost a tooth.

While fondly thus you strive to shine
    In all the charms of youth,   10
Your face and figure are divine,
    But O! you've lost a tooth.

Ah! why that angry frown? for shame!
  I only speak the truth:
It cannot hurt Eliza's fame
  To say she's lost a tooth.

But search some hearts, perhaps you'll find
  A greater fault, forsooth;
O! it were well for womankind
  Were all their loss a tooth!   20

(1790)

287   *A Young Lass's Soliloquy*

An' so it seems it is reported
That I hae ne'er been woo'd nor courted,
    But de'il speed lies;
The bonny lads came flocking round me,
Enough in conscience to confound me,
    Like hives of bees.

But I was cald as winter snaw,
An' nae return would ever shaw
    For a' their favours;
An' now ye see ye hae been wrang,   10
Nae mair o' me ye'll make a sang,
    But ha'd ye'r clavers.

Yet out o' spite I'll tell the rest,
An' which o' them I likèd best,
    Wha was sae clever
To melt this icy breast o' mine,
To take my heart without design,
    An' keep it ever.

It was a lad wi' yellow hair,
Wi' rosy cheeks, an' forehead fair,   20
    An' light blue een;
The like o' him on hill or dale,
In borough's town, or country vale,
    Was never seen.

287 ha'd] hold   clavers] chatter

O vow but he was proud an' saucy,
An' better loo'd anither lassy,
    Wha had some siller;
But I hae five an' five good nails,
An', ere my strength or courage fails,
    I'll wi' them till her.   30

(1790)

ANN FRANCIS (née GITTINS)
(1738–1800)

She was the daughter of the Revd Daniel Gittins (d. 1761), Rector of South Stoke, near Arundel, Sussex, and Vicar of Leominster, who educated her in the classical languages and in Hebrew, in which she became a 'great proficient'. She married the Revd Robert Bransly Francis, Rector of Edgefield, near Holt, Norfolk. Although 'the greater part of her life was passed in domestic retirement', she was 'honoured with the friendship and correspondence of many very eminent and learned men', including William Jones of Nayland and John Parkhouse, author of a Hebrew lexicon. *A Poetical Translation of the Song of Solomon, From the Original Hebrew* (1781), dedicated to Parkhouse, is in dramatic form. Her preface clearly anticipates the reaction that a woman would lack the learning for such a translation, and that such erotic (albeit allegorical) material was unfit 'for the exercise of a *female* pen'. She later published *The Obsequies of Demetrius Poliorcetes: A Poem* (1785) and *A Poetical Epistle from Charlotte to Werther* (1788), one of many responses by women in the 1780s to Goethe's novel.

Her *Miscellaneous Poems, By a Lady* (Norwich, 1790), including several by her husband, are mostly on less ambitious and more domestic subjects. Subsequently she published a broadside ballad, *A Plain Address to My Neighbours* (1798), a stern warning of the consequences of a French invasion to liberate the British working classes. She died at Edgefield Parsonage on 7 November 1800, praised in an obituary not merely for her 'mental acquirements', but as a daughter, wife, and mother.

288   from *An Elegy on a Favourite Cat*

WHEN cats like him submit to fate,
    And seek the Stygian strand,
In silent woe and mimic state
    Should mourn the feline band.

For me—full oft at eventide,
    Enrapt in thought profound,
I hear his solemn footsteps glide,
    And startle at the sound!

siller] silver   till] to

Oft as the murmuring gale draws near
  (To fancy's rule consigned),   10
His tuneful purr salutes my ear,
  Soft-floating on the wind.

Among the aerial train, perchance,
  My Bully now resides,
Or with the nymphs leads up the dance—
  Or skims the argent tides.

Ye rapid Muses, haste away,
  His wandering shade attend,
Hunt him through bush and fallow grey,
  And up the hill ascend;   20

O'er russet heath extend your view,
  And through th' embrowning wood;
On the brisk gale his form pursue,
  Or trace him o'er the flood:

If he a lucid Sylph should fly,
  With various hues bedight,
The Muse's keen pervading eye
  Shall catch the streaming light. . . .

(1790)

ANN RADCLIFFE (née WARD)
(1764–1823)

Born in London, she was the only daughter of William Ward, a haberdasher, and his wife Ann Oates. Her origins in 'trade' may explain her later uneasiness in fashionable society, as well as the emphasis placed by her early biographers on the fact that her parents were related to the distinguished medical families of Jebb and Cheselden. Her uncle Thomas Bentley was a partner of Josiah Wedgwood, which is no doubt why, when she was 8, her father moved to Bath to manage a shop selling Wedgwood china. In January 1787 she married at Bath William Radcliffe, a recent graduate of Oriel College, Oxford. Although admitted to the Middle Temple, he lived at first on translating and journalism, editing *The Gazette* from 1791 to 1793. It is possible that she turned to fiction to supplement their income, although it was also suggested that, without children, she found it an occupation in the evenings when her husband was working late on his newspaper.

   The Castles of Athlin and Dunbayne (1789) and *A Sicilian Romance* (1790) were followed by three novels which made her reputation as the most prominent writer of

'Gothic' fiction: *The Romance of the Forest* (1791), *The Mysteries of Udolpho* (1794), and *The Italian* (1797). She also published an *Account of a Journey . . . through Holland and the Western Frontier of Germany* (1795). Such was her popularity that she was able to sell the copyright of *The Mysteries of Udolpho* for £500 and of *The Italian* for £800 (which may have enabled her husband in that year to become the proprietor and editor of *The English Chronicle*). After a decade of increasing celebrity, however, she stopped publishing, although *Gaston de Blondeville*, written in 1802, appeared posthumously in 1826. Charlotte Smith reported in 1802 that Mrs Radcliffe had been 'restrained by the authority of her husband from calling any more "spirits from the vasty deep" of her imagination'; but, having inherited property from her parents in 1798 and 1800, she may have had less financial motivation, and she also suffered from an old-fashioned uneasiness about being a professional author.

According to an early biographer, the 'old gentility' of her relatives fostered 'a natural repugnance to authorship, which she never entirely lost, even after her splendid success was assured'. Although she is said to have met Elizabeth Montagu and Hester (Thrale) Piozzi, and Elizabeth Carter tried in vain to meet her, she played no part in literary society: 'The very thought of appearing in person as the author of her romances shocked the delicacy of her mind.' She could not 'publish *herself*' or sink 'the gentlewoman in the novelist'. She 'rarely alluded to her novels', disliked 'the increasing familiarity of modern manners', and 'confined herself, with delicate apprehensiveness, to the circle of domestic duties and pleasures'. She was also 'tremblingly alive' to reflections on 'the personal character she valued far above literary fame', as is clear from her hypersensitive reaction to references to herself in the published letters of Elizabeth Carter (1809) and Anna Seward (1811). Lacking 'that confidence which is necessary to mixed society', her greatest pleasure was travelling in England, mostly near the south coast, which she usually did with her husband once or twice a year. Her notes on these journeys between 1797 and 1812 were published posthumously. For one who had such impact on her contemporaries, her life was remarkably uneventful, without important incidents or friendships. Secluded from society throughout her life, she became even more of a recluse in her last twelve years, when she suffered increasingly from asthma and depression. Unsurprisingly, there were rumours that she had gone mad through brooding on Gothic horrors, or that she was already dead. In fact she died in London on 7 February 1823, survived by her husband.

She had often introduced verse into her novels and after 1802 seems to have written mainly poetry, including a long narrative poem, 'St. Alban's Abbey', a Metrical Tale', published posthumously with some shorter pieces as Vols. III and IV of *Gaston de Blondeville* (1826). These were reprinted as *Poetical Works* (2 vols., 1834). An unauthorized collection of verse from her fiction had appeared as *Poems* (1815), and was several times reprinted. Leigh Hunt said unsympathetically in 1847 that 'in her verse she is a tinselled nymph in a pantomime, calling up commonplaces with a wand', but the following poem would have had some freshness in the early 1790s.

289   *Song of a Spirit*

IN the sightless air I dwell,
  On the sloping sunbeams play;
Delve the cavern's inmost cell,
  Where never yet did daylight stray:

Dive beneath the green sea-waves,
  And gambol in the briny deeps;
Skim every shore that Neptune laves,
  From Lapland's plains to India's steeps.

Oft I mount with rapid force
  Above the wide earth's shadowy zone;   10
Follow the day-star's flaming course
  Through realms of space to thought unknown:

And listen oft celestial sounds
  That swell the air unheard of men,
As I watch my nightly rounds
  O'er woody steep, and silent glen.

Under the shade of waving trees,
  On the green bank of fountain clear,
At pensive eve I sit at ease,
  While dying music murmurs near.   20

And oft, on point of airy clift,
  That hangs upon the western main,
I watch the gay tints passing swift,
  And twilight veil the liquid plain.

Then, when the breeze has sunk away,
  And ocean scarce is heard to lave,
For me the sea-nymphs softly play
  Their dulcet shells beneath the wave.

Their dulcet shells! I hear them now,
  Slow swells the strain upon mine ear;   30
Now faintly falls—now warbles low,
  Till rapture melts into a tear.

The ray that silvers o'er the dew,
  And trembles through the leafy shade,
And tints the scene with softer hue,
  Calls me to rove the lonely glade;

Or hie me to some ruined tower,
  Faintly shown by moonlight gleam,
Where the lone wanderer owns my power
  In shadows dire that substance seem;   40

In thrilling sounds that murmur woe,
  And pausing silence make more dread;
In music breathing from below
  Sad solemn strains, that wake the dead.

Unseen I move—unknown am feared!
  Fancy's wildest dreams I weave;
And oft by bards my voice is heard
  To die along the gales of eve.

(1791)

MARIA (b. 1771?) and HARRIET (b. 1774?) FALCONAR

In December 1786, at the age of 15, Maria Falconar contributed two poems to the *European Magazine*, and during 1787 contributed again with her sister Harriet, who would be aged no more than 13. The number of precocious children who were finding their way into print at this period may be evidence of rising standards of education or of the decadence of fashionable poetic styles, which could be so easily mimicked. (Mrs Lennox's 11-year-old son George and 13-year-old John Drewitt contributed to magazines; in 1788 12-year-old John Morrison of Wolverhampton published a translation of two books of the *Aeneid*, and John Browne of Crewkerne, also aged 12, published his *Poetical Translations*. In 1789 14-year-old 'Susannah' published her *Poems* and in 1791 13-year-old Elizabeth Ogilvy Benger *The Female Geniad*. The 16-year-old Henry Francis Cary, whose *Sonnets and Odes* appeared in 1789, was unusual in going on to a prominent literary career.)

Joseph Johnson published the *Poems* of the Falconar sisters in 1788, when they were aged about 17 and 14, their 400 subscribers including the Duke of Northumberland, Hugh Blair, William Beloe, Richard Cosway, William Roscoe, Anna Seward, Helen Maria Williams, as well as Robert Falconar of Nairn in Scotland and James Falconar of Drakies, near Inverness, the only clue to the origins of the young authors. The uninformative preface states that since they were children 'these lisping Sapphos' had stolen from 'the necessary refreshments of repose those hours which others appropriate to rest; and these they employed in such studies and meditations as their little fancies suggested to them'. The volume consists mainly of ballad narratives and verses on such topics as Fancy and Remorse. Also in 1788 they published a collection of *Poems on Slavery*, a subject on which More, Williams, and Yearsley were also writing at this time. Their *Poetic Laurels* (1791), when they would be aged about 20 and 17, had fewer subscribers, but shows them adapting to the new poetic tastes of the 1790s: Harriet's 'A Fragment', for example, is a visionary poem full of spectres, frenzy, and despair. Thereafter they seem to have fallen silent: perhaps, as the following (untypically facetious) lines to their reviewers may suggest, they were ready for the anonymity of marriage, but they could have continued publishing under their unidentified married names.

290   *A Prefatory Epistle [to the Reviewers]*

STAY, gentle Child of Taste! who'er thou art,
Listen, for mercy's sake, and take our part;
See where the critics, poring o'er our book,
Threat with each motion, kill with every look,
Growl o'er the titlepage—'What's here, Miss Flirt?
You'd better make a pudding—or a shirt;
Poetic Laurels! there's a pretty puff!
Poor silly wenches, what a string of stuff!
Sure madness rages now with every woman,
And, when one favourite scheme has grown too common,   10
With matchless art she strikes some novel's plan,
To soothe her pride and tyrannise o'er man;
Tells an affected, sentimental story,
Or prates in senseless rhymes of Fame and Glory.
These modern Sapphos are conceited creatures,
They sport their thoughts as others do their features;
These but coquette it with a different part,
And seize the head, while others charm the heart.
'Twere best would each young woman mend her life,
And learn to be a decent, careful wife.'   20
      There goes my work—I'll find some fair pretence
To face the Board, and make my own defence:
'May't please ye, reverend sirs, we own the crime,
So long to trespass on your precious time;
And since you seem to think domestic fetters
Become us better than the love of letters,
Assist us, dear messieurs—have you no friend,
Your sons, perhaps yourselves, to recommend?
Myself or sister, blest with such a mate,
Will quit ambition and the tuneful state;   30
Conform ourselves to be whate'er ye choose,
And cease to plague you with the jabbering Muse;
Nay, the last gleam of our poetic rays
Shall shine an Ode in quarto to your praise.'

(1791)

JANET LITTLE (later RICHMOND)
(1759–1813)

She was the daughter of George Little of Nether Bogside, Ecclefechan, Dumfries. She had only 'a common education' and became a servant to a local clergyman, but she loved reading and had acquired some reputation as a 'rustic poetess' by 1788, when she sought a post as chambermaid or nurse with Mrs Frances Dunlop of Dunlop House, Ayrshire, the friend and correspondent of Robert Burns. Mrs Dunlop recommended her to her daughter, recently married to James Henri, a French refugee, who from 1789 rented Loudoun Castle. She was eventually put in charge of the dairy at Loudoun, from where she wrote to Burns on 12 July 1789, enclosing a poem addressed to him and hoping for his 'favour and friendship'. Mrs Dunlop also wrote on her behalf to Burns on the following day: 'Her outside promises nothing; her mind only bursts forth on paper.' (Another source describes her as 'a very tall masculine woman, with dark hair, and features somewhat coarse'.) All too aware of the number of humble Scottish poets who were trying to imitate his own recent success, Burns was at first cautious, but later advised Mrs Dunlop about the publication of Janet's poems, and helped with the accompanying subscription. Of Janet Little's hopes for financial independence, Mrs Dunlop wrote (23 September 1790) that 'ten guineas would make her as happy as worldly circumstances could do . . . since her modest wishes are placed within such humble bounds'. Another poet praised by Mrs Dunlop for his 'disinterested, generous conduct' to Janet was Alexander Wilson (1766–1813), the pedlar poet, later a famous ornithologist in America.

Among the subscribers to *The Poetical Works of Janet Little, The Scotch Milkmaid* (Ayr, 1792) were Burns, Mrs Dunlop (who, with relatives, took twenty copies), and James Boswell, to whom she had hoped to dedicate the book. Boswell had advised her to dedicate it instead to a titled lady, who turned out to be the 11-year-old Flora, Countess of Loudoun (who took twelve copies), then under the guardianship of the Countess of Dumfries. Janet Little is said to have made £50 from the subscription. Her poems include 'On a Visit to Mr. Burns' (in 1791, when he came home with a broken arm; pp. 111–12); 'An Epistle to a Lady' (pp. 125–8), in which she describes the activities of the 'lower class' at Loudoun, and refers to herself as 'Our crazy-pated dairy-maid'; 'An Epistle to Mr. Robert Burns' (pp. 160–3); and some amiable lines 'To My Aunty' (pp. 164–6). After Mrs Henri's departure from Loudoun (her husband had died in June 1790), Janet Little married John Richmond (c.1741–1819), a labourer at the Castle, who was a widower with five children and some eighteen years her senior. She died at Loudoun on 15 March 1813, after a short illness described as 'a cramp in the stomach'. She had been a member of the dissenting congregation at Galston and some religious poems were printed after her death.

291 *Given to a Lady Who Asked me to Write a Poem*

'In royal Anna's golden days,
Hard was the task to gain the bays:
Hard was it then the hill to climb;
Some broke a neck, some lost a limb.
The votaries for poetic fame
Got aff decrepit, blind an' lame:
Except that little fellow Pope,
Few ever then got near its top:
An' Homer's crutches he may thank,
Or down the brae he'd got a clank.   10

'Swift, Thomson, Addison an' Young
Made Pindus echo to their tongue,
In hopes to please a learned age;
But Doctor Johnson, in a rage,
Unto posterity did show
Their blunders great, their beauties few.
But now he's dead, we weel may ken;
For ilka dunce maun hae a pen,
To write in hamely, uncouth rhymes;
An' yet forsooth they please the times.   20

'A ploughman chiel, Rab Burns his name,
Pretends to write; an' thinks nae shame
To souse his sonnets on the court;
An' what is strange, they praise him for't.
Even folks, wha're of the highest station,
Ca' him the glory of our nation.

'But what is more surprising still,
A milkmaid must tak up her quill;
An' she will write, shame fa' the rabble!
That think to please wi' ilka bawble.   30
They may thank heaven auld Sam's asleep:
For could he ance but get a peep,
He, wi' a vengeance wad them sen'
A' headlong to the dunces' den.

'Yet Burns, I'm tauld, can write wi' ease,
An' a' denominations please;

souse] pour

454

Can wi' uncommon glee impart
A usefu' lesson to the heart;   40
Can ilka latent thought expose,
An' Nature trace whare'er she goes:
Of politics can talk wi' skill,
Nor dare the critics blame his quill.

   'But then a rustic country quean
To write—was e'er the like o't seen?
A milkmaid poem-books to print:
Mair fit she wad her dairy tent;
Or labour at her spinning-wheel,
An' do her wark baith swift an' weel.   50
Frae that she may some profit share,
But winna frae her rhyming ware.
Does she, poor silly thing, pretend
The manners of our age to mend?
Mad as we are, we're wise enough
Still to despise sic paultry stuff.

   'May she wha writes, of wit get mair,
An' a' that read an ample share
Of candour every fault to screen,
That in her doggerel scrawls are seen.'

                                                          60

   All this and more, a critic said;
I heard and slunk behind the shade:
So much I dread their cruel spite,
My hand still trembles when I write.

                                        (1792)

ELLEN TAYLOR
(*fl.* 1792)

She was the daughter of 'an indigent Cottager'. Formerly a servant, she was keeping a small school by the time her *Poems* appeared at Dublin in 1792 in a pamphlet of a mere fourteen pages. They were published without her knowledge to raise money for her, but only forty subscribers are listed, including Thomas Tickell, probably the grandson of the early eighteenth-century poet. Some of her poems had previously appeared in newspapers. One of them, 'To a Gentleman who had lent her some books', mentions her reading of Milton, Thomson and Young.

          quean] lass   tent] tend

292 *Written by the Barrow side, where she was sent to wash Linen*

THY banks, O Barrow, sure must be
　The Muses' choicest haunt,
Else why so pleasing thus to me,
　Else why my soul enchant?

To view thy dimpled surface here,
　Fond fancy bids me stay;
But Servitude, with brow austere,
　Commands me straight away.

Were Lethe's virtues in thy stream,
　How freely would I drink,　　　　　　　10
That not so much as on the name
　Of books I e'er might think.

I can but from them learn to know
　What misery's complete,
And feel more sensibly each blow
　Dealt by relentless fate.

In them I oft have pleasure found,
　But now it's all quite fled.
With fluttering heart, I lay me down,
　And rise with aching head.　　　　　　20

For such a turn ill suits the sphere
　Of life in which I move,
And rather does a load of care
　Than any comfort prove.

Thrice happy she, condemned to move
　Beneath the servile weight,
Whose thoughts ne'er soar one inch above
　The standard of her fate.

But far more happy is the soul,
　Who feels the pleasing sense;　　　　　30
And can indulge without control
　Each thought that flows from thence.

Since naught of these my portion is,
    But the reverse of each,
That I shall taste but little bliss,
    Experience doth me teach.

Could cold insensibility
    Through my whole frame take place,
Sure then from grief I might be free:
    Yes, then I'd hope for peace.   40

(1792)

HENRIETTA O'NEILL (née BOYLE)
(1758–93)

She was the only child of Charles Boyle, Lord Dungarvon (son of the 5th Earl of Cork and Orrery) and his wife Susanna Hoare of Stourhead, the daughter of Henry Hoare the banker. Her parents had married in 1753 but are said to have been unhappy together. After her father's death in 1759 at the age of 30, her mother (whom Horace Walpole in 1776 described as 'mad') married Thomas Brudenell-Bruce, later 1st Earl of Ailesbury. In October 1777 Henrietta married John O'Neill, Irish politician, of Shane's Castle, Antrim. Her two sons, described in the poem below, were born in 1779 and 1780. She was an excellent amateur actress, wrote an epilogue for a performance of *Cymbeline* in which she acted with Lord Edward Fitzgerald, and was a friend and patroness of Mrs Siddons. During her visits to London she became friendly with Charlotte Smith (see nos. 237–43), for whom she wrote her 'Ode to the Poppy', first published in Mrs Smith's *Desmond* in 1792. By then she appears to have been suffering from poor health and to have visited Portugal in an attempt to recover from it. In September 1791 she was at Shane's Castle, having 'lately returned from Portugal in perfect health'. (There seems to be no evidence to confirm later rumours that her problem was an addiction to the opium she celebrated in verse.) She must soon have returned to Portugal, since she died there at the Caldas de Rainha near Lisbon on 3 September 1793. William Withering, physician and scientist, described her as 'a lady of fascinating manners and exquisite poetical taste', who had been friendly with his family at St Jozé, and further details of her residence in Portugal and her monument in the English Cemetery at Lisbon (near the grave of Henry Fielding) were recorded by Robert Bisset Scott in 1833. Scott records that she had presented a copy of W. J. Mickle's translation of Camoens' *Lusiad* to the library of the Abbey of Alcobaça, 'with an elegant letter affixed, of thanks for the courtesies she had experienced from the Fathers of St Bernard and St Dominic'.

Her 'Ode to the Poppy', often reprinted in magazines, was called 'perhaps the most beautiful lyric production of the age' in an obituary in the *Anthologia Hibernica* in October 1793, which also describes her as 'a lady whose elegance of mind could only be surpassed by the charms of her person: uniting with the polish of courts the brilliancy of genius, she shone pre-eminent in the fashionable world', while remaining devoted, as a wife and mother, to 'domestic duties'. Charlotte Smith, who had already addressed her friend in a sonnet, included a poem on her death, as well as Mrs O'Neill's verses on her sons, in her *Elegiac Sonnets* in 1797. Mrs Smith described her friend's early death as 'a deprivation which has rendered *my* life a living death'. Her husband, who was created Baron O'Neill a few weeks after her death, and Viscount O'Neill in 1795, was killed in the rebellion in Ireland in 1798.

293   *Ode to the Poppy*

NOT for the promise of the laboured field,
Not for the good the yellow harvests yield,
      I bend at Ceres' shrine;
For dull, to humid eyes, appear
The golden glories of the year,
        Alas!—a melancholy worship's mine.

I hail the goddess for her scarlet flower!
      Thou brilliant weed,
      That does so far exceed
      The richest gifts gay Flora can bestow: 10
Heedless I passed thee, in life's morning hour,
      Thou comforter of woe,
Till sorrow taught me to confess thy power.

In early days, when Fancy cheats,
      A varied wreath I wove
Of laughing Spring's luxuriant sweets,
      To deck ungrateful Love:
The rose, or thorn, my labours crowned,
As Venus smiled, or Venus frowned;
But Love, and Joy, and all their train, are flown;   20
      E'en languid Hope no more is mine,
And I will sing of thee alone,
Unless, perchance, the attributes of Grief,
The cypress bud, and willow leaf,
      Their pale funereal foliage blend with thine.

      Hail, lovely blossom!—thou canst ease
      The wretched victims of Disease;
      Canst close those weary eyes in gentle sleep,
      Which never open but to weep;
      For, oh! thy potent charm   30
      Can agonizing Pain disarm;
Expel imperious Memory from her seat,
And bid the throbbing heart forget to beat.

Soul-soothing plant! that can such blessings give,
By thee the mourner bears to live!
    By thee the hopeless die!
Oh! ever 'friendly to despair,'
Might Sorrow's pallid votary dare,
Without a crime, that remedy implore,
    Which bids the spirit from its bondage fly,   40
I'd court thy palliative aid no more;

    No more I'd sue that thou shouldst spread
    Thy spell around my aching head,
    But would conjure thee to impart
    Thy balsam for a broken heart;
And by thy soft Lethean power,
    Inestimable flower,
Burst these terrestrial bonds, and other regions try.

                                        (1792)

294   *Written on Seeing her Two Sons at Play*

SWEET age of blest illusion! blooming boys,
Ah! revel long in childhood's thoughtless joys,
With light and pliant spirits, that can stoop
To follow, sportively, the rolling hoop;
To watch the sleeping top with gay delight,
Or mark, with raptured gaze, the sailing kite;
Or, eagerly pursuing Pleasure's call,
Can find it centred in the bounding ball!
Alas! the day *will* come, when sports like these
Must lose their magic, and their power to please;   10
Too swiftly fled, the rosy hours of youth
Shall yield their fairy-charms to mournful Truth;
Even now, a mother's fond prophetic fear
Sees the dark train of human ills appear;
Views various fortune for each lovely child,
Storms for the bold, and anguish for the mild;
Beholds already those expressive eyes
Beam a sad certainty of future sighs;
And dreads each suffering those dear breasts may know
In their long passage through a world of woe: 20
Perchance predestined every pang to prove,
That treacherous friends inflict, or faithless love;
For, ah! how few have found existence sweet,
Where grief is sure, but happiness deceit!

                                (Wr. by 1793; pub. 1797)

                        459

MARY LOCKE (later MISTER)
(*fl.* 1786–1816)

She was an orphan, brought up from about 1786 by her uncle, Edward Taylor of Hill House, Steeple Aston, Oxfordshire. Educated at Eton and Cambridge, Taylor had legal qualifications but, after travelling in Europe, settled in the country at the age of 30, in about 1771. *Cursory Remarks on Tragedy* (1774) has been attributed to him, and he wrote an unpublished play and some verse. His niece depicts him in her poem, *Eugenius: Or, Virtue in Retirement* (1791), in which his love of rural peace and virtue is contrasted with a boorish fox-hunting squire. In her 'Advertisement', Mary Locke describes herself as unworthy of 'the Attention of a World, with which a Life of Retirement has left her but little acquainted . . . the Author is young, uneducated, and inexperienced'. In September 1791 she began contributing verse, mostly sonnets, to the *Gentleman's Magazine*, often taking the increasingly fashionable subjectivity and melancholy to alarming extremes. One might have expected her uncle to be disconcerted to find 'Miss Locke' so frequently wandering alone through the 'black congenial Night' ('Envelop'd in her gloom, I love . . . to rove'). By July 1796 she had contributed twenty such poems. The series may have ended because of her uncle's ill health. He died in December 1797, 'after a most agonizing illness', leaving his niece substantial property at Steeple Aston and Middle Barton. She wrote the inscription on a tablet in the church: 'An orphan who for eleven years found an asylum beneath his hospitable roof raises this simple and sincere Memorial of gratitude to the Memory of her beloved and generous Benefactor.' She later sold her property and by 1808 had married a Welshman, William Mister. (In that year, she and her husband, who had a share of the advowson of Steeple Barton, presented to the vicarage Robert Wright, who is said never to have entered the church in the forty-two years he held the living.)

Under her married name of Mary Mister (the connection with Mary Locke has not hitherto been made) she published a series of children's books, including *Mungo, The Little Traveller* (by 1811), *Tales from the Mountains* (1811), *Little Anecdotes for Little People* (1814), and *The Adventures of a Doll* (1816).

295 *Sonnet*

I HATE the Spring in parti-coloured vest,
    What time she breathes upon the opening rose,
When every vale in cheerfulness is dressed,
    And man with grateful admiration glows.
Still may he glow, and love the sprightly scene,
    Who ne'er has felt the iron hand of Care;
But what avails to me a sky serene,
    Whose mind is torn with Anguish and Despair?
Give me the Winter's desolating reign,
    The gloomy sky in which no star is found;   10

Howl, ye wild winds, across the desert plain;
  Ye waters roar, ye falling woods resound!
Congenial horrors, hail! I love to see
All Nature mourn, and share my misery.

(1792)

296   *Sonnet*

'TIS dead of night; storms rend the troubled air:
  Fell Murder takes his solitary round,
Yet shrinks affrighted from the meteor's glare,
  And starts while falling trees and rocks resound.
From Alpine woods, his hunger to allay,
  Rushes the wolf, and tears the new-made grave;
Yet, though half-famished, quits his bloody prey,
  And slinks reluctant back to his lone cave.
But who is she, who 'mid the dreadful scene,
  Fearlessly treads the cliff's extremest verge,   10
Surveying all around with looks serene,
  The prostrate towers, rent rocks, and foaming surge?
'Tis Virtue—conscious she of blameless life,
  Nor shuns nor fears the elemental strife.

(1794)

MARY ALCOCK (née CUMBERLAND)
(*c.*1742–98)

She was the youngest daughter of Dr Denison Cumberland, Vicar of Stanwick, Northamptonshire, and his wife Joanna, daughter of Richard Bentley, classical scholar and Master of Trinity College, Cambridge. She accompanied her parents to Ireland when her father became Bishop of Clonfert in 1763. He became Bishop of Kilmore in 1772 but died in 1774, her mother dying in the following year. Her brother, Richard Cumberland (1732–1811), the dramatist, stated in his *Memoirs* (1807) that 'One surviving sister, the best and most benevolent of human beings, attended them in their last moments'. He also mentions his efforts to obtain compensation, 'for my sister's use', from the new Bishop for his father's expenditure on improvements in the diocese. At her death she was described as the widow of 'the late Archdeacon Alcock', perhaps John Alcock, who entered Trinity College, Dublin in 1750 and became Archdeacon of Raphoe. After his death she settled at Bath, where she contributed to Lady Miller's poetry sessions at Bath Easton in 1781. According to her niece Joanna Hughes, 'She never held herself up as a writer: when she resorted to her pen, it was either to amuse a leisure hour, to gratify an absent friend, or for the sublimer purpose of pouring out her heart in praise and thanksgivings to God.' Her niece also states that she had endured 'afflictions . . . of a very

461

peculiar nature' and had 'a corporeal frame so extremely feeble and defencless, that every blast of the climate might be supposed to threaten it with extinction'. In spite of this, she became 'the benefactress and protectress of a whole orphan family of dependent Nieces', of whom Joanna Hughes was one. She published *The Air-Balloon* (1784), an early reaction in verse to the current craze for aeronautics, and *The Confined Debtor. A Fragment from A Prison*, for the relief of debtors at Ilchester, as a result of which 'many debtors were liberated out of their confinement at Ilchester, and fourteen out of Newgate'. She died on 28 May 1798, while travelling from Bath to visit relatives in York, at the age of 56: 'Exhausted by long illness, which she endured with undiminished patience, she expired, without pain or struggle, in the house of her beloved friends and affectionate relatives, Mr. and Mrs. [George] Ashby, of Haselbeach, in Northamptonshire, and was buried in the parish church of that village.' Her *Poems* were posthumously published in 1799, edited with a short memoir by Joanna Hughes. The subscribers included the Prince and Princess of Wales, the Princesses Sophia and Amelia, Elizabeth Carter, William Cowper, John Kemble, Hannah More, Samuel Rogers, and George Romney.

297   *Instructions, Supposed to be Written in Paris, for the Mob in England*

> OF Liberty, Reforms and Rights I sing,
> Freedom, I mean, without or Church or King;
> Freedom to seize and keep whate'er I can,
> And boldly claim my right—The Rights of Man:
> Such is the blessèd liberty in vogue,
> The envied liberty to be a rogue;
> The right to pay no taxes, tithes or dues;
> The liberty to do whate'er I choose;
> The right to take by violence and strife
> My neighbour's goods and, if I please, his life;   10
> The liberty to raise a mob or riot,
> For spoil and plunder ne'er were got by quiet;
> The right to level and reform the great;
> The liberty to overturn the state;
> The right to break through all the nation's laws,
> And boldly dare to take rebellion's cause:
> Let all be equal, every man my brother;
> Why have one property, and not another?
> Why suffer titles to give awe and fear?
> There shall not long remain one British peer;   20
> Nor shall the criminal appallèd stand
> Before the mighty judges of the land;
> Nor judge nor jury shall there longer be,
> Nor any jail, but every prisoner free;

All law abolished and, with sword in hand,
We'll seize the property of all the land.
Then hail to Liberty, Reform and Riot!
Adieu, Contentment, Safety, Peace and Quiet!

(Wr. *c*.1792; pub. 1799)

298　　*The Chimney-Sweeper's Complaint*

A CHIMNEY-SWEEPER's boy am I;
　　Pity my wretched fate!
Ah, turn your eyes; 'twould draw a tear,
　　Knew you my helpless state.

Far from my home, no parents I
　　Am ever doomed to see;
My master, should I sue to him,
　　He'd flog the skin from me.

Ah, dearest madam, dearest sir,
　　Have pity on my youth;　　　　　　　　　10
Though black, and covered o'er with rags,
　　I tell you naught but truth.

My feeble limbs, benumbed with cold,
　　Totter beneath the sack,
Which ere the morning dawn appears
　　Is loaded on my back.

My legs you see are burnt and bruised,
　　My feet are galled by stones,
My flesh for lack of food is gone,
　　I'm little else but bones.　　　　　　　　20

Yet still my master makes me work,
　　Nor spares me day or night;
His 'prentice boy he says I am,
　　And he will have his right.

'Up to the highest top,' he cries,
　　'There call out *chimney-sweep*!'
With panting heart and weeping eyes,
　　Trembling I upwards creep.

But stop! no more—I see him come;
  Kind sir, remember me!   30
Oh, could I hide me under ground,
  How thankful should I be!

               (1799)

299   *Written in Ireland*

How blest would be Iërne's isle,
Were bigotry and all its guile
  Chased as a cloud away;
Then would Religion rear her head,
And sweet Contentment round her spread,
  Like a new dawn of day.

Come then, oh come, thou Truth divine!
With double radiance deign to shine,
  Thy heavenly light expand;
'Tis thine to chase these clouds of night,   10
Which darken and confound the sight
  In this divided land.

Attendant on thy prosp'rous train
I see sweet Peace with honest gain
  Spread wide her liberal hand,
While Discord, masked in deep disguise,
Abashed from forth her presence flies,
  Struck by her magic wand.

Around, where now in ruins lie
Thy sacred altars, I espy   20
  Fair Order rear each pile,
Whilst o'er thy wilds forlorn and waste,
Lo, Industry with nimble haste
  Makes hill and valley smile.

No more thy sons in fell despite,
A murderous band *arrayed in white*,
  Shall deal destruction round;
Each man beneath his vine shall rest,
No more by bigotry oppressed,
  But Truth by Peace be crowned.   30

Then shall Iërne tune her lyre,
And with united voice conspire
   To hail her happy state;
All hail, Iërne, Nature's pride,
No more shall wars thy land divide,
   Wert thou as good as great.

(1799)

300   *Modern Manners*

'OF modern Manners let me sing,'
   The gay Flirtilla cries—
'Manners, my dear! there's no such thing'—
   Her grandmamma replies.

'You say,' cries Miss, 'in days of yore
   People were highly bred;
But, thank my stars, those days are o'er,
   Those people are all dead.

'The world is now at ease and gay,
   Improved in every art,   10
Fraught with diversions night and day
   To charm and fire the heart.

'To live in these enlightened days
   Is surely life indeed;
Long may they last, Flirtilla prays,
   And joy to joy succeed!

'The mind, left free and uncontrolled,
   Makes pleasure all its aim;
Youth will not now by age be told,
   "My dear, you are to blame".   20

'Such Gothic parents, thanks to Heaven,
   Are now but rarely found;
Those, whom the fates to me have given,
   Live but in Pleasure's round.

'No tedious hours at home they pass
   In dull domestic care;
To think, they say, would soon, alas!
   Bring wrinkles and grey hair.

'Oft have I heard them jeer and joke
　　At wedlock's galling chain;
Then cry, "Thank Heaven, 'tis now no yoke;
　　We wed to part again".   30

'In former times, indeed, 'twas said
　　That hearts were joined above,
That women to their husbands paid
　　Obedience, truth and love.

'But title, pin-money and dower
　　Now join our hands for life;
No other ties than these have power
　　To couple man and wife.   40

'To these alone my thoughts aspire,
　　On these I fix my heart;
A wealthy husband I require—
　　I care not when we part.'

(1799)

301   *A Receipt for Writing a Novel*

WOULD you a favourite novel make,
Try hard your reader's heart to break,
For who is pleased, if not tormented?
(Novels for that were first invented.)
'Gainst nature, reason, sense, combine
To carry on your bold design,
And those ingredients I shall mention,
Compounded with your own invention,
I'm sure will answer my intention.
Of love take first a due proportion—   10
It serves to keep the heart in motion:
Of jealousy a powerful zest,
Of all tormenting passions best;
Of horror mix a copious share,
And duels you must never spare;
Hysteric fits at least a score,
Or, if you find occasion, more;
But fainting-fits you need not measure,
The fair ones have them at their pleasure;

dower] dowry

466

Of sighs and groans take no account,   20
But throw them in to vast amount;
A frantic fever you may add,
Most authors make their lovers mad;
Rack well your hero's nerves and heart,
And let your heroine take her part;
Her fine blue eyes were made to weep,
Nor should she ever taste of sleep;
Ply her with terrors day or night,
And keep her always in a fright,
But in a carriage when you get her,   30
Be sure you fairly overset her;
If she will break her bones—why let her.
Again, if e'er she walks abroad,
Of course you bring some wicked lord,
Who with three ruffians snaps his prey,
And to a castle speeds away;
There, close confined in haunted tower,
You leave your captive in his power,
Till dead with horror and dismay,
She scales the walls and flies away.   40

    Now you contrive the lovers' meeting,
To set your reader's heart a-beating,
But ere they've had a moment's leisure,
Be sure to interrupt their pleasure;
Provide yourself with fresh alarms
To tear 'em from each other's arms;
No matter by what fate they're parted,
So that you keep them broken-hearted.

    A cruel father some prepare
To drag her by her flaxen hair;   50
Some raise a storm, and some a ghost,
Take either, which may please you most.
But this you must with care observe,
That when you've wound up every nerve
With expectation, hope and fear,
Hero and heroine must disappear.
Some fill one book, some two without 'em,
And ne'er concern their heads about 'em:
This greatly rests the writer's brain,
For any story, that gives pain,   60
You now throw in—no matter what,
However foreign to the plot;

467

So it but serves to swell the book,
You foist it in with desperate hook—
A masquerade, a murdered peer,
His throat just cut from ear to ear—
A rake turned hermit—a fond maid
Run mad, by some false loon betrayed—
These stores supply the female pen,
Which writes them o'er and o'er again,   70
And readers likewise may be found
To circulate them round and round.

Now, at your fable's close, devise
Some grand event to give surprise—
Suppose your hero knows no mother—
Suppose he proves the heroine's brother—
This at one stroke dissolves each tie,
Far as from east to west they fly:
At length, when every woe's expended,
And your last volume's nearly ended,   80
Clear the mistake, and introduce
Some tattling nurse to cut the noose;
The spell is broke—again they meet
Expiring at each other's feet;
Their friends lie breathless on the floor—
You drop your pen; you can no more—
And ere your reader can recover,
They're married—and your history's over.

(1799)

MARY ROBINSON (née DARBY)
(1758–1800)

She was born at College Green, Bristol, the younger daughter of Captain John Darby
and his wife (maiden name Seys), who had five children. In the 1760s her father's
absence for three years on a project of establishing a whaling station on the coast of
Labrador left the family in financial difficulties. Mary was educated first at the school
in Bristol run by the sisters of Hannah More (see nos. 215–21) and later, after the
family's removal to London, at a school in Chelsea. Here her literary interests were
stimulated by a cultivated teacher, Mrs Meribah Lorrington, whose father had given
her a 'masculine education', but who also had an 'unfeminine propensity' to alcohol.
As she was often in 'a state of confirmed intoxication', the school had to be closed.
Lack of regular financial support from Captain Darby forced her mother to open her
own school for girls in Chelsea, at which Mary assisted in her early teens. On one of
his reappearances (her parents were eventually to separate) her father objected to

this occupation and she was sent to a finishing school in Marylebone run by a Mrs Hervey. Through Hussey, the dancing-teacher, who was also a ballet-master at Covent Garden Theatre, she met Thomas Hull, Arthur Murphy, and David Garrick, the last of whom encouraged her to take up acting.

On 12 April 1774, however, at the age of 15 she married Thomas Robinson, an articled clerk at Lincoln's Inn, whom her mother believed to be a man of means. For a time they lived fashionably, although she had to cope with the harrassment of her husband's libertine friends, such as the notorious Lord Lyttelton. Eventually her husband, as careless about money as about his wife, had to leave London to escape his creditors, and their daughter Mary Elizabeth was born in Wales on 18 November 1774. In 1775 he was arrested for debts of £1,200 and for some ten months she lived with him and her daughter in the King's Bench Prison. She had already planned a volume of *Poems* (1775), a copy of which she sent to the Duchess of Devonshire, from whom she received some assistance. She later wrote bitterly about the indifference of her other women friends to her plight: 'From that hour I have never felt the affection for my own sex which perhaps some women feel. . . . Indeed I have almost uniformly found my own sex my most inveterate enemies; I have experienced little kindness from them; though my bosom has often ached with the pang inflicted by their envy, slander, and malevolence.' During this period she also published *Captivity. A Poem; and Celadon and Lydia. A Tale* (1777), but was later embarrassed by these conventional early writings.

On his release her husband encouraged her ambitions as an actress and through Garrick and Sheridan she was engaged at Drury Lane Theatre, appearing first with great success as Juliet in December 1776. She continued to act for four seasons until her retirement from the stage in May 1780. Her second child died not long after her acting career began. In April 1778 her musical farce *The Lucky Escape* was performed. Late in 1779 she appeared as Perdita in *The Winter's Tale* and her beauty attracted the 17-year-old Prince of Wales (later George IV). After some negotiation through Lord Malden, 'Perdita' agreed to become the mistress of 'Florizel', on payment of a bond for £20,000 when the Prince came of age. After about a year the Prince lost interest, the royal bond was unpaid and, after a relationship which had been followed with intense interest in the press, she felt unable to resume her stage career. She accordingly demanded £25,000 for the return of the Prince's passionate letters to her. George III told Lord North in August 1781 that, after protracted negotiations, she had settled for £5,000, 'an enormous sum, but I wish to get my son out of this shameful scrape'. Subsequently she had affairs with Lord Malden (whose mistress, according to the Duchess of Devonshire and others, she had been before meeting the Prince) and Charles James Fox, who in 1782 secured for her an annuity of £500 in return for the surrender of the Prince's bond.

Although her husband turned up from time to time in the following decade, her longest relationship began in about 1782 with Colonel (later Sir) Banastre Tarleton, an army officer recently returned from action in North America and later MP for Liverpool. Another debt-ridden gambler, Tarleton left for the Continent in 1783 and it was during her journey to join him that she had the miscarriage which led to the partial paralysis from which she suffered thereafter. (Mrs Piozzi later recorded, albeit sceptically, the inevitable rumour that her disability was the result of her 'Venereal Indulgencies'.) In the mid-1780s she was with Tarleton in Aix-la-Chapelle, where she read a report of her death in the *Morning Post* of 14 July 1786. Three weeks later she published her reply to the biographical inaccuracies in her 'obituary' (there had been persistent rumours that she was the illegitimate child of a nobleman), admitting only to a 'trifling lameness', and reporting the recent death of her father, as a Captain in the Russian navy, in December 1785. Although she wrote some verse in these years, she was probably preoccupied for a time with helping Tarleton with his *History of the Campaigns of 1780 and 1781 . . . in North America* (1787), just as she later helped to write his parliamentary speeches.

In January 1788 she returned with her daughter to England, living for some years in Clarges St. (where she would have been a neighbour of Elizabeth Carter in the winters). Soon after her return she began contributing as 'Laura' and 'Laura Maria' to the florid Della-Cruscan poetical exchanges with Robert Merry and others in *The World* and *The Oracle*. When she published her *Poems* in 1791, her 600 subscribers, headed by several members of the Royal Family, included many aristocratic and military names. A few months later Tarleton tried to end their relationship and the renunciatory 'Stanzas' given below were written in July 1792 when she briefly crossed to Calais with her mother and daughter. A reconciliation with Tarleton lasted only until his marriage to a youthful heiress in 1798. Financial problems now forced her, in spite of poor health, into unflagging literary activity. During 1793 she published a second volume of *Poems*, *Modern Manners*, a satire which included an ineffective reply to William Gifford's attacks on Della-Cruscan poetry, and *Sight, The Cavern of Woe, and Solitude*. In 1796 *Sappho and Phaon*, a collection of sonnets, and *The Sicilian Lover; A Tragedy* appeared. More reliably profitable was a series of novels, whose popularity was partly due to her notoriety and to their semi-autobio-graphical aspects. (Several were rapidly translated into French and German.) *Vancenza* (2 vols., 1792), which is said to have sold out on the day of publication, was followed by *The Widow* (2 vols., 1794), *Angelina* (3 vols., 1796), *Hubert de Sevrac*, a 'Gothic' romance (3 vols., 1796), *Walsingham* (4 vols., 1797), *The False Friend*, which included a hostile characterization of Tarleton, who had finally deserted her (4 vols., 1799), and *The Natural Daughter* (2 vols., 1799). (Her daughter, Mary Elizabeth, had also written a novel, *The Shrine of Bertha*, in 1794.) She also published, under the name of Anne Frances Randall, *A Letter to the Women of England, on the Injustice of Mental Insubordination* (1799).

Between 1798 and 1800 she became a regular paid contributor of verse (with Robert Southey) to the *Morning Post*, under a variety of pseudonyms (such as 'Tabitha Bramble', 'Bridget', 'Laura', etc.). A long poem in blank verse, 'The Progress of Liberty', appeared in seven parts between 7 April and 2 August 1798 and, in spite of seriously deteriorating health, she contributed some forty-five poems in the first four months of 1800. At this period she aroused the admiration of Coleridge, another contributor, who called her 'a woman of undoubted Genius' and showed her the unpublished 'Kubla Khan', to which she made detailed allusions in a poem addressed to him. Her *Lyrical Tales* (1800) reflect the early influence of the *Lyrical Ballads*. She also began writing her autobiography, which was unfinished at her death on 26 December 1800, at the age of 42, while staying with her daughter at Englefield Cottage in Windsor Park. Her daughter edited her *Memoirs, with some Posthumous Pieces* (4 vols., 1801) and her *Poetical Works* (3 vols., 1806).

The more notorious aspects of her career and the affectations of her early poetry have led to neglect of her writings, although her later verse can be vigorous and socially aware, perhaps under the influence of Godwin and Mary Wollstonecraft, whom she knew in the 1790s. As attitudes hardened in the new century, readers had to be warned against sympathy for her. As Arthur Aikin cautioned, in a review of her *Poetical Works* in 1806: 'Before a tender-hearted young lady has committed to memory the invocation to "Apathy," or learned to recite with tragic emphasis the "Ode to Ingratitude," let her at least be aware from *what reflections* the author wished to take shelter in insensibility, and for *what favours* her lovers had proved ungrateful.'

302 *Stanzas. Written between Dover and Calais, in July, 1792*

BOUNDING Billow, cease thy motion;
  Bear me not so swiftly o'er!
Cease thy roaring, foamy Ocean!
  I will tempt thy rage no more.

Ah! within my bosom beating,
  Varying passions wildly reign!
Love, with proud Resentment meeting;
  Throbs by turns of joy and pain!

Joy, that far from foes I wander,
  Where their arts can reach no more;   10
Pain, that woman's heart grows fonder,
  When the dream of bliss is o'er!

Love, by fickle fancy banished,
  Spurned by Hope, indignant flies!
Yet, when love and hope are vanished,
  Restless Memory never dies!

Far I go, where Fate shall lead me,
  Far across the troubled deep!
Where no stranger's ear shall heed me;
  Where no eye for me shall weep.   20

Proud has been my fatal passion!
  Proud my injured heart shall be!
While each thought and inclination
  Proves that heart was formed for thee!

Not one sigh shall tell my story;
  Not one tear my cheek shall stain!
Silent grief shall be my glory,
  Grief that stoops not to complain!

Let the bosom, prone to ranging,
  Still, by ranging, seek a cure!   30
Mine disdains the thought of changing,
  Proudly destined to endure!

Yet ere far from all I treasured,
  ********! ere I bid adieu,
Ere my days of pain are measured,
  Take the song that's still thy due!

Yet believe no servile passions
   Seek to charm thy wandering mind;
Well I know thy inclinations,
   Wavering as the passing wind!   40

I have loved thee, dearly loved thee,
   Through an age of worldly woe!
How ungrateful I have proved thee,
   Let my mournful exile show!

Ten long years of anxious sorrow,
   Hour by hour I counted o'er;
Looking forward till tomorrow,
   Every day I loved thee more!

Power and Splendour could not charm me;
   I no joy in Wealth could see;
Nor could threats or fears alarm me—   50
   Save the fear of losing thee!

When the storms of fortune pressed thee,
   I have sighed to hear *thee* sigh!
Or when sorrows dire distressed thee,
   I have bid those sorrows fly!

Often hast thou smiling told me
   Wealth and Power were trifling things,
While Love, smiling to behold me,
   Mocked cold Time's destructive wings.
      60
When with thee, what ills could harm me?
   Thou couldst every pang assuage!
Now, alas! what Hope shall charm me?
   Every moment seems an age!

Fare thee well, ungrateful rover!
   Welcome Gallia's hostile shore;
Now the breezes waft me over;
   Now we part—to meet no more!

                      (1792)

303   *London's Summer Morning*

WHO has not waked to list the busy sounds
Of summer's morning, in the sultry smoke
Of noisy London? On the pavement hot

303 list] hear

The sooty chimney-boy, with dingy face
And tattered covering, shrilly bawls his trade,
Rousing the sleepy housemaid. At the door
The milk-pail rattles, and the tinkling bell
Proclaims the dustman's office; while the street
Is lost in clouds impervious. Now begins
The din of hackney-coaches, waggons, carts;   10
While tinmen's shops, and noisy trunk-makers,
Knife-grinders, coopers, squeaking cork-cutters,
Fruit-barrows, and the hunger-giving cries
Of vegetable-vendors, fill the air.
Now every shop displays its varied trade,
And the fresh-sprinkled pavement cools the feet
Of early walkers. At the private door
The ruddy housemaid twirls the busy mop,
Annoying the smart 'prentice, or neat girl,
Tripping with band-box lightly. Now the sun   20
Darts burning splendour on the glittering pane,
Save where the canvas awning throws a shade
On the gay merchandise. Now, spruce and trim,
In shops (where beauty smiles with industry)
Sits the smart damsel; while the passenger
Peeps through the window, watching every charm.
Now pastry dainties catch the eye minute
Of humming insects, while the limy snare
Waits to enthral them. Now the lamp-lighter
Mounts the tall ladder, nimbly vent'rous,   30
To trim the half-filled lamps, while at his feet
The pot-boy yells discordant! All along
The sultry pavement, the old-clothes-man cries
In tone monotonous, and sidelong views
The area for his traffic: now the bag
Is slyly opened, and the half-worn suit
(Sometimes the pilfered treasure of the base
Domestic spoiler), for one half its worth,
Sinks in the green abyss. The porter now
Bears his huge load along the burning way;   40
And the poor poet wakes from busy dreams,
To paint the summer morning.

                              (Wr. *c.*1794; pub. 1804)

         pot-boy] servant in a tavern

304 *January, 1795*

PAVEMENT slippery, people sneezing,
Lords in ermine, beggars freezing;
Titled gluttons dainties carving,
Genius in a garret starving.

Lofty mansions, warm and spacious;
Courtiers cringing and voracious;
Misers scarce the wretched heeding;
Gallant soldiers fighting, bleeding.

Wives who laugh at passive spouses;
Theatres, and meeting-houses;   10
Balls, where simpering misses languish;
Hospitals, and groans of anguish.

Arts and sciences bewailing;
Commerce drooping, credit failing;
Placemen mocking subjects loyal;
Separations, weddings royal.

Authors who can't earn a dinner;
Many a subtle rogue a winner;
Fugitives for shelter seeking;
Misers hoarding, tradesmen breaking.   20

Taste and talents quite deserted;
All the laws of truth perverted;
Arrogance o'er merit soaring;
Merit silently deploring.

Ladies gambling night and morning;
Fools the works of genius scorning;
Ancient dames for girls mistaken,
Youthful damsels quite forsaken.

Some in luxury delighting;
More in talking than in fighting;   30
Lovers old, and beaux decrepid;
Lordlings empty and insipid.

Placemen] those appointed to court or government posts without regard to merit

Poets, painters, and musicians;
Lawyers, doctors, politicians:
Pamphlets, newspapers, and odes,
Seeking fame by different roads.

Gallant souls with empty purses,
Generals only fit for nurses;
School-boys, smit with martial spirit,
Taking place of veteran merit.   40

Honest men who can't get places,
Knaves who show unblushing faces;
Ruin hastened, peace retarded;
Candour spurned, and art rewarded.

(Wr. 1795; pub. 1806)

305   *Stanzas*

IN this vain, busy world, where the good and the gay
By affliction or folly wing moments away;
Where the false are respected, the virtuous betrayed,
Where Vice lives in sunshine, and Genius in shade;
With a soul-sickened sadness all changes I see,
For the world, the base world, has no pleasure for me!

In cities, where wealth loads the coffers of pride,
Where talents and sorrow are ever allied;
Where dullness is worshipped, and wisdom despised,
Where none but the empty and vicious are prized;   10
All scenes with disgust and abhorrence I see,
For the world has no corner of comfort for me!

While pale Asiatics, encircled with gold,
The sons of meek Virtue indignant behold;
While the tithe-pampered churchman reviles at the poor,
As the lorn, sinking traveller faints at his door;
While Custom dares sanction Oppression's decree—
Oh, keep such hard bosoms, such monsters, from me!

While the flame of a Patriot expires in the breast,
With ribbands, and tinsel, and frippery dressed;   20
While Pride mocks the children of Want and Despair,
Gives a sneer for each sigh, and a smile for each prayer;
Though he triumph his day, a short day it must be—
Heaven keep such cold tyrants, oh, keep them from me!

art] cunning   **305** Asiatics] i.e. those who have made fortunes in Asia, especially India

While the lawyer still lives by the anguish of hearts,
While he wrings the wronged bosom, and thrives as it smarts;
While he grasps the last guinea from Poverty's heir,
While he revels in splendour which rose from Despair;
While the tricks of his office our scourges must be,
Oh, keep the shrewd knave and his quibbles from me!   30

While the court breeds the sycophant, trained to ensnare;
While the prisons re-echo the groans of Despair;
While the State deals out taxes, the Army dismay;
While the rich are upheld, and the poor doomed to pay;
Humanity saddens with pity to see
The scale of injustice, and trembles like me!

While patriots are slandered, and venal slaves rise;
While Power grows a giant, and Liberty dies;
While a phantom of Virtue o'er Energy reigns,
And the broad wing of Freedom is loaded with chains;   40
While War spreads its thunders o'er land and o'er sea,
Ah, who but can listen and murmur like me?

While the bosom which loves, and confesses its flame,
By the high-titled female is branded with shame;
While a coronet hides what the humble despise,
And the lowly must fall that the haughty may rise;
Oh, who can the triumphs of infamy see,
Nor shrink from the reptiles, and shudder like me?

Ah world, thou vile world, how I sicken to trace
The anguish that hourly augments for thy race!   50
How I turn from the worst, while I honour the best,
The enlightened adore, and the venal detest!
And, oh! with what joy to the grave would I flee—
Since the world, the base world has no pleasure for me.

(1797)

306   *The Birth-Day*

HERE bounds the gaudy, gilded chair,
    Bedecked with fringe and tassels gay;
The melancholy mourner there
    Pursues her sad and painful way.

306 Birth-Day] the elaborate annual celebration of a royal birthday

Here, guarded by a motley train,
　　The pampered Countess glares along;
There, wrung by poverty and pain,
　　Pale Misery mingles with the throng.

Here, as the blazoned chariot rolls,
　　And prancing horses scare the crowd,　　　　10
Great names, adorning little souls,
　　Announce the empty, vain and proud.

Here four tall lacqueys slow precede
　　A painted dame in rich array;
There, the sad, shivering child of need
　　Steals barefoot o'er the flinty way.

'Room, room! stand back!', they loudly cry,
　　The wretched poor are driven around;
On every side they scattered fly,
　　And shrink before the threatening sound.　　20

Here, amidst jewels, feathers, flowers,
　　The senseless Duchess sits demure,
Heedless of all the anguished hours
　　The sons of modest worth endure.

All silvered and embroidered o'er,
　　She neither knows nor pities pain;
The beggar freezing at her door
　　She overlooks with nice disdain.

The wretch whom poverty subdues
　　Scarce dares to raise his tearful eye;　　　　30
Or if by chance the throng he views,
　　His loudest murmur is a sigh!

The poor wan mother, at whose breast
　　The pining infant craves relief,
In one thin tattered garment dressed,
　　Creeps forth to pour the plaint of grief.

But ah! how little heeded here
　　The faltering tongue reveals its woe;
For high-born fools, with frown austere,
　　Condemn the pangs they never know.　　　　40

'Take physic, Pomp!', let Reason say:
  'What can avail thy trappings rare?
The tomb shall close thy glittering day,
  The beggar prove thy equal there!'

(Wr. by 1800; pub. 1806)

307   *The Haunted Beach*

UPON a lonely desart beach
  Where the white foam was scattered,
A little shed upreared its head
  Though lofty barks were shattered.
The sea-weeds gathering near the door
  A sombre path displayed;
And, all around, the deafening roar
Re-echoed on the chalky shore,
  By the green billows made.

Above, a jutting cliff was seen
  Where sea-birds hovered, craving;   10
And all around, the crags were bound
  With weeds—forever waving.
And here and there, a cavern wide
  Its shadowy jaws displayed;
And near the sands, at ebb of tide,
A shivered mast was seen to ride
  Where the green billows strayed.

And often, while the moaning wind
  Stole o'er the summer ocean,   20
The moonlight scene was all serene,
  The waters scarce in motion:
Then, while the smoothly slanting sand
  The tall cliff wrapped in shade,
The fisherman beheld a band
Of spectres, gliding hand in hand—
  Where the green billows played.

And pale their faces were as snow,
  And sullenly they wandered:
And to the skies with hollow eyes   30
  They looked, as though they pondered.
And sometimes, from their hammock shroud,
  They dismal howlings made,
And while the blast blew strong and loud
The clear moon marked the ghastly crowd,
  Where the green billows played.

And then, above the haunted hut,
   The curlews screaming hovered;
And the low door with furious roar
   The frothy breakers covered.   40
For, in the fisherman's lone shed,
   A murdered man was laid,
With ten wide gashes in his head,
And deep was made his sandy bed
   Where the green billows played.

A shipwrecked mariner was he,
   Doomed from his home to sever,
Who swore to be through wind and sea
   Firm and undaunted ever!
And when the wave resistless rolled,   50
   About his arm he made
A packet rich of Spanish gold,
And, like a British sailor, bold,
   Plunged where the billows played!

The spectre band, his messmates brave,
   Sunk in the yawning ocean,
While to the mast he lashed him fast
   And braved the storm's commotion.
The winter moon upon the sand
   A silvery carpet made,   60
And marked the sailor reach the land,
And marked his murderer wash his hand
   Where the green billows played.

And since that hour the fisherman
   Has toiled and toiled in vain!
For all the night, the moony light
   Gleams on the spectred main!
And when the skies are veiled in gloom,
   The murderer's liquid way
Bounds o'er the deeply yawning tomb,   70
And flashing fires the sands illume,
   Where the green billows play!

Full thirty years his task has been
   Day after day more weary;
For Heaven designed his guilty mind
   Should dwell on prospects dreary.

Bound by a strong and mystic chain,
   He has not power to stray;
But, destined misery to sustain,
He wastes, in solitude and pain,   80
   A loathsome life away.

(1800)

MARIA LOGAN
(*fl.* 1793)

Her *Poems on Several Occasions* enjoyed two editions at York in 1793. Most of the subscribers were local, but the list also includes John Aikin and his sister, Mrs Barbauld, and Henry Mackenzie of Edinburgh, the novelist. The expanded list in the second edition includes the name of Gamaliel Lloyd of Bury St Edmund's, whose copy (in the Bodleian) contains a transcript of part of a letter from the author Capel Lofft (1751–1824), praising Miss Logan's poems in contrast to the 'fashion to overload our Poetry with the false Glitter of uninteresting embellishment, which never touches the Heart, and is sure to pall upon the Fancy'. William Enfield also praised her in the *Monthly Review*, 11 (1793), 214.

Her volume includes lines to her brother in 1784, on his going to London to complete his training as a surgeon, a sonnet 'On the Spring of a Seventh Year of Uninterrupted Sickness', and a poem 'To Opium', on which she evidently depended for alleviation of her sufferings.

308   *Verses on Hearing that An Airy and Pleasant Situation, Near a Populous and Commercial Town, was Surrounded with New Buildings*

THERE was a time! that time the Muse bewails,
When Sunny Hill enjoyed refreshing gales;
When Flora sported in its fragrant bowers,
And strewed with liberal hand her sweetest flowers!
Now sable vapours, pregnant with disease,
Clog the light pinions of the southern breeze;
Each verdant plant assumes a dusky hue,
And sooty atoms taint the morning dew.
No more the lily rears her spotless head,
Health, verdure, beauty, fragrance, all are fled: 10
Sulphureous clouds deform the rising day,
Nor own the power of Sol's meridian ray;
While sickly damps, from Aire's polluted stream,
Quench the pure radiance of his parting beam.

These are thy triumphs, Commerce!—these thy spoils!
Yet sordid mortals glory in their toils,
Spurn the pure joys which simple Nature yields,
Her breezy hills, dark groves, and verdant fields;
With cold indifference view her blooming charms,
And give youth, ease and health to thy enfeebling arms.   20

(1793)

ISABELLA KELLY (née FORDYCE, later HEDGELAND)
(c.1759?–1857)

Although she was a prolific novelist at the turn of the century, little has hitherto been known about her. She was the third daughter of William Fordyce of Aberdeen and his wife Elizabeth Fraser, niece of Alexander Fraser, Lord Strichen. Although both her parents were from wealthy Scottish families, their secret marriage in romantic circumstances in the early 1750s offended their relatives and left them impoverished. Her father obtained a commission in the Royal Marines in 1755 through Lord Adam Gordon, was a Captain by 1761, and endured 'the vicissitudes of a military life, and many distant wanderings' before becoming Groom of the Bedchamber to George III. Her mother died in 1785. In 1789 Isabella, who later said that 'she was born in a Castle (that of Cairnboro'), nursed in a cottage by one of the family cotters, and bred at Court', married Robert Kelly, son of Colonel Robert Kelly, who since 1760 had been in the service of the East India Company in Madras. (Her sister Margaret had married the adventurer Sir Richard Perrott in 1782; her other sister Amelia married Major-Gen. William Souter of the Marines in 1797.)

By 1794, when she published her *Collection of Poems and Fables*, Isabella Kelly had suffered 'a variety of domestic calamities . . . a father injured and oppressed by the unfeeling hand of Power, a husband neglected by those on whom he had hereditary claims of protection, and a beloved child untimely snatched away'. Her father had been listed as one of the four Grooms of the Bedchamber in the Royal Household in 1785, but his name had been removed, for unknown reasons, by the following year. Little more is known of her husband's misfortunes. His father had died in India in 1790 and he may have been the natural son who had joined Col. Kelly in Madras in 1786 but evidently failed to inherit his wealth. If the following poem is taken literally, he had eventually been imprisoned. The first poem in her volume is in memory of Robert Hawke Kelly, the 'dear departed infant'. (A note, which refers to her father-in-law as formerly 'a hero, worship in the East', and to the 'honor, worth, and grace' of her own family, complains that the child was refused burial for a day because neither clergyman nor sexton was present in the churchyard.) Her husband had evidently become an army officer (the subscribers include a number of officers of the Marines at Plymouth and Chatham) and several poems suggest that the Kellys had had marital problems ('Extempore after a Dispute at Dunkerque', 'To a Wandering Husband from a Deserted wife').

Driven to support herself and her two children by her pen, Mrs Kelly published a long sequence of novels, beginning with *Madeline* (4 vols., 1794). Several were dedicated to members of the nobility and had short subscribers' lists. *Joscelina* (2 vols., 1797), her fourth novel, lists only some eighty names, but they include the Duke and Duchess of York, the Duchess of Devonshire and her sister, the Countess of Bessborough. The dedication to the Duchess of York refers to her personal problems: 'while the trembling wife venerates the Royal munificence which may extricate a husband from distress, the anxious mother blesses that gracious hand which preserves her infants!' Several works were dated from King's Road, Chelsea, including a new edition of her *Poems and Fables on Several Occasions* (Chelsea, 1807) in which she adds to the account of her calamities in her original preface that 'that Father is gone to eternal rest,—that Husband lies in a foreign land,—the Orphan, the Widow, still survives—survives to feel the wrongs, to feel the anguish accumulated in her struggles for an infant family'. Her husband had evidently gone to Madras and had died there with the rank of Major.

By 1813 she had published some fourteen books, mostly novels in the Gothic mode, but including *The Child's French Grammar* (Brentford, 1805). By 1816 she had married a wealthy merchant named Hedgeland, and although he had died by about 1820, she was in relatively comfortable circumstances thereafter. Under her new name she published only *Instructive Anecdotes for Youth* (1819), which appears to indicate that she had for a time run or taught at a school for girls. Her son, who is said to have been 'in early life a grocer's assistant', entered Lincoln's Inn in 1819 and, as Sir Fitzroy Kelly (1796–1880), eventually had a distinguished legal and political career, becoming in turn Solicitor-General, Attorney-General, and Lord Chief Baron of the Exchequer.

Her last work has not previously been attributed to her. A *Memoir of the Late Mrs. Henrietta Fordyce* (1823) is an anonymous account of the widow of Dr James Fordyce, a cousin of her father. It contains a detailed narrative of a visit in about 1821 to Mrs Fordyce by a newly widowed Mrs H———— and her daughter, who were then living near Bath, and includes references to a son as the 'young Templar' (i.e. Fitzroy). Mrs Fordyce recalled Mrs H————'s family background, including her parents' romantic marriage in Scotland. Mrs Fordyce later invited Mrs H———— and her daughter (who had been educated in a French convent and was to marry a clergyman) to live with her, but died in January 1823, aged 89. Mrs Kelly-Hedgeland, who insists that she could have lived independently, may have published the memoir partly to make clear to those aware of the situation that she had not simply taken advantage of an elderly woman. Her son's growing prosperity and distinction must have made her later years increasingly comfortable. She was said to have been aged 90 in 1849 and died on 25 June 1857, 'At a very advanced age, from the effects of an accident, after leaving the house of her son, Sir Fitzroy Kelly'.

309   *To an Unborn Infant*

BE still, sweet babe, no harm shall reach thee,
    Nor hurt thy yet unfinished form;
Thy mother's frame shall safely guard thee
    From this bleak, this beating storm.

Promised hope! expected treasure!
   Oh, how welcome to these arms!
Feeble, yet they'll fondly clasp thee,
   Shield thee from the least alarms.

Loved already, little blessing,
   Kindly cherished, though unknown,   10
Fancy forms thee sweet and lovely,
   Emblem of the rose unblown.

Though thy father is imprisoned,
   Wronged, forgotten, robbed of right,
I'll repress the rising anguish,
   Till thine eyes behold the light.

Start not, babe! the hour approaches
   That presents the gift of life;
Soon, too soon thou'lt taste of sorrow
   In these realms of care and strife.   20

Share not thou a mother's feelings,
   Hope vouchsafes a pitying ray;
Though a gloom obscures the morning,
   Bright may shine the rising day.

Live, sweet babe, to bless thy father,
   When thy mother slumbers low;
Slowly lisp her name that loved him,
   Through a world of varied woe.

Learn, my child, the mournful story
   Of thy suffering mother's life;   30
Let thy father not forget her
   In a future, happier wife.

Babe of fondest expectation,
   Watch his wishes in his face;
What pleased in me mayst thou inherit,
   And supply my vacant place.

Whisper all the anguished moments
   That have wrung this anxious breast:
Say, I lived to give thee being,
   And retired to endless rest.   40

          (1794)

ANNE BATTEN CRISTALL
(b. *c*.1768)

She was the elder daughter of Joseph Alexander Cristall, mariner, and his wife Anne Batten, daughter of a merchant of Penzance, who married on 29 April 1767. Her father, a Scotsman from Arbroath, for a time had his own ship and later became a sail-, mast-, and block-maker, with yards at Fowey and Penzance in Cornwall and subsequently at Rotherhithe. She was probably born in about 1768, since in most accounts she is said to have been older than her brother Joshua, who believed himself to have been born in 1769. She also had a younger sister Elizabeth. Their father was 'of an extremely jealous disposition, and his time ashore was usually a period of trouble and discomfort in the family'. Their education was left to their more cultivated mother, who had a small private income. The Cristalls moved to London when the children were small, and Joshua and Anne were closely attached: 'They studied together as children, and hand in hand did they daily walk to London and back for their schooling when the family lived at Rotherhithe.' Later the family moved to Blackheath.

Relatively little is known about Anne, who evidently became a teacher. Joshua was at first apprenticed in the china and glass retail trade, but his artistic ambitions led to some years of wavering about his career during which he had a variety of jobs. For a time in the 1790s his sister Elizabeth lived with him when they were both planning to become engravers. Eventually he won some reputation as an artist and became a founder-member of the Society of Painters in Watercolours in 1804, although he seems always to have been hard-pressed financially. Anne had probably met Mary Wollstonecraft and her sister by 1788 and there are several references to her in Wollstonecraft's letters to Joshua in 1790. In March Wollstonecraft wrote sternly to Joshua, then employed at Thomas Turner's china factory in Shropshire, about the risks of an artistic career: 'I know that you earnestly wish to be the friend and protector of your amiable sister and hope no inconsiderate act or thoughtless mode of conduct will add to her cares— for her comfort very much depends on you.' On 9 December 1790 (in a letter not included in the recent edition of her *Collected Letters*) she warned Joshua that, if he continued wavering, he would, 'instead of being useful to your sisters, become a burden to yourself'. He must decide, 'like a man', whether art was to be 'the business or the amusement of your future life'. Of Anne, Wollstonecraft said: 'I have seldom seen your sister since you left town. I fear her situation [at home?] is very uncomfortable. I wish she could obtain a little more strength of mind. If I were to give a short definition of virtue, I should call it fortitude.'

Little else is known about Anne before the appearance of her *Poetical Sketches*, published by Joseph Johnson, in 1795, with a vignette on the title-page by her brother. The circles in which she moved are suggested by the subscribers' list, which includes Mary Wollstonecraft, Mrs Godwin, Mrs Barbauld, and John Aikin, as well as John Wolcot, Samuel Rogers, Richard Porson, William Beloe, and George Dyer, the friend of Lamb and Southey. (Anne's name appears in a similar list in the *Poems* of Mrs Sarah Spence in the same year.) Her volume caused little stir, although two of her poems were reprinted in the *Gentleman's Magazine* in 1795, and William Enfield in the *Monthly Review* found originality and imagination, but also faulty versification and obscurity, in her book. There is evidence of social contact with the Godwin circle later in the decade but it was George Dyer who became the closest friend of the

Cristalls: he is said to have been 'a constant visitor; and . . . to have conceived a platonic affection for Miss Cristall', presumably the elder sister. In about 1796 Dyer tried to persuade the feminist Mary Hays, who had just published *Emma Courtney*, to collaborate on a 'poetical novel' with Anne Cristall, 'I mean a novel with occasional poetical effusions introduced. A.C. has a very fine talent for poetry: one or two of her songs are, I think, as beautiful as any I know. She is indeed a little incorrect and luxuriant, "her poetical vine wants trimming.". . . . A. Crystall's poetry, if she writes, will, I doubt not, display more judgement and correctness. But these can only be acquired by practice.' In 1797 Dyer introduced Robert Southey to Anne Cristall and Marys Hays, as Southey told Joseph Cottle on 13 March: 'But Miss Christal,—have you seen her poems?—a fine, artless, sensible girl! . . . Her heart is alive, she loves poetry, she loves retirement, she loves the country: her verses are very incorrect, and the literary circles say she has no genius; but she has genius, Joseph Cottle, or there is no truth in physiognomy. . . . You see I like the women better than the men. Indeed, they are better animals in general, perhaps because more is left to nature in their education.' In May 1799 Dyer promised a poem by her for Southey's *Annual Anthology* (1799–1800), but in the end she seems not to have contributed. There is, indeed, only an undated 'Song' in an unidentified newspaper to add to her collection of 1795. Dyer included her in 1801 in a list of prominent women poets, which includes Smith, More, Williams, Robinson, Carter, Seward, and Opie, but so far nothing more about her later life has come to light, surprisingly in view of the circle of friends she knew in the 1790s. Early death or the anonymity of marriage are, as always, possible explanations, although it may be noted that she is listed under her own name in the *Biographical Dictionary of Living Authors* (1816), p. 80. Her brother died in 1847 and her sister was still alive aged about 80, in 1851.

310   *Morning. Rosamonde*

WILD midst the teeming buds of opening May,
Breaking large branches from the flowery thorn,
   O'er the ferned hills see Rosamonda stray,
Scattering the pearls which the gay leaves adorn!
   Her ringlets o'er her temples play,
Flushed with the orient splendour of the morn.
The sun broke forth—and wide its glories threw,
Blushing along the sky, and sparkling in the dew.
   The plains gay-glittered with ethereal light,
      And the field-melody,   10
      Nature's wild harmony,
   Breathed love, and sang delight!

Fresh Rosamonde the glowing scene surveys,
   Her youthful bosom inly stung with pain;
Early amid the shadowy trees she strays,
   Her shining eyes the starting tears restrain;
While tyrant Love within her pulses plays,
   O'er the wet grass she flew with wild disdain.

She flew from thought, and far
She sang, and hailed the morning star.   20
  Her voice was pinioned on the wind,
Which wafts her notes around;
Encircling zephyrs caught each sound,
And bore them echoing through the wood,
Where pleased offended Urban stood,
  With archest smile, yet musical and kind:
Conquering the sigh, she gaily sung,
And scorn loud-trembled on her wiry tongue.

While Urban stood, and held her in his eyes,
He to his lips applies   30
  The soft-breathed flute;
Whose notes, when touched with art,
Steal to the inmost heart,
And throw the tyrannizing spirit down—
  While vanity and pride are charmed and mute.

Those lays reached Rosamonda's ear,
She fluttering, like a bird whom fear
Has drawn within the fascinating serpent's fangs,
Unable to conceal the pangs
Of pride, conflicting with returning love,   40
To hide her blushes, darts amid the grove:
  Sweet showers fast sprinkle from her lovely eyes,
Which drown her short-lived scorn;
  But as she moves the young musician flies,
Leaves her all wild, sad, weeping, and forlorn.

                                                     (1795)

311   *Evening. Gertrude*

    IN clouds drew on the evening's close,
    Which 'cross the west in ranges stood,
    As pensive Gertrude sought the wood,
    And there the darkest thicket chose;
    While from her eyes amid the wild briar flows
    A sad and briny flood.
        Dark o'er her head
    Rolled heavy clouds, while showers,
    Perfumed by summer's wild and spicy showers,
        Their ample torrents shed.   10

              wiry] thin-sounding

                      486

Why does she mourn?
   Why droop, like flowret nipped in early spring?
Alas! her tenderness meets no return!
   Love hovers round her with his airy wing,
And warms her youthful heart with vain delight:
While Urban's graceful form enchants her sight,
   And from his eyes shoots forth the poisonous sting,
Another's charms th' impassioned youth inspired,
The sportive Rosamonde his genius fired.

The drops which glide down Gertrude's cheeks   20
Mid bitter agonies did flow;
And though awhile her pallid lips might glow,
'Twas as a blossom blighted soon with woe:
   Her disregarded tresses, wet with tears,
Hung o'er her panting bosom straight and sleek;
   Her faithful heart was all despondency and fears.

The skies disgorged, their last large drops refrain,
   The cloudy hemisphere's no more perturbed;
The leafy boughs, that had received the rain,
   With gusts of wind disturbed,   30
Shake wild their scattering drops o'er glade and plain;
They fall on Gertrude's breast, and her white garments stain.
Sighing, she threw her mantle o'er her head,
And through the brakes towards her mansion sped;
Unheedingly her vestments drew along,
Sweeping the tears that to the branches hung:
      And as she passed
O'er the soaked road, from off the shining grass,
In clods around her feet the moist earth clung.

The clouds dispersed, again to sight   40
The evening sun glowed lambent bright;
And, forcing back the lowering shades,
Spread its enlivening beams, and kindled mid the glades:
With high-wrought verdure every object glowed,
And purple hills their glittering mansions showed.
   The universal gleam invites to sport,
      For toil and care cease with the ebbing day;
Th' industrious youths to plains or groves resort,
   Dance on the lawn, or o'er the hillocks stray.

Gertrude, wandering up a lane,   50
From among the winding trees,
Fanned by a refreshing breeze,
   Ascends upon the glistening plain.

Across gay Iris flung her bow,
  Reflecting each celestial ray;
  As if the flowers that decked the May
Were there exhaled, and through its watery pores did glow.

From a fair covert, Urban's gay resort,
  A whistling pipe in warbling notes respired;
The well-known sound invites each youth to sport,   60
  And every heart its harmony inspired;
      While from each mead,
      So thick with daisies spread,
The bounding nymphs with fairy lightness sprung,
And gaily wild their sportive sonnets sung;
The air was scented by the odorous flowers,
Bright sprinkled with the dews of fresh-fall'n showers.

Of lively grace, and dimpled smiles,
  Slim Cynthia, the refined,
Came, with neat Phillis, full of tricksome wiles;   70
  While Silvius strolled behind,
  Chased by the marble-hearted Rosalind:
The loud and witty large-mouthed Madge,
With her obsequious servant Hodge.

Blithe from the mill, which briskly turning round
Made the young zephyrs breathe a rural sound,
Leaped Charles, gay-glowing with industrious heat,
Active to lead in every rustic seat:
Back from his brows he shook his wavy locks,
  And turning quick his lively eyes,   80
  His lovely, modest Peggy spies,
Returning with her aged father's flocks.
Straight with his hand he gave his heart sincere,
Devoid of order danced, and whistled loud and clear.

Hebe, a blooming, sprightly fair,
With shallow Ned, an ill-matched pair;
Simple Daphne, rosy John,
And ever-blundering Heleson;
From a large mansion, gloomed by shading trees,
Forth sprung the star-eyed Luisse;   90
Graceful her tresses flowed around,
  Like scattered clouds, that catch the moon's pale beams;
Scarcely she seemed to touch the verdant ground,
  But, as inspired, along the plain she streams.

More join the flock—they spring in air,
Light as winged doves, and like to doves they pair;
The sun's last ray now lingered o'er their head,
And sweets delectable around were spread.

Poor Gertrude, hid amongst the trees, surveyed
Each ardent youth, each blooming maid;   100
    And as she gazed,
Pleasure by slow degrees within her senses steals:
    Her eyes, with tears impearled, she raised,
Her heart each sweet sensation feels;
    Lightly her feet the grassy meadows tread,
While music's power deludes her from her cares;
    Among the nymphs, by its soft influence led,
Her sympathetic breast their raptures shares.

Thus while she felt, and joined the lively throng,
    Lo! quick ascends the plain   110
    The glory of each swain,
Urban, with sportive song,
    Whose cheerful notes in frolic measures fled;
        While Rosamonde,
    Fleet-footed Rosamonde, he led:
The rapture of the lark her voice sent forth,
Too well, ah! Gertrude knew its worth;
Dire tremblings soon her spirits seize:
Could she, vain untaught nymph, aspire to please?
Her body owns no grace,   120
No smiles, no dimples, deck her eyes or face:
    She feels that she has naught to prize;
Yet, totally devoid of art,
    Expression's charm was hers, with beaming eyes,
A voice soul-reaching, and a feeling heart.

She turned around—
The flying breezes loosened to the air
Her ill-beseeming vests, her scattered hair:
    So sad she looked, so artless was her woe,
As from a thinking mind had drawn a tear;   130
But joy through every vein had stole,
    And mirth shut out the sympathetic glow.
The heart's gay dance admits of no control,
Sweet joys but seldom through our senses steal;
'Tis pity then we should forget to feel.

vests] vestments, garments

Gay wicked wit amid the circle spread,
And wanton round the lively sallies sped;
Each neat-trimmed maiden laughed with playful glee,
Whom whispering swains divert with mimicry.
    Fair Rosamonde, whose rival bosom burned,   140
With taunting mirth directs young Urban's eyes;
    He, with mischievous archness, smiles returned,
Amid whose circles wounding satires rise;
    Their sportive feet still beat the flowering ground,
While wicked looks, and jests, and jeers went round.

Pierced by their insults, stung with bitter smart,
Sad fell poor Gertrude's tears, high heaved her heart.
Distant she flew and, sitting on a stone,
Concealed, gave sorrow vent, and wept alone:
    Till mid her grief, a virtuous just disdain   150
    Came to her aid, and made her bosom glow;
    With shame she burns, she blushes at her woe,
And wonders at her weakness and her pain.

'Unhappy maid!', she cried, 'thou art to blame,
Thus to expose thy virtuous breast to shame:
    Poor heart! thy love is laughed at for its truth;
Yet 'tis a holy treasure, though disdained,
And wantonly by thoughtlessness profaned;
    Ah! why then waste the blessings of thy youth?
No more fair reason's sacred light despise;   160
    Thy heart may blessings find
That dwell not in the eyes,
    But in the virtues of the feeling mind.'

        (1795)

312   *A Fragment. The Blind Man*

S AY, reverend man, why midst this stormy night
Wander'st thou, darkling and exposed, alone?
Alas! I would assist thee, though unknown.

  'Rash youth! that God which robbed my eyes of sight
Darts through my mind a ray of sacred light:
The winds I heed not, nor the lashing shower,
My sinewy frame is firm, my soaring mind has power.
This oaken staff feels out the dangerous way:
'Twas Heaven's fierce fire which swept my eyes away,
And left an orbless trunk, that knows nor night nor day.   10

Yet strong ideas rooted in my brain
Form there an universe, which doth contain
Those images which Nature's hand displays,
The heavenly arch, the morning's glowing rays;
Mountains and plains, the sea by tempests hurled,
And all the grandeur of this glorious world!'

But, ah! how wild drives on the rapid storm,
Dashing the rain against thy reverend form!
Yon swelling river, foaming towards the main,
Smokes midst th' advancing waves and falling rain: 20
O, father! my young soul is shook within;
O! let me lead you from this horrid scene.

   'I yield;—but let not fear thy mind deform:
Hark! 'tis God's voice which urges on the storm;
He to this world of elements gave form.
From them he moulded all, yet gave not peace,
   But broke the harmony, and bade them rage;
He meant not happiness should join with ease,
   But varied joys and pains should all the world engage.'

                                             (1795)

313   *Song*

THROUGH springtime walks, with flowers perfumed,
   I chased a wild capricious fair,
Where hyacinths and jonquils bloomed,
   Chanting gay sonnets through the air:
Hid amid a briary dell,
   Or 'neath a hawthorn tree,
Her sweet enchantments led me on,
   And still deluded me.

While summer's splendent glory smiles,
   My ardent love in vain essayed;   10
I strove to win her heart by wiles,
   But still a thousand pranks she played;
Still o'er each sun-burnt furzy hill,
   Wild, playful, gay and free,
She laughed and scorned, I chased her still,
   And still she bantered me.

When autumn waves her golden ears,
   And wafts o'er fruits her pregnant breath,
The sprightly lark its pinions rears,
   I chased her o'er the daisied heath;   20
Sweet harebells trembled in the vale,
   And all around was glee;
Still, wanton as the timid hart,
   She swiftly flew from me.

Now winter lights its cheerful fire,
   While jests with frolic mirth resound,
And draws the wandering beauty nigher,
   'Tis now too cold to rove around:
The Christmas game, the playful dance,
   Incline her heart to glee;   30
Mutual we glow, and kindling love
   Draws every wish to me.

                 (1795)

ANNABELLA PLUMPTRE
(1761–1838)

She was the third daughter of Dr Robert Plumptre, Prebendary of Norwich, and from 1760 President of Queens' College, Cambridge, and his wife Anne Newcome, who had ten children. An account of her in 1816, probably supplied by herself, states that her father 'gave her an education very different from what generally falls to the lot of even well instructed females . . . he took a delight in cultivating the inclination of his daughters, who became by his tuition proficients in several modern languages'. After Dr Plumptre's death at Norwich in 1788, her elder sister Anne, about whom rather more is known, went to London and, under the influence of Helen Maria Williams (see nos. 267–71), became an ardent enthusiast for the French Revolution. William Beloe, a Norwich contemporary, described Anne at this period as 'generally obnoxious, to those alone excepted, who considered all as deserving of the burning fiery furnace, who did not fall prostrate before the shrine of Bonaparte, and adore the Briarean Idol of the French Revolution'. The following spirited attack on moderate opinion in an age of revolution suggests that Annabella, for a time at least, shared her sister's views. Reporting on the election at Norwich in July 1794, Sarah Scott described to her sister Elizabeth Montagu a large political meeting of 'Jacobins' at the Town Hall, which was addressed by 'a young woman of uncommon talents', probably Amelia Alderson (later Mrs Opie), while 'two daughters of a late Doctor of Divinity stood one on each side of her to encourage her in her proceeding'. These were no doubt the Plumptre sisters, who were later friendly with Mrs Opie.

   Annabella evidently stayed for some years in Norwich, where her poem appeared anonymously in *The Cabinet*, a radical periodical published there in 1794–5. (The attribution is from a marked copy and, given the similarity of their names, it is possible that Anne was the author. This was, no doubt, why Annabella later published some of her works under the name of Bell Plumptre, and also signed letters, 'A.B. Plumptre'.) It may have been to support themselves after their father's death, as well as to spread liberal views, that Anne and Annabella both published novels and translations from the mid-1790s. (Their brother James (1770–1832) was a dramatist but later became a clergyman.) Anne was always the more prominent and was especially prolific in translating the plays of Kotzebue in 1798–9. Annabella published a novel, *Montgomery* (2 vols., 1796), various translations from German authors, *The Western Mail* (1801), and *Stories for Children* (1804). Apart from the fact that Anne was in France between 1802 and 1805 (described in her *Narrative of Three Years' Residence in France*, 3 vols., 1810), little is known of their later years. One explanation may be Anne's willingness to disconcert her acquaintance with her political views. Henry Crabb Robinson met her in February 1810:

With an ugly person, she was revolting in her sentiments. She said to-day: 'People are talking about an invasion. I am not afraid of an invasion. I believe the country would be all the happier if Buonaparte were to effect a landing and overturn the Government. He would destroy the Church and the aristocracy, and his government would be better than what we have.'

'I said nothing', Robinson noted, but was staggered when Anne went on to speak highly of a French book which he himself had found 'so filthy and obscene that I was not able to finish it'. (When Charles Lamb learned later that Anne Plumptre was dead, he exclaimed: 'Dead! . . . What an ugly ghost she will make!')

That Annabella no longer shared the interests of her uncompromising sister is suggested by her publication in the same year of *Domestic Management; or, The Healthy Cook-Book* (1810; 2nd edn., 1812), of which she spoke with modest pride in a letter in 1813 to Francis Douce, the antiquarian. A note of the same period from Anne to Douce indicates that her tastes were not solely political, since she invites him to a musical party ('Mr & Mrs Nathan, Signor Sola with his flute, and M. Canongia with his clarinet, about a dozen in all'). In 1818 the sisters jointly published *Tales of Wonder* (3 vols.), but Anne died later in the year at Norwich. Of Annabella's remaining years nothing is known, except (as seems not previously to have been noted) that she died at the age of 77 at Rennes in France, on 18 December 1838.

314   from *Ode to Moderation*

> To thee, whose cautious step and specious air
>   Deceive the world; who, simulating *good*,
> Drop'st from thine oily tongue the pitying prayer
>   T'avert the ills of man and spare his blood:
> 'To thee I call, but with no friendly voice',
>   I am no dupe to thine insidious art,
>   The vaunted mercy of thy traitor heart,
> Nor in thy promises can I rejoice.
> For well I know thee, hypocrite!—I know
> Thou art the fatal source of human woe;   10
> Thine is the shield that bloodiest tyrants bear,
> Foul harbinger of death, black herald of despair.

Why groans yon hapless, violated land,
   With such continued sufferance and long care?
'Tis that, deceiver! there thou giv'st command,
   That moderate justice, moderate truth are there.
The poor not quite destroyed, though doomed to toil
   From day to day unceasing, yet must hide
   Their soul's deep anguish from the gaze of pride,
And greet with smiles the plunderers of the soil.   20
The sad seditious thoughts that fire the brain
Must be subdued;—'tis treason to complain;
For order, peace, tranquillity require
They suffer all *unmoved*,—then silently expire.

O rather bear me fury, vengeance wild!
   To the red scene of slaughter and dismay,
Where the bold multitude, no more beguiled,
   The deathful banners of their rage display.
Ah! let *their* generous ardours burn for me;
   Their fiercest energies my bosom steel,   30
   Who learn to vindicate, when taught to feel
And dare th' extreme of all things to be free.
Better by far at once the conflict end,
The general *foe* prevail or general *friend*.
Than that faint hope should languish with the throng,
Who love the right but half, but half detest the wrong.

Mark, how the desolating tempest flies,
   And rends the groaning forest from its base;
Its bursting thunders wreck the powerless skies,
   Its lightnings nature's loveliest scenes deface.   40
Anon, behold its transient fury sped,
   More fresh the flowers their vivid tints disclose,
   With richer pride the yellow harvest glows,
More soft the air, more sweet the odours spread.
Thus, from the storms of intellectual strife
The moral system wakes to purer life,
The passions harmonize which late were hurled,
And reason's fairer beams illume a happier world.

'Tis true, seductive is thy mild discourse,
   With dainty terms of soft benevolence   50
And honeyed phrases filled, abjuring force,
   Trusting to time, and to progressive sense.

Thus the wild jargons of submissive peace,
  Of calm endurance, petrify the heart,
  Check the bold tear of manhood ere it start,
And bid the holy animation cease.
By due and slow degrees, by sober zeal,
Profess to rectify the public weal,
Which, by confusing parts, confound the whole,
Disorganise the will, and dislocate the soul.   60

'Tis thine to boast of long-existing laws,
Blame the *effect* of ill, but not the *cause*;
'Tis thine to call it mad erroneous rage,
  When Indignation's spirit nobly glows,
  When, smarting with the sense of bitterest woes,
The mass of man the war of nature wage;
'Tis thine with horror then to paint the scene,
As barbarous tyranny had never been,
Of ruthless anarchy alone complain:
Then if thy victims pause, prepare th' eternal chain.   70

(1795)

ANONYMOUS ('ELIZA')

Only a few scraps of information can be gleaned about 'Eliza', who published her *Poems and Fugitive Pieces* in 1796 at the urging of her friends. She had previously contributed verse to *The Star* newspaper, including some lines about Ramsgate Pier by moonlight, written in September 1790 'by way of amusement in ill health' (pp. 21–5). Other poems had excited admiring replies from readers with such Della-Cruscan names as 'Alphonzo' and 'Henry', which she also reprinted. Both her parents were dead and she lived in the country near the Thames: she refers to her 'humble roof' and 'the unassuming height' of her 'rural cot', which may have been near the Earl of Abergavenny's new house at Erridge, since several of her poems are addressed to her friend the Countess of Abergavenny, who died later in 1796 at Bristol aged 36. 'Eliza' was a not uncommon signature for women poets of the period: there is nothing, for example, to link her with *Adversity: or, The Tears of Britannia, A Poem, by a Lady* (1789), signed 'Eliza'. Her amusing account of her exhausting journey from Geneva to Chamonix and her adventures on the glaciers, from which an extract follows, makes an instructive contrast to the Duchess of Devonshire's more elevated description of her journey in the Alps published three years later (see no. 323).

315   from *A Tour to the Glaciers of Savoy*

An Epistle to John Waller, Esq.

WHEN we parted with you at Genève,
    The road was enchantingly various;
We began for to laugh in our sleeve,
    When they talked of the things that would scare us.

The Arve it flowed winding along
    Cultured vales, as we viewed them askance;
Enraptured we chatted and sung,
    Till arived at the town of Sallenche.

Ah me, then our troubles began,
    For our carriage no further could go,   10
So we stuffed in a vile charabanc,*
    Be-jerked from our top to our toe.

O, Gemini me! what a squalling,
    As along the rough muleteer banged us;—
'O, hold fast, be sure'—each kept bawling,
    As through the wild torrents he twanged us.

'Look here! and see there!'—cried each one,
    As over such steeps we were twitched;
But I vow in the midst of the fun,
    I thought our mule-driver bewitched!   20

Such twistings and jerkings there were,
    Predetermined to heartily bump us,
Zig-zag, like a dog in a fair,
    To all the four points of the compass.

However, to shorten my story,
    In very few words may be said,
When you get to the vale of Chamouny,
    All your twitches and jerks are repaid.

---

* *Charabanc*, a wooden machine to convey passengers over the mountains, in shape like the long carriages for musical instruments; it is open on the sides, and the travellers sit back to back, on benches placed length ways, with a footboard, or plank, in the same direction, to prevent their falling out; it is drawn by mules, and having no springs, the motion is inexpressibly rough, over very uneven and stony roads.

---

in our sleeve] to ourselves   twanged] pulled

For though many a vale we had passed,
  And o'er mountains, whose heads were gigantic,   30
Yet this vale of all vales, at the last,
  Was beyond every thing most romantic.

I wished for a genius of fire,
  I wished for a thousand of quills,
Of paper far more than a quire,
  To sketch out each beauty it fills.

For though I no genius was born,
  From such wishes I am not exempt;
Your pen would the subject adorn:
  You might soar,—but I must not attempt.   40

From this vale you ascend the Glaciers;
  On our ten toes we braved the fatigues;
That day laid aside female fears,
  And trudged there and back full eight leagues.

O, such puffing, and breathing, and blowing,
  Some languishing, faint, half-expiring!
Some danced, others sung, as a-going,
  Melting airs!—for we all were perspiring.

The guides they stumped first, looking big,
  With a prong, we each one scrambled after;   50
Though they all talked of dancing a jig,
  I protest I was far off from laughter.

Curiosity nudged me in vain,
  For slipping I looked to my feet;
Though expiring, I durst not complain,
  But with ecstasy cried—'Lord, how sweet!'

Such chasms there yawned on the plain,
  As fearful I peeped o'er the rocks,
Ay, if ever you catch me again,
  I deserve to be clutched in your stocks.   60

Then sliding and trembling again,
  Each wonder fresh frights on us heaping,
Each silently grunting through pain,
  Though forewarned, we must all pay for peeping.

ANONYMOUS ('ELIZA')

Arrived at the Maison de Blair,
   A hut that is not over-nice,
Yet pleased, although homely the fare,
   Then went on to the ocean of ice.

If to wonder it makes you look old,
   Such wonder of wonders are in it,   70
Muse but how those billows are rolled,
   You'd be ninety years old in a minute.

Suppose the sea heaving and swelling,
   Arrested in act of that motion,
With colours the rainbow excelling,
   And you'll faintly conceive the Ice Ocean.

The torrents that scare you withal,
   The deep fissures that strike ye with wonder,
The immense rocks of ice, as they fall,
   With reverb'rating noise loud as thunder.   80

Yet though 'twas enchantingly fine,
   Très superbe, magnifique, the rude murmur,
Still the part I thought nearest divine,
   Was when my feet touched *terra firma*.

Down the mountain we trudged it again,
   Each anxious to see the dear valley;
The whole party were hopping through pain,
   Like a group of lame ducks in an alley.

But oh, woe on woe, on the plain,
   Three good miles had we yet for to go;   90
We were caught in a deluge of rain,
   And besoused from our top to our toe.

The lightning it flashed in our faces,
   The hail it bespattered us round;
We all made most direful grimaces,
   To hear the hoarse thunder resound.

Had you seen but the droop of our hats,
   Not a thread 'mongst us all of dry linen;
Though we looked like a parcel of rats,
   'Midst our troubles we could not help grinning.   100

besoused] soaked

498

Arrived at our inn at the last,
  Our kind hostess she thought it so handy,
Before any other repast,
  To drench us all round with some brandy.

Then in our hot beds we reclined,
  Each served with a basin of whey;
Yet withal, 'twas a wonder to find,
  We had none of us colds the next day.

(1796)

MATILDA BETHAM
(1776–1852)

She was baptized Mary Matilda, the eldest of the fourteen children of the Revd William Betham (1749–1839) and his wife Mary Damont. Her father was head-master of a school at Stonham Aspel, Suffolk, from 1784 to 1833, and thereafter Rector of Stoke Lacy, Herefordshire. Six of her eight brothers entered the East India Company. She was educated spasmodically by her father and by access to his library (he published antiquarian works). She wrote of her childhood:

In our quiet and unorganized household sometimes the arts were all in all—sometimes learning unlocked her abstruse stores and people talked, albeit without pedantry, as if in the house of a philosopher. Sometimes plays were read and listened to with enthusiasm, or poems, followed in succession by the criticism of admiration. . . . We had loads of books in my father's library, and new ones, with reviews, etc., from the book-club every month. We were heard if we carried our lessons to my father's study, at least the boys were, but if they did not an occasional sarcasm or prophecy of what would become of them was all the punishment.

She came to London in 1794, staying with an uncle, and attempted to support herself in various ways while hoping for marriage. In 1796 she was in Cambridge, learning Italian from Agostino Isola, a well-known teacher, and in the following year published her *Elegies and Other Small Poems* at Ipswich. By 1799 she was engaged on a translation and also writing a novel, about which her friend Lady Bedingfield was encouraging: 'nothing goes down the Public throat like that sort of writing—any stuff will do, and small profits do to build on'. But a year later she was at home at Stonham, planning to support herself by painting miniature portraits, although her preparations for this career were hampered by her mother's insistence that she help in running the household. She later exhibited at the Royal Academy and also gave public readings from Shakespeare, but continued writing and in 1804 published her *Biographical Dictionary of the Celebrated Women of every Age and Country*, on which she had worked since 1798. According to her proposals for this work (1801), it was to have been in four volumes, but she had reduced its scale after the appearance of Mary Hays' *Female Biography* (1803), of which she speaks disparagingly in her preface. (As J. M. S. Tompkins has pointed out, Mary Hays, ardent feminist of the 1790s, did not include Mary Wollstonecraft Godwin in her work, whereas Matilda Betham did, pp. 374–7.) Her morale often flagged in her battle for independence. Lady Bedingfield in about 1804 referred to Matilda's 'disagreeable' feelings about her life as a journey 'across the fields and thickets', with 'brambles and rough paths' impeding her progress, and encouraged her to believe that an independent life could also lead into more 'delightful Glens, and Grottoes' than the 'beaten road' of marriage.

Coleridge admired one of her poems and addressed her in verse in 'To Matilda Betham from a Stranger', sent from Keswick on 9 September 1802. They did not meet for several years, by which time she was friendly with Robert Southey, Mrs Barbauld, and other writers. In 1808 she published a new volume of *Poems* and was by then having some success with her portraits. Southey, who described George Dyer as her 'agent', invited her to stay at Keswick in the summer of 1809 and she painted five portraits of members of his family. He and Charles Lamb both encouraged her literary ambitions, Lamb reading in MS her *Lay of Marie*, published (with scholarly appendices) in 1816. In about 1818, when her *Vignettes in Verse* appeared, family problems and her own ill health obliged her to leave London for the country, and she may have had some kind of nervous breakdown. In June 1820 Southey met 'poor Miss Betham' at Lamb's, 'perfectly sane in her conversation and manner, tho she has written me the maddest letters I ever saw'. She again settled in London in the 1830s and remained a familiar figure in literary circles until her death on 30 September 1852.

316 *In a Letter to A.R.C. on her Wishing to be Called Anna*

FORGIVE me, if I wound your ear
  By calling of you Nancy,
Which is the name of my sweet friend,
  The other's but her fancy.

Ah, dearest girl! how could your mind
  The strange distinction frame?
The whimsical, unjust caprice,
  Which robs you of your name.

Nancy agrees with what we see,
  A being wild and airy;   10
Gay as a nymph of Flora's train,
  Fantastic as a fairy.

But *Anna*'s of a different kind,
  A melancholy maid;
Boasting a sentimental soul,
  In solemn pomp arrayed.

Oh ne'er will I forsake the sound,
  So artless and so free!
Be what you will with all mankind,
  But *Nancy* still with me.   20

(1797)

Written on Whitsun-Monday, 1795

AT an open window sitting
    On this day of mirth and glee,
'Cross a flowery vista flitting,
    Many passing forms I see.
Ah! lovely prospect, stay awhile!
    And longer glad my doting eye
With poverty's delighted smile,
    And lightened step, as passing by;

With labour's spruce and ruddy train,
    Decked out in all their best array,   10
Who months of toil and care disdain,
    Paid by the pleasures of a day.
The village girl still let me view,
    Hastening to the neighbouring fair;
Her cap adorned with pink or blue,
    And nicely smooth her glossy hair;

With sparkling eye and smiling face,
    Tinged o'er with beauty's warmest glow;
With timid air and humble grace,
    With clear and undepressèd brow.   20
Go! lovely girl, and share the day
    To thy industrious merit due;
There join the dance or choral lay;
    Thou blooming village rose, adieu!

And thou, O youth, so blithe and free,
    Bounding swiftly o'er the plain,
Go, taste the joys of liberty,
    And cheer thy spirit, happy swain!
How different to the lonely hour,
    When slowly following the plough;   30
Self-buoyant joy forgets the power,
    Which warms thy gladdened bosom now.

If, some rural prize desiring,
    Or ambitious of applause,
Loud huzzas thy wishes firing,
    Thy steady hand the furrow draws;
Ne'er a victor famed in story
    Greater praise and reverence drew
Than thou, attired in humble glory,
    So, guiltless conqueror, adieu!   40

Oh, here a charming group appears!
  A cottage family, so gay,
Whose youthful hopes, unchecked by fears,
  In smiles of thoughtless rapture play.
Here, borne in fond, parental arms,
  The infant's roving eye we view;
Boasting a thousand, thousand charms,
  Endearing innocents, adieu!

They go! no more with beating heart,
  And lively, dancing step to tread;   50
Unwillingly will they depart
  To seek again their homely shed.
Ah! Eve, I love thy veil of grey,
  Which will conceal them from my view,
For, bending home their weary way,
  How sad would be our last adieu!

                                          (1797)

318   [*The Power of Women*]

WE wish not the mechanic arts to scan,
But leave the slavish work to selfish man!
He claims alone the privilege to war,
But 'tis our smiles that must reward the scar!
We need not these heroic dangers brave,
Who hold the laurelled conqueror a slave.
We need not search the world for sordid gain,
While we its proud possessors can enchain,
When their pursuit is only meant to prove,
How much they'd venture to deserve our love;   10
For wealth and honours they can only prize,
As making them more worthy in our eyes.
Their insufficiency they would supply,
And to these glittering resources fly!
Let the poor boasters then indulge their pride,
And think they o'er the universe preside;
Let them recount their numerous triumphs o'er,
And tell the tales, so often told before;
Their own much-doubted merit to enhance;
And gain the great reward—a favouring glance!   20
Let them, in bondage, fancy themselves free;
And while fast fettered, vaunt their liberty!
Because they do not massy chains behold,
Suppose that they are monarchs uncontrolled!

How vain! to hope 'twould be to them revealed
The flame burns strongest that is most concealed!
Then with what potent, what resistless art,
Those hidden bonds are twined about the heart,
So that the captive wanders unconfined,
And has no sovereign but o'er his mind!   30
The prize is mutual, either power or fame;
We have the substance, *they* may keep the name!

(Wr. *c.*1798; pub. 1905)

ANNA SAWYER
(*fl.* 1794–1801)

From the contents of her *Poems on Various Subjects* (Birmingham, 1801), it is evident
that she had formerly lived near Rowberrow, Somerset, a few miles from Cheddar
(on which she wrote a poem) and from Wrington, which explains her knowledge of
Hannah More. Some unspecified misfortune associated with her husband had
forced them to leave the Mendips for Birmingham. The 'Preface, By a Friend'
explains that the book is 'the first production of her unpractised Muse'. Some of the
verse had been written much earlier, 'partly for the amusement of a private circle, but
chiefly to dissipate unavoidable sorrow'. Her friends had urged her to publish them,
'in the fond hope of dispersing the clouds that hovered over her worthy Husband in
his declining years'. They had been corrected by 'a gentleman of erudition and taste'.
The volume was shorter than promised to her subscribers, as 'the unexpected duty
on paper obliged her to contract her original design'. A prefatory 'Address to the
British Public' (pp. vii–viii) by Charles Collins of Christ Church, Oxford, also refers
to her husband's misfortunes:

> From life's gay morn, to sober evening gray,
> Contented has she trod his luckless way.

Her subscribers accounted for some 700 copies, which would have brought her
about £175. They included Hannah More, Anna Seward, Dr Jenner, and the Revd
T. S. Whalley, as well as the Society of Artisans, Birmingham.

319 *Lines, Written on Seeing my Husband's Picture,*
painted when he was young

> THOSE are the features, those the smiles,
>   That first engaged my virgin heart:
> I feel the pencilled image true,
>   I feel the mimic power of art.

For ever on my soul engraved
  His glowing cheek, his manly mien;
I need not thee, thou painted shade,
  To tell me what my Love has been.

O dearer now, though bent with age,
  Than in the pride of blooming youth!
I knew not then his constant heart,
  I knew not then his matchless truth.

Full many a year, at random tossed,
  The sport of many an adverse gale,
Together, hand in hand, we've strayed
  O'er dreary hill, and lonely vale.

Hope only flattered to betray,
  Her keenest shafts misfortune shot;
In spite of prudence, spite of care,
  Dependence was our bitter lot.

Ill canst thou bear the sneer of wealth,
  Averted looks, and rustic scorn;
For thou wert born to better hopes,
  And brighter rose thy vernal morn.

Thy evening hours to want exposed,
  I cannot, cannot bear to see:
Were but thy honest heart at ease,
  I care not what becomes of me.

But though, my Love, the winds of woe
  Beat cold upon thy silver hairs,
Thy Anna's bosom still is warm;
  Affection still shall soothe thy cares.

And Conscience, with unclouded ray,
  The cottage of our age will cheer;
Friendship will lift our humble latch,
  And Pity pour her healing tear.

(Wr. 1796; pub. 1801)

Sunday Schools

'BRING little children unto me,'
　　The God of our Salvation cries:
The good and wise obey the call,
　　And lay up treasures in the skies.

Oft have I seen, with pensive eye,
　　Children in groups our streets disgrace,
Exposed to infamy and vice,
　　With shameless, yet with ruddy face.

Along the fields, along the lanes,
　　Rambled the giddy, giggling throng,　　　　　10
Eager to strip the flowering thorn,
　　Or rob the poor bird of its young.

No fears had they of God above,
　　No reverence for the Sabbath Day;
But thought those hallowed hours were meant
　　For naught but frolic—naught but play.

For play and mischief: out they flew,
　　The plague of many an honest clown,
Who, muttering, mourned his broken fence,
　　And clovered meadow trampled down.　　　　　20

Their toil-worn parents, sore distressed
　　To feed and clothe each luckless child,
No schooling could afford; their minds
　　Were like the weedy garden wild.

No bounds their insolence restrain,
　　No check the little urchins know;
None, save the beadle's lifted staff,
　　Or stern church-warden's angry brow.

Compassion bled at every pore
　　To hear their rude noise rend the sky:　　　　30
Oh! have not these immortal souls?
　　For these did not a Saviour die?

Celestial Charity advanced,
　　Instant their idle clamour ceased;
Smiling, she seized each vagrant's hand,
　　And let them to the 'paths of peace'.

How changed the scene! in decent garb,
　　With sober step and serious air,
Obsequious to their tutor's voice,
　　To church the cherub-train repair.　　　　　　40

The power of discipline has checked
　　The wild-fire of impetuous youth;
And heaven-taught Charity disclosed
　　The sacred Oracles of Truth.

What joy to view the infant tribes,
　　With eyes that glisten, cheeks that glow,
Fixed steady on their bible-tasks,
　　Or hammering out their chriss-cross row!

Ye more than parents of the poor,
　　How great, how god-like is your plan!　　　　50
To snatch from fire the 'flaming brand,'
　　And hew the rough block into man.

And oh! 'twill soothe the hours of pain,
　　And brighten your declining days,
That ye have taught the poor, forlorn,
　　To know their God, and hymn his praise.

　　　　　　　　　　　　　(Wr. *c.*1796; pub. 1801)

ANONYMOUS ('A LADY')

Poems on Various Subjects. By a Lady (1798) are dedicated to her 'Generous Patrons'.
Necessity, she explains, had driven her to publish verses written to amuse a mind in
danger of becoming 'a prey to serious and settled melancholy: early cut off from that
class of society it had been accustomed to associate with'. She admits to being
'totally unskill'd,—untutor'd in the art of poetry'. One of her poems also describes
her as banished 'Far from those scenes of elegance and ease,| (My natal rights)'. The
contents of her volume, though generalized, suggest that she had been deserted, and
left with a child, by a lover or husband.

321　　　*On my own little Daughter, Four Years old*

　　SWEET lovely infant, innocently gay,
　　　　With blooming face arrayed in peaceful smiles,
　　How light thy cheerful heart doth sportive play,
　　　　Unconscious of all future cares and toils.

　chriss-cross row] Christ-Cross row, alphabet (from the figure of a cross prefixed to the
alphabet in early hornbooks for children)

With what delight I've seen thy little feet
   Dancing with pleasure at my near approach!
Eager they ran my well-known form to meet,
   Secure of welcome, fearless of reproach.

Then happy hast thou prattled in mine ear
   Thy little anxious tales of pain or joy;   10
Thy fears lest faithful Tray thy frock should tear,
   Thy pride when ladies give the gilded toy.

How oft, when sad reflection dimmed mine eye,
   As memory recalled past scenes of woe,
Thy tender heart hath heaved the expressive sigh
   Of sympathy, for ills thou could'st not know.

Oft too in silence I've admired that face,
   Beaming with pity for a mother's grief,
Whilst in each anxious feature I could trace
   Compassion eager to afford relief.   20

E'en now methinks I hear that artless tongue,
   Lisping sweet sounds of comfort to mine ear:
'Oh! fret no more—your Fanny is not gone—
   She will not go—don't cry—your Fanny's here.'

If, ere her mind attains its full-grown strength,
   Thy will consigns me to an early tomb,
If in Thy sight my thread's near run its length,
   And called by Thee I cannot watch her bloom—

Oh heavenly Father, guard my infant child;
   Protect her steps through this wide scene of care;   30
Within her breast implant each virtue mild,
   And teach her all she ought to hope or fear.

(1798)

ANONYMOUS ('A LADY')

This poem was published in March 1799, in response to Robert Southey's 'Written on Sunday Morning', in his *Poems* (1797), pp. 129–31. Southey seems not to have reacted to it.

322   *[A Rebuke to Robert Southey]*

'Go thou and seek the House of Prayer,
I to the woodlands wend', &c.

Southey's *[Written on] Sunday Morning*

YES, Southey, yes, I to the House of Prayer,
Each Sabbath Day, will duly bend my step,
For God himself requires my presence there:
The sacred fane at his command arose,
And one blest day in seven he calls his own.
On Sinai's holy mount th' Almighty said,
'Make me a Sanctuary', in mystic state:
There, with his people, high communion held;
There, from the mercy-seat, his voice was heard,
Revealing hallowed truths to favoured man.   10

And when, among the wise and good, the time
That man refused to join in holy worship?
The heathen temple, and the Turkish mosque,
The Jewish synagogue, and Christian church,
Have all resounded with a *social* praise.
Shall I then go like thee, in churlish, wild,
Or solitary mood, to the lone vale,
The silent glen, or unfrequented grove,
When from the neighbouring spire the cheerful bells
Call us in sweet society to join,   20
And offer holy prayer?—With grateful love,
Father of Spirits, hail! behold I come!
Filled be my soul with reverential awe,
When in thy House I hear thy Sacred Word,
Disclosing truths majestic, strong, severe,
Such as may make Vice tremble; while, in strains
Of heavenly sweetness to the troubled heart,
It whispers comfort and eternal rest.

Yet too, like thee, Southey, I deem it sweet
Widely to rove, where by no human eye   30
My footsteps may be traced; down the deep dell,
Where rocks on rocks are piled above my head,
To penetrate, and mark where, through their clefts,
The fibrous roots of some old elm or yew
Shoot bare and rugged; whilst their trunks ascend
In shape grotesque and rude, excluding day.
How does my pensive soul, in these lone scenes,

Remote from mortal tread, delight to dwell,
Where I on Nature, and on Nature's God,
In calm repose, can meditate profound!   40

   Sweet also to my ear, sweet as to thine,
Are Nature's melodies: the lowing herd,
The distant bell, that speaks the fold at rest;
The gushing rill which, through the creviced rock,
Distills its freshness; the low-murmuring bee,
And cooling stockdove; all awake my heart,
Southey, like thine, to tenderness and love.

   Yet on that day, hallowed by ages past,
To which exhausted Labour looks for rest,
And Tumult for the hour of sacred peace,   50
My feet shall hasten from their sylvan haunt,
Though sweet as fabling poets ever sung;
Mine ear thy warbling Philomel forego,
And all the woodland harmony of spring,
To raise with man a nobler strain of praise:
Man who alone, of all creation, knows
His Maker to adore with vocal praise.

   Whether the village church attracts my steps,
Whose simple bell calls from the hamlets round
Their meek inhabitants, to praise their God,   60
Where all is decent, quiet, plain, and fit,
And untaught voices hymn their Maker's praise;
Or whether, in some old cathedral pile,
I find myself enclosed, with cloistered pillars,
Long Gothic aisles, and windows richly dim,
Where, slowly rising to the pealing sound
Of swelling organ, the loud-echoing chant,
And lofty anthem, raise th' enraptured soul:
Alike I own thy presence, hear thy word!
Nor would I, Southey, for the world forego   70
This dearest privilege to man allowed,
Due, as the sun each Sabbath Day shall shine,
To meet, with kindred man, the Parent God.

                  (1799)

GEORGIANA CAVENDISH (née SPENCER),
DUCHESS OF DEVONSHIRE
(1757–1806)

She was the eldest daughter of John, 1st Earl Spencer, and his wife Georgiana Poyntz. Brought up at Althorp, she was reported to be a beauty at the age of 15, and two years later married 'the first match in England', William Cavendish, 5th Duke of Devonshire. She soon became a prominent hostess, 'the empress of fashion', as Walpole repeatedly called her. As he wrote soon after her marriage, 'her youth, figure, flowing good nature, sense and lively modesty, and modest familiarity, make her a phenomenon'. Many years later she herself wrote: 'Before you condemn me remember that at seventeen I was a toast, a beauty, and a Duchess, and wholly neglected by my husband.' She had friends among the intelligentsia, and admired Samuel Johnson, whose 'cynic moroseness', according to Wraxall, 'seemed to dissolve under so flattering an approach', and he visited the Devonshires at Chatsworth in September 1784, shortly before his death. She was also friendly with R. B. Sheridan and C. J. Fox, for whom she boldly canvassed among the lowest class of voters (to the delight of the purveyors of satirical prints) in the famous Westminster election of 1784, giving a butcher what has been called 'the most famous kiss . . . in the history of electioneering'.

Her marital difficulties found a solution of a kind with the arrival in 1782 of Lady Elizabeth Foster, recently separated from her husband, with whom the Duke and Duchess lived for much of the rest of their lives in an amicable *ménage à trois*, both of them bearing children to the Duke, at one point only some two weeks apart. The Duchess was a spectacular gambler from early in her marriage, her debts amounting to almost £60,000 by 1789. In 1791 what appears to have been her only sexual indiscretion led to pregnancy by Charles Grey, the future Prime Minister, as a result of which she was ordered by the Duke to leave the country. She travelled in France, Switzerland, and Italy between November 1791 and September 1793, when the Duke allowed her to return. Although she led a quieter life thereafter, domestic arrangements were not simple. By 1797 the Duke was supporting two daughters and a son by his wife, his two children by Lady Elizabeth Foster, and Lady Elizabeth's two children by her original marriage, while his and the Duchess's two illegitimate daughters were brought up elsewhere. Her gambling debts, about which she was never entirely honest even to herself, weighed heavily on her to the end of her life. Of her recklessness she said: 'With a head not bad (I humbly trust) I have an instability of nature that is sometimes madness.' She was 44 when her mother, Lady Spencer, always her severest critic, told her: 'Your motives in everything are generous and benevolent, but you have never accustomed yourself to any degree of order or regularity, on the contrary you rather hold it in contempt.' She died at Devonshire House in March 1806. The Duke married Lady Elizabeth Foster in October 1809, but died in 1811.

She wrote light verse throughout her life, some of which found its way into print. *The Sylph* (1779), a novel, has often been attributed to her and, although she never claimed its authorship, she never denied it. Her only serious published poem describes her journey from Italy into Switzerland in 1793, when she was returning from 'exile' to the children from whom she had been separated for twenty months (lines 117–20). It may have been first printed for private circulation in 1799 as an undated quarto pamphlet. She was 'mortified and distressed' when it appeared in a number of newspapers and magazines in December 1799: 'I really have given so few away that I cannot guess in what manner it became so public.' Coleridge admired it and immediately addressed a poem to her in the *Morning Post* of 24 December 1799 ('O Lady, nursed in pomp and pleasure! | Whence learn'd you that heroic measure?', lines 5–6). It was soon translated into French and Italian and Lady Elizabeth Foster published an edition in 1816 illustrated with her own drawings.

323   *The Passage of the Mountain of St. Gothard.*
To my Children

YE plains, where threefold harvests press the ground,
    Ye climes, where genial gales incessant swell,
Where Art and Nature shed profusely round
    Their rival wonders—Italy, farewell!

Still may thy year in fullest splendour shine!
    Its icy darts in vain may Winter throw!
To thee a parent, sister, I consign,
    And winged with health, I woo thy gales to blow.

Yet pleased Helvetia's rugged brows I see,
    And through their craggy steeps delighted roam;   10
Pleased with a people, honest, brave, and free,
    Whilst every step conducts me nearer home.

I wander where Tesino madly flows,
    From cliff to cliff in foaming eddies tossed;
On the rude mountain's barren breast he rose,
    In Po's broad wave now hurries to be lost.

His shores neat huts and verdant pastures fill,
    And hills where woods of pine the storm defy;
While, scorning vegetation, higher still
    Rise the bare rocks, coeval with the sky.   20

Upon his banks a favoured spot I found,
    Where shade and beauty tempted to repose:
Within a grove, by mountains circled round,
    By rocks o'erhung, my rustic seat I chose.

Advancing thence, by gentle pace and slow,
    Unconscious of the way my footsteps pressed,
Sudden, supported by the hills below,
    St. Gothard's summits rose above the rest.

Midst towering cliffs, and tracts of endless cold,
　　The industrious path pervades the rugged stone,　　30
And seems—Helvetia! let thy toils be told—
　　A granite girdle o'er the mountain thrown.

No haunt of man the weary traveller greets,
　　No vegetation smiles upon the moor,
Save where the floweret breathes uncultured sweets,
　　Save where the patient monk receives the poor.

Yet let not these rude paths be coldly traced,
　　Let not these wilds with listless steps be trod:
Here fragrance scorns not to perfume the waste,
　　Here charity uplifts the mind to God.　　40

His humble board the holy man prepares,
　　And simple food and wholesome lore bestows;
Extols the treasures that his mountain bears,
　　And paints the perils of impending snows.

For whilst bleak Winter numbs with chilling hand,
　　Where frequent crosses mark the traveller's fate,
In slow procession moves the merchant band,
　　And silent treads where tottering ruins wait.

Yet, midst those ridges, midst that drifted snow,
　　Can Nature deign her wonders to display;　　50
Here Adularia shines with vivid glow,
　　And gems of chrystal sparkle to the day.

Here, too, the hoary mountain's brow to grace,
　　Five silver lakes in tranquil state are seen;
While from their waters many a stream we trace,
　　That, 'scaped from bondage, rolls the rocks between.

Hence flows the Reuss to seek her wedded love,
　　And, with the Rhine, Germanic climes explore;
Her stream I marked, and saw her wildly move
　　Down the bleak mountain, through her craggy shore.　　60

My weary footsteps hoped for rest in vain,
　　For steep on steep in rude confusion rose:
At length I paused above a fertile plain,
　　That promised shelter, and foretold repose.

Adularia] feldspar, a crystalline mineral

Fair runs the streamlet o'er the pasture green,
    Its margin gay, with flocks and cattle spread;
Embowering trees the peaceful village screen,
    And guard from snow each dwelling's jutting shed.

Sweet vale! whose bosom wastes and cliffs surround,
    Let me awhile thy friendly shelter share!   70
Emblem of life! where some bright hours are found
    Amidst the darkest, dreariest years of care.

Delved through the rock, the secret passage bends,
    And beauteous horror strikes the dazzled sight;
Beneath the pendent bridge the stream descends
    Calm—till it tumbles o'er the frowning height.

We view the fearful pass—we wind along
    The path that marks the terrors of our way—
Midst beetling rocks, and hanging woods among,
    The torrent pours, and breathes its glittering spray.   80

Weary at length, serener scenes we hail—
    More cultured groves o'ershade the grassy meads;
The neat though wooden hamlets deck the vale,
    And Altorf's spires recall heroic deeds.

But though no more amidst those scenes I roam,
    My fancy long each image shall retain—
The flock returning to its welcome home,
    And the wild carol of the cow-herd's strain.

Lucernia's lake its glassy surface shows,
    Whilst Nature's varied beauties deck its side;   90
Her rocks and woods its narrow waves enclose,
    And there its spreading bosom opens wide.

And hail the chapel! hail the platform wild!
    Where Tell directed the avenging dart,
With well-strung arm, that first preserved his child,
    Then winged the arrow to the tyrant's heart.

Across the lake, and deep embowered in wood,
    Behold another hallowed chapel stand,
Where three Swiss heroes lawless force withstood,
    And stamped the freedom of their native land.   100

Their liberty required no rites uncouth,
  No blood demanded, and no slaves enchained;
Her rule was gentle, and her voice was truth,
  By social order formed, by laws restrained.

We quit the lake—and cultivation's toil,
  With Nature's charms combined, adorns the way;
And well-earned wealth improves the ready soil,
  And simple manners still maintain their sway.

Farewell, Helvetia! from whose lofty breast
  Proud Alps arise, and copious rivers flow;   110
Where, source of streams, eternal glaciers rest,
  And peaceful Science gilds the plain below.

Oft on thy rocks the wondering eye shall gaze,
  Thy valleys oft the raptured bosom seek—
There, Nature's hand her boldest work displays,
  Here, bliss domestic beams on every cheek.

Hope of my life! dear children of my heart!
  That anxious heart, to each fond feeling true,
To you still pants each pleasure to impart,
  And more—O transport!—reach its home and you.   120

(1799)

SOURCES AND NOTES

THE notes are keyed to the texts by poem-number and not by pagination. Sources for the biographical headnote appear first, followed by sources of the texts of individual poems and, where necessary, concise explanatory notes on factual matters. The following abbreviations are used in the biographical sources:

Ballard, *Memoirs*	George Ballard, *Memoirs of Several Ladies of Great Britain who have been Celebrated for their Writings* (Oxford, 1752)
Biographia Dramatica	David Erskine Baker, *Biographia Dramatica or A Companion to the Playhouse* (2 vols., 1764); revised Isaac Reed (2 vols., 1782); revised Stephen Jones (4 vols., 1812)
Boswell, *Life*	James Boswell, *The Life of Samuel Johnson*, ed. G. B. Hill, revised L. F. Powell (6 vols., Oxford, 1934–64)
Cokayne, *Baronetage*	G. E. Cokayne, *The Complete Baronetage* (6 vols., Exeter, 1900–9)
Cokayne, *Peerage*	G. E. Cokayne, *The Complete Peerage* (revised edn., 13 vols., 1910–59)
Coleridge, *Letters*	*Collected Letters of Samuel Taylor Coleridge*, ed. E. L. Griggs (6 vols., Oxford, 1956–71)
DNB	*Dictionary of National Biography*
Dodsley, *Collection*	*A Collection of Poems by Several Hands*, ed. Robert Dodsley (6 vols., 1748–58)
Foxon, *Catalogue*	D. F. Foxon, *English Verse 1701–1750: A Catalogue* (Cambridge. 1975)
Garrick, *Letters*	*The Letters of David Garrick*, ed. D. M. Little and G. M. Kahrl (3 vols., 1963)
Gent. Mag.	*The Gentleman's Magazine* (1731–)
Nichols, *Anecdotes*	John Nichols, *Literary Anecdotes of the Eighteenth Century* (9 vols., 1812–15)
Nichols, *Illustrations*	John Nichols, *Illustrations of the Literary History of the Eighteenth Century* (8 vols., 1817–58)
Poems by Eminent Ladies	*Poems by Eminent Ladies*, ed. George Colman and Bonnell Thornton (2 vols., 1755; revised edn., 2 vols. [1780?])
Pope, *Correspondence*	*The Correspondence of Alexander Pope*, ed. G. Sherburn (5 vols., Oxford, 1956)
Shiells, *Lives*	Robert Shiels or Shiells, *The Lives of the Poets of Great Britain and Ireland* (5 vols., 1753; attributed to Theophilus Cibber on the title-page)
Swift, *Correspondence*	*The Correspondence of Jonathan Swift*, ed. H. Williams (5 vols., Oxford, 1963)
Thraliana	*Thraliana: The Diary of Mrs. Hester Lynch Thrale (Later Mrs. Piozzi)*, ed. K. C. Balderston (2 vols., Oxford, 1942; revised edn., 1951, cited)
Todd, *Dictionary*	*A Dictionary of British and American Women Writers 1660–1800*, ed. J. Todd (1984)

Walpole, *Correspondence*   Horace Walpole, *Correspondence*, ed. W. S. Lewis *et al.* (48 vols., New Haven, 1937–83)

Wordsworth, *Letters*   *The Letters of William and Dorothy Wordsworth* (2nd edn., revised by C. L. Shaver, M. Moorman, and A. G. Hill, 7 vols., Oxford, 1967–88)

MARY, LADY CHUDLEIGH (1–3). See Bodleian MS Rawl. Letters 90, fos. 61–2; E. Thomas, *Miscellany Poems* (1722), pp. 145–51, 275–80, and *Pylades and Corinna* (1731–2), i. 264–8, ii. 247–55; *Miscellaneous Poems*, ed. R. Savage (1726), pp. 213–14, for Martha Sansom's poem; Ballard, *Memoirs*, pp. 409–13; Shiells, *Lives*, iii. 177–86; *Poems by Eminent Ladies* (1755), i. 179–226; Cokayne, *Baronetage*, i. 206; M. Ferguson, *First Feminists* (Bloomington, 1985), pp. 212–38, for the full text of *The Ladies Defence*.

    1. Text from *The Ladies Defence* (1701), pp. 14–16.

    2–3. Texts from *Poems on Several Occasions* (1703), pp. 40, 104–5.

ANNE, COUNTESS OF WINCHILSEA. (4–18). See Shiells, *Lives*, iii. 321–5; the biographical introduction to *Poems*, ed. M. Reynolds (Chicago, 1903); *Victoria County Hist. of Hampshire*, iv (1911), 254; Cokayne, *Peerage*, XII. ii. 780–1; H. S. Hughes, 'Lady Winchilsea and her Friends', *London Mercury*, 19 (1929), 624–35; *Pope's Own Miscellany*, ed. N. Ault (1935); D. G. Neill, 'Studies for an Edition of the Poems of Anne, Countess of Winchilsea' (unpub. thesis, Oxford, 1954); Pope, *Correspondence*, i. 203; Swift, *Poems*, ed. H. Williams (3 vols., Oxford, 1958), i. 119–21; Wordsworth, *Letters*, iii. 154, v. 157, 237–9, 259–60; Wordsworth, *Prose Works*, ed. W. J. B. Owen and J. W. Smyser (3 vols., Oxford, 1974), iii. 74, 94; E. Hampsten, 'Poems by Anne Finch' and 'Petticoat Authors 1660–1720', *Women's Studies*, 7 (1980), 5–19, 34–8; A. Messenger, 'Publishing Without Perishing: Lady Winchilsea's *Miscellany Poems* of 1713', *Restoration*, 5 (1981), 27–37; J. Gay, *Dramatic Works*, ed. J. Fuller (2 vols., Oxford, 1983), i. 440–2.

    4. Published in *A New Collection of Poems on Several Occasions*, ed. C. Gildon (1701); text from *Miscellany Poems* (1713), pp. 92–5. Lines 15–16 allude to the biblical story of Balaam and the ass, Num. 22: 21–35. Lines 57–8 refer to tea and coffee.

    5. Text from Richard Steele's *Poetical Miscellanies* (1714), pp. 45–6. She may have omitted it in 1713 because it had often been reprinted with a parody ('A Fart'), as in the anonymous *Poems on Several Occasions: Together with Some Odes* (1703).

    6. Published in Delariviere Manley, *Secret Memoirs . . . from the New Atlantis* (1709), pp. 169–71; text from *Miscellany Poems* (1713), pp. 259–62. For Moses' view from Pisgah (lines 8–10), see Deut. 34: 1–4.

    7–8. Published in *Poetical Miscellanies*, vi (1709), 225–32; texts from *Miscellany Poems* (1713), pp. 123, 179–83.

    9. Text from *Miscellany Poems* (1713), pp. 145–50. Lines 31–4 characterize the reign of Charles II. Lines 54–66 refer to six of her literary contemporaries and perhaps acquaintance: Matthew Prior, poet and diplomat; Sir John Vanbrugh, dramatist and architect; Nicholas Rowe, poet and tragedian; John Philips, author of the pseudo-Miltonic *The Splendid Shilling* (1705); Elizabeth Singer (later Rowe) as 'Philomela', identified in a note as 'Author of several excellent Poems'; herself as 'Ardelia'; and Edmund 'Rag' Smith, poet and dramatist. Maro (line 70) is Virgil, rewarded for his poetry by Augustus. Maecenas (line 73) is the patron of Horace. Line 97 refers to Wentworth Dillon, Earl of Roscommon, respected Restoration poet and critic.

10. Text from *Miscellany Poems* (1713), pp. 33–40. For Solomon and the Queen of Sheba (lines 58–63), see I Kgs. 10: 1–13: a long note to these lines from Josephus has been omitted. For Jacob wearing Esau's coat (lines 76–85), see Gen. 27. A note to lines 89–96 states, 'These Circumstances are related by *Plutarch* in the Life of *Sylla*.' Lucullus (*c.* 114–57 BC) was a successful Roman general.

11–16. Texts from *Miscellany Poems* (1713), pp. 110–12, 154–6, 200–2, 227–9, 252–3, 291–3. In **16** the compliment in lines 19–20 is to Anne Tufton, Countess of Salisbury.

17. In the Wellesley MS: text as printed in the article (1929) by H. S. Hughes cited above, pp. 627–9. She addressed two other poems to Catherine Fleming at Coleshill, Warwickshire, the seat of Lord Digby. Birnam (line 71) alludes to the witches' prediction in Macbeth, fulfilled in Act V.

18. Text from British Library, MS Lansdowne 852, fo. 208; printed in *The Hive* (1724), i. 96. Many women were among the credulous investors in the South Sea Bubble in the summer and autumn of 1720.

SARAH EGERTON. **(19–23).** See Delariviere Manley, *Secret Memoirs . . . from the New Atlantis* (1709), pp. 158–63, and *Memoirs of Europe* (1710), pp. 289–90; *Gent. Mag.* (1780), 562 and (1781), 121–2, 455; *Records of Buckinghamshire*, 8 (1903), 34; P. B. Anderson, 'Mistress Delariviere Manley's Biography', *Modern Philology*, 33 (1936), 271–2; F. A. Nussbaum's edition of *Satires on Women* (Augustan Reprint Society No. 180, Los Angeles, 1976), which includes *The Female Advocate*; J. Medoff, 'New Light on Sarah Fyge (Field, Egerton)', *Tulsa Studies in Women's Literature*, 1 (1982), 155–75; F. A. Nussbaum, *The Brink of All We Hate* (Lexington, 1984), pp. 30–4; M. Ferguson, *First Feminists* (Bloomington, 1985), pp. 152–70. Texts from *Poems on Several Occasions* (1703), pp. 25–7, 34–5, 42–3, 97–8, 108–9.

23. The Pentateuch (line 12) is the first 5 books of the Old Testament, supposedly written by Moses. The 'ten celestial females' (line 36) are Minerva, goddess of wisdom, and the Nine Muses.

ELIZABETH THOMAS **(24–32).** See Bodleian MS Rawl. Letters 90, for some of the material sold to Curll; *Memoirs of William Congreve*, ed. C. Wilson (1730), pt. ii, pp. 1–10; *Pylades and Corinna* (2 vols., 1731–2); Pope, *Dunciad* (1743 edn.), ii. 69–76; W. Ayre, *Memoirs of Alexander Pope* (2 vols., 1745), i. 292; Shiells, *Lives*, iv. 146–63; J. Dryden, *Critical and Miscellaneous Prose Works*, ed. E. Malone (1800), I. i. 353–5n.; W. M. Thomas, 'Dryden, Pope, and Curll's "Corinna" ', *Notes and Queries*, 1st ser., 12 (1855), 277–9; *Letters of John Dryden*, ed. C. E. Ward (Durham, NC, 1942), pp. 125–8, 132, 186; Pope, *Correspondence*, i. 57n., ii. 437, 439–41, iii. 458–9; J. V. Guerinot, *Pamphlet Attacks on Alexander Pope* (1969), pp. 153–6. Texts from *Miscellany Poems on Several Subjects* (1722), pp. 174–9, 79–85, 98, 181–6, 193–5, 218–19, 267–8, 294–5. See also p. 539 below.

24. 'Clemena' was Anne Osborne, her cousin. Locket's and Pontack's (line 72) were popular taverns.

26. Line 31 refers to Lord Foppington in Vanbrugh's *The Relapse* (1696) and Justice Overdo in Jonson's *Bartholomew Fair*, which was still performed. At Marathon (line 61) the Athenians defeated the Persians in 490 BC.

28. Lines 70–3 refer to Anne Dacier (1654–1720), translator and critic of Homer and other classical authors.

30. See Ruth Perry, *The Celebrated Mary Astell: An Early English Feminist* (Chicago, 1986).

ELIZABETH ROWE **(33–6).** See the biography by Theophilus Rowe and Henry Grove in *Miscellaneous Works* (1739), i. pp. i–xcvi; Shiells, *Lives*, iv. 326–41;

E. H. Plumptre, *Life of Thomas Ken* (2 vols., 1889), ii. 173–4; *The Early Diary of Frances Burney*, ed. A. R. Ellis (2 vols., 1907), i. 9; Boswell, *Life*, i. 312; H. S. Hughes, *The Gentle Hertford* (New York, 1940) and 'Elizabeth Rowe and the Countess of Hertford', *Publications of the Modern Language Association*, 59 (1944), 726–46; H. B. Wright, 'Matthew Prior and Elizabeth Singer', *Philogical Quarterly*, 24 (1945), 71–82; M. Prior, *Literary Works*, ed. H. B. Wright and M. K. Spears (2nd edn., 2 vols., Oxford, 1971), i. 199–202, 247, ii. 888, 949; H. F. Strecher, *Elizabeth Singer Rowe, the Poetess of Frome* (Berne, 1973).

33. Text from *Divine Hymns and Poems* (1704), pp. 11–13.

34. Text from *Miscellaneous Works* (1739), i. 92–3. Another poetic version of this song, which derives from John Scheffer's *Lapponia* (Frankfurt, 1673; English trans. 1674), ch. 25, has been attributed to Ambrose Philips: see *Spectator*, No. 366, 30 Apr. 1712 (ed. D. F. Bond, Oxford, 1965, iii. 376).

35. Text from A. Pope, *Eloisa to Abelard* (2nd edn., 1720 [for 1719], pp. 47–52. For Thomas Rowe see headnote.

36. Text from *Miscellaneous Works* (1739), i. 131–2.

OCTAVIA WALSH (37). T. R. Nash, *Collections for the History of Worcestershire*, i. (1781), 2–3; Peter Murray Hill, Cat. 82 (1962), item 31. Text from Bodleian MS Eng. poet. e. 31, fo. 26.

LADY MARY WORTLEY MONTAGU (38–49). She has been unusually well served by modern scholarship: see R. Halsband, *The Life of Lady Mary Wortley Montagu* (Oxford, 1956); *Complete Letters*, ed. R. Halsband (3 vols., Oxford, 1965–7); *Essays and Poems and Simplicity. A Comedy*, ed. R. Halsband and I. Grundy (Oxford, 1977). Texts usually follow the MSS as printed in *Essays and Poems* (1977), but in a few cases texts printed in her lifetime, in which metrical and grammatical irregularities have been eliminated, have (with some hesitation) been preferred.

38. Text from *The Plain Dealer*, 27 Apr. 1724, followed with minor variants in *Six Town Eclogues* (1747), p. 47.

39. Published in *Six Town Eclogues* (1747); text from *Essays and Poems*, pp. 201–4. For her own illness from smallpox, see headnote. In line 21 Charles Lillie was a perfumer in the Strand and Peter Motteux, also an author, sold oriental goods in Leadenhall St.

40. Written 26 Dec. 1717; published, through her uncle William Fielding, in *A New Miscellany*, ed. A. Hammond (1720), from which the title is adopted; text from *Essays and Poems*, pp. 206–10. The Fanar or Phanar (line 68) was the Greek quarter of Constantinople.

41. Written in 1718, in response to Pope's epitaphs on the two lovers struck by lightning at Stanton Harcourt, where he was staying (see *Minor Poems*, ed. N. Ault and J. Butt, 1954, pp. 197–201); published in her *Letters* (1763); text from *Essays and Poems*, pp. 215–16.

42. Written in the early 1720s; published in *Six Town Eclogues* (1747); text from *Essays and Poems*, pp. 235–6.

43. Written *c.* 1725; text from *Essays and Poems*, pp. 242–4. For the personality and interests of Allen, Lord Bathurst (1684–1775), see M. Mack, *Alexander Pope* (1985), pp. 371–3, 382–4. Andrea Palladio (1508–80), the neo-classical Italian architect (line 3), admired Vitruvius Pollio (line 9), Roman author (*fl.* 40 BC) of *De Architectura*.

44. Written in the 1720s; published in *London Mag.* 19 (1750); text from *Essays and Poems*, pp. 244–6.

45. Written *c*.1730; text from Dodsley, *Collection*, iii. 312–13. It was evidently addressed to, and answered by, Lady Anne Irwin (see headnote to **102**).

46. Text from *Verses Address'd to the Imitator of . . . Horace* (1733), lines 55–112. For her quarrel with Pope, see headnote, and for a more detailed account, Halsband, *Life* (1956), pp. 129–32, 135–52. Lines 3–4 allude to Gen. 3: 15 and lines 58–9 to Gen. 4: 15. Some lines from Pope himself are adapted: in lines 26–7, *Epistle to Burlington*, 107–8, and in 31–3, the *First Satire of the Second Book*, 118, 69, 79–80.

47. Written 1736, perhaps in despair at Algarotti's departure from England (see headnote); printed in *London Mag.* 18 (1749), 284, as 'Verses on Self-Murder', with an editorial note disclaiming its contents; text from *Essays and Poems*, pp. 290–1. Tully (line 13) is Cicero.

48–9. Written by 1740; printed in *London Mag.* 19 (1750); texts from *Essays and Poems*, pp. 300–1.

MARY MONCK (**50–2**). See short accounts of her in Ballard, *Memoirs*, pp. 418–22, and Shiells, *Lives*, iii. 201; G. Jacob, *Historical Account of the English Poets* (1720), pp. 106–8; Cokayne, *Peerage*, xi. 31–2; *Hist. MSS Comm.: Various Reports*, viii. (1913), 243–68, 318–19.

50–1. Texts from *Marinda. Poems and Translations upon Several Occasions* (1716), pp. 23–5, 124. In **51** she refers to Madeleine de Scudéry's *Artamène: ou le Grand Cyrus* (Paris, 1649–53; English trans., 1653–5).

52. Text from *Poems by Eminent Ladies* (1755), ii. 195, where it seems to have been first printed. It noticeably fails to reflect her husband's recent problems. See also p. 539 below.

JANE HOLT (**53**). See G. Jacob, *Poetical Register* (1719), p. 301. Text from *A Fairy Tale* (1717), pp. 28–30. The 'good Bishop' (1) is St Valentine, Bishop of Terni. Line 15 refers to William, Earl Cowper, the Lord Chancellor.

SUSANNA CENTLIVRE (**54–5**). See G. Jacob, *Poetical Register* (1719), pp. 31–4; Shiells, *Lives*, iv. 58–61; J. W. Bowyer, *The Celebrated Mrs. Centlivre* (Durham, NC, 1952); J. H. Mackenzie, 'Susan Centlivre', *Notes and Queries*, 198 (1953), 386–90; J. E. Norton, 'Some Uncollected Authors: Susanna Centlivre', *Book Collector*, 6 (1957), 172–8, 280–5; F. P. Lock, *Susanna Centlivre* (Boston, Mass., 1979); F. Morgan, *The Female Wits* (1981), pp. 51–61, 449.

54. Text from *An Epistle to the King of Sweden* (1717), pp. 5–8. Charles XII of Sweden (1682–1718), the ascetic military leader, remained a bachelor in spite of repeated promises to marry. He intrigued with the Jacobites against the Elector of Hanover ('Brunswick', line 68) when he became George I, and there were rumours that he would invade Britain. At line 50 'young James' is the Young Pretender.

55. Text from *A New Miscellany*, ed. A. Hammond (1720), pp. 326–30. The poem is addressed to Nicholas Rowe (1674–1718), the dramatist, who died later in the year. It refers to his wife Anne as Nancy (line 39); to Dr James Wellwood (1652–1727), physician and author (line 46), who wrote the memoir of Rowe in his posthumously published translation of Lucan (1718); and to Carr, Lord Hervey (1691–1723) (line 46), who subscribed for 4 copies of Rowe's Lucan.

JANE BRERETON (**56–7**). See the memoir prefixed to *Poems on Several Occasions* (1744), pp. i–xxix; *Gent. Mag.* (1737), 316, (1741), 224, 392, 664, (1742), 224, 392, 664, (1744), 344, 680; Swift, *Correspondence*, iv. 320–2. Texts from *Poems* (1744), pp. 33–5, 53–60.

56. Lines 19–30 condemn Aphra Behn (1640–89), dramatist and novelist, Delariviere Manley (1663–1724), dramatist, journalist, and author of 'scandal novels', and Eliza Haywood (1693–1756), dramatist, novelist, and journalist; and praise Katherine Philips (1631–64) ('The Matchless Orinda'), Elizabeth (Singer) Rowe (see 33–6), and Anne Finch, Countess of Winchilsea (see 4–18).

57. Thomas Griffith was no doubt related to Nehemiah Griffith, a Welsh friend of the Breretons, author of *The Leek. A Poem on St. David's Day* (1717). Lucy (line 4) was her elder daughter. Lines 23–8 allude to the Jacobite Rebellion of 1715, after the failure of which there were expectations that Charles XII of Sweden (line 43) might invade Britain (see **54**). Carolina (line 71) was the Princess of Wales, the future Queen. Joseph Addison (lines 94–101) had celebrated Marlborough's victory at Blenheim in *The Campaign* (1705).

ANONYMOUS. (**58**). From *A New Miscellany*, ed. A. Hammond (1720), p. 123.

MARTHA SANSOM (**59–63**). See G. Jacob, *Historical Account of Our Most Considerable English Poets* (1720), p. 326, and *Human Happiness . . . with Several Other Miscellaneous Poems* (1721), p. 43; *Clio: Or, A Secret History of the Life and Amours of the Late celebrated Mrs. S–n—m. Written by Herself, in a Letter to Hillarius* (1752); A. Hill, *Works* (1753), i. 338, ii. 180, iii. 6, 41, 45–6, 50, iv. 96–8, and *Dramatic Works* (1760), ii. 389–404; *Gent. Mag.* (1781), 22; Bolton Corney in *The Athenaeum* (16 July 1859), p. 78; *English Army Lists 1661–1714*, ed. C. Dalton, vi (1904), 243; C. Tracy, *The Artificial Bastard* (1953), pp. 61–8, and *The Poetical Works of Richard Savage* (Cambridge, 1962), pp. 26–30, 53, 73, 250, 276; James Thomson, *Letters and Documents*, ed. A. D. McKillop (Lawrence, Kan., 1958), pp. 34–5; James Thomson, *The Seasons*, ed. A. J. Sambrook (Oxford, 1981), p. 309.

59–60. Texts from *A New Miscellany*, ed. A. Hammond (1720), 258–60, 264–6. In **59** Bucelia (line 24) is presumably a playful personification of 'buckle'. Isaac (line 40), who was a well-known dancing-master of the period, is my emendation of 'Isaiah' in the original text, which seems meaningless. In **60** lines 15–22 allude to the love-poetry of Edmund Waller and to Milton's *Paradise Lost*.

61–2. Texts from *Miscellaneous Poems* (1726), ed. Richard Savage, pp. 182–6, 191–2. In **61** line 45 refers to Sir Anthony Van Dyck (1599–1641), the celebrated portrait-painter. In **62** 'melancholy Bateman' (line 23) refers to the popular chapbook, *Bateman's Tragedy: Or, The Perjur'd Bride Justly Rewarded*, in which the rejected lover hangs himself outside the girl's bedroom door.

63. Text from *Clio* (1752), p. 165.

CONSTANTIA GRIERSON (**64**). See A. C. Elias, 'A Manuscript Book of Constantia Grierson's', *Swift Studies*, 2 (1987), 33–56, which supersedes all previous accounts. Text from Laetitia Pilkington, *Memoirs*, i (Dublin, 1748), 29–32, where she explains: 'I being in a Country-Town at the Assizes Time, had writ her an Account to *Dublin* of the principal Entertainments I met with there and in the rest of the Country.'

JUDITH MADAN (**65–7**). See J. Brereton, *Poems on Several Occasions* (1744), pp. 88–9; *Poems by Eminent Ladies* (1755), ii. 135–44; *London Mag.* 28 (1759), 101–2, 155–7; 29 (1760), 99; *Poetical Calendar* (1763), iii. 17–30; F. Madan, *The Madan Family* (Oxford, 1933), pp. 55–103, 264–72; Pope, *Correspondence*, ii. 136, 138, 142–4, 148–50, 155–6, 174–5, 179–80, 194–6, 201–3, 209–10. Texts from F. Madan, *The Madan Family* (Oxford, 1933), pp. 100, 102.

65. Howe (line 12) refers to her friend Mary Howe (d. 1749), a Maid of Honour, later Countess of Pembroke.

67. The son was Martin Madan (1725–90), Methodist clergyman and author.

ELIZABETH TOLLET (**68–74**). See J. Hanway, *Translations of Several Odes, Satyrs, and Epistles of Horace* (1730), pp. 262–3; A. Hill, *Works* (1753), iii. 51–2; *Monthly*

Review, 13 (1755), 373–7; *Biographia Dramatica* (1782), i. 449–50; J. Nichols, *Select Collection of Poems*, vi (1782), 64–81; *Gent. Mag.* (1815), ii. 484. Texts from *Poems on Several Occasions* (1724), pp. 21–2, 54–5, 57, 62–3 and (1755), pp. 131–3, 152.

68. Her brother Cooke Tollet entered St John's College, Cambridge from Westminster School in June 1716, became a Fellow-Commoner in 1721, married in 1732, and died in 1739. In Greek mythology, Cadmus of Tyre (line 3) civilized the Boeotians and taught them the use of letters. Tully (line 9) is Cicero. Line 31 probably refers to Mary Villiers, Lady Lansdown, and Catherine Wyndham, daughter of Charles Seymour, Duke of Somerset, and wife of Sir William Wyndham, Tory politician. The poets Abraham Cowley and Matthew Prior (line 56) had been members of Trinity and St John's Colleges. Line 60 may be a joke, suggesting that her brother praise *not* the rival university, but Robert Harley, Earl of Oxford, the recently deposed Tory statesman.

71. Hypatia was a famous Neo-platonic philosopher, who was murdered by the Alexandrian mob in AD 415: she taught astronomy, as well as the philosophy of Plato and Aristotle.

74. This unusually compressed short poem alludes to the new Westminster Bridge, opened in 1750: to Cassibelan or Cassivelaunus (line 9), commander of the British forces resisting Julius Caesar's second invasion of Britain in 54 BC; and (lines 13–14) to the replacement of the calendar established by Julius Caesar in 46 BC with the Gregorian Calendar, finally adopted in Britain in 1752.

MARY DAVYS (**75**). See G. Jacob, *Historical Account of Our Most Considerable English Poets* (1720), p. 290; *Biographia Dramatica* (1782), i. 118–19; Swift, *Correspondence*, iv. 83–4, 107; W. H. McBurney, 'Mrs. Mary Davys: Forerunner of Fielding', *PMLA* 74 (1959), 348–55, and *Four Before Richardson* (Lincoln, Neb., 1963), p. xxix. Text from *Works* (2 vols., 1725), i. 277–80. The omitted rhymeword (line 36) may be 'piss-bowl'.

ARABELLA MORETON (**76**). From *A New Miscellany . . . Written Chiefly by Persons of Quality* [1726?], p. 71. See also p. 539 below.

FRANCES SEYMOUR, COUNTESS OF HERTFORD (**77–8**). See H. S. Hughes, 'Thomson and the Countess of Hertford', *Modern Philology*, 25 (1928), 439–68 and 28 (1931), 468–70, *The Gentle Hertford* (New York, 1940), and 'Elizabeth Rowe and the Countess of Hertford', *PMLA* 59 (1944), 726–46; Walpole, *Correspondence*, xxxii. 283; J. Thomson, *The Seasons*, ed. J. Sambrook (Oxford, 1981), pp. xliii, xlv–vi, 2, 300–1.

77. First published in *A New Miscellany . . . Written Chiefly by Persons of Quality* [1726?]; text, slightly revised, from *The Story of Inkle and Yarico* (1738). The narrative in Steele's *Spectator*, No. 11 (13 Mar. 1711) derived from Richard Ligon's *True and Exact History of the Island of Barbados* (1657). Several later poets retold the story from different viewpoints.

78. Text from a letter to Lady Pomfret, 1 July 1740, in the Hertford–Pomfret *Correspondence* (3 vols., 1805), ii. 37–9. Richkings (or Riskins) was later known as Percy Lodge (see headnote). Lines 9–11 refer to the religious writers John Scott (1639–95) and Samuel Clarke (1675–1729), and to John Gay's *The Shepherd's Week* (1714). Lines 12–14 refer to incidents in Tasso's *Jerusalem Delivered*, Bks xii–xvi. Sir Robert Walpole's opponents were demanding a war with Spain (line 34) at this time.

MEHETABEL WRIGHT (**79–82**). See *Gent. Mag.* (1736), 155, 740; *Poetical Calendar* (1763), vi. 79–89; *Letters from Dr. Thomas Herring, Archbishop of Canterbury*, ed. J. Duncombe (1777), p. 131; A. Clarke, *Memoirs of the Wesley Family* (1823),

SOURCES AND NOTES

pp. 486–510; *The Bards of Epworth: Or, Poetic Gems from the Wesley Cabinet* (1856), pp. 244–63; Samuel Wesley, *Poems on Several Occasions*, ed. J. Nichols (1862), pp. 548–50, 554–6; John Wesley, *Letters*, ed. F. Baker (2 vols., Oxford, 1980–2), i. 151–2, 161, 176–7, 185, 189, 199–205, 207, 219–20, 231, ii. 99, 112, 642.

79. Text from A. Clarke, *Memoirs of the Wesley Family* (1823), pp. 491–3.

80. Text from Samuel Wesley, *Poems on Several Occasions*, ed. J. Nichols (1862), pp. 553–4.

81. Text from *Gent. Mag.* (1733), 542.

82. Text from *Poetical Calendar* (1763), vi. 89.

ANONYMOUS. **(83)**. From *The Flower-Piece. A Collection of Miscellany Poems*, ed. M. Concanen (1731), pp. 237–9. Lines 51–62 refer to Salmacis in Greek myth, who loved Hermaphroditus, son of Hermes and Aphrodite. When he rejected her, the gods granted her prayer that they be joined in one body (hence 'hermaphrodite').

MARY BARBER **(84–90)**. See British Library, Stowe MS 748, fo. 191, for an undated letter to Edward Cave, about their common ailment of gout, and sending him a poem, probably that in *Gent. Mag.* (1737), 179; Ballard, *Memoirs*, pp. 461–4; L. Pilkington, *Memoirs*, iii (1754), 65; *Poems by Eminent Ladies* (1755), i. 7–50; *Autobiography and Correspondence of Mary Granville, Mrs. Delany*, ed. Lady Llanover (6 vols., 1861–2), i. 330–1, 383, 402, 554, ii. 306, 316; *The Orrery Papers*, ed. Countess of Cork and Orrery (2 vols., 1909), i. 223–5, ii. 103, 107; *Alumni Dublinienses*, ed. G. D. Burtchaell and T. V. Sadleir (Dublin, 1935), p. 38; R. W. I. Smith, *English-Speaking Students of Medicine at the University of Leyden* (Edinburgh, 1932), p. 14; W. M. Sale, *Samuel Richardson: Master Printer* (Ithaca, 1950), pp. 114–15; Swift, *Correspondence*, iii. 430, 449, 457, 478–81, 501, iv. 80, 92–3, 185–6, 191–2, 224, 333, 456, 538–41; T. C. D. Eaves and B. D. Kimpel, *Samuel Richardson* (Oxford, 1971), pp. 122, 144; A. C. Elias, 'A Manuscript Book of Constantia Grierson's', *Swift Studies*, 2 (1987), 33–56.

84. Text from *The Flower-Piece. A Collection of Miscellany Poems*, ed. M. Concanen (1731), pp. 228–30. In infancy both boys and girls wore frocks. Constantine Barber (*c.*1713–83) entered Trinity College, Dublin, in 1730, studied medicine at the University of Leiden from 1738, became a professor at Trinity College in 1740, and was later three times President of the College of Physicians in Dublin.

85. Text from *Poems on Several Occasions* (1734), pp. 17–19. Guido (line 24) is Guido Reni (1575–1642), the Bolognese painter much admired in the 18th century.

86. Text from *Poems* (1734), pp. 58–62. For 'Con.' (line 2), still at school when these lines were written in the early 1720s, see note to **84** above. St Patrick (lines 13–14) supposedly banished snakes from Ireland. Poets were to have been excluded from Plato's *Republic* (lines 16–18). For the allusion to Sir Thomas More (lines 24–7 and note) see *Guardian*, No. 163 (17 Sept. 1713), which translates some Latin verses by More on the choice of a wife ('May she be learned, if possible, or at least capable of being made so!'). They were addressed, however, not to a son but to a friend.

87. Text from *Poems* (1734), pp. 126–7. The poem was said to be '*positively*' hers by a member of Swift's circle in 1732 (*Autobiography and Corresp. of Mrs. Delany*, i. 372) and she herself refers to it in 'To A Lady', line 81 (see **90**). A mistaken attribution to Jabez Earl in Dodsley's *Collection*, v. 110, has led some recent scholars to the damaging and unjustified conclusion that she was in the habit of printing poems by others as her own: see H. Williams's note in Swift, *Correspondence*, iv. 192, and the article by A. C. Elias cited above, p. 43 and n. The 1782 edn. of Dodsley's *Collection*, v. 118–19, withdrew the attribution to Earl, admitted that the poem was generally attributed to Mrs Barber, but suggested that it was really by Mrs Pilkington who seems, however, never to have claimed it.

88. Text from *Poems* (1734), pp. 151–3. Frances Arabella Kelly, a correspondent of Swift and member of his circle, had in fact died in November 1733 'in the Flower of her Youth and Beauty, of a consumptive Illness' (Swift, *Correspondence*, iv. 203 n.). Ovid described the head of Medusa, the Gorgon, which turned to stone whatever met its gaze in *Metamorphoses*, Bk. iv (lines 4–10).

89. Text from *Poems* (1734), pp. 233–5.

90. Text from *Poems* (1734), pp. 275–81. Both Swift and Lord Dorset (lines 16–17) did indeed subscribe for 10 copies. For *The Widows Address* (1725) (lines 20–1) see headnote. Lines 44–8 refer to the intense interest in the London musical world in 1733 in Handel's engagement of Carestini to replace another highly paid Italian singer, Senesino, with whom he had quarrelled.

MISS W—— **(91)**. Text from *The Gentleman's Study, In Answer to The Lady's Dressing-Room* (Dublin, 1732).   Lines 97–110 refer to remedies for venereal disease. For Mrs Pilkington's mother see her *Memoirs*, iii (1754), 161.

ELIZABETH BOYD **(92)**. See *Biographia Dramatica* (1782), ii. 90–1. Text from *The Humorous Miscellany; Or, Riddles for the Beaux* (1733), p. 18.

ANONYMOUS **(93)**. Text from *Gent. Mag.* (1733), 371, where it is followed by 'The Answer. By a Gentleman' ('How happy is a woman's fate', etc.).

LAETITIA PILKINGTON **(94–5)**. See *Memoirs of Mrs. Laetitia Pilkington* (Vols. i–ii, Dublin, 1748–9; Vol. iii, London, 1754), *passim* (and also the modern edition by Iris Barry, 1928); Shiells, *Lives*, v. 315–25; *Poems by Eminent Ladies* (1755), ii. 235–68; F. E. Ball in *Notes and Queries*, 11th ser., 6 (1912), 65–6; Swift, *Correspondence*, iii. 411–12, 495–6, iv. 57, 61–2, 74–5, 95, 209, 232, 532, v. 95; T. C. D. Eaves and B. D. Kimpel, *Samuel Richardson* (Oxford, 1971), pp. 175–9; Bodleian MS Add. C. 89 fo. 29, cited by W. H. Epstein, *John Cleland: Images of a Life* (New York, 1974), pp. 97–8; A. C. Elias, 'A Manuscript Book of Constantia Grierson's', *Swift Studies*, 2 (1987), 38–9. Texts from *Memoirs*, i (1748), 137–9 and 238–41.

95. Written after her separation from her husband in 1737. On his first visit to her in London, Colley Cibber burst into tears reading this poem, which was also admired by Wordsworth. He included it in an album presented to Lady Mary Lowther in 1819, and recommended it to Alexander Dyce in 1830: 'The first and third Paragraph[s] are very affecting' (*Letters*, v. 236 and n.).

JEAN ADAMS **(96–8)**. See R. H. Cromek, *Select Scottish Songs* (1810), i. 67–70, 189–99. Texts from *Miscellany Poems* (Glasgow, 1734), pp. 25–6, 174–6, 188–9.

ANONYMOUS **(99–101)**. Texts from *Caribbeana* (2 vols., 1741), i. 314–15, 360–2, ii. 29–30 (originally in the *Barbados Gazette*, 20 Apr. and 29 June 1734, 1 Mar. 1735).

99. Dr Richard Busby (1606–95) (line 15) had been a notoriously severe head-master of Westminster School. John Dennis (1657–1734) (lines 25–6), dramatist and critic, had been satirized by Pope.

ANNE, LADY IRWIN **(102)**. See *Gent. Mag.* (1764), 602; *Hist. MSS Comm.: Carlisle MSS* (1897), pp. 71, 77, 97–8, 105–6, 163–5, 184–6; Lady Mary Wortley Montagu, *Complete Letters*, ed. R. Halsband (3 vols., Oxford, 1965–7), i. 211, iii. 162; Walpole, *Correspondence*, vii. 73, xxxviii. 475. Text from *Gent. Mag.* (1736), 745.

MARY CHANDLER **(103–4)**. See Shiells, *Lives*, v. 345–56, for an account of her by her brother Dr Samuel Chandler (1693–1766), Nonconformist divine and author; O. Doughty, 'A Bath Poetess of the 18th Century', *Review of English Studies*, 1 (1925),

404–20; W. M. Sale, *Samuel Richardson: A Bibliographical Record* (New Haven, 1936), p. 156; B. Boyce, *The Benevolent Man: A Life of Ralph Allen* (Cambridge, Mass., 1967), pp. 57–60, 82, 87. Texts from *A Description of Bath* (3rd edn., 1736), pp. 40–1, and (6th edn., 1744), pp. 81–5.

104. Her poem, 'A Wish' (lines 40–1), had appeared in *A Description of Bath* (3rd edn., 1736), pp. 65–7. If she was 54 at the time (line 54), the proposal was made in about 1741.

MARY JONES (**105–9**). See, for quotations from her letters, *Miscellanies in Prose and Verse* (Oxford, 1750), pp. 254, 267–8, 293–7, 300–2, 310–13, 320–2; Bodleian MS C. 89, fos. 171–6; D. Isles in *Times Literary Supplement*, 5 Aug. 1965, for her letter to Lennox; *London Mag.* 20 (1751), 567–8, 21 (1752), 320–1, 428, 475; *Monthly Review*, 6 (1752), 213–23, 470–81; *European Mag.* 19 (1791), 247–8; Cockayne, *Peerage*, viii. 235; Boswell, *Life*, i. 322–3, vi. 489; *Correspondence of James Boswell with Certain Members of The Club*, ed. C. N. Fifer (1976), p. 233; Walpole, *Correspondence*, xviii. 258, xx. 327. Texts from *Miscellanies* (Oxford, 1750), pp. 1–7, 87, 88–90, 100–3, 133–8.

105. Sir William Bowyer of Denham Court, Bucks., married Anne, daughter of Sir John Stonehouse, in 1733. She died in 1785, aged 75. Nevill, 6th Baron Lovelace (line 84), Martha Lovelace's brother, died unmarried in 1736, when the barony became extinct. For Mary Jones's mother and father (lines 111–12) see headnote. The passage suggests she had been reading Pope's recent tribute to his parents in *Epistle to Dr. Arbuthnot* (1734), 388 ff. For Charlot Clayton (line 123) see headnote.

107. Line 8 adapts Dryden, *Absalom and Achitophel*, 548. The 'mad Macedonian' (line 15) was Alexander the Great.

108. Wildey and Pinchbeck were fashionable London shopkeepers (line 39). Payne (line 40) was probably John Payne, the London bookseller and friend of Johnson, but there were other booksellers of the same name.

109. The friends in Brooke Street (lines 30, 94) were probably the Lovelaces.

ELIZABETH CARTER (**110–12**). See *Gent. Mag.* (1766), 27–30, (1806), i. 190–1; Matthew Pennington's *Memoirs* of her (2 vols., 1807, vol. ii collecting her poems, including some previously unpublished); and his editions of her correspondence with Catherine Talbot (4 vols., 1809) and Elizabeth Montagu (3 vols., 1817); Boswell, *Life*, i. 122–3, 203, etc.; E. Rohe, 'Thomas Birch, Samuel Johnson and Elizabeth Carter', *PMLA* 73 (1958), 491–500; *Poems of Gray, Collins and Goldsmith*, ed. R. Lonsdale (1969), pp. 549, 552.

110. The text in *Gent. Mag.* (1737), 247 is preferred to the longer version in *Gent. Mag.* (1739), 152. For Elizabeth Rowe, who had died in 1737, see **33–6**.

111. Text from *Poems on Several Occasions* (1762), pp. 25–7; first printed in *Gent. Mag.* (1741), 46, with notes later omitted: 'The Head' (line 7); 'The Thoughts' (line 10), 'The Stomach' (line 13), 'The Spirits' (line 14), 'Death' (line 33).

112. Text from *Poems on Several Occasions* (1762), pp. 85–90; it appeared first (see headnote) in Richardson's *Clarissa* (Letter 54) in 1747. A note to the corrected text in *Gent. Mag.* (1747), 585, stated that 'We have had the following beautiful ODE above a year, under an injunction, which was general on all the copies given out, not to print it', an embargo unwittingly broken by Richardson. 'Ilissus' (line 61) is the river flowing to the south of Athens.

MARY COLLIER (**113**). See M. Ferguson, *First Feminists* (Bloomington, 1985), pp. 257–65, and her edition of *The Woman's Labour* with Duck's *The Thresher's Labour* (Augustan Reprint Society No. 230, Los Angeles, 1985); D. Landry, 'The

Resignation of Mary Collier' in *The New Eighteenth Century*, ed. F. Nussbaum and L. Brown (New York, 1987), pp. 99–120. Text from *The Woman's Labour* (1739), pp. 12–15.

SARAH DIXON (114–19). Texts from *Poems on Several Occasions* (Canterbury, 1740), pp. 18, 49–50, 68–70, 96, 168–9, 179–81. See also p. 539 below.

116. Melpomene (line 29) and Thalia (line 41) are respectively the Muses of Tragedy and Comedy.

118. The reference to the South Sea Bubble of 1720 (line 13) may indicate that a number of the poems date from the 1720s.

ELIZABETH AMHERST (120–4). See British Library, Add. MS 28543, fos. 174–220 (letters to da Costa); *London Mag.* 31 (1762), 434; Shenstone, *Works* (1764), ii. 376–8, and *Letters*, ed. M. Williams (Oxford, 1939), p. 589; *Gent. Mag.* (1779), 271; E. Halsted, *History of Kent* (3 vols., 1797–1801), iii. 93–5; *Biographia Dramatica* (1812), ii. 176. Texts from Bodleian MS Eng. poet. e. 109, fos. 4, 20–1, 47–50, 51, 77–9.

124. Mr Adams had been reading G. H. Bougeant, *Amusement philosophique sur le langage des bestes* (Paris, 1739): 'Les chats sont perfides & ingrats . . . Les chiens son envieux . . . Les ames des Bêtes sont des esprits rebelles qui se sont rendus coupables envers Dieu' (pp. 45, 49).

ANNABELLA BLOUNT (125). See Cokayne, *Baronetage*, iii. 218–19; J. Kirk, *Biographies of English Catholics in the Eighteenth Century* (1909), p. 27; *Raymond and Guise Memoirs*, ed. G. Davis (Camden Society, 3rd ser., 28 (1917), 142–3); Pope, *Correspondence*, esp. i. 337–8, ii. 85–6, 89, 176, 296–7, 319–20. Text from *Correspondence between Frances, Countess of Hertford, and Henrietta Louisa, Countess of Pomfret, between . . . 1738 and 1741* (3 vols., 1805), ii. 348–54. Winkle and Guiret (lines 13–14) are unidentified.

CHARLOTTE BRERETON (126). See Cokayne, *Peerage*, v. 605–6. Text from *Gent. Mag.* (1742), 103. The '*Mag.*' (line 38) is, of course, the *Gent. Mag.* itself. While she uses her pseudonym within the poem (line 33), 'Ch——ly' (line 49) points to her real name.

FRANCES GREVILLE (127–8). See Frances (Burney) D'Arblay, *Memoirs of Dr. Burney* (1832), i. 55–9; Walpole, *Correspondence*, xi. 2, 47, xvii. 186, xxx. 328; *Shenstone's Miscellany*, ed. I. Gordon (Oxford, 1953), pp. 5–7; R. Lonsdale, *Dr. Charles Burney* (Oxford, 1965), pp. 19–21; *Percy–Shenstone Correspondence*, ed. C. Brooks (New Haven, 1977), p. 15.

127. Text from *Gent. Mag.* (1784), i. 123–4, where the explanatory notes given with the text appeared.

128. Text from *Poetical Calendar* (1763), vi. 76–8. For Lady Carlisle's reply, see e.g. *London Mag.* 40 (1771), 167.

MARY LEAPOR (129–44). See *London Mag.* 16 (1747), 45; *Monthly Review*, 2 (1749), 14–25 and 5 (1751), 23–32; Smart, *The Midwife* (16 Nov. 1750), i. 81–4; the prefatory memoir by Fremantle and Leapor's letters in *Poems Upon Several Occasions. The Second and Last Volume* (1751); *Biographia Dramatica* (1782), i. 278–9; *Gent. Mag.* (1784), ii. 650, 702 (by 'Crito', i.e. John Duncombe) and 806–7 (by 'W'); G. Baker, *History of Northamptonshire* (1822), i. 579; T. C. D. Eaves and B. D. Kimpel, *Samuel Richardson* (Oxford, 1971), pp. 460, 531; B. Rizzo, 'Christopher Smart, the 'C.S.' Poems, and Molly Leapor's Epitaph', *The Library*, 6th ser., 5 (1983), 22–31. I am grateful to Richard Greene for advice about Mary Leapor's life.

129–30. Texts from *Poems* (1748), pp. 101–3, 104–6.

131. Text from *Poems* (1748), pp. 175–7. Lines 39–42 refer to Homer's *Iliad* (in Pope's translation, xxi. 255–357).

132–3. Texts from *Poems* (1748), 247–9, 258–61. A longer version of 133 appeared in *Poems*, ii. (1751), 100–10.

134. Text from *Poems*, ii (1751), 7–10.

135. Text from *Poems*, ii (1751), 47–53. For Bridget Fremantle ('Artemisia'), see headnote. The subtitle, quoted from an earlier passage of the poem, suggests a consciously ironic contrast on her part with Pope's tribute to his literary mentors in *Epistle to Dr. Arbuthnot*, lines 135–46. Line 66 alludes to Samuel Butler, *Hudibras*, II. iii. 383–4: 'His *Sonnets* charm'd th' attentive Crowd, | By wide-mouth'd Mortal trol'd aloud'.

136–8. Texts from *Poems*, ii (1751), 54–6, 64–7, 68–71.

139. Text from *Poems*, ii (1751), 118–20. Crumble Hall may describe Weston Hall, where she is said to have worked (see headnote).

140. Text from *Poems*, ii (1751), 123–4. The play was 'The Unhappy Father', included in *Poems*, ii (1751). The Monument, erected in memory of the Great Fire, and the lions at the Tower (lines 19–20) were popular attractions for visitors to London.

141. Text from *Poems*, ii (1751), 123–4.

142. Text from *Poems*, ii (1751), 295–8. An anxious note appeared at the end of the poem: 'This Description of her Person is a Caracature'. Fremantle (ii, pp. xxxi–xxxii) had explained that 'her Person . . . was very far from being shocking. . . . The Poem was occasioned by her happening to hear that a Gentleman who had seen some of her Poems, wanted to know what her Person was'.

143. Text from *Poems* (1748), pp. 8–10.

144. Text from *Poems* (1748), pp. 38–41. Tycho Brahe and Copernicus (line 3) were famous 16th-century astronomers. For her mother's death (lines 49–52) see headnote.

ELIZABETH TEFT (**145–8**). Texts from *Orinthia's Miscellanies* (1747), pp. 8–10, 54, 56, 102.

CHARLOTTE LENNOX (**149–50**). See L.-M. Hawkins, *Memoirs* (2 vols., 1824), i. 70; F. Burney, *Diary and Letters* (6 vols., 1904), i. 86; Boswell, *Life*, iv. 275, 524; M. R. Small, *Charlotte Ramsay Lennox* (New Haven, 1935); Walpole, *Correspondence*, ix. 74; D. Isles, on the Lennox MSS in *Times Literary Supplement*, 29 July and 5 Aug. 1965, pp. 666 and 685, also 'Johnson and Charlotte Lennox', *New Rambler* (June 1967), pp. 34–48, and his edition of *The Female Quixote* (1970), which has an important 'Chronology' superseding M. R. Small (above) in some respects; *Poems of Gray, Collins and Goldsmith*, ed. R. Lonsdale (1969), p. 667.

149. Text from *Poems on Several Occasions* (1747), pp. 35–6.

150. Originally in *Poems on Several Occasions* (1747), but the corrected text in *Gent. Mag.* (Nov. 1750), 518–19, has been preferred.

HENRIETTA KNIGHT, LADY LUXBOROUGH (**151–2**). See the collections of letters cited in the headnote; *The Letters of William Shenstone*, ed. M. Williams (Oxford, 1939), *passim*; H. S. Hughes, *The Gentle Hertford* (New York, 1940), pp. 121–81; Walpole, *Correspondence*, xi. 64–6, xxviii. 233, xxxii. 243–4. Texts from Dodsley's *Collection*, iv. 316–17, 313–14.

ESTHER LEWIS (**153–5**). **153.** Text from Samuel Bowden, *Poems on Various Subjects* (Bath, 1754), pp. 325–32, where it is dated 1748; in her *Poems* (Bath, 1789), pp. 162–9, it is revised as 'Slander delineated'.

154. Text from *Gent. Mag.* (1752), 234–5; in *Poems* (1789), pp. 83–7.

155. From *Poems* (1789), pp. 299–300: the identity of her addressee is revealed only in the 'Contents', p. ix, where the title is 'To Miss Fielding, in London, the writer of David Simple and other Publications'.

CATHERINE JEMMAT (**156**). See *Gent. Mag.* (1756), 595; British Library, Add. MS 32908, fo. 276; J. Starkey, 'Two Poets of Old Dublin', in his *Essays and Recollections by Seumas O'Sullivan* (Dublin, 1944), pp. 14–23, which assumes that she was a native of Dublin. Her mother's name was either Corham or Harris. A MS note in the British Library copy of her *Memoirs* (2 vols., 1762) states that one of her mother's sisters married Dr Huxham of Plymouth, identifiable as John Huxham, MD (1692–1768), who married (1) Ellen Corham and (2) Elizabeth Harris (*DNB*). Text from *Gent. Mag.* (1750), 517, revised in *Miscellanies* (1766), pp. 58–62.

HESTER MULSO (**157**). See *Gent. Mag.* (1761), 43, 430, (1775), 87–8; *Johnsonian Miscellanies*, ed. G. B. Hill (Oxford, 1897), ii. 251–2; T. C. D. Eaves and B. D. Kimpel, *Samuel Richardson* (Oxford, 1971), pp. 343–9, 446; J. L. Clifford, *Dictionary Johnson* (1979), pp. 75, 113–14, 120–1, 216–17. Text from *Miscellanies* (1775), 146–9. 'Stella' was Susanna Highmore, another member of Richardson's circle, who later married John Duncombe.

ANNA WILLIAMS (**158–9**). See *Gent. Mag.* (1750), 432; A. T. Hazen, *Johnson's Prefaces and Dedications* (New Haven, 1937), pp. 213–16; Johnson, *Letters*, ed. R. W. Chapman (Oxford, 1952), i. 54–5, 122–3, iii. 70; T. C. D. Eaves and B. D. Kimpel, *Samuel Richardson* (Oxford, 1971), pp. 336–7; J. L. Clifford, *Dictionary Johnson* (1979), pp. 92–5, 101, 162, 265.

158. Text from *Gent. Mag.* (1754), 40: the MS, with corrections in Johnson's hand, is in the Forster Collection in the Victoria and Albert Museum. The poem alludes to Richardson's novels, *Pamela* (1740), *Clarissa* (1747–8), and *Sir Charles Grandison* (1754), in the last of which Harriet Byron and Clementina Porretta (lines 41–2) feature. Line 23 refers dismissively to Fielding's *Tom Jones* (1749) and to Capt. Booth, the male protagonist in his *Amelia* (1751). *Clarissa* was translated into German 1748–52 (line 28).

159. Text from *Miscellanies in Prose and Verse* (1766), pp. 107–10. See Bridget Hill, 'A Refuge from Men: The Idea of a Protestant Nunnery', *Past and Present*, 117 (1987), 107–30, for the prevalence of the idea from the 16th century and its revival by Mary Astell in 1694. Samuel Richardson had promoted the idea in *Grandison* (1754). Anna Williams's poem has, however, been curiously misdescribed as 'longing for the security of the cloister to be made available to English women' (Todd, *Dictionary*, p. 323).

ANONYMOUS ('Ophelia') (**160**). From *Gent. Mag.* (1754), 135.

CLARA REEVE (**161–3**). See *Gent. Mag.* (1786), i. 15–17, 117–18, 288–9, (1807), ii. 1233; A. Seward, *Letters* (1810), i. 135, 149–50; W. Scott, 'Prefatory Memoir' to her novels in Ballantyne's Novelist's Library, v (1823), pp. lxxix–lxxxviii. Texts from *Original Poems on Several Occasions* (1769), pp. 8–11, 23, 58–60.

ANONYMOUS (**164**). From *Gent. Mag.* (1758), 82.   Line 8 probably refers to the recent court martial of Sir John Mordaunt for the failure of the British fleet to attack Rochefort in the autumn of 1757. Lines 56–8 refer to Voltaire's *Siècle de Louis XIV*, translated into in English in 1752.

MARY LATTER (**165**). See *Monthly Review*, 21 (1759), 82, 24 (1761), 444; *Gent. Mag.* (1761), 136; *Biographia Dramatica* (1812), i. 439; *Private Correspondence of David*

Garrick, ed. J. Boaden (1831), i. 633–4; Garrick, *Letters*, iii. 927; B. Rizzo in Todd, *Dictionary*, p. 190. Texts from *Miscellaneous Works* (Reading, 1759), pp. 152–3, 163–4.

MARY WHATELEY (**166–9**). I am indebted for information about her birth, marriage, and death to Anne Messenger. In addition to material in *Gent. Mag.* cited in the headnote, see also tributes to her in (1766), 188–9 and (1788), ii. 133; *Monthly Review*, 30 (1764), 445–50; J. Darwall, *Political Lamentations Written in the Years 1775 and 1776* (doggerel printed amateurishly on his own press at Walsall); W. Shenstone, *Letters*, ed. M. Williams (Oxford, 1939), pp. 588–9.

166. Text from *Gent. Mag.* (1759), 538.

167–8. Texts from *Original Poems on Several Occasions* (1764), pp. 13–16 and 102–5.

167. Galen and Hippocrates (lines 16–17) are ancient medical authorities; lines 22 and 24–5 list modern British and Continental medical writers. Lines 39–43 refer to legal authorities. In the list of Augustan literary names (line 44), Hill is presumably Aaron Hill (1685–1750), poet and dramatist. Line 57 probably refers to the landowner John Russell, 4th Duke of Bedford (1710–71) and the Jewish financier Sampson Gideon (1699–1762).

169. Text from *Poems on Several Occasions* (Walsall, 1794), ii. 55–7. Erato (line 11) is the Muse of the Lyre; Pierian (line 14) refers to the Muses (of Pieria).

ALISON COCKBURN (**170**). See R. Chambers, *The Scottish Songs* (2 vols., Edinburgh, 1829), i. 118–19; J. G. Lockhart, *Life of Sir Walter Scott* (7 vols., Edinburgh, 1837–8), i. 86–8; *Letters and Memoir of her own Life by Mrs. Alison Rutherford or Cockburn*, ed. T. Craig-Brown (Edinburgh, 1900); Scott, *Minstrelsy of the Scottish Border*, ed. T. F. Henderson (4 vols., 1902), iii. 407–11; Scott, *Letters*, ed. H. J. C. Grierson (11 vols., 1932–7), i. 244; T. Crawford, *Society and the Lyric* (Edinburgh, 1979), pp. 177, 183; Burns, *Letters*, 2nd edn., ed. G. R. Roy (2 vols., Oxford, 1985), ii. 220. Text from the autograph transcript made for Lady Helen Hall and annotated, 'A real picture of the Authors feeling', reproduced in *Letters and Memoir* (1900), p. 112.

JANE ELLIOT (**171**). See Burns, *Works*, ed. J. Currie (4 vols., Liverpool, 1800), i. 185; R. Chambers, *The Scottish Songs* (2 vols., Edinburgh, 1829), i. 118 n.; Scott, *Minstrelsy of the Scottish Border*, ed. T. F. Henderson (4 vols., 1902), iii. 402–3; Scott, *Letters*, ed. H. J. C. Grierson (11 vols., 1932–7), i. 121, ix. 242–3; N. H. Russell, 'New Letters of Sir Walter Scott', *Review of English Studies*, NS 14 (1963), 61–5; T. Crawford, *Society and the Lyric* (Edinburgh, 1979), p. 176. Text from Scott, *Minstrelsy* (2 vols., Kelso, 1802), ii. 158–9.

LADY DOROTHEA DUBOIS (**172**). See *DNB*, 'Richard Annesley'; Cokayne, *Peerage*, i. 136–8; *Gent. Mag.* (1774), 94. Text from *Poems on Several Occasions* (Dublin, 1764), pp. 102–4.

CHRISTIAN CARSTAIRS (**173–6**). See *Gent. Mag.* (1768), 398, and (1794), ii. 1154; T. G. Stevenson, *The Bibliography of James Maidment* (Edinburgh, 1883), p. 9. Texts from *Original Poems. By a Lady* (Edinburgh, 1786), pp. 14, 27, 43, 56.

173. Lines 3–8 refer to Mary Queen of Scots, who after her deposition in 1567 was confined in Loch Leven Castle, but escaped from the island in 1568. In 1768–9 Carstairs wrote a longer poem about Queen Mary (pp. 9–14).

MARIA COWPER (**177–8**). See F. Madan, *The Madan Family* (Oxford, 1933), pp. 121–3, 129; *Letters of William Cowper*, ed. J. King (5 vols., Oxford, 1979–86), i. pp. xvi, xxxvii, iv, pp. xx, 332–3.

177. Text from Bodleian MS. Eng. poet. c. 51, fos. 278–9.
178. Text from *Original Poems* (1792), pp. 7–8.

PRISCILLA POINTON (179–81). What is known of her derives mostly from the prefaces, by John Jones and Joseph Weston, to her two volumes, and from her verse itself.

179. Text from *Poems* (Birmingham, 1794), i. 2–3. Lines 1–2 allude to Pope, *Essay on Criticism*, line 216. The Pierian spring was sacred to the Muses.

180. Text from *Poems on Several Occasions* (Birmingham, 1770), pp. 31–2. Diuretics (line 8) relax the bladder.

181. Text from *Poems* (Birmingham, 1794), i. 20–3. The lines are addressed to her sister Maria. Barnes (line 5) was probably a brother-in-law. Shotwick (line 9), Saughall (line 10), and Parkgate (line 27) are all near Chester.

LADY ANNE LINDSAY (182). See Lord Lindsay, *Lives of the Lindsays* (3 vols., 1849), esp. ii. 300–38, for her memories of her early life at Balcarres; C. Rogers, *The Modern Scottish Minstrel* (Edinburgh, 1855), i. 59–61; D. Fairbridge, *Lady Anne Barnard at the Cape of Good Hope* (Oxford, 1924); Boswell, *Life*, v. 401, 575–6; *Thraliana*, i. 335; Walpole, *Correspondence*, xxiii. 418–19, xli. 311; M. Masson, *Lady Anne Barnard* (1948); A. M. L. Robinson, *The Letters of Lady Anne Barnard to Henry Dundas 1793–1803* (Cape Town, 1973). Text from Walter Scott's edition of *Auld Robin Gray* for the Bannatyne Society (Edinburgh, 1825).

SUSANNA BLAMIRE (183–91). All information about her derives from the investigations of Patrick Maxwell and Henry Lonsdale cited in the headnote. Texts from *Poetical Works* (Edinburgh, 1842), pp. 1–12, 88–9, 153–8, 191–4, 203–4, 208–10, 218–19, 234–5.

183. The date of the poem is suggested by line 140, i.e. 5 years after her sister's marriage to Col. Graham in 1767. Admiral Sir Hugh Palliser (1723–96) (lines 31–3) had been Governor and Commander-in-Chief at Newfoundland 1764–6. Lines 157–62 adapt Prior's 'Epitaph' on 'Saunt'ring Jack, and Idle Joan', lines 9–12.

184. Stoklewath, properly Stockdalewath, is some 8 miles south of Carlisle near Raughton Head. Thackwood Farm lay just outside the village.

189. Line 20 refers to Thomas Paine's *The Rights of Man* (1792) and line 36 to the harsh Game Laws which restricted the taking of game to substantial property-owners.

ANNE PENNY (192). See *Biographia Dramatica* (1812), i. 566, ii. 58; Nichols, *Illustrations*, vi. 187, vii. 541; Walpole, *Correspondence*, xvi. 181–2. Texts from *Poems* (1780), pp. 158–60. The purpose of the Marine Society was to maintain a supply of seamen for the navy. Within 6 years of its foundation, it had fitted out 5,451 boys and 4,787 landsman volunteers for the navy (*DNB*, 'Jonas Hanway').

ANONYMOUS (193–4). Text from *Original Poems, Translations, and Imitations, From the French, &c. By a Lady* (1773). A recent suggestion, based on a copy with the book-plate of Middleton Park (Quaritch, Bulletin 45, 1987, item 91), that the author might be Frances Villiers, Countess of Jersey (1753–1821), later mistress of the Prince of Wales, does not carry great force. There seems no reason why, three years after her marriage, she should publish such a volume. The book-plate may indicate that the author was a friend of the Countess.

ANNA BARBAULD (195–203). See A. L. Breton, *Memoir of Mrs. Barbauld* (1874), drawing on an unpublished account of her aunt by Lucy Aikin; F. A. Pottle, *Literary Career of James Boswell* (Oxford, 1929), p. xxxiv; Walpole, *Correspondence*, xi. 169,

320, xxxi. 357–8, 361–2; B. Rogers, *Georgian Chronicle: Mrs Barbauld and Her Family* (1958); *Boswell for the Defence*, ed. W. K. Wimsatt and F. A. Pottle (1960), p. 107.

195. Text from *Poems* (1773), pp. 9–12. James Boswell's *Account of Corsica* (1768) had popularized the issue of Corsican liberty in Britain and rendered General Pasquale Paoli (1725–1807), leader of the revolt against Genoa, a heroic figure. After the French conquest of the island in 1769, Paoli fled to Britain.

196. Text from *Poems* (1773), pp. 37–40. For Joseph Priestley (1733–1804), see headnote.

197–201. Texts from *Works* (1825), i. 146, 180–2, 185–7, 192–3, 199–201. In **198** Briareus (line 17) is the hundred-handed giant of Greek mythology. **199** is a somewhat ambivalent response to Mary Wollstonecraft's *Vindication of the Rights of Woman* (1792).

202–3. Texts from *Monthly Magazine*, 4 (1797), 452, and 7 (1799), 231–2. In **202** Guatimozin (line 30) was a King of Mexico tortured by Cortés in an attempt to discover his treasure (W. Robertson, *History of America*, 2 vols., 1777, ii. 126–7). Erebus (line 38) is the darkness between earth and Hades in Greek mythology. Lines 82–3 refer to the pioneering experiments with hot-air balloons by the Montgolfier brothers in France from 1783. **203** was no doubt written after a visit by the 24-year-old Coleridge to Mrs Barbauld in Bristol in Aug. 1797 (Coleridge *Letters*, i. 341 n.). Her shrewd assessment of his gifts and temperament may explain his later condescending remarks about her.

ANNA SEWARD (**204–12**). See *Letters* (6 vols., Edinburgh, 1811); T. S. Whalley, *Journals and Correspondence* (2 vols., 1863); M. R. Mitford, *Life . . . Told by Herself*, ed. A. G. L'Estrange (2 vols., 1870), i. 242; M. Ashmun, *The Singing Swan: An Account of Anna Seward* (New Haven, 1931); Boswell, *Life*, ii. 467; Walpole, *Correspondence*, xxxi. 271, xxxiii. 463, 475, 533; J. L. Clifford, 'The Authenticity of Anna Seward's Published Correspondence', *Modern Philology*, 39 (1941), 113–22.

204–5. Texts from *Original Sonnets* (1799), pp. 12, 16. **205** had appeared earlier in the *Gentleman's* and *European Magazines* in Mar. 1789. For Honora Sneyd, see headnote.

206. Text from *Gent. Mag.* (1791), ii. 1140. In *Poetical Works* (1810), ii. 55–7, 'Stella' is identified as 'Mrs. C——'. With the American War going badly, the general fast, 'To pray for a divine blessing on His Majesty's arms by sea and land', was observed in England on 21 Feb. 1781. Lines 33–4 allude to Joseph Warton's 'The Dying Indian', in Dodsley's *Collection*, iv. 209–10, which begins: 'The dart of Izdabel prevails! 'twas dipt | In double poison—'. Até (line 41) was the Goddess of Vengeance. Atreus, King of Mycenae (lines 45–6), served his brother Thyestes, who had seduced his wife, a dish containing the flesh of Thyestes' children. For the trial and execution of Capt. John Donellan for the murder of Sir Theodosius Boughton (lines 51–2), see *Gent. Mag.* (1780), 445–6, (1781), 156–8, 190, 209–11. Laurel-water, distilled from the leaves of the cherry-laurel, contains prussic acid.

207–8. Texts from *Original Sonnets* (1799), pp. 42, 65. There is a longer version of **208** in *Poetical Works* (1810), ii. 314–19, from which an excerpt is given in the *New Oxford Book of Eighteenth Century Verse* (1984), p. 754. Early in the century Abraham Darby had established his ironsmelting works in the picturesque Severn gorge at Coalbrookdale in Shropshire. Artists in the later 18th century frequently depicted the contrast of the pastoral idyll and the Darby furnaces and coke hearths: see A. Briggs, *Iron Bridge to Crystal Palace* (1979), pp. 7–9; *Coal: British Mining in Art 1680–1980* (1982), pp. 10–12.

209. Text from *Llangollen Vale, With Other Poems* (1796), pp. 37–40. It had been first published in the *European Mag.* 22 (1792), 308–9. There is a MS in Bodleian MS Pigott d. 12, fos. 10–12. For Thomas Seward, to whose senility the poem alludes, see headnote: he remained Rector of Eyam until his death in 1790. Anna Seward was an ardent music-lover and, when possible, concert-goer.

210–11. Texts from *Original Sonnets* (1799), pp. 73, 84.

212. Text from *Gent. Mag.* (1792), i. 364.

MARY SCOTT (**213**). See *Gent. Mag.* (1783), i. 519–20, (1787), ii. 1024, (1793), i. 579; *Monthly Review*, 79 (1788), 277–8; A. Seward, *Letters* (1811), i. 133, 185, ii. 88, 118–19, 228, 344, iii. 149–51, 310–11; *DNB*, 'John Edward Taylor'; *The Female Advocate*, ed. G. Holladay (Augustan Reprint Society, Los Angeles, 1984); M. Ferguson, *First Feminists* (Bloomington, 1985), pp. 349–67. Text from *The Female Advocate* (1774), lines 437–64.

ANONYMOUS ('A Female Hand') (**214**). Text from *Literary Amusements: Or, Evening Entertainer. By a Female Hand* (1782), ii. 96. I have located only copies of the Dublin edition, although the work was evidently first published in London.

HANNAH MORE (**215–21**). See John Langhorne in *Monthly Review*, 49 (1773), 202–4 and 54 (1776), 89–99; W. Roberts, *Memoirs of the Life and Correspondence of Mrs. Hannah More* (4 vols., 1834); J. Cottle, *Reminiscences of Coleridge and Southey* (1847), pp. 52–4, 260; Boswell, *Life*, i. 75 n., iii. 293, iv. 341; G. H. Spinney, 'Cheap Repository Tracts', *The Library*, 20 (1939), 295–340; M. A. Hopkins, *Hannah More and Her Circle* (New York, 1947); *Thraliana* (1951), i. 331, ii. 1000 n. 3; H. W. Liebert, 'We Fell upon *Sir Eldred*', in *New Light on Johnson*, ed. F. W. Hilles (New Haven, 1959), pp. 233–45; Garrick, *Letters*, iii. 1108, 1115, 1355–8.

215. Text from *The Search after Happiness* (3rd edn., Bristol, 1774), pp. 42–4 (the title was slightly emended from *A Search* etc. after the 1st edn.). Lines 27–32 refer to Elizabeth Carter (see **110–12**), Anna Laetitia Aikin (later Barbauld) (see **195–203**), Elizabeth Montagu (1720–1800), author of *An Essay on the Writings and Genius of Shakespear* (1769), Frances Brooke (1724–89), novelist and dramatist, and Catherine Macaulay (1731–91), author of a *History of England* (6 vols., 1763–83).

216. Text from *The Search after Happiness* (4th edn., Bristol, 1774), pp. 45–7. The poem has been taken to evoke the estate of Edward Turner, her ex-fiancé (see headnote) at Belmont, Wraxall, near Bristol.

217. Text from *Sacred Dramas . . . to which is added, Sensibility, A Poem* (1782), pp. 282–4. Lines 17–20 refer to Thomas Otway, the Restoration dramatist, best known for his tragedy *Venice Preserv'd* (1682); to *Jane Shore* (1714), an admired tragedy by Nicholas Rowe; to Samuel Richardson's *Clarissa* (1747–8), and to Clementina Porretta in his *Sir Charles Grandison* (1754).

218. Text from *Florio: A Tale . . . and, The Bas Bleu; Or Conversation: Two Poems* (1786), pp. 72–5. Line 12 alludes to Pope, *Rape of the Lock*, i. 123–4. Rhodope (line 18) is a mountain range in Thrace. The 'affected Peer' (lines 21–2) was the Earl of Chesterfield, whose *Letters to his Son* (2 vols., 1774) had aroused much discussion. Alcides (line 50) is a designation of Heracles or Hercules, son of Zeus and Alcmene (line 54) in Greek legend.

219. Text from *Slavery, A Poem* (1788), pp. 4–6, 15–16. Hannah More had met William Wilberforce, who was to become a prominent anti-slavery campaigner, in 1787. Line 34 refers to Hernando Cortés (1485–1547), conqueror of Mexico.

220–1. Texts from the original broadsheets (1795) in the Cheap Repository Tracts. Another in the series, 'The Riot', can be read in *The New Oxford Book of Eighteenth Century Verse* (1984), pp. 808–10.

ANONYMOUS (**222**). Text from *Gent. Mag.* (1775), 394. Aldermen (lines 43–4) traditionally relished turtle soup at their feasts.

ANONYMOUS ('A Lady') (**223**). For Harford, see *Gent. Mag.* (1771), 566; J. G. Morris, *The Lords Baltimore* (Baltimore, 1874), pp. 52–3; Sir N. W. Wraxall, *Historical and Posthumous Memoirs*, ed. H. B. Wheatley (1884), v. 137–8; Foster, *Alumni Oxonienses*, 2nd ser., ii. 607. Text from *Poems by a Lady* (1781), pp. 95–7.

LADY SOPHIA BURRELL (**224–6**). See *Gent. Mag.* (1788), ii. 758, 834; *Biographia Dramatica* (1812), I, i. 79; *DNB*, 'Sir William Burrell'; Cokayne, *Baronetage*, v. 177; Walpole, *Correspondence*, xii. 236. Texts from *Poems* (1793), ii. 36–7, 46–8, 292–3.

224. Lady Mary Wortley Montagu wrote in 1752 that 'Ever since I knew the World, Irish Patents have been hung out to Sale' like second-hand clothes, for 'those who had rather wear shabby Finery than no Finery at all', *Complete Letters*, ed. R. Halsband, ii (Oxford, 1966), 457–8.

225. The love of Paris (line 22) for Helen led to the Trojan War, the subject of Homer's Iliad, in Bk. vii of which Ajax's shield is described.

226. Dumergue (line 21) was a celebrated dentist. Medusa (line 47) was the Gorgon whose gaze turned the beholder to stone.

MARY SAVAGE (**227–30**). See *Gent. Mag.* (1772), 391, (1807), i. 635, (1816), ii. 184; *Eton College Register 1753–90*, ed. R. A. Austen-Leigh (1921), pp. 464–5. Texts from *Poems on Various Subjects and Occasions* (1777), i. 10–16, ii. 8–12, 69–75, 79–85.

227. The Pump Room (line 66) was the social centre of Bath.

ANNE WILSON (**231**). Text from *Teisa* (Newcastle, 1778), pp. 30–2.

FRANCES BURNEY (**232**). See J. Hemlow, *The History of Fanny Burney* (Oxford, 1958); R. Lonsdale, *Dr. Charles Burney: A Literary Biography* (Oxford, 1965). Text from *Evelina, Or, A Young Lady's Entrance into the World* (1778), i, pp. iii–iv.

ANN MURRY (**233**). The only wine-merchant I have found in the *London Directory* in the period is Isaac Murray of Love Lane, Eastcheap. See *Monthly Review*, 60 (1779), 476 and *London Mag.* 48 (1779), 277; *Biographical Dictionary of Living Authors* (1816), pp. 246–7. Text from *Poems on Various Subjects* (1779), pp. 119–28.   John Harrison (line 8) was found guilty of defrauding the London Assurance Office by forgery in 1777 but was reprieved on a point of law (*Gent. Mag.*, 1777, pp. 349, 458). Charles would have gone to Bombay or Madras (line 79) in the service of the East India Company. 'Superstition' (line 87) is Roman Catholicism.

ANN THOMAS (**234**). Text from *Poems on Various Subjects* (Plymouth, 1784), pp. 4–7. See *Monthly Review*, 73 (1785), 389. The combined French and Spanish fleets lay off Plymouth on 16–18 Aug. 1779 and attacked the British man-of-war *Ardent*. The fortifications and garrison were strengthened during the scare. Major-General Simon Fraser (1726–82) (lines 11–16) had raised a regiment of Highlanders at the outbreak of the war with America.

ANNE HUNTER (**235–6**). See R. Nares in *Gent. Mag.* (1821), i. 89–90; *DNB* for articles on her husband and brother; *Thraliana*, i. 533–4; R. C. Robbins Landon, *Haydn in England 1791–95* (1976), pp. 179, 257, 285, 394–6; T. Crawford, *Society and the Lyric* (Edinburgh, 1979), p. 177. Texts from *Poems* (1802), pp. 79–80, 110–11.

235. In 1782 Mrs Thrale recorded that it was William Seward who had come across the original music of the 'Death Song'. Mrs Hunter herself in 1802 (p. 80 n.) stated that she heard a gentleman who had lived among the Cherokees 'sing a wild air, which he assured me it was customary for those people to chaunt with a barbarous jargon, implying contempt for their enemies in the moments of torture and death'.

CHARLOTTE SMITH (237–43). See *Gent. Mag.* (1786), i. 333–4, ii. 619, 713, (1794), ii, 1035, (1806), ii. 1250; A. Seward, *Letters* (1811), i. 162–3; Coleridge, *Poetical Works*, ed. E. H. Coleridge (1912), ii. 1139; F. M. A. Hilbish, *Charlotte Smith, Poet and Novelist* (Philadelphia, 1941); M. Bishop, *Blake's Hayley* (1951), pp. 172–3; A. D. McKillop, 'Charlotte Smith's Letters', *Huntington Library Quarterly*, 15 (1951–2), 237–55; Wordsworth, *Letters*, i. 68, 381 n.; Cowper, *Letters and Prose Writings*, ed. J. King and C. Ryskamp (5 vols., Oxford, 1979–86), iv. 170–2, 181–2, 189–90, 249, 281, 308–9, 318–19, 336, 341–2; Burns, *Letters*, 2nd edn., ed. G. R. Roy (2 vols., Oxford, 1985), i. 435, ii. 37.

237. Text from *European Mag.* 2 (Dec. 1782), 472.

238. Text from *Elegiac Sonnets* (5th edn., 1789), p. 44. According to a note, 'Middleton is a village on the margin of the sea, in Sussex, containing only two or three houses. There were formerly several acres of ground between its small church and the sea, which now, by its continual encroachments, approaches within a few feet of this half-ruined and humble edifice. The wall, which once surrounded the church-yard, is entirely swept away, and many of the groves broken up, and the remains of bodies interred washed into the sea: whence human bones are found among the sand and shingles on the shore' (pp. 101–2).

239. Text from *Elegiac Sonnets* (6th edn., 1792), pp. 82–5. This uncharacteristic piece may be a response to pleas, mentioned in her preface, that she should include some 'more cheerful' poems.

240. Text from *The Emigrants* (1793), pp. 41–4. Louis XVI had been executed in Jan. 1793 (lines 19–20). Lines 43–4 quote *Henry V*, Prol., 7–8.

241. Text from *Elegiac Sonnets*, ii (1797), 78–81: the 'Fragment' came from *The Emigrants* (1793), pp. 55–8, which she otherwise did not reprint.

242–3. Texts from *Elegiac Sonnets*, ii. (1797), 11, 24.

JANE CAVE (244–9). See *Gent. Mag.* (1813), i. 88.

244–5. Texts from *Poems on Various Subjects* (Winchester, 1783), pp. 47–9, 49–51.

246–7. Texts from *Poems on Various Subjects* (2nd edn., Bristol, 1786), pp. 149, 151–2.

248–9. Texts from *Poems on Various Subjects* (4th edn., Bristol, 1794), pp. 150–2, 153–5.

JANE WEST (250–1). See *Gent. Mag.* (1791), i. 68–9, (1793), ii. 1134–5, (1795), i. 422, (1799), ii. 881, 1128–9, (1800), i. 318, 370, 465–6, (1802), i. 7, 99–100, (1823), i. 183; A. Seward, *Letters* (1811), iii. 113, 132; *Biographia Dramatica* (1812), i. 742; Nichols, *Illustrations*, vii. 88–9, 592–3, 597–601, viii. 326–31, 424–34. See also p. 539 below.

250. Text from *Poems and Plays* (1799), ii. 170–2. For Martha (line 57), who became the patron saint of good housewives, see Luke 10: 38–42.

251. Text from *Miscellaneous Poems* (York, 1791), pp. 115–21. Mrs West's addressee and benefactor is identified in the subscriber's list as the Hon. Mrs Cockayne, wife of the Hon. William Cockayne. Line 38 refers to the frequently ridiculed versifications of the Psalms by Thomas Sternhold (d. 1549) and the poetry of Francis Quarles (1592–1644).

HANNAH COWLEY (252–4). See *St. James's Chronicle*, 7, 14, 17 Aug. 1779; *Gent. Mag.* (1779), 407–8, (1798), i. 170; *Monthly Review*, 62 (1780), 352–4; W. C. Oulton, *History of the Theatres of London* (1796), pp. 83 ff.; *Biographia Dramatica* (1812), i. 152–4; 'Preface' to *Works* (1813), i. pp. v–xxi; *Thraliana*, ii. 709, 716; Garrick, *Letters*,

iii. 951–3, 955, 1165–6, 1172; J. E. Norton, 'Some Uncollected Authors: Hannah Cowley', *Book Collector*, 7 (1958), 68–76.

252. Text from *Gent. Mag.* (Aug. 1784), ii. 613–14, where it is attributed to Mrs Cowley or Miss Seward, the latter denying her authorship in Sept. 1784 (p. 693); also attributed to Cowley in *European Mag.* 6 (Sept. 1784), 238.

253–4. Texts from *Works* (1813), iii. 111–12, 191–2.

HESTER PIOZZI **(255).** See J. L. Clifford, *Hester Lynch Piozzi (Mrs. Thrale)* (Oxford, 1941; with new introd. by M. A. Doody, 1987). Text from *Thraliana*, ii. 641–2, where she transcribed it on 27 June 1786, 'having given away some Copies & lost others'. It had been written in the previous Sept. or Oct. She printed it in *Observations and Reflections* (1789), i. 369–71, with minor changes, introducing it with the passage quoted in the headnote. Lines 27–37 refer to the 'Bluestocking' circles headed by Elizabeth Montagu, who had recently built a handsome house in Portman Square. Staffa (line 40) is in the Hebrides. Hetruria (line 46) is a variant of Etruria (misspelt or mistranscribed as 'Hetraria' in *Thraliana* in 1942, but 'Hetruria' in 1789). The 'one friend' (lines 67–9) is, of course, Gabriel Piozzi.

ANN YEARSLEY **(256–9).** See R. Griffiths to Yearsley, 23 Aug. 1793, Bodleian MS Add. C. 89, fo. 371; *Gent. Mag.* (1784), ii. 897, (1785), i. 304, (1806), i. 485; *Monthly Review*, 6 (1791), 347; A. Seward, *Letters* (1811), i. 121–2, 394–6, ii. 364; *Biographia Dramatica* (1812), i. 764, iii. 182–3; W. Roberts, *Memoirs of Mrs. Hannah More* (1834), i. 361–75, 383–91; J. Cottle, *Reminiscences of Coleridge and Southey* (1847), pp. 47–51; R. Southey, *Letters*, ed. C. Southey (6 vols., 1849–50), ii. 24; J. M. S. Tompkins, *The Polite Marriage* (Cambridge, 1938), pp. 58–102; Walpole, *Correspondence*, xxxi. 218, 253–4, 283, xxxiii. 462, 475, 533, 537–8, 550; M. Mahl and H. Kroon, *The Female Spectator: English Women Writers before 1800* (Bloomington, 1977), pp. 177–86 (for More's MS letters in the Huntington Library); M. Ferguson, 'Resistance and Power in the Life and Writings of Ann Yearsley', *The Eighteenth Century*, 27 (1986), 247–68.

256. Text from *Poems on Several Occasions* (1785), pp. 101–6. For Elizabeth Montagu's patronage of Yearsley through Hannah More ('Stella', line 28), see headnote. Montagu's admired *Essay on the Writings and Genius of Shakespear* (1769) had defended him against the strictures of Voltaire (lines 22–7). Cacus (line 25) in classical mythology was a monster slain by Hercules.

257–8. Texts from *The Rural Lyre* (1796), pp. 69–72, 117–19.

259. Text from *The Rural Lyre* (1796), pp. 60–4. Lines 1–2 allude to the preceding poem, 'The Consul C. Fannius to Fannius Didius' (pp. 47–59), in which Tellus, his wife Nisa, and the aged Fulvia also appear. Fulvia had tried to dissuade the Consul from seducing Nisa, but it was in fact the 'artless Virtue' of the sleeping Nisa which had disarmed him. Criminals were executed by being hurled from the Tarpeian rock (lines 25, 33–4). The Tartarean realms (line 59) were the underworld.

ELIZABETH MOODY **(260–3).** See Bodleian MS Add. C. 89, fos. 252–3, 258, 261–2; *Monthly Review*, 73 (1785), 432–5, 81 (1789), 455–7, New Series 3 (1790), 400–2; *Gent. Mag.* (1788), i. 249–50, (1814), ii. 613, (1815), ii. 643, (1816), i. 635; B. C. Nangle, *The Monthly Review: First Series* (Oxford, 1934), pp. 29–30 and *Second Series* (Oxford, 1955), pp. 45–7.

260. Text from the *General Evening Post*, 18–21 Mar. 1786. Boswell's *Journal of a Tour to the Hebrides* (1785) aroused disapproval in some quarters by the unprecedented detail and frankness of its portrayal of Johnson, who had died in Dec. 1784. The poem is a parody of David Mallet's popular 'William and Margaret'. Boswell recorded Johnson's hostile remarks about John Knox, the 16th-century reformer (line 40), while they were in St Andrew's on 19 Aug. 1773. Ulysses met the ghost of Ajax (lines 55–6) in Homer's *Odyssey*, Bk. xi.

261–3. Texts from *Poetic Trifles* (1798), pp. 19, 33–4, 52–4.

263. Elizabeth Greenly, as she would then be, had an unusual taste for early Italian poetry (lines 5–10). She also alludes to Pope's translation of Homer and his 'Eloisa to Abelard' (lines 41–8).

HANNAH WALLIS (**264–6**). See *Monthly Review*, 80 (1789), 279. Texts from *The Female's Meditations* (1787), pp. 87–90, 144–50, 153–4.

264. For Moses on Pisgah (lines 25–6), see Deut. 34: 1–4.

265. Bromfield Hall (line 14) had been the seat of Sir Richard Everard in 1751, and was later occupied by John Olmius, grandson of a London merchant, but the period to which she is referring is unclear. (See *England's Gazetteer*, iii (1751); P. Morant, *History of Essex* (1768), ii. 75–8). The 'late Hon. Edward Hatton' (lines 17–24 and note) may have been the Hon. Edward Finch Hatton (1697–1771), diplomat and MP for Cambridge University 1727–68, although at first sight he had no obvious connection with Bromfield.

HELEN MARIA WILLIAMS (**267–71**). See *Monthly Review*, 67 (1782), 26–30, 71 (1784), 12–20; *Gent. Mag.* (1784), ii. 613, (1793), i. 108–10; A. Seward, *Letters* (1811), i. 171–3; L. D. Woodward, *Une adhérente anglaise de la Révolution française, Hélène-Maria Williams et ses amis* (Paris, 1930); *Thraliana*, ii. 849, 885, 894–5, 910, 922; Boswell, *Life*, iv. 282 n.; Wordsworth, *Letters*, i. 68–9.

267. Text from *Poems* (2nd edn., 1791), i. 55–6. For her correspondence with Burns from 1787, see Burns, *Letters*, 2nd edn., ed. G. R. Roy (2 vols., Oxford, 1985), i. 95–6. Line 1 adapts line 19 of Burns's 'To a Mountain Daisy' (1786).

268. Text from *Julia. A Novel* (1790), i. 204. Wordsworth (to Dyce, c.22 Apr. 1833) considered it had 'great merit'.

269. Text from *Poems on Various Subjects* (1823), pp. 222–4.

270. Text from *Letters from France*, ii (2nd edn., 1792), 10–13. Dr John Moore (1729–1802), physician and author, published accounts of his travels on the Continent, and three novels, the most successful being *Zeluco* (1789). After visiting Paris in 1792, he published *A Journal During a Residence in France* (2 vols., 1793–4). In 1797 he edited the *Works* of his friend Tobias Smollett, with a biography. Lines 11–26 describe a scene near Orleans.

271. Text from *Gent. Mag.* (1796), i. 66. For Dr Andrew Kippis (1725–95), a much-respected Nonconformist divine and author, see headnote. He had died on 8 Oct. 1795. William Godwin and Samuel Rogers had been his pupils at Hackney Dissenting Academy. 'Th' ignoble Tyrant' (line 31) is Robespierre. Lines 41–2 quote Pope, *Epistle to Arbuthnot*, lines 201–2.

HELEN LEIGH (**272**). Text from *Miscellaneous Poems* (Manchester, 1788), pp. 10–12.

ELIZABETH HANDS (**273–7**). See *Monthly Review*, 3 (1790), 345–6; W. K. R. Bedford, *Three Hundred Years of a Family Living, being a History of the Rilands of Sutton Coldfield* (Birmingham, 1889), pp. 112–14. Texts from *The Death of Amnon* (Coventry, 1789), pp. 86–7, 113, 115–16, 47–55.

276. Line 31 refers to *The Whole Duty of Man* (1658), probably by Richard Allestree, a popular devotional work.

277. Lines 31–50 refer to the title-poem of her volume, based on the rape of Tamar by her brother Amnon, son of King David, in II Sam. 13. Line 53 refers to the novel (1754) by Samuel Richardson. For the 'mad cow' (lines 89–90) see **275**.

JOANNA BAILLIE (**278–85**). See *Monthly Review*, 6 (1791), 266–9; M. S. Carhart, *The Life and Work of Joanna Baillie* (New Haven, 1923). Texts from *Poems* (1790), pp. 1–4, 27–33, 42–8, 56–61, 78–81, 170–9.

278. In *Fugitive Verses* (1840), she explained that a 'hind' (line 7) was more than 'a common labourer,—the tenant of a very small farm, which he cultivates with his own hands. . . . A class of men very common in the west of Scotland, ere political economy was thought of' (p. 1 n.).

REBEKAH CARMICHAEL (**286–7**). The quoted letter and the lines on Forbes are inserted in the British Library copy. For David Ramsay Hay, see *DNB*. Texts from *Poems* (Edinburgh, 1790), pp. 12–13, 52–3.

ANN FRANCIS (**288**). See *Gent. Mag.* (1800), ii. 1190; *Biographia Dramatica* (1812), i. 771; J. Dalloway, *Western Sussex* (1832 edn.), ii. 223. Text from *Miscellaneous Poems* (Norwich, 1790), pp. 251–2. A note (p. 22) to a poem about the poet William Collins refers to his supposed insanity in Chichester, during her own early years in Sussex, and may be based on first-hand knowledge: 'Collins was, at times, *quite* raving, and noisy, though Dr. Johnson thought otherwise [in his *Lives of the Poets*].'

ANN RADCLIFFE (**289**). See *Annual Biography and Obituary*, 8 (1824), 89–105, which became the basis of Walter Scott's 'Prefatory Memoir' in her *Novels* (1824), pp. i–xxxix, and was expanded in the 'Memoir' by T. N. Talfourd prefixed to *Gaston de Blondeville* (1826), i. 3–132; L. Hunt, *Men, Women, and Books* (1847), ii. 145–6; A. D. McKillop, 'Charlotte Smith's Letters', *Huntington Library Quarterly*, 15 (1951–2), 255; A. Grant, *Ann Radcliffe* (Denver, 1952); E. B. Murray, *Ann Radcliffe* (New York, 1972); E. R. Napier, 'Ann Radcliffe', in *British Novelists 1660–1800*, ed. M. C. Battestin (2 vols., Detroit, 1985), ii. 363–72. Text from *The Romance of the Forest* (1791), ii. 129–31.

MARIA and HARRIET FALCONAR (**290**). See *European Mag.* 10 (1786), 457, and 11 (1787), 108–9, 286–7. They may have been related to a Magnus Falconar, who published medical works in the 1780s. Text from *Poetic Laurels* (1791), pp. ix–x.

JANET LITTLE (**291**). See James Paterson, *The Contemporaries of Burns* (Edinburgh, 1840), pp. 78–89; William Wallace, *Robert Burns and Mrs. Dunlop* (1898), esp. pp. 126–7, 185–6, 283–4, 346; Burns, *Letters*, 2nd edn., ed. G. R. Roy (2 vols., Oxford, 1985), i. 438–9, ii. 21–2, 61–2, 129; F. Brady, *James Boswell: The Later Years* (1984), p. 464. Text from *Poetical Works* (Ayr, 1792), pp. 113–16. Lines 11–17 and 31 refer to Samuel Johnson's *Lives of the Poets* (1779–81) and his death in 1784. Burns (lines 21–6) had won sudden fame with his *Poems* (Kilmarnock, 1786).

ELLEN TAYLOR (**292**). Text from *Poems* (Dublin, 1792), pp. 8–9. The River Barrow in south-east Ireland meets the sea at Waterford.

HENRIETTA O'NEILL (**293–4**). See *Anthologia Hibernica*, 2 (1793), 319–20, 384–5; C. Smith, *Elegiac Sonnets*, ii. (1797), 74–7, 115; W. Withering, *Miscellaneous Tracts* (1822), i. 137; *Gent. Mag.* (1833), ii. 130–2; Cokayne, *Peerage*, iii. 423, x. 61–2; D. J. O'Donoghue, *The Poets of Ireland* (Dublin, 1912), p. 365; Walpole, *Correspondence*, xxiv. 218.

293. Text from Charlotte Smith, *Desmond* (1792), iii. 165–6.

294. Text from Charlotte Smith, *Elegiac Sonnets*, ii (1797), 72–3. Her two sons, Charles (1779–1841) and John (1780–1855), in turn became Viscount O'Neill.

MARY LOCKE (**295–6**). See *Gent. Mag.* (1797), ii. 1076; W. Wing, *Annals of Steeple Barton* (Oxford, 1866), pp. 51–2, and *Annals of Steeple Aston* (Oxford, 1875), pp. 72–3; C. Brookes, *A History of Steeple Aston* (Long Compton, 1929), p. 157; *Victoria*

County History of Oxfordshire, xi (1983), 63, 72. The texts of the two sonnets are from *Gent. Mag.* (1792), i. 72 and (1794), i. 462.

MARY ALCOCK (**297–301**). See *Gent. Mag.* (1798), i. 539; R. Cumberland, *Memoirs* (1807), i. 241, 375, 378. Texts from *Poems* (1799), pp. 22–4, 48–9, 78–83, 89–93.

299. Iërne (line 1) is a form of Hibernia, one of the Latin names for Ireland. Line 26 alludes to the 'White Boys', members of an Irish agrarian association, responsible for disturbances in Munster in the 1780s, when the poem may have been written.

MARY ROBINSON (**302–7**). See *Gent. Mag.* (1800), ii. 1300; *Annual Review*, 5 (1806), 516–19; *Memoirs of Mary Robinson*, ed. J. F. Molloy (1930); M. Steen, *The Lost One* (1937); *Thraliana*, ii. 830; Walpole, *Correspondence*, xxv. 154 n., xxxv. 523 n.; Coleridge, *Letters*, i. 562–3, ii. 669; Earl of Bessborough, *Georgiana* (1955), p. 290; R. D. Bass, *The Green Dragoon: The Lives of Banastre Tarleton and Mary Robinson* (New York, 1957); R. S. Woof, 'Wordsworth's Poetry and Stuart's Newspapers, 1797–1803', *Studies in Bibliography*, 15 (1962), 152.

302. Text from *Poems*, ii (1793), 70–3. First printed in *The Oracle*, 3 Aug. 1792, it was addressed to Banastre Tarleton (see headnote).

303–4. Texts from *Poetical Works* (1806), iii. 223–4, 274–6.

305. Text from *Gent. Mag.* (1797), i. 62–3.

306. Text from *Poetical Works* (1806), ii. 338–40. Line 41 quotes *King Lear*, III. iv. 33.

307. Text from *Lyrical Tales* (1800), pp. 72–6; originally in the *Morning Post*, 26 Feb. 1800. For the incident which suggested the poem, see *Memoirs* (1930), pp. 168–70. Coleridge considered it 'a poem of fascinating Metre', *Letters*, i. 575–6.

MARIA LOGAN (**308**). Text from *Poems on Several Occasions* (York, 1793), pp. 45–6.   The River Aire (line 13) flows through Leeds and the West Riding of Yorkshire, where industrialization was proceeding rapidly.

ISABELLA KELLY (**309**). See *Gent. Mag.* (1782), 149, (1789), ii. 1208 (where her husband's name is given as Thomas Kelly, contrary to other sources), (1857), ii. 229; *The Royal Kalendar for 1785* (1785), p. 89; J. Watkins, *Biographical Dictionary of Living Authors* (1816), p. 152; *Memoir of the Late Mrs Henrietta Fordyce* (1823), pp. 88–133; J. Mill, *History of British India* (5th edn., 10 vols., 1858), v. 249; E. Foss, *Biographical Dictionary of the Judges of England* (1870), p. 381; A. D. Fordyce, *Family Record of the Name of Dingwall Fordyce* (Toronto, 1885), pp. xlii–xliii, xlvii–xlviii; *Lincoln's Inn: Admissions Register* (1896), ii. 81; *Hist. MSS Comm.: Palk MSS.* (1922), pp. 106, 114–15, 406. Text from *A Collection of Poems and Fables* (1794), pp. 21–3.

ANNE BATTEN CRISTALL (**310–13**). See British Library, 11621.k.3 (22), for the undated 'Song'; *Gent. Mag.* (1795), i. 325, ii. 861; *Monthly Review*, 20 (1796), 98–100; G. Dyer, *Poems* (1801), p. 301 n.; R. Southey, *Life and Correspondence*, ed. C. C. Southey, i (1849), 305–6, ii (1849), 16; R. and S. Redgrave, *A Century of Painters of the English School* (1866), i. 508–14; J. L. Roget, *A History of the Old Water-Colour Society* (1891), i. 178–91; *The Love-Letters of Mary Hays*, ed. A. F. Wedd (1925), pp. 238–9; W. G. S. Dyer, *Joshua Cristall* (Plymouth, 1959; revised, Camborne, 1962); M. Wollstonecraft, *Collected Letters*, ed. R. M. Wardle (Ithaca, 1979), pp. 172, 188–9, 194, 196, 379–80, 384, 421–2. Texts from *Poetical Sketches* (1795), pp. 9–11, 20–9, 115–17, 147–8.

ANNABELLA PLUMPTRE (**314**). See Bodleian MSS Douce d. 22, fo. 137 and d. 31, fos. 65–7; *Biographical Dictionary of Living Authors* (1816), p. 277; W. Beloe, *The Sexagenarian* (2nd edn., 1818), i. 362; *Gent. Mag.* (1818), ii. 571, (1839), i. 334;

C. L. Brightwell, *Memorials of Amelia Opie* (2nd edn., Norwich, 1854), pp. 77, 96; R. Blunt, *Mrs. Montagu, 'Queen of the Blues'* (1923), ii. 304; *The Love-Letters of Mary Hays*, ed. A. F. Wedd (1925), p. 238; W. Graham, 'The Authorship of the Norwich *Cabinet*, 1794–5', *Notes and Queries*, 162 (1932), 294–5; *Henry Crabb Robinson on Books and their Writers*, ed. E. J. Morley (3 vols., 1938), i. 14–15. Text from *The Cabinet*, iii (Norwich, 1795), 117–19. The quotation in line 5 is from Milton, *Paradise Lost*, iv. 35–6.

ANONYMOUS ('Eliza') (**315**). Text from *Poems and Fugitive Pieces, by Eliza* (1796), pp. 163–8.

MATILDA BETHAM (**316–18**). See *Selections from the Letters of Robert Southey*, ed. J. Warter (1856), ii. 67, 153–4, 175; E. Betham, *A House of Letters* (1905), *passim*; J. M. S. Tompkins, *The Polite Marriage* (Cambridge, 1938), p. 186; *New Letters of Robert Southey*, ed. K. Curry (1965), i. 514–18, ii. 215.

316–17. Texts from *Elegies and Other Small Poems* (Ipswich, 1797), pp. 22–3, 45–8.

318. Text from E. Betham, *A House of Letters* (1905), pp. 55–6. She gave these lines in about 1798 to Lady Boughton, as a 'little continuation of some verses I had met with', which began: 'Since 'tis superior skill in arts refin'd, | That ranks the male above the female kind; | Ye fair, each meaner vanity controul, | And study how to ornament the soul!', etc.

ANNA SAWYER (**319–20**). Her husband was just possibly the William Sawyer, 'formerly a resident at Bristol', who died in Birmingham on 23 May 1808 (*Gent. Mag.*, i. 561). Texts from *Poems on Various Subjects* (Birmingham, 1801), pp. 37–9, 56–9.

320. She would have been familiar with the rise of the Sunday School movement in Gloucestershire in the 1780s, especially the Cheddar school established by Hannah More and her sisters.

ANONYMOUS (**321**). Text from *Poems on Various Subjects* (1798), pp. 73–4.

ANONYMOUS (**322**). From *Gent. Mag.* (1799), i. 237. Lines 6–7 refer to Exod. 25: 8: 'And let them make me a sanctuary; that I may dwell among them.'

GEORGIANA, DUCHESS OF DEVONSHIRE (**323**). See Walpole, *Correspondence*, v. 280, 292, xxiii. 562, xxv. 411, xxxii. 232; Boswell, *Life*, iii. 425 n., iv. 357; B. Masters, *Georgiana, Duchess of Devonshire* (1981). Text from the undated quarto edition, where it is heavily annotated. A selection from these notes is given below. The earliest of the unauthorized texts may have been that in the *Morning Chronicle*, 20 Dec. 1799. The parent and sister (line 7) were Lady Spencer and Lady Bessborough. Lines 13–28: 'On the 9th [August] we embarked, upon the Lago Maggiore, at the little town of Sesto situated where the Tesino runs out of the lake. . . . On the evening of the 10th, we landed at Magadino. . . . we set out, on the evening of the 12th, to enter the mountain, and ascended gradually by a road which nearly followed the course of the Tesino. . . .' Lines 45–6: 'When any lives have been lost from the falls of snow, a small cross is erected.' Lines 47–8: 'The whole trade from Switzerland to Italy, passes over this mountain; and they often travel in bands of forty laden mules.' Lines 55–6: 'The Rhine, the Rhone, the Aar, the Tesino, and the Reuss, all rise in the mountain of St. Gothard.' Lines 63–4: 'The valley of Ursera, is celebrated for its fertility and verdure; and the placid manner in which the Reuss runs through it.' Lines 73–6: 'The Devil's Bridge is one of the five bridges that distinguish this road . . .' Line 84: 'The Revolution, known by the name of the Swiss League, began in its smallest canton, Switz; but the chief events happened at Altorf, capital of the canton of Uri. . . .' Lines 93–6: a long note relates the familiar legend of William Tell shooting the apple off his son's head in the 14th century. Lines 97–100: another long note describes the three 'friends of liberty' who also helped to liberate Switzerland from Austrian oppression.

ADDITIONAL NOTES

ELIZABETH THOMAS (24–32). For discussion of the evidence of Pope's contact with her in 1708 and a rejection of the assumption that she was Cromwell's mistress, see T. R. Steiner, 'Young Pope in the Correspondence of Henry Cromwell and Elizabeth Thomas' and 'The Misrepresentation of Elizabeth Thomas', *Notes and Queries*, 228 (1983), 495–7, 506–8. See also Joanna Lipking, 'Fair Originals in Male Commendatory Poems', *Eighteenth Century Life*, 12 (1988), 67–70.

MARY MONCK (50–2). 52 appears anonymously in a MS collection compiled by Gabriel Lepipre in 1749 (Bodleian MS Eng. poet e. 40, fo. 18), with a note: 'This Coppy of Verses was gave me by Miss Carbonnel. 1747.' The attribution to Mary Monck in 1755, forty years after her death, awaits final confirmation.

ARABELLA MORETON (76). I am indebted to Mrs E. E. Duncan-Jones for the identification of 'B–ll M–rt–n' to whom the poem was attributed in *A New Miscellany* [1726?]. She was Arabella Moreton, daughter of Matthew Ducie Moreton (*c*.1662– 1735), Lord Ducie (1720), who had married Arabella Prestwich in 1690. He was MP for Gloucestershire 1708–13 and 1715–20 and died at Tetworth, Glos., in 1735 (Cokayne, *Peerage*, iv. 474). Arabella had died unmarried by 1741. Her poem appears anonymously in Ashley Cowper's *Norfolk Poetical Miscellany* (1744), ii. 83, but in the Cowper family album is attributed to her sister Penelope (British Library, Add. MS 28101 fo. 49). Another text attributed to 'Miss Morton' appears in Bodleian MS Eng. poet e. 40, fo. 6 (see the preceding note).

SARAH DIXON (114–19). I am indebted to Professor Ann Messenger, whose investigations in Canterbury have brought to light Sarah Dixon's dates. She was born in 1672, the daughter of James Dixon of Newnham, Kent, and she died on 23 April 1765 aged 93. (There is evidently no basis for the Bodleian annotation suggesting that she was a widow.) The brother at University College, Oxford, who died young, was apparently James Dixon, who matriculated there on 17 Feb. 1694 aged 17, but did not take a degree. Some of her poems were no doubt written much earlier in the century than had previously seemed likely.

JANE WEST (250–1). A belated visit to St Nicholas' Church, Little Bowden, in July 1989 revealed that her maiden name was Iliffe. She erected a gravestone in the churchyard to her parents ('late of Desborough'), which records that her mother Jane died in 1796 aged 77 and her father John in 1805 aged 79. Another memorial reveals that her husband was aged 67 at his death in 1823. I subsequently realized that some of these facts had been brought to light by Pamela Lloyd in 'Some New Information on Jane West', *Notes and Queries*, 229 (1984), 469–70, who adds the names of her sons Thomas (1783–1843), John (1787–?), and Edward (1794–1821). Lloyd also reveals from local records that in 1812 she sold the property she had inherited from her father for £3000. Her MSS, left in her will (1846) to her grandson, the Revd Edward West, have not been traced.

INDEX OF TITLES AND FIRST LINES

References are to the numbers of the poems

INDEX OF TITLES AND FIRST LINES

INDEX OF TITLES AND FIRST LINES

INDEX OF TITLES AND FIRST LINES

INDEX OF TITLES AND FIRST LINES

INDEX OF AUTHORS

References are to the numbers of the poems. Cross-references are supplied only for authors who published under or are known by both unmarried and married names

INDEX OF SELECTED TOPICS

OXFORD

MORE OXFORD PAPERBACKS

Details of a selection of other Oxford Paperbacks follow. A complete list of Oxford Paperbacks, including The World's Classics, Twentieth-Century Classics, OPUS, Past Masters, Oxford Authors, Oxford Shakespeare, and Oxford Paperback Reference, is available in the UK from the General Publicity Department, Oxford University Press (RS), Walton Street, Oxford, OX2 6DP.

In the USA, complete lists are available from the Paperbacks Marketing Manager, Oxford University Press, 200 Madison Avenue, New York, NY 10016.

Oxford Paperbacks are available from all good bookshops. In case of difficulty, customers in the UK can order direct from Oxford University Press Bookshop, 116 High Street, Oxford, Freepost, OX1 4BR, enclosing full payment. Please add 10 per cent of the published price for postage and packing.

THE NEW OXFORD BOOK OF EIGHTEENTH-CENTURY VERSE

Chosen and Edited by Roger Lonsdale

'a major anthology: one of the best that Oxford has ever produced' *The Times*

'a major event . . . forces a reappraisal of what 18th-century poetry is' *Sunday Times*

'the most important anthology in recent years' *The Economist*

'indispensable' Kingsley Amis

BRITISH WRITERS OF THE THIRTIES

Valentine Cunningham

This wide-ranging discussion of British writing and writers in that momentous and notorious decade offers interpretations of central texts of the period, not in linguistic isolation, but in the contexts—social, political, historical, ideological, personal—in which they were written.

'*British Writers of the Thirties* must be acknowledged a success. The immense strings of citations, marshalled with care and often with wit, eventually weave together an enormous design.' *Times Literary Supplement*

'This rich book . . . independent-minded, iconoclastic and articulate' *Sunday Times*

'*British Writers of the Thirties* is by far the best history of its kind published in recent years . . . it will become required reading for those who wish to look back as a society and a culture in which writers, for all their faults, were taken seriously.' Peter Ackroyd, *The Times*

'Cunningham's extraordinary assiduousness . . . makes it hard to see how *British Writers of the Thirties could be surpassed as a reading of what has become—probably now more firmly than ever—the 'canonical' literature of the period.' Times Higher Education Supplement*

THE COURTSHIP OF ROBERT BROWNING
AND ELIZABETH BARRETT

Daniel Karlin

Daniel Karlin's exciting and imaginative book gives a fresh account of one of the most celebrated romances of literary history. Based on a much closer study of the love letters than has been attempted before, shows how significant they are for an interpretation of the work of both poets.

'A well written and very perceptive study of a love affair that was as much a literary event as a private emotional experience' *New Statesman*

'A rewarding study . . . Karlin's sensitive guidance enables us to appreciate the poignancy of what Browning achieved for Elizabeth.' *Times Higher Education Supplement*

THE LADY INVESTIGATES

Women Detectives and Spies in Fiction

Patricia Craig and Mary Cadogan

In the early chapters of this book, the authors examine the crime novels of Wilkie Collins, George R. Sims, Grant Allen, and Anna Katherine Green, and discover the splendid and daunting lady detective Miss Van Snoop. Later they explore the period this century in which women writers made the detective story their own—Christie, Sayers, Allingham, Marsh, and many more.

'Patricia Craig and Mary Cadogan . . . explore a rich vein of fantasy, eccentricity, humour, and social comment in this comprehensive survey of women in the detective story and spy thriller . . . and in their saga present for our edification and delight a splendidly mixed bunch of amateur and professional sleuths.' P. D. James, *The Times*

THE LIFE OF KATHERINE MANSFIELD

Antony Alpers

Until recently it has not been possible to deal freely and frankly with all the events of Katherine Mansfield's life. Conventional mores, respect for the privacy of her lovers, family, and friends, and the lack of some crucial material, have all prevented it. Little was known, for example, of her disastrous one-day marriage, her elopement with her childhood friend, Garnett Trowell, and her subsequent affair with Ida Baker. Now, drawing on newly opened manuscript collections, private papers, and personal contacts to which he has had exclusive access, Antony Alpers has been able to expand his 1953 biography in a new, award-winning interpretation of this volatile and vulnerable genius.

'This is in the way of being a definitive biography, and as such utterly engrossing, simply because Katherine Mansfield herself is always engrossing.' Kay Dick, *The Times*

Oxford Lives

CHARLOTTE BRONTË

The Evolution of Genius

Winifred Gérin

Winner of the James Tait Black Memorial Prize, the William Heinemann Award, and the British Academy's Rose Mary Crawshay Prize.

'surely one of the great biographies of recent times' *Sunday Times*

'a book to end all books about the Brontës' *Sunday Telegraph*

Oxford Lives